W9-AOO-865
MRAC

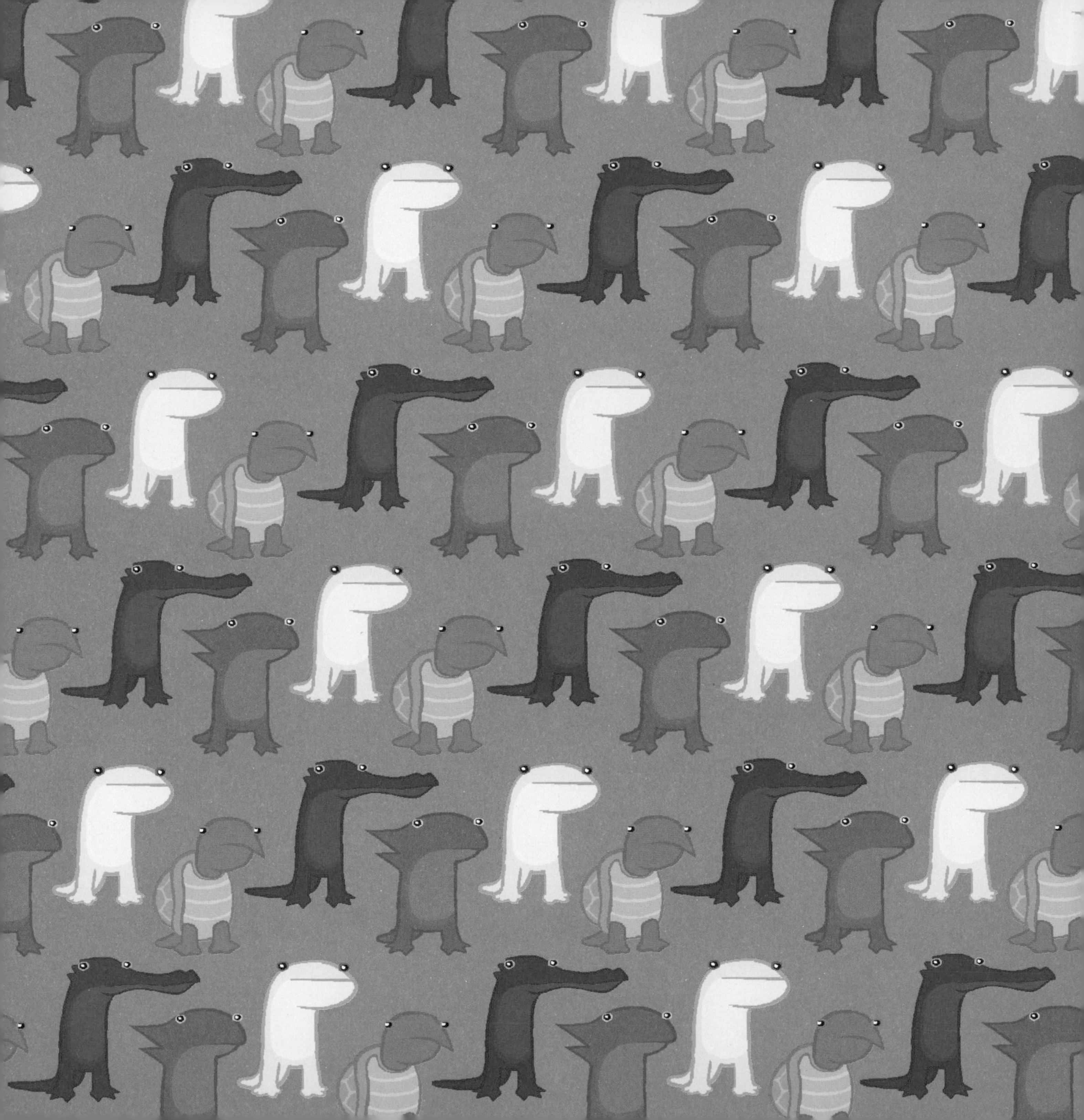

BY ANDREW HUSSIE

BOOK 5

PART 2

ACT 5 ACT 2 PART 1

Act 5 Act 2

"He is already here."

import universe U2;

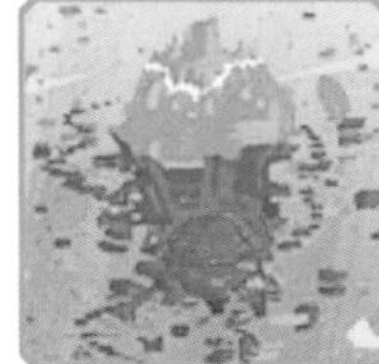

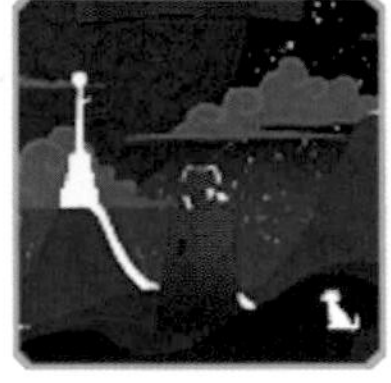

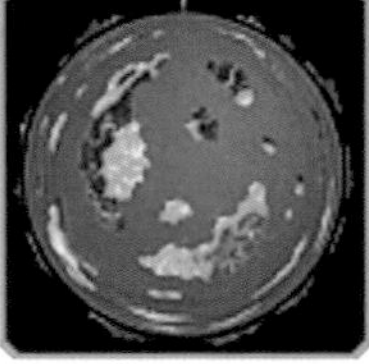

ACT 5 ACT 2
HE IS ALREADY HERE.

SBURB
LOADING...

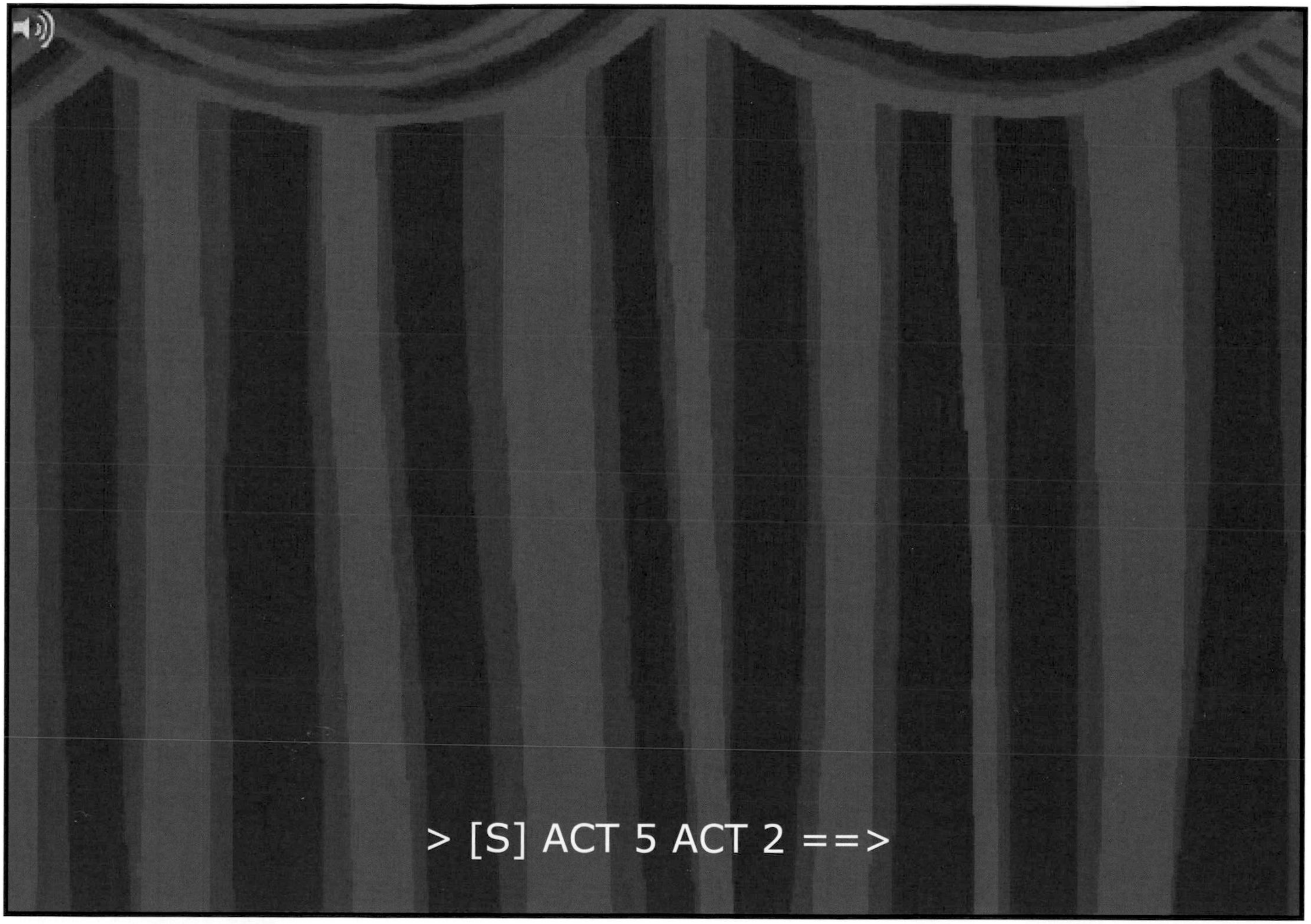

> [S] ACT 5 ACT 2 ==>

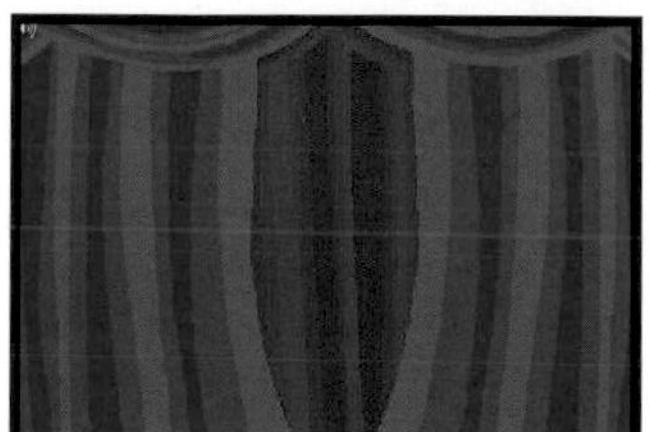

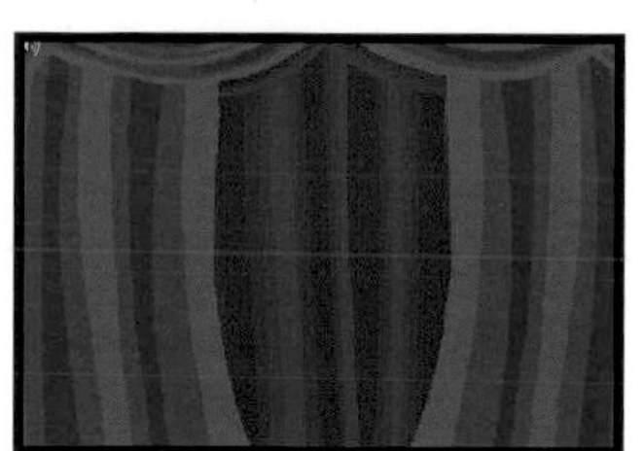

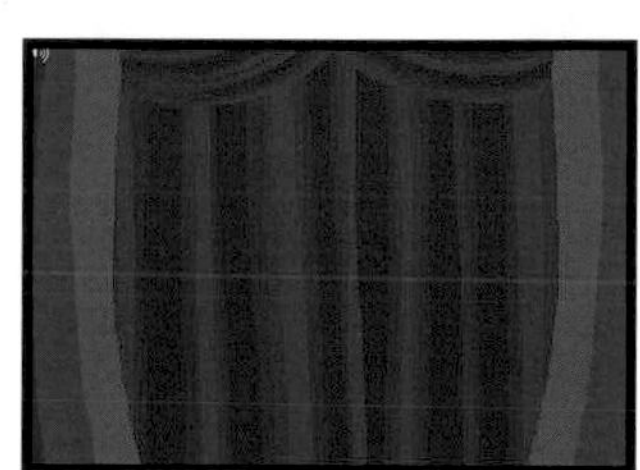

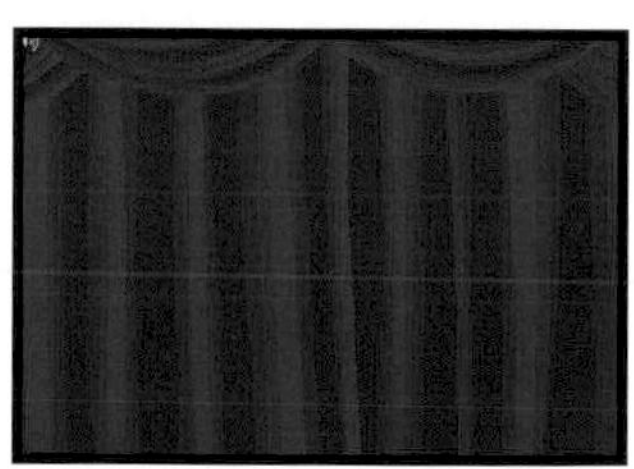

Here it is, yet another book hopelessly clogged with your favorite webtoon series, *Homestuck*. It's Book 5, which covers Act 5 Act 2. So in other words, a rare moment where the book number coincides with the act number. Don't worry though, that won't last long since this volume covers only half of Act 5 Act 2. So I guess it's...Act 5 Act 2 Part 1? I think I'm already getting a headache. Hey, is it too late to cancel these books? What's that? You're telling me it's too late for everything? We're all going down on this ship together? I see people in the crowd nodding their heads. Is what I'm doing by making jokes down here tantamount to what those guys were doing in playing classical music on the deck of the *Titanic*? Wait, I'm being handed a note from offstage. It says...yes. Yes, that's exactly what I'm doing. It also says I should keep it up, if I know what's good for me, Joke Boy. Joke Boy?? Come on, guys. This book is 480 pages long, so I've got my work cut out for me. Maybe jokes are overrated. Maybe I'll start with a poem instead. Here goes: Curtains are red. Curtains are blue. Here's some more curtains. Instead of one, there are two.
/Bows, ducking under brick thrown at head./

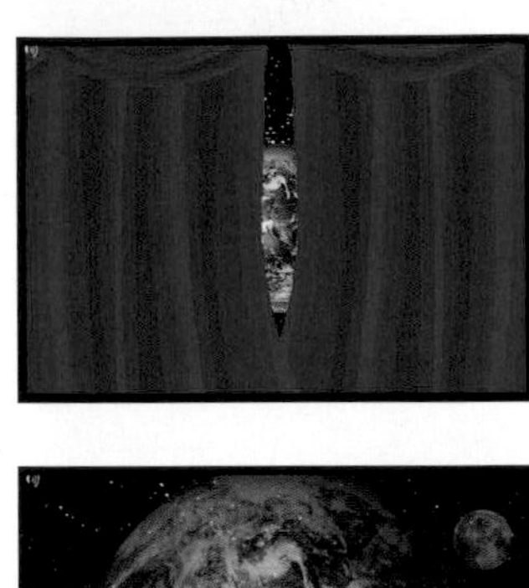

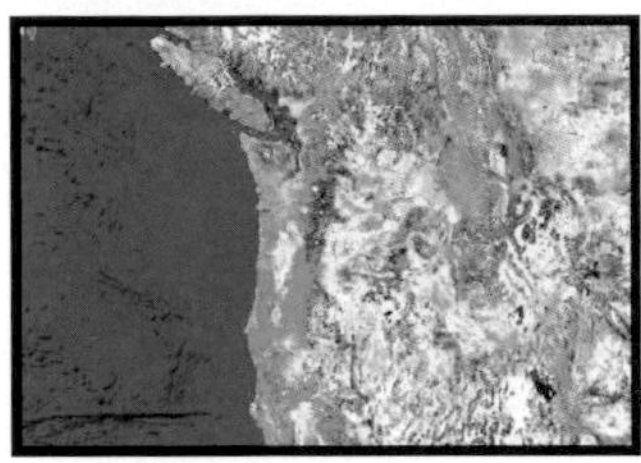

Can we start over? The note on the first page probably sounded a bit unhinged. Time to pull my shit together, splash a glass of cold water on my face, and add some fucking VALUE to this book. I promise I will do my very best to be coherent, articulate, and funny on every single page from now on. Oh, what's that? NOW you start laughing? Here's an idea. I'll start making some remarks about *Homestuck*, and you can all chill out. Deal? A5A2 opens with a stately, low-key animation reintroducing us to all the plot threads and characters we put on hold for what must have seemed like an eternity but in truth was only a few months of real-time updating. It's a piece conveying narrative integration, a montage of transmission, redirecting the energy just generated by the engine of Hivebent into torque, which then begins turning the wheels of the greater plot. When this animation ends, we finally take our foot off the brake and peel outta here. Since we just took such a long detour, we need little reminders of where we left off, which was **[S] Descend**. One such reminder is delivered by showing direct evidence that baby John has, in fact, literally murdered his grandmother with the huge joke book he rode down from space after getting shot through a portal during the Reckoning. Perhaps I should add that ending the life of another human being via a vast collection of corny jokes is a proposition I can identify with on a very personal level.

The old threads we're being reminded of wind into the new threads we just caught up with, by way of reviewing the life and times of John Egbert through the eyes of our new and favorite buddy, Karkat. The old and the new coming together like this lets us know what we're in for over the remainder of Act 5, which by now we can infer is a Whopper Act by previous standards, because we've just been modestly informed that the rest of this act is labeled with an entirely new subdivision called Act 2. Layering acts within acts is a thing that we didn't even know *Homestuck* could do. But really, we *should* have known, because *Homestuck* is always trying to let us know it can do anything it wants, but we just keep not listening. When I do things like drop the label "Act 5 Act 2" on readers, maybe it seems like I'm just clowning on you as usual. Maybe it's all a big goof. If you think that, fair. But there's real purpose here. By signaling that this is the beginning of an entirely new act unto itself, yet one still contained within another act, I'm letting you know the remainder of the arc is likely to be substantial. The process of merging two major narrative rivers into one huge river is itself going to be a very substantial narrative undertaking, and the story isn't going to bother pretending otherwise. Fooling around with the story's partitioning system in this whimsical way is actually a direct, totally up-front mechanism for dropping that pretense. It is literally using bullshit in order to stop bullshitting you.

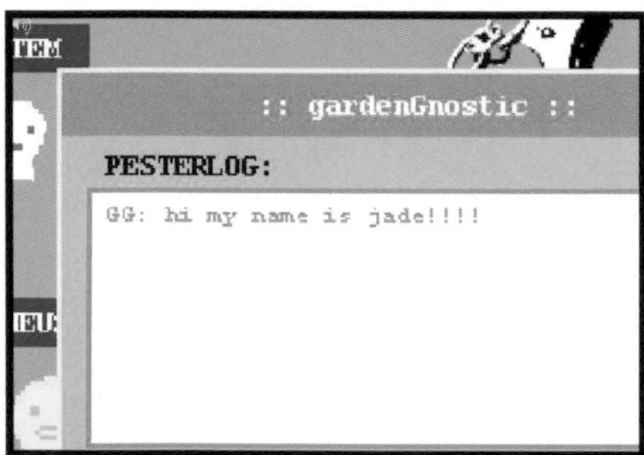

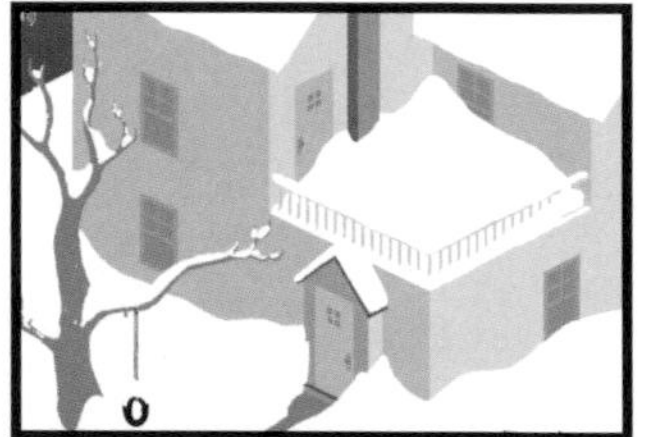

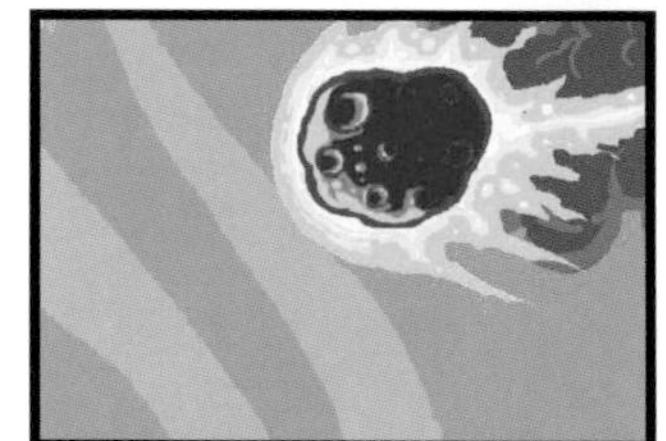

Every little morsel of John's life, no matter how mundane or foolish, is absorbed by an absolutely captivated Karkat. Every tiny increment of this strange and exciting alien boy's journey through childhood is feeding into Karkat's brewing hatred just a little bit more. We coast through a few endearing moments we hadn't seen before, such as when John met Jade for the first time. As one might expect, it was a simple "hi im jade! hi i'm john!" type of transaction that got their friendship rolling. We also get a peek at John's ludicrous Harry Anderson wallpaper. A few weeks before I typed this note, Harry Anderson tragically passed away. R.I.P. to this magician guy who barely anyone knows of, or cares about. We hardly knew ye, or cared about ye.

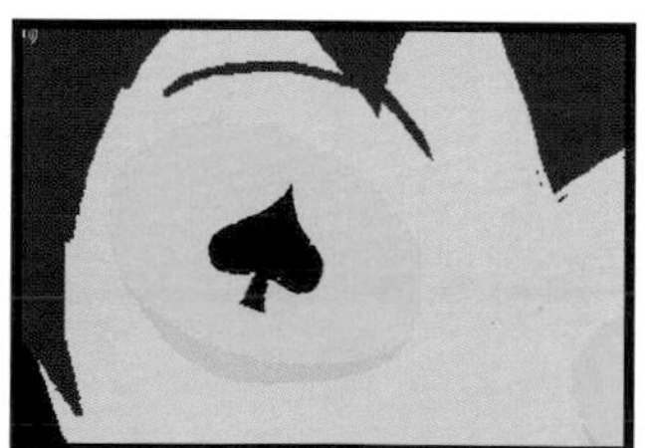

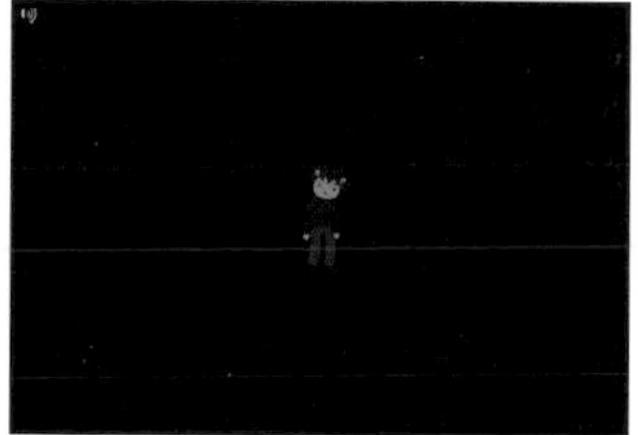

The gag here—okay wait, this isn't even a gag, it's serious as hell... Whatever this is, here's what's up with it. Basically, when Karkat discovers John for the first time, when he connects the dots and decides that this is the boy who is directly responsible for all his failures and problems, it's "hate at first sight." Even though this may not be a gag, it does serve as a pretty good punchline of sorts to all the buildup we just went through: getting to know Karkat through a long detour/review of his journey, learning about troll romance and how that system works, etc. Then we finally return to the A-plot, and we see the spades in Karkat's eyes, and...ah, yes. We get it now. This is why Karkat is infatuated with John and spews impotent rage through a clumsy reverse-linear deluge of hate-flirting. In a way, this is something readers can relate to, since we've had a similar experience in following John's journey and growing to love him. But for Karkat, that love transmutes into hate, due to his displaced anger and his culture. It must be very confusing for love and hate to be almost interchangeable emotions. When you add being a stupid teen to the equation, it's no wonder all the trolls are such hot disasters. And now we know all this, and so have valuable context for fully appreciating the A5A2 arc. It only took getting steamrolled by hundreds of pages of Hivebent to enjoy these dividends.

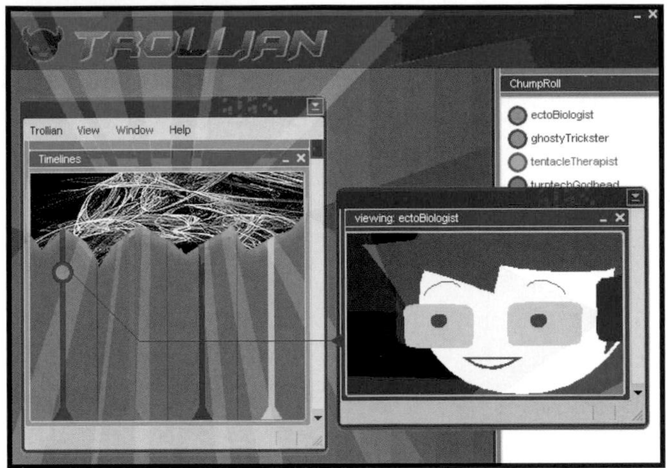

You finally found him. After hours of searching.

No.

SWEEPS of searching.

> Karkat: Troll this worthless human.

carcinoGeneticist [CG] **began trolling ectoBiologist [EB]**

CG: ATTENTION WORTHLESS HUMAN.
CG: THIS IS YOUR GOD SPEAKING.
CG: IT IS A WRATHFUL GOD WHO DESPISES YOU MORE THAN YOU COULD HAVE POSSIBLY DARED TO FEAR.
CG: I HAVE WATCHED YOUR ENTIRE PATHETIC LIFE UNFOLD.
CG: I HAVE OBSERVED YOU WHILE YOU WOULD QUAKE AND TREMBLE IN PERSONAL PRAYERS OF SHAME.
CG: WHILE YOU PLEADED FORGIVENESS FOR BEING SUCH A WRETCHED DISGUSTING FAILURE ON EVERY CONCEIVABLE LEVEL.
CG: PROSTRATE BEFORE THE STUPID AND FALSE CLOWN GODS YOU HAVE SCRIBBLED ON THE WALLS OF YOUR BLOCK.
CG: BOGUS DEITIES WORSHIPED BY A PRIMITIVE "PARADISE" PLANET.
CG: BUT YOUR PRAYERS WILL NOT BE ANSWERED.
CG: THERE ARE NO MIRACLES IN STORE FOR YOU, HUMAN.
CG: ONLY MY HATE.
CG: IT IS A HATE SO PURE AND HOT IT WOULD CONSUME YOUR SAD UNDERDEVELOPED HUMAN THINK PAN TO EVEN CONTEMPLATE.
CG: IT IS A HATE THAT TO FATHOM MUST BE PUT INTO SONG.

CG: SHRIEKED BY THE TEN THOUSAND ROWDY SHOUT SPHINCTERS PEPPERING THE GRUESOME UNDERBELLY OF THE MOST TRUCULENT GOD THE FURTHEST RING CAN MUSTER.
CG: IT IS A HATE THAT MADE YOU AND WILL SURELY DESTROY YOU.
CG: MY HATE IS THE LIFEBLOOD THAT PULSES THROUGH THE VEINS OF YOUR UNIVERSE.
CG: IT IS MY GIFT TO YOU.
CG: YOU'RE WELCOME FOR THAT.
CG: YOU UNGRATEFUL PIECE OF SHIT.
EB: hi karkat!
CG: WHAT

Is there something incongruous, or emotionally dissonant, about the fact that this adorable, pajama-wearing Future John has his head sandwiched by a device emblazoned with the image of a grotesque rapist? Maybe I should change the subject. There's so much to talk about here, it would be a shame to get hung up on the sexual crimes of John's favorite celebrities. Anyway, this panel is a great and exciting way to get into the arc of A5A2. Just this single shot of Future John and a few points of dialogue tell us so much. Cool new outfit, plans are being hatched, everybody's friends now... It's a future-plot snapshot imbued with optimism and intrigue. It lets us know very swiftly what the ultimate narrative purpose of A5A2 is going to be: to bring us to this moment and reveal what happens along the way. Some of the energy from Hivebent's intense nonlinear storytelling patterns are carrying over to the next sub-act. A5A2 isn't quite as freewheeling as Hivebent in terms of "show literally anything, from any point on the timeline, literally any time," but it jumps around enough to keep things interesting and unpredictable.

CG: HOW DO YOU KNOW MY NAME.
EB: oh man.
EB: this is it, isn't it?
EB: i've been looking forward to this!
CG: WHAT IS IT.
CG: ME HATING YOU IS WHAT'S IT.
CG: IF THAT'S WHAT YOU MEAN, YEAH, BINGO.
EB: no, i mean this is the first conversation between us, from your perspective.
EB: right?
CG: YEAH.
CG: ARE YOU SUGGESTING WE'VE SPOKEN BEFORE.
EB: yeah, lots of times!
EB: actually...
EB: i should introduce myself properly.
EB: hi karkat, i am john!
CG: JOHN, WHY WOULD I GIVE A PUNGENT WHIPPING LUMPSQUIRT WHAT YOUR NAME IS.
EB: because we are buddies!
CG: I ADMIT I AM NEW TO HUMAN SOCIAL CONSTRUCTS
CG: BUT I REFUSE TO BELIEVE OUR RELATIONSHIP CAN OR WILL EVER BE DESCRIBED AS "EARTH HUMAN BUDDIES".
EB: yup, we totally are.
EB: we just became earth human buddies in a kind of weird way.
EB: you decide to keep talking to me backwards through my adventure.
EB: and then when you are done with that you come back and talk to me more recently on the timeline for a while.
EB: you talk to my friends a whole bunch too.
EB: you and your alternian troll buddies help me and my earth human buddies hatch a plan!
EB: which we are busy putting into motion right now, as you can see.
CG: THESE ARE LIES.
CG: I KNOW WHEN I AM BEING TROLLED, WHO DO YOU EVEN THINK YOU ARE TALKING TO HERE.
CG: I AM YOUR GOD, REMEMBER.
EB: yeah yeah, i know.
CG: WHY WOULD I TROLL YOU BACKWARDS? THAT DOESN'T MAKE ANY FUCKING SENSE.
CG: AND WHY WOULD I HELP YOU AND YOUR IDIOT FRIENDS?
CG: I WOULD JUST BE HELPING YOU BLUNDER DOWN THE PATH THAT ENDS WITH YOU OPENING THE RIFT LIKE A BUNCH OF MORONS.
EB: you mean the scratch?
CG: WHATEVER.
EB: yes! that is the plan.
EB: you yourself said it was the only hope now.
CG: RIDICULOUS.
CG: I DIDN'T WRIGGLE OUT OF A PUDDLE OF SLIME YESTERDAY.
CG: THAT WAS SEVERAL WEEKS AGO, OK?
EB: heheheh.
CG: I DO NOT THINK YOU APPRECIATE THE GRAVITY OF MY ANTIPATHY, JOHN HUMAN.
EB: egbert.
CG: OK, HUMAN EGBERT.
CG: I FUCKING LOATHE YOU, AND I HAVE TUNED INTO YOUR CHANNEL MOMENTS BEFORE THE ERADICATION OF YOUR TIMELINE AND THAT SMUG LOOK ON YOUR FACE, WITH JUST ENOUGH TIME FOR ME TO BASICALLY COMPLETELY FUCKING DESTROY YOU WITH HOSTILE RHETORIC.
CG: THERE IS NO CHANCE I WILL EVER HELP YOU.
CG: YOU CAN'T POSSIBLY UNDERSTAND HOW MUCH I HATE YOU OR WHY I HATE YOU.
CG: I WASN'T JOKING WHEN I SAID I WAS YOUR GOD, LIKE THAT WASN'T JUST A LOT OF BRAVADO AND USELESS PISSING AROUND.
CG: I AM LITERALLY RESPONSIBLE FOR YOUR EXISTENCE.
CG: WE BEAT THE GAME YOU ARE PLAYING AND CREATED YOUR UNIVERSE.
CG: WE WERE GOING TO ENTER YOUR UNIVERSE AND RULE OVER IT.
CG: LIKE TYRANTS.
CG: IT WAS TO BE OUR PLAYTHING, JOHN.
CG: YOU HAVE NO IDEA HOW SWEET IT WAS GOING TO BE.
CG: BUT THEN WE COULDN'T CLAIM OUR PRIZE BECAUSE OF THAT MONSTROSITY YOU SPRUNG ON US.
EB: man...
EB: i knoooow.
EB: none of this is news to me, karkat!
EB: but to be quite honest, it doesn't sound like your intentions were all that great.
EB: wanting to be tyrants and all.
EB: maybe you got what you deserved, you stutid fuckass!
CG: STUTID?

The time-hopping here isn't purely narrative trickery, or me being whimsical by pointing the camera at whatever I want, whenever I want. There's a good in-story reason for scattering nonlinear focal points throughout A5A2. Which is that, unlike in the acts prior to Hivebent, now we have the luxury of seeing events from a troll point of view. And the trolls are all accessing human events through Trollian, which lets them bounce around the human timeline like maniacs. So we get to see what they see sometimes, which isn't necessarily the order in which we would be viewing things if we didn't have their POV at our disposal.

CG: WOW, YOUR SPECIES REALLY IS BRAINDEAD.
EB: eh, it's an in-joke, never mind.
EB: anyway, hey!
EB: i thought this was supposed to be the conversation where you do all that AMAAAAAZING TROLLING!
EB: come on bro, flame me!
EB: i have been really excited about this.
CG: YOU ACTUALLY WANT ME TO TROLL YOU?
CG: I MEAN
CG: DON'T WORRY, I CAN AND I WILL, AND IT WILL BE A GODDAMN BLOODBATH WHEN I GET STARTED.
CG: IT'S JUST KIND OF WEIRD YOU'RE EXCITED ABOUT IT, IS THAT NORMAL FOR YOUR RACE?
EB: um...
EB: i don't know, probably not.
EB: i just think it's kind of funny when you do it.
CG: THAT'S REALLY CONDESCENDING AND IT'S HARD TO CONVEY HOW MUCH MORE I JUST GOT PISSED OFF THAN I ALREADY WAS.
CG: BUT MAYBE IT MAKES SENSE ACTUALLY
CG: THAT YOU WELCOME MY ACRIMONY SO READILY
CG: ON ACCOUNT OF PROBABLY SOME WEIRD GLAND HUMANS HAVE, LIKE A PUNISHMENT THROBBER OR SOME SILLY SOUNDING THING LIKE THAT.
CG: IT MIGHT MEAN THAT I'M RIGHT ABOUT YOU.
EB: right about what?
CG: I MEAN THAT IT SEEMS LIKE WE ARE CONNECTED IN SOME WAY, DON'T YOU THINK JOHN.
CG: SORT OF COSMICALLY.
CG: LIKE OUR HATE FOR EACH OTHER IS SO STRONG IT MUST HAVE BEEN WRITTEN IN THE STARS.
CG: YOU KNOW, THE ONES I FUCKING MADE FOR YOU.
EB: ha ha, i don't hate you!
CG: HOW CAN YOU POSSIBLY CLAIM TO HAVE TALKED TO ME A LOT ALREADY AND NOT HATE ME, SEE IT DOESN'T ADD UP.
EB: wait...
EB: are you saying that we are kisme-whatevers?
CG: WHAT, NO.
CG: WHAT DO YOU TAKE ME FOR, THAT WOULD BE SUCH A BRAZEN SOLICITATION.
CG: IT'S INSULTING.
CG: I MEAN
CG: OK I'M NOT SAYING I'M RULING OUT THE IDEA OR ANYTHING.
CG: LIKE IF LATER OVER TIME YOU STARTED REALLY HATING ME MORE
CG: LIKE REALLY GOT TO KNOW ME AND FOUND OUT ABOUT HOW MUCH THERE WAS TO HATE
EB: er...
CG: BUT... IN THE PAST I GUESS? I'M JUST SAYING WHO KNOWS WHAT COULD HAPPEN.
CG: OR HAS ALREADY HAPPENED.
EB: uh.
CG: FUCK WHAT AM I BABBLING ABOUT.
CG: THIS IS FUCKING RIDICULOUS, WE JUST MET FOR FUCK'S SAKE.
CG: AND IT'S NOT LIKE WE'RE EVER GOING TO MEET IN PERSON, SO IT'S ALL A MOOT POINT.
CG: SO FORGET I SAID ANYTHING.
CG: GOD, WHAT IS WRONG WITH ME.
EB: well...
EB: i just didn't really have any idea that you had any sort of feelings like that, so i am kind of caught off guard.
CG: WHAT FEELINGS, THERE ARE NO FEELINGS, END OF DISCUSSION.
EB: hey, i don't have a problem with your weird sort of alien hate-love thing!
EB: it is just that, uh...
CG: WHAT
EB: i am not a homosexual.
CG: WHAT THE HELL IS THAT?
EB: it is like, when a boy likes another boy.
EB: or i guess hates, in this case.
CG: HUMANS HAVE A WORD FOR THAT?
EB: yes.
CG: HOW IS THAT EVEN A THING?
EB: shrug. it just is.
CG: HUMAN ROMANCE SURE IS WEIRD.
EB: i am just as confused by your troll shenanigans.
EB: so many shenanigans!
EB: anyway, i kind of got the impression that you and terezi were a thing.
CG: WHAT DO YOU MEAN A THING.
EB: like, i dunno.
EB: going on weird fight dates and beating the crap out of each other, and being in hate-love or love-hate.
EB: isn't that how it works?
CG: YOU ARE SUCH AN IGNORAMUS I COULD SHIT MILES

Because of the intriguing Future John pajama panel, I'm launching into some bigass paragraphs on storycraft. Frankly, since the last book, that's basically what this gutter has been used for. So be it. But in doing so, I'm almost missing the chance to reflect on this really epic screed that Karkat introduces himself to John with, which, as we now know, might as well be a love letter. John says he's not gay. I mean, sure, I guess he technically is "not a homosexual." But aside from that, who are we trying to kid? Everything going on here is really quite spectacularly gay. All of the trolls' involvement with the humans originates from one poorly thought-out, helplessly hate-smitten and gay overture made by a cranky teen boy. Karkat had this whole tirade bottled up inside, ready to unload, but because John is totally expecting it, and already knows Karkat well, he is able to completely disarm, flummox, and redirect all of the hostile energy. The ensuing backwards-chatting idiot spiral is a direct result of John affably and naively sabotaging Karkat's high-strung, breathlessly romantic overture. The lesson is clear: the entire *Homestuck* universe turns exclusively on the axis of of gay teen follies.

OF RAGE SNAKE TO CHOKE YOU TO DEATH.
EB: ew.
CG: WHO HAVE YOU BEEN TALKING TO, WHAT HAVE YOU HEARD ABOUT THAT.
EB: um, i talked to you...
EB: and her...
EB: and some others. i don't know! like i said it's just a sense i got.
EB: sorry!
CG: OK FIRST OF ALL, IF THERE WERE A "THING" WITH HER, AND THAT'S A HUGE IF
CG: IT WOULD BE A TOTALLY DIFFERENT QUADRANT THAN WHAT WE WERE JUST TALKING ABOUT.
EB: oh god, the quadrants...
CG: SECOND, WHETHER SHE AND I HAVE A THING OR DON'T HAVE A THING, OR TOOK A ROMANTIC HOT AIR BALLOON RIDE SUSPENDED IN A GODDAMN FILIAL PAIL TOGETHER
CG: IT'S DEFINITELY NONE OF YOUR FUCKING EARTH BUSINESS, EGBERT HUMAN JOHN.
CG: GOT IT????????
EB: ok, sheesh!
EB: karkat, i am going to be honest...
EB: this first conversation is not going how i thought it would at all!
EB: it is really kind of...
EB: awkward.
CG: YEAH
CG: WOW, IT IS
EB: yeah...
CG: HUH.
EB: well...
EB: um...
CG: OK, LOOK.
CG: LET'S JUST AGREE TO NEVER BRING IT UP AGAIN.
CG: THE STUFF I WAS BABBLING ABOUT EARLIER.
EB: yeah, well we never really talked about it in the past, so i guess we do agree to that.
CG: BUT IF I TALK TO YOU AGAIN
CG: IN YOUR FUTURE, LIMITED THOUGH IT IS
CG: YOU'LL REMEMBER MY EMBARRASSING SHIT
CG: SO I GUESS
CG: I'LL HAVE TO TROLL YOU BACKWARDS?
EB: told you bro!!!!!!!
EB: hahahaha.
CG: YOU REALLY ARE A SMUG NOOK WHIFFER, JOHN EGBERT.
CG: I THINK WE NEED TO GET BACK ON POINT HERE.
CG: WHICH IS ADDRESSING THE MATTER OF WHAT INCOMPREHENSIBLY PUTRID GARBAGE YOU AND YOUR FRIENDS ARE AND HOW MUCH I HATE YOU.
EB: you mean platonic hate?
CG: SHUT THE FUCK UP, WE AREN'T TALKING ABOUT THAT, REMEMBER.
EB: oh yeah.
CG: SO YOU WANTED TO GET TROLLED, WELL YOU GOT IT.
CG: PREPARE TO GET YOUR PUNY HUMAN BULGE FLAMED INTO NUCLEAR HATEBLIVION.
CG: WELCOME TO THE TROLLOCAUST. THE PAINSTAKING GENOCIDE OF YOUR FRAGILE SELF ESTEEM WILL BE MY SWAN SONG.
EB: oh boy, this sounds great.
EB: but...
EB: we're out of time!
EB: i have to go put this plan into motion.
CG: OH I SEE, TAKING THE COWARD'S WAY OUT.
CG: SCAMPERING OFF TO GET ANNIHILATED BY A DEADLY RIFT, HOW CONVENIENT.
CG: WELL FINE, SAYONARA YOU WORTHLESS CROTCHSTAINED BARFPUPPET.
CG: I WILL BID YOU ONE FIRST AND FINAL FUCK YOU.
CG: FUCK YOU, JOHN EGBERT.
CG: FUCK YOU AND FUCK THE JOKE BOOK YOU RODE IN ON.
CG: FUCK.
CG: FUCKING.
CG: YOU.
EB: :D
EB: see you soon!
CG: WAIT
CG: WHAT

ectoBiologist [EB] ceased pestering carcinoGeneticist [CG]

> Terezi: Open memo.

Everything John is saying here, his whole attitude, and lines like "oh god, the quadrants..." reflect the fact that he clearly knows considerably more about the trolls than he did when we last saw him. In other words, it's almost like he just got done with the onerous process of reading Hivebent, just like we did. And he probably has about the same take on most of that material as we do. In this story, the characters literally never stop behaving as stand-ins for the readers in various ways. This conversation winds down in the fairly predictable manner we've come to expect from Karkat, with his stubborn commitment to ongoing gestures of self-humiliation and outlandish insults. But then there's a curveball at the end. People really got a kick out of John's final line. But "soon," as we're going to gradually learn, is a pretty relative concept. Sometimes you need a lot of patience when waiting for stuff that's coming soon.

CURRENT gallowsCalibrator [CGC] **RIGHT NOW opened memo on board R41NBOW RUMPUS P4RTYTOWN.**

CGC: WH4T DO YOU GUYS TH1NK 4BOUT K4RK4TS N3W PL4N
CGC: TO TROLL TH3S3 K1DS
CGC: P3RSON4LLY 1 TH1NK H3 H4S F1N4LLY SN4PP3D 4ND 1T DO3SNT M4K3 4NY S3NS3
CGC: 1 F1GUR3D M4YB3 W3 COULD T4LK 4BOUT 1T H3R3 1N S3CR3T WH1L3 H3 ST4NDS OV3R TH3R3 M4K1NG H1S BOR1NG 1NSP1R4T1ON4L SP33CH
CGC: 1M PR3TTY SUR3 H3S STOPP3D BOTH3R1NG TO 1NV4D3 P4RTYTOWN, H3 H4S L34RN3D H1S L3SSON >:]
CGC: OBV1OUSLY TH1S 1S JUST FOR US H3R3 1N TH3 PR3S3NT TO R3M4RK ON
CGC: 1F YOU 4R3 FROM TH3 P4ST 4ND 4R3 CUR1OUS 4BOUT TH1S 4ND W4NT TO S4Y SOM3TH1NG YOU W1LL NOT B3 B4NN3D 4S 1S TH3 G3N3R4L RUL3 H3R3
CGC: BUT 1 W1LL POL1T3LY 4SK YOU TO K33P YOUR 1NT3RJ3CT1ONS TO 4 M1N1MUM!
CGC: 1 W1LL H4V3 ORD3R 1N TH1S RUMPUSBLOCK >:D
PAST carcinoGeneticist [PCG] **7 MINUTES AGO responded to memo.**
PCG: YOU THINK I STOPPED KEEPING TABS ON YOUR VAPID, SEDITIOUS BULLSHIT???
PCG: THINK A FUCKING GAIN.
CGC **banned** PCG **from responding to memo.**
CGC: TH3 TOP1C 1S NOW OP3N FOR 4RGUM3NT4T1ON
CGC: *H3R TYR4NNY Y13LDS TH3 FLOOR W1TH 4 M1GHTY B4NG OF H3R G4V3L*
CGC: B4NG B4NG B4NG!
CGC: THR33 M1GHTY B4NGS
CGC: WH4T DO YOU H4V3 TO SUBM1T ON TH3 SUBJ3CT OF K4RK4TS T3NUOUS GR1P ON TH3 T4TT3R3D R3M41NS OF H1S S4N1TY, COUNS3LOR N3P3T4?
CURRENT arsenicCatnip [CAC] **RIGHT NOW responded to memo.**
CAC: :33 < *the especially impurrtant pouncellor looks really serious and thoughtful as she scoots her chair out from under the official courty looking table and begins to pace around thoughtfurry*
CAC: :33 < *she doesnt understand why
CAC: :33 < i dont understand why we are doing this!
CAC: :33 < what was the point again?
CGC: 3XC3LL3NT QU3ST1ON M1SS POUNC3LLOR

PAST carcinoGeneticist 2 [PCG2] **5 MINUTES AGO responded to memo.**
PCG2: ARE YOU FUCKING RETARDED.
PCG2: I CAN PLAINLY SEE YOU ARE GOING TO START WRITING THIS MEMO IN FIVE MINUTES.
PCG2: ALL I HAVE TO DO IS GO MAKE MY "BOR1NG 1NSP1R4T1ON4L SP33CH" AND THEN WALK OVER TO YOUR COMPUTER AND START FUCKING WITH YOU.
PCG2: GO AHEAD, BAN ME ALL YOU WANT.
CGC **banned** PCG2 **from responding to memo.**
CGC: *H3R TYR4NNY 3XPR3SS3S D1SD41NFUL Y3T 4UTHOR4T1V3 1NT3R3ST 1N OTH3R OP1N1ONS ON TH3 STUP1D3ST PL4N 3V3R CONC31V3D*
CGC: 4NY THOUGHTS?
CAC: :33 < i dont s33 why karkat has to always be banned from these memos!
CAC: :33 < what if he promises to behave himself?
CGC: W3 H4V3 B33N OV3R TH1S >:[
CAC: :33 < what if i talk to him in the past and told him he could post here as long as he was not purrticularly disagr33able?
CAC: :33 < thats a good idea! brb
CGC: OH GOD!
PAST carcinoGeneticist 3 [PCG3] **10 MINUTES AGO responded to memo.**
PCG3: THANK YOU NEPETA, FOR ALERTING ME TO THE PRESENCE OF YET MORE OF THIS TAWDRY ROLEPLAY-INFESTED CLOAK AND DAGGER RUBBISH.
PCG3: HOW VERY INTERESTING.
CGC: *H3R TYR4NNY F4C3 P4LMS 1N 4 R34LLY D1GN1F13D 4ND 1NT1M1D4T1NGLY JUD1C14L M4NN3R*
CGC **banned** PCG3 **from responding to memo.**

The R41NBOW RUMPUS P4RTYTOWN is one of the more "Terezi" contributions Terezi has made to the story. Possibly only second to the time she uses her own blood to write instructions that rewrite the whole story to bring Vriska back to life, or when she preemptively convinces herself to dump Karkat before anything even starts. This whole memo is made primarily to troll Karkat, roast him for his own self-important memos, and provide a fun environment everyone likes better—a nice, easy-going space where they can have a good time and do some roleplaying (which is also meant to own Karkat). Also, he's not allowed to post. Of course, if Terezi *really* knew what was going on, she wouldn't have to work that hard to own him at all about his plan to troll the humans. She could just keep mercilessly pointing out that the only reason he wants to do it at all is because he has a hate-crush on the nerdy human boy.

CGC: *TH3 D1ST1NGU1SH3D POUNC3LLOR R3C31V3S 4 HUNDR3D B1LL1ON RUMPUS D3M3R1TS FOR 1NV1T1NG UNCOUTH R4BBL3 1NTO H3R ORD3RLY BLOCK*
CAC: :33 < :((
CURRENT twinArmageddons [CTA] **RIGHT NOW responded to memo.**
CTA: ii already told KK what ii thought about thii2 awful iidea.
CTA: iit ju2t make2 NO 2en2e, you can count me out.
CTA: you all can troll the2e iincompetent aliien2 all you want, iit won't change anythiing.
CTA: ii'll ju2t be over here waiitiing two diie wiith diigniity, ok well maybe iit'2 two late for that, but ju2t diie ii gue22, and y'all can 2uck iit biitche2.
CGC: TH3 M4G1STR4T3 FROM TH3 D3L1C1OUS 4PPL3B3RRY JUR1SD1CT1ON M4K3S 4N 3XC3LL3NT PO1NT 4BOUT TH3 OV3R4LL SH1TT1N3SS OF TH3 PROPOS1T1ON
CGC: 4ND 4BOUT M4N4G1NG TO B3 4N 3V3N GRUMP13R P41N 1N TH3 4SS TH4N OUR F34RL3SS L34D3R SOM3HOW
CTA: ii don't get why you're RP'iing about thii2, iit doe2n't make 2en2e, you're all out of your fuckiing 2ponge2.
CTA: why don't you ju2t u2e our name2.
CGC: >:O
CGC **banned** CTA **from responding to memo.**
CGC **unbanned** CTA **from responding to memo.**
CGC: OK SORRY 4BOUT TH4T
CGC: THOLLLLUUUUUUXXXXTHHHH
CGC: TH3R3 4R3 YOU H4PPY
CTA: whatever.
PAST carcinoGeneticist 4 [PCG4] **4 MINUTES AGO responded to memo.**
PCG4: YOU BASTARD, IS IT REALLY SO MUCH TO ASK TO TAKE A FEW TOOLS OUT BEHIND THE GRUBSHED.
PCG4: ALL I'M ASKING YOU TO DO IS HASSLE SOME ALIENS, GOD.
PCG4: AFTER ALL THOSE TIMES I SAVED YOUR LIFE YOU THINK YOU COULD DO ME ONE LITTLE SOLID.
CTA: yeah after you got me kiilled iin the fiir2t place.
PCG4: HOW CAN YOU THROW THAT IN MY FACE AGAIN, I THOUGHT WE WERE COOL.
CTA: ii 2aiid whatever.
CGC: UUUGH
CGC **banned** PCG4 **from responding to memo.**
CURRENT apocalypseArisen [CAA] RIGHT NOW responded to memo.
CAA: i will n0t be participating
CAA ceased responding to memo.
PAST carcinoGeneticist 5 [PCG5] **3 MINUTES AGO responded to memo.**
PCG5: OH MY GOD, WHAT ARE WE GOING TO DO NOW.
PCG5: THAT'S IT GUYS, THE PLAN IS CANCELED.
PCG5: ARADIA ISN'T GOING TO MOPE AT THESE LOSERS FOR US, THE WHOLE PLAN HINGED ON THAT.
CGC **banned** PCG5 **from responding to memo.**
CURRENT cuttlefishCuller [CCC] RIGHT NOW responded to memo.
CCC: I still don't quite understand t)(e plan eit)(er.
CCC: I mean, I don't really mind talking to t)(em! It could be fun and t)(ey look interesting.
CCC: But I really don't t)(ink t)(is is all t)(eir fault.
CCC: Can't we say nice t)(ings to t)(em instead of troll t)(em?
CCC: Maybe even)(-ELP t)(em! 38)
PAST carcinoGeneticist 6 [PCG6] **2 MINUTES AGO responded to memo.**
PCG6: NO, FUCK.
PCG6: YOU CAN'T BE NICE TO THEM.
PCG6: YOU ARE COMPLETELY MISSING THE GLUBBING POINT, FISH PRINCESS.
CGC **banned** PCG6 **from responding to memo.**
PAST carcinoGeneticist 7 [PCG7] **2 MINUTES AGO responded to memo.**
PCG7: HEY TEREZI I'M ABOUT TO MAKE THIS AWESOME SPEECH AND INSPIRE THE FUCK OUT OF YOU GUYS.
PCG7: WHEN I'M DONE I'M COMING OVER TO YOUR STATION AND THEN YOUR ASS IS MINE.
PCG7: ENJOY THIS GARBAGE DUMP OF A MEMO WHILE IT LASTS.
CGC: BL444444R >XO
CGC **banned** PCG7 **from responding to memo.**
CGC: TH1S 1S WHY W3 C4NT H4V3 N1C3 TH1NGS
CGC: 1M T3MPT3D TO CLOS3 TH1S M3MO NOW >:\
CGC: 1F 4NYON3 H4S 4NYTH1NG TO S4Y S4Y 1T QU1CK!
PAST carcinoGeneticist 8 [PCG8] **2 MINUTES AGO responded to memo.**
CGC **banned** PCG8 **from responding to memo.**
CGC: NOT YOU
PAST terminallyCapricious [PTC] 420 HOURS AGO

Even though the trolls are at the end of their adventure, the attitude of everyone under Karkat's leadership is pretty much the same as it was when they began: much skepticism and ridicule surrounding his orders, with no one particularly inclined to take him all that seriously. Maybe it's because they're just used to acting this way by now. But the deeper reason is that all of Karkat's orders, everything he insists on as being "urgent," revolve around some unwitting need to serve his own objectives rather than something that serves everyone's needs in a clear way. At the beginning, he was desperately trying to pull the team together to play *Sgrub*, but mainly so he could prove himself as a great leader and a ruthless warrior. Here he's trying to get everyone on board with harassing some alien kids they don't know, basically for some combination of satisfying his own petty grievances and wanting an excuse to hate-crush on John some more. So when everyone's response to his "plan" is some variation on "Dude, this makes no sense at all," it's because...it doesn't.

responded to memo.
PTC: YeAh iM NoT FoLlOwInG ThIs mOtHeRfUcKiN PlAn uP At aLl
PTC: wHo aRe wE TrOlLiNg
CGC: G4MZ33 TH1S CONV3RS4T1ON 1S T4K1NG PL4C3 W33KS 1N TH3 FUTUR3
CGC: 1T DO3S NOT CONC3RN YOU!
PTC: oH
PTC: WeLl mOtHeR FuCk i gUeSs
CGC: DONT WORRY 4BOUT 1T >:P
CGC: JUST SCROLL 4ROUND 4ND LOOK FOR ON3 OF TH3 RRPT OP3N CH4T M3MOS
PTC: oKaY
PTC: HoNk :o)
CGC: LKSD;GDKNLN
CGC: ASDM SDFSFD9W30
CGC: DFD;
CGC: GH
CGC: EUHFHSDKLNVSDJKLSJKBSDJKF
PTC: wHoA
CGC: K4RK4T IS M4SHING MY K3YBOSDVFDNFLBLGBGSDGFSB['A
CGC: AKJFA
CGC: SEUFHWEUIONDN
CGC: AUIHDF
CGC: SDSAD
CGC: 4444UGH H3 1S SUCH 4 L1TTL3SDKJGBSDJKBG
CGC banned herself from responding to memo.
CGC unbanned herself from responding to memo.
CGC banned herself from responding to memo.
CGC unbanned herself from responding to memo.
CGC banned herself from responding to memo.
CGC unbanned herself from responding to memo.
CGC: FUUUUUUUUCK!!!!!
CURRENT carcinoGeneticist [CCG] RIGHT NOW responded to memo.
CCG: OH NOW WHAT'S UP???????????
CGC: GOD D4MM1T H3 LOGG3D ON TO MY COMPURO3IHHGRNVNFSDKS'SD
CGC: 4ND H3S ST1LL M4SH1NG M3!!! >:[
CGC: SDKLFSDK FHS
CGC: YUGUFY
CGC: G3T OFF!!!!!!!!!SFBSDJB
CGC banned herself from responding to memo.
CGC unbanned herself from responding to memo.
CGC banned herself from responding to memo.
CGC unbanned herself from responding to memo.
CCG: WHY ARE YOU BANNING YOURSELF TEREZI????
CCG: PRETTY FUCKING MENTAL IF YOU ASK ME.
CCG: REALLY FUCKED UP OF YOFDIHFNGNJKGLJS
CCG: ASKJSKF89UG
CCG: YDRHHGH
CCG: WEFOWEGWLKNGNIOV
CCG: SDIJS
CCG banned himself from responding to memo.
CCG unbanned himself from responding to memo.
CGC banned CCG from responding to memo.
CCG unbanned himself from responding to memo.
CCG banned CGC from responding to memo.
CGC unbanned herself from responding to memo.
CGC banned herself from responding to memo.
CGC unbanned herself from responding to memo.
CCG banned CGC from responding to memo.
CCG unbanned CGC from responding to memo.
CGC banned CCG from responding to memo.
CGC unbanned CCG from responding to memo.
CCG banned himself from responding to memo.
CGC banned herself from responding to memo.
CGC unbanned herself from responding to memo.
CCG unbanned himself from responding to memo.
CCG: OK QUIT THADJKNFSDK
CCG: FUCK OW GOD DAMFFJKSNFBGB
CCG: OW!!!!! FUCKALKLKDNJJV
CGC: 1 4M GO1NG TO SH4RP3N YOUR STUP1D LOOK1NG NUBBY HORNS 1N YOUR SL33P!!!
CGC: TH3N TH4TS WH4T W1LL B3 UP, BY3 BY3 NUBS
CCG: WHY DON'T YOU JUST FILE THEM ALL THE WAY DOWN.
CCG: SINCE YOU'RE RUNNING OUT OF WAYS TO EMASCULATE ME IN FRONT OF MY TEAM.
CGC: W1LL YOU G1V3 YOUR BOR1NG L34D3R COMPL3X 4 R3ST FOR ONC3
CGC: 1TS G3TT1NG SO OLD!
CURRENT arachnidsGrip [CAG] RIGHT NOW responded to memo.
CAG: Hahahahahahahaha!!!!!!!!
CAG: You are 8oth ridiculous.
CCG: HEY VRISKA, YOU'RE DOWN WITH MY TROLLING PLAN.
CCG: WHY DON'T YOU TELL EVERYONE IN RAINBOW ASSGRAB JUNCTION WHAT A GREAT IDEA IT IS.
CAG: I'm 8usy.
CCG: WHAT THE FUCK COULD YOU BE BUSY WITH???
CAG: I'm making my own plans! I'm a pretty 8ig

Terezi tells a confused Gamzee from weeks ago to go peruse other memos. Perhaps ones that get started on the meteor in the future? Ones written during more fraught and suspenseful circumstances than this? How much advance reading has Gamzee been doing? How much studying? Planning? Biding his time? Makes you wonder, is all I'm saying. But it doesn't make you wonder too much, because we quickly get distracted by about 500 consecutive lines of Karkat and Terezi banning each other as they fight over the same keyboard. In the last book, I told you we would be reaping great rewards from these memos. I would never lie to you. Not ever, about anything. I would never risk jeopardizing this special bond of trust we have.

deal, remem8er Karkat?
CGC: 1T LOOKS L1K3 YOU FORGOT HOW M4NY 1RONS SH3 H4S 1N TH3 F1R3
CAG: Exactly!
CCG: WHAT IS SO HARD ABOUT GOING ALONG WITH MY SIMPLE PLAN TO SERVE A FEW PINK SKINNED DOUCHE BAGS A PIPING HOT NUTRITION PLATEAU FULL OF FUCK YOU.
CGC: M4YB3 W3 W1LL BUT W3 4LL JUST K1ND OF W4NT TO DO OUR OWN TH1NG!
CCG: THERE IS A WORD FOR THAT, IT IS CALLED GROSS INSUBORDINATION.
CGC: TH4TS TWO WORDS R3T4RD >:P
CAG: Do you guys realize you are sharing a key8oard and taking turns to argue with each other?
CAG: That is kind of cute. ::::)
CTA: yeah ii hate to 2ay iit, but iit really 2ort of ii2.
CCG: OK FUCK THIS.
CCG: EVERYONE IS OFFICIALLY BANNED FROM THIS TRAIN WRECK.
CCG **banned CAG from responding to memo.**
CCG **banned PTC from responding to memo.**
CCG **banned CCC from responding to memo.**
CCG **banned CAA from responding to memo.**
CCG **banned** CTA **from responding to memo.**
CCG **banned** CAC **from responding to memo.**
CCG **banned** CGC **from responding to memo.**
CCG **unbanned** CGC **from responding to memo.**
CCG: YOU C4N'T B4N M3 FROM MY OWN M3MO!
CCG: WHOOPS >:[
CGC: YOU C4N'T B4N M3 FROM MY OWN M3MO!
CGC: LOOKS LIKE I JUST DID.
CGC: SHIT. D:B
CCG: LOOKS LIKE I JUST DID.
CGC: F1N3 1 W1LL JUST SHUT TH3 M3MO DOWN
CGC: SO YOU W1LL G3T TH3 H3LL OUT OF H3R3!
CCG: FINE, I'M GONE.
CCG **banned himself from responding to memo.**
CGC: UUUUUUUUUUUGH
FUTURE gallowsCalibrator [FGC] **6:12 HOURS FROM NOW responded to memo.**
FGC: H3Y!
CGC: OH H3Y!
FGC: 1 JUST THOUGHT 1 WOULD 4DD ON3 L4ST R3M4RK TO TH1S S1LL1N3SS
FGC: 4 R3M4RK OF R34SSUR4NC3!
CGC: OHH >:?
FGC: Y3S, YOU SHOULD TROLL TH3 HUM4NS
FGC: 1T W1LL B3 FUN >:]
CGC: W3LL, W3 BOTH KNOW TH4T 1 W4S PL4NN1NG TO 4NYW4Y
FGC: OF COURS3! 1 TRUST YOUR JUDGM3NT ON TH3 M4TT3R
FGC: JUST H3R3 TO S4Y YOU WONT R3GR3T 1T
CGC: TH4T 1S N1C3 TO KNOW!
CGC: 1 TRUST YOUR JUDGM3NT 4S W3LL
FGC: Y3S!
FGC: 4NOTH3R TR1UMPH OF SOUND JUDGM3NT 4ND GOOD T1M3S FOR T34M PYROP3 4ND TH3 LOY4L SUBSCR1B3RS OF R41NBOW RUMPUS P4RTYTOWN
CGC: HOOR4Y! >:D
FUTURE carcinoGeneticist [FCG] **6:12 HOURS FROM NOW responded to memo.**
FCG: I'M GOING TO BE FUCKING SICK.
CGC **banned** FCG **from responding to memo.**

CGC closed memo.

~~~~~~

> John: Land already.

They have a point here. While it's funny to see the results of their keyboard mashing and mutual banning warfare in the form of the resulting memo text, we don't really get to see them do all this. We can only imagine what it looks like. So we also have to picture them typing these entire statements to each other on the same keyboard. And there's no way that can possibly work unless they take turns, where one troll waits patiently while the other is composing a testy remark to the other, right in front of them. It's a completely absurd way to have an argument. It probably also qualifies as another log on the Karezi fire, for those keeping score at home. It's important to keep score of all those logs. That way, you'll know the precise quantity of precious shipping lumber that gets erased from history once I retcon-shitcan their entire relationship off the website.
~~~~~~

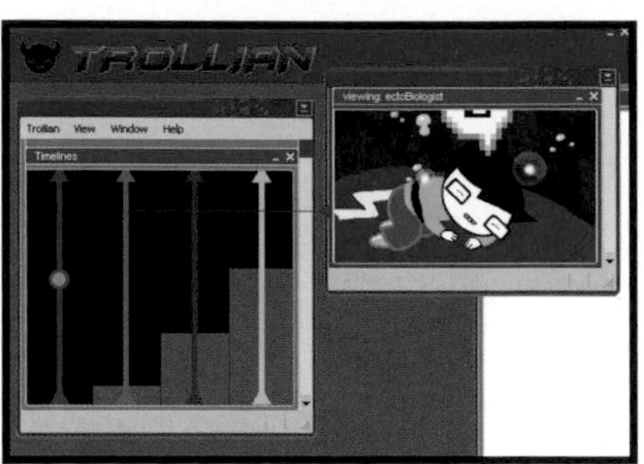

> Vriska: Manipul8 this worthless human.

Okay, time to cut the baloney. This here is the real purpose of all that Hivebent nonsense. After **[S] Descend**, instead of just getting to the damn point, we had to go through a very long backstory sequence. And I may say a lot of stuff about a lot of things, but if you need one guiding principle to simplify everything for you, just remember this: everything boils down to Vriska in the end. We needed to cut away and do a huge backstory song and dance just so we could establish the alien setting in which Vriska exists, so we could introduce Vriska and bring her into the story. Then, once all that was said and done, only one question remained, and only one question mattered: How does Vriska fit into all this? What does Vriska think of these human kids? How is she messing with them? That's the important stuff. Even before Hivebent, we could tell already that Karkat was completely useless and full of hot air. But Vriska? Wow. We know a lot about her now. We know she's a striking combination of being extremely dangerous and extremely effective. This should be good, right? Of course it's going to be good. We know this because we just learned the golden rule of *Homestuck*: everything boils down to Vriska in the end.

It is no use. It seems your abilities cannot cross between sessions. Or cannot influence his species. Or both.

Or MAYBE you just aren't TRYING HARD ENOUGH.

You wonder what this goofball is dreaming about. Too bad these stupid viewports can't see into dreams. This software SUCKS!!!!!!!!

The answer to "How does Vriska fit into all this?" should have been obvious. Of course she's going to latch onto the most "important" character, which is John. Why would she settle for anything less? If her fate becomes inseparably entwined with John's, that guarantees she gets to be important. And since all their correspondence is so mixed up with predestination due to their nonlinear chatting methods, she's basically trapped Paradox Space into making sure she stays important throughout the entire remainder of the human session. We quickly see that her attachment to John starts bordering on obsessive for these reasons. In fact, she hardly ever talks to the other kids and seems to have a noticeable disdain for the very idea of even bothering to interact with them. She even uses one of them as a guinea pig to test her psychic abilities on, which SURE DOES retroactively explain the sporadic sleeping habits of the character in question.

> John: Reunite with your loving father, and also scarf lady.

> Vriska: Try harder.

Content Warning: Entering Sadstuck Zone. Sometimes it's easy to lose track of one small piece of John's arc, which is basically the "poignant quest to reunite with Dad." When John entered the Medium, his dad quickly went missing, and I think this set up the expectation that the search for Dad would be an integral part of John's journey. It's only a minor refrain though, and as the story goes on, it becomes less about legitimate reunification with his father and more about presenting his father as a figure that keeps receding into the distance, further and further out of John's reach. Which culminates in Dad's death, and visions of his ghost staying tantalizingly beyond John's ability to engage with. The guardians are presented more like parental abstractions than real people, and this partly means they symbolize some idealized form of the parent-child relationship, as well as the previous life that embodies for the kids. Or in other words, they symbolize childhood itself. Abstract, authority figure-like touchstones for the life of innocence the kids can never return to, which only seems to get further away from them whenever they try.

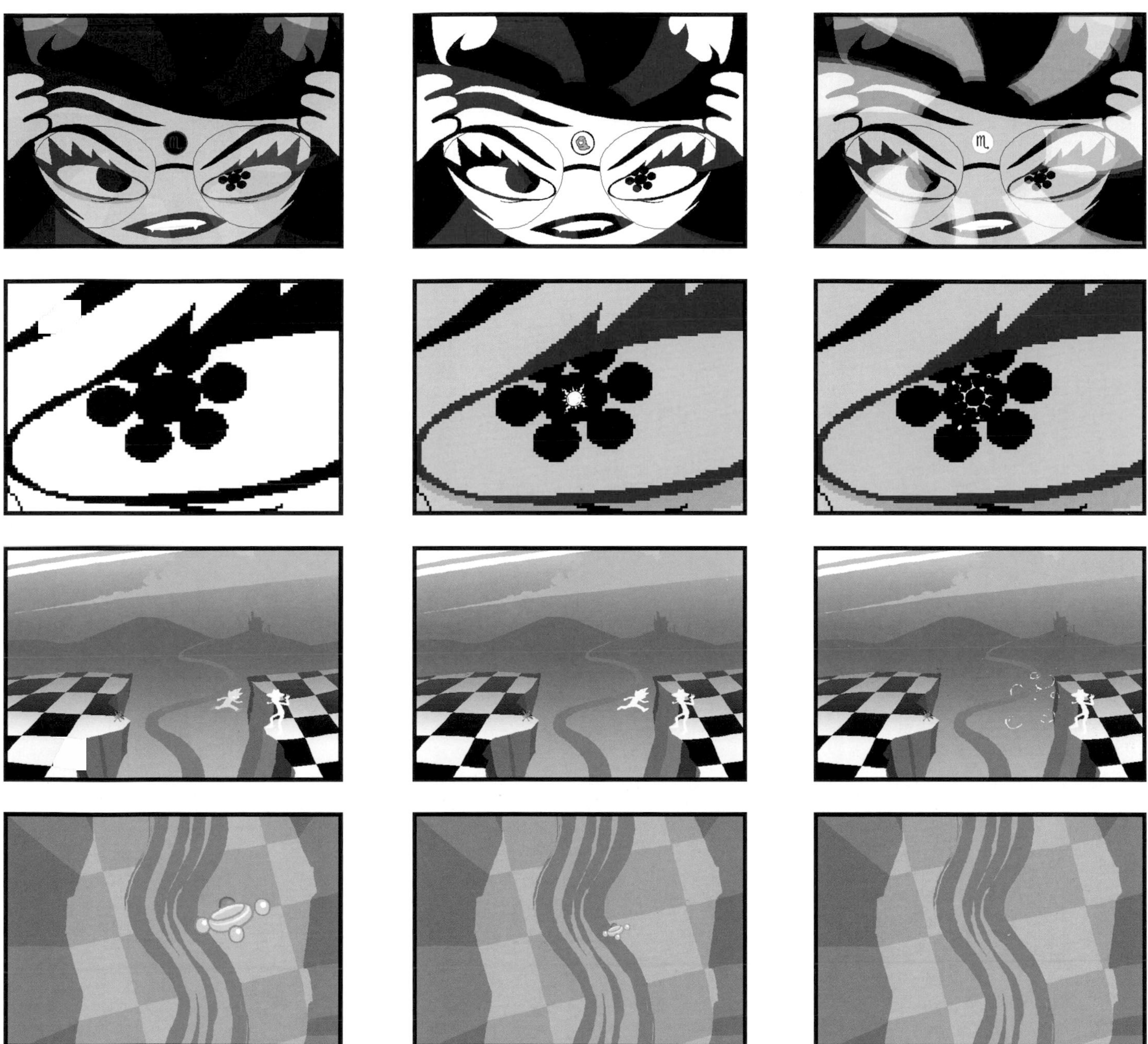

So, looking at it that way, John's striving to reunite with Dad is less about his relationship with a specific person he cares about, and more about clinging to the simpler and joyful times of his childhood. In fact, Dad hardly *is* a specific person. He's an explicitly faceless, stylistic expression of a certain platonic ideal of Fatherliness, easily recognized as such by the culture he grew up in. John plays it cool through a lot of adversity and trauma, but his great desire to reunite with his dad shows how much he misses the peaceful life of childhood, and how alarmed he feels by his sudden departure into this life of uncertainty and danger. It's one of his few tells, a window into heavily masked trauma. Even when he finally reunites with his dad in the end, it's not actually his specific dad. It's Jane's peculiar doppeldad. Any dad will do, when Dad himself is an intrinsically nonspecific entity. John's not reuniting with his father in that case, he's reuniting with the IDEA of a father. The idea of a comfort and peace long left behind, which maybe can begin to be restored in some sense through their victory.

> John: Answer troll.

It seems Roxy Lalonde has been biding her time for many years. And now she finally makes her move. These two are abstract parental figures, but from another angle, they're also real people who lived lives and had feelings about stuff. I think Mom is signaling an implied understanding of what's going on here, from both her perspective as a parent and on a certain metatextual level. He did his job as a father. She did her job as a mother. They brought their kids here, got them this far, and now it's time to let them go. Why not let loose a little? The Battlefield in a way is like their retirement home in Florida.

arachnidsGrip [AG] began trolling ectoBiologist [EB]

AG: Joooooooo
AG: oooooooo
AG: oooooooo
AG: oooooooo
AG: oooooooo
AG: oooooooo
AG: oooooooo
AG: ooooooooohn!
AG: W8ke up!!!!!!!!
EB: heheh. i am pronouncing that like a really long "june".
EB: that is so many o's.
AG: It is 8ight groups of 8ight. I specifically counted them.
AG: It's sort of a thing I do.
EB: you typed my name in 64 bit.
AG: Wow. What a nerd!
EB: have i talked to you before?
AG: Um, possi8ly? This is the first time I have contacted you that I am aware of.
EB: i'm pretty sure i remember you. you hassled me a long time ago.
EB: i think you threatened to kill me at some point.
AG: John, give me a 8r8k! That was o8viously just my way of getting to know you.
AG: Or it will 8e, whenever I get around to it.
EB: well, yeah, i know that about you guys by now.
EB: but also i know that it is probably not exactly an empty threat!
EB: since one of you already managed to trick me into getting myself killed.
EB: well, in another timeline at least.
AG: Man.
AG: That was pro8a8ly Terezi! I should have known she would pull something like that. What a meddler.
EB: terezi?
AG: Yes. The pesky 8lind troll who licks her monitor and smells words and stuff. The one who got you killed. I'm sure of it!
EB: huh. it never really occurred to me to ask what your names are.

EB: kinda rude of me!
EB: what is yours?
AG: Marquise Spinneret Mindfang. ::::)
EB: man, that sounds so made up!
EB: but if you say so, marquise.
AG: Spinneret! Marquise is a title, stupid.
EB: oh, ok.
AG: And you don't have to worry a8out me manipul8ting you to your death!
AG: It is completely 8eneath me. Unlike her, I plan on taking the high road.
AG: You see John, you and I actually have some things in common, 8ut you couldn't possi8ly understand why yet.
AG: So I'm planning on helping you!
EB: ok, i will be sure to let my guard down.
EB: psyche!!!!!!!!!
EB: oh damn, that was 9 !'s.
EB: !!!!!!!1
EB: shit!
EB: never mind.
AG: Hahahahahahahaha.
EB: anyway, nice meeting you spinneret.
EB: if you don't mind, i would like to try to go back to sleep.
EB: i was dreaming about something important.
AG: You can't sleep now, John!
AG: What a8out J8de????????
EB: oh god, i forgot!
EB: poor jade... :(
EB: i hope she is alright.

The way Vriska introduces herself to John says everything about her, and about their relationship, and really, her relationship with everyone. She forcefully interrupts a moment that is deeply important and emotional to him, thereby probably denying that opportunity from ever happening again, just so she can insert herself into his life and force him to pay attention to her. Now here she is again, being kind of rude (e.g. calling him stupid), but more than that, being vaguely obsequious overall, which is something about her I was harping on in the last book. Vriska cozies up to certain kinds of people, namely those she wants something from or feels will elevate her status by association. John's the perfect mark for the manipulative, ass-kissing games she plays.

AG: She's fine. I can see her right now!
AG: 8ut she will not 8e for long if you don't get her into your session.
EB: yeah, you're right.
EB: i have to hurry and go save her!
EB: see ya!
AG: Wait!!!!!!!!
AG: Where the hell do you think you're going to go? You don't even have your copy of the game yet!
EB: oh yeah...
EB: duh, stupid stupid dumb.
EB: do you know where i am supposed to get it?
AG: Easy! Just w8 around for a few minutes.
EB: hmm...
EB: ok?
AG: See, John? You need me to advance.
AG: Even though you were going to do this stuff anyway, it turns out I am the reason you were going to do it anyway in the first place!
AG: Your timeline is my we8, and suddenly you are all tangled up in it, wriggling and helpless.
AG: Isn't that cooooooool????????
EB: meh.
EB: so, you seem to like 8's a whole bunch, and i guess you are like, kind of spidery themed or something?
AG: Yeah!
EB: haha, spiders are gross!
AG: Fuck you!!!!!!!!

> John: W8 around for a few minutes.

Since we're in the Vriska Zone now and forever, I'll just keep talking about her. It bears more examination of how her manipulation strategy seems to deftly blend ass-kissing and aggression. Successfully manipulative, sociopathically charismatic people tend to have this balance down to a science. The strategy seems to involve controlling the interplay between flattery, appealing to common interests, charming or flirtatious rhetoric, and little jabs, negs, or outright insults to keep the target off-balance. The target gets sort of hooked by the fascinating spectacle, intrigued, and strangely disarmed. Too much flattery results in suspicion, too much negativity is a turn-off (or taken to an extreme like Karkat, results in not being taken seriously at all). The barbs mixed in with the flattery are effective because they lead the target to think, "If this person really wants something from me, why would they insult me?" Of course, this is how pick-up artists operate, which isn't far off from Vriska's mindset when pursuing her goals—which, although more broad than romantic goals, are still mixed in with them, with the end result being part of the overall power play. Over the course of her tactics focused on John to make herself more relevant, when actual romantic designs start seeping into the fabric of her manipulation campaign, that's when it all starts to get...A Little Bit Weird.

You got the server copy of the SBURB BETA!

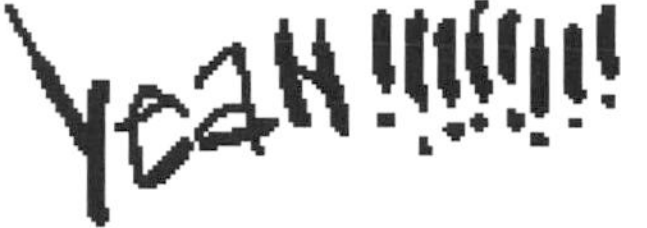

> Jade: Land already.

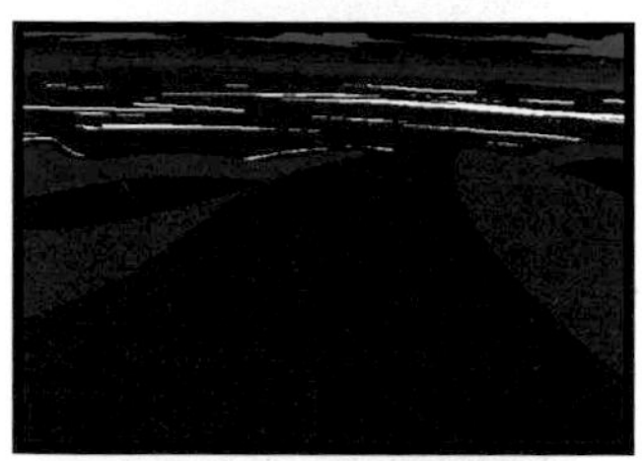

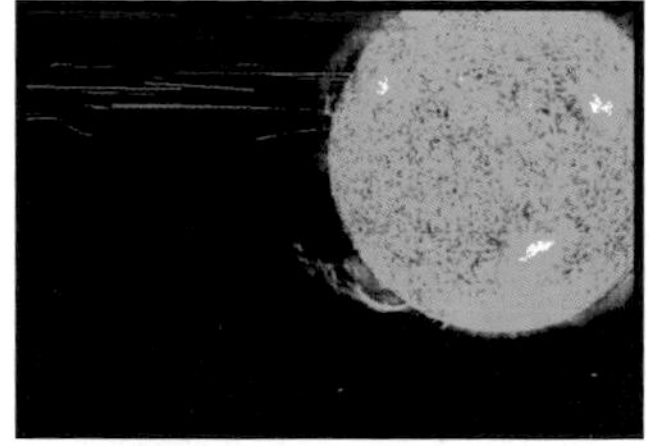

We've already seen a lot of Vriska's tactics on display in Hivebent, with mixed results. By now she's had a lot of practice, and she's bringing all her skills to bear on the perfect rube for her schemes, this nerdy, gullible Egbert kid. The romantic angle that surfaces from this effort, as I just implied, is vaguely troubling. How else to describe it...? Icky, maybe? Something is off about it, and we feel that more than John does, obviously because we know a lot more about her than he does. For Vriska, are the romantic desires real? Is she such a mess inside that she wouldn't be able to tell whether the feelings are genuine or not? It's more likely that it's all about the ego boost, the power trip involved with grooming this hapless fool into the thing she wants him to be, and hoodwinking him into feeling something for her. But for him, it's probably more sincere. His first awkward experience with romance, albeit one contrived by a manipulator. Too bad he has no idea that none of this even has anything to do with him. It's still just about Vriska's gamesmanship with Terezi, who is another person exhibiting many of the aforementioned qualities of a manipulator. Terezi just uses hers to target a different boy. Both are highly successful with their boywork, but they take very different approaches.

> WV?: Survey casualties.

Everyone is dead.

Everyone except you.

[S] Descend left Jade's plot thread in a state of suspense, with her plummeting through the air after her dreambot exploded due to the death of her dream self. The resolution wasn't that surprising though: Bec just mask-zapped her bed under her to break her fall. We've already seen him use this ability to protect Jade, or otherwise herd her to where she needs to be, like a sort of sheep dog. First Guardians are said to protect the planets they inhabit, but that's a bit of an oversimplification. They mainly protect the apparatus that is needed to begin the *Sburb* session and complete all the time loops leading to their arrival on the planet in the first place. This also means protecting the players of the session before they enter. It turns out the guardians have no qualms about sacrificing the well-being of the planet if it helps them achieve their primary objective. (Consider how unconcerned Doc is with Alternia's fate as he's doing what he needs to do.) Similarly, when the time comes, Bec doesn't hesitate to throw the planet under the bus when it's time to help Jade enter.

Your RAG OF SOULS begins to soak in the BLOOD OF THE FALLEN. You suppose it could be poetic?

No, instead you think it is just sad.

You were very foolish to believe you could be a leader of men. Look at what bearing that flag has wrought.

Perhaps one day you will find something new to bear. A burden befitting of the peasant you truly are.

Oh my what's that shiny thing in the water.

> John: Prepare for flight.

EB: jade is not answering!
EB: are you sure she's ok?
AG: She's asleep!
AG: She sure seems to sleep a lot. She sort of reminds me of my goo8er teamm8.
AG: He napped through most of the adventure, and was practically useless.
EB: oh...
EB: you mean carcino geneticist?
AG: Hahahaha, no way! Karkat is so up tight, he hardly slept a wink over the whole 600 hour span of our quest.
AG: He didn't even wake up on the moon until AFTER we won the game, hahahahahahahaha.
AG: What a loser.
EB: heheh. car cat. that is how i am saying that.
EB: beep beep, meow!
EB: i will have to remember to give him a hard time about that.
AG: John, you are pretty weird! I can see why you would piss him off so much.
EB: it is really not hard to do that.
AG: Tell me a8out it!
AG: Speaking of telling me a8out things...
AG: Why don't you tell me what you were just

dreaming a8out that was so important, fellow Prospit dreamer????????
AG: Prospit is the 8est. Derse is where all the rejects hang out. Am I right?
EB: i never even saw prospit.
EB: aside from flaming bits and pieces of it i guess.
EB: something happened, and it blew up, and dream jade died, and then i was wandering around this place that was like a chess board with a huge

Considering that Vriska originally wanted to be on the blue team (Derse) and felt bitterly betrayed when it turned out that was never the plan, she sure came around to feeling the Prospit Pride. She probably doesn't even have any real opinions on which one is better. The one that's better is whichever one she ended up on. Just like in her upcoming boy-manipulation contest with Terezi, she probably doesn't have a real opinion on whether John is better than Dave. She only thinks John is better because that's the horse she bet on. The rule is simple: the best team or affiliation of any sort is always the one most closely associated with Vriska. I know this is the rule I live by, and you should too.

crater in it, with loads of dead black and white guys everywhere.
AG: Yes, I know all that! That place is the 8attlefield, which is where your dream self lives now. You will appear there any time you go to sleep.
AG: Prospit dreamers are supposed to end up there eventually. If they're any good, that is. ::::)
AG: 8ut you got there so much sooner. Normally a dreamer's journey to the 8attlefield will not 8e so spectacularly sudden and violent. Meteoric, if you will!
EB: oh, huh.
AG: 8ut you didn't answer my question! What was so important that you wanted to go 8ack to sleep again for?
EB: my dad was there.
AG: What's that?
EB: um, you know...
EB: my guardian?
AG: Oh, you mean the adult male human who lived in your hive?
EB: yes. if by hive you mean house.
AG: Haha, I was wondering a8out that. I was like, what the hell is this guy doing in this kid's hive? Where is his lusus? Is he an orphan contending with some sort of meddlesome grownup squatter????????
EB: um...
EB: these observations are very alien of you.
EB: but that's pretty cool i guess, seeing as you are an alien.
AG: Yes, I just chalked it up as generic alien weirdness and didn't think too much a8out it. Just another series of strange exhi8its from an inferior civiliz8tion.
EB: the funny thing is, he is not even really my dad.
EB: i mean, i was adopted by him, although we are not actually unrelated, i think.
EB: he is the son of my grandmother, who isn't really my grandmother...
EB: nanna is sort of like my biological mother, and my biological father would be jade's grandpa, sorta.
EB: both of which i just created, with slime and stuff, and sent back in time as babies.
EB: so i guess, if anything, that makes my dad...
EB: my half brother???
AG: ::::\
EB: tell me about it!

When we met a few trolls in Act 4, they were mysterious kids who knew a lot more about this game than our heroes, figures who could serve as cantankerous guides and foul-mouthed sources of exposition when the narrative needed to expand everyone's understanding of the situation. Karkat was the one mostly playing that role. But now that we've gone through all the material introducing Vriska and showing her trying to get to know John, it looks like she's the one stepping into that role instead, continuing to help pad out our understanding of the story and confirm various details and points of lore—to some extent, she's playing the role of an ambassador in an alien cultural exchange. Unlike when Karkat was ranting in Act 4, we actually know a lot about troll culture now. Watching the clash between the kids and trolls in their understandings of society and what it means to grow up is going to be a big part of the narrative from now on. The Vriska/John dialogues are probably at the forefront of this cultural exchange, since Vriska's objective is to try to genuinely connect with him and win him over.

AG: W8! 8efore you wander too far off course like a doofus, you need to know how to get to a return node!
AG: So you can get 8ack to your computer. Here, hang on, I am making you a map.
EB: but i know where i'm going!
EB: terezi already made me a map.
AG: What!!!!!!!!
EB: first she made a really crappy one, then a really nice one that works kind of like google.
EB: she started helping me after she tried to kill me.
AG: Ugh. She is still trying to one up me I see. Even preempting my awesome helpfulness!
AG: When did she do that? I mean from my perspective? Do you think she already did it, or hasn't done it yet?
EB: wow, how could i possibly know that!
AG: I don't know. Forget it.
AG: I will show her though. I will show her the meaning of helpfulness.
AG: I will help this little human nerd under the ta8le. The very same ta8le you dined at, while I w8ted on you prong and fucking nu8.
EB: you mean like a candle light hate date?
AG: God, no!!!!!!!! With a human? Gross.
EB: oh...
EB: well then, thanks, i guess?
EB: why do you want to be so helpful, anyway?
EB: i mean, with her i got the sense she was being kind of jokestery about it, which is something i can understand.
EB: but why bother helping, if we aren't going to win anyway?
AG: You won't win? Says who?????????
EB: you guys.
EB: it is practically all you ever say.
AG: Well, ok yes, you are screwed. And so are we.
AG: 8ut so what!
AG: Just 8ecause you are going to fail doesn't mean it won't 8e any fun along the way!
AG: 8y the looks of things, you have a very exciting 24 hours ahead of you.
AG: It'll 8e one hell of a reckoning!

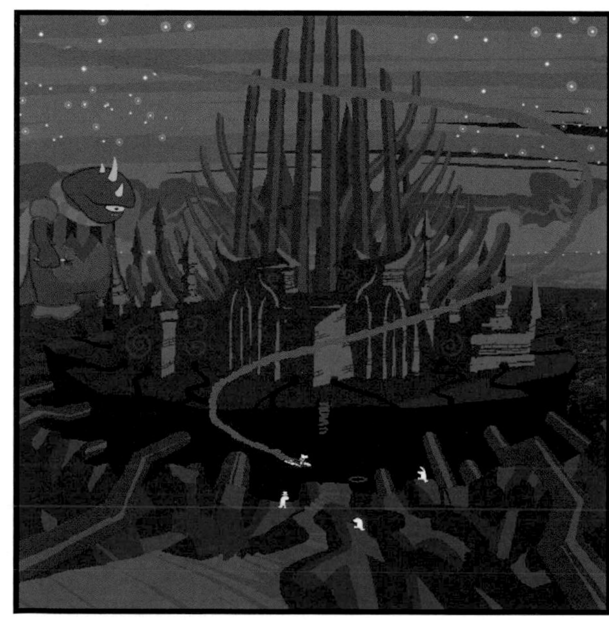

The fact that Vriska's attempting to genuinely form a connection with John, even if it's for cynical purposes, means that some of these exchanges on their cultural differences will actually get pretty sincere, at least by her standards. This allows her to open up on some deeply rooted stuff that shaped her brutal upbringing. When she starts getting more real with him about her issues, it starts blurring the line on whether their romantic entanglement is just a means to an end for her or something grounded in mutual feelings between them. Very confused feelings, but maybe legit nonetheless, regardless of her original intentions. John is someone who appreciates sincere communication, no matter who it's with. Vriska is someone who never had a sympathetic listener, a person to talk to who wouldn't also regard her upbringing as "culturally normal." There's a nexus of mutual sympathy here. That stuff all takes shape later in Act 5, though. All that's going on here right now is that Vriska's starting to catch wind of Terezi's competitive meddling. Which wasn't even competitive until Vriska heard Terezi was doing it and decided to MAKE it competitive.

EB: that is nice to know.
AG: Yes, and 8esides. Continuing on this path and 8ringing Jade into the game I think you will agree is very important!
AG: And not just 8ecause she is your friend and you would 8e kind of upset if she died.
AG: Again.
EB: yes, i think i would be.
EB: but why else?
AG: 8ecause you need to complete your prototyping chain!
AG: Only when all players have entered with a prototyped kernel does the 8attlefield assume its final form.
AG: That form prepares Skaia to grow the new universe you will cre8te.
AG: Or in this case, fail to cre8te. 8ut whatever!
AG: That is no reason to deter you from completing worthwhile game o8jectives.
EB: we are supposed to create a universe?
AG: Yeah! You didn't realize that yet?
EB: no!
AG: 8oy. How clueless can you get.
EB: why are we supposed to do that?
AG: What a stupid question! It is the point of the game. It's what happens when you win, and winning is the only point of anything.
EB: oh. that's true, i guess.
AG: Anyway, you should 8e glad it's the point. And you should 8e glad your predecessors were not such a sad sack group of players like you guys.
AG: Otherwise your universe would not exist, seeing as we cre8ted it 8y 8eing incredi8le in every way.
EB: you did?
AG: Yep. You're welcome. ::::D
EB: hmm...
EB: i don't know what to think about that.
AG: Not knowing what to think a8out things appears to 8e your specialty!
EB: hurrrrr oh man what a burn!
EB: (j/k it was actually lame.)
AG: ::::P
EB: well to be honest, i never really believed any of your guys's doom and gloom nonsense.
EB: not because i think you are lying...
EB: i just feel like there must still be a way to win!
AG: That's the spirit, John!
AG: That is a winner's attitude, and there is always hope for someone who has that.
EB: yes, i agree.
EB: also, there is always hope for someone who has good friends to count on!
AG: Pff.
AG: Laaaaaaaame.

> John: Return.

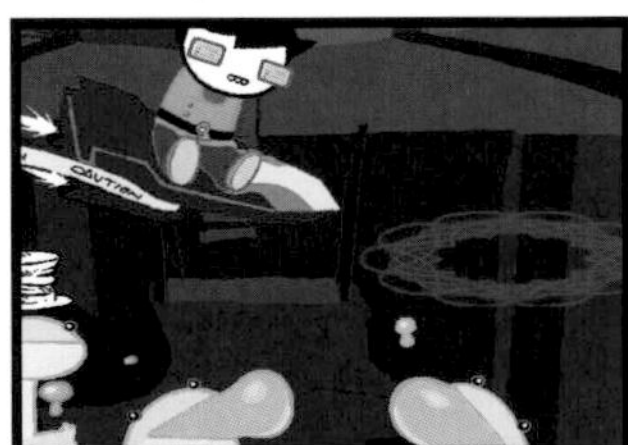

Now that the purpose of the game has been revealed to be the creation of universes, the characters have the luxury of casually blurting out what they're ultimately supposed to be trying to do here. Which feels blunt compared to how cagey the story has been about that fact right up until the reveal. Vriska hammers that home here. "You didn't realize that? How clueless can you get. LOL." She's kind of right. It *is* crazy that they/we didn't know that information until recently. It was protected, but not all that artificially. Karkat could have said it at any time in Act 4, but he didn't bother to because he was working backwards. He already gave his whole initial spiel to John at the end of John's timeline (I AM YOUR GOD! I CREATED YOU! BLAH BLAH BLAH!). Why would he want to repeat himself, especially after he felt like he made a fool of himself with that speech? But now that Vriska's on the scene, of course she just comes out and *says* it. She's much more blunt, always walks in the front door, always looks for the shortcut. If she were around in Act 4, there'd probably be no way she'd be able to keep that secret for the purposes of narrative convenience. Which was a pretty good reason to hold her back as a character until now. That, along with the fact that she hadn't been created yet.

IIIIIIIIIIIIIIIIIIIIMPS!

> John: Dispatch these pests.

That is IT.

EVERYBODY OUT.

You are *DEAD SERIOUS.*

> John: Examine room.

Look at this mess.

Will you just LOOK at this slightly bigger mess than usual.

> John: Examine computer.

John telling all the sad imps to GTFO is probably one of the better gags in this act. Is it just a gag though? No! Nothing is ever just an anything, obviously. John ordering the imps to get out understatedly helps signal that the characters aren't really in the business of monster-killing anymore. By this point in the story, imps and other types of underlings are so trivial to the heroes that they might as well be regarded as bothersome house guests. It's a reminder that the game is no longer the game we once thought it was. There's too much intrigue to keep track of now to bother caring about the mundane, low-level gameplay hurdles native to *Sburb*.

They chucked it out the window. Little oily bastards. You'll have to get your hands on a new one somehow.

> John: Examine Posters.

This is just insult to injury. You almost want to cry.

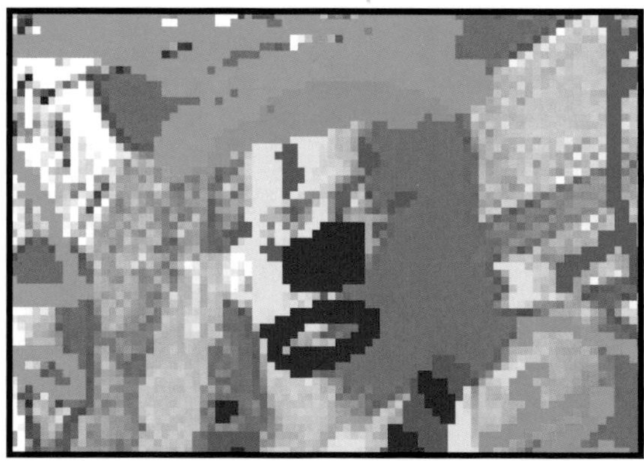

Just look at that face.

A sad face. A forlorn face.

> Vriska: What's his deal????????

Continuing from the previous note, unless we're talking about a truly nasty or rare underling, they don't pose physical threats to the players at all by now. The worst that they can do is create logistical impediments, like trashing John's room and throwing his computer out the window. Which isn't even that inconvenient for him, since he's already made plenty of backup computers. But hey, they tried. Once the players are past the point of low-level creatures posing a threat, things like imps fall back on doing what imps do best, which is a lot of impish, mischievous behavior to create impediments for players. Hold the fucking phone. I just realized "imp" is part of "impediment." I'm blowing my own damn mind here.

AG: John, why are you standing around wasting time????????
EB: um, i don't know. you can see my future, can't you?
EB: how much time am i wasting?
AG: Enough to make me wonder what the hell your deal is!
EB: then i would venture to guess i am wasting time because you chose to pester me just now!
AG: Dammit, John.
AG: Stop sounding smarter than me. It is un8ecoming of someone so inferior.
EB: i mean, i was just pausing for a moment...
EB: to look at my trashed movie posters.
EB: they bring back memories, of a life that i guess is long gone now.
EB: but you probably know what that is all about.
AG: Yeah, I know.
EB: it wasn't even that long ago, but it already seems like forever since i was on earth!
EB: it was a pretty nice place, i bet you would have liked it.
AG: It seems a little too sunny for my liking.
EB: well, what about you? do you miss your planet, and your parents and such?
AG: The life I left 8ehind wasn't so hot, to 8e honest.
EB: oh. that's too bad.
AG: Why don't we not talk a8out that!
AG: What are these movies, anyway? They look just awful.
EB: but you see, that is where you are wrong. these films are the finest earth has to offer!
AG: Are they a8out clowns?
EB: no, no. i drew those clowns in my sleep, for some reason.
AG: ::::|
EB: this one here is so great. it is about this street tough renegade who did hard time behind bars, and wants nothing more in the world than to reunite with his loving wife and daughter. but not so fast! he has to go on crazy and dangerous escapades through the sky with a motley assortment of rogues led by john malkovich, who is wise to cage's heroic nature and pure heart. they tether a grumpy police man's awesome car to

the plane and smash it, and then later they crash into some casinos. cage gets out of the wreckage and hugs his family, and i usually tear up a little.
EB: that is my working troll title for the movie, i hope it was ok.
AG: John, even though your title is quite amusing and pro8a8ly kind of cute, that movie sounds hilariously 8ad!
EB: yeah, well you are hilariously WRONG!
EB: here, hang on, i will show you.
EB: http://tinyurl.com/hullohumminburr
EB: oh, but you will probably have to use your troll thingy to rewind time or whatever, to before the earth internet blew up so you can watch it.
AG: Is this like the Earth equivalent of Gru8tu8e or something?
EB: i guess??
AG: Man. I am not watching this shitty video. It looks so 8ad!
EB: ok, suit yourself.
EB: but there it is, in case you are ever hankering after some incredible movie magic.
AG: Ok, I will 8e sure 8ookmark it and la8el it "dum8 kid's retarded nonsense."
EB: ok, good idea.
AG: 8y the way! Why aren't you using your computer glasses to talk suddenly????????
AG: This device seems less efficient, and doesn't look as cool!

That tinyurl link maps to a real YouTube video of the moment in *Con Air* when Nic Cage finally reunites with his wife and daughter. Except I'm pretty sure that video got taken down years ago, seeing as I just linked to a video in some random guy's account rather than bothering to host it myself. Ironically, just after John shares the link, he warns Vriska she might have to view it through an older version of the internet, from a time before Earth's servers were all destroyed. Which is the situation we find ourselves in now, with the gradual decay of the internet making it harder to consume the patchwork media comprising *Homestuck* in its original totality. The gradual entropy eating away at *Homestuck* and its myriad formats is a very real phenomenon. I expect this will continue and eventually all the content will fade away. In the future, these books won't even contain the original panels and text. They will be completely displaced by author notes, as the bottom margin creeps higher and higher, totally drowning out the comic you once knew and loved.

EB: oh, the goggles are cool and all, but they kind of restrict my vision stupidly when i'm using them!
EB: i should remember to make a new hands-free device, that is less obtrusive.
EB: maybe after i make a new computer so i can install this game.
AG: How will you duplic8 it? Isn't it smashed out there on your lawnring?
EB: yeah, but i can use one of my old previously punched cards.
AG: Oh, gr8.
AG: Uh........
AG: John?
EB: what?
AG: Ok, I will slide you a 8r8k 8ecause clearly your 8lock was just ransacked.
AG: 8ut may8e you want to put that away? Somewhere discreet, where you usually keep it?

AG: There is at least one girl spying on you right now, you know.
EB: put what away? what are you talking about?
AG: Your pail is showing, stupid!!!!!!!!

EB: my pail?
EB: you mean this bucket here?
AG: Yes! Come on, will you take a hint and show some decorum????????
EB: umm...
EB: i'm really not following. what do you have against buckets?
AG: Man! Nothing, really. It's just........
AG: Ok, may8e humans don't really have any sense of shame over this sort of thing?
EB: shame over what?
EB: it's just a bucket! you know, for putting soapy water in and cleaning stuff with.
EB: why, what do trolls use them for?
AG: Oh.
AG: Haha, yeah, of course!
AG: That's what I was talking a8out. Your cleaning 8ucket.
AG: In troll culture we consider cleaning products to 8e really indecent or something!
AG: I am 8lushing furiously a8out it right now. Please try to 8e sensitive to my cultural ways

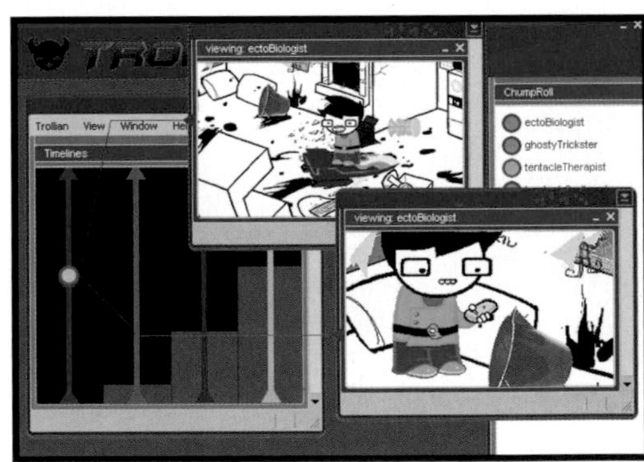

and understandings.
EB: wow... uh. that is definitely pretty odd.
EB: but ok, i'm sorry you saw my bucket. i will just chuck it out the window i guess.
AG: Thank you, John. That is very gentlemanly of you.
AG: Now will you quit shitting around and get on with it!!!!!!!! God.

Okay, so the imps throwing John's computer out the window did pose a *minor* inconvenience, since to run *Sburb* he needs a legit PC, not Dad's dinky fucking Blackberry or whatever. But John reminds us how trivially easy it is to just make a brand-new computer any time he wants, so once again: nice try, imps. Anyway, here John and Vriska waste little time in bellyflopping directly into some of the more awkward parts of the troll/human cultural exchange process. When Vriska finally understands the nature of the misunderstanding, she can't even level with him about what pails are really for on her planet, so she makes up a weak story about how trolls think cleaning supplies are indecent. She likes to broadcast a lot of swagger about practically everything, but when it comes to lewd content or bold romantic overtures, she folds like a cheap suit. She *wants* to have swagger in that arena, like her ancestor, but her fairy stunt with Tavros and other similar interactions show that she's not cut out for it. It's a window into Insecure Vriska's psyche, and as we should all know by now, Insecure Vriska is the root of all Vriskas.

EB: well i was GOING to but you started babbling at me!
EB: jeez, spinneret.
AG: That isn't my real name, you dope!
EB: ok, then what is it!
AG: I ain't telling you that!
AG: It's a sekret. :::;)
EB: *ROLLS EYES*
EB: all eight gross spidery eyes!
EB: oops i mean !x8.
AG: You don't even need to say that. I can see you rolling your eyes, remem8er?
EB: oh yeah.

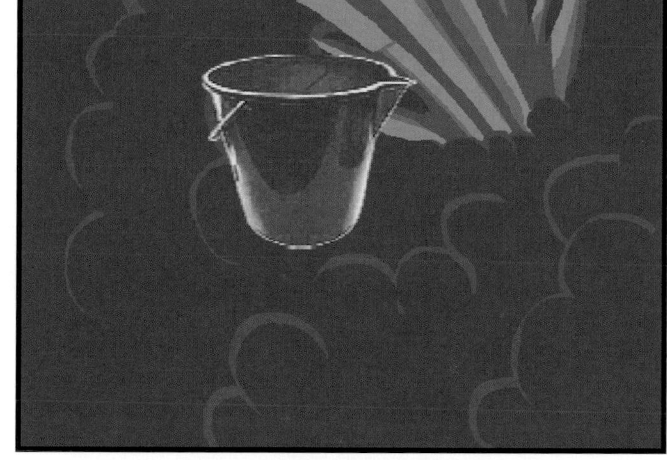

> John: Discard sordid receptacle.

> John: Exit to balcony.

Precedent says that any time we watch an object fall and disappear into the gray clouds, it's not the last we've seen of it. Does this bucket come up again later? If so, I can't remember how at this exact moment. If you're a superfan, maybe you know? I guess you have a leg up on me THIS TIME, cool guy. Note that Vriska gives John a non-subtle little clue about her real name, saying it's a "sekret," a minor jumble of "Serket." John can tell something's fishy, and I think he repeats this word to her later, signaling the fact that he wasn't really fooled by it. This exchange also shows that Vriska is the type of person who gets antsy about keeping a secret. Someone who would say, "Ah, wouldn't YOU like to know!" and you go, "Actually, I don't care much," and she's like, "Okay fine, I'll give you ONE hint, but that's IT!" I think she was similarly antsy about her "secret present" for Aradia, and similarly frustrated by the latter's apathy about it (which in part was due to the fact that Aradia already knew what it was).

What a surprise, more lousy imps having their way with the place. You wonder where nanna could be. Someone needs to get this motley assortment of rogues under control.

Now what in the hell is going on over there??

Oh no, more embarrassing cleaning apparatus. You've got to hide it before Sekret Spinneret or whatever her name is sees it and gets upset.

> John: Assail rogue.

GET THAT SHIT OUTTA HERE!!!

Here's a really good sitcom-style running gag based on John's misunderstanding that trolls find cleaning products unseemly. You can easily imagine an entire sitcom episode revolving around this premise. You're probably doing it now, actually.

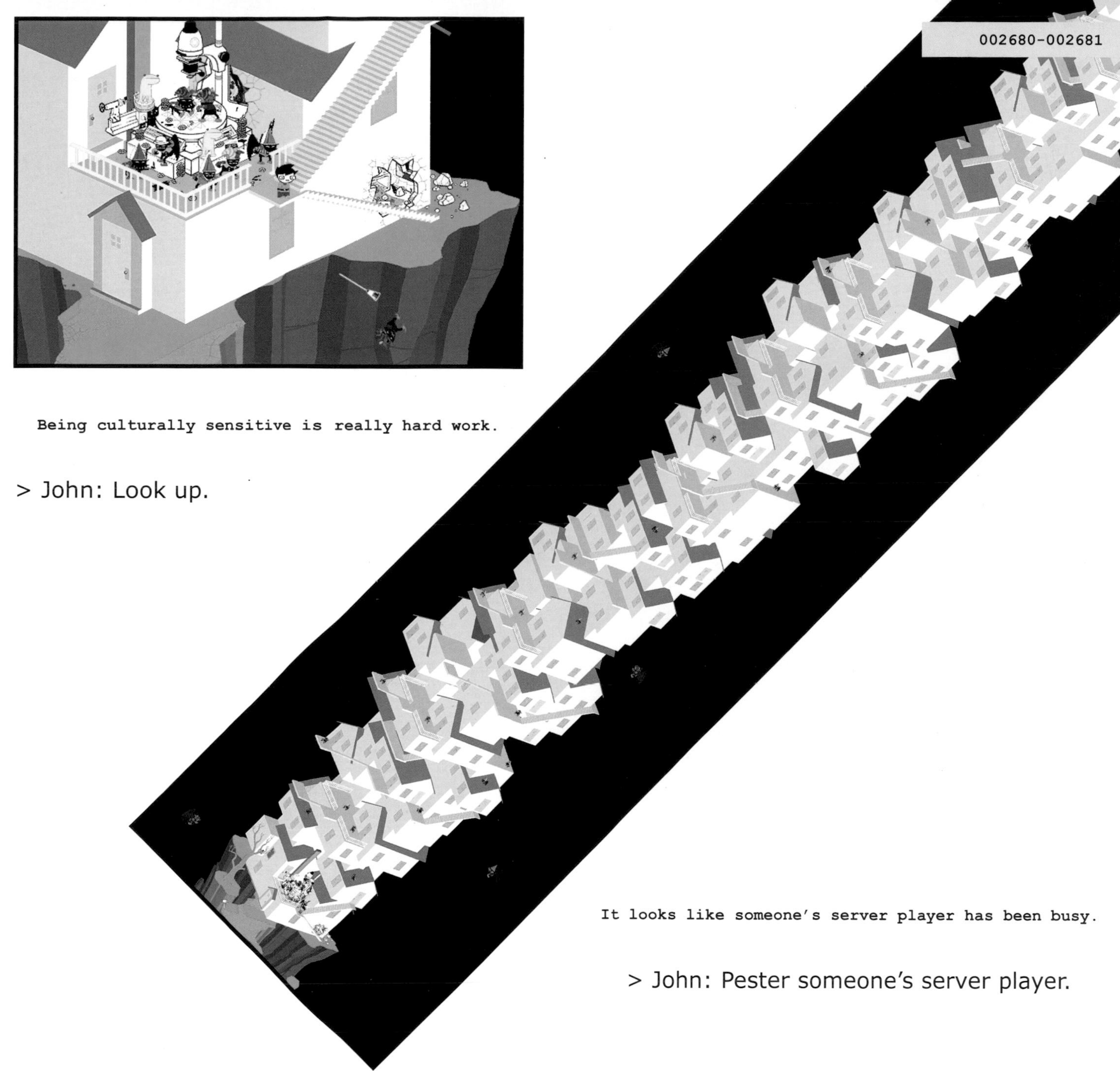

Being culturally sensitive is really hard work.

> John: Look up.

It looks like someone's server player has been busy.

> John: Pester someone's server player.

That house image was just TOO FUCKING TALL. We had to tilt it like that. HAD TO. Sorry. We're finally getting a look at some real building progress. By now we can see some repetitive structural patterns, making it clear that Rose has discovered the value of the copy/paste feature.

-- ectoBiologist [EB] began pestering tentacleTherapist [TT] --

EB: hey rose!
TT: Hi.
EB: how are you doing? i don't even remember the last time we talked.
EB: i have been so busy.
EB: and it looks like you have been too.
EB: i mean, hopy shit!
EB: my house is HUUUUUUUUUUUUUUUUUUUUUUUUGE!
TT: Actually, building up your house has been one of the more trivial ways I've passed the time.
TT: Great swaths of the structure may be copied and pasted with little architectural consideration.
TT: I've only bothered to do so while in contemplation.
TT: It's relaxing.
EB: oh.
EB: well, it must have cost a fortune!
TT: We have a lot of grist.
EB: how much?
TT: I don't recall any hard figures off hand.
TT: Last I checked, more than a million units of several different types.
TT: Torrented between the three of us.
EB: torrented?
TT: Shared, through an application.
TT: I unlocked the disc from your registry, and deployed it.
TT: I convinced your nanna to install it on your computer.
TT: Before an imp threw it out the window, that is.
EB: you got her to do that? but she's an old lady! also, a ghost.
TT: My methods of persuasion have been improving.
EB: also, she is really tricky, and plays lots of pranks.
EB: did she try to prank you?
TT: No.
EB: huh.
EB: i guess you enjoyed the prankster's gambit on that exchange then.
TT: ?
EB: oh yeah...

EB: what's up with the alchemiter?
EB: it looks weird.
TT: Upgrades.
EB: did you get nanna to do that too?
TT: No, your consorts were utilized for that.
EB: the salamanders??
TT: Yes. They seem eager to receive simple instruction.
TT: I'm guessing they find their way back to your house to allow the client player to remain productive while the server player is away.
EB: they aren't very smart...
TT: No, they aren't.
EB: i'm surprised they even understand what to do.
TT: Like I said.
TT: Coercion hasn't been much of a problem.
EB: yeah...
EB: uh...
EB: what exactly does that mean?
EB: what have you been doing this whole time???
TT: Why don't you tell me what you've been up to first?
TT: I've been curious, but too preoccupied to inquire.
EB: well,
EB: i have been talking to a lot of trolls, for

Lest *Homestuck*'s vast, tendrilous corpus gradually fade from memory entirely, "hopy shit" is a reference to a line from a *Sweet Bro and Hella Jeff* comic, wherein Jeff exclaimed "hopy shit" to communicate astonishment at the size of a large, yellow dog named Peaches. I put that line in the *SBaHJ* comic originally because one time, probably days prior to making it, I overheard a young child saying, "Holy shit, that dog is HUGE!" and thought it was a funny line because the dog he was talking about wasn't even that big. Oh also, Rose just comes out and admits she's copy/pasting the house structure now, thereby stealing the thunder from my note on the previous page. I feel like this happens a lot??

one thing.
EB: they sure are a talkative bunch!
TT: I've noticed.
EB: and then i cloned some slime babies in the veil.
TT: Did you?
EB: yes. um...
EB: ok, long story short is, jade is my slime clone sister, and dave is your slime clone brother, and we were all born today!
TT: Yes.
EB: yes?
TT: I figured that out.
EB: oh.
TT: Anything else?
EB: umm...
EB: then i fell asleep, and woke up on the battlefield.
EB: oh!
EB: rose, i am fairly sure i saw your mom!
TT: You did?
TT: Are you sure it was her?
EB: well, it was a nice and proper looking lady, with a pink scarf, so...
EB: i dunno, who else would that be!
TT: That was likely her.
TT: How was she?
EB: fine, i guess...
EB: she was with my dad.
TT: That's interesting.
EB: yeah!
TT: Did she seem happy?
EB: happy?
EB: wow, i dunno.
EB: i don't really know her well enough to say, i guess?
EB: plus, i was a little distracted.
EB: maybe i will find out next time i go to sleep.
TT: Fair enough.
EB: now stop being so spookily mysterious and tell me what you've been doing!
TT: Investigating, mostly.
EB: investigating what?
TT: Everything there is to investigate.
TT: Information hidden in the lore of our lands, concealed in ruins and riddles.
TT: I'm looking for whatever there is to discover about the game, and more importantly, whatever exceeds its boundaries.
TT: The cloaked traces of myth beyond its scope.
EB: its scope?
EB: oh, rose, did you know that we are supposed to be creating a universe with this game?
TT: Yes.
EB: i think that's pretty neat!
TT: It is, in principle.
TT: But it won't happen.
EB: so you believe the trolls then?
TT: It's not a matter of believing them.
TT: The writing is on the wall. Literally.
EB: it is?
TT: This session was never meant to bear fruit.
TT: It's barren, so to speak.
EB: that's a bit of a bummer!
EB: i am still skeptical about that, though.
TT: That's why you're our leader, John.
EB: huh?
TT: Optimism through stalwart skepticism is a defect not everyone is lucky enough to be cursed with.
EB: that's stupid.
EB: i'm not your leader, i am your FRIEND, there is a BIG difference!
TT: Statements like that are also why you're our leader.
EB: pff.
EB: laaaaaaaame.
TT: Yes, kind of.
EB: so, if you're sure that we are going to fail...
EB: what is the point of everything we're doing?
TT: Simple.
TT: The objective is no longer to win.
EB: um...
EB: i mean, what are we actually shooting for here?
TT: To do as much damage to the game as possible.
TT: To rip its stitches and pry answers from the seams.
TT: We will snatch purpose from the jaws of futility.
TT: Are you ready to wreak some havoc, John?
EB: i suddenly don't understand anything.

On the previous page, Rose talks of "methods of persuasion" and "coercion" when it comes to getting Nanna and the consorts to do things for her. This seems like a pretty ominous way of putting it. Is she... Is she TORTURING John's grandmother and a bunch of cute salamanders?? Dear God. I mean, probably not? But it sort of hints that something's up with Rose. We'll cut to her soon to find out what. And be like, "Oh I see, it's just her goth phase." Sounds about right.

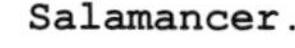

Salamancer.

Wand, please.

Thank you, Viceroy.

It's way more dramatic relying on a familiar than a boring old sylladex.

Rose definitely thinks this outfit is EXTREMELY cool. Oh, I see, you were never a thirteen-year-old child? I guess you're just too good for everything, aren't you? Hey, here's a hot take for you: I actually think this outfit is pretty badass by ANY standard. I'll understand if you'll need to start fanning yourself after being exposed to that take. We never see Rose make this outfit, though. The reason why is that the story is still building up to its previous level of steam after the Hivebent slog, and in reintroducing the human plotline we're also establishing a new pacing rhythm for events, a faster rhythm that allows us to skip over much bigger chunks of the action. When we come back to a character and they're wearing a new outfit we didn't see them make, doing stuff we have no basis for understanding, we intuit that there may be a lot going on offscreen now. It's kind of exciting, isn't it? Tuning into a character's part in the story and thinking, hey, *that's* a cool new outfit, nice. What did we miss? Let's find out through inference and implication. In other words, we're taking bigger strides to cover more narrative ground. This new rhythm, combined with a whole bag of nonlinear story-hopping tricks, gives us a really versatile toolkit for making the rest of the act a wild ride.

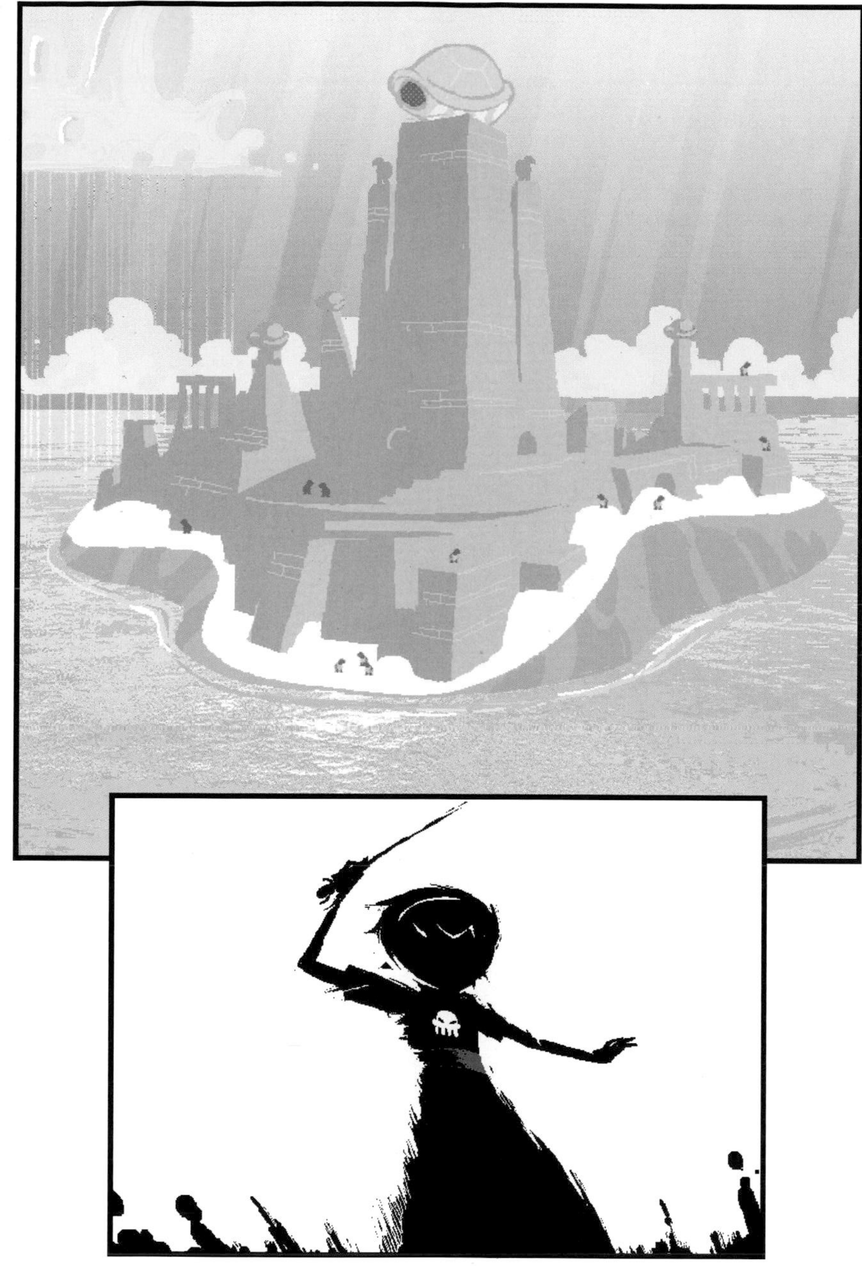

> Rose: Investigate.

The pink turtle ruins are actually really nice looking, aren't they. They're probably also a lot of fun to explore. Too bad Rose immediately decides to just FUCK this thing up. Back to one of my old saws: *Sburb* ruins, mythic challenges, and personal quests generally tend to come off as shallow busywork, stage props, or set pieces in a spurious Hero's Journey. Rose either faintly glimpses this truth at this early stage, or she's just hitting her rebellious teen stride. Either way, she doesn't take the surface value of the quest seriously at all, and only wants to smash it apart and loot the secrets. My sense is that the average reader reacts to this impulse unfavorably. Because readers watch the formula play out so often, they are trained heavily to respect the journey of the hero, to anticipate and crave its fulfillment, to see it as something verging on contractual in their relationship with a story. So a gut-response to this recklessness is like, "ROSE, NO! STOP THAT! You simply *must* complete your quest and play the rain!" What comes with this view is the feeling that her evolution as a character is only being delayed for a bit while she gets some anti-narrative foolishness out of her system, and *then* we'll get down to business and watch her do her quest, play a whole BUNCH of rain, and reap the narrative satisfaction. There's just one problem: she never does that. This candy-coated Kiddie Kwest is at no point ever taken seriously by Rose or the narrative itself, nor should it be. -->

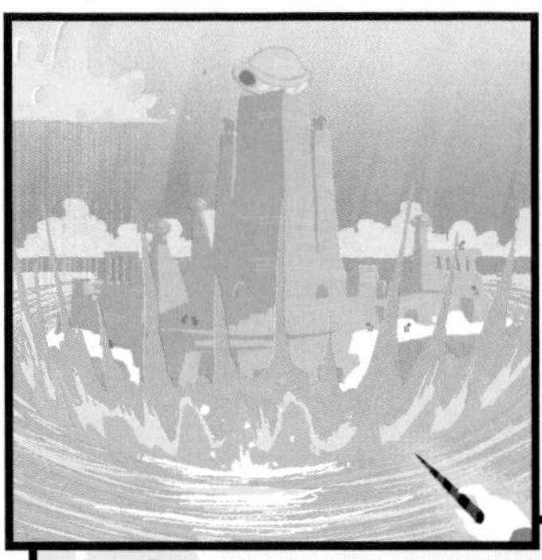

> Rose: Answer.

--> Has this topic been covered in my notes in previous books? Almost certainly. I'll keep hitting it though, because it's so deeply connected to *Homestuck*'s nature as a narrative and why there are so many screwball progressions that don't sync up with familiar patterns in fiction. When trying to parse character arcs, we look out for certain beacons. So when we hear "play the rain," we're like, ah, GOT IT. That's Rose's arc. Once she finally gets over this destructive teen bullshit, she can wise up, play the rain, and her arc will be finished. *Wrong.* This is almost a red herring arc. Her quest on this planet, its patronizing presentation, its intrinsic shallowness, is a mirage surrounding her that represents a fully regimented series of milestones for achievement and personal growth, much as society dubiously presents to young people in many forms. The true arc-within-the-arc is actually an upside-down version of what it appears to be. What Rose is doing now, which seems to be misguided recklessness taking her further *away* from the truth of herself, is actually better seen as a good start to her real journey: breaching the mirage of regimented growth, exposing it for the charade it is, and pulling the truth out of it. The real conflict in her arc comes not from the fact that she refuses to take it seriously, by destroying it and taking shortcuts. It's the opposite. It's that, upon trashing her planet, she continues to have this nagging sense that she *should* be taking this quest seriously, much like how a young adult may have a nagging sense of guilt that they aren't "being an adult right" by the time they approach adulthood. And this nagging, unanswerable guilt arises from the truth that the regimentation of adulthood is completely fake. It was always a mirage. Learning this, making peace with it, is part of the growing process for many, and it is for her too. -->

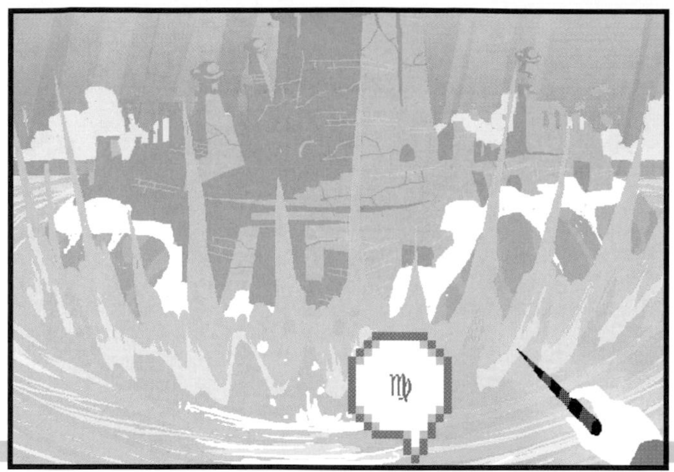

-- grimAuxiliatrix [GA] began trolling tentacleTherapist [TT] --

GA: Okay This Will Probably Strike You As An Odd Moment For Me To Mention This
GA: But Actually
GA: There Are Not Many Moments Ive Observed On Your Timeline Which Wouldnt Qualify As Odd
GA: And Somehow
GA: Your Idle Moments Seem To Invite Interruption The Least
GA: And This Is A Difficult Topic For Me To Broach
GA: For Reasons That You Probably Wont Understand
TT: You're rambling again, Kanaya.
GA: Okay Sorry
GA: Ive Just Been Meaning To Say
GA: That I Read Your Instructional Guide

> Rose: Be the troll girl.

You are suddenly the troll girl.

In a different game session.

In the past.

> Kanaya: Confer with leader.

--> These story arcs often involve a character overcoming something that's holding them back, and they tend to be more compelling when it's something internal to the character that needs to be confronted or overcome. There are failed (a.k.a. tragic) arcs, where a character struggles to overcome flaws inside them but doesn't succeed, suffering miserably or dying as a result. Successful arcs are ones where the character does make the transformative journey and surmounts those internal obstacles. The things to identify are: what is the internal obstacle, how is it holding the character back, and what's the *real* process (not the presumed one) by which this actually takes place over a full story. So when we hear "play the rain," if we take it at face value as a story arc element the supposition is: Rose struggles internally with an impulse to destroy, to cheat, to take shortcuts, and must overcome these immature impulses, take her rain quest seriously, enjoy the magical yields of doing so, and release her inner greatness. Okay, that's the presumed arc, and importantly, Rose *herself* presumes it's her arc too. But let's flip the whole thing around: Rose falsely diagnoses her own arc, "rebels" against it with acts of teen vandalism, obsesses over the knowledge it yields, becomes "corrupted" by said knowledge, struggles with depression, and later, alcoholism, and feels like something is wrong. Like resisting the quest was a mistake, a rejection of her designated path for growth. The guilt of resisting the false quest is the struggle. Letting go of that guilt and all cerebral intensity surrounding it is the overcoming process Rose needs to go through. Her arc is literally her deliverance from what she falsely perceives as her own arc. Confused yet??? Well, she sure was. Oh, Kanaya's here, let's pause all this arctalk for a minute and get her into the mix.

grimAuxiliatrix [GA] began trolling
carcinoGeneticist [CG]

GA: Your Speech Was Really
GA: Emotional
CG: OK I DEFINITELY DON'T NEED YOU BUSTING MY BULGE ABOUT THE SPEECH NOW.
CG: I'VE TAKEN ENOUGH SHIT. I GOT A LITTLE WORKED UP OK?
CG: AND IF YOU HAVE SOMETHING TO SAY, WHY DON'T YOU COME SAY IT TO MY FACE.
CG: I'M FED UP WITH THESE BACK DOOR NOOKBITING SHENANIGANS.
GA: I Dont Mean To Critique Your Speech
GA: I Just Wanted To Ask You Something In Confidence
GA: About The Humans
CG: OK, WHAT IS IT?
GA: Are You Sure Theyre Responsible For Our Misfortune
CG: YES. THERE IS NO DOUBT ABOUT IT.
GA: Was It On Account Of Malice Or Incompetence
CG: I DON'T KNOW. MAYBE BOTH?
CG: WHY DOES IT MATTER.
GA: It Sort Of Does
GA: Im Not Even That Sure Why
GA: This Is A Difficult Topic For Me To Broach
GA: For Reasons That You Probably Wont Understand
CG: GOD DAMMIT.
CG: NO MORE MYSTERIES, PLEASE.
CG: YOU'D THINK WE'D HAD OUR FILL OF THEM BY NOW.
CG: IF I HAVE TO SOLVE ONE MORE RIDDLE, I'M GOING TO...
CG: I DON'T KNOW.
GA: Will Your Response Involve An Athletic Maneuver Of Some Sort
CG: NO
CG: ABSOLUTELY NOT.
CG: I WILL JUST GO OVER THERE AND WEEP GENTLY IN THE HORN PILE.
CG: SERIOUSLY, WHAT IS THIS ABOUT?
GA: Um
CG: WHAT I CAN TELL YOU IS
CG: THEY ARE ALL LUDICROUSLY INCOMPETENT.
CG: SOFT, PINK FRAGILE THINGS WHO DO NOTHING BUT WASTE TIME.
CG: THEY DON'T EVEN HAVE HORNS!
GA: What
GA: Really
CG: YEAH, I WAS LIKE, WHOA DID THEY GET FILED DOWN OR SOMETHING
CG: BUT NO IT TURNS OUT THAT'S JUST HOW THEY ARE.
GA: Weird
CG: THEY'RE A MISERABLE POINTLESS CROP OF LIFEFORMS FROM A MEANINGLESS BORING PUSTULE OF A PLANET.
CG: IT'S INFURIATING THEY WERE SOMEHOW ALLOWED TO HAVE ANY INFLUENCE OVER US.
GA: It Is Pretty Disheartening
GA: But
GA: You Are Absolutely Sure They Are All Failures
GA: And That They Have No Chance Of Succeeding
CG: YEP.
CG: IT'S ALL RIGHT HERE.
GA: Im Not Sure Which Depresses Me More
GA: The Sabotage Of Our Session Or The Futility Of Theirs
CG: WHAT ARE YOU TALKING ABOUT.
CG: YOU'RE BEING REALLY WEIRD ABOUT THIS.
GA: Well I Havent Asked What I Wanted To Ask
CG: THEN ASK!!!
GA: Its About TentacleTherapist
CG: YEAH. THAT'S THE ROSE HUMAN.
CG: SHE'S APPARENTLY PRETTY SARCASTIC.
CG: IT'S IN MY NOTES.
GA: You Have Notes On Them
CG: YES.
GA: I Guess
GA: Thats Why Youre Our Leader Karkat
CG: NO, I'M YOUR LEADER BECAUSE OF MY INCREDIBLE TACTICAL SKILLS AND MY ABILITY TO MOBILIZE AND MOTIVATE A BUNCH OF USELESS PEOPLE TOWARD A COMMON GOAL, AND BECAUSE I'M EXTREMELY AMBITIOUS AND INTREPID. ALSO BECAUSE LEADERSHIP IS IN MY BLOOD. WE'VE BEEN OVER THIS.
GA: Statements Like That Are Also Why Youre Our Leader
CG: OK, I'LL ACCEPT THAT.
GA: Have You Talked To Her
CG: WHO

We're about to start going harder into the Rose/Kanaya material. They're two characters who absolutely revolve around each other for most of this act, and *Homestuck* in general, like a sort of lesbian binary star system. But before we do that, we need to hop back to Hivebent for a little more setup reference, specifically the "trolling" plan and how Kanaya ended up talking to Rose, which was basically due to Kanaya's prior admiration of her resulting from the walkthrough study. Which we could already surmise from Hivebent, but hey, now we're more formally telling the story of Kanaya and Rose, so we might as well start at the beginning again. Their interaction was never was genuinely antagonistic, it only went in that direction due to some misfires which we saw in Act 4. It was always grounded in admiration. This feature of their relationship, Kanaya's natural gravitation toward Rose, links easily to the topic of Rose's arc on previous pages. The intensity of Rose's focus on ripping the game apart, finding answers, and telling her quest to fuck off, and the level of empowerment and control over her fate that seems to embody, signals a certain degree of self-confidence. And confidence is something we've seen Kanaya struggle with. Rose's newfound flair for destruction and recklessness is also captivating to her. Remember that Kanaya's a sucker for "meddling" with dangerous girls. Their confidence pulls her in, the intellectual intensity and danger keep her hooked, and then her mothering need to "protect" starts kicking in. These dynamics provide most of the fuel for the Rosemary fire, which, unlike virtually every other ship in the story, literally never stops burning.

GA: The Rose Human
GA: Also
GA: Do We Really Have To Say Things Like The Rose Human
CG: OF COURSE WE DO.
CG: IT SOUNDS SUITABLY DISDAINFUL.
CG: I MEAN, IF A BUNCH OF ALIENS STARTED HASSLING YOU, YOU WOULD EXPECT THEM TO ACT REALLY HIGH AND MIGHTY, AND SUPERIOR IN EVERY WAY, RIGHT?.
CG: WHICH WE ARE, OF COURSE.
GA: Uh Okay
CG: AND NO, I HAVEN'T TALKED TO HER.
CG: I WILL PROBABLY STEER CLEAR OF HER FOR THE MOST PART.
CG: I HAVE MY SIGHTS SET ON THE JOHN HUMAN, AND PROBABLY ALSO THE JADE HUMAN, SHE'S A HUGE CULPRIT TOO.
GA: It Just
GA: Feels Really Silly When We Say Things Like The John Human In Confidence Amongst Ourselves
CG: WE HAVE TO COMMIT TO THIS. STAY IN CHARACTER, YOU KNOW?
CG: REMEMBER THE SPEECH.
GA: The Speech Has Become Emblazoned On My Think Pan
GA: Virtually Ensconced In The Fold Of My Personal Mythology
CG: DID YOU WANT TO TROLL HER? ARE YOU VOLUNTEERING?
CG: BECAUSE THAT WOULD BE GREAT, I'D REALLY APPRECIATE THAT.
GA: I Dont Know
GA: Im Not Sure If Ive Got It In Me Right Now
CG: COME ON. YOU'LL BE GREAT AT IT.
CG: PLEASE JUST DO THIS ONE THING FOR ME. WE'VE GOT TO STAY COORDINATED ON THIS.
CG: TOO MANY OF THESE FUCKS ARE GOING ROGUE.
CG: LIKE WHAT ARE WE EVEN DOING.
GA: Fine
CG: GREAT! THANKS KANAYA.
CG: I'LL EXPECT A FULL REPORT SOON.
GA: A Report About What
CG: LIKE
CG: HOW HASSLED YOU GOT HER TO BE
CG: BUT LESS STUPID SOUNDING THAN THAT.
GA: Is There A Metric For That Concept
CG: NO
CG: WELL THERE COULD BE
CG: WE CAN GAUGE YOUR RESULTS WITH THE "FLIGHTY BROADS AND THEIR SNARKY HORSESHITOMETER".
GA: That Seems Just As Disparaging To Me As It Is To Her
CG: YEAH WELL
CG: USE IT AS MOTIVATION
CG: I GOTTA GET CRACKING HERE, LATER.

> Kanaya: Troll the Rose human.

Notice, if you will, that Karkat and Kanaya are having this entire conversation via computers while standing in the same room. Should this surprise us by now? Probably not. It's not as absurd as it might seem, since this is a pretty good way to have some chats in confidence between two people in a crowded room full of nosy friends. Like two kids in a classroom texting each other. Which I assume is a thing that happens these days. It didn't really happen when I was in school, because I crawled out of a puddle of amino-sludge some time in the late Proterozoic era, and the technology to do that wasn't quite as common back then.

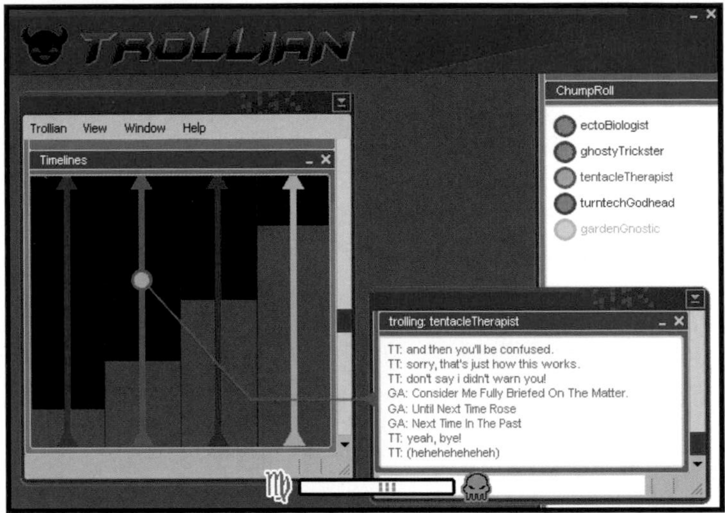

You begin trolling the Rose human, even though you aren't really feeling this at all.

You can't seem to figure out how to get the viewport feature to work. You muddle through the FIRST CONVERSATION blind.

She does not prove to be the intellectual adversary you anticipated. But this is no longer all that surprising, now knowing the true fate of her team.

Nethertheless, you manage to find yourself vehemently fondling the short end of the antagonism stick. The FLIGHTY BROADS AND THEIR SNARKY HORSESHITOMETER ticks a few notches in her favor. Your aggravation and curiosity are simultaneously piqued. You wish you could get a look at her.

> Kanaya: Open viewport.

There she is.

How underwhelming. No horns. Skin as white as a ghost! You wonder how she manages to look in a mirror without falling asleep.

You resume your stance of alien complacency. The SNARKY HORSESHITOMETER ticks back in your favor.

> Kanaya: Keep viewing.

Are we deep enough into the pit of hell to start lurching into the onerous topic of Racestuck? There's probably no turning back now. I should probably put a flashlight under my face like I'm telling a fucking horror story whenever I get into this. Okay, imagine me doing that now. Kanaya says Rose is "white as a ghost." Well, *Kanaya* doesn't, the narrative does, which puts the statement at least one layer removed from actual observation. So, is this observation literally true about Rose? To our eye, her skin definitely appears to be paper-white. But then, so is her hair (observed to be blonde once). So are her clothes, desk, computer, floor, etc. This opens up the question of what here is meant to be understood as *literally white* versus what is shown as *representationally white*, i.e. a non-literal expression of "blankness" that the imagination can fill in as it pleases. This is a pretty interesting avenue of thought, involving certain philosophical inquiries into the subject of blankness, how blankness can be visually represented, what blankness means, and whether a truly blank abstraction can even really exist. -->

You continue to spy on the Rose human. What's that nonsense she wrote on her walls? What did she do to her totem lathe?? Idiot.

OH DEAR GOD.

The exhibit of depravity maxes out your side of the HORSESHITOMETER.

You had this girl wrong all along. She is an utter buffoon.

--> Focusing on the abstraction issue, the question becomes: Is what we're seeing an abstract presentation of a general idea, with a fungible set of characteristics that remain intrinsically unassigned, and therefore are open to interpretation? Or is the presentation meant to be taken literally, with concrete depictions telling us what is truly intended to be taken as unalterable fact, and therefore not open to interpretation? A good example of the latter is eye color. Later, we see through deliberate close-up shots that the eye colors of the humans correspond to their text colors. The specificity and delivery of that information basically kills any interpretive latitude. That is what their eye colors literally are, whereas previously their eyes were just represented by black dots, which was the symbolic presentational default that came with their paper-doll avatars. This tells us that a simple presentation can begin with nonliteral attributes (like color), and then become assigned literal specificity later under certain conditions. It happens with the characters' eyes, but the same thing never happens with their skin tones. Which means they're all either literally white as ghosts, as the dubious narration suggests, or they're deliberately never assigned specificity, leaving precise tonal designation ambiguous. The only visual exception to this is a flagrantly satirical wind-up of this very issue that takes place in what is indisputably the hottest fucking mess in *Homestuck* by far, the Trickster arc. -->

You hope nobody caught you looking at that.

The horseshitometer swings back to her side, as she has inadvertently caused you to flush with the shame of one thousand cocoon-wetting children.

You win this round, Lalonde.

> Kanaya: View the past.

You need to put some distance between yourself and that egregious display.

These look like simpler times. Probably better to mess with her earlier on the timeline rather than later.

Hmm.

> Kanaya: Enter name.

--> I'm breezing past a truly choice example of Blurry Gamzee to keep talking about this shit. Sorry, I just need to wrap this up, then I'll get back to the jokes (i.e. more long-ass posts). So, while the kids' clothing colors change from the original paper-doll white, denoting progression from nonliteral blankness to literal specificity, and their eyes do the same, their skin colors never do (Tricksters notwithstanding), even when the kids are rendered more "realistically." If paper-white blankness is truly meant to denote an interpretive reality, then that interpretation depends on the reader, the walk of life they're from, their associations with certain social cues, the way they parse the signals of racial coding and how much stock they put in it. If someone has hard ideas about character depictions always needing to be specific and fixed—that there's no such thing as interpretational freedom or reader agency in creating the meaning of a text—then it won't matter if you draw a cartoon face on a paper plate and shout, BEHOLD: ABSTRACTION! They won't get it, let alone accept it. -->

Why Ms. Lalonde. It does appear you have once again fallen out of favor with the FLIGHTY BROADS AND THEIR SNARKY HORSESHITOMETER.

Your move, Therapist.

This is boring. Where's the challenge in teasing a mentally retarded alien girl? Her stupid walkthrough was probably plagiarized from another more advanced civilization or something.

Maybe bothering her friends will be more interesting.

> Kanaya: Troll the John human.

--> Certain people may conclude something like, "Well, my head is spinning a bit from all this equivocation about abstraction and race, I don't care that much, and truth be told, they always just seemed like a bunch of white American kids to me, so I think I'm just gonna say they're all white. Peace out." And that's valid. But it's just as valid to interpret the kids as belonging to any other race, considering their depictions are abstract to the point that sometimes they don't have things like arms. I would look at the previous notes of dissertation on this as sort of like an extensive mathematical proof just to formally prove a theorem that sounds like it should be obvious, but for some stupid reason just isn't. But if you're a mathematician, you live for this shit, doing a deep dive into the rigors of a proof, discovering exactly why a problem is more complex than it seems. And if you're whatever the math guy analogue is for whatever the hell it is we're talking about here, you're probably getting a kick out of all this too. Are you feeling wiser now? More enriched? Eh, you probably wish I'd just made a short joke about the FLIGHTY BROAD gag up there instead. Fair enough.

grimAuxiliatrix [GA] began trolling ghostyTrickster [GT]

GA: Hello
GT: hi...?
GA: Allow Me To Make This Simple
GA: I Am A Troll From Another Universe Using A Chat Client Utility Which Is Capable Of Contacting You And Your Friends At Any Point Of Your Lives Which I Choose Up To And Including The Moment Of Your Own Incompetence Fueled Self Destruction
GA: Im Looking For Evidence Of Intelligence In Your Species
GA: A Reason
GA: Any Reason At All Really
GA: To Justify Wasting The Few Precious Remaining Moments Of My Life On You
GA: It Has Fallen On Your Shoulders To Supply Me With That Reason John Human
GA: Go
GT: ha ha, what?
GA: What Indeed
GA: I Was Just Leaving
GT: so you're a time traveler?
GA: No
GA: We Dont Actually Travel Through
GA: Uh
GA: Well
GA: Not All Of Us Do
GA: One Of Us Does Though
GA: Thats Not What We Are Talking About Here And Is Aside From The Point
GT: so let me see if i have this straight...
GT: you are a time traveling space alien from the future, sent here to study humans?
GA: No
GT: are you from mars? is it a mission of peace?
GA: No John You Werent Listening
GT: what does your time machine look like? a phone booth? phone booths are a popular thing for some reason.
GA: Damn It
GT: were you lured to earth by a huge gyroscopey thing that jodie foster piloted in contact, while matthew mcconaughey sort of acted as her spiritual guide i guess...

GA: What The Hell
GT: and then he kind of preached to her about having faith instead of believing in the sciences so hard all the time, and i guess in the end she believed him, maybe?
GT: actually, im not even sure what the point of mcconaughey was in that movie. but he was still awesome.
GT: and then jodie found her dad on an alien planet... but i think he was a ghost or something? or maybe an alien in disguise.
GT: and then she went home and nobody believed her, but you just KNOW mcconaughey believed her.
GT: because he had all the faith. and i mean ALL OF IT.
GT: anyway, does that have any applicability to your cosmic interstellar astrojourney?
GA: Okay Youre Even Dumber Than The Rose Human Thats Incredible Really
GT: pff, i know i'm dumber than rose, that is not much of a burn, dude!
GA: Im A Girl Not A Boy
GT: oh, sorry.

John proves once again he's actually a better troll than most of the trolls are. What most of them don't get, especially Karkat, is that the most effective way of trolling someone is to come across like you're not trying to troll them at all, or even antagonize them. Innocent questions, an agreeable demeanor, and painfully naive "attempts to understand" are all tactics that, when harnessed by someone the right way, can cause certain kinds of aggressors to have total meltdowns.

GT: i don't know why i thought you were.
GA: It Happens
GT: were you trolling rose too?
GT: TIME TRAVEL TROLLING???
GA: Yes As A Matter Of Fact
GT: oh boy, let me go put on my quantum space hat, and extra terrestrial adventure boots, and you can tell me all about it.
GA: If You Werent So Stupid Id Suspect You Were Being Insincere For The Benefit Of Your Amusement
GT: ha ha ha. i don't follow!
GA: I Just Spoke To Her In The Future
GA: Shes An Imbecile And Conveying How Much I Dislike Her At This Point Presents An Overwhelming Gauntlet Of Personal Expression
GA: But Regardless She Said To Paste Something From Our Conversation
GA: To Get You To Understand Whats Going On
GA: I Have Strong Doubts It Will Be Effective But Here Goes
GA: GA: I Should Figure Out How The Viewport Feature Of This Application Works
GA: GA: So I Can See What Such A Primitive Creature Looks Like
GA: TT: haha, well i know what you guys look like.
GA: TT: you look kind of like...
GA: TT: howie mandel from little monsters.
GA: TT: even though, to be perfectly frank, he was kind of a big monster.
GA: TT: because he was a big goofy adult.
GA: TT: and fred savage was like his child prankster sidekick.
GA: GA: Is This An Adversary You Have Encountered On Your Quest
GA: TT: no, it's a movie.
GA: TT: you should ask john about it, because he thinks it's awesome, which it is.
GT: hahaha! oh man, you blew it!
GT: now i know for sure you're trolling me. rose hates that movie.
GA: Are You Suggesting
GA: I Was Being Trolled
GA: That It Was A Charade Meant To Make Me Look Foolish
GT: possibly! i know that sure didn't sound like her.
GT: but i think it's more likely that you made it all up cause you know i like that movie.
GT: so i tip my cap to you, well played miss troll!
GA: Now Im Wondering If You Might Be Trolling Me As Well
GT: ok well, just between you and me...
GT: SOMEONE here is getting trolled.
GT: and it just might be all three of us.
GA: Okay
GT: but you shoulda told me you liked little monsters!
GT: we could jam about that. what was your favorite part?
GA: Suspicions Pitching Once Again Toward The Conclusion That You Are Just Very Stupid
GT: i really want to get a little monsters poster, but they're hard to find!
GT: i asked my dad for one for christmas. fingers crossed!
GA: Im Guessing Thats The Human Equivalent Of 12th Perigees Eve
GA: Will Your Adult Human Custodian Forage For Leavings As Ours Do
GT: yup, that sure keeps sounding alien of you.
GT: keep up the good work!
GT: listen, i'm kind of busy, i have to wrap this present and mail it in a hurry.
GT: so i'm going to block you!
GT: but i might unblock you again soon, because you're kinda cool.
GA: Your Blocks Mean Nothing But Dont Worry You Wont Hear From Me Again
GT: yeah well...
GT: you might just hear from me!
GT: also, you should give rose another chance.
GT: she is really great! whatever she did, she was probably just pulling her mind games on you, it's all in fun.
GT: there is more to her than that, you'll see.
GT: bye!

ghostyTrickster [GT] blocked grimAuxiliatrix [GA]

This flashback was long ago enough that it's very likely John didn't remember this exchange when it came time to type Rose's end of that pasted conversation himself. But he still doesn't miss a beat in taking the opportunity to troll Kanaya about the film *Little Monsters*. This is what makes John such an excellent prankster by nature. Unlike Karkat, who's his own worst enemy, John is his own best ally. He's always on the same page with himself when it comes to pranking instincts, so his past and future selves require minimal direct coordination when it comes to dunking on unsuspecting rubes.

AUGH. Stupid trolls.

Looks like this package is going to be late.

The conversations with the other two humans didn't go that well either.

Must be something about the human intellect, and a specific posture it assumes. Particularly when a certain subject is broached.

And yet...

Your curiosity. It remains piqued.

How maddening.

John's flashback spade shirt may seem like an oddity here, or something he'd be unlikely to wear. It's hard to say, because we don't know much about his wardrobe habits outside of an established tendency to wear that green ghost shirt all the time. But in this flashback section, having the kids wear shirts with card suit symbols on them is a nod to the way the trolls began meeting them and started engaging with them, most notably Karkat's "spades at first sight" moment with John. Later we see Jade associated with a diamond (a Skaianet logo), and Dave associated with a heart (which his bro appropriated from the fallen Maplehoof corpse, the pony that Dave rode down from space).

Earth is surprisingly pretty.

It seems very...

Bright.

Ok, you will have to admit that is a nice outfit. Humans get points for fashion too.

You begrudgingly concede a single SNARKTICK to the stylish human and her loyal snowlusus.

> Kanaya: Troll Rose human again.

In a little while, she is back in her hive.

You prepare an ambush. This time, the fashionable, hand-crafted gloves are coming OFF.

These flashbacks also present convenient opportunities to portray the houses we've already seen in different weather environments. Rose's house covered in snow, Dave's house on a rainy day instead of being scorched by an oppressive sun. It helps unflatten the portrayal of the kids' lives a little bit. When you start by setting up characters and settings that have an inherently abstracted flatness to the presentations, finding strategies to gradually provide depth to all aspects of the story becomes a key objective.

You proceed to have your SECOND CONVERSATION.

You feel pretty good about your effort. It was a measured balance of barbs and condescension. Your leader will be pleased with the report.

And yet...

It seems the John human was right. This is not the same Rose human you dealt with before. She has been toying with you all along. Oh, the curiosity. How it persists. The maddening, maddening curiosity.

Your arbitrating gauge decides on a draw. Snark reaped and sown in equal distribution.

This is far from over.

> Kanaya: Explore this human emotion called friendship.

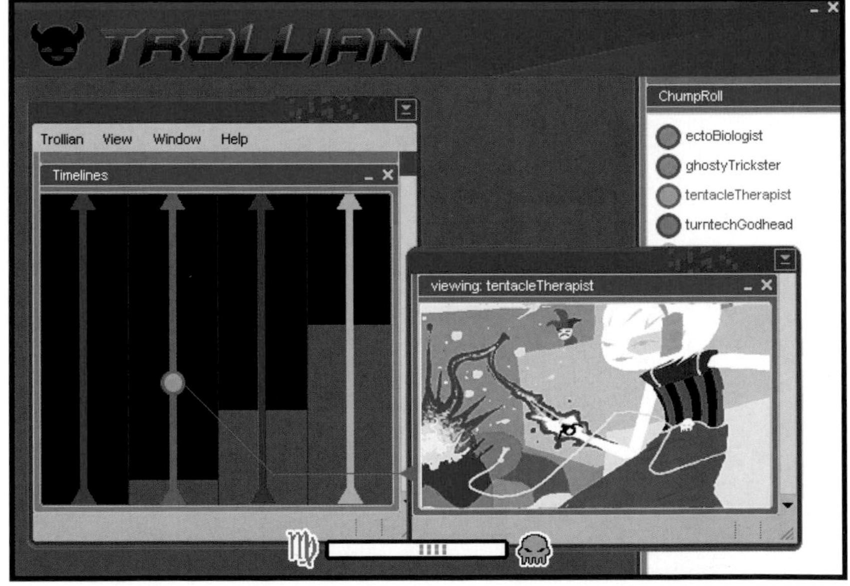

You can only assume this is a somewhat typical way for human relationships to blossom. It seems friendship for some humans is a basic aggregation of shallow and insincere hostilities. Human friendship sure is complicated.

You skip ahead to a point on her timeline when you suspect friendship may plausibly have been established already. You have your THIRD CONVERSATION. It does not go as well as you'd hoped.

Rose takes the lead.

The "THIRD CONVERSATION" refers to one we've already read in Act 4. Gotta stay on the ball here, dig it out of our memories. It was the one where Rose owned Kanaya basically just by going "I'm too busy for you. Get back to me, k?" A real power move. Rose might not even realize what she's doing—or maybe she does. She's setting Kanaya up to fall hard for her through a consistent pattern of blowing her off and acting too cool for her. It's possible Rose is doing this instinctively to set herself up for a pretty sweet position in ALIEN GIRLFRIEND CITY. She is a Seer of Light after all, which means she has a natural affinity for seeing the most fortuitous path toward success, however success is defined. Surely she would agree drunkenly making out with Kanaya on a dark staircase several years from now as hitting the jackpot.

Your FOURTH, FIFTH, AND SIXTH CONVERSATIONS don't fare much better. This friendship is stalling fast. What are you doing wrong?

You are now getting your ass handed to you on a silver nutrition plateau. You are in serious need of a ploy to turn the tables in this duel of snarky one-upsmanship.

Some advice couldn't hurt, you suppose.

> Kanaya: Troll the Dave human.

You decide to SEEK COUNSEL from the Rose human's dark spectacled friend.

You believe you understand how to proceed.

> Kanaya: Have seventh conversation.

Lest we not give props where they are due, the "Snarky Horseshitometer" is clearly just an adaptation of an earlier construct: John's "prankster's gambit," which quantified the lopsided state of the jape-based rivalry between him and his dad. It's a good way of gauging the score in a silly contest surrounding a silly idea that doesn't matter much. I don't think it's used again after this for anything else? Which maybe is a shame, since it easily could have been. But some horses just need to be put out to pasture sometimes. *Homestuck* has many horses, and a very big pasture.

You put into motion a cunning plan in your SEVENTH CONVERSATION, in which you have attached a MISSION CRITICAL TEXT DOCUMENT.

-- grimAuxiliatrix [GA] began trolling tentacleTherapist [TT] --

GA: Im Supposed To Antagonize A Few Members Of Your Trivial Species
GA: I Have To Start Somewhere
GA: And Somewhen
GA: So I Am Starting With You
GA: And Now
GA: Its Going To Be Pointless And Unpleasant
GA: Mostly For Me
GA: [Tactical Omission]
GA: [Tactical Omission]
GA: [Tactical Omission]
TT: she's not here right now, she's asleep!
TT: but ok, see you.
TT: And Then I Proceed To Make This Brainless Remark To Complement My Many Others
TT: Or Do I
GA: Is This
GA: Your Human Sarcasm That Ive Heard About
GA: That You Always Use
GA: And That Is Basically A Terrible Way To Communicate
TT: umm... no?
GA: I Thought That Was The Thing You Did
GA: The Rose Human Specifically
TT: oh, yeah.
TT: that's me! i am the rose human. look at me, i am so smart with all these snooty words and complicated things to say.
TT: i am the queen of books.
TT: I Am Also Infuriatingly Aloof
TT: And Difficult To Engage With
TT: When Maybe All The Other Person Wants To Do Is Maybe To Try To Be My Friend
TT: Has That Ever Occured To Me
TT: Probably Not
GA: Okay These Are Definitely Insincere Statements
GA: Why Do You Work So Hard At Being So Awful
TT: fffuuhhhhhhhh
TT: i'm so burned, these burns are crazy.
TT: can we just cut to the chase and be friends already??
TT: these cat and mouse games are so dumb, you know we're just going to all be friends at some point anyway.
GA: Have We Spoken Before

I have to admit, when I first got to this part of the book, I thought this was a mistake, and some text was left uncolored here. Actually though, on the site, a link is provided beneath this panel which opens a text file containing her earlier conversation with Rose, including several "[Tactical Omissions]." It was very clear what was happening on the site, because it was a link to a distinct file, but here it's probably a little confusing. Is this a conversation taking place now? No, we are reading a text file Kanaya created and shared with Rose in the "SEVENTH CONVERSATION" cited above. Maybe you recall that when we read that conversation in Act 4, we only saw the attached conversation referred to as "ConversationWithAVeryStupidGirl.Txt," but we didn't see the contents of it. We only saw Rose say "TT: I guess being forced to cooperate with a stable time loop is the only plausible explanation for my remarks." Which deepened the mystery of the file, and we could only speculate on what was in it.

TT: i don't know, uh, maybe???
TT: it's hard to keep track with all your time nonsense.
TT: Am I Being Sincere Here
TT: In Retrospect It Will Probably Seem Unlikely To My Current Conversational Partner
GA: Now That I Think About It It Is Pretty Conceivable That I Will Talk To You Again In The Past After This Conversation
TT: that's because you guys always do things the hard way.
TT: and the dumb way.
GA: I Should Figure Out How The Viewport Feature Of This Application Works
GA: So I Can See What Such A Primitive Creature Looks Like
TT: haha, well i know what you guys look like.
TT: you look kind of like...
TT: howie mandel from little monsters.
TT: even though, to be perfectly frank, he was kind of a big monster.
TT: because he was a big goofy adult.
TT: and fred savage was like his child prankster sidekick.
TT: Why Would I Even Be Saying Things Like This
TT: Of Course
TT: I Have Been So Foolish
TT: It Is Because I Am Trolling You
TT: I Wonder Where I Could Have Possibly Gotten The Idea To Do That In The First Place
TT: Whoops There Goes My Human Sarcasm Again
TT: It Is Like A Regrettable Bodily Function
GA: Is This An Adversary You Have Encountered On Your Quest
TT: no, it's a movie.
TT: you should ask john about it, because he thinks it's awesome, which it is.
GA: It Seems [Tactical Omission]
GA: [Tactical Omission]
GA: [Tactical Omission]
TT: yeah, i got him this really cool bunny for his birthday, and it's really nicely knitted and everything.
TT: because i am basically in love with him, you are right.
TT: It Is At This Point I Admit To Flushed Longings For The Ignoramus Who Likes Terrible Films
TT: I Am Doing This Only To Bother You
TT: I Openly Acknowledge This Here Specifically To Improve The Chances That We Will Develop A More Favorable Relationship In The Future
GA: [Tactical Omission]
GA: I Think Ill Talk To Someone Else Now
TT: why don't you talk to john?
GA: Maybe
GA: When Along His Timeline Would You Recommend Communicating With Him
TT: oh man, i don't know.
TT: why don't you pick the time that will make the most complicated mess out of everything imaginable?
TT: you know that's what you're gonna do anyway.
TT: I Said Smugly
GA: [Tactical Omission]
GA: [Tactical Omission]
GA: [Tactical Omission]
GA: [Tactical Omission]
GA: Im Going To Talk To Your Comrades
GA: This John Human
GA: And Figure Out Whats Going On
TT: ok.
TT: if you talk to him in the past...
TT: he'll understand even less buggywhipped fuckall about time, and he'll be confused.
TT: so maybe paste something from this conversation to him? i don't know.
TT: and if you talk to him in the future...
TT: he'll probably know all this stuff, like things you've said to him but haven't said yet!
TT: and then you'll be confused.
TT: sorry, that's just how this works.
TT: don't say i didn't warn you!
GA: Consider Me Fully Briefed On The Matter.
GA: Until Next Time Rose
GA: [Tactical Omission]
TT: yeah, bye!
TT: (hehehehehehehe)
TT: The Last Thing I Said There Definitely Doesnt Make Any Sense Especially Given The Context I Now Have For Authoring The Remark
TT: I Feel Really Stupid For Having Typed It Along With Many Other Things I Just Typed

-- grimAuxiliatrix [GA] ceased trolling tentacleTherapist [TT] --

But now we can see the full transcript, including omissions, which makes it clear why Rose reacts the way she does to the contents. Because John was posing as her and making her sound dumb. Of course we already know that by now, because we saw him do it. Still, for the sake of a sort of excruciatingly thorough completionism, now we have the full transcript of the file and can see which lines Kanaya decided to omit in order to control the flow of information from the future into the past, for strategic effect. To be honest, it's getting a bit exhausting trying to keep up with the mind games of these hyper-intellectual girls, even for me. But since *technically* I am responsible for this morass of cerebrally flirtatious girlwank, I still feel a sense of duty to walk you through it.

Lalonde has finally been outmaneuvered. The horseshitometer is lopsided in your favor. And most delightfully of all, this fiendish ploy has ensured that all previous snarkticks against you have been rendered completely irrelevant. It turns out they were just a consequence of your future design all along.

You cannot hope to beat Kanaya Maryam in a snark-off. She is simply the best there is.

(heheheheheheh)

> Kanaya: Hop to 8=8.

You scan her timeline for the right moment to sync up both your sides of the dialogue. Ideally she will have long since discarded her train of thought.

You will finally reap the spoils of all your careful subterfuge. You will reap them good.

I like to think the fact that it takes a full eight conversations for Kanaya to become obsessed with Rose indicates that even while she's courting the affection of an entirely new dangerous girl, she still can't seem to get Vriska out of her head.

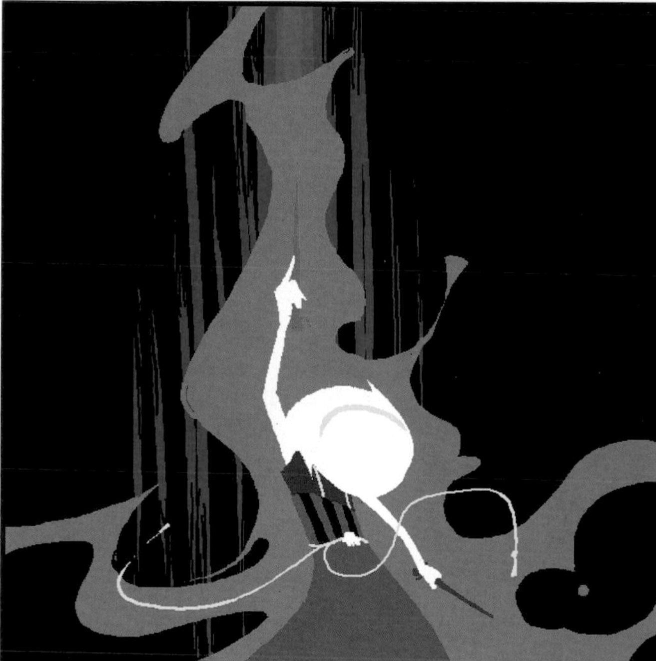

Uhh...

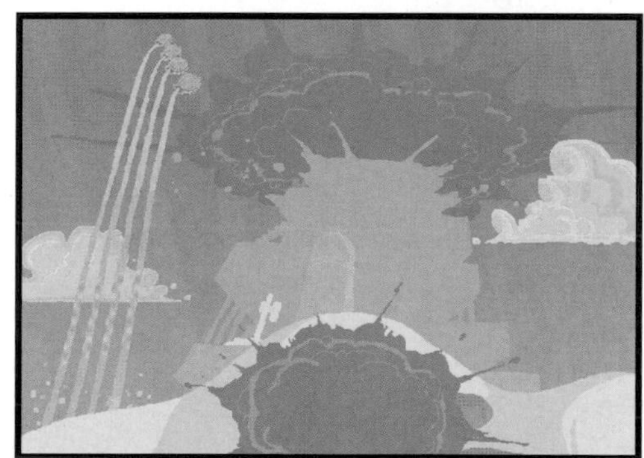

The FLIGHTY BROADS AND THEIR SNARKY HORSESHITOMETER explodes.

It simply cannot take this much horseshit.

Possibly the reason the meter device never returns in any form again (save for the prankster's gambit, I think), is that it's been completely destroyed here by Rose's finishing move in their vaguely defined rivalry. Rose basically owns Kanaya so hard at...whatever it is they're dueling about here, that it utterly obliterated the entire mechanism by which success was measured. And by "owned," I guess I mean did something so thoroughly badass and dangerously attractive that Kanaya had no choice but to admit defeat forever, fall in love with Rose, and never question this decision even once until the end of the story and beyond.

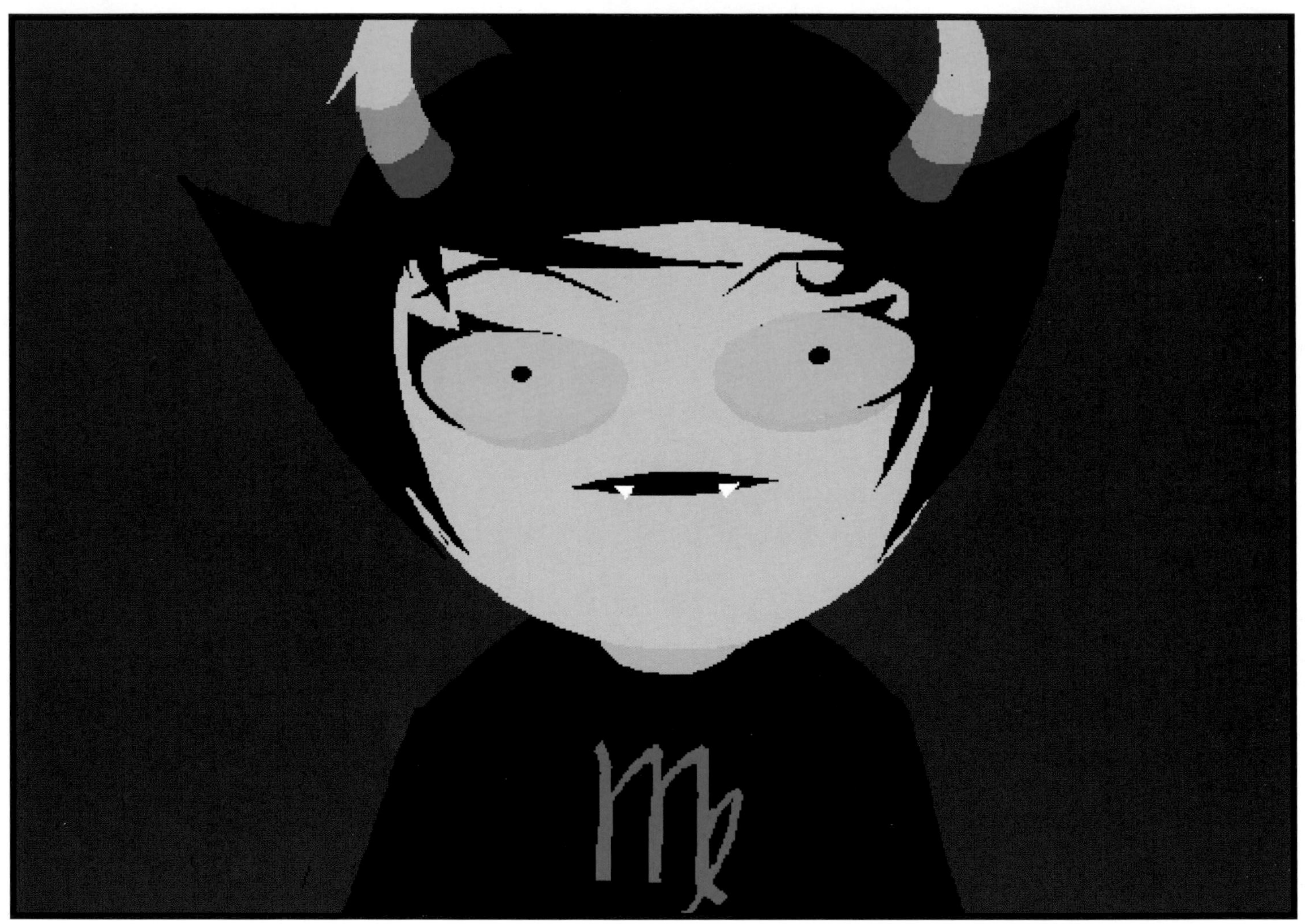

> Kanaya: Have eighth conversation.

I think this is the first one of these "wide-eyed reaction shot" memes. Or visual callbacks. I'm not sure which to even call them anymore. But there are a whole bunch of these later on. And due to the precedent established here, future instances can be read to imply the subject is not only flabbergasted by what they just saw, but also possibly a little aroused.

-- **grimAuxiliatrix** [GA] **began trolling tentacleTherapist** [TT] --

GA: What
GA: The Hell
GA: Did You Just Do
TT: Hi there.
GA: You Actually Did It
GA: Blew It Up I Mean
GA: I Had Begun To Believe That Was Embellishment
TT: This is it, isn't it?
GA: What Is It
TT: This is the eighth conversation between us, from your perspective.
TT: As well as mine.
GA: Yeah
TT: I've been looking forward to this.
GA: Really
TT: Yes.
TT: I have some questions for you.

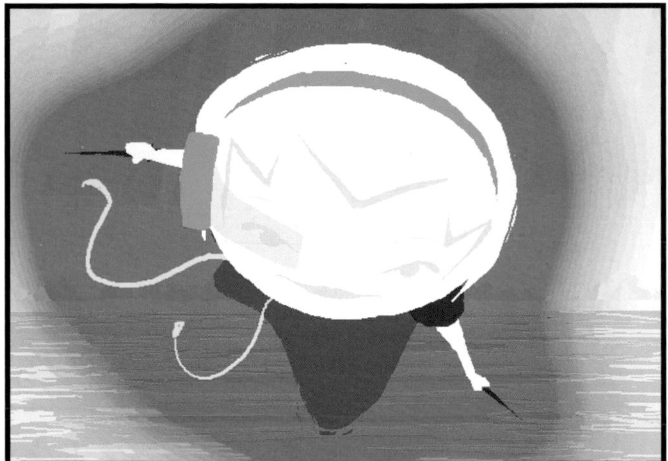

GA: What Questions Do You Have
TT: I'll start with a simple one.
TT: Do trolls have names?

> John: Make backup computer.

Rose is pretty full of herself. But maybe at this exact moment in time, she's earned a little latitude in the smugness department. Her demeanor here makes it pretty clear that from her point of view, Kanaya just passed some sort of test by jumping over all the hurdles comprised of the past eight conversations. The prize for passing the test seems to be something like: "Congrats. You are now worthy of being allowed to know me."

You make a new COSBYTOP so you can do some serious computing on the go. You barely got a chance to mess around with the first one you made before it was pilfered by a scurrilous imp. Ok it was actually a sylladex mishap but whatever.

Remember how that happened? That didn't stop being a thing that happened or anything.

> John: Reunite with loving fatherly comedian themed laptop.

arachnidsGrip [AG] began trolling ectoBiologist [EB]

AG: What.
AG: The hell........
AG: Are you doing!!!!!!!!
EB: oh hey.
AG: John, stop kissing that adult 8rown male human computer at once.
EB: but...
EB: it is bill cosby.
EB: he's back.
EB: in laptop form.
AG: Man. It is just another waste of time.
AG: Everything you do is a huge waste.
AG: A stupid pointless 8unch of w8stey w8stey w8stes.
EB: excuse me, but spending just a little quality time with my man bill here is not a w8stey w8ste at all.
EB: no amount of 8's in words will make that true.

AG: You have important things to do!
AG: Remem8er Jade????????
EB: of course i do! jeez!
EB: ok, i'm going.

John, no. Just...please don't go down that road. Trust me.

Oh, whoops, I got so distracted by the fact that Bill Cosby has since retconned his profile in popular culture to that of a notorious rapist that I missed pointing out a funny line. The one saying that an imp stole John's Cosbytop, when in fact John picked up a hat that, due to inventory overflow, launched the Cosbytop out of the sylladex and tragically knocked the imp in question over the ledge. I guess Cosby's victim count just keeps on growing.

AG: Noooooooo!!!!!!!!
AG: XXXXO
EB: what?!?!?!
AG: What the fuck are you doing now!
EB: i am going to blast off and fly a little higher, to see if i can find nanna up there!
EB: and then i will install the game.
EB: it will only take a second!
AG: No, that's not what I mean!
AG: I know that's what you're going to do.
AG: You're just not supposed to do it now!
AG: You are supposed to do something else first. And then fly up. It's right here on your timeline. 8y attempting to do the thing you're not supposed to do yet, you are just wasting more of our time!!!!!!!!
EB: jeez!!!
EB: you are incredibly bossy.
EB: more like marquise bossyfangs.
AG: I told you, that's my role playing name, not my real one! So your weak 8urn means nothing.
EB: no, you did not tell me that you like to play troll dungeons and dragons.
AG: Oh, yes John. I am really going to know what that stupid Earth game is, just 8ecause you put troll in front of it. Stupid.
EB: i will find out what your name is, i am tricky and i have ways.
AG: Pffffffff, dou8t it.
AG: Now shut up and do what you are going to do next!
EB: i don't know what i'm going to do next!
EB: apparently what i thought i was going to do next was wrong, so why don't you tell me?
AG: 8ecause.
AG: That's ridiculous!
AG: That would 8e a ridiculous way for us to do things.
EB: has it occurred to you that i might be wasting so much time because you keep pestering me telling me how much time i'm wasting?
EB: and then when i'm about to make progress you tell me i am doing the wrong thing!
EB: if it weren't for you i would be playing this game already.
AG: Okaaaaaaaay, shut up!

AG: Fine. I will hold your hand every step of the way, since that's apparently how you want to do this.
EB: but it isn't!
AG: I said shut up!
AG: Look, you are a8out to make yourself a new outfit, and THEN you will fly up and install the game.
EB: oh...
EB: but why would i do that? my ecto labsuit is rad!
AG: 8ecause you look like an idiot!
EB: :(
AG: Seriously, it's a good thing I did decide to 8other you now. Otherwise you would go through the game looking like a little weenie 8oy-Skylark.
EB: what is a boy skylark?
AG: It is the most terri8le, gutless class for wimpy losers, ones who have no idea how to handle themselves when a girl talks to them and stuff.
EB: actually, i think i remember passing that rung on my echeladder a while ago.
AG: Yes, exactly! It is 8eneath you, John.
AG: You are clearly much 8etter than that. You should dress like it.
EB: who cares what i dress like? it is what's inside the adventurer that counts.
AG: Hahahahahahahaha!
AG: I watched you actually say that with a str8 f8ce. Oh my god.

"8y attempting to do the thing you're not supposed to do yet, you are just wasting more of our time!!!!!!!!" Another candidate for *Homestuck's* tagline? I don't know, but it's a good line. When you're being guided by someone who can see your future, especially someone bossy like Vriska, it can be a little like having a back seat driver. Except you're both on a train instead, and the back seat driver is trying to boss around the passenger sitting in front of them.

EB: why are you taking such an interest in my fashion, anyway?
AG: Trolls are an extremely fashion-minded race, John. You should make a note of this, since you pretend to 8e a scientist or something.
EB: ha ha, it sounds like you have a really lame culture.
AG: John, that is an outr8geous thing to say. You don't even know how important the fashions are, so 8e quiet.
EB: laaaaaaaame.
AG: Look at that! You counted out 8 a's for me, John! That is so thoughtful of you.
EB: oh, ha ha...
EB: i didn't even count. it just...
EB: turned out like that.
AG: Really????????
EB: yeah.
AG: <33333333
EB: er...
EB: ok, anyway, i will make a new suit, but i am not ditching my ectosuit!!!
EB: it is so sweet, i look like link, if zelda was a quest about an elf scientist.
EB: i am the wind waker. it's me.
AG: I know you are, John.
AG: Now empty out your sylladex and let's see what sort of killer gear we can make for you. 8ut do it fast!

> Kanaya: Have sixteenth conversation.

-- grimAuxiliatrix [GA] began trolling tentacleTherapist [TT] --

GA: Okay This Will Probably Strike You As An Odd Moment For Me To Mention This
GA: But Actually
GA: There Are Not Many Moments Ive Observed On Your Timeline Which Wouldnt Qualify As Odd
GA: And Somehow
GA: Your Idle Moments Seem To Invite Interruption The Least
GA: And This Is A Difficult Topic For Me To Broach
GA: For Reasons That You Probably Wont Understand
TT: You're rambling again, Kanaya.
GA: Okay Sorry

GA: Ive Just Been Meaning To Say
GA: That I Read Your Instructional Guide

Here's Obsequious Vriska in full force. Obsequious Vriska shows up when someone has her full attention as a target for the purpose of advancing all of her immediate personal goals, which usually revolve around making herself feel important or exonerated of guilt. And right now that's John. Look how all he has to do is accidentally type "lame" with 8 a's, and she starts slobbering all over him, and drops a fat 8-layer heart to jumpstart this vaguely offputting campaign of flirtation. Bluh bluh, huge slut.

TT: Oh?
GA: Yeah
TT: Sorry to hear you were subjected to that.
GA: Why
TT: It was a little melodramatic in retrospect. Heavy-handed.
TT: But now it's stuck on that server forever, broadcasting the notes of very confused girl sifting through the aftermath of just another pedestrian apocalypse somewhere in paradox space.
TT: Have you ever written a message you regretted instantly upon sending?
GA: Lately
GA: Almost Perpetually
TT: That line included?
GA: Wow Yeah Kind Of
GA: Also
GA: That One
TT: I'm sure you must regard the walkthrough as pretty quaint.
TT: As a veteran of the game.
GA: Actually
GA: At The Time Of Reading It Lent Some Useful Insight
GA: Into The Nature Of The Game I Hadnt Yet Considered
GA: And
GA: The Author I Guess
TT: At the time?
TT: When exactly did you read it?
GA: Uh
GA: By The Way
GA: What Are You Doing Here
GA: Is This Part Of Your Ongoing Investigation
TT: Yes.
GA: Are These Tactics Really Necessary
TT: It's faster this way.
TT: If there's one thing you and your friends regularly remind us, it's that time is not on our side.
GA: I Know
GA: But I Thought Our Methods Earlier Were Effective
GA: In Illuminating The Underpinnings Of The Game
GA: You Ask Some Questions
GA: And I Answer

GA: If I Can
TT: Yes, that has been effective.
TT: But you don't know everything, do you?
GA: No
TT: My current strategy is comprehensive.
TT: Your notes have been helpful, but the facts you've supplied are being cross-referenced with understandings I already have, and data gathered by the sort of means presently on display.
TT: I still have more questions for you, which I will ask in time.
GA: Okay
GA: But These Means Presently On Display
GA: Are Making Me A Little Nervous
GA: I Think Its Kind Of A Reckless Use Of
TT: Of what?
GA: These Forces
TT: Dark magic, you mean?
GA: Yes
GA: Well
GA: Influence By The Gods From The Furthest Ring
GA: The Communion You Seem To Have Developed With Them I Find Kind Of Troubling
TT: I don't think they are as nefarious as you might imagine.
TT: Many of them seem to be intent on helping us.
GA: How Exactly Do You Know That
TT: From their whispers in my dreams.
GA: How Much Time Have You Really Spent Sleeping
GA: Since You Began Playing
TT: Not much.

Kanaya has been wringing her hands, waiting for the exactly right moment to fangirl all over Rose's GameFAQ walkthrough. Another way of looking at Kanaya's blossoming friend-mance with Rose is that it's a little like when someone who deems themself an "unworthy rando" starts getting access to someone internet-famous, such as a notable fanfic writer or content creator of some sort. Once they have an "in," they work the angles a little bit to solidify it as a real friendship (see: the eight-conversation "trial" that Rose essentially subjects Kanaya to in order to confirm her worthiness). Then, once the friendship has been cemented, the fan still needs to figure out some way of finally putting it out there how much she loves the creator's work, but without blowing her cool too much. She can't risk going full fangirl before the friendship deal is sealed, because that could fuck up the befriending process. Once she determines it's safe, she can start revealing traces of the hero worship a little more, but while still showing some restraint, as Kanaya's doing here. Like, "Oh, yeah. It was pretty good. I mean, it helped me out and stuff. And it told me about the author. Who, I GUESS, is also pretty cool? Yeah." Note how Kanaya also has to calibrate the tone of her praise in response to Rose's self-deprecating remarks. Like, "Oh, that old fucking thing? God, don't REMIND me about that," when all Kanaya probably wants to do is gush about it. Does any of this sound familiar? I'm hitting a little too close to home for some of you out there, I know it.

TT: But quite a lot in a failed timeline.
TT: And now and then, memories surface from that alternate reality.
TT: Vague memories, but unmistakable in familiarity, like spontaneously remembering a dream from years ago by some inexplicable catalyst.
TT: In that reality, they spoke to me in my sleep and told me much of what I needed to know.
TT: Including what to do to reset our timeline and create the present reality.
GA: That Makes Me No Less Nervous
GA: Our Understanding Is That Influence From Doomed Timelines
GA: Though Seemingly Necessary To Advance In The Alpha Reality
GA: Is Generally Inauspicious
GA: Travelers From Such Branches Are Marked For Death
GA: And Though It Was Only An Insubstantial Part Of You Which Traveled
GA: Just Memories I Suppose
GA: Its Still Troubling
TT: I have assurances I'm on the right track.
TT: Surely you must have spoken to the gods by now.
TT: What did they tell you to make you so suspicious?
GA: Actually
GA: I Havent
GA: I Have Never Visited Derse Or Traveled Beyond The Veil
GA: Prospits Moon Was My Home
GA: For Most Of My Dreaming Life
TT: It was?
GA: Yes
TT: This surprises me.
GA: Why
TT: ...
TT: Good question.
GA: Skaia Was Always The Foil For My Curiosity
GA: But It Only Showed Me What I Needed To See
GA: It Very Much Had The Presence Of Something Sentient
GA: And
GA: Benevolent
GA: But Silent
GA: Not Something To Converse With Or Be Instructed By
GA: Or Anything With An Agenda Beyond Which It Knows To Be Manifest Already
GA: Like A Very Clear Mirror
GA: That Has Everything There Is To See Inside It
GA: But Only Some Things Are Visible At Any Given Moment
GA: I Always Trusted It
GA: And I Dont Trust Gods That Would Eschew Its Light
TT: You didn't actually answer my question.
TT: When was it exactly that you read my walkthrough?
GA: Oh
GA: A While Ago
TT: Before you first contacted me?
GA: I Have To Confess That
GA: Ive Been Experiencing Something Like
GA: Impression Whiplash
GA: Since That Time
TT: What do you mean?
GA: At First I Thought You Were Foolish And Incompetent
TT: My apologies for whatever misstep I may have taken to dispel that impression.
TT: It was an honest mistake, I swear.
GA: You See Thats What Im Talking About
GA: That Was A Very Snarky Remark That Happened Just Now
GA: Stratified By Your Signature Varieties Of Insincerity Which Cut Through The Literal

Though they're printed small here, I think this was a pretty evocative sequence of panels. Again, it always goes back to "the thing that should be the real quest is never the real quest." These ruins could have been explored the "right" way, and we would have learned about the mysteries of the Green Sun as *Sburb* intended in a slow and methodical manner. But who the fuck has time for that? Rose clearly doesn't, and frankly, neither do we. So when the game is hacked in various ways, such as in this particularly blatant example, it deconstructs things for us and spreads the pieces out for us to study. We can see an almost architectural cross section of these mysterious ruins, take note of the spherical green stone structure embedded within them that represents the sun, and we can infer what this dungeon-crawling part of Rose's quest may have been like if she'd played straight, how the epiphany about the Green Sun might have been experienced the "right" way. That's what makes this a great example of how *Homestuck* works. This entire chunk of very important ruins is used as a passive stage prop, pushed into the background as a visual aid for educating the reader/characters on points of lore while allowing the story the liberty of foregrounding what it really considers important, which is the evolving relationship and interaction between these two characters.

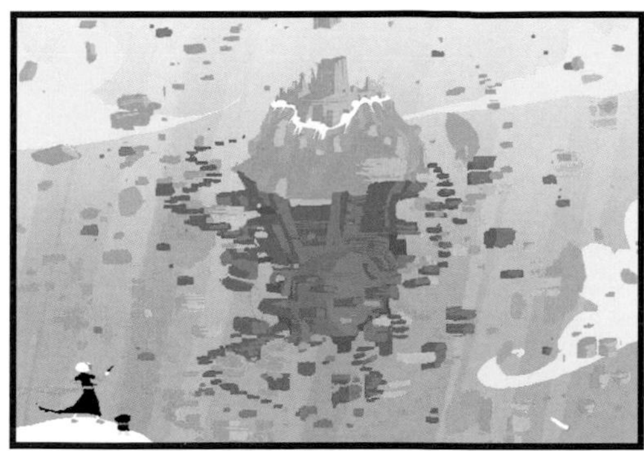

Meaning Of The Statement Like Colorful Ribbons
GA: And The Net Intent Is Something Maddening To Try To Know
GA: Its Meaning I Think Exists At The Inscrutable Nexus Of Semantic Space Where Humor Chafes Against Soft Malice
GA: A Place Perhaps The Human Mind Occupies More Comfortably I Dont Know
GA: Xenopsychology Isnt My Strong Suit
GA: Or Even A Real Word
TT: ...
GA: Uh Yeah I Know Im Babbling Again
GA: The Point Is Its Not The Type Of Behavior A Very Stupid Person Can Perpetrate
GA: And So My Impression Has Thrashed Around From Conversation To Conversation
GA: And Now
GA: Rather Than Suspecting You Of Incompetence
GA: I Have Begun To Fear Just The Opposite
GA: I Think You Might Be Dangerous
TT: To whom?
GA: Maybe Not Knowing That Is What Really Bothers Me
GA: Why Dont You Put The Turtle Ruins Down
GA: And Return To Your House
GA: I Have Sketched Some New Outfits For You That I Think Are Nice
GA: We Could Try To Make Them
GA: It Will Be Fun
TT: You seem to have taken quite an interest in my wardrobe decisions.
TT: Are all trolls so fashion-minded?
GA: Urrgh No
GA: Sadly
TT: Maybe later.
GA: What If There Isnt A Later
TT: Well, we already know there won't be.
TT: That's nothing new.
GA: I Mean
GA: There Not Being A Later Might Happen Sooner Than You Think
TT: Wow, what?
GA: I Mean
GA: For You Specifically
GA: Okay
GA: This Was Something Else I Wanted To Say
GA: Or Ask About
GA: But Im Afraid My Asking Might Play A Role In The Outcome
GA: And I Dont Know If I Want That
TT: The outcome will happen one way or another.
TT: Whether you have something to do with it or not.
TT: You might as well ask me.
TT: At least when it happens, you'll understand what it is that's happening.
TT: And just maybe, if we're really lucky, so will I.
GA: Um
TT: I have a question for you too.
TT: Let's swap ignorance, ok?
GA: Alright
GA: I Cant See You In The Future
GA: The Viewport Wont Let Me After A Certain Point

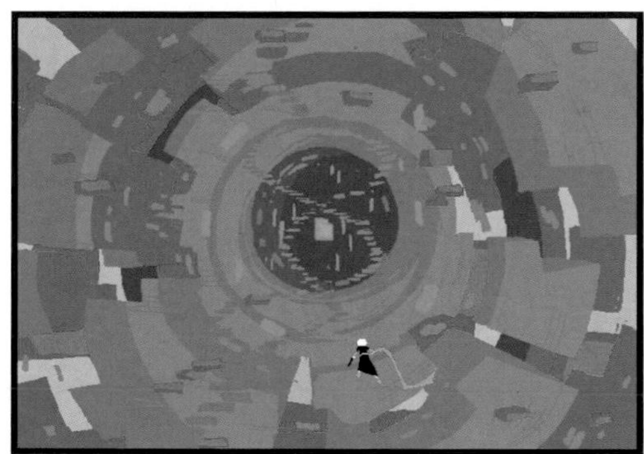

There's a John arm in the mess of pink blocks. Think Rose notices it? I doubt it. She's got a lot on her plate right now. Despite Kanaya's best efforts to play it cool, she's basically giving everything away here. "Hey, I just want you to know, I think you might be dangerous. And that's bad. Yeah that, um, really sucks. It sucks so much I think I'm going to need to spend lots and lots of time keeping an eye on you and talking to you. And protecting you from yourself. And also sort of being your mom? Can I be your mom too? Is that cool? Great. Also btw I drew lots of nice outfits for you already. Maybe later you can try them on? I'll watch, and tell you how great my clothes look on you." Also note earlier in the conversation how Kanaya is being cagey about exactly when she read the walkthrough. Rose asks when she read it, and Kanaya changes the subject. If Kanaya copped to the time, she'd have to admit that she studied Rose well in advance of meeting her, which reframes her actions up to this point as a little stalker-ish, and much, much less cool than she was making herself out to be. But then she finally cops to it obliquely on the previous page. Which may have spurred this breach in composure, where she literally pitches Rose on trying on the fan outfits she made for her.

GA: Its Black
GA: But Only For You
GA: Not The Others
TT: When?
GA: Several Hours From Now
GA: Do You Know Why This Could Be
TT: I have no idea.
TT: I can't see the future.
TT: I'm a disreputable Derse Dreamer, remember?
TT: But I promise that if I have a hand in it, it won't be because you told me.
TT: Does that make you feel better?
GA: Sort Of
GA: But It Remains Ominous
TT: Is that why you want to dissuade me from my admittedly zealous investigation to go play dress-up again?
TT: Because our time here is almost up?
TT: And you hope what's on the other side of the dark curtain for me is not some sort of corruption or damnation?
GA: Also Sort Of
TT: That's thoughtful of you.
TT: To strive to pacify me as I scuffle down this black corridor.
GA: Wait
GA: Is That What Im Doing
TT: Is it?
GA: On Second Thought
GA: Thats Not What I Want To Do
TT: Oh.
TT: That's a pity.
TT: Who will make sure my soul isn't forfeit in service of gods then?
GA: Well
GA: I Hope That Doesnt Happen
GA: But Id Rather Not Get Stuck In That Kind Of Pattern Again
GA: So If You Want To Wreck Turtle Villages And Tear Your Planet Apart On The Counsel Of Dark Gods
GA: Fine With Me I Guess
TT: What do you mean, "again?"
GA: Ur
GA: Ill Do The Thing You Do When You Dont Say Anything
GA: "..."
TT: One simple word can so easily begin a story in a very thick book.
TT: But I guess we won't open this one?
GA: What Was Your Question
GA: I Believe Youre Owed Some Compensatory Ignorance
TT: Yes.
TT: I was wondering.
TT: What do you know about the Green Sun ?
GA: Ive Never Heard Of It
TT: Thank you.
TT: The transaction was very tidy.
GA: Agreed

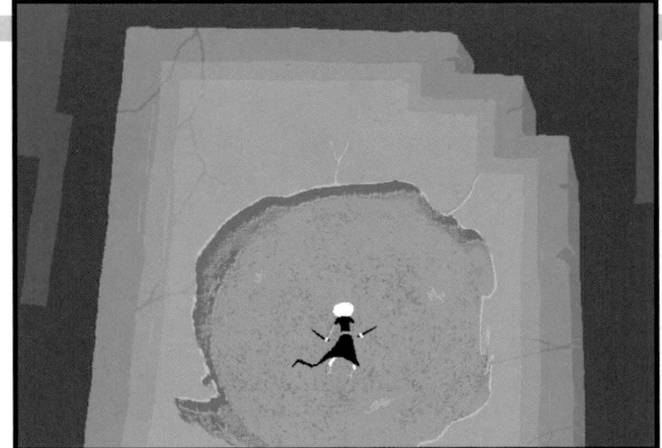

> John: Empty sylladex.

Learning about the Green Sun is a pretty big deal, because it functions as the cosmological focal point for Paradox Space, or at least for the full scope of everything relevant that happens inside it for the purposes of this story. Kind of like how Skaia is the cosmological focal point for any given session. In other words, the addition of this celestial body signifies a massive broadening of the cosmic scale of the story. This is not just being pulled out of a hat here, by the way, even if it may seem so. There are signs of it back in Act 3, when Jade is dueling Bec. You can see flickers of the sun, if you pay attention. The Green Sun, in addition to its many other intriguing qualities, along with an origin story that has convoluted entanglement with story events all throughout this act, serves as the unlimited power source for First Guardians, which is technically what makes them "omnipotent." I know this was an idea I had when initially conceiving of First Guardians. But I'm also sure that after revealing Bec, I began gathering ideas for how to weave this vast cosmic body into the greater lore of the story, how it relates to the other First Guardian we know, like Doc, and then how this all comes together to tilt the plot in a certain grandiose direction. So this isn't just some wild-ass curve ball being slung at the reader out of nowhere. This chartreuse behemoth has been lurking in the shadows as a narrative construct for the last several acts, biding its time, waiting to make its move. This is its move. And you can tell it's Very Serious, because Rose said it with a special green flashing GIF inserted into her dialogue.

AG: This is the most ridiculous pile of useless crap I have ever seen.
AG: Why did you pick up all this junk????????
Rocks, mushrooms, shoes........
AG: Jegus, John.
EB: jegus?
AG: Yes. Jegus!
EB: how do you know about jegus? do you even know what that is?
AG: I have no idea! It's something Terezi has 8een saying non stop for some reason.
AG: It is weirdly infectious.
AG: What is it, some sort of human profanity?
EB: no. well, yeah kind of.
EB: it is a misspelling of an adult male bearded human, who was magic.
AG: 8oooooooooring.
EB: shrug!
AG: John! Is that a frog I see there?
EB: uh, yes. it is.
AG: How do you have a frog already????????
EB: i dunno. i found it, and i decided to captchalogue it for some reason.
EB: frogs are pretty cool.
AG: It seems awfully early in your game for you to 8e finding frogs. Your session sure is weird!
EB: huh. ok...
EB: apparently it is considered illegal contraband.

EB: why would a frog be illegal?
AG: John, shut your trap! We are in a hurry here.
EB: bossy!!!!!!!!
AG: Ok, I think I can make you a completely faaaaaaaa8ulous outfit using this trash, and may8e some other stuff around your hive.
AG: 8ut you have to do exactly what I say!
EB: bossy bossy bossy bossy bossy bossy bossy bossy.
EB: to the eighth power.
EB: times eight infinities!!!
AG: H8RRY 8P!!!!!!!!!
EB: that was nine !'s.
AG: Oops.

> John: Hurry up!

If you actually played the minigame at the start of Act 3, you resonate deeply with this useless pile of crap, because you were literally the one who scrambled around the map to pick it all up. And as such you will take more offense at Vriska's slander of your carefully gathered booty than John appears to. Vriska continues feeding him a steady diet of negs, which John parries adroitly by not really caring about anything she says, and offers his own goofy comebacks. Her aggressive flirtation strategy wildly mixes negwork and minor points of flattery, but John's retort patterns clearly throw her off her game. Her nine !'s indicate this better than anything. She very rarely misses her 8-character mark. This may actually be the only time it ever happens? It surely convinces her beyond any reasonable doubt that John is a worthy adversary.

EB: so, uh...
EB: red sneakers, some jeans, a tee shirt, and another shirt...
EB: this is the fabulous outfit you had in mind?
AG: Yes! Isn't it awesome?
EB: it's pretty cool and all...
EB: i was just picturing something...
EB: more elaborate? like maybe more adventurey.
AG: Fuck that.
AG: This is a really hot look for you, John. It makes you look a million times more cool, instead of some kind of overa8sconding daggerlance fl8ling pansy.
EB: what?
AG: Now move your ass!
AG: Go go go go go go go go!!!!!!!!
EB: ok, jeeeeeeeez.

> John: Blast off.

EB: pchoo.
AG: D::::
EB: ha ha, just messin' with ya.

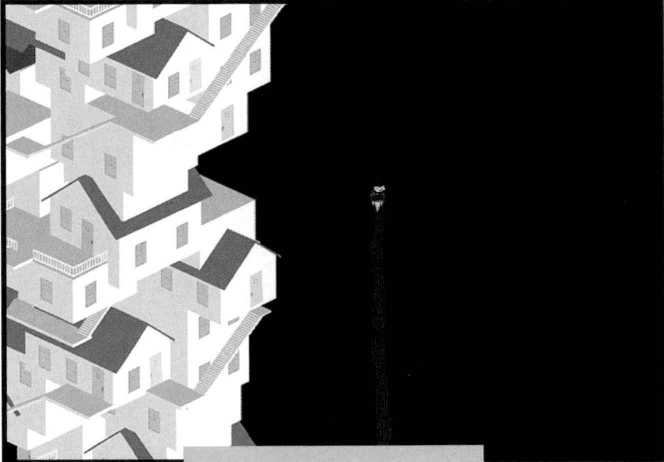

EB: pchoooooooo!
AG: Yesssssss.

Vriska does John the ultimate favor, in her own mind, which is to make him look just a little more like Vriska. The gradual Vriskafication of John is her true objective, almost like marking her territory, or branding the most important kid of this session as "hers" so no one gets any ideas. She also alludes to the fact that this makeover has the added benefit of making him look less like the Pupa edition of her loathsomely weak and cowardly ex-boyfriend (if you can even call him that). I guess it's like coming out of a shitty relationship and meeting a new guy who seems much better, but through no fault of his own, the poor guy bears a few stylistic similarities to your bad, lame ex. So of course all that has to go. So you rummage through your own closet, give him some of *your* cool clothes, and say there, much better. Now you remind me of a cool person instead of a lame person. People do this, right? Alright, maybe not. But VRISKA does it, and I think we're in agreement that whatever Vriska does is all that really matters.

EB: ok...
EB: marquise bossyfangs mcsekret, this has been a lot of fun...
EB: but i have to go talk to my pals now, and also rescue jade!
AG: Yes, I know that, dummy! I am in complete command of your timeline, remem8er?
E8: oh yeah. sure, if you say so.
AG: We will not speak again for a while. 8ut for me it will only 8e a moment.
AG: I do not envy the Serketless coldspell you are a8out to endure, John.
EB: that's too bad.
EB: how long will it be?
AG: Man, calm down! It will only 8e a couple of hours or so.
AG: Sweet Jegus, I have clearly done a num8er on you to engender such a frothing o8session so quickly.
AG: Not surprising. It's just the 8urden that comes with 8eing so damned awesome. 8ut you will figure that out soon enough John, 8ecause I have you well on your way.
EB: ha ha, i guess...
AG: Phase two of my program for you 8egins in a little while.
AG: In the meantime, try not to get corrupted 8y anyone too lame. Especially no8ody with 8rown text or gray text, or any shit ugly color at all for that matter.

EB: ok, i will try.
EB: thanks for all the help. bye, ms. serket!
AG: 8ye, John........
AG: W8.
AG: John what?
EB: Anderson.
AG: Ok. Til next time, Mr. Anderson.
EB: (hehehehehehehehe)

-- arachnidsGrip [AG] ceased trolling ectoBiologist [EB] --

> John: Pester someone's server player's server player.

-- ectoBiologist [EB] began pestering turntechGodhead [TG] --

EB: hey dave!
TG: hey
EB: wow, it's been a while since we talked, hasn't it.
TG: has it
EB: i think the last time i talked to you, i was doing exactly what im doing now...
EB: which is blasting off from my house.
EB: or was it?
EB: wow, i can't remember...
TG: man who cares
TG: i mean thats great and all
TG: but i talked to you plenty more times since that from where im standing
TG: ive got to make this quick
EB: oh.
EB: you mean like the trolls?

Most spoken lines can be read as metatextual missives addressing the reader as well. "I do not envy the Serketless coldspell you are a8out to endure" certainly counts as one. This line was my way of saying, whew, I really feel sorry for you guys, but we have to take a little break from Vriska for a while. I know, it's tough. Stay strong, and we'll get through this. But the fact that John is about to talk to Dave sort of softens the blow. They are the Original Pals. It feels comforting to return to their jocular repartee. The quality of their boybanter will never let you down.

EB: are you using the troll time chat gizmo?
TG: fuck no fuck that trollian horseshit
TG: its just regular old time travel
TG: im from the future
EB: oh ok. is this dave sprite?
TG: no
TG: just regular ordinary dave from the fucking future nothing special dude come on
EB: well, excuse me, but i still think time travel sounds kind of special.
EB: sorry you are so jaded by awesome shit!
TG: yeah ok it is awesome but im in a hurry
EB: what is it?
TG: i need to borrow some boondollars off you
EB: boondollars? i thought they didn't do anything.
TG: no they do do something
EB: what do they do?
TG: what do you think they buy shit its fucking money
EB: what do they buy?
TG: i cant answer all these questions dude youll find out anyway its not like youll even really need your money
TG: you you might as well give it to me
EB: uh...
EB: how much do you need?
TG: all of it
EB: oh, fuck that!!!
TG: man you just said you thought it was useless why do you care
EB: but you just said it wasn't useless!
TG: ill pay you back
EB: really? when?
TG: in the future
TG: if theres one thing im not short on its the fuckin future
EB: how far in the future are you from?
EB: i thought we only had something like 24 hours until, like...
EB: game over.
TG: yeah we do
TG: but chronologically ive been around for at least triple that
EB: wow. how...
EB: i don't get how that works!
TG: no shit your deal is wind not time

TG: youre on easy street what is there even to think about with wind
TG: like what angle to blow it at to fly a damn kite or how gentle its gotta be to make a picnic go swimmingly
TG: its kiddie bullshit time is serious fucking business
TG: leave it to the pros ok
EB: but, doesn't going back in time make an alternate reality?
EB: i thought that's what happened with dave sprite, he came back to make sure i didn't die and this is a new timeline now.
TG: yeah it can work that way
TG: or not
TG: ive been very careful
TG: this whole operation is strung together with stable time loops
TG: no timeline offshoots cause thats when daves start dying and that isnt no good for nobody
EB: daves, plural?
TG: yeah
TG: there are a bunch of daves running around the timeline
EB: oh, man.
TG: but they are all me
TG: i mean they will all become me and ill become

There's a very noble tradition in *Homestuck* involving characters rambling in a ridiculously casual way about completely extraordinary topics. Things such as the end of the world, death and resurrection, alternate selves, and time travel. Like, "u time travelin dude?", "yeah guess so", "oh that's cool i guess. hey let's spend the next 50 lines arguing about money", "yeah totally". But even this principle is being a little bit spoofed by John (again, very casually) reminding Dave that he sounds jaded about his own kickass time adventures. So part of this overly casual pattern is for straight-up comedic effect, I guess. That probably goes without saying. I think it also functions as a corollary to HS treating "awesome background lore and puzzles" with a sense of frivolity, dismissing them as things unworthy of much overt scrutiny or interest by the characters. It's the backgrounding of the extraordinary, and the foregrounding of the mundane, in order to focus on relationships, character profiles, and arcs. If the kids were always flying off the deep end about how INSANE it is that the world ended, or how CRAZY it is that Dave can time travel now, that would absorb way too much of the conversational focus and we would not be experiencing the story and characters as intended.

them one way or another
TG: thats how stable time loops work shit takes a lot of planning and precise choreography
TG: ive got some help though
EB: help?
EB: sounds like you have been talkin' to some trolls!
TG: yeah
EB: they seem to be getting more talkative lately.
TG: man dont even get me started with that
TG: the 24 hour span of the reckoning is like some kind of critical spike in us dealing with troll bullshit
TG: i guess its just when the most shit is going down so they figure thats the best time to mess with us
EB: yeah, that makes sense.
EB: i guess since you've lived three days in one day, you've just been hassled that much more?
TG: i dont know man they seem to flock to me
TG: ive been laying waste to chumps nonstop
TG: its like they heard somebody over here was handing out asses and theyve known nothing but years of bitter ass famine
EB: heheh.
EB: so what is the future like?
EB: or uh, the 3x future...
EB: do we win???
TG: oh you know
TG: noirs outta control
TG: rose is crazy jades crazier and youre
TG: well youre you
TG: and together were up to our bulges and miscellaneous bullshit alien physiology in hot sloppy shenanigans while hatching plans under our feathery asses like a bunch of cage free farm fresh motherfuckers
TG: but im not about to get into specifics cause this is complicated enough as it is
TG: and if i started ranting too much about the future id start sounding like one of these smug alternian shitheads and im not about to drop that retarded science on my good bro
TG: so im staying on track here
TG: speaking of which
TG: give me your money
EB: but...
EB: i worked hard saving up that money!
EB: i have a whole boonbuck now.
TG: oh christ
TG: only one
TG: well fuck nevermind then
TG: i thought youd have more by now but thats goddamn peanuts
EB: :(
TG: i mean
TG: ill take it anyway but damn
EB: tell me what you want with it!
TG: im working the system here
TG: using time loops to manipulate the incipispheres financial sector
TG: making a goddamn killing in the lohacse
EB: lohacse?
TG: lohac stock exchange
EB: um...
EB: lohac?
TG: my planet
TG: land of heat and clockwork dude come on
TG: you know like gears and lava and shit
EB: oh, huh.
EB: that sounds unpleasant.
TG: wrong it kicks ass
EB: your unpleasant face is what kicks ass!
EB: or DOESN'T, more like.
TG: egbert stfu and give me your goddamn boonbuck j3gus fuck
TG: ill turn it into a boonmint in an hour and youll get it back ok
EB: j3gus?
EB: *narrows eyes suspiciously...*
TG: no comment
EB: i don't even know how to give it to you!
EB: they are just more weird gaming abstractions, how do we do this?
TG: you can wire it to my account
TG: ill send you the app
EB: i'm really pretty busy you know. i have to help jade!
TG: i know
TG: but this takes like two seconds
EB: bluh...
EB: fiiiiiiiine.
TG: dude

The "years of bitter ass famine" line sounds like a euphemism for one of the comic's longer pauses over its tenure. Like the gigapause. Everybody was just *starving* for ass by the time that was about to end. I had stored up an awful lot of ass to hand out by then too. But enough about GAME OVER. That's probably going to be printed about ten books from now, when I am a senior citizen. Anyway, on a more substantive note, a key takeaway from this conversation is that, after arguing uselessly about money for a couple pages, John and Dave are twigging onto the influence their respective Scourge Sister allies are starting to have on them, in speaking habits and otherwise. Neither boy is that approving of what they observe from the other, sowing the seeds of a bro-schism. This probably does more than anything to help convey the fact that Vriska and Terezi primarily view these two boys as conduits for their own rivalry and use them as such. They basically looked at both John and Dave and took that "choose your fighter" meme very literally.

TG: dont do the vriska thing ok
TG: shes messed up we talked about this
TG: or will talk
EB: who?
TG: whatever
TG: alright app incoming
-- turntechGodhead [TG] sent ectoBiologist [EB] the file "virtualporkhollow.exe" --
TG: gotta go later

-- turntechGodhead [TG] ceased pestering ectoBiologist [EB] --

> Dave: Make a goddamn killing in the LOHACSE.

It is the perfect crime.

> Dave: Receive transfer from John.

There probably aren't many panels that capture "quintessential *Homestuck* shenanigans" better than these. Is *any* of this bullshit strictly necessary to accomplish whatever financial caper Dave is trying to pull off? Of course not. But this is what happens when you're well past the point of no return in a scheme Terezi is closely involved with. John learns this too much later, during his jaunt through canon informally known as Scarf Quest.

Looks like Egbert came through. He wires you his measly BOONBUCK. It's not much, but it is immediately funneled into the pipelines of your various investment scams, and quickly begins paying dividends.

The figures are tight.
You have this shit on fiduciary lockdown.
The economy belongs to you.

> Dave: Answer.

-- gallowsCalibrator [GC] began trolling turntechGodhead [TG]

GC: H3Y D4V3
GC: B1G N3WS
TG: hey
TG: have i made enough money yet
GC: OF COURS3 YOU H4V3
GC: MOR3 TH4N W3 COULD 3V3R POSS1BLY F1GUR3 OUT WH4T TO DO W1TH
GC: BUT TH4T 1S NOT TH3 B1G N3WS! >:]
TG: ok
GC: 1 M4D3 YOU 4NOTH3R COM1C
TG: fuck

"Virtual PORKHOLLOW v41.3" looks pretty slick. Totally ironed out all the kinks that were plaguing earlier versions. v41.1 was complete trash. Don't even get me started on v40.7. Any version under v37.2 literally made its users want to commit suicide. The perils of this shitty application resulted in one of the greatest losses of crocodile life in LOHAC history. Okay, enough of that. Dave's amount of money there really is outrageous. 216 trillion trillion. It's such a ludicrous sum, it really reframes Dave's solicitation of John for money as especially preposterous. How much money could he assume that John possibly could have at this point in his adventure, knowing full well that John isn't engaging in the same stock market scams that made Dave this rich? Even if John had a BILLION boonbucks, it wouldn't put the slightest dent in Dave's total as an overall percentage. In fact, this makes it clear it was so illogical for Dave to go hitting John up for cash, that there's no way there wasn't some other motive. I think he just wanted any excuse to go chat up his good buddy. Given the chats we've seen in the past, it certainly wouldn't be the first time.

002742

TG: bout time
TG: what took so long
GC: 1 R3S3NT TH3 1MPL1C4T1ON D4V3
GC: TH4T 1 4M NOT WORK1NG T1R3L3SSLY ON YOUR B3H4LF 4S W3LL 4S ON B3H4LF OF TH3 F1N3 4RTS
GC: JUST B3C4US3 YOU GO FOR HOURS W1THOUT H34R1NG FROM M3
GC: DO3SNT M34N 1 4M NOT SL4V1NG 4W4Y H3R3 4T M4K1NG YOU R1CH
GC: F1N4NC14LLY 4ND 4RT1ST1C4LLY
GC: 1TS JUST 1 DONT H4V3 TH3 LUXURY OF YOUR 3XP4ND3D T1M3FR4M3
GC: M1ST3R THR33 D4YS 1N ON3 >:[
TG: k cool lets see it
GC: 1S TH3R3 4NYTH1NG TH4T 4 HUM4N COOLK1D C4NNOT DO???
GC: http://tinyurl.com/T34CHM3D4V3

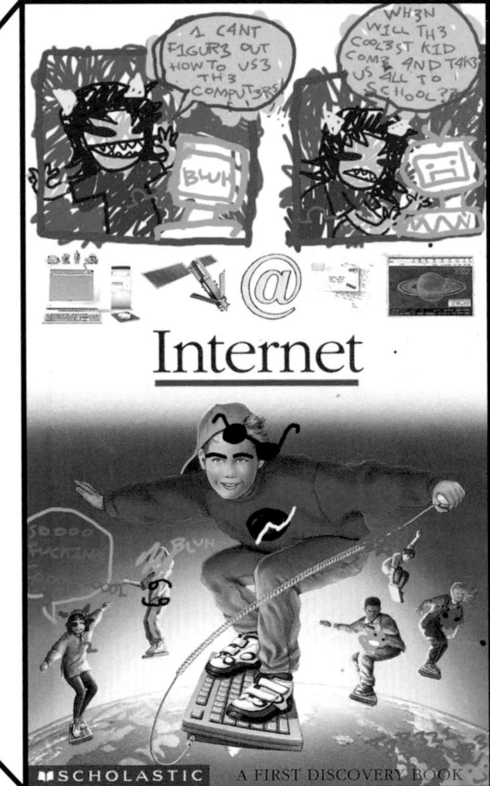

GC: 1 DOUBT 1T! >8D
TG: damn
TG: thats incredible
GC: TH3 PH3NOM3NON OF TH3 COOLK1D 1S 4 F4SC1N4T1NG ON3 D4V3
GC: 1 H4V3 STUD13D 1T
GC: D1D YOU KNOW TH4T W3 DO NOT H4V3 COOLK1DS ON 4LT3RN14?
TG: oh shit really
TG: that loud sound of shock you just smelled was my jaw hitting the floor
GC: 1TS TRU3
GC: SOM3 TRY TO B3 1 TH1NK, W1THOUT 3V3N B31NG 4W4R3 OF TH3 T3MPL4T3 TH3Y 4R3 STR1V1NG FOR
GC: 1T 1S 4 S4D SP3CT4CL3
GC: BUT 1 TH1NK YOU 4R3 PROB4BLY TH3 COOL3ST COOLK1D D4V3
GC: 4LL TH3S3 OTH3R HORNS3S 4SS3S SURF1NG ON K3YBO4RDS 4ND PUTT1NG H4TS ON TURNW4YS 4R3 4 BUNCH OF STUT1D NUMPNUTS
GC: TH3Y H4V3 NOTH1NG ON TH3 ON3 TRU3 STR1D3R
TG: yeah i mean
TG: i cant possibly argue with any of that
TG: so are we done making money yet or what
GC: OH 1 DONT KNOW
GC: T3CHN1C4LLY W3 W3R3 4 LONG T1M3 4GO
TG: yeah i kinda figured
GC: BUT 1TS 4 FUN W4Y TO STR3TCH OUT TH3 T1M3 YOUV3 GOT L3FT, 1SNT 1T?
GC: >:]
TG: im not complaining
TG: but you said there was something specific we were working toward here
TG: i mean aside from buying up all the nastiest fraymotifs
GC: Y3S BOTH 4R3 TRU3
GC: 4ND TH3R3 4R3 SOM3 YOU H4V3NT BOUGHT Y3T!
GC: TH4T 1S 1MPORT4NT, W3 N33D TO K33P YOU COMP3T1T1V3 W1TH JOHN
TG: competitive
TG: man
TG: dont matter what i do im not gonna outpace egbert
GC: DONT S4Y TH4T! YOUV3 GOT TO B3L13V3 1N YOURS3LF D4V3

There's apparently an entire genre of ridiculous "coolkid art" out there, either illustrations or photos, featuring extremely cool boys doing rad things in order to promote a company, product, or in this case, apparently the Internet itself? I don't remember exactly when it started... But I began hoarding these graphics because they reminded me of Dave, or more specifically, the type of image one of Dave's friends would show him, perhaps strategically altered like this, in order to give him a hard time. Terezi is the perfect foil for this idea, of course. And since Dave is a true coolkid, he can't let it be known that he feels owned by it, and just rolls with it instead. In fact, due to their high compatibility with his own sense of humor, there's no way he isn't being genuine when he says these things are incredible. He really means it. And he's right, this shit absolutely is incredible. Top-shelf content by literally any standard.

TG: hey its not like the futures a mystery or anything weve both seen it
TG: well
TG: ive seen it
TG: youve just caught a whiff of it
TG: like a hungry beggar loitering cross the street of an olive garden
TG: just cause a filthy vagrants barred from entry dont mean a dude doesnt know italian foods nearby its a fucking fact to his nose
GC: DO NOT D1STR4CT FROM TH3 1SSU3 W1TH YOUR S4SSY R3M4RKS 4BOUT 34RTH 1T4L14N FOOD
GC: Y34H OK, JOHN M4Y S3RV3 YOU YOUR OWN BULG3 ON 4 S1LV3R TURN T4BL3 PR3 SCR4TCH
GC: BUT WH4T 4BOUT 4FT3R TH4T?
GC: W3 N33D YOU TO K33P P4C3
GC: 1T 1S TH3 CL4SS1C STRUGGL3, TH3 HUM4N 34RTH COOLK1D V3RSUS TH3 34RTH HUM4N N3RD
GC: WHO W1LL W1N??????? >:O
GC: (D4V3 D4V3 D4V3)
TG: yeah fine
TG: so whats the other thing we were accomplishing here
TG: does that get to be not an obnoxious secret yet
GC: Y3S, NOW 1S TH3 T1M3
GC: YOU MUST W1R3 YOUR BOONDOLL4RS TO MY 4CCOUNT
TG: ok so this was your game
TG: to get rich off me
GC: Y3SSSSSSSSSSSS >8]
GC: BUT S3R1OUSLY 1TS 1MPORT4NT!
GC: 1T 1S CR1T1C4L TO 4LL OUR PL4NS
TG: alright well its not like i even have a problem parting with this useless bullshit money
TG: how much do you need
GC: 413 BOONBONDS
TG: thats all
TG: i can afford to give you a fuckload more than that
TG: how bout i give you an even boonbank
GC: NO!!!
GC: 1T MUST B3 3X4CTLY TH4T 4MOUNT
TG: ok just to be clear
TG: thats 413
TG: not "aie"
GC: Y34H
GC: J3RK >:P
TG: whats up with that number
TG: ive seen it around
GC: TH3Y 4R3 TH3 NUM3R4LS OF TH3 BL1ND PROPH3TS
TG: whats that mean
GC: 1 DONT KNOW >:?
TG: ok awesome
GC: 4LSO
GC: 4T TH3 3X4CT 3ND OF TH1S CONV3RS4T1ON
GC: YOU MUST W1R3 TH3 MON3Y TO MY 4CCOUNT 3X4CTLY 6 HOURS 4ND 12 M1NUT3S 1NTO TH3 P4ST
GC: MY P4ST! R3L4T1V3 TO MY PR3S3NT MOM3NT 4S OF TYP1NG TH1S
TG: you mean i can do that
TG: then
TG: why werent we just wiring money into the past for these investment escapades instead of doing all this time traveling
GC: B3C4US3!
GC: TH4T W4SNT TH3 PL4N
GC: W3 H4D TO PL4Y 4LONG W1TH TH3 ST4BL3 T1M3 LOOPS W3 W3R3 PR3S3NT3D W1TH
GC: YOU KNOW, M4K3 SUR3 4LL THOS3 D4V3S RUNN1NG 4ROUND 3X1ST3D 1N TH3 F1RST PL4C3
TG: oh yeah
TG: i knew that its just frustrating sometimes its like paradox space makes you do everything the hard way
GC: Y34H T3LL M3 4BOUT 1T
GC: BUT H3Y 1TS B33N FUN PL4Y1NG 4LONG, H4SNT 1T?
TG: sure
GC: W3V3 GOT TO K33P B31NG D3L1C4T3 W1TH T1M3
GC: 1F YOU ST4RT B3ND1NG TH3 RUL3S 4ND T4K1NG SHORTCUTS
GC: TH4TS WH3N D34D D4V3S ST4RT P1L1NG UP
GC: D34D D4V3S 4R3 TH3 3N3MY!
GC: 4S D3L1GHTFUL 4S 1T 1S TO SM3LL TH31R SW33T C4NDY BLOOD 3V3RYWH3R3
TG: yeah
TG: reminds me
TG: i made you a comic a while ago
GC: YOU D1D???

Compared to the John/Vriska conversations, this exchange gives the sense that Dave and Terezi get along a little more organically than the other two. There's a similar teasing, neggy dynamic here, but they seem to at least be starting on a similar wavelength, with both being interested in bad comics, scamming rubes out of loot, and talking about how cool Dave is. Terezi has a similar purpose as Vriska, to use this guy as an extension of their rivalry, but it also feels like she'd be just as fine dropping the rivalry aspect and instead just making a cool new friend. Vriska's solicitation feels like a higher-stake game, more heavy-handed. She's a bit more forced in the way that she tries to mold John in her image, and more overt or desparate-seeming in her flirtatious methods. She gets flustered, whereas Terezi does not. Certain things seem to come easier for Terezi, which is part of what fuels the old rivalry. Vriska seems to have some jealousy issues about it, which were expressed in Hivebent through Terezi's more cunning manipulation methods, which don't need any special powers. Since Vriska's insecurity tells her this stuff doesn't come as easy to her as it does for Terezi, she feels like she has to cheat through use of mind control and such. The insecurity over "things come easy for her, but not for me" seems to be a lot of what's behind Vriska's brute-force approach to certain things, which includes completely dominating John's attention for most of the remaining act.

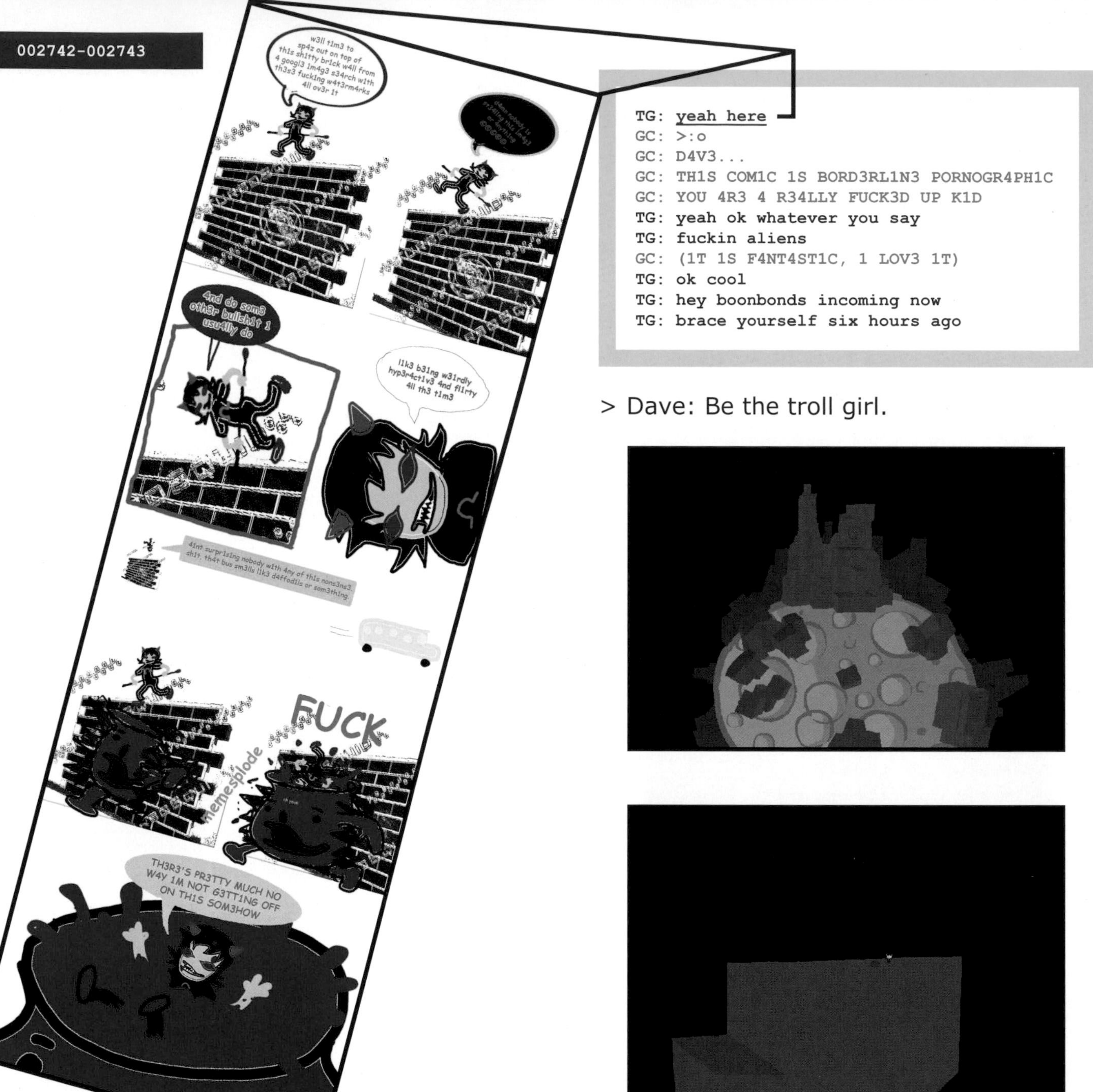

TG: yeah here
GC: >:o
GC: D4V3...
GC: TH1S COM1C 1S BORD3RL1N3 PORNOGR4PH1C
GC: YOU 4R3 4 R34LLY FUCK3D UP K1D
TG: yeah ok whatever you say
TG: fuckin aliens
GC: (1T 1S F4NT4ST1C, 1 LOV3 1T)
TG: ok cool
TG: hey boonbonds incoming now
TG: brace yourself six hours ago

> Dave: Be the troll girl.

Dave pretends he doesn't understand how this masterpiece he just made could be interpreted as pornographic, even though the final panel literally has Terezi acknowledging that she is sexually aroused by the act of splashing into the top of the Kool-Aid Man's head. Maybe Dave knows exactly what he's doing. Maybe he's being "too cool" to admit it. Maybe everybody here low-key knows the score when it comes to all *kinds* of subtext. Maybe low-key knowing the score in virtually all situations is the very definition of "being cool." And hence, you have just understood what my secret is to being so cool. Which is definitely a thing a cool person would say.

You are suddenly the troll girl.

In a different game session.

In the past.

> Terezi: Sniff Skaiaward.

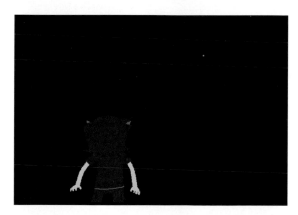

You have recently retreated to the Veil to hide from a mysterious demon which appears to be bent on your destruction. Suddenly nobody understands anything.

There is not much to do but wander around the laboratory while the others squabble amongst each other and search for answers. You point your nose Skaiaward. It is a refreshing blue minty dot against the Medium's dark canvas. It is very far away from this meteor though. It is hard to pick up its scent clearly.

> Terezi: Deploy smelloscope.

You make use of your trusty SMELLOSCOPE, an item you crafted during your adventure. It came in handy so many times.

> Terezi: Take a whiff.

A highly rewarding and hard-earned gambit from having cleared Hivebent is that we now have the ability to hop over to the troll meteor literally any time, for any reason. We don't need to be cagey with that environment anymore, because we know who all the trolls are, and we know most of their backstories, with only a few key omissions which we are working to fill in as a significant narrative objective for the rest of the act. This gives us (by which I mean, me) a lot of firepower to work with. Let's say I feel like having Terezi flash back to an earlier point where she goes up to the roof to use a smelloscope for some damn reason? Sure, we can do that. We can do *anything*. Just as long as it doesn't incidentally involve providing the answer to any of your most important, burning questions about the story.

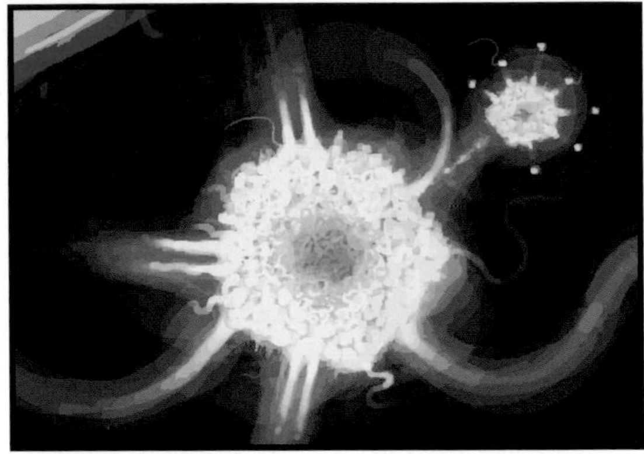

Your keen nose penetrates deep into the Insniffisphere I mean Incipisphere and zeroes in on the familiar honey-sweet smell of Prospit.

Thank goodness it is still safe. It would be terrible if the demon were to...

OH NO!

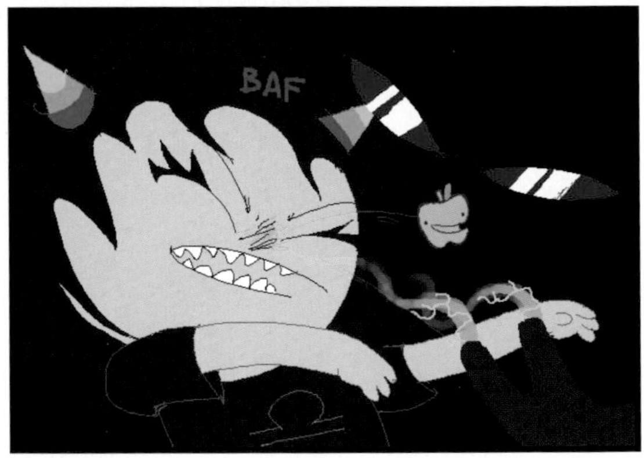

You take the brunt of the stellar smellsplosion like a sour apple punch to the snout!

> Terezi: Return to party.

Okay, I guess I was lying. Almost right away, I'm using the ability to cut away to any point on the meteor's timeline to fill in some critical gaps in the history and thus answer a few burning questions by providing a more complete picture of what happened. Here's the placement of a key event somewhere on the timeline, well before Terezi works with Dave but a little after the trolls have arrived on this meteor to escape this "demon." The event is the destruction of Prospit, through a huge burst of what we should recognize as Green Sun energy from either Doc, Bec, or (possibly??) Lord English himself. We also get another cameo from our friendly apple buddy, who sure is a sight for sore eyes. There's no way you don't love the dancing fruit buddies. If you were to disagree, I'd simply call you a fraud.

You suppose you'd better report this to your teammates. Perhaps a memo is in order. But today, there will be little reason for rumpus in your partytown. Today is a very sad day. You are all in bigger trouble than you suspected.

Unsurprisingly, you return to a room full of commotion.

What is this guy staring at? Always with the staring. He is so weird.

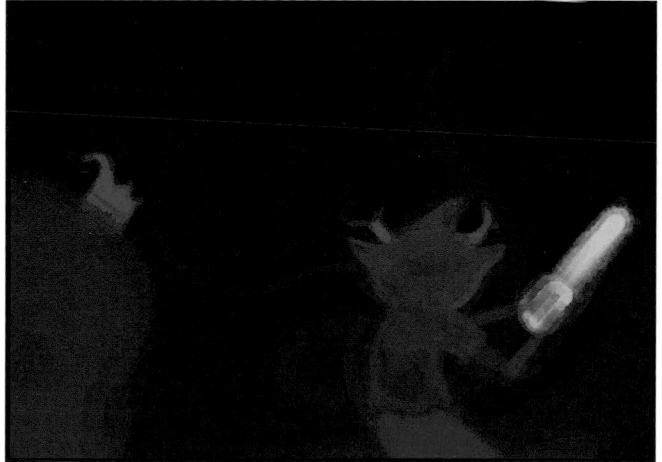

And what is she doing with that chainsaw over there?? The rich scent of chocolatey blood fills the room.

Good grief. You can't turn your back on these lunatics for a second!

Keying this new event to just before a known event from Hivebent (Kanaya's undoubtedly medically-sound procedure here) screws together the chronology of everything just a little tighter. There is lots and lots of this chronology backfill in A5A2. For example, a couple of details in this scene that we didn't know about before. We knew Equius was watching like a creep, but we didn't know Gamzee was even further behind him, lurking in the darkness, awestruck by the bloody display. Think it's giving him some ideas??

And here is your bold leader, passed out on the floor. He is sleeping like a wiggler.

You wonder what he could be dreaming about? Prospit is gone now, and he never even had the chance to wake up. Poor guy.

> Terezi: Report news to partytown subscribers.

It is important to keep your loyal subscribers of the past and future informed. It is your duty as a dedicated bulletin administrator.

Still, it's hard to find the words to break this to them. The partytown has been host to nothing but bad news lately.

> Terezi: Open memo.

Sleeping Karkat is another critical timeline marker, including the moment he falls asleep, and the moment he wakes up. In fact, Karkat waking up from this snooze is such a key event to track that the command **[S] Past Karkat: Wake up** presides over an entire playable game that takes up almost 150 pages of this book. Wait, really? Dear God. That CAN'T be right.

CURRENT gallowsCalibrator [CGC] **RIGHT NOW opened memo on board R41NBOW RUMPUS P4RTYTOWN.**

CGC: B4D N3WS 3V3RYON3!
CGC: UM
FUTURE gallowsCalibrator [CGC] **3 MINUTES FROM NOW responded to memo.**
FGC: T3R3Z1 SOM3TH1NG H4S COM3 UP
CGC: OH?
FGC: Y3S YOU W1LL N33D TO CUT TH1S M3MO SHORT
FGC: 3V3RYON3, TH3 BOTTOM L1N3 1S TH4T PROSP1T W4S JUST D3STROY3D
FGC: 1 4M SORRY TO S4Y
FGC: >:[
CGC: >:[
FUTURE adiosToreador [FAT] **3:14 HOURS FROM NOW responded to memo.**
FAT: iS,
FAT: tHAT WHAT HAPPENED,
FGC: Y3S T4VROS
FAT: }:(
FGC: WOW 1T TOOK YOU THR33 HOURS TO F1GUR3 TH4T OUT?
FGC: WH4T TH3 H3LL H4V3 YOU B33N DO1NG
FAT: mOSTLY,
FAT: gETTING USED TO THESE LEGS,
FAT: fALLING DOWN STAIRS, aND THINGS LIKE THAT,
FUTURE centaursTesticle [FCT] 3:14 HOURS FROM NOW responded to memo.
FCT: D --> I'm quite sure I warned you about attempting to navigate stairs while adjusting to the new equipment
FUTURE arachnidsGrip [FAG] 3:14 HOURS FROM NOW responded to memo.
FAG: Yes, you told him 8ro!
FAG: I distinctly remem8er you telling him a8out stairs. 8ut he didn't listen.
FAG: He never listens! None of you do, really.
FAG: And now all of your extra lives are waaaaaaaasted.
FAG: What a 8unch of losers! I'm outta here.
FAG banned herself from responding to memo.
CGC: W3LL
CGC: NOT 4LL OF TH3M
CGC: TH3 D3RS3 DR34M3RS 4R3 F1N3 4S F4R 4S 1

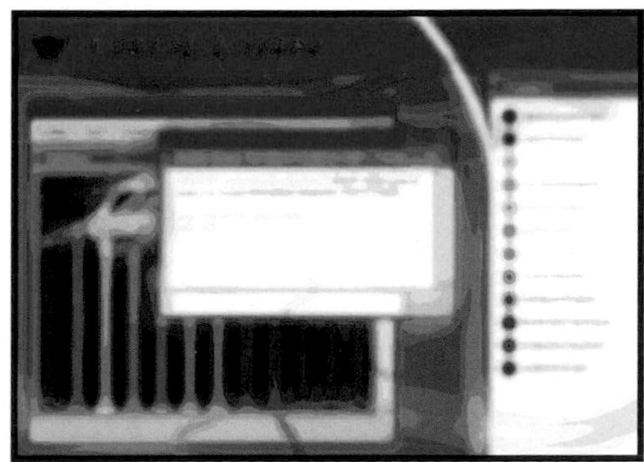

KNOW
FUTURE arsenicCatnip [FAC] **3:14 HOURS FROM NOW responded to memo.**
FAC: :33 < ummm no not quite :((
FAC: :33 < she is refurring to the fact that derse was just destroyed too
FAC: :33 < i saw him during my catnap, he blew it right on up!
CGC: >8C
FAC: :33 < :'CC
FAC: :33 < feferi was sl33ping too, and now she will not wake up!
FAC: :33 < i am very purrturbed by this
FGC: 3V3RYON3, PL34S3!
FGC: P4ST T3R3Z1 H4S SOM3TH1NG 1MPORT4NT TO 4TT3ND TO 1N 4 MOM3NT
FGC: SO 1 4M 4FR41D 1 MUST CLOS3 TH1S M3MO!
FGC: PL34S3 SC4N TH3 BULL3T1N FOR FUTUR3 M3MOS TO CONT1NU3 D1SCUSS1NG TH1S 4ND OTH3R 1NTR1GU1NG TOP1CS
FGC: 4S 4LW4YS, 1T H4S B33N 4 PL34SUR3 S3RV1NG YOUR TR4NST1M3L1N3 D1SCUSS1ON N33DS H3R3 4T TH3 R41NBOW RUMPUS P4RTYTOWN
FAG unbanned herself from responding to memo.
FAG: You doofus!!!!!!!!
FGC: SHUT TH3 FUCK UP!
FGC **banned FAG from responding to memo.**

FGC **closed memo.**

~~~~~~

> Terezi: Wait for this important thing to happen.

Note how, in response to all the dream selves being killed, Vriska says all *your* extra lives are wasted. Not *our* extra lives. Hmm, interesting clue there, one that implies Vriska didn't have a dream self at the time of the explosion. Meaning it was killed earlier, or... I won't spoil it! It's too exciting. Haha, just joking around, I know you know what I'm referring to. This memo is useful because it gives us a bunch of new pins to put in our timeline chart, including a moment 3:14 hours from now, wherein Tavros falls down stairs and Vriska is feeling kind of bitchy, incredibly enough. ALSO, according to my good friend Nepeta, Derse blows up at that timestamp, meaning the "demon" took about three hours to fly from Prospit to Derse. Feferi was sleeping during the explosion and now can't wake up, just like Karkat isn't waking up after Prospit exploded. Implying that if your dream self dies while you're sleeping, you're kind of locked in sleep for a while? Guess we'll see. Note that we already have an example of this: Jade's dream self died in **[S] Descend** while Jade was sleeping, and we haven't returned focus to her yet to see what's up with that. These tidbits are all noticeably converging to result in a question which appears to demand an answer.
~~~~~~

On the instruction of yourself from three minutes in the future, you wait for something to happen.

You wonder what could possibly happen that will cause you to become your future self in three minutes and interrupt your past self's memo and tell her to wait for three minutes doing nothing but wondering what could possibly happen that will cause her to become her future self in...

Hey. Someone just wired you some money. That's odd.

> Terezi: Accept transfer.

Huh. 413 boonbucks. The numerals of the blind prophets. A sign, perhaps? A secret message? But from who? This makes no sense.

Wait... those are not boonbucks. Some of the digits are obscured. You need to take a closer look. Which is to say, a closer lick.

> Terezi: Lick screen.

This explicit visualization of the way Terezi "sees" through smell and taste feels like a nice window into the way she perceives the world. I didn't have to go there. I could have left it totally vague and abstract, allowing the reader to imagine it, the way so many other things are. But I did, so you're welcome for that. Is it all right if I remind you to never stop thanking me for everything I do? Sure, it's fine. I think it was probably just a question nagging at me personally, so I addressed it fully, which was: it's easy to guess how Terezi can walk around and recognize forms, using something like nasal sonar, but how the hell does she read a *screen*? What is the resolution like? Is it really that clear? The answer is, she can vaguely smell rough shapes of light and color. But to really enhance the resolution, she needs to lick the screen, which dramatically sharpens the text and other shapes. Note how the screen here already appears bleary and smeared with saliva from previous lickings. Which implies she's just constantly licking her devices while having conversations.

413 boon*bonds*???

This is an absolutely preposterous amount of money.

> Terezi: Confer with network administrator.

Look how sharp those characters get. This means her sense of taste is very powerful and nuanced, more so than her nose, which just huffs in the atmosphere around her to provide vague outlines of her surroundings. Which is comparable to how those senses work for us. Smelling a hot pepper is quite a different experience from tasting one. Also here's the first callback to that Stunned Kanaya panel, which wasn't even that long ago. I warned you about this, and also said this particular panel format had become tied to the concept of someone acting stunned in a way associated with romantic attraction. Viewed in that light, this would imply Terezi gets a little worked up over people with very deep pockets. Not too surprising, really.

gallowsCalibrator [GC] **began trolling** twinArmageddons [TA]

GC: SOLLUX 1 N33D YOU TO TR4C3 4 MON3Y TR4NSF3R
TA: 2omeone 2ent you money?
GC: Y3S
TA: why'2 2omeone 2endiing you money.
TA: and why now of all tiime2, liike we can even u2e iit.
TA: who'2 thii2 doucebag?
GC: TH4TS WH4T 1 W4NT YOU TO F1GUR3 OUT!
TA: ok.
TA: bam, done.
TA: ii am fuckiing iincrediible.
GC: WHO 1S 1T?
TA: 2omeone iin our uniiver2e.
GC: C4N YOU B3 MOR3 SP3C1F1C?
GC: UN1V3RS3S 4R3 K1ND OF HUG3.
GC: SOM3ON3 FROM 4LT3RN14?
TA: no no, ii mean 2omeone from OUR uniiver2e, the one we ju2t made.
GC: WOW, 4LR34DY?
GC: TH4T W4S F4ST
GC: W3 JUST M4D3 1T!
TA: yeah 2ure but we are completely out2iide iit2 temporal envelope remember.
TA: the entiire hii2tory of the thiing exii2t2 already iin iit2 entiirety from our per2pectiive, iit2 flow of tiime mean2 nothiing two u2.
TA: 2o we don't have two waiit for anythiing, iit'2 all already there.
GC: Y34H TH4TS TRU3
GC: ST1LL S33MS W31RD THOUGH >:?
TA: 413 boonbond2? damn.
TA: 2omeone here ha2 been playiing 2grub ii gue22. wonder why they'd 2end u2 money.
TA: maybe they know we made them? maybe iit'2 liike a tiip. liike thank2 dude2 for makiing u2 exii2t.
GC: >:???
TA: why 413, why that number.
TA: any iidea?
GC: NUM3R4LS OF TH3 BL1ND PROPH3TS
GC: OTH3R TH4N TH4T, DONT KNOW
TA: well, 2eeiing a2 we don't know 2hiit about

the guy...
TA: bliind 2eem2 liike the operatiive concept.
TA: kiinda liike a bliind donatiion.
TA: and now we're fuckiing riich.
TA: 2o ii gue22 you could 2ay...
TA: they're the numeral2 of the bliind profiit2.
TA:
GC: HURRR >8P
GC: SO TH3N 1 GU3SS 1TS FROM 4N 4L13N
TA: yeah.
GC: M4YB3 W3 SHOULD T3LL K4RK4T
GC: WH3N3V3R H3 W4K3S UP
TA: ehhhhh, thii2 2hiit'2 probably not iimportant enough two bother hiim wiith.
TA: iif he fiind2 out, he'll probably want two hatch 2ome dumba22 plan that make2 no 2en2e.
TA: and badger me iintwo doiing a lot of miindnumbiing bu2ywork.
TA: ii'd leave hiim alone.
GC: WH4T DO3S H3 LOOK L1K3
GC: OUR BL1ND DONOR
TA: here come here ii'll open hiim up iin a viiewport.
GC: OK
TA: let'2 2hed 2ome...
TA: LIIGHT on the 2ubject.
TA:
GC: H4H4H4 TH4T W4SNT 3V3N 4NY SORT OF PUN YOU DOOFUS
TA: that wa2 the joke 2hut the fuck up.

Naturally, Terezi immediately hits up her hacker friend to teach her how bitcoin works, so she can start spending all this sweet cash. Come to think of it, the boondollar symbol is quite similar to the bitcoin symbol. But bitcoin wasn't shit back in 2010, so it's not like I was trying to riff on it. The bitcoin riff comes deep in Act 6 when Caliborn starts dabbling in his own cryptocurrency. I half-assedly tried to get some people to bring the calcoin to life, but it never really went anywhere. Which is a shame, because if I followed through with that, it almost certainly would have have accrued some appreciable value by now. I guess that minor endeavor was a microcosm of much of what *Homestuck* turned out to be for me: something which always confusingly blurring the line between being a complete joke, and a lucrative business opportunity. Come to think of it, that sounds like a pretty good tagline for bitcoin as well.

Who'th thith douthchebag?

> Terezi: Examine douthchebag.

The youngster receives striking new eyewear. Quite a handsome set. Perhaps it is customary for this species after emerging from the trials in the brooding caverns?

Or just MAYBE, this is some sort of coolkid you are dealing with here.

Now we see the whole point of this odd boondollar escapade was to help Terezi establish first contact with the human kids to begin with. At the time, I felt like these were two important dots to connect. How *did* the trolls first find out about the humans, given they have an entire universe full of countless planets and lifeforms to peruse? That's a good question. A decent answer is to establish a simple signal from a human, prompted by a stable time loop situation fulfilled by Terezi herself. Not in an obligatory way, either. She gets to have a lot of fun with her money-making scams and with hassling this adorable coolkid she just discovered. The one who apparently rode a pony down to Earth as a baby. Here he appears with a heart symbol, similar to how Karkat first viewed John through hate-spade goggles. But Terezi is enamored by her first flush with this alien boy, rather than indignantly aggrieved, and thus Dave's juxtaposition with a pink heart on a dead pony's ass has just been adroitly retconned from "curiously arbitrary" to "strikingly appropriate." How does this guy fucking do it, I can hear you ask? I'm no hero, folks.

It seems the child's lusus was slain in the collision. He will grow up an orphan, just like you.

This adult alien male appears to be taking on the role of his custodian, instead of killing the boy outright. What a fascinating culture.

The fellow retrieves the lusus carcass. This appears to be a gentleman who knows better than to let good pony meat go to waste.

> Terezi: Observe coolkid.

You learn much of this young creature's civilization and its customs.

The adult's puppet assistant commences the standard feeding ritual.

Bro wastes no time in branding his cool new brotherson babyboy in his own image, with the anime shades and all. Also the pony heart is a nice branding touch for Dave's early years, and perhaps reflects a certain love that Bro has for the child, which he otherwise fails miserably to communicate through his parenting methods. By showing how early in his life Dave was subjected to Dirk's self-obsessed projections of certain ideals, coolness, martial prowess, and such, this sequence helps us see how deeply ingrained all these things are for Dave. It's a clear challenge for him to throw off these shackles, or escape out from under this large, looming shadow. Dave starts the process of figuring out how to define himself as an individual, rather than a Bro-clone protégé, through interacting with his friends. The most notable symbolic gesture being John giving him a different style of shades, which helps him establish forever after his own new and distinctive brand of coolness. -->

The little coolkid is making a mess of his lovely new horseleather bib. It is about as adorable as it gets.

This race appears to be quite martially adept, even from early childhood. They must have proven to be very powerful Sgrub players. No wonder they managed to make so much money.

You suddenly understand everything.

> Sollux: Enter name.

--> Still, even though his friends help Dave liberate himself from these unfortunate circumstances, all of it sticks with him forever psychologically. Dave's full trajectory through Act 6 delves deeper into these issues and results in him confronting things a lot more head-on than he allowed himself to previously, due to the effect of meeting Dirk. The sequences here convey a couple things. Obviously the situation is Bad. This is not how you raise a child. But we also gather there was some value to it, a hardening through combat training that will prove to be useful later, when the stakes are high and Dave's skills are needed. And however fucked-up and misguided Bro's methods are, there does appear to be some warped sense of affection driving these practices, as is true of many abusive situations. But in the long run, these methods appear to backfire on Dirk's plans for Dave. The negative associations he forms with combat and violence instill in Dave a certain pacifist quality, which makes him deeply adverse to fighting and results in strong resistance toward any calls for acts of heroism. -->

You cannot name him yet, no matter how inthufferable you find this coolkid to be! You will need to wait until his wriggling day, when he turns six solar sweeps.

Mr. Appleberry Blast needs to step off. This kid is yours to mess with. You smelled him first!

> Terezi: Troll this awesome coolkid.

--> Pardon the silly panels above, as DAVE ARCTALK continues. Clearly Dave is Terezi's favorite character at this moment, so she won't mind as we indulge in this meta. Basically, his childhood training-trauma results in aversion to violence that fuels his "resistance to the call" feelings. Resistance to the call is a common step in the hero's journey. What's probably less common is the resistance being due to abusive conditioning from the training for that (supposed) journey. Usually in such arcs, the hero resists but then stops resisting in some triumphant moment, overcoming the inner obstacle that caused the resistance. But with Dave, it doesn't quite pan out that way. There isn't this moment where he says "SCREW my abusive past, I need to MAN UP and KILL LORD ENGLISH!" The resolution progresses through a more psychological manner than that. It's similar to the structure of Rose's arc in that way. Both characters know there's this thing they *should* be doing, as informed by their understanding of how heroic narratives work, so they feel some guilt and struggle with their reluctance or inability to rise to the challenges of the regimented journey of personal growth. The resolution isn't about finding the inner grit to complete their plainly evident arcs by rote (which would therefore validate certain things about them, such as, if Dave fully embraced his destiny as a warrior, maybe that just vindicates Bro's methods?). It's more about finding release from the psychological burden of these narrative-mandated pressures and becoming more complete not as a warrior or a hero, but as a person. Someone who can make peace with their flaws, forgive themselves and others, and move forward in life with a greater understanding of themselves and a better adjusted sense of priorities.

gallowsCalibrator [GC] began trolling turntechGodhead [TG]

GC: H3Y 34RTH BOY
GC: W41T...
GC: 1 JUST 4SSUM3D YOU W3R3 4 BOY
GC: M4YB3 YOUR3 4 G1RL?
GC: 1 DONT KNOW MUCH 4BOUT YOUR W31RD HORNL3SS SP3C13S, 1 GU3SS YOU COULD B3 >:\
TG: yes im a girl
GC: OH R34LLY?
GC: 34RTHL1NGS 4R3 R34LLY B1Z4RR3
GC: NO OFF3NS3
GC: WH4T 1S YOUR SP3C13S C4LL3D
TG: north american hollering phallus baboon
GC: >:?
GC: 1 TH1NK YOU M1GHT B3 PULL1NG MY FROND, F3M4L3 34RTHL1NG
TG: no its true we are highly endangered
TG: when our territory is threatened thats when the indiscriminate fucking begins
TG: could fuck a circus tent down a gas tank
TG: bunch it up in there good
TG: slam the lid and drive away
TG: beep beep albino hairless dickmonkey coming through
GC: 1M NOT SUR3 WH4T TH4T M34NS
GC: BUT 1 SUSP3CT 1T W4S SOM3TH1NG H1GHLY L4SC1V1OUS >:|
TG: the glittering civilization before you was built on angry apefuck power alone
TG: stand agog and marvel bitch
GC: H4H4H4 OK TH1S 1S NONS3NS3, YOU 4R3 4 JOK3R
GC: L1K3 M3 >:]
GC: MY N4M3 1S T3R3Z1, WH4TS YOURS
TG: shaggy 2 dope
GC: OK SH4GGY, S33
GC: 1 C4N SM3LL D3C31T
GC: L13S H4V3 4 SUBTL3 ODOR, 34SY TO M1SS 4T F1RST
GC: BUT TH3 MOR3 TH3Y P1L3 UP TH3 MOR3 TH3Y ST1NK!
GC: TH4T 1S NOT YOUR R34L N4M3
TG: ok sorry
TG: its ben stiller
GC: 4LSO 1 DONT TH1NK YOUR3 R34LLY 4 G1RL
TG: nope
TG: sorry to disappoint you dude
GC: 1 4M 4 G1RL NOT 4 BOY!
TG: dont care
GC: >:[
GC: TH1S F1RST 3NCOUNT3R 1S NOT GO1NG 4S W3LL 4S 1 HOP3D
TG: oh man another failed trolling attempt
TG: i had such high hopes trapezi it started out brilliantly
GC: T3R3Z1!!!!!!!!
GC: 4ND 1 4M NOT TROLL1NG YOU, 1 4M JUST TRY1NG TO G3T TO KNOW 4 L1TTL3 4BOUT YOU 4ND YOUR SP3C13S
GC: 1 JUST D1SCOV3R3D 1T 4ND 1 4M CUR1OUS
TG: excuse me but it says right in the header of this conversation that youre trolling me
TG: persterchum always knows
GC: OH...
GC: OH Y34H
GC: BUT
GC: OK TH1S M1GHT B3 H4RD FOR 4N 34RTH B4BOON TO UND3RST4ND
GC: BUT TROLL 1S 4 V3RB TH4T H4S 4 LOT OF NU4NC3
GC: TH3 WORD C4N M34N 4 LOT OF TH1NGS
GC: FOR 1NST4NC3, 1 4M 4 TROLL!
TG: no shit
GC: NO 1 M34N
GC: TH4TS WH4T MY SP3C13S 1S C4LL3D
TG: ok

In the most fevered days of *Homestuck* fandom, there were hordes of teens who would roleplay online constantly, casually, for no reason at all, in anyone's direction. They used troll quirks, faithfully mimicked characters, the works. I only bring this fact up now because it occurs to me that this conversation does a great job capturing what it's like when you're minding your own business as Dave is doing, and some rando comes out of nowhere and starts roleplaying a troll at you, and you don't have the slightest fucking clue what's going on, what *Homestuck* is, or what this annoying child is trying to accomplish. Dave handles it the way I assume many guys would, which is through a vaguely detached series of counter-trolling measures.

TG: let me just set aside some time to be stupid enough to believe that
TG: hey looks like next month is chemical lobotomy month youre in luck
GC: OH GOD WH4T 4 SM4RT4SS!
GC: SM4RT4SS13ST 4L13N 3V3R
TG: so what do you think
TG: time to block you yet or what
GC: NO!
GC: L3TS K33P T4LK1NG
GC: UM
GC: WH4T 4R3 YOU DO1NG NOW
TG: drawing a comic
GC: H3Y 1 L1K3 TO DR4W TOO
GC: 1M R34LLY QU1T3 GR34T 4T 1T
TG: awesome
GC: C4N YOU SHOW M3 YOUR COM1C
TG: nah
GC: COM3 ON
GC: 1 W1LL DR4W YOU SOM3TH1NG 1N R3TURN
GC: 1T W1LL B3 4 CULTUR4L 3XCH4NG3
TG: i dunno
TG: you seem kinda young to me and this thing is like
TG: borderline pornographic
TG: how old are you
GC: 6
TG: goddamn
TG: ok now youre messing with me arent you you arent 6
GC: NO 1TS TRU3!
TG: whatever thats bullshit
TG: ok fuck it
TG: just dont tell your parents
GC: WH4T 4R3 P4R3NTS
TG: thats just about the saddest thing i ever heard get said
TG: here
TG: http://tinyurl.com/CDandSL 
GC: 1 4M NOT SUR3 WH4T 1S PORNOGR4PH1C 4BOUT TH4T
GC: 1TS JUST K1ND OF STR4NG3
TG: i guess
GC: 1TS PR3TTY GOOD THOUGH
TG: its ok
TG: im not thrilled with this direction though i think its too much like my bros stuff
TG: need to figure out my own ironic statement to make
TG: spread my wings you know
GC: Y3S
GC: 1 TH1NK YOU C4N DO TH4T
GC: YOU JUST H4V3 TO F1GUR3 OUT WH4T TH3 TRUTH 1S 1NS1D3 YOU
TG: pretty deep troll girl
GC: 1TS TRU3!
GC: TH3R3 1S 4 LOT 1N YOUR M1ND WH1CH 1S CONC34L3D FROM YOUR SURF4C3 P3RC3PT1ON
GC: YOU JUST N33D TO TRY TO B3COM3 4W4R3 OF 1T
GC: CLOS3 YOUR 3Y3S
GC: 4ND T3LL M3 WH4T YOU S33 1N YOUR M1NDSP4C3
TG: ok
TG: i see

Here comes the good shit. Thank god I put this comic in here. What would *Homestuck* be without award-winning decisions such as this? I mean, aside from respectable. *Cool Dude and Stoner Lou* was the precursor comic to *Sweet Bro and Hella Jeff*. And both comics were made specifically to spoof other people's bad comics involving this sort of content. Much like with *SBaHJ*, I bestowed that creation upon Dave and designated him as the fictional creator of the content that in truth I was responsible for before *Homestuck* began. Same thing here with *CDaSL*. Note how Dave's presenting this work in a flashback, casting it as a precursor work to *SBaHJ,* which he still considers to be a "vision" he is tinkering with, which is roughly true of the IRL progression of this content. (Though I wasn't taking this shit nearly as seriously as Dave is here, on an artistic basis. For me this was ludicrous shitpost stuff taking place on old forums.)

TG: that fucking puppet
GC: H4H4 Y3S YOUR 4DULT CUSTOD14NS S3RV4NT PUPP3T
TG: uh what
GC: WH4T 3LS3 DO YOU S33
TG: man i dunno
TG: wheres this drawing you promised me
GC: OH Y34H
GC: H4NG ON
GC: OK H3R3 YOU GO B3N ST1LL3R
GC: http://tinyurl.com/FORB3NST1LL3R

TG: oh my fucking hell
TG: that is horrendous
TG: in the most beautiful way
GC: TH4NK YOU B3N >:]
TG: god damn
TG: that mouth
TG: its like
TG: i dont know
TG: a fucking pork chop
TG: jegus
TG: i mean jesus
TG: so overwhelmed i cant even damn type
GC: Y3S W3LL
GC: B3N 1 4M DR4W1NG W1TH 4 MOUS3 YOU KNOW
TG: is there even any other way to draw on a computer
TG: fuckin doubt it
GC: 1M ST4RT1NG TO TH1NK YOUR N4M3 1SNT B3N
GC: 1 TH1NK TH4T W4S 4NOTH3R RUS3
GC: T3LL M3 YOUR R34L N4M3!!! >:[
TG: ok lets say its
TG: dave why not
GC: D4V3!
GC: TH4T SM3LLS L1K3 TRUTH
GC: 1 W1LL D3C1D3 TO B3L13V3 1T >:]
TG: fuck
GC: OK D4V3, 1 H4V3 4 LOT TO DO
GC: BUT 1 W1LL G3T B4CK TO YOU
TG: what the hell could you possibly have to do
TG: doesnt seem like youre into trolling us as much as your numbnut friends
GC: MY FR13NDS?
GC: 4R3 YOU SUGG3ST1NG OTH3RS L1K3 M3 H4V3 TROLL3D YOU
TG: yeah what didnt you get the memo
GC: 1 WR1T3 TH3 M3MOS!!!
GC: 1 M1GHT NOT H4V3 WR1TT3N TH1S ON3 Y3T THOUGH...
GC: 1 SHOULD PROB4BLY RUN TH1S BY
GC: UH
GC: MY L34D3R
TG: your leader
TG: thats a retarded thing to say even by the standard of your own bullshit made up vernacular
GC: SM4RT4SS!
TG: whos he really
TG: your boyfriend or something
GC: PFFFFFFFF Y34H R1GHT
GC: W3LL OK
GC: 1 M34N
GC: 1TS B33N SORT OF COMPL1C4T3D W1TH H1M
TG: ok asking for an explanation on that is pretty much the exact opposite of what im doing
TG: and interesteds the opposite of what im being
GC: SM4RT
GC: 4SS
GC: >:P
GC: 4CTU4LLY H3S K1ND OF SM4RT4SSY L1K3 YOU NOW TH4T 1 TH1NK 4BOUT 1T
GC: BUT YOU S33M C4LM 1NST34D OF SHOUTY 4LL TH3 T1M3
GC: 4LSO
GC: YOU TYP3 1N BR1GHT BOLD R3D
GC: YOU DONT H1D3 TH3 COLOR OF YOUR BLOOD L1K3 4 STUP1D W1GGL3R >:]
TG: ok that remark was almost as boring as it was weird
GC: OH P1P3 DOWN D4V3, 1 4M TRY1NG TO P4Y YOU 4 COMPL1M3NT!

It seems Terezi provides the kernel of inspiration for Dave's next artistic endeavor, *SBaHJ*. Which also somewhat tracks reality, since originally *SBaHJ* stemmed from a playful roast of some guy's bad gamer comic, and in particular isolated certain peculiarities about the style, like the strange way the mouths were drawn. That's just how it happens. We all inspire and influence each other, even with our bad stuff. Sometimes our bad stuff gives people more to think about and find unlikely inspiration from than our good stuff. My bet is the guy who was the original subject of my roast is a thousand times more pleased to see his crappy comic left a lasting legacy in the way it did, than he felt any real lasting sense of pride or attachment to his bad comic. There is no way I wouldn't feel the same way if I were in his position.

GC: 1 4M HOLD1NG OUT TH3 1NT3RSP3C13S OL1V3 BR4NCH H3R3, 4ND YOU 4R3 G1V1NG 1T 4 GOOD F1RM S4SS GR4B
TG: haha
GC: ON3 D4Y YOU W1LL RU3 4LL TH1S S4SS YOU H4V3 D1SH3D D4V3
GC: YOU M4Y NOT B3 4 G1RL, BUT YOU W1LL CRY L1K3 ON3 WH3N 1 4M THROUGH W1TH YOU
TG: i dont cry
GC: YOU W1LL
GC: TH3R3 W1LL B3 T34RS
GC: TH3Y W1LL SM3LL S4LTY, 4ND TH3N YOUR CH33KS W1LL B3 MY S4NDY B34CH >8]
TG: oh god
GC: OK, 1 W1LL G3T B4CK TO YOU 4FT3R YOU B3G1N PL4Y1NG
GC: TH4T W1LL B3 N3XT SOL4R SW33P FOR YOU
GC: TRY NOT TO B3 TOO 1MP4T13NT FOR MY R3TURN
TG: i plan on forgetting about you instantly after this conversation
GC: Y34H R1GHT
GC: YOU KNOW 1 H4V3 L3FT MY M4RK
GC: 1 4M S33R3D 1NTO YOUR R3T1N4S
GC: L1K3 4 B1G R3D SUN
TG: well maybe
TG: even if thats the case
TG: ill just forget on principle
GC: TH4T SOUNDS L1K3 SOM3TH1NG TH4T 4 COOL K1D WOULD TRY TO DO
TG: yeah
TG: pretty cool guy here
TG: case you hadnt noticed
GC: 1 MOST C3RT41NLY D1DNT H4DNT NOT1C3D >:]

gallowsCalibrator [GC] **ceased trolling turntechGodhead [TG]**

> Terezi: Be the awesome coolkid.

You are suddenly the awesome coolkid.

In a different game session.

In the future.

> Dave: Pester Terezi.

Cry like a girl? Terezi, we need to have a talk about this internalized misogyny, which your planet supposedly doesn't even have. This was an important line though, because it established that Terezi had the objective of making Dave cry, which she finally succeeds in doing when we hop back to the "present." Some might say that bamboozling him into a vat of soup surrounded by crocodiles chopping onions actually constitutes a desperate measure. But hey, it gets the job done. This is another very good panel, incidentally. This scene, combined with the LOHACSE moneycrime antics, all paint a picture of Dave's adventure as a nonstop parade of utterly ridiculous shenanigans, mostly fueled by Terezi's whims.

-- turntechGodhead [TG] began pestering gallowsCalibrator [GC] --

TG: what the fuck was the point of this again
GC: WHY D4V3
GC: WH4T 1S TH1S TH4T MY NOS3 D3T3CTS
GC: COULD 1T B3
GC: T34RS??? >:O
TG: this is bullshit
TG: this was a setup all along
GC: 1 TOLD YOU YOU WOULD CRY D4V3
GC: 1 TOLD YOU BRO................ >8y
TG: ok jegus
TG: dont say it
TG: if you say i warned you about tears or something one more time
TG: i swear to gog
GC: DONT!
GC: DONT S4Y YOUR3 GO1NG TO DO 4N 4CROB4T1C SOM3RS4ULT OR P1RHOU3TT3 OFF OF SOM3TH1NG, J3GUS
GC: 1 G3T 1T 4LR34DY!
TG: ok fine
TG: our memes can cancel each other out this time
GC: Y3S 4GR33D
GC: NOW DRY THOS3 SORRY 3Y3S D4V3
GC: TRY NOT TO B3 SUCH 4 FUCK1NG W1MP
GC: 1T 1S UNFL4TT3R1NG B3H4V1OR FOR 4 COOLK1D OF YOUR ST4TUR3
TG: god dammit
TG: im not actually crying
TG: its the fucking onions
TG: these piece of shit crocodiles are lambasting me with them
GC: TH4TS TH3 L4M3ST 3XCUS3 1V3 3V3R H34RD
GC: WHO 3V3R H34RD OF 4 S1LLY L1TTL3 ON1ON M4K1NG SOM3ON3 CRY, 1T 1S 4BSURD
TG: i guess the stench of onions is covering up the smell of the truth how convenient
TG: also your nose sux youre not even any good at smellin at all
GC: >8O TH4T 1S OUTR4G3OUS
GC: BUT 1 KNOW YOU 4R3 JUST TRY1NG TO G3T MY 34RTH GO4T
GC: FOR HUM4N 1RON1C PURPOS3S
TG: the only thing im getting
TG: is out of this goddamn idiot cauldron here
GC: NO D4V3 DONT! YOU 4R3 GO1NG TO M4K3 TH3 MOST

D3L1C1OUS SOUP
GC: 1T 1S M4K1NG M3 HUNGRY JUST TH1NK1NG 4BOUT 1T >:O~
TG: the only thing im going to make
TG: is like banana and split
TG: out of this bubbling pail of misery
GC: OH GOG...
GC: YOUR3 R1GHT
GC: YOU 4R3 S1TT1NG 1N 4 HUG3 P41L >:o
TG: why whats the relevance of that
TG: tell me its more alien nonsense it will be so awesome to hear more of that
GC: 1 4M NOT GO1NG TO 3XPL41N 1 WOULD B3 TOO 3MB4RR4SS3D
TG: man
TG: why did i ever agree to go along with this horseshit
GC: B3C4US3 YOU H4D TO, 1T W4S 1N YOUR FUTUR3
GC: 4ND B3S1D3S YOU MUST US3 D1PLOM4CY TO W1N OV3R YOUR CONSORTS
GC: S33 LOOK D4V3, TH3Y 4LL LOV3 YOU NOW! YOU 4R3 TH3 H3RO, 1TS YOU >:]
GC: NOW TH3Y W1LL G1V3 YOU 4LL TH3 S3CR3TS OF TH3 L4ND
TG: what secrets
TG: they dont have any secrets
TG: look at them theyre morons
TG: the only secret theyve got is how many times a day they accidentally flush their medical alert bracelets down the toilet
GC: D4V3, TH3Y 4R3 STUP1D 4ND Y3T V3RY W1S3
GC: YOU H4V3 MUCH TO L34RN 4ND 1 W1LL K33P H3LP1NG YOU L34RN 1T!

They're already getting sick to fucking death of each other's memes. I insist this is relatable to you. You agree and we move on. After a lot of bullshit, Terezi finally seems to imply that the point of this soup incident is to boost Dave's status among the crocodiles so they will help him by giving him their secrets and such. The rationalization is so flimsy, there's no way we can't conclude in hindsight that she contrives this entire thing just to mess with him. In fact, we start to suspect that the vast majority of Dave's time in this session is spent fulfilling predestined actions that have all been traps orchestrated by Terezi to perpetually dunk on him. It is also clear that this is her one and only method of flirtation, much like Vriska tends to have very clear and predictable patterns when it comes to her own dubious methods of courtship.

GC: 3V3N 1F YOU 4R3 4 HUG3 CRYB4BY WHO 1S 34S1LY UPS3T BY CHOPP3D V3G3T4BL3S
TG: ok im gonna change out of this wet suit
TG: and into a dry shut your fucking mouth
GC: >8Y BLUHHHHHHH

> Dave: Change into Four Aces Suited.

TG: there now i wont be satisfying your crazy red fetish either
GC: >:'C
GC: NOW 1 4M CRY1NG TOO YOU S33 WH4T YOU D1D
TG: all you get to smell is black
TG: like licorice or something
TG: you hate licorice right
GC: 1 LOV3 L1COR1C3
TG: shit
TG: ok lets say i dont smell like licorice then
TG: i smell like
TG: a coal miners asshole
GC: TOO L4T3!
GC: 1T 4LR34DY SM3LLS L1K3 L1COR1C3 S1NC3 YOU S41D TH4T, 4ND NOW 1 C4NT UNSM3LL 1T
TG: whatever
TG: anyway
TG: probably bout time i got on with this game
TG: sans these pointless sidequests you want drag me through for kicks
TG: later terezi nice knowing you
GC: W41T!
GC: YOU C4N'T D1TCH M3, W3V3 GOT 1MPORT4NT STUFF TO DO TOG3TH3R
TG: unlikely
GC: OH
GC: H3Y >:o
GC: HOW DO YOU KNOW MY N4M3?
TG: you told me remember
GC: Y34H, BUT 1 THOUGHT YOU FORGOT!
TG: why would i forget
GC: YOU S41D YOU W3R3 GO1NG TO M4K3 4 PO1NT OF FORG3TT1NG!
TG: oh
TG: i guess i forgot i was supposed to forget
GC: W3LL TH3N
GC: M1ST3R D4V3 STR1D3R
GC: 1 4M GL4D TH4T YOU FORGOT TO FORG3T >:D
TG: uh alright
GC: OH!!!
GC: SP34K1NG OF FORG3TT1NG TO NOT FORG3T TH1NGS
GC: 1 FORGOT TO SHOW YOU TH1S
GC: PR3TTY SPOT ON DONT YOU TH1NK
GC: http://tinyurl.com/SPOTONSTR1D3R

TG: what the hell

Another doctored coolkid image, featuring some old cartoon. I forget what it is now but probably knew at one point. It's good base material because the kid already had a broken record-like symbol on a red shirt. It's impossible to pass up, and Terezi agrees. Note how she has contemptuously crossed out the girl whom she's designated as Rose, which seems to imply that she views Rose as her chief romantic rival in pursuit of Dave, despite the incestuous implications. Of course trolls don't have the same hang-ups about incest, and don't even seem to understand the idea. Which of course makes them the perfect mouthpieces for the text to exploit in order to continue forcing the idea of some of these incestuous matchups into our awareness, thus making us all slightly uncomfortable. It's almost as hard to pass up an opportunity to achieve this result as it is to pass up a good coolkid image to modify in this manner.

GC: H4H4H4H4H4H4H4H4H4H4H4H4H4H4H4H4H4
GC: 4BSOLUT3 P3RF3CT1ON!
GC: 4ND TH3R3 GO3S TH3 B1G M4N 1N H1S 34RTH SPORT, DR1V1NG TH3 HOOP THROUGH TH3 P41NT........
GC: DOWN TOWN!!!!!!!!!!!!!!!!!!!!
TG: whats your obsession with making this goofy bullshit anyway
TG: is it troll irony
GC: 1 H4V3 D3V3LOP3D 4 P4SS1ON FOR COMB1NG YOUR 1NT3RN3T FOR TH3 COOL K1DS
GC: 4ND M4K1NG TH3M COOL3R
GC: BY STR1D3RFY1NG TH3M >:]
TG: dont get me wrong its awesome
GC: TH4NK YOU D4V3
GC: HON3STLY 1 TH1NK 1 4M 4 B3TT3R 4RT1ST TH4N 1 H4V3 PR3S3NT3D SO F4R
GC: 1F ONLY 1 COULD DR4W YOU SOM3TH1NG W1TH MY CH4LK >:\
GC: OH!!!
GC: 1 KNOW, 1 C4N BORROW MY FR13NDS DR4W1NG T4BL3T
GC: 1 W1LL DO TH4T 1N 4 L1TTL3 WH1L3
TG: thats cool
GC: D4V3 W3 SHOULD TR4D3 SOM3 DR4W1NGS
GC: YOU 4ND M3
TG: sure thats fine
TG: im still gonna go off and do my own thing though
TG: later
GC: W41T!!!!!!!!!!!!!!!!!
TG: dammit what
GC: OK 1 G3T TH4T YOU 4R3 TH1S R4D LON3R 4ND YOU TH1NK YOU H4V3 1T 4LL F1GUR3D OUT
GC: BUT HOW 4BOUT TH1S
GC: 1F 1 4M M34NT TO H3LP YOU, TH3N YOUR FUTUR3 S3LF OUGHT TO V1S1T YOU R1GHT NOW 4ND G1V3 YOU 4 THUMBS UP, R1GHT?
GC: 1T W1LL B3 YOUR W4Y OF CONF1RM1NG TO YOURS3LF TH4T 1 C4N B3 TRUST3D
GC: TH3R3 1S NO W4Y YOU WOULD PL4N TO DO TH4T 1N TH3 FUTUR3 1F YOU 3ND UP R3GR3TT1NG MY H3LP
GC: DO3S TH4T SOUND F41R?
TG: yeah fine but i doubt that i
TG: oh fuck there i am hiding behind that column
GC: >8D

As with any work, it's always fair to wonder how many offscreen conversations are taking place, omitted for style or brevity or narrative purposes. Did these two cool guys exchange any words? Or was the simple exchange of deeply cool and knowing looks sufficient to say everything that needed to be said? It will remain an enigma forever. Just like all coolkids. Also note the first appearance of Dave's red-sleeved baseball shirt, arguably the most popular of all of Dave's many fashion statements. For a few years after this panel showed up in the comic, this exact shirt was pretty hard to keep in stock consistently.

TG: ok so whats the plan
GC: 1 THOUGHT YOU WOULD N3V3R 4SK
GC: TH3R3 4R3 SO M4NY PL4NS
GC: W3 4R3 GO1NG TO B3 SO BUSY D4V3, YOU H4V3 NO 1D34
TG: thats cool
TG: but whats the answer that doesnt have anything to do with meaningless bullshit
GC: 1SNT 1T OBV1OUS?
GC: NOW TH4T W3 4R3 4 T34M D4V3
GC: YOU 4ND M3
GC: 1T 1S T1M3
TG: time
TG: for
GC: T1M3
TG: for
TG: come on
GC: FOR............
TG: ......
TG: ....
GC: ....
GC: FOOOOOOOOOOORRRRRRRRRRRRRRRRRR..............
TG: god dammit
GC: 4 MOTH3R FUCK1NG D4NC3 P4RTY!!!!!!!
>:O!!!!!!!!!!!!!!!!!!!!!
GC: http://tinyurl.com/OMGD4NC3P4RTY

TG: whoa
TG: its like
TG: watching a miracle made of nothing but twitching schroder legs

GC: YOU S33 D4V3
GC: 1 TOLD YOU, YOU W1LL NOT R3GR3T H1TCH1NG YOUR SH1TTY JP3GGY FOUR WH33L D3V1C3 TO MY CONST3LL4T1ON
GC: TH1S 1S WH3R3 TH3 P4RTYS 4T
TG: look at us go
TG: i cant stop watching
TG: damn
TG: those moves
GC: TRUST M3
GC: TH3S3 MOV3S DONT STOP K33P T4K1NG PL4C3
GC: NOT 4T TH1S P4RTY
TG: i can see im going to have to drop everything
TG: drop it like its simultaneously hot and i just tripped over the rug
TG: dedicate my undivided attention to this shit
GC: D4V3, WHY TR1P OV3R TH4T RUG...
GC: WH3N YOU C4N CUT 1T????? >:]
GC: T4PP4 T4P T4P 4 P4P!
GC: SHOOSH SHOOSH!
TG: damn youre right
TG: truth be told everyone will be tripping when im done
TG: once i upset this biznasty with my swift cuts
TG: dudes will phalanx themselves agape like theyre offerin to store my shit in their mouths for the night
TG: rows of glasseyed human fly catchers beholding categorical fucking domination of the dance floor
TG: but they wont catch none cause the flys all mine

It's completely impossible to fully appreciate the frenetic energy of these Dancing Schroder GIFs without actually watching them on a screen. I'll rarely do this, even for Flash animations, but at this point I think you should find a device, go to Homestuck.com, and point it to page number 2779 in the url to watch the magic. I believe there was discussion at the time in some circles about how young Ricky Schroder was a solid pick for a headcanon Dave, which I didn't disagree with. And thus more coolkid media was harvested for exploitation, and additionally served to bond Dave's thematic identity with Schroder, thereby resulting in some Schroder/Schrödinger's paradox material. Which maybe doesn't make a whole lot of sense, now that I'm actually typing this out, but that's fine, since I'm about to deflect by changing the subject. "dudes will phalanx themselves agape like theyre offerin to store my shit in their mouths for the night"... Yeah, okay, Dave. Nothing gay about what you just said there at all. You're literally 100% straight.

GC: YOU H4V3 4LL TH3 D3L1C1OUS FL13S
TG: theres not any i dont have
TG: im crafting a new dance move
TG: to shock the shit out of asses in pants
TG: fred astaires ghost will weep in the arms of his own nimble rotting corpse
GC: WH4T 1S YOUR N3W MOV3 D4V3 >:?
TG: its called
TG: the smug cracker parlor wiggle
GC: >:O
GC: 1 1M4G1N3 TH3S3 GYR4T1ONS W1LL SM3LL QU1T3 FR3SH
GC: L1K3 R3C3NTLY L34V3N3D GRUBLO4F
TG: of course
TG: and just when the scene thought it was startin to recover from its ridiculous erection over that
TG: thats when i bust out another fierce move
TG: i call it rageclock me in the douche smirk plz
TG: cut out to the rude jam "askin 4 it!"
GC: HOW RUD3 WOULD YOU S4Y TH1S J4M 1S D4V3
TG: id say if i had to take an educated guess it was outright goddamn unmannerly
TG: needs to get worked over by some stuffy prude at finishing school
GC: W1LL YOU T34CH M3 TH3S3 MOV3S
TG: i dont know about that
GC: PL34S3 D4V3

GC: YOU ST4ND TH3R3 4ND DO TH3 UNM4NN3RLY MOV3S, 4ND 1 W1LL OBS3RV3 STUD1OUSLY
TG: i dont know if you can keep up with me kid
TG: no offense
TG: theres just magic in these shoes and the coy gnome i ransacked wants them goddamn back
GC: COM3 ON
GC: YOU T4K3 TH3 L34D
GC: 4ND 1 W1LL FOLLOW
GC: L1K3 TH1S
GC: http://tinyurl.com/T34CHM3YOURMOV3SD4V3
TG: ahahahahahaha

There's a lot I could say about whatever down here, but I think the bottom line is this is just a very funny conversation. There's not much I can do to compete with it really. At the end of the day, much like Dave himself, my own greatest artistic competition is another version of myself somewhere else on the timeline. And also like Dave, different versions of myself also serve as my own greatest hype man. Neither he nor I would have it another way.

TG: i feel like i should be offering some visual rebuttal here
TG: you arent giving me any time though dammit
GC: TH4T 1S B3C4US3 1 H4V3 YOU 4T TH3 T3MPOR4L D1S4DV4NT4G3
GC: 1 C4N P4US3 4ND DO WH4T3V3R 1 L1K3 4ND TH3N CONT1NU3 OUR CONV3RS4T1ON W1THOUT M1SS1NG 4 ST3P!
GC: BUT DO NOT WORRY D4V3
GC: 1T WOULD B3 4 SH4M3 TO H4V3 TO WH1FF YOUR FR4GR4NT T34RS 4G41N
GC: 3V3NTU4LLY TH3 T4BL3S W1LL TURN 4ND TH3 4DV4NT4G3 W1LL B3 YOURS
GC: YOU W1LL H4V3 4LL TH3 T1M3 1N TH3 PR3N4T4L UN1V3RS3 4T YOUR D1SPOS4L
GC: B31NG TH3 KN1GHT OF T1M3 4ND 4LL
TG: oh yeah
TG: i keep forgetting i can time travel
TG: thats fine i guess
GC: 4ND ONC3 YOU H4V3 TH3 UPP3R H4ND
GC: 4ND TH3R3 4R3 MOR3 D4V3S SCR4MBL1NG 4ROUND

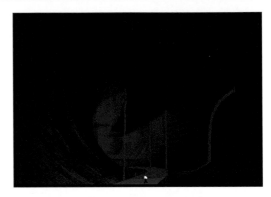

TH4N YOU C4N SH4K3 4 BROK3N SWORD 4T
GC: TH3N YOU W1LL G3T YOUR CH4NC3 TO 1MPR3SS M3 >;]
GC: L1K3 SO
GC: http://tinyurl.com/TH3FLO4R-1SONF1R3

TG: see
TG: i cant compete with this
GC: H3H3H3H3H3
TG: but seriously what is the real plan here
TG: that has to do with not fucking around
GC: TH3R3 1S NO PL4N TH4T DO3S NOT 1NVOLV3 FUCK1NG 4ROUND
GC: BUT W3 W1LL M4K3 SUR3 4LL OF OUR FUCK1NG W1LL B3 4PPL13D 1N 4 CONSTRUCT1V3 D1R3CT1ON
TG: ok could you try to be somehow even less subtle when you hit on me thanks
GC: WH4T

On the previous page I remarked on how I couldn't really compete with the humorous content generated by my past self, and now Dave is lamenting that he can't compete with the humorous content generated by Terezi, which somehow simultaneously extolls yet roasts Dave's dance moves and coolkid flavor. But Terezi's content was actually produced by me, as were her words, and so are Dave's words, so really this is just the same thing happening: me openly lamenting how I can't compete with my own great shit. It's a perpetual and paradoxical self-escalation of quality material which all at once eggs me on to do better yet serves to demoralize me because how the fuck can I compete with this?? Even though I'm the one who makes the very stuff that starts to seem unapproachable. But then, I guess when you splinter off your own creative capabilities and make it appear that your own fictional characters are responsible for the material rather than you, then you have manufactured the illusion that competing with the quality of your own artistic undertaking now seems like a tall order. Welcome to "Doing Art," or as I like to call it, Endlessly Dissociative Identity Jerkoff Theater For Self Absorbed Fuckheads. I like to call it that because I just made it up now for the purpose of this note, and I will stop liking to call it that the moment this note is over, which means the euphemism will be retired forever. In fact, I already forgot what I just said. R.I.P.

GC: WH4T D1D 1 S4Y?
TG: man
TG: nevermind
GC: YOU W1LL H4V3 TO FORG1V3 M3 D4V3, 1 TH1NK SOM3T1M3S TH3 M34N1NG OF WORDS 1S LOST THROUGH OUR CULTUR4L D1FF3R3NC3S
TG: no shit
TG: im going to infer that your species reproduces by having sex with a grub in a bucket or something
TG: am i close
GC: D4V3
GC: TH4T 1S 4BSOLUT3LY TH3 F1LTH13ST TH1NG 1 H4V3 3V3R H34RD 4NYON3 S4Y >:\
TG: ok sorry
TG: back on point
TG: what are we doing
GC: W3LL, W3 N33D TO ST4RT M4K1NG YOU SOM3 MON3Y
GC: LOTS 4ND LOTS 4ND LOTS OF 1T!
TG: ok
GC: WH3N YOU H4V3 S4V3D UP 3NOUGH
GC: W3 W1LL BUY YOU YOUR F1RST FR4YMOT1F
GC: TH3N YOU C4N ST4RT CUTT1NG OUT TRULY TH3 FLY3ST OF MOV3S
GC: 4ND TH4T 1S WH3N W3 W1LL B3G1N TH3 MOST POORLY B3H4V3D D4NC3 P4RTY OF 4LL >:D
TG: sounds cool
GC: D3MONS 4ND D3N1Z3NS 4L1K3 W1LL TR3MBL3 B3FOR3 YOUR F1DG3TY GYR4T1ONS
GC: 4ND MOST 1MPORT4NTLY, YOU W1LL PROV3 YOURS3LF TO B3 TH3 B3ST HUM4N BOY OF 4LL
GC: W4Y B3TT3R TH4N TH4T DORKY 3GB3RT 4ND WHO3V3R M1GHT B3 M3DDL1NG W1TH H1M 4T 4NY G1V3N MOM3NT
TG: huh what an odd thing to say
TG: it demands no explanation whatsoever
GC: NO OF COURS3 NOT
TG: so how do i start making all this money
GC: P4T13NC3!
GC: R3M3MB3R HOW 1 S41D YOU H4V3 PL3NTY OF T1M3
TG: tell me anyway
GC: OK W3LL T4K3 WH4T YOU H4V3 S4V3D UP FROM CL1MB1NG YOUR 3CH3L4DD3R TO ST4RT W1TH
GC: HOW MUCH DO YOU H4V3?
TG: dont know
TG: i never even looked at it
GC: D3RRRRP, N1C3 JOB 4C3 G4M3R

GC: M4YB3 YOU SHOULD H4V3 4 LOOK 4T 1T
TG: k
GC: 4ND TH3N 1 W1LL 4DV1S3 YOU L4T3R 4FT3R OBS3RV1NG TH3 GR4ND SCH3M3 OF 4LL TH1NGS 4ND 4LL D4V3S
GC: 1 W1LL L34V3 YOU 4LON3 FOR 4 L1TTL3 WH1L3 TO W4ND3R 4ND 3XPLOR3
GC: BUT 1 W1LL B3 B4CK!
GC: 4ND 1 W1LL COM3 B4CK W1TH 4 DR4W1NG T4BL3T
GC: 4ND TH3N YOU W1LL S33 SOM3 TRU3 M4ST3RP13C3S
TG: ok after all this hype you better be prepared to fucking dazzle me
TG: are you gonna bring it?
GC: 4LLOW M3 TO PROV1D3 4N 4NSW3R THROUGH 1NT3RPR3T1V3 D4NC3
GC: http://tinyurl.com/H3LLFUCK1NGY3S

TG: awesome
TG: peace out t-z
GC: >:)
TG: oh shit
GC: >:?

Daverezi is a legit ship. It's Valid, as they say. Which means it's worth digging into. Is it "endgame material"? Are they going to get hitched? No, that won't happen. Let's not be ridiculous. But it does have narratively load-bearing structural capacity. In the previous book I went on a pretty good jag about Karezi, its merits and flaws. Dave is like the guy Terezi gravitates toward after a completely exhausting, emotionally draining experience. Karkat's like her extremely high-maintenance, temperamental ex. Not a bad guy necessarily, and she doesn't dislike him or anything, but there comes a time when enough's enough, and a new person without that baggage serves as a refreshing counterpoint. Dave is fun and casual, and isn't tied up in a hundred different knots over everything imaginable. They quickly establish a rapport, share a sense of humor, and even though *technically*, yes, she is using him as a pawn in a game of one-upmanship with her one true psycho-romantic vice, Vriska, it still feels easygoing, and their repartee rings true to that of a decent rebound date after a trying experience with a very uptight boy. Perhaps this is the most fundamental contrast with Vriska's courtship of John. Terezi actually seems to *want* a real friend, or maybe more than a friend, whereas Vriska's chief objectives are victory, conquest, relevance—all the sort of things that don't lend themselves to being the foundation of a quality relationship. Daverezi, being an authentic relationship, has real legs and makes some pretty deep headway into Act 6 before it slams into a brick wall of pure clown lust. But that's a very different issue.

002783-002784

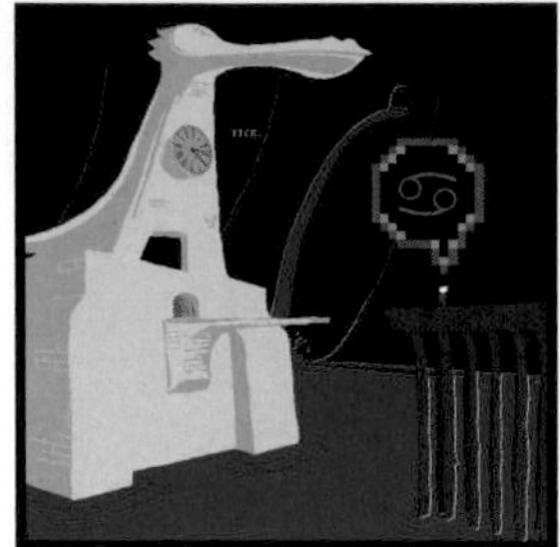
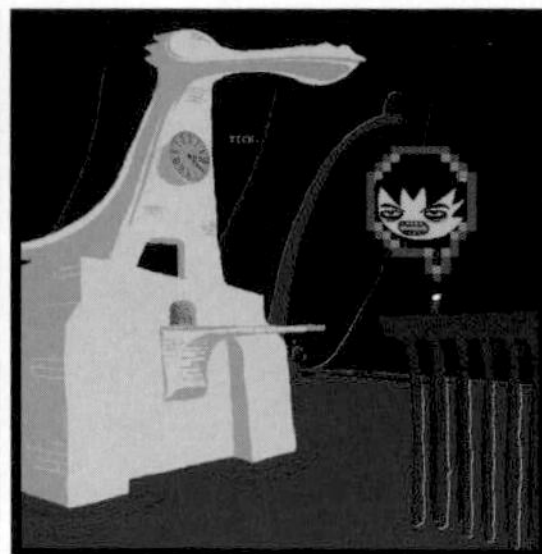
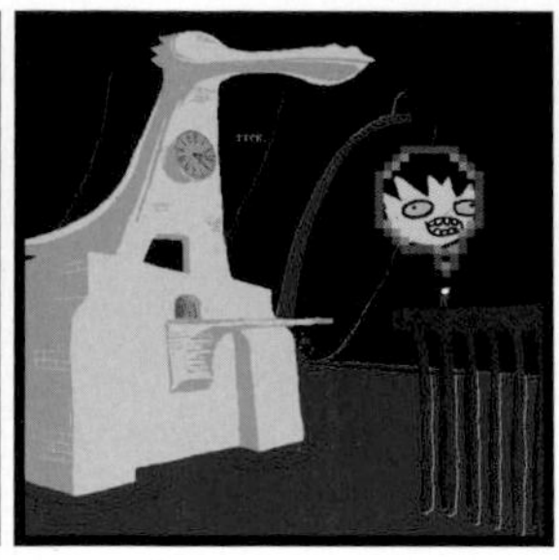

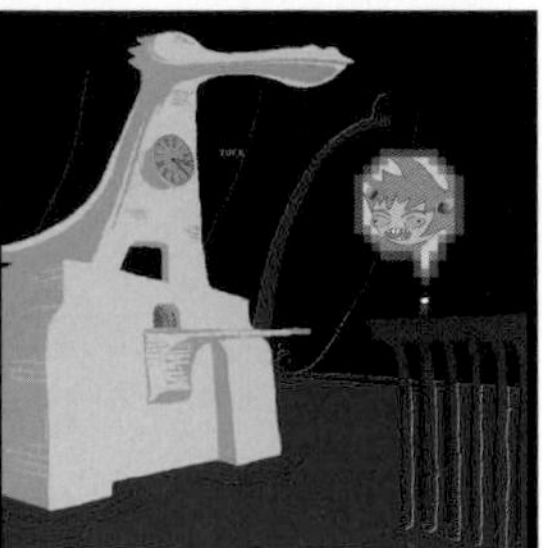

GC: WH4T 1S 1T?????
TG: fuck

> John: Pester Vriska.

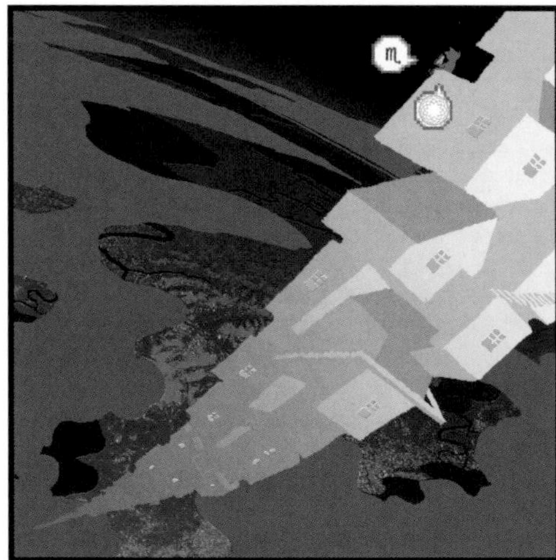

-- ectoBiologist [EB] began pestering arachnidsGrip [AG] --

EB: hey vriska!
EB: ok, i still cannot find my nanna up here, so now i am just installing this game.
EB: what are you up to?
AG: John! What the hell. There are so many things wrong with what you just said.
AG: First of all, who told you you could just hassle me without warning like this? That's not how this works!
EB: why not? you guys do it all the time.
AG: Yes, 8ecause we are trolling you! Those are the rules. We get to 8ug you any time we feel like, and you have to sit there and t8ke it like a chump.
EB: bluh...
AG: I am too 8usy to 8e fielding your nonsense at the drop of one of your a8surd human hats. I have a ridiculous num8er of irons in the fire. You will speak to me only when I am ready to contact you, is that clear????????
EB: that's dumb. i'm going to talk to you whenever i want!
AG: Secondly, I am very pissed off that you figured out my name.
EB: well, i didn't know it was your name for sure until you just told me now.
EB: so, haha.
AG: Dammit!
AG: Who told you?
EB: heheh, i am not telling.

Speaking of Terezi's crabby ex, here he comes barging in at the tail end of the conversation, setting us up to expect that chat to happen soon. (It lives up to the hype, IIRC.) It's almost like that long, fun chat between Dave and Terezi was inviting us to wonder...what would Karkat think of this? By now we know this complete bitch of a little boy so well that we can almost fill in the lines of this conversation using our own imaginations, and probably none of us would be that far off. "DAVE, I'M SIMPLY DELIGHTED TO SEE YOU PHILANDERING WITH MY MURDEROUS OLD FLAME! I WISH YOU BOTH THE BEST!" Yeah, it doesn't go like that. Oh, and speaking of Karezi drama, now we switch to a panel of John talking to Vriska, which calls back to that same composition used when Terezi was sitting on her tall house, having an emotional conversation with Karkat. As is true with many of these visual echoes, we've been trained to associate a certain idea with the first use of this particular template. And that idea is roughly, "a private romantic discussion is taking place." But now knowing what we know of the Karezi situation, there's an additional layer, which is, "the romance in question isn't actually that good."

EB: a true wise guy never reveals his tricks.
AG: I will find out who told you. And then I will m8ke them p8y.
EB: nuh uh!
EB: anyway, i was just wondering if you had a chance to watch that awesome video i linked you to?
AG: What video?
EB: you know...
EB: the one about the renegade hero who busted loose from the slammer to save the day.
AG: John, the way you descri8e movies makes them sound extremely stupid. Why would I want to watch this crap????????
EB: just do it, you won't be sorry.
EB: i mean, when you are not so busy and have less irons in the fire or whatever.
EB: ok, i am starting this game now and saving jade, like a street tough maverick with nothing to lose.
EB: see ya, vriska!
AG: XXXX|
EB: oh, damn...
AG: ::::?

AG: What is it now!
EB: fuck.

John is suddenly preoccupied with something. How dare he bother you and then leave you hanging like this.

You guess you can spare a moment to watch this terrible video. Why does that nerdy kid have to be so persuasive?

> [S] Vriska: Watch street tough maverick with nothing to lose

Blurry Gamzee alert. My duty is to point this out. Every. Time. Meanwhile, John gets the same spastic notification from Karkat that Dave got, suggesting this is probably a memo between the three, which is how we know it's going to be good. Also, let's do our best to yet again avoid acknowledging Bill Cosby's presence on this page. Or Gamzee's, for that matter. Wait... It's too late for both of those things? I already blew it? Well, excuse me, buckos but what the FUCK else is new. Ironically, in the time since these panels were created, events have conspired both inside and outside the story to retroactively recast this entire page as one of readers being passively and pleasantly leered at by two totally unrelated yet perhaps equally repugnant sexual predators. Hold on. I'm getting another message from my producer through my earpiece. Yeah, this is awful. I'm being told this note is just utterly fucking abysmal, and they want to pull the plug. The note is hemorrhaging sponsors now. Christ. Okay, I'll work on drafting an apology...wait. No. My producer just wants me to stop talking. I'm literally and quite rudely being told to shut the fuck up. The stock price of the parent company is plummeting with each additional word. Whew, rough crowd. I think I'm starting to understand how Bill must have felt. Wow, okay, now there's actual screaming in my earpiece. Let's all just watch this Youtube video, okay??

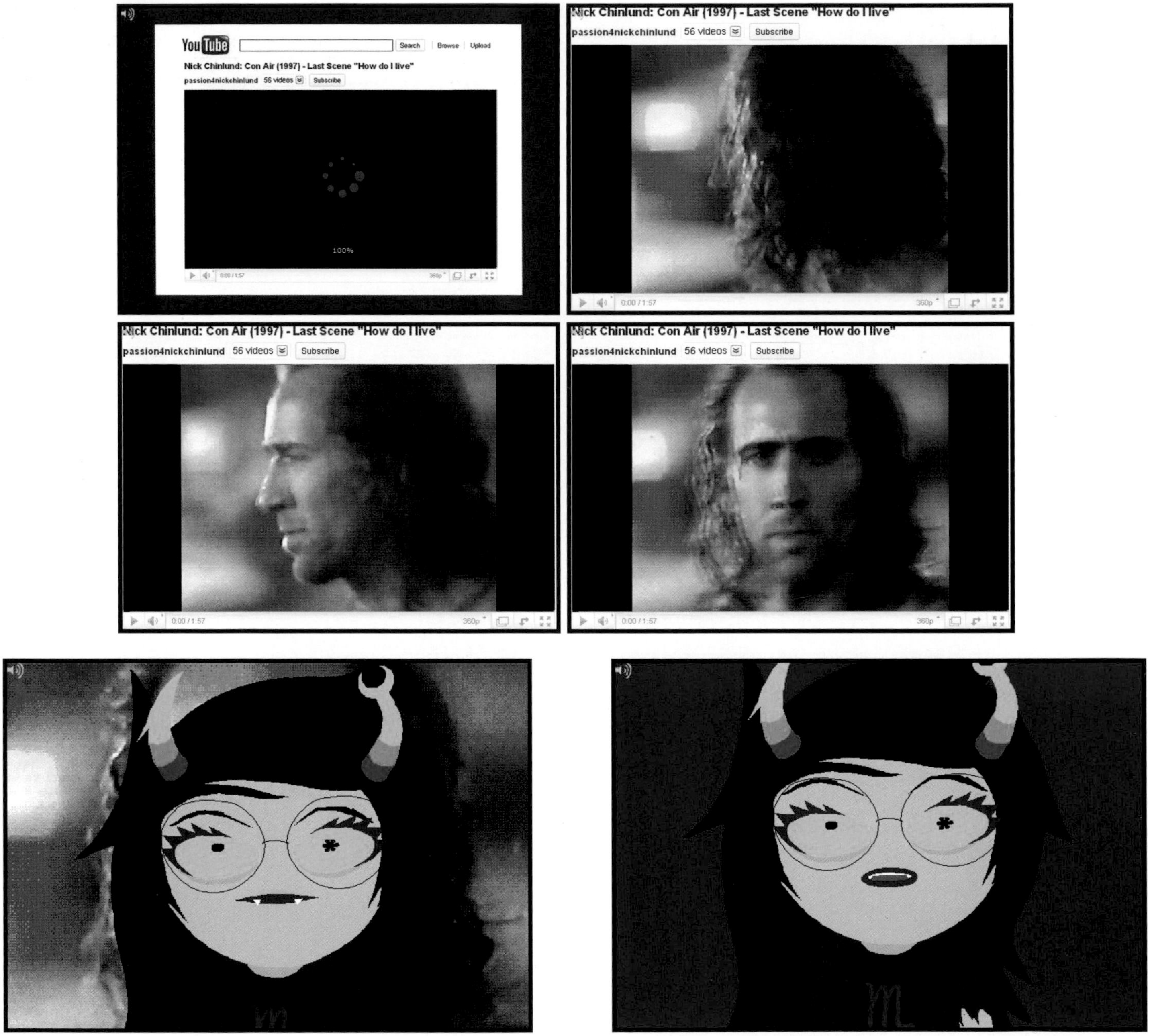

There's that Stunned Kanaya panel callback again. If it wasn't clear the first couple times, by now it should be blatantly obvious. When we see this composition, it means the person has just been amorously astounded. Unsurprisingly, our boy Nic did the trick.

I used Flash to cobble together a shitty reconstruction of a YouTube version of the final scene in *Con Air*, when Nic Cage reunites with his family. "How Do I Live" plays while Vriska swoons, and it's all a bit silly. This is the smoking gun confirmation that not only does Vriska now have a thing for Cage, but also is likely potently attracted to Equius, at least physically. She may get a kick out of pushing around impressionable nerds like Tavros and John, but what really gets her fired up is a filthy, sweaty slab of beef with a mullet and a wife beater. In a way, it's almost surprising that during the dress-up session with John, she didn't take the opportunity to make him look like Nic Cage. Instead she gave him the Vriska Look. Which just goes to show, if there's one person she loves more than anyone, it's herself.

002787 [S]

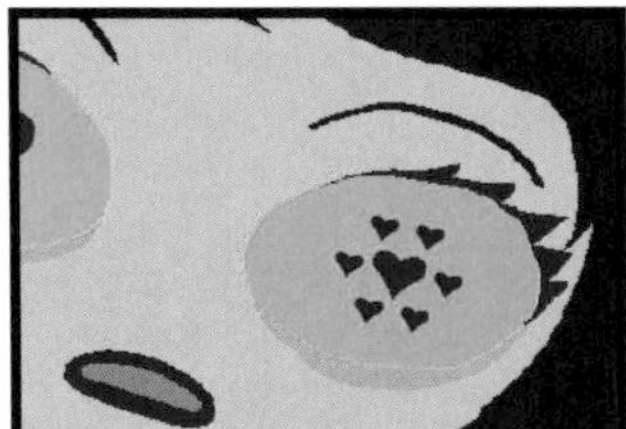

> John: Answer Karkat.

We're already calling back to the opening animation of A5A2, when Karkat hateswoons over John. That scene is "important," but this animation is "just a joke." Actually the real joke is what I just said, because nothing is just a joke, and everything is important. (Except Tavros.)

carcinoGeneticist [CG] began trolling ectoBiologist [EB]

CG: HEY SHITHEAD YOU ARE IN HUGE TROUBLE.
CG: A WORD WITH YOU AND YOUR FRIEND.
EB: oh no.
EB: which conversation is this for you? your second or so?
CG: WHAT ARE YOU TALKING ABOUT
EB: i mean...
EB: the second time you have spoken to me?
EB: or first??
CG: JOHN, FOR ALL INTENTS AND PURPOSES, THIS IS OUR TEN MILLIONTH CONVERSATION.
EB: oh.
EB: i thought you were going backwards though.
CG: I WAS
CG: GOT BACK TO THE BEGINNING
CG: AND THEN JUMPED AHEAD AGAIN A BUNCH OF TIMES.
CG: STOP BEING SO LINEAR, IT'S GETTING OLD.
CG: NOW I NEED YOU TO JOIN THIS MEMO SO WE CAN DISCUSS SOMETHING IMPORTANT.
EB: memo?
CG: CLICK THE AWESOME BANNER I MADE.
CG:

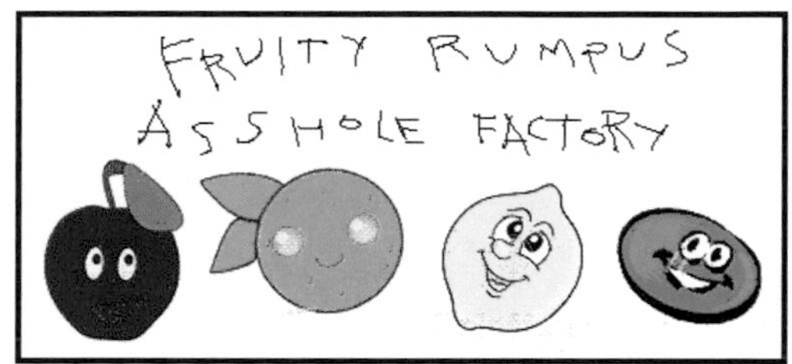

EB: uh...
EB: ok.

> Dave: Answer Karkat.

carcinoGeneticist [CG] began trolling turntechGodhead [TG]

CG: HEY SHITHEAD YOU ARE IN HUGE TROUBLE.
CG: A WORD WITH YOU AND YOUR FRIEND.
TG: i thought you were asleep
CG: YES DAVE, I WAS ASLEEP AT ONE POINT.
CG: IT STANDS TO REASON I AM NOW AND WILL ALWAYS BE ASLEEP AT EVERY POINT ON ALL TIMELINES.
CG: THAT REALLY MAKES A LOT OF FUCKING SENSE.
CG: NOW YOU, ME, AND EGBERT NEED TO HAVE A CHAT.
CG: HERE I MADE A COOL BANNER USING SOME OF YOUR SHITTY EARTH CLIP ART.
CG: CLICK IT.
TG: not cool
TG: luring me into your cyber boobytrap with shitty clip art who told you my weakness
CG: IT'LL WORK, WON'T IT?
TG: obviously

> John and Dave: Respond to memo.

Karkat is brilliantly spoofing Terezi's bulletin board with bad fruit clip art, which I'm going to double-count as a return of our friendly fruit buddies, even though they look like absolute shit. Possibly the funniest thing about this is that Karkat didn't need to make it at all and simply could have just linked to his memo via URL. This sick Terezi burn is for no one's benefit but his own. Also note how Dave acknowledges that the banner is serving as effective bait, i.e. his "weakness," to lure him in. This is not only (I think) the first interaction between Dave and Karkat but also the first stealth-foreshadowing of Davekat itself. Now THERE is some endgame-worthy shit, which at this point was on exactly zero people's radar.

?CG AT ?:?? opened memo on board FRUITY RUMPUS ASSHOLE FACTORY.

CURRENT turntechGodhead [CTG] RIGHT NOW responded to memo.
CTG: what
CURRENT ectoBiologist [CEB] RIGHT NOW responded to memo.
CEB: ok, i am here.
CEB: oh, hi dave!
CTG: hey
CEB: what is going on in here?
CTG: some kinda asshole rumpus looks like
?CG: EVERYBODY SHUT THE FUCK UP, I HATE YOU BOTH, ETC. ETC. ETC.
?CG: NOW THAT THE PLEASANTRIES ARE OUT OF THE WAY, THERE IS IMPORTANT BUSINESS TO DISCUSS.
?CG: THIS MEMO IS NOT ABOUT WHICH GUY CAN MANAGE TO BE THE HEFTIEST SACK OF SHAME GLOBES TO ONE ANOTHER.
?CG: IT IS NOT ABOUT WHICH ONE OF US WILL MOST DECISIVELY ESCORT THE OTHERS "TO SCHOOL", WHERE THEY WILL RECEIVE A VAST HELPING OF "OH SNAP" RAMMED DOWN THEIR INSATIABLE IGNORANCE SHAFTS.
?CG: THIS IS AN IMPORTANT CONVERSATION WHICH I BELIEVE NEEDS TO TAKE PLACE HERE AND NOW, SO YOU WILL BOTH SHAPE YOUR SHIT UP AND PERHAPS BEGIN TO APPROXIMATE PEOPLE WHO AREN'T EXCRUCIATINGLY RETARDED.
CTG: ok later windbag
?CG: STRIDER FUCK OFF
?CG: AND BY FUCK OFF I MEAN FUCK OFF RIGHT BACK HERE AND LISTEN, YOU INSUFFERABLE PRICK.
CEB: yeah, dave, don't go!
CEB: i think we should listen to what he has to say.
?CG: YES, LISTEN TO YOUR LEADER DAVE.
?CG: AS DUMB AS EGBERT IS, HE IS SMARTER THAN YOU AND IS THE RIGHTFUL SUPERIOR AMONG YOUR DREARY LITTLE PARTY.
?CG: BUT I AM THE SUPERIOR OF BOTH OF YOU AND WHAT YOU REALLY NEED TO BE DOING IS LISTENING TO ME.
?CG: SO DAVE, TRY TO KEEP ALL THOSE SICK FIRES CHECKED AND THOSE STOIC LIPS PURSED FOR A GOD DAMNED SECOND
?CG: AND TAKE THIS SIMPLE BIT OF HATEFRIENDLY ADVICE:

?CG: STOP HITTING ON TEREZI IMMEDIATELY, IT'S FUCKING EMBARRASSING TO WATCH.
CTG: nah
CEB: haha, dave you're hitting on terezi? really??
CTG: no
CTG: but whatever he thinks im doing im not going to stop
CTG: the guys jealous obviously he thinks his girlfriend has a thing for me and you know what hes probably right
CTG: but what else is new just another lady from outer space mackin on me whatever chance she gets
?CG: OH, HA HA! IF SMUG WAS A MOTORCYCLE, IT JUST JUMPED OVER A FUCKING CANYON.
?CG: THE CROWD GOES WILD WITH DISMAY, AND THEN COMMITS MASS SUICIDE.
CEB: karkat, is terezi really your girlfriend?
?CG: GUESS WHAT THIS CONVERSATION IS ABOUT! NOT THAT PARTICULAR TOPIC.
?CG: ALSO GUESS WHOSE BUSINESS THAT STILL ISN'T, FUCKING YOURS, THAT'S RIGHT.
CTG: pretty sure she is
CTG: or he thinks she is or something
CTG: made it pretty obvious when he started ranting at me months ago
CTG: back when i suspected these trolls were full of shit
CTG: but now look how far weve come
CTG: theres not any doubt left about that at all
?CG: EVEN IF THERE WAS ANYTHING GOING ON, WHICH THERE DEFINITELY [OOPS TIME TO MIND YOUR OWN BUSINESS AGAIN, ASSHOLE!]

I distinctly remember feeling relieved that for troll-to-human memos, I could just leave the timestamp at ?:?? due to trolls not being anchored to the human timeline. Which meant I didn't have to bother doing any mind-bending calculations. That freed me up to focus on what's really important here, which is boys yelling at each other about romance problems.

?CG: OUR ROMANCE IS MUCH MORE COMPLICATED THAN THE JOKE THAT PASSES FOR YOUR UNDERSTANDING OF THE CONCEPT.
?CG: YOU ONLY HAVE ONE QUADRANT! THAT'S JUST ABSURD.
CTG: right
CTG: sounds like its time to get a clue she is over you dude
CEB: what is so different about your romance?
CEB: what's a quadrant? how many do you have?
CTG: john god dammit stop embarrassing us
CTG: first of all weve got to be on record here as not giving a shit about that
CTG: second obviously theres gonna be 4 quadrants come on
?CG: JOHN, I TAKE BACK EVERYTHING I SAID ABOUT YOU BEING THE SMART ONE.
?CG: DAVE IS NOW THE LEADER, EVEN THOUGH HE'S A SMUG SHITSTAIN WITH SHADES AND A POKER FACE.
?CG: IF THERE WERE FIVE, THEY'D BE CALLED QUINTDRANTS, GET IT???
CEB: wow, okay!
CEB: who cares, jeeeeeeeez.
?CG: YES, EXACTLY. WHO CARES?
?CG: AS FASCINATING AS A LECTURE ON ALL THAT WOULD BE, IT'S NOT WHAT THIS IS ABOUT.
?CG: WHICH BRINGS ME TO A RELATED POINT OF BUSINESS.
?CG: JOHN, DON'T THINK I DIDN'T NOTICE HOW MANY E'S YOU JUST TYPED THERE.
?CG: THAT'S GOT TO STOP TOO.
CEB: what does?
?CG: STOP TALKING TO VRISKA. I'M FUCKING SERIOUS.
CEB: what!
CEB: no way. vriska's cool, i'll talk to her all i want!
?CG: HAHAHAHAHAHAHAHA.
?CG: YOU JACKASSES HAVE NO IDEA WHAT YOU'RE GETTING YOURSELVES INTO.
?CG: THEY'RE DANGEROUS, AND YOU'RE JUST BLUNDERING RIGHT INTO THEIR HYPERCOMPETITIVE MINDFUCK MURDER-THICKET.
?CG: THESE PSYCHO GIRLS HAVE ALREADY GOTTEN EACH OF YOU KILLED AT LEAST ONCE TO MY KNOWLEDGE.
CEB: well, yeah...
CEB: but terezi killed me in an alternate timeline, so that isn't too bad i guess.
CEB: plus, i am pretty sure that she is sorry about it.
?CG: OH GOD, YOU EVEN KNOW ABOUT IT?
?CG: AND YOU'RE STILL GETTING UP TO THESE ANTICS
?CG: YOU ARE BOTH FUCKING HOPELESS, I GIVE UP.
CTG: k then bye
?CG: SHUT YOUR SQUAWK GAPER AND STAY PUT.
?CG: I'M NOT DONE.
CTG: sounds like a loudmouth inferiority thing going on here to me
CTG: like you dont want to acknowledge that your troll ladies find a couple of human dudes irresistible
?CG: YOU DON'T GET IT.
?CG: I DO ACKNOWLEDGE THAT AS MUCH AS IT MAKES ME SICK TO MY VARIOUS BITS OF ALIEN PHYSIOLOGY YOU'VE NEVER HEARD OF, THESE GIRLS ARE CLEARLY FLIRTING WITH BOTH OF YOU PRETTY HARD.
?CG: THE FACT THAT THEY HAVE SWEPT YOU BOTH INTO THEIR SICK ASSASSINATION GAMES IS SADLY WHAT MAKES THIS OBVIOUS.
?CG: THAT'S WHAT THEY DO.
CEB: wait...
CEB: are you saying that vriska is interested in me?
CEB: like, romantically?
?CG: EGBERT JUST EARNED A FEW BRAIN POINTS!
?CG: HE HAS REACHED A NEW RUNG ON HIS ECHELADDER, "EASILY OUTFOXED BY SIMPLE UTENSILS"
?CG: "BUCKAROO"
?CG: OR SOMETHING LIKE THAT
CTG: smooth
CEB: oh man.
CEB: uh...
?CG: YES LET'S ALL HAVE A GREAT BIG OH MAN OVER THAT
?CG: AND THEN FUCKING CUT THE HORSESHIT FOREVER. SOUND GOOD?
CEB: i'm not sure what to think about this.
CEB: dave, what do you think i should do?
CTG: i dunno
CTG: do you like her
CEB: well, like i said, i thought she was pretty cool...
CEB: kinda bossy! but also pretty friendly.
CTG: yeah ok
CTG: but i mean

There's so much happening here, it gets overwhelming to try to document it. Which was also true of the memos in Hivebent. Let's go for a swim through this slurry of red, blue, and gray and see what morsels we find. Dave telling John they have to be on record as not caring, then dunking on him for not knowing that quadrants come in fours... First of all, that's obviously funny. Let's all have a laugh for a second. Okay, that's done. It also reveals a feature of Dave's conversational strategy that doesn't become exposed until he's forced to participate in an exchange that's not one-on-one. He projects an appearance of not caring as a matter of policy to establish tone and control the conversational agenda. Don't give the opponent any ammunition to use against you. This breaks down when a conversational ally is present, but isn't on the same page. John is way too eager to learn about troll romance, which is ruining Dave's flow, making his weapons against Karkat less effective. Then it all quickly spirals out of control to become a reasonably earnest jam between bros about girls they may or may not like, while Karkat looks on in horror. Then what happens?

CTG: anything more than that
CTG: like
CTG: if earth wasnt destroyed and she werent in some other universe on a planet full of unspeakable frothing dipshits
CTG: and she was on earth visiting your town or something
CTG: would you want to ask her to go see one of your dumbass movies
CTG: like the new maconnohey jam where he smirks and like all but deliberately draws the audiences ire like a goddamn magnetron
CEB: mcconaughey!!!!!!!!
CEB: um, wow, i don't know.
CEB: i mean, yeah, sure it would be fun to do something like that with her, i think.
CEB: but...
CEB: beyond that, it's a little confusing!
CEB: i don't think i have ever actually liked a girl before in that way, so i am not really sure what i am supposed to feel or do...
?CG: HOLY FUCK WHAT AM I EVEN READING HERE?????
CTG: doesnt concern you dude
?CG: OK JOHN, ARE YOUR FEELINGS QUITE SORTED OUT YET?
?CG: ARE YOU QUITE DONE SLOGGING THROUGH THE EMOTIONAL MORASS OF ADOLESCENCE, EMERGING FROM THE SLUDGE IN YOUR JUNIOR ECTOBIOLOGY WADERS?
?CG: ARE WE FEELING JUST A LITTLE BIT WISER? DID WE GROW TODAY? THAT WOULD BE WONDERFUL!
?CG: YOU WOULD THINK WARNING YOU GUYS THAT FRATERNIZING WITH THESE FEMALES IS PUTTING YOUR LIVES IN DANGER WOULD BE ENOUGH.
?CG: REALLY, DANGER YOU SAY? OH GOODNESS, WE NEARLY MADE A HUGE MISTAKE! WHY THANK YOU, MR. TROLL, HOW GRACIOUS OF YOU TO ALERT US TO OUR FOOLISHNESS.
CTG: i dunno man doesnt sound like you really got our interests in mind here
CTG: you just sound kinda bitter
CTG: did one of the human ladies reject you
?CG: OF COURSE NOT.
CTG: how did it go did you stand in a quadrant like you were playing four square
CTG: holding a bucket full of flowers or slime or whatever and jade was like no thanks bro
CTG: is that how it went down
?CG: YES, YOU FIGURED IT OUT! YOU ARE A SAVANT OF XENOBIOLOGY DAVE AND I SALUTE YOU WITH ONE OF MY MANY INTERGALACTIC SPACE TENDRILS
?CG: (THAT'S FAKE, I MADE THAT UP TO FUCK WITH YOU)
CTG: or maybe it was a guy who rejected you
?CG: FUCK OFF.
CTG: haha wow bingo
CTG: see how i look right now thats a poker face might want to take some notes
?CG: I SEE NOTHING BUT A COWARD BEHIND DARK EYEWEAR CLEARLY DESIGNED FOR WOMEN AND A PAIR OF IMPUDENT LIPS PURSED SO TIGHT IT'LL SOUND LIKE AIR SQUEALING OUT OF A BALLOON WHEN I PUNCH YOU IN THE GUT.
CTG: oh god stop talking about my lips thats the second time
CTG: ok youre clearly gay and youve probably got some issues about it dude
CTG: john just a heads up in the future i think youre gonna spurn one of his awkward advances
CEB: uh oh!
?CG: JOHN DON'T LISTEN TO THIS FUCKER, HE'S THE WORST GUY AT GIVING ADVICE I'VE EVER SEEN.
CEB: yeah, i dunno dave, i have talked to karkat a lot and i really don't think he has a thing for me.
?CG: EXACTLY. JOHN ONCE AGAIN IS FLYING HIGH AS SMARTEST HUMAN.
?CG: AND JOHN, PURELY HYPOTHETICALLY, IF ONE OF US IN THE FUTURE DOES MAKE SOME SORT OF SOLICITATION YOU DON'T QUITE UNDERSTAND...
?CG: BECAUSE OF PERHAPS SOME CULTURAL DIFFERENCES
?CG: I MEAN NO ONE IN PARTICULAR HERE
?CG: MAYBE TRY TO UNDERSTAND THAT PERSON MIGHT NOT BE THINKING TOO CLEARLY AT THAT MOMENT
CEB: uh...
?CG: IT MIGHT BE THE CASE THAT THIS PERSON HAS GOTTEN TOO WRAPPED UP IN A SORT OF CALIGINOUS IDEAL
?CG: AND GET CARRIED AWAY, POSSIBLY SO MUCH SO THEY WERE BLIND TO HOW COMPLETELY FUCKED UP AND WEIRD IT WOULD BE TO PURSUE ANYTHING LIKE THAT WITH ANOTHER SPECIES
?CG: ESPECIALLY ONE THAT DIDN'T EVEN UNDERSTAND

What happens is that Dave starts sussing out John's interest in Vriska in a fairly innocent way, as if he's ready to tell John to go for it, if he's feeling it. But remember that earlier, Dave was warning John to stay away from Vriska. Bear in mind, though, that was a future Dave, and we've been backtracking to his earlier exploits with Terezi. Eventually, Dave comes around to Karkat's view that Vriska is not to be toyed with, even though it's unlikely Karkat will get any credit for this advance warning. So what happens between now and then to change Dave's tune? Anti-Vriska propaganda from Terezi...or something else? It's worth keeping an eye out for. There's still way too much to talk about here, so I won't even bother. Except to point out that Karkat and Dave say more gay stuff, Karkat keeps talking about Dave's lips, and Dave accuses Karkat of being gay, and he's right, Karkat is gay, but also Dave is gay too, and they're both gay, and they both definitely end up kissing each other years from now. Sorry, that's the only other thing I wanted to point out about this.

THE CONCEPT OF A CALIGINIOUS RELATIONSHIP
CTG: what
CTG: the fuck
CTG: are you talking about
?CG: BUT I'M NOT THAT PERSON. I HAVE A FIRM GRASP ON HOW DERANGED AND UNNATURAL ANY SORT OF INTERSPECIES RELATIONSHIP WOULD BE, WHETHER CALIGINOUS OR CONCUPISCENT.
?CG: SO I ASK
?CG: NO I'M FUCKING BEGGING YOU BOTH
?CG: TO QUIT CHATTING UP THESE SHITHIVE BROADS AND LEAVE WELL ENOUGH ALONE.
CTG: thats obviously not gonna happen
?CG: FUCK.
?CG: LOOK.
?CG: ALRIGHT I ADMIT THIS ISN'T PURELY MAGNANIMOUS CONCERN FOR YOUR SAFETY HERE.
?CG: WE'RE ALL SORT OF COOKING UP A PLAN RIGHT NOW.
?CG: MY RIGHT NOW.
?CG: WHICH IF SUCCESSFUL, MAY, AND I DO STRESS MAY, END UP WITH ALL OF US MEETING FACE TO FACE.
?CG: AND WHAT I'D LIKE TO AVOID IF AT ALL POSSIBLE
?CG: IS TO HAVE THIS RENDEZVOUS INSTANTLY DETERIORATE INTO A LOT OF REVOLTING TROLL/HUMAN SLOPPY MAKEOUTS.
?CG: THAT WOULD JUST RUIN IT FOR ME, OK?
?CG: REALLY THE ONLY SCENARIO THAT I AM SURE WOULD CAUSE ME TO REGRET SUCCESS. GOT IT?
CEB: er...
CEB: do...
CEB: you think that vriska is going to try to make out with me?
?CG: SHUT UP.
?CG: I'M NOT ANSWERING YOUR DUMB QUESTIONS ABOUT HOW MUCH SNOGGING YOU'RE IN FOR AND I'M NOT PLAYING INTERSPECIES MATCH MAKER HERE.
?CG: SERIOUSLY, WHAT IS WRONG WITH YOU GUYS?
?CG: I SHOULDN'T EVEN NEED TO BE SAYING THIS.
?CG: GOD DAMMIT, IT'S NOT EVEN LIKE YOU DON'T HAVE ACTUAL HUMAN FEMALES NEARBY FOR ACTUAL BIOLOGICALLY VIABLE MATESPRITSHIPS!
?CG: DO I HAVE TO DRAW YOU A DIAGRAM???
CEB: rose and jade?
CEB: so, uh...
CEB: you want us to like, date them?
?CG: WOULD IT REALLY FUCKING KILL YOU TO CONSIDER IT??????
?CG: I MEAN GOD. WHAT DO YOU EVEN THINK YOU'RE DOING HERE IN THIS GAME?
?CG: YOU'RE CREATING YOUR OWN UNIVERSE TO GO LIVE IN.
?CG: AND JUST HOW DO YOU THINK YOUR SPECIES IS SUPPOSED TO REPOPULATE ITSELF??????????? IDIOTS.
CTG: dude
CTG: no
CTG: just
CTG: stop
?CG: OH OK, SO THE ALIEN HERE IS THE ONLY ONE CONCERNED WITH THE PROPAGATION OF YOUR SPECIES.
?CG: THAT MAKES A LOT OF FUCKING SENSE. WHY DON'T YOU WISE THE FUCK UP, COOLDOUCHE?
CEB: i think he is right, i think we are all a little young to be thinking about that!
?CG: WELL NO SHIT, NOW YOU ARE OBVIOUSLY.
?CG: BUT WHAT ABOUT LATER? THINK ABOUT THE BIG PICTURE.
?CG: HOW DID HUMANITY GET AS FAR AS IT GOT BEING SO DUMB?
CEB: um, also,
CEB: we are kinda all related! sort of. through shared ghost slime genes. right?
CEB: so, uh...
?CG: OH RIGHT, THE BIZARRE HUMAN ANATHEMA OF INCEST, I FORGOT.
CTG: oh my fucking god
CTG: please let this conversation not be taking place
?CG: OK WELL LET'S SAY THAT'S HYPOTHETICALLY A PROBLEM, EVEN THOUGH I'M RACKING MY BRAIN TO UNDERSTAND WHY IT WOULD BE.
?CG: I GUESS I WILL HAVE TO DRAW YOU A DIAGRAM, BECAUSE YOU ARE JUST THAT STUPID.
?CG: HERE

I probably don't even have to bother stating for the record that Karkat's shipping diagram is the stuff of legends. It bluntly illustrates the truth that any reader must have confronted by now, which is that the human hetero shipping matchups can only result in one configuration by default. Of course, it doesn't play out quite this way (except Dave x Jade, but that's sort of a sideshow involving Davesprite). The incest pairings are stated as non-viable, although at least for Dave and Rose, the topic just seems to keep getting dragged back into the spotlight more than you might expect, or want. It disregards troll-human matchups (Karkat actively campaigning against them here is probably the best evidence we have at this point that they are *definitely* going to happen), and also ignores Beta-Alpha Kid matchups, because nobody knows yet that they're all going to meet kid versions of their parents, let alone consider dating them. Karkat makes a valiant effort here, and if nothing else reveals himself to be one of the most entertaining Bad Artists in the story. That is, until Caliborn comes along, who has a similar aesthetic, is *much* worse (but gets better), and uses his skills for similar purposes. The fact that Karkat and Caliborn have a bit of overlap in personality and typing style may correlate somewhat with their artistic sensibilities as well. Like there's a certain part of the brain that's overactive in both kids, and possibly in all very special boys of their ilk.

?CG: http://tinyurl.com/MATINGDIAGRAMFORMORONS

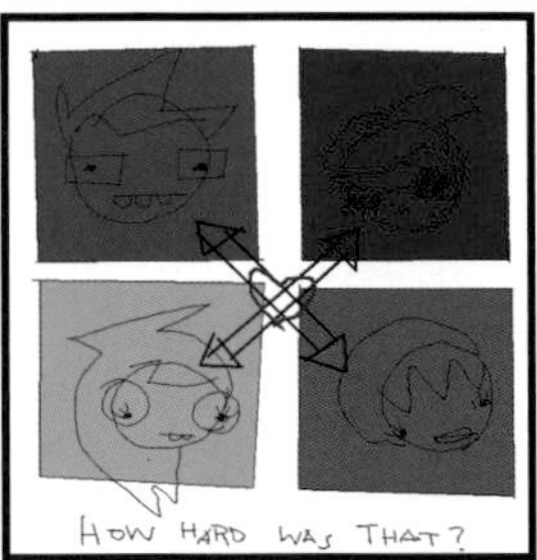

CTG: ok youre by far the worst artist out of any of us
CTG: and thats saying something
?CG: SHUT UP I DREW IT FAST
?CG: NOW
?CG: AS YOU CAN CLEARLY SEE, THERE ARE ONLY TWO SETS OF COMPATIBLE QUADRANTS HERE FOR LEGITIMATE CONCUPISCENT PAIRINGS.
?CG: DAVE AND ROSE ARE "RELATED"
?CG: JADE AND JOHN ARE "RELATED"
?CG: THAT ONLY LEAVES TWO PAIRS.
?CG: ONCE AGAIN, THE DECISIONS PERTAINING TO HUMAN ROMANCE REMAIN STUNNINGLY SIMPLE.
?CG: AND YET I STILL HAVE TO SPELL IT OUT FOR YOU.
YOU'RE WELCOME.
?CG: NOW GO HASSLE YOUR FUTURE MATESPRITS AND LEAVE THE TROLL GIRLS ALONE.
CTG: thx for the shipping grid bro imma drop everything and go have a baby with jade right now
CTG: no peeking k
CEB: wow, i have to marry rose?
CEB: uh...
CEB: wow.
?CG: AND NOW THAT I HAVE SAVED YOUR ENTIRE WORTHLESS SPECIES WITH MY IMPECCABLE ROMANCE BROKERING SKILLS
?CG: I WILL BID YOU A BITTER FUCKING FAREWELL.
?CG: JEGUS I AM SO TIRED.
CTG: you should go back to sleep
CTG: it was so much cooler when you were asleep and i basically never had to listen to you ever
?CG: I CAN'T GO TO SLEEP
CEB: why not?
?CG: BECAUSE I'M TOO TIRED TO EXPLAIN WHY IS WHY.
?CG: YOU'LL FIGURE IT OUT LATER.
?CG: MEMO OVER.
?CG: GET OUTTA HERE.
?CG banned CEB from responding to memo.
?CG banned CTG from responding to memo.

?CG closed memo.

> Karkat: Be Past Karkat.

You cannot be Past Karkat because in the past, Past Karkat is asleep!

> [S] Past Karkat: Wake up.

It's possible that one of the more entertaining results of Karkat's grid is that John appears to take the advice seriously on some level. Dave blows it off (yet actually does end up dating Jade in some capacity), whereas John, who plainly has *no* romantic traction with Rose at any point in the story, seems to take it to heart, as if this really is his duty if they want to advance the human race. Nothing ever really comes of that, but there are moments where you can tell it's still on his mind, like in the **[S] Seer: Descend** game, where you play as John and Grimdark Rose. Speaking of playable games, it's time for the first instance of these RPG-style behemoths. They're monstrously big in print, at least. This one picks up on a key point in the timeline that the story has already led us to wonder about: when does Karkat wake up, why was he asleep for so long, and what did he see in his dreams? The player gets to walk around, talk to all the trolls in the lab, and find out the answers at their own pace. It ends up being *a lot*. But that's what makes the format engaging, in its native medium, conveying a feeling that there is much to freely explore. Does it work in a book? Well, let's find out.

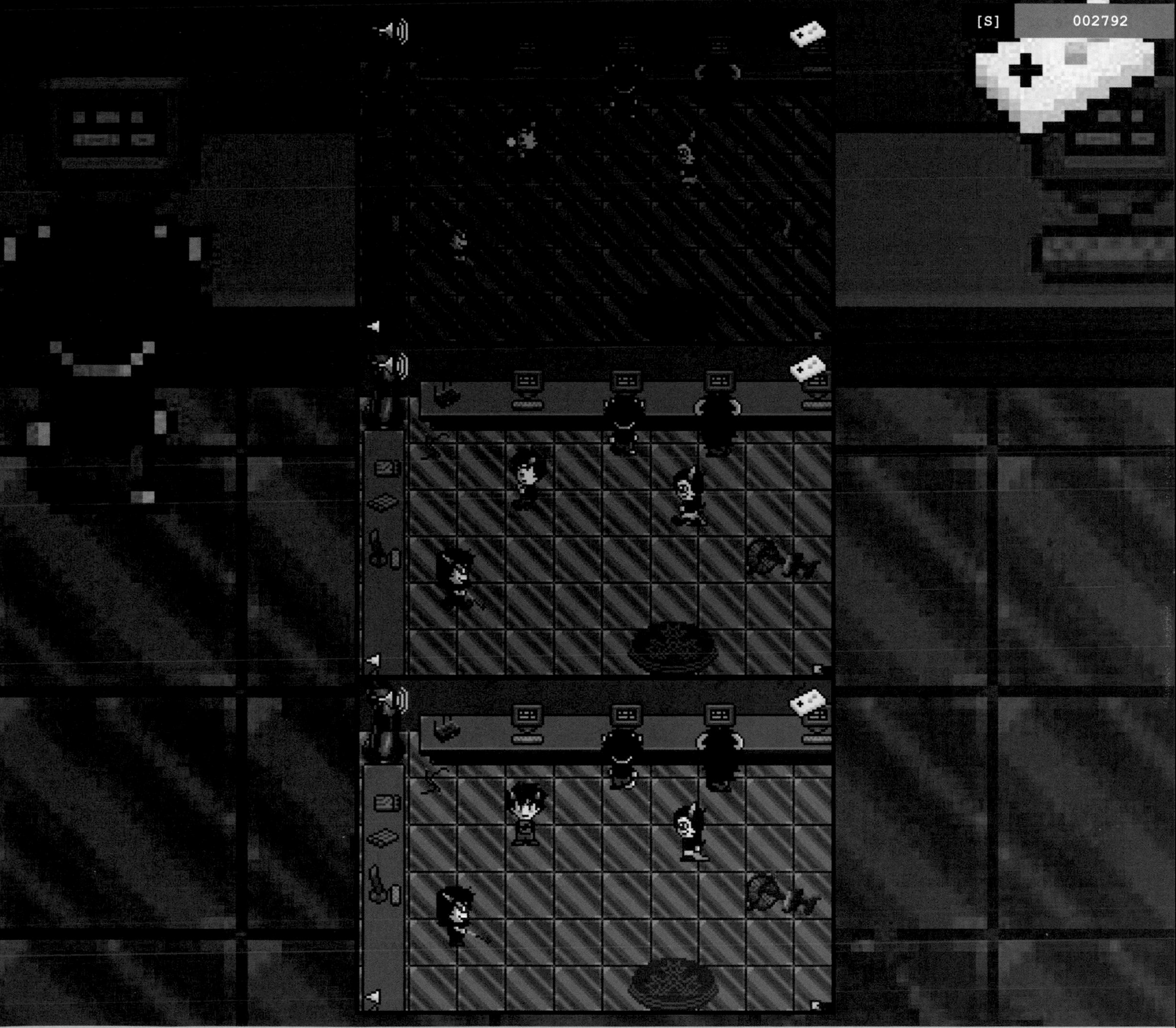

As the command implies, you wake up as Karkat after a long, grim nap. He was asleep when Prospit was destroyed, killing his dream self and trapping him in his sleep for a while, for mysterious reasons. Regardless of the narrative purpose it serves or the questions it answers, this game was an EXCITING *HOMESTUCK* MOMENT when it was released, dropping in out of nowhere. It was another one of those instances where readers had no idea a certain format was in *Homestuck*'s arsenal, then it dropped without any warning at all, and with barely any pause preceding it (maybe a few days in this case). And just like that, a new type of content became "something *Homestuck* is capable of doing, and may continue doing in the future." And that did turn out to be true. There are at least another three games like this. One later in this book where John explores a village, the aforementioned one with Rose and John, and another one involving Equius, Nepeta, and Gamzee during the throes of Murderstuck. Each has different tonalities and story purposes. The Rose/John one has a melancholy atmosphere, a sense of dramatic irony over slain parents on a roof. The latter one is essentially purely in the horror genre. But in this one here, the atmosphere is mainly, HEY LOOK! THIS IS A THING WE CAN DO NOW! IT'S PRETTY COOL! By my recollection, there were few who disagreed.

Immediate dividends of this format included the introduction of the "talksprite." People loved these things, made their own, and looked forward to any additional representations of the characters that looked like this. They added some flavor to the dialogue, showing facial expressions to go along with certain lines, which I think definitely changed the feel of the dialogue compared to the previously unillustrated pesterlogs. Since this was a new idea, and also since these games got made with such INSANE speed by a variety of artists without the luxury of style sheets or anything, they come across as a little wonky in this first game. All over the place in terms of style. But that's *Homestuck* for you. The sprites served their purpose and were all pretty good on their own terms.

FEFERI: W)(en Derse is destroyed, I am going to go to sleep and prove it.
FEFERI: I will prove it to you, and to t)(em as well.
KARKAT: THEM?
FEFERI: Our new friends! You'll see. -Everyt)(ing is going to be ok.
FEFERI: T)(IS IS PR-ETTY -EXCITING! Don't you t)(ink???
KARKAT: "M-E)("

You can talk to anyone you want when you gain control of Karkat, but here in the book it sorta makes sense to check with Feferi first, since it gets right to the point of what happens when you go to sleep without a dream self. Karkat ominously advises against this. Feferi is a good foil for this topic, because it reminds us that in an earlier memo we saw, three hours after Karkat wakes up, Derse is destroyed too, which traps Feferi in her sleep like Karkat just was. In fact, she knows this already, because she got the memo too and wants to trap herself in the nap deliberately. We'll keep tabs on that. Another key element of this game is Karkat waking up to everyone buzzing about these new alien kids they found. So this gives us insight into Karkat's first exposure to the humans, and the origin of his decision to organize a trolling effort against them. It's kind of an interesting wrinkle to the troll timeline. It shows the rest of the trolls were pretty deep into interacting with the kids before Karkat even knew about them, which is not the impression we got when we first heard from Karkat. He's actually pretty late to the party, which shouldn't surprise us by now.

The horn pile is established through this game as a critical fixture in the troll lab, referenced repeatedly and almost always in the context of being used as a bed. There is no reason for its existence aside from the fact that Gamzee is a sloppy, useless, clowny piece of complete garbage. He dances by the pile perpetually throughout this game, also for no reason. One thing this game can do, which *Homestuck* in general can also do, is spontaneously hop to another point in the timeline to check something out. In this case, "Be Future Feferi" hops three hours ahead to when she's sleeping on the horn pile, trapped in her Dark Nap. And we quickly return from that future vignette to resume play. This is one way we flesh out the full series of timeline events.

Time to catch up with Terezi now. Due to the expanded nature of this format, on this page we make it...a full SIX lines deep into this conversation before we have to turn the page. Perhaps it's time to address the elephant in the room. This game (again, a single page on the website), occupies about ONE HUNDRED AND FIFTY PAGES in this book. Was there a better way to do this, to save space? Probably. Maybe we could have made like, maps? Compressed the conversations into a linear, non-illustrated text format by omitting some of the talksprites? Maybe we could have cut the page count in half or such. Would that have been worth it? We *would* lose a few things, the flavor to the conversations that the talksprites add and such. Also, the more you mess around with trickery like that, the more the layout decisions start piling up. And pretty soon you realize, it's just easier to start charging through this material with pure screencaps alone, and maybe at the end of the day, that's fine, and it's a decent way to read all this in a book, and nobody's actually complaining, except me. And even I'm not really. I'm just typing longass posts down here as usual, which for some unfathomable reason I have taken to calling "posts."

002792 [S]

But there's a predictable consequence to having this one game take up so many pages: it means suddenly I have to make A LOT OF EXTRA NOTES. And I'm sorry, folks, but I just don't think I can in good conscience come up with unique notes for when Karkat finds a fucking bottle of Faygo or a couple boondollars in a chest next to a transporter after walking down five flights of stairs or something. This is as good an excuse as any to begin reinstituting the GENIUS policy I introduced in the previous book, which can be summarized as, "not doing notes for certain pages, if I don't feel like it." I can just skip those pages! It's totally fine. Sure, you'll miss me on those pages, but you know what they say about absence making the heart grow fonder. And when I finally come back to say something stupid, you may feel slightly less inclined to throw the book across the room.

I'm about to start skipping notes like a madman. But first, here's Karkat bringing up the "demon" again. It's supposed to be this huge mystery, but come on. Let's be grown-ups here. It's just Bec Noir. We all know it. But the story toys with this mystery through its nonlinear presentation. Karkat seems to *suspect* it's Jack (without the text being totally clear about that), but he's not sure, since Bec Noir looks so different. He needs to do more research to confirm it for himself, but he will. Which means that later on, he knows the demon is Jack, but the story dexterously weaves around having him spill this info to the reader, using methods like we're seeing above. When the time is exactly right (**[S] Jade: Enter**) the information is revealed to us in grand fashion, a device otherwise known as a "major plot development." I find that's a pretty good way to reveal things, because having people just say the things can be a little boring. And it would be a shame to waste even a single precious drop of your boredom until I have you exactly where I want you, which is trapped with me, right down here in the Laugh Gutter. Anyway, on that note, bye for a while.

KARKAT: I NEED TO SEARCH FOR MORE ANSWERS BEFORE I KNOW FOR SURE.

TEREZI: STOP B31NG MYST3R1OUS 4ND T3LL M3!
TEREZI: 4RGH, F1N3

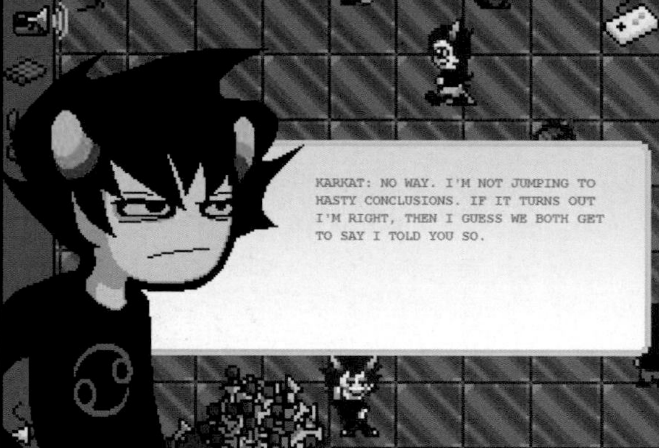
KARKAT: NO WAY. I'M NOT JUMPING TO HASTY CONCLUSIONS. IF IT TURNS OUT I'M RIGHT, THEN I GUESS WE BOTH GET TO SAY I TOLD YOU SO.

TEREZI: SO, YOU S4W H1M JUST B3FOR3 H3 D3STROY3D PROSP1T?

KARKAT: YEAH. AND THAT WASN'T EVEN THE BAD PART OF THE DREAM.

TEREZI: TH4T W4S 4N HOUR 4GO! WH4T H4V3 YOU B33N DR34M1NG 4BOUT S1NC3?
KARKAT: THE BOTTOM LINE IS, EVERYONE HERE IS FORBIDDEN FROM GOING TO SLEEP.
KARKAT: YES, AS YOUR LEADER, I AM ORDERING ALL PROSPIT DREAMERS TO STAY AWAKE, NO MATTER HOW TIRED YOU GET.

KARKAT: I DON'T WANT TO TALK ABOUT IT.
TEREZI: FORB1DD3N?
TEREZI: UM, 4LR1GHT >:/

KARKAT: DO YOU EVER EVEN GET TIRED?

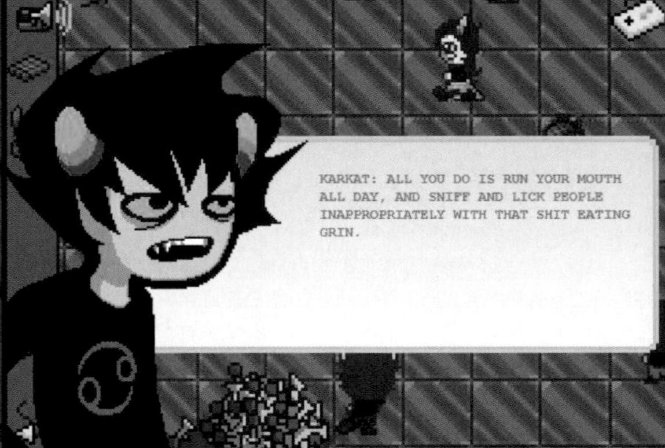
KARKAT: ALL YOU DO IS RUN YOUR MOUTH ALL DAY, AND SNIFF AND LICK PEOPLE INAPPROPRIATELY WITH THAT SHIT EATING GRIN.

TEREZI: 1M G3TT1NG PR3TTY T1R3D R1GHT NOW 4S 4 M4TT3R OF F4CT

TEREZI: WH4TS TH4T SUPPOS3D TO M34N!
KARKAT: I DON'T THINK I'VE EVER EVEN SEEN YOU YAWN.
TEREZI: T1R3D OF YOUR BULLSH1T!

KARKAT: GOD I'M TIRED.

> Talk To Terezi
Get lowdown from Terezi.
> Be Terezi.
> Cancel

TEREZI: SO GU3SS WH4T

TEREZI: W3V3 B33N 1N CONT4CT W1TH SOM3 4L13NS FROM TH3 UN1V3RS3 W3 CR34T3D

KARKAT: OK. SO?

TEREZI: DONT YOU TH1NK TH4TS K1ND OF N34T?

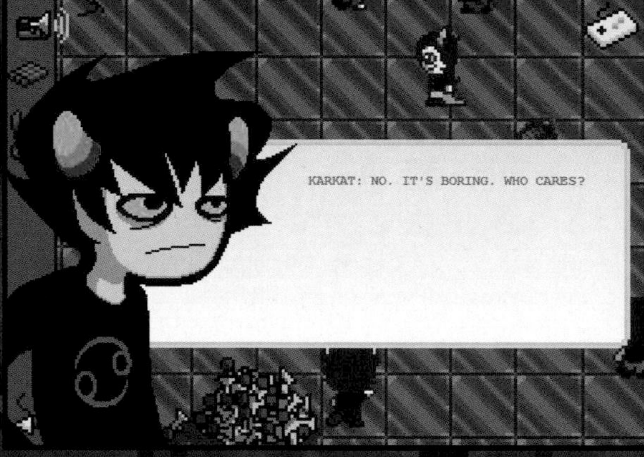
KARKAT: NO. IT'S BORING. WHO CARES?

TEREZI: 1 THOUGHT 4S OUR 1NTR3P1D L34D3R TH4T W4S SOM3TH1NG YOU M1GHT W4NT TO KNOW

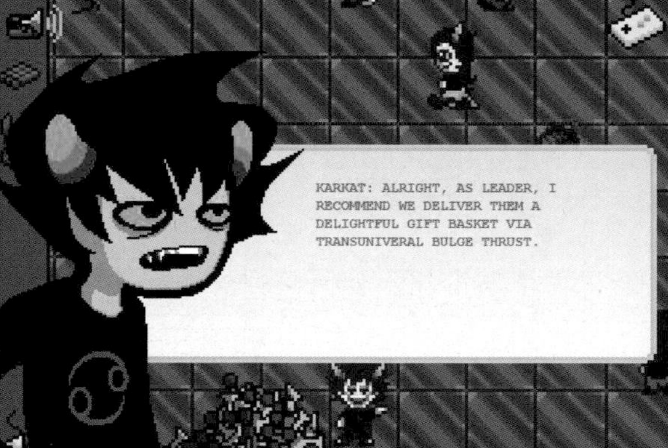
KARKAT: ALRIGHT, AS LEADER, I RECOMMEND WE DELIVER THEM A DELIGHTFUL GIFT BASKET VIA TRANSUNIVERAL BULGE THRUST.

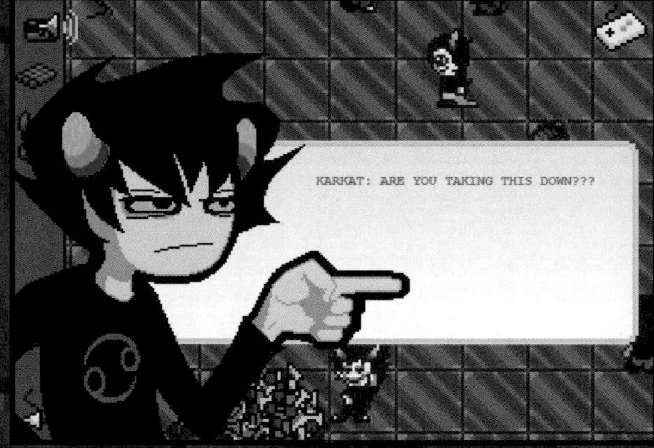
KARKAT: ARE YOU TAKING THIS DOWN???

TEREZI: >:P

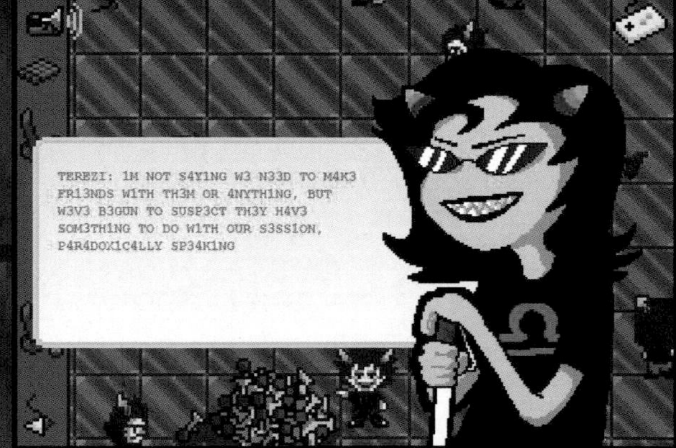
TEREZI: 1M NOT S4Y1NG W3 N33D TO M4K3 FR13NDS W1TH TH3M OR 4NYTH1NG, BUT W3V3 B3GUN TO SUSP3CT TH3Y H4V3 SOM3TH1NG TO DO W1TH OUR S3SS1ON, P4R4DOX1C4LLY SP34K1NG

KARKAT: IS ANYTHING EVER NOT PARADOXICALLY SPEAKING?
KARKAT: NOPE. I ALREADY TOLD YOU. WE'RE DOOMED. A MEANINGLESS RACE OF ALIENS WON'T CHANGE THAT.

TEREZI: M4YB3 W3 C4N F1GUR3 OUT 4 W4Y TO G3T OURS3LV3S OUT OF TH1S J4M?

KARKAT: NOW IF YOU'LL EXCUSE ME, I'VE GOT A LOT OF IMPORTANT SHIT TO DO.

TEREZI: YOU M34N 4 LOT OF 1MPORT4NT W4ND3R1NG 4ROUND 41ML3SSLY 4ND T4LK1NG TO P3OPL3?

KARKAT: YES, EXACTLY.

> Finish responding to Kanaya in memo.
> Cancel
CURRENT carcinoGeneticist [CCG] RIGHT NOW responded to memo.
CCG: OK.
CCG: EVERYTHING'S FINE I GUESS.
PGA: What Happened
CCG: I PASSED OUT FOR ABOUT AN HOUR.

Returning to say: You can go up to that computer and "Finish responding to Kanaya in memo." So even though we see their talksprites, this isn't actually an in-person conversation. It's Current Karkat and Past Kanaya. This initiates part of a memo conversation we read in the previous book (Book 4, page 404, if you care to go back and review the context, or page 2567 on Homestuck.com). Back then, we already caught a glimpse of this moment just after Karkat woke up, through a very narrow sliver of what takes place in this game. It reminds us that his entire critical nap was precipitated by the fact that he passed out when Kanaya cut off Tavros's legs. When he woke up, he finally decided to close the book on this memo to clean up the loose ends, which he's doing here. Very tidy of him, and me.

CCG: FUCKING EMBARRASSING.

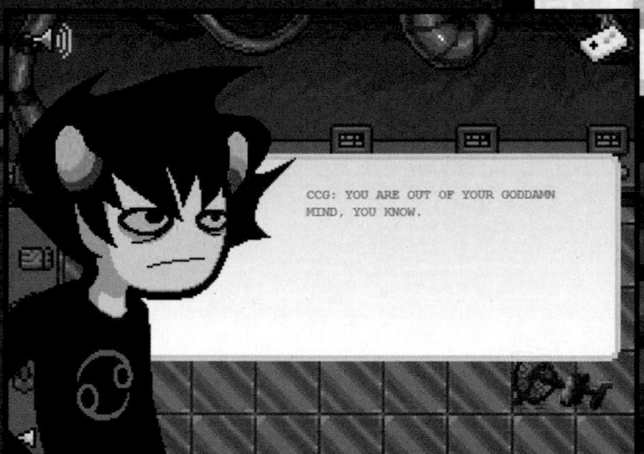
CCG: YOU ARE OUT OF YOUR GODDAMN MIND, YOU KNOW.

PGA: Shithive Maggots You Mean

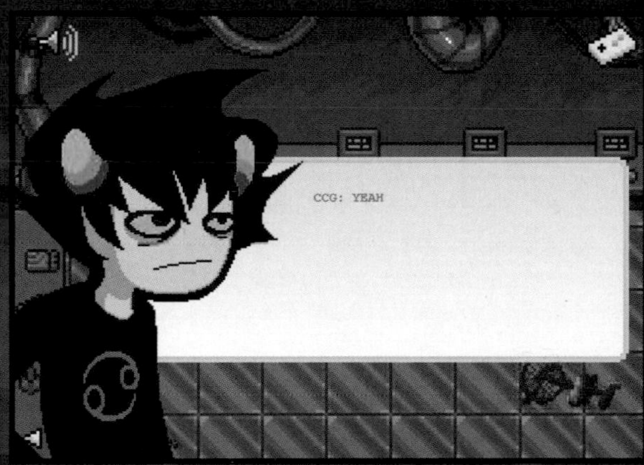
CCG: YEAH

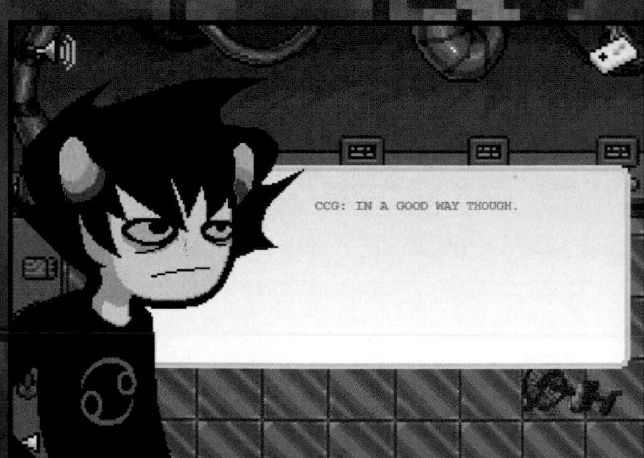
CCG: IN A GOOD WAY THOUGH.

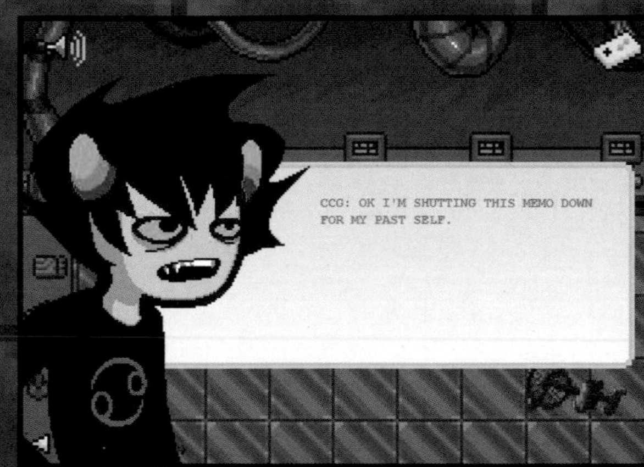
CCG: OK I'M SHUTTING THIS MEMO DOWN FOR MY PAST SELF.

CCG: SINCE HE'S CURRENTLY LYING UNCONSCIOUS ON THE FLOOR AN HOUR AGO.
CCG: SEE YOU IN THE FUTURE-NOW.
PGA: Til Then
CCG banned CGA from responding to memo.
CCG banned PCG from responding to memo.
CCG closed memo.
> Talk to Sollux.
> Cancel
SOLLUX: hey kk mo2t of the2e computer2 are 2hiit.

SOLLUX: 2o unle22 youve got a real good rea2on ii dont thiink iim gonna bother fiixiing them.

KARKAT: I'M FINE, THANKS FOR ASKING MAN. YOUR CONCERN IS REALLY APPRECIATED, I APPRECIATE IT.

SOLLUX: fuck you and your priimadonna garbage, iim not goiing two break down 2obbiing becau2e you pa22 out at the 2iight of a liittle blood, why dont you man up.

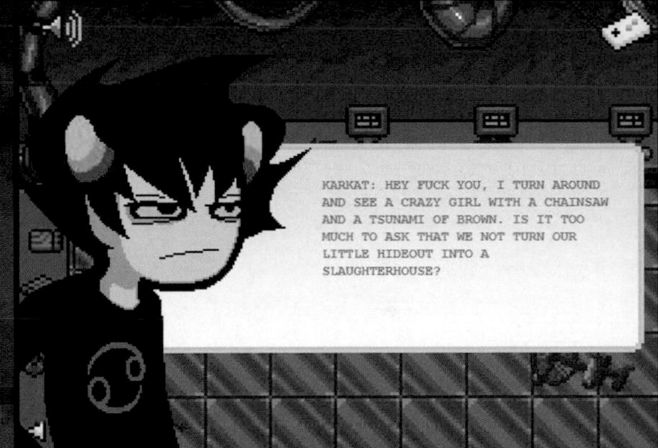
KARKAT: HEY FUCK YOU, I TURN AROUND AND SEE A CRAZY GIRL WITH A CHAINSAW AND A TSUNAMI OF BROWN. IS IT TOO MUCH TO ASK THAT WE NOT TURN OUR LITTLE HIDEOUT INTO A SLAUGHTERHOUSE?

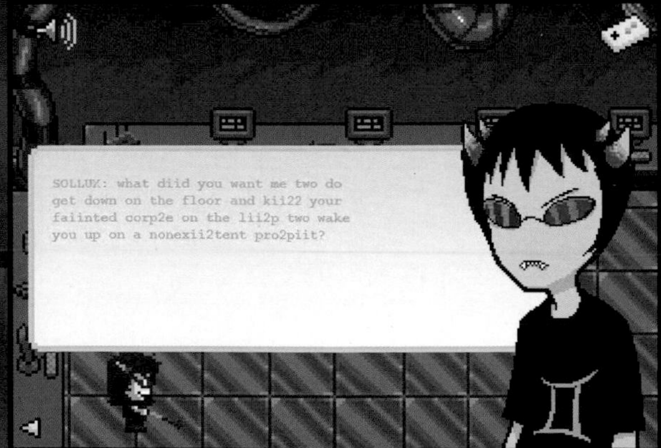
SOLLUX: what diid you want me two do get down on the floor and kii22 your faiinted corp2e on the lii2p two wake you up on a nonexii2tent pro2piit?

KARKAT: LET'S NOT DO THIS, OK MAN? JUST THIS ONCE. I DON'T HAVE THE ENERGY.

[S]

SOLLUX: yeah ok fiine.

KARKAT: SO WHAT'S THE DEAL WITH THESE ALIENS, IS IT ANYTHING I SHOULD GIVE A SHIT ABOUT?

SOLLUX: no not at all, theyre u2ele22 and uniintere2tiing liike iim 2ure you already gathered.

SOLLUX: ii recommend we dont bother wiith them, though aradiia 2eem2 two thiink well all be iin each other2 2ponge2 iineviitably.

SOLLUX: whatever, iim pretty commiitted two not haviing anythiing two do wiith them ever.

KARKAT: GOOD, THAT'S WHAT I LIKE TO HEAR.

A lot of these conversations mainly involve Karkat insisting he thinks these aliens are boring and he'll want nothing to do with them. The lens of dramatic irony of course frames these proclamations as ridiculous, and even Sollux finds it laughable, because he is privy to the same sense of dramatic irony we are through reading the future memos. He brings this up, and Karkat naturally pounces on the opportunity to lambaste Future Karkat. And oh yeah, also Past Karkat, he's even worse, and maybe while he's at it, Current Karkat too, because wow, fuck that guy. Since we learn that Karkat is initially reluctant to troll the humans, it retroactively sets up a punchline to this joke that asks "what made him change his mind?" And we already know the punchline. It's because he falls in hate with John.

SOLLUX: ehehehehehehe.

Talk to Eridan.
> Cancel

ERIDAN: wwhat a fuckin vvulgar display this is

ERIDAN: airin out all his dirty laundry like that puttin a big fuckin pile a horns in the middle of the room

ERIDAN: at least i got the upright basic decency to hide my shitty wand pile somewwhere in the lab you wwont find it dont evven bother lookin

GAMZEE: sLeEp iN ThE HoRn pIlE? oNlY 420 bOoNdOlLaRs

Gamzee allows you to sleep on the horn pile for 420 boondollars. In this sense, he's like an RPG innkeeper. Except the service he is offering is worse than useless. Just like him.

KARKAT: BESIDES, I JUST BANNED EVERYONE FROM SLEEPING, SO DON'T GO PULLING THIS HORN PILE INN KEEPER SHIT, GOT IT?

GAMZEE: Ok wEll If yOu gEt yOuR MiNd aLl cHaNgEd aBoUt tHaT ThEn yOu kNoW WhErE To fInD ThE PiLe, BeSt fRiEnD

GAMZEE: HoNk hOnK HoNk hOnK HoNk!
:o)

Talk to Kanaya.
> Cancel

KARKAT: HEY I JUST GOT DONE TALKING TO YOU IN THE PAST. REMEMBER YOU WERE FUCKING AROUND WITH THE VOLCANO AND I PASSED OUT FOR AN HOUR?

KANAYA: Vaguely

KARKAT: THAT WAS NOW. HEY GUESS WHAT, NEW ORDERS. NO MORE IMPROMPTU AMPUTATIONS, OK?

KANAYA: Impromptutations

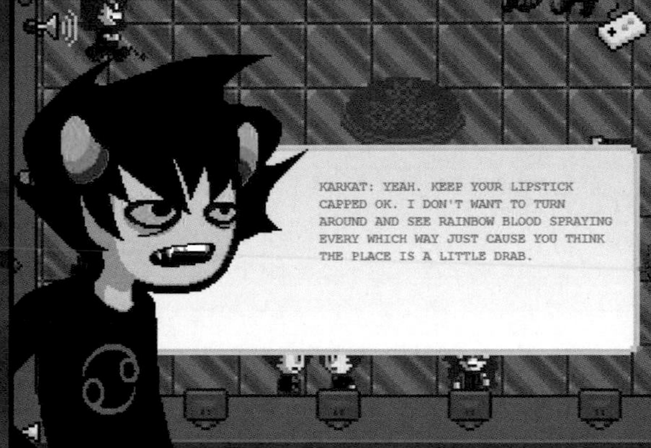
KARKAT: YEAH. KEEP YOUR LIPSTICK CAPPED OK. I DON'T WANT TO TURN AROUND AND SEE RAINBOW BLOOD SPRAYING EVERY WHICH WAY JUST CAUSE YOU THINK THE PLACE IS A LITTLE DRAB.

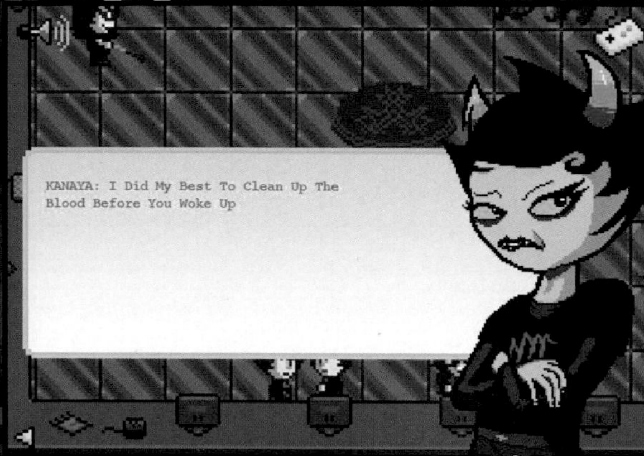
KANAYA: I Did My Best To Clean Up The Blood Before You Woke Up

KARKAT: THANKS FOR THAT. ALSO ANOTHER NEW ORDER. DON'T GO TO SLEEP.

KANAYA: Dont Worry I Dont Really Want To Find Out What Happens If I Do

KANAYA: Any Other Orders

KANAYA: Such As Those Which Might Pertain To These Alien Children

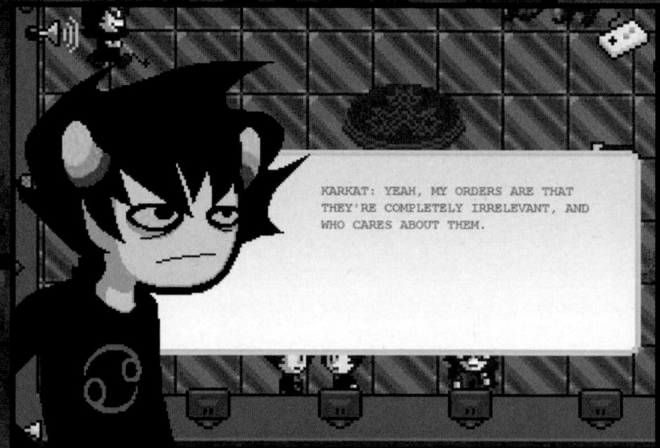
KARKAT: YEAH, MY ORDERS ARE THAT THEY'RE COMPLETELY IRRELEVANT, AND WHO CARES ABOUT THEM.

Translation of that last panel: I think you should consider scoping out that Egbert kid's sweet ass before you write them all off as a waste of time.

Here's another key point, which I'm not sure if I referenced yet: Karkat's Big Speech. It's a moment on the timeline that we've seen numerous allusions to already. We have no idea how good the speech is, because we don't get to read it. Some trolls seem to think it's good, like Kanaya. But one thing is indisputable. It is directly inspired by how hot Karkat thinks John is.

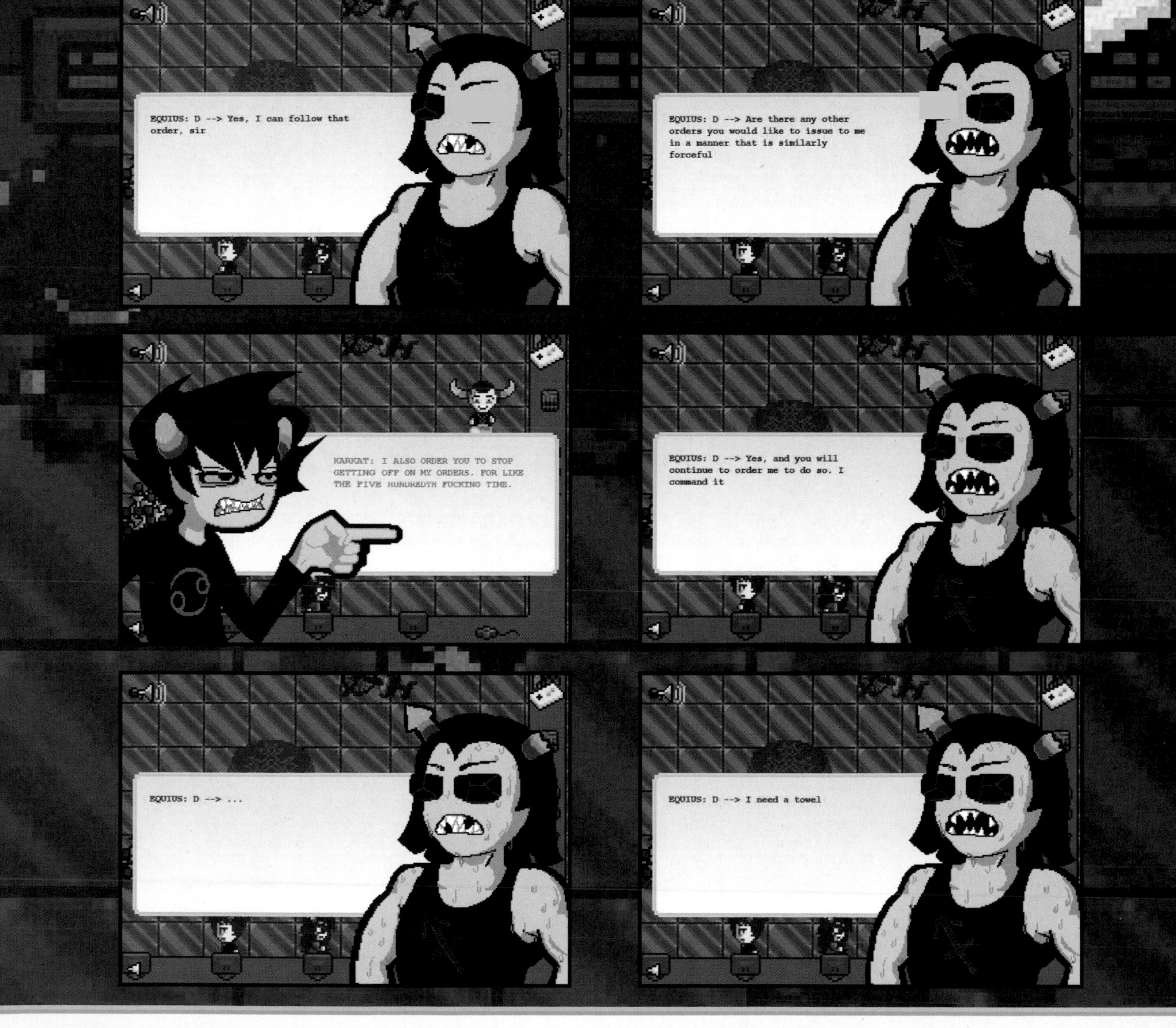

Karkat orders Equius never to give anyone horse legs. Which I believe is an order he manages to follow. His ancestor Horuss, however, is a different story. I doubt Kankri ever specifically ordered Horuss not to give Rufioh horse legs. Or maybe he did, but Horuss didn't listen, because people somehow take Kankri even less seriously than Karkat.

I'm just going to use this conversation as an excuse point out that one reason why this game format is really good is that it gives practically everyone an excuse to talk to everyone else without making a huge deal out of it and wildly inflating the online page count. God, I'm so clever. All I *really* managed to do was wildly inflate the book page count, many years later.

EQUIUS: D --> I will be as gentle as possible
KARKAT: DON'T TOUCH ME.
> Examine host plush.
> Cancel
Looks like SOMEONE needs to stop playing games for girls.
Talk to Tavros.
> Cancel
TAVROS: hEYYY, yOU'RE AWAKE,

KARKAT: HEY, YOU KNOW WHAT WOULD HAVE BEEN AN AWESOME TIME TO TAKE THE OPPORTUNITY TO SAW YOUR LOWER TORSO OFF AND REPLACE IT WITH ROBO LEGS?
TAVROS: nO,
KARKAT: ANY GODDAMN TIME BEFORE NOW. YOU KNOW, DURING OUR WHOLE ADVENTURE WHEN THEY MIGHT HAVE COME IN HANDY.
KARKAT: ALSO WHEN I DIDN'T HAPPEN TO BE STANDING AROUND. THAT WOULD HAVE BEEN SO SWEET.
TAVROS: oHH, sORRY, i MEAN i WAS KIND OF ASLEEP TOO, sO, i DIDN'T HAVE A LOT OF SAY,
TAVROS: iN THE MATTER,

Karkat makes a pretty good point. If Tavros was going to get robo-legs at all, why not during the session, which would have allowed him greater mobility in a physically demanding environment? And Tavros makes a pretty disturbing point. He didn't actually consent to having his legs sawed off and replaced. These people are disasters. It does make you wonder about Kanaya's motivation. Mothering gone overboard? Erasing the most major lasting effect of Vriska's bullying, which she continues to use as ammunition against Tavors for years after, including during the session? Perhaps the answer to this second question also answers the first posed by Karkat. Kanaya and Equius never got around to the leg transplant during the session because they could never find a moment alone with Tavros without Vriska looming over him. They got to this meteor, found their chance, and took it.

The rest of the conversation is dedicated to making sure we all know that Tavros doesn't have the slightest idea what's actually going on right now. Sounds about right.

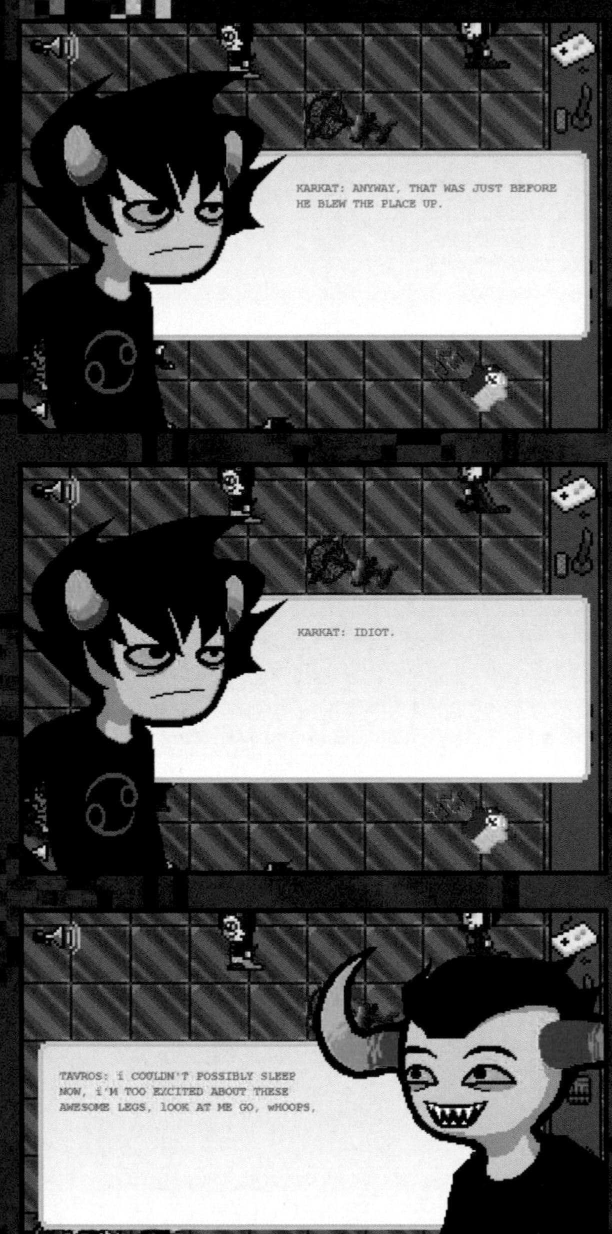
KARKAT: ANYWAY, THAT WAS JUST BEFORE HE BLEW THE PLACE UP.
KARKAT: IDIOT.
TAVROS: i COULDN'T POSSIBLY SLEEP NOW, i'M TOO EXCITED ABOUT THESE AWESOME LEGS, lOOK AT ME GO, wHOOPS,

TAVROS: wHOA, iS THAT WHAT HAPPENED,
KARKAT: JUST DON'T GO TO SLEEP. SPREAD THE WORD.

> Examine UNIREAL AIR.
> Cancel

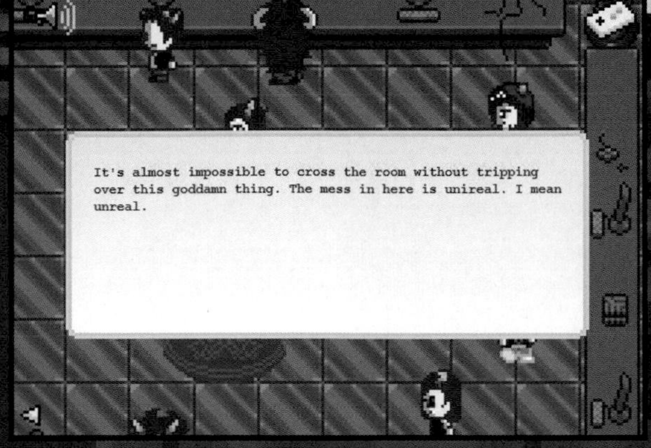
It's almost impossible to cross the room without tripping over this goddamn thing. The mess in here is unireal. I mean unreal.

Talk to Nepeta.
> Cancel

NEPETA: :33 < oh god this is so great, they look like they are so much fun!

KARKAT: WHO

NEPETA: :33 < the humans!!!

KARKAT: WHAT'S A HUMAN
NEPETA: :33 < the alien kids! come on karcat, you need to stop taking all these silly naps and get up to sp33d
KARKAT: WAIT, WHAT HAVE YOU BEEN DOING
KARKAT: YOU HAVEN'T BEEN PULLING YOUR RP NONSENSE ON THEM HAVE YOU? TALK ABOUT A SHITTY FIRST ENCOUNTER.
KARKAT: OK AS LEADER, I FORBID YOU FROM RP'ING WITH THEM.
NEPETA: :33 < but equius already furbid me from doing that :((

Nepeta is understandably one of the trolls most excited about the human discovery. Possibly more excited than anyone. And she's forbidden from talking to them, which causes Karkat, out of spite for Equius, to order her to talk to them *a lot*. So given that Nepeta is excited about the humans and has been COMMANDED by her crush to interact with them, it's a little surprising that we barely ever see her talk to the humans on-screen. Or is it? It probably just means she has dozens of offscreen conversations with all of them, all throughout the timeline, but they aren't important enough to show because they're just a bunch of useless roleplaying, and also Nepeta is a borderline useless character with nothing that important to say about anything. Sorry, Nep, but your metatextually exaggerated uselessness as a minor character has been well-established as a critical feature of your profile in many of these author notes by now. Haven't you been paying attention?

002792
[S]
KARKAT: TROLL WHO?
ARADIA: never mind
ARADIA: lets pretend i didnt say that and lets als0 pretend it isnt inevitable
KARKAT: WHAT THE FROND BUCKLING NOOK STENCH ARE YOU TALKING ABOUT.
ARADIA: n0thing. its n0t like a decisi0n y0u are ab0ut t0 make will invariably lead t0 every pr0blem we have and will ever face as well as the great und0ing itself
ARADIA: just keep listening t0 y0ur angry impulses it will all be fine

We don't get a lot of banter from Aradiabot before this. Aside from her vicious beatdown of Vriska, which characterizes her pretty well through action alone, we don't have much of a sense for what she's like verbally, in contrast with her ghost self and formerly alive self. She's incredibly moody, angry, and fatalistic. She lets timeline "spoilers" slip casually but doesn't care due to both her intense nihilism and the fact that nothing can really be changed. She is one of the striking early examples of revealing the full depth of a character's comprehensive personality by showing different facets of them through different "versions" of the character.

Aradia is kind of a linear example of that concept, though. She goes from alive --> ghost --> frog --> robot to alive again, all in sequence in the same timeline. Which means these facets come across as character evolution, not hypothetical alternate presentations. Distributed characterization approaches happen a lot more later in the story, through methods using splintered alternate selves, such as Dave–Davesprite–Davepeta, Jade–Jadesprite, Dirk–AR Dirk–Arquiusprite, or Vriska–(Vriska). Aradia serves as a pretty good trial run for some of these ideas, partly by illustrating how different one person can be under different circumstances.

Another quick hop-to-the-future vignette establishing another key point on the timeline to keep track of, which is "Aradiabot Explodes." Similar to how we had a "Jadebot Explodes" key moment to track earlier that's revealed in **[S] Descend**, which covers the "when" and "why" about it. So we're possibly set up to expect a similar type of revelation concerning this moment. Its revelation is nearly on the same energy wavelength of narrative sensationalism as **Descend**, broadcast through an animation covering the destruction of Prospit and Derse. This is around when A5A2 starts going full blast. There's a significant period in this sub-act when the crazy intense stuff just never seems to let up. But these stockpiled little mysteries have to be seeded like this for those revelations to have the right impact.

By now we know that Karkat's "trolling campaign," which seemed like it was the Whole Point of the trolls back in Act 4, is completely trivial and comically meaningless. And we have a great appreciation for why that is now, because we know two facts. 1) There are several trolls on this roster who are much more ruthless and cunning than Karkat is, mainly revolving around the Scourge Sister dynamic we didn't know about before. And 2) Karkat spent a long time asleep on the floor before he even heard of the humans, enabling the troublemakers to run wild hatching plans and messing with humans before he had a chance to do anything. So the real "shadow plan" related to the troll engagement with humans was always overwhelmingly focused on Vriska and Terezi's intense meddling efforts. But we had no appreciation for this at all in Act 4, because our gateway to learning about the trolls was presented through Karkat's screaming. In a way, his blustering trolling effort was a great decoy for Vriska and Terezi to use as cover while they went about their scheming sort of under the radar.

VRISKA: They are........

VRISKA: IN

VRISKA: THE

VRISKA: FIIIIIIIIRE!!!!!!!! ::::)

KARKAT: GOD FUCKING DAMMIT.

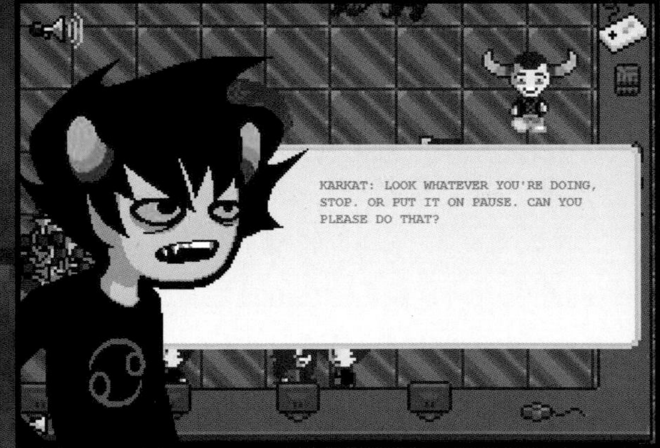
KARKAT: LOOK WHATEVER YOU'RE DOING, STOP. OR PUT IT ON PAUSE. CAN YOU PLEASE DO THAT?

KARKAT: I WASN'T GOING TO BOTHER WITH THE HUMANS BUT NOW YOU'RE MAKING ME NERVOUS. JUST GIVE ME THE CHANCE TO LOOK INTO THIS MATTER, AND THEN I'LL BRIEF EVERYBODY.

KARKAT: MAYBE WITH A SPEECH OR SOMETHING. CAN YOU DO THAT?

KARKAT: PLEEEEEEEEASE? I JUST SAID THAT WITH EIGHT E'S.

VRISKA: Fine, I will take a 8r8k, Karkat. 8ut only 8ecause you were so polite a8out it.

VRISKA: It will give me a chance to go get some stuff done!

> Talk to Vriska.
> Be Vriska.
> Cancel

Being able to switch characters is an important part of the "feel" you get from these games. Loses a *little* something here. (But what doesn't?) When you assume control of a new character, the song changes, and it alters the perspective a little. Now you go around talking to people as Vriska instead of Karkat, and you have to switch your psychology a bit. Vriska is going to offer a very different side to these conversations now, and the responses and attitudes she elicits from others is going to be different too. These are pretty obvious points I'm making, but they're still worth noting, because splashing this type of content into the rest of the story really illustrates how it differs as a storytelling tool, what kind of things you can do with it, and the many interesting ways it shapes reader perception as compared to the more static content.

Looks like Kanaya's still a little frosty from their breakup. You know, because of the relationship they had, which never took place anywhere except for in Kanaya's mind. The breakup also took place in her mind. You can understand why she's a bit upset.

VRISKA: Nothing really! It's just you haven't said one word to me since we got here.

KANAYA: Oh Sorry I Hadnt Really Noticed

KANAYA: Do You Want Me To

VRISKA: In fact, we've hardly spoken in weeks! Not since you gave me that nice dress.
VRISKA: That was gr8, remem8er that? What happened to all that? You used to meddle and 8ug and fuss over me all the time. It was annoying, 8ut kinda fun!
VRISKA: I don't know. It would 8e cool if we could catch up some time though.

KANAYA: Whats There Really To Catch Up On

VRISKA: Whatever! Stuff. Anything!

VRISKA: You are really strange, fussyfangs. I don't get you anymore.

KANAYA: Okay

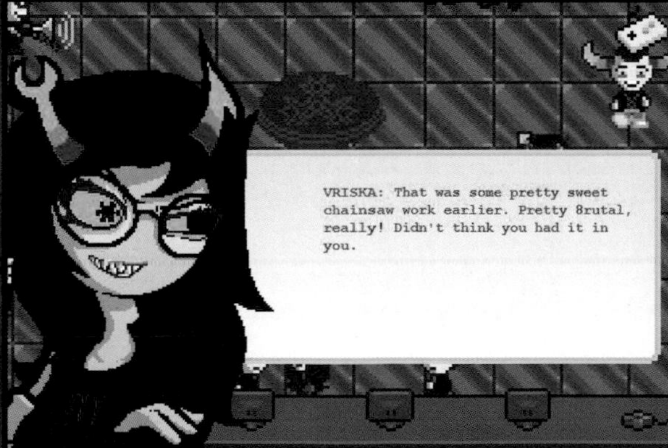
VRISKA: That was some pretty sweet chainsaw work earlier. Pretty 8rutal, really! Didn't think you had it in you.

VRISKA: Hey, you weren't settling a score with him there 8y any chance?

002792
[S]
KANAYA: What
VRISKA: I've got a pretty keen nose for revenge. Could it 8e that you had a thing for him and were upset when he went for me instead? Hmmmmmmmm?
KANAYA: Did He Really "Go" For You
KANAYA: Thats Not How I Remember It
VRISKA: Yes, I think I must 8e on to something here! Anyway if that's the case, sorry a8out the 8ad 8r8k!
KANAYA: Could You Leave Me Alone

Vriska unsurprisingly is quite obtuse about why Kanaya has been standoffish since she gave her the fairy dress. I'm sure I commented on this at the time, but Vriska speculating that Kanaya had a thing for Tavros is just a shout-out to the bold individuals who speculated the same thing when she saw them kiss. It's about as humorously dense for a reader to make that speculation as it is for Vriska to do the same thing here.

The best explanation for why Gamzee says he's scared of Vriska, in my opinion, is this: he's flat-out lying. It's a good way for him to maintain his cover as "Soft Gamzee." It also provides some ammunition for those who, against all sense of good taste and judgment, want to continue to believe and assert that Gamzee is a decent guy with sensitive emotions and vulnerabilities before he undergoes his Murderstuck awakening. He was none of those things, ever.

VRISKA: Aww. ::::)
Talk to Eridan.
> Be Future Eridan.
> Cancel
VRISKA: Hey.
ERIDAN: hey
VRISKA: So........
ERIDAN: wwhats up

VRISKA: Nothing.
VRISKA: Standing by the old horn pile I see.
ERIDAN: yup
VRISKA: Yeah........
VRISKA: Ok then. Carry on I guess.
ERIDAN: god damn vvris wwhys it still got to be so flippin awwkwward like this come on

Vriska's brief conversations with Kanaya and Eridan in close vicinity help convey a likely truth about her. Most of the "relationships" she has tend to take place inside the minds of the people she messes with. The only one for whom this definitively proves not to be true in the long run is Terezi.

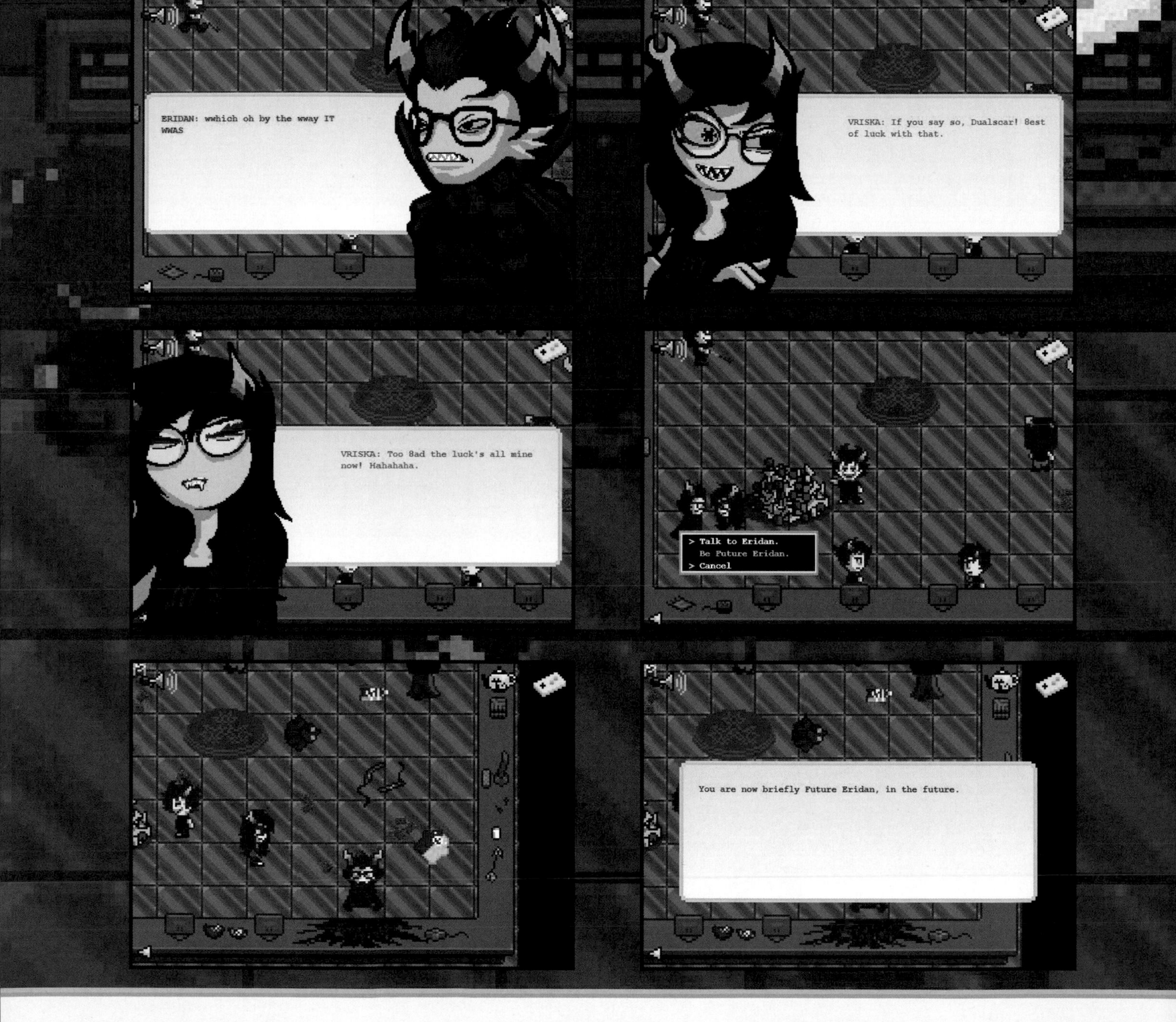

Another future time hop, another explosion to track. Put another pin on the insane timeline you've got scattered all over your wall like a lunatic, and continue. All of this will be explained. This incident involves Rose, in response to conduct from Eridan that will in no way come as surprising.

> Talk to Vriska.
ERIDAN: fuck that fuckin wwitch bleww up my computer
ERIDAN: ok not literally the wwitch as in thats not literally her title or anythin
ERIDAN: the seer i guess
ERIDAN: fuckin lousy no good goddamn rotten seer
VRISKA: Eridan! Do I detect 8lack romance in the air????????

Actually...it's basically explained here. What I mean is, we will get to read this conversation in due time. Also, no, Vriska does not detect blackrom in the air. Rose isn't interested either. No one is, or ever will be. Wait, I take that back. Cronus is the only exception.

VRISKA: <3< <3< <3< <3< <3< <3< <3< <3<
ERIDAN: shut yer spidertrap wwitch there are serious emotions happening ovver here
Talk to Equius.
> Cancel
VRISKA: I must say, I am really disgusted 8y how you've resorted to following orders from that low class slo8 with the hideous mutant 8lood.
VRISKA: I thought you were 8etter than that! I thought WE were 8etter than that.
EQUIUS: D --> I...

One of Vriska's many great attributes is how she just genuinely does not give the slightest fuck about so many things. The "cutting through the bullshit" part of her personality is mainly what's behind her power as a narrative driver who can turbocharge the plot and move things along in compelling, albeit chaotic ways. But another advantage to this quality is it allows me to bring certain conversational trains of thought to a dead stop sometimes. We really don't need to read more of this shit right now, Equius. Sorry, man.

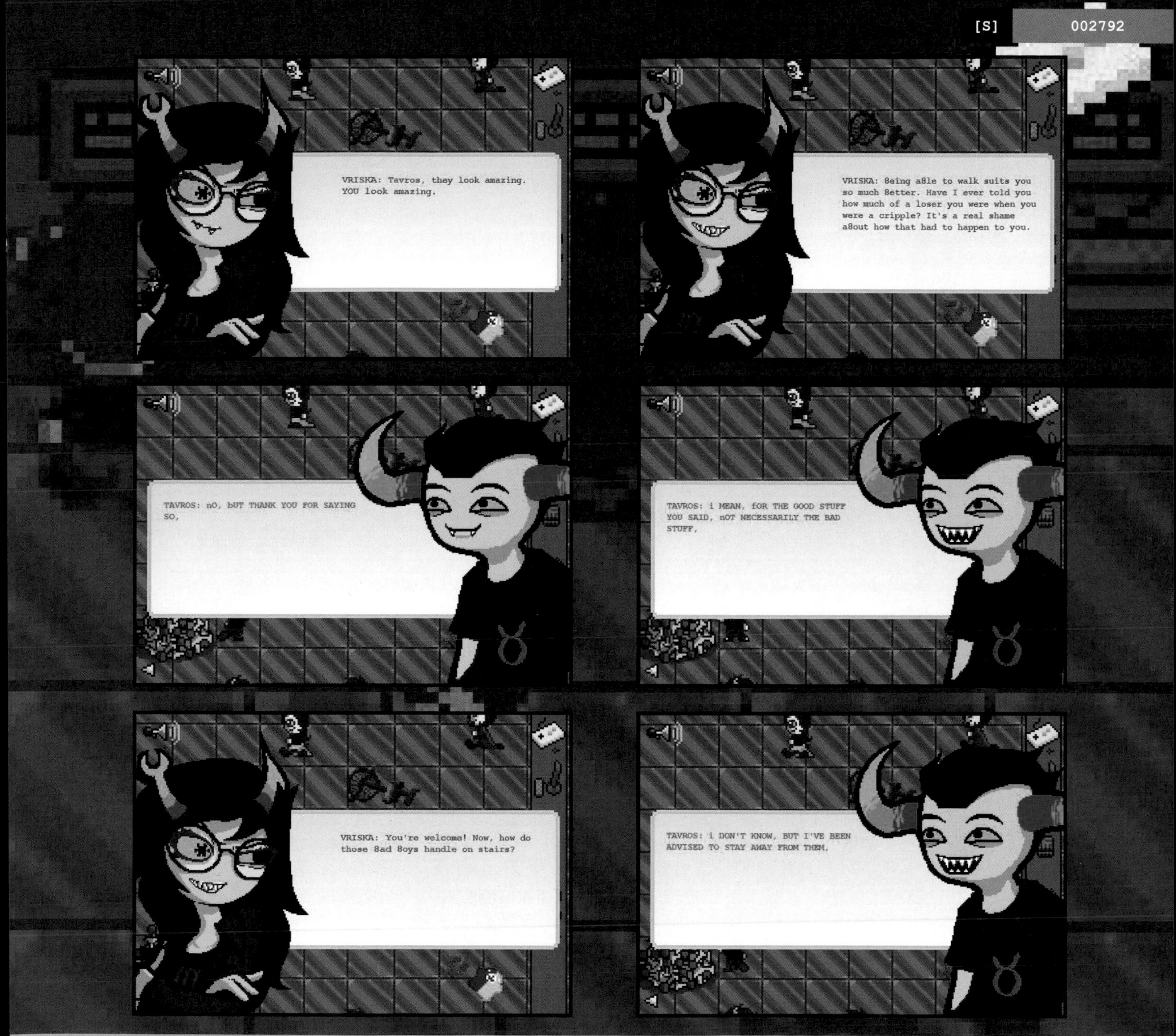

VRISKA: Tavros, they look amazing. YOU look amazing.

VRISKA: 8eing a8le to walk suits you so much 8etter. Have I ever told you how much of a loser you were when you were a cripple? It's a real shame a8out how that had to happen to you.

TAVROS: nO, bUT THANK YOU FOR SAYING SO,

TAVROS: i MEAN, fOR THE GOOD STUFF YOU SAID, nOT NECESSARILY THE BAD STUFF,

VRISKA: You're welcome! Now, how do those 8ad 8oys handle on stairs?

TAVROS: i DON'T KNOW, BUT I'VE BEEN ADVISED TO STAY AWAY FROM THEM,

What an incredible line in that second panel. Sometimes I have to sit back and just marvel at the great things I made her say. Or was she the one who made me make her say the things? I wouldn't be surprised if that were true. I think the next self-insert segment raises this possibility implicitly, by putting her little icon over my forehead. What's the truth? Is she the one writing all this? I think we start to see, as her plan with human meddling starts to play out, that this is exactly what she's trying to do, at least in a retroactive sense. Overwriting the actions of others with her own intent, putting her "brand" on things, casting herself as "responsible" in hindsight for actions that she technically did not author. Though it seems like a cheap trick, it really does have the effect of blurring original intent, and we can lose our bearings on who exactly was responsible for what. So I'll ask again. Who's more real, Vriska or me? Not so sure now, are you???

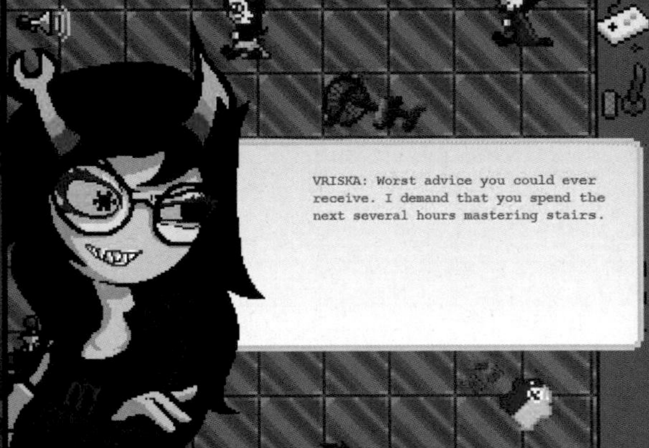
VRISKA: Worst advice you could ever receive. I demand that you spend the next several hours mastering stairs.

TAVROS: uHHHH,

VRISKA: Come on, what would that fakey 8ullshit fantasy asshole Rufio say a8out this?

TAVROS: oH, mAN, hE WOULD MOST SURELY BE ALL ABOUT ME CLIMBING LOTS OF STAIRS,

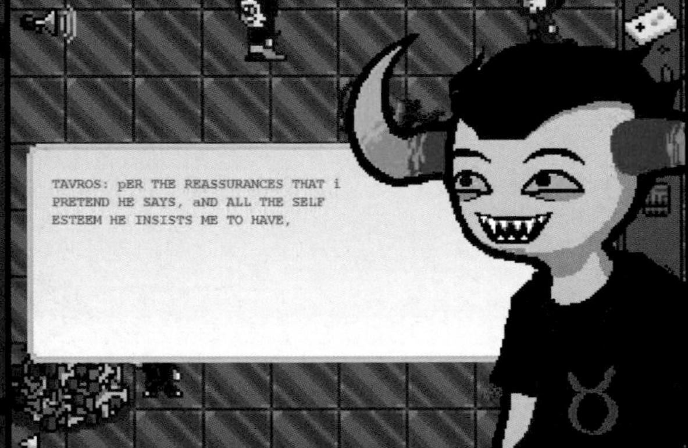
TAVROS: pER THE REASSURANCES THAT i PRETEND HE SAYS, aND ALL THE SELF ESTEEM HE INSISTS ME TO HAVE,

VRISKA: Exactly! Now hop to it, and don't think twice a8out it, or I'll know. We don't want to have to do it the hard way now, do we?

[S]
002792

TAVROS: oH MY GOD,

> Talk to Nepeta.
> Cancel

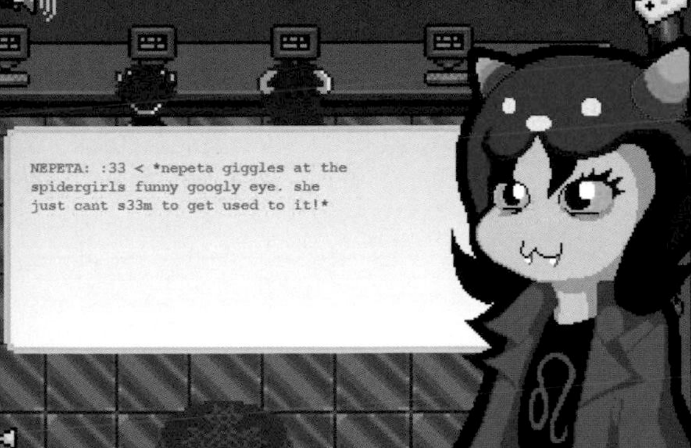
NEPETA: :33 < *nepeta giggles at the spidergirls funny googly eye. she just cant s33m to get used to it!*

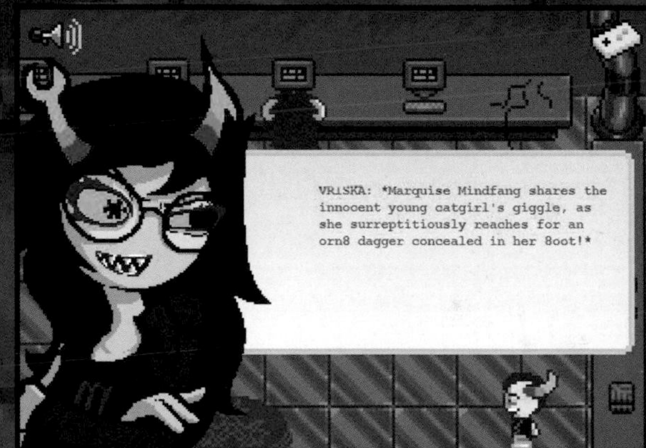
VRiSKA: *Marquise Mindfang shares the innocent young catgirl's giggle, as she surreptitiously reaches for an orn8 dagger concealed in her 8oot!*

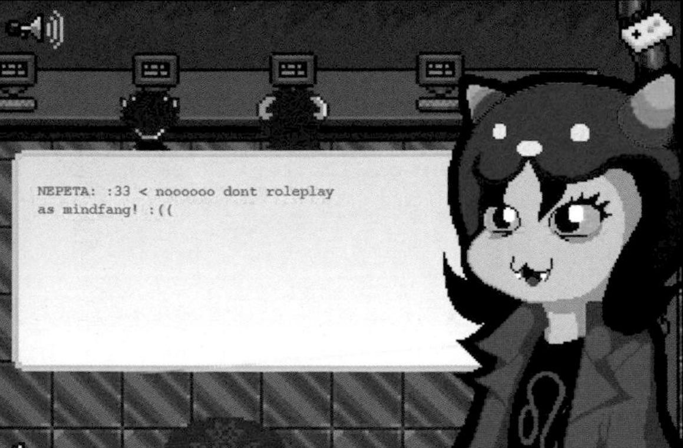
NEPETA: :33 < noooooo dont roleplay as mindfang! :((

NEPETA: :33 < you only do terrible things when you are her

Nepeta, how fucking DARE you stifle Vriska's creativity. Her spidersona is probably GREAT. You see? Shit like this is why you get such a raw deal in this story. Maybe if you were cooler and played ball with her spidersona and Mindfang a little more, things could have turned out differently for you. It didn't have to be this way...it's just sad.

VRISKA: Oh?

FEFERI: T)(e w)(ole t)(ing doesn't seem like it's wort)(getting worked up about, to be)(onest.

VRISKA: ::::|

FEFERI: Sig)(. T)(ey're just kind of dull.

FEFERI: Life is dull and uninteresting.

FEFERI: I don't know, maybe I'm just a little depressed.

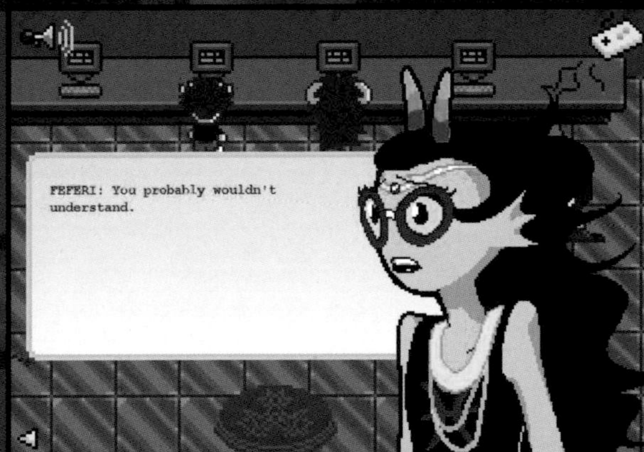
FEFERI: You probably wouldn't understand.

VRISKA: Sure I would! We all have our off days. Hey, if you need someone to talk to, I'm...

FEFERI: Pfffffffffffffffffff)(-E)(-E)(-E)(-E!

FEFERI: PSYYYYYYC)(-E)(-E-E)(-E-E)(-E-E)(-E-E)(OO)(OO)(OO! 38D

FEFERI:)(oly crap did I get you good!)(ey, Sollux! Did you catc)(any of t)(at?
FEFERI: A live one jumped rig)(t into my boat! A real suckerfis)(! Woo)(oo)(oo.)(ow do you like t)(at, spider)(ag! Sea dwellers represent!!!
VRISKA: That was...
VRISKA: Surprisingly nasty of you.
VRISKA: I'm impressed!
FEFERI: T)(anks. I)(ope I didn't jeopardize our friends)(ip wit)(t)(at little stunt! 38)

This conversation provides a very rare glimpse into the possibility that Feferi may have a more interesting personality than she gets credit for. Playing mind games to own Vriska, even if it's just in a meaningless throwaway conversation, isn't a bad thing to have on your resume. But again, it's my sad duty to remind you that, whatever other surprises may exist in the full range of her profile, Feferi just doesn't last much longer than this. She and Nepeta really can't catch a break. Luckily, they both experience profound narrative redemption much later, in the form of Fefeta. I believe Fefeta's stirring, ten-page soliloquy after she gets created really captures the pathos behind their mutual struggle with narrative irrelevance. Keep an eye out for that.

VRISKA: Friendship? I don't know if...

VRISKA: W8 a minute. Why you!!!!!!!!
You almost got me AGAIN!

VRISKA: Have I ever told you how awesome you are, Peixes?

Talk to Aradia.
> Cancel

VRISKA: Hey dead girl! How's 8eing dead treating you?

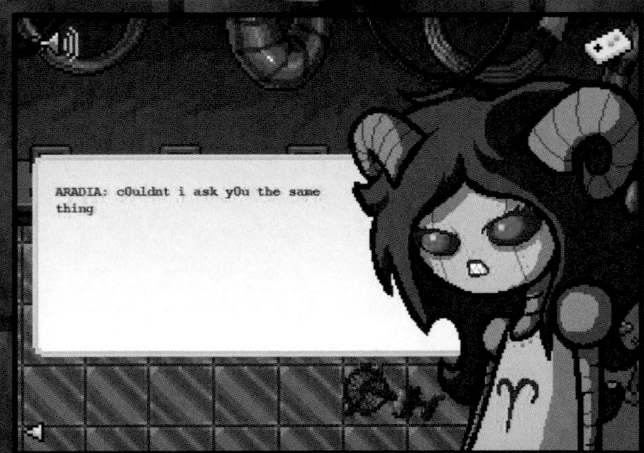
ARADIA: c0uldnt i ask y0u the same thing

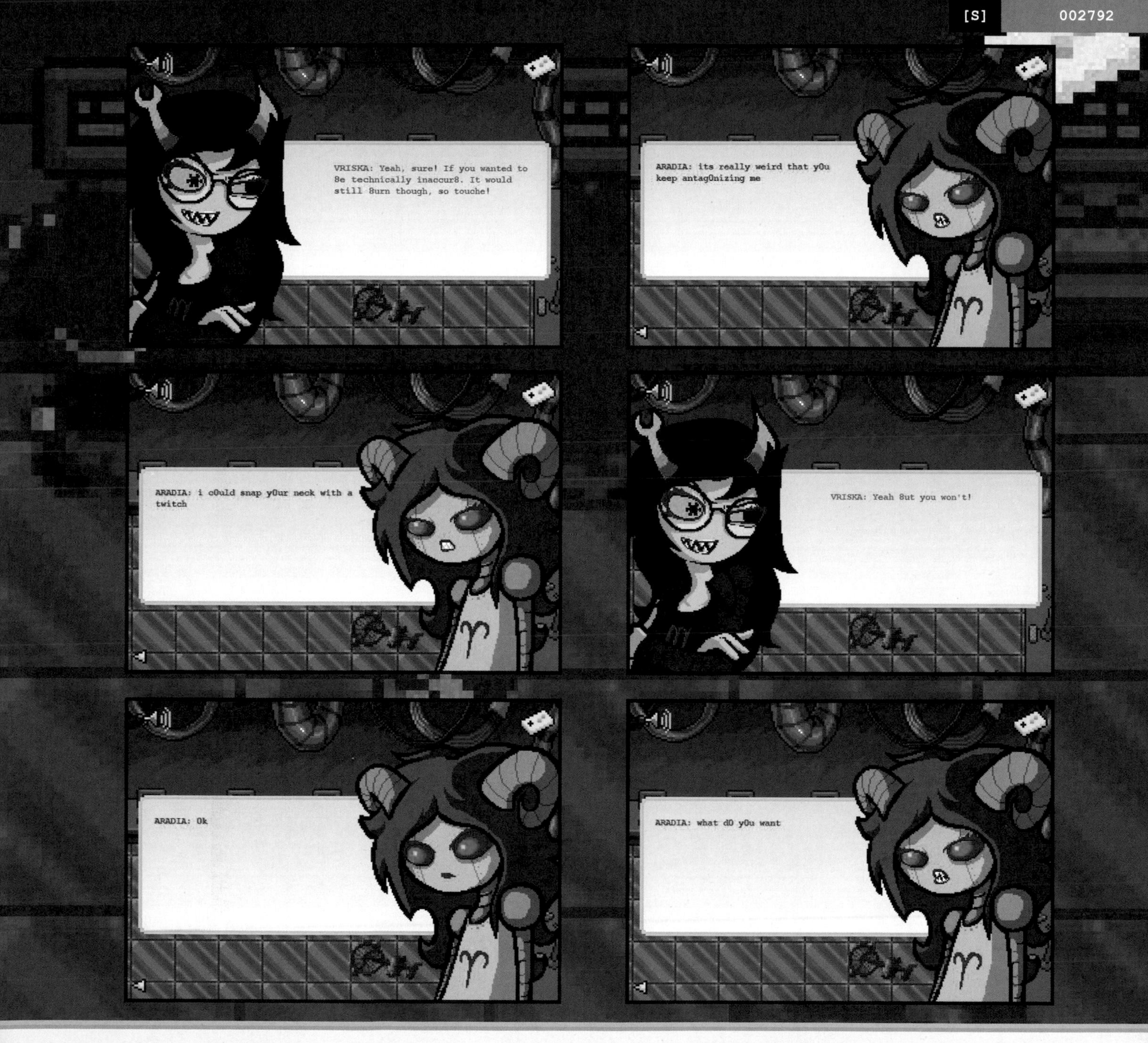

Sure, Aradiabot could probably break her neck. But what we aren't supposed to know yet is that Vriska is god tier. So would it be a Just Death? I guess it depends on how sick the burn is that warrants having her neck snapped by Aradia. Maybe that's why Aradia doesn't bother? These burns are kind of weak, so she knows Vriska would just come back to life.

VRISKA: You saw the demon up close, right? You fought him! Or at least your doppelgangers did.

ARADIA: yes

VRISKA: What was he like!

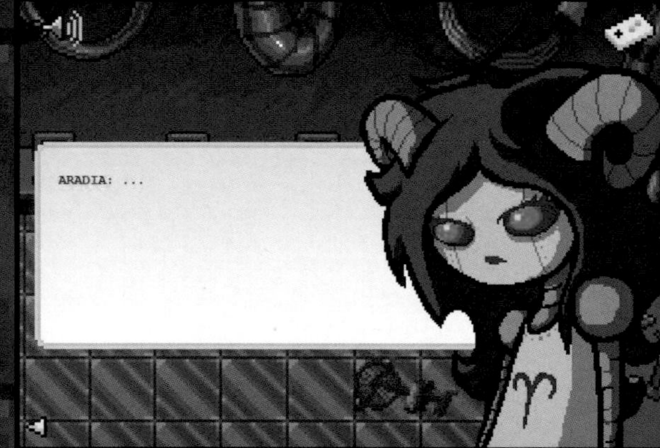
ARADIA: ...

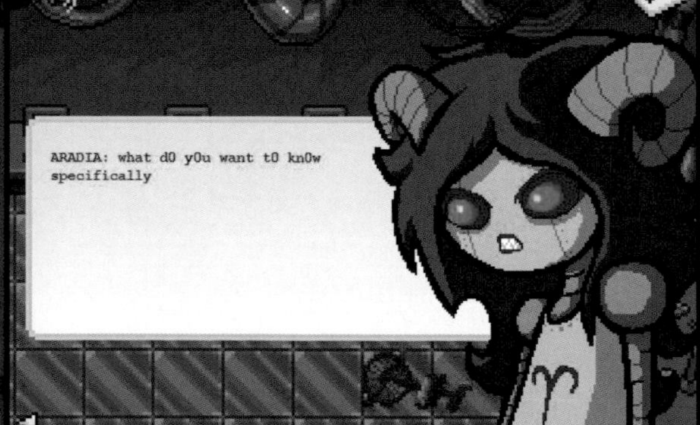
ARADIA: what d0 y0u want t0 kn0w specifically

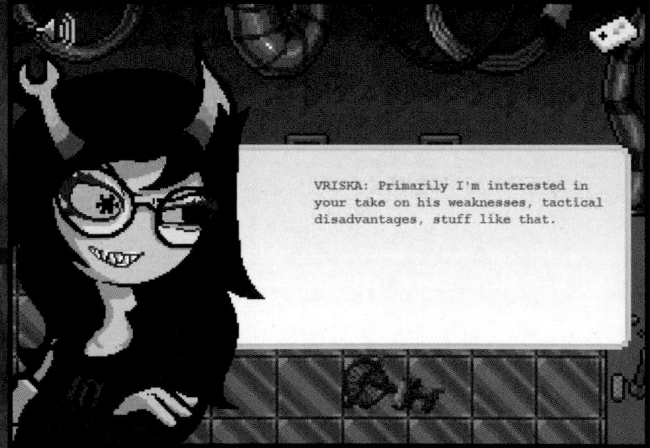
VRISKA: Primarily I'm interested in your take on his weaknesses, tactical disadvantages, stuff like that.

ARADIA: 0_0
VRISKA: Wouldn't you like to know!!!!!!!!

ARADIA: are y0u seri0usly intending t0 fight him

ARADIA: n0t especially

Talk to Sollux.
> Cancel

VRISKA: Sollux, I never got to simultaneously thank you and reprimand you for tracing that money transfer.

VRISKA: On the one hand, it made Terezi rich, and now she won't stop lording it over me!
SOLLUX: ok, ii'm pretty much 100% po2iitiive 2he'2 not actually doiing that, but ok.
VRISKA: Shh! 8ut on the other hand, you've opened up a whole world to me with this discovery. So many people to meddle with, so many plans to hatch.
VRISKA: So really, my reaction to it is twofold. Somewhat 8ipolar if you will. Don't you think that's appropri8?
SOLLUX: man, ju2t...
SOLLUX: go away.

Sollux x Feferi is a romance that in my view is quite deftly handled offscreen. You see hints of it, like in how Feferi's fishspeak slips into Sollux's language. Some people notice, like Vriska, and get annoyed. Which is a thing that's been going on in a larger sense, actually, characters detecting traces of other character's speech patterns rubbing off on another, and using this as a clue that something romantic is brewing. Vriska with John, Terezi with Dave. Even Jade starts flagrantly swearing more than she typically does after more interaction with Karkat. Rose and Kanaya already basically talk like each other, so they can't really tip other people off to what's going on there. Although I guess you could infer that the moment Rose Starts Talking Like This, maybe it's a sign that they both finally went all the way. Not that this ever actually happens. Although to be fair, by the time they're both in a position for anything like that to hypothetically take place, Rose is drunk off her ass anyway.

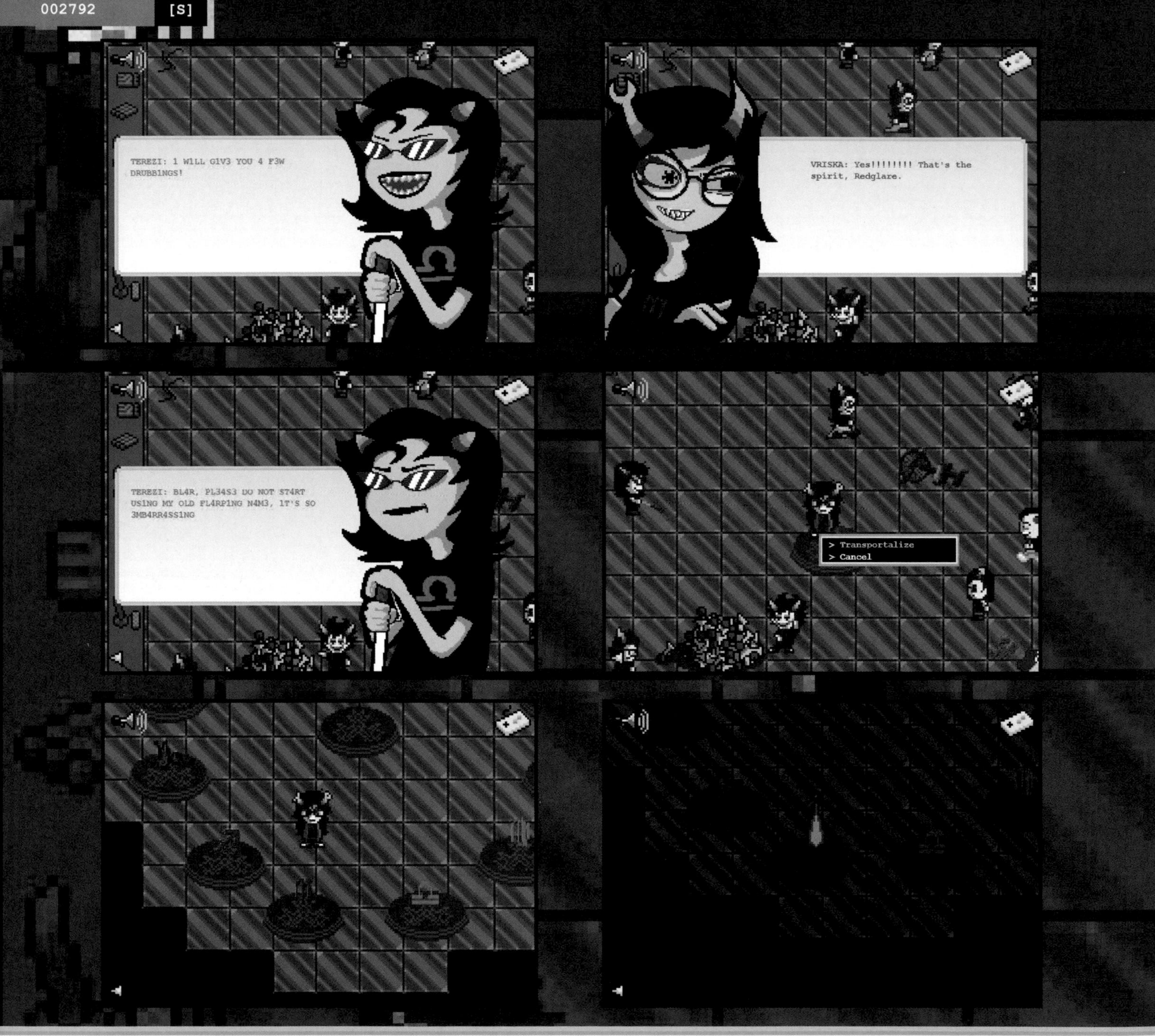

You can transportalize to another room full of transporters, each one labeled with a troll sign. Only the troll of that sign can use it, as if each one took the time to specifically claim one and lock everyone else out. When did they find the time to do this? It seems very organized of them, to secure their own private spaces on the meteor. Especially considering their hasty getaway, which was forced by a crisis. Maybe trolls have such a strong instinctive sense of private space, groups of trolls always do this any time they find a new space to commonly settle into? It would make sense, since they all grow up solo in their own very personalized hives. Yeah, let's say that's the explanation for this ridiculous feature of this game map.

Okay, there's a lot to keep up with on this page. I know this comic gets pretty dense sometimes, but hang in there. If you really take the time to study it, you'll get it all eventually. Keep an eye out for the Author Notes Expansion Pack later, wherein I expound upon this page with the thoroughness it deserves.

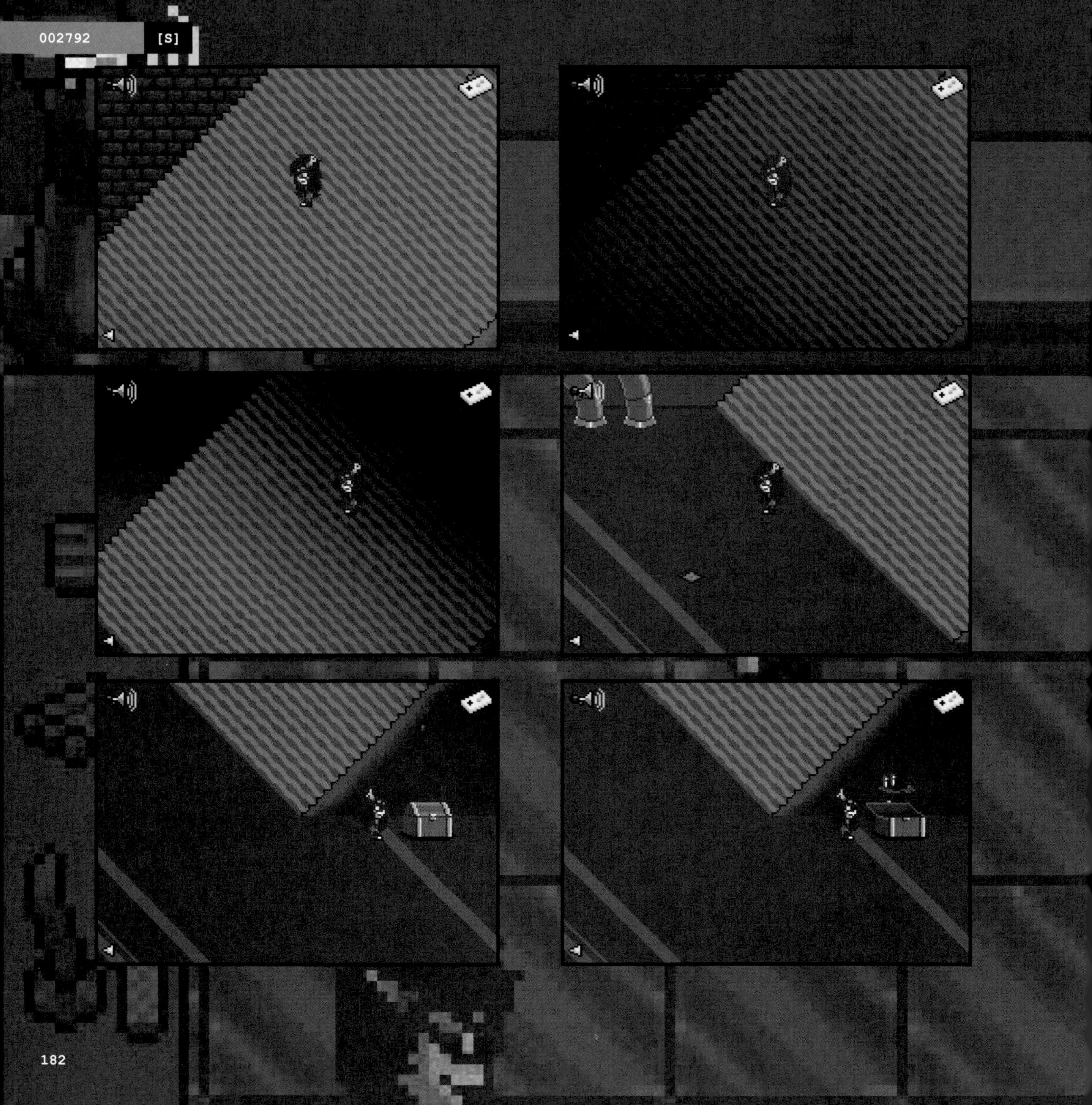

You got TAVROS'S SEVERED LEGS!
Why...
Why would you keep these in a chest?
> Examine equipment.
> Cancel
Another dodecascreen. Seem to be a lot of these things lying around.

Vriska keeps the Tavros's severed legs in a chest because...she just does. She's Vriska. She gets to do stuff like that, and we don't get to ask why. Any questions? You aren't allowed to have questions. Here's a tangential consideration that you may not want to think about it, but let's just consider this your punishment for daring to question Vriska's motives. If you take into account Tavros's lower torso, which has been hoarded here, and the existence of alchemy, I think we can begin to see the basic constituents for the origin of the bull penis cane. An item which, like many things on this meteor, eventually finds its way to the Felt Mansion in the future. Now, did you *need* to be forced to think about how Vriska may have quite literally used the mutilated remains of her ex-boyfriend to make a bovine dildo? No, you didn't. But as I said, you brought this upon yourself.

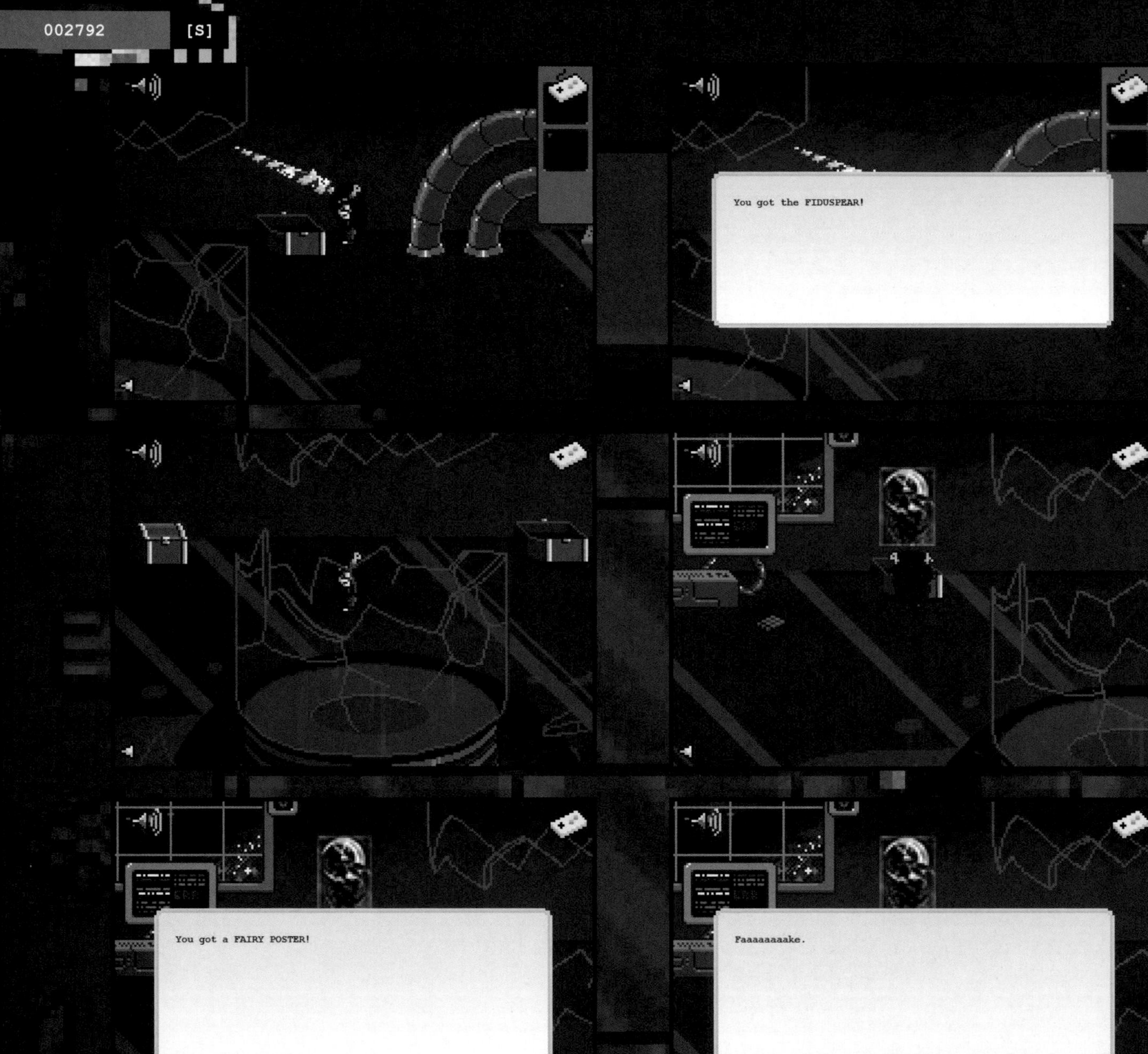
002792
[S]
You got the FIDUSPEAR!
You got a FAIRY POSTER!
Faaaaaaaake.

Examine equipment.
> Cancel
A monitor with a map of some place on Alternia, displaying impact sites. It looks like it crashed and froze at some point during the reckoning.
> Examine huge broken container.
> Cancel
Looks like a terrible monster has escaped. Better be careful!

We've already spent a little time on a similar meteor in the Veil in the human session. So we know stuff like this is lying around, big glass tubes full of test subjects, usually big mutant chess freaks that get deployed on the Battlefield. Here's one that's busted. We're getting foreshadowed at here, in a way that games commonly do. Uh-oh! There should be a monster safely contained here, and yet it seems to have escaped! Suuuure hope you don't have to confront this beast in some way later!

Haha, yeah right. You're gonna murder this thing if it crosses you.
ERR_
ERR
Transportalize
> Cancel

> Who's this douche baq?
> Cancel
Aqqress
> Steal
You 8n't got your dice on you!
SO STUPID!!!!!!!!

Here's a boss battle. It's not real, of course. There's no combat or anything. You just choose some options and it sort of plays itself. Who has time to "make real games" when the games in question take several days to make? This was a pretty fun diversion, though. We even switched the sprite style briefly, from what is usually an *Earthbound*-inspired look to what I believe was mimicking the sprite style in a *Scott Pilgrim* game. If this were a real battle, it would probably be pretty strenuous. I'm guessing the boss's udder would be some sort of weak point? But Vriska just cheats her way through it, which is fine, because we don't have all day.

Vriska is the Thief of Light. So she literally steals his luck, and gives it to herself. This makes it much more likely something bad will happen to him, all on its own.

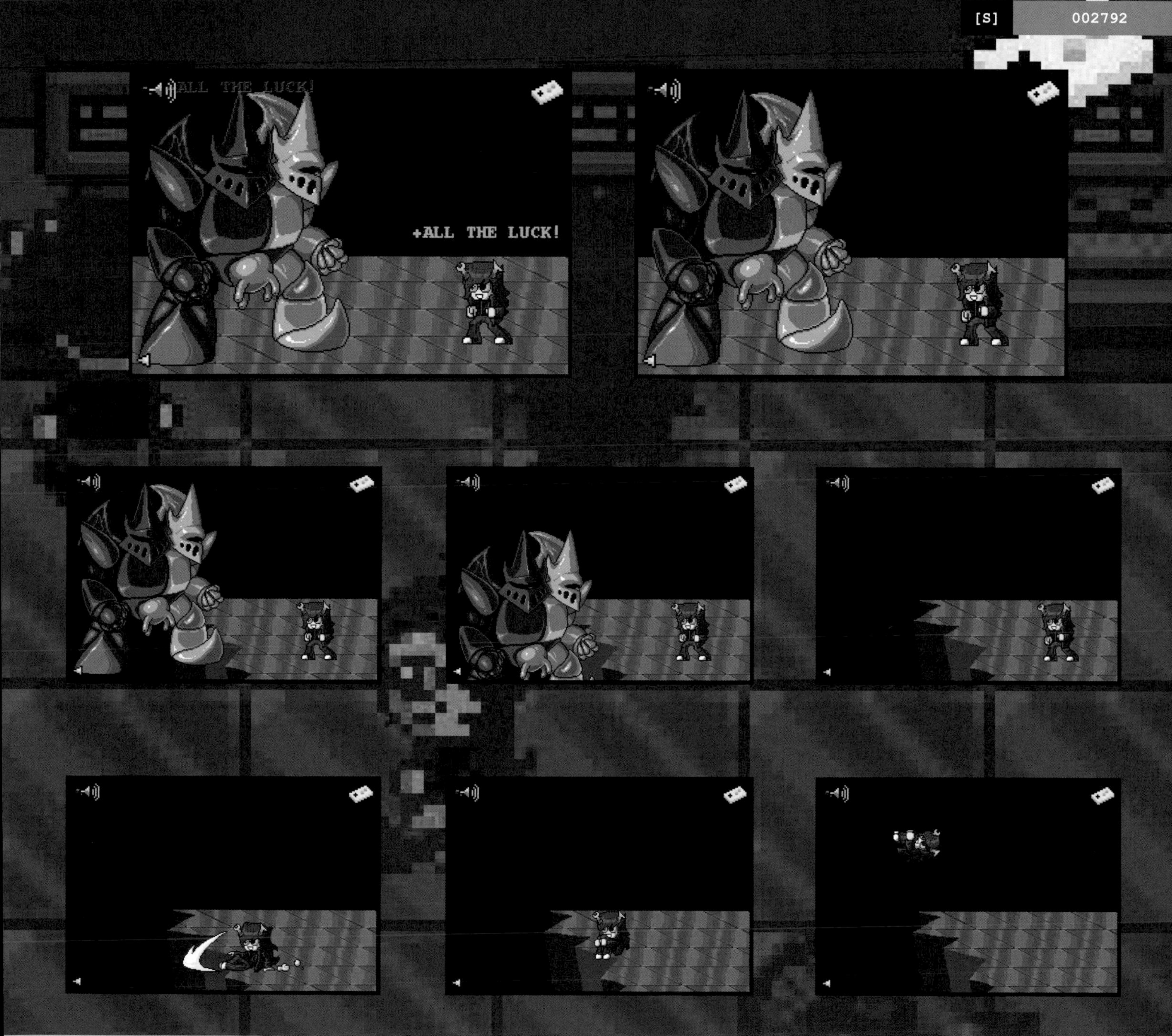

Like this. He falls in a pit, and that's the end of this guy forever. Take a note of this pit she just created, though. Remember the context and the shape of those jagged edges. This precipitous venue comes back into play during a critical showdown with Tavros, wherein dramatic happenings take place. (FYI: she just throws the dude off another fuckin' cliff.)

Open Chest
> Cancel
You got the FLOURITE OCTET!
Maybe you should keep these on you in the future.
> Open Doors
> Cancel

The items are a bit ridiculous. Finding them in chests serves no purpose at all, except to sort of amusingly emulate the feel of playing an RPG. Otherwise there's very little logic to it. Why *wouldn't* she keep her dice on her all the time? Especially since a sylladex allows you to do this very easily, without feeling encumbered. The answer is, these are all completely ridiculous people who like to hoard things in their secret, locked-away parts of the meteor, especially the ones who have a flair for treasure and the hunting thereof. Bear in mind that Vriska originally found her cool dice in a chest on a ship. Maybe she just likes to relive the magic of that experience now and then?

[S]
002792
> Examine boondollar pile.
> Cancel
Lousy stupid goddamn Terezi, finding all those boonbonds and instantly rendering your fortune worthless. You'll show her. That snotty rich kid too.

Speaking of treasure, here's her secret pirate's trove. Which, yes, due to inflation is now completely worthless. But it was already worthless, since she was never going to use it to buy anything ever again anyway. Let's try to imagine how much more money Terezi has than this now. If this is the size of Vriska's stockpile, then Terezi's would be...the size of the sun? Bigger? Probably bigger. No wonder Vriska's steamed. Time to spend the rest of the act radically overcompensating.

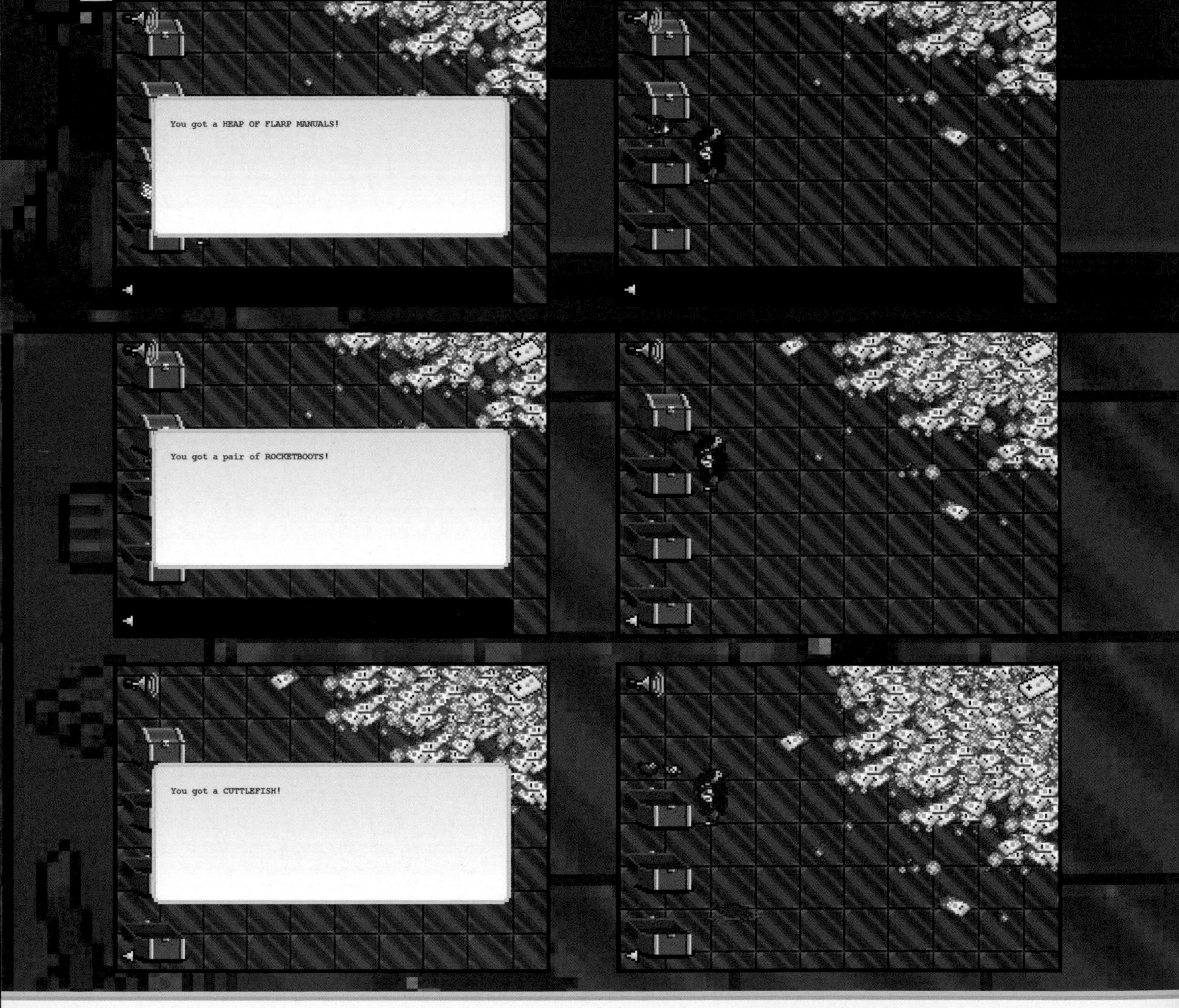
You got a HEAP OF FLARP MANUALS!
You got a pair of ROCKETBOOTS!
You got a CUTTLEFISH!

W...wow?

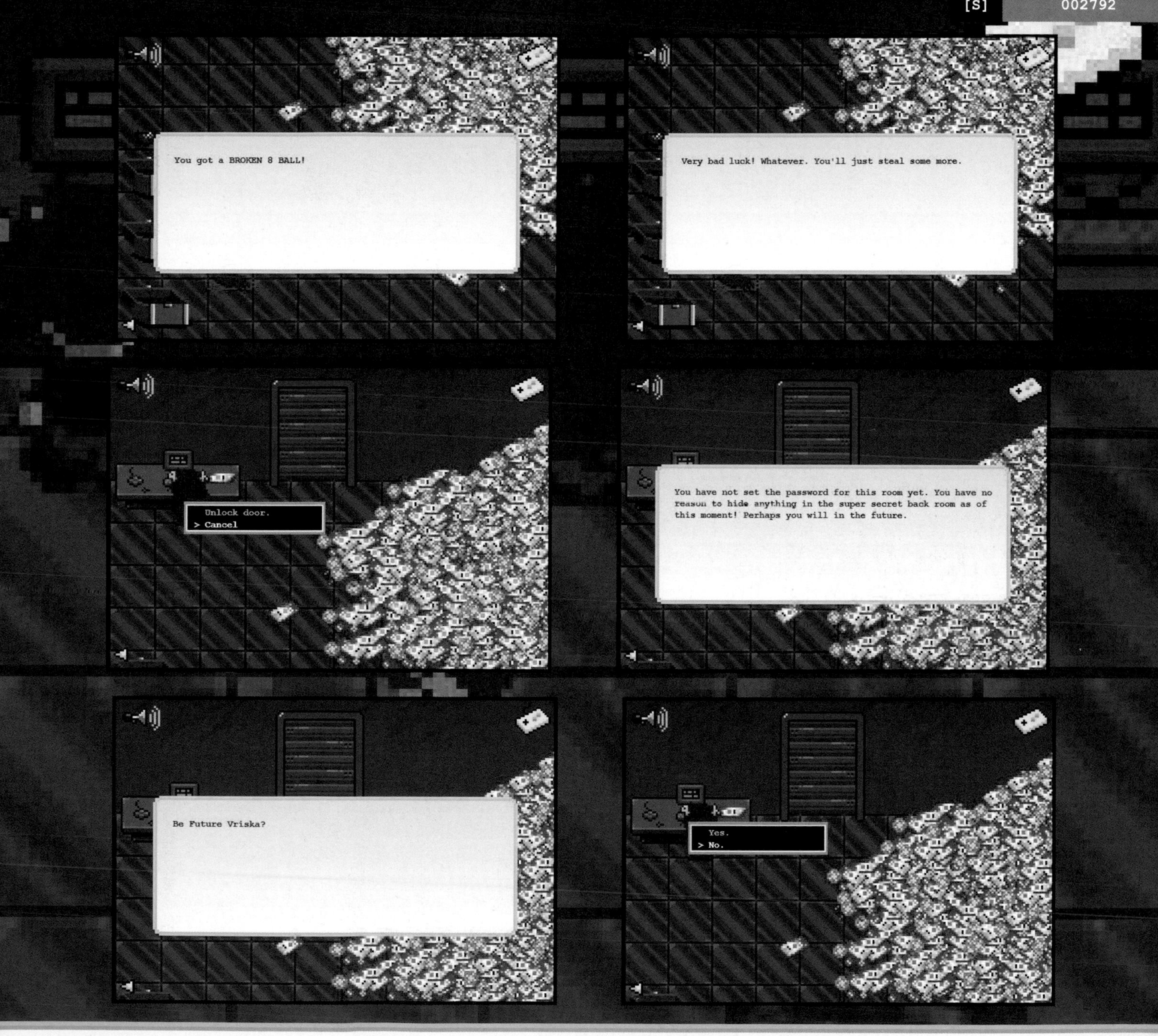

More Strong Content.

In the future I guess Vriska cleans out her whole supply of boondollars. I forget what happened... Possibly she gives it all to John to help him compete with Dave? That sounds about right, even if it's not. Let's just say it is. I believe this time hop forward triggers some poignant music, because she's about to express her undying love for Nic Cage again.

Vriska has stashed a dreamy Cage bust away in here, understandably. And also...a salamander? Okay. I guess she...kidnapped one? Again, let's remind ourselves we aren't allowed to question anything Vriska does. It's totally fine she trapped a helpless salamander in this chest for many hours.

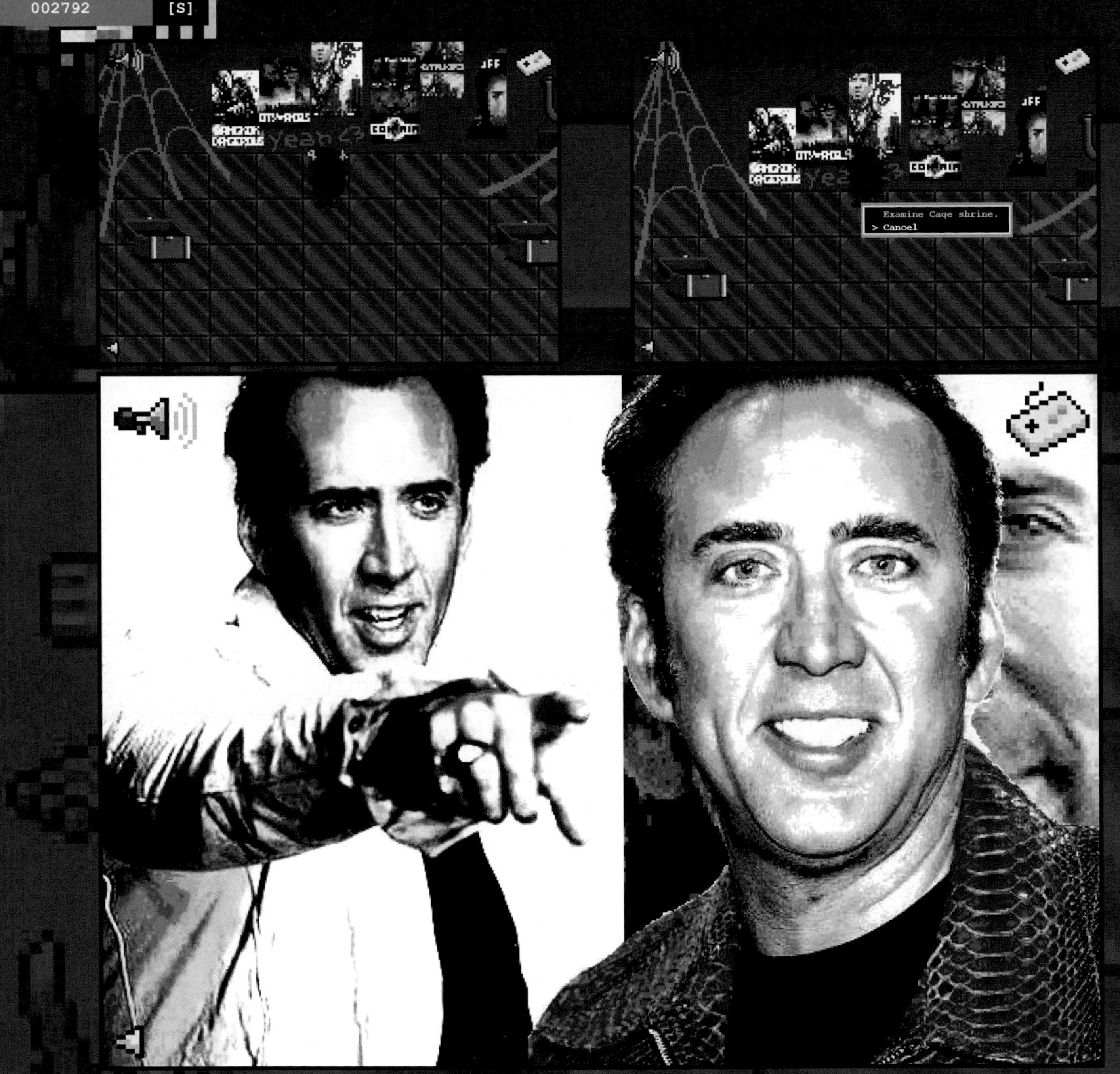

Vriska's Cage Shrine is where she goes to be alone with her most private thoughts, and to put in some good swooning time over her main boy, Nic. Examining the wall triggers this...I'm not sure what it is. Some half-assed Flash garbage jittering about. Nic Cage, in terms of the mythological language and symbolism native to *Homestuck*, conforms to the archetype of "Human Shitpost."

We're back. That was the completion of a minor "arc" on this minigame's terms. You get to the Cage room, and that's that for Vriska. It unlocks another part of the game you can play, which starts here.

Terezi is frustrated beyond words that her bonehead ex-almost-boyfriend doesn't see what the big deal is about a moon made of gold. Just another indication that what she really values is a partner who has a deep appreciation for the value of riches. Dave easily beats Karkat in that regard. But it also sheds a little more light on the fact that no one will ever truly be able to compete with Vriska when it comes to Terezi's fixation.

You have to be pretty alert to tell when someone is hitting on you in the clubs quadrant. It's subtle enough to miss easily. "Hey, could you tell that bastard over there he's a bastard for me? And don't you DARE think of watering down my message of hate for me, so as to moderate this unpleasant rivalry I'm placing you in the middle of!" Okay, that's an obvious clubs solicitation. But usually they don't sound like that. You know how sometimes in bar fights, there's the guy who wants to start a fight, but he tries to get his friends to "hold him back"? That's textbook solicitation in the ashen quadrant. Apparently rowdy, drunken bros do it all the time.

TEREZI: 1F YOUR3 W4X1NG 4SH3N FOR M3, F1N3, 1... GU3SS 1M FL4TT3R3D???

TEREZI: BUT H3S TOT4LLY NOT 3V3N 1NT3R3ST3D 1N TH3 TYP3 OF

TEREZI: UH...

TEREZI: R1V4LRY YOU W4NT W1TH H1M, OK?

ERIDAN: swweet stinkin murder i am truly pathetic arent i

TEREZI: Y3S, 4BSOLUT3LY

Take note of the phrase “unexpected honk jump” as a sign of oblique, yet retroactively blatant foreshadowing for the Gamrezi ship.

TEREZI: SORRY BUT WH3N 4 G1RL H4S TO G3T H3R HONK JUMP ON TH3R3 1S JUST NO STOPP1NG H3R

TEREZI: NO PROM1S3S!

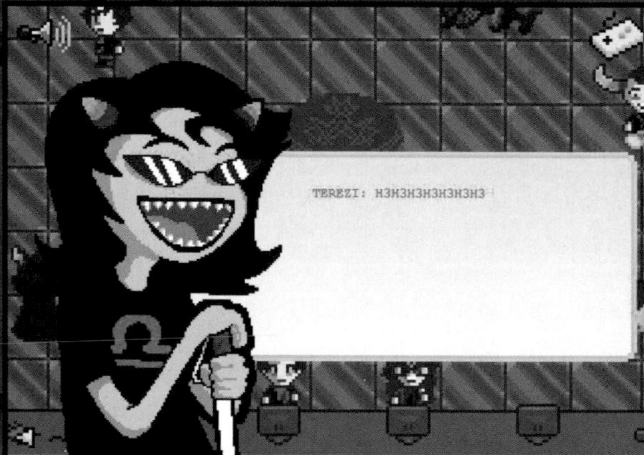
TEREZI: H3H3H3H3H3H3H3

GAMZEE: OkAy wElL MaYbE WaRn mE ThEn mAyBe.
GAMZEE: :o(
> Talk to Kanaya.
> Be Future Kanaya.
> Cancel

TEREZI: H3Y K4N4Y4, 4R3 YOU ST1LL OGL1NG H3R?

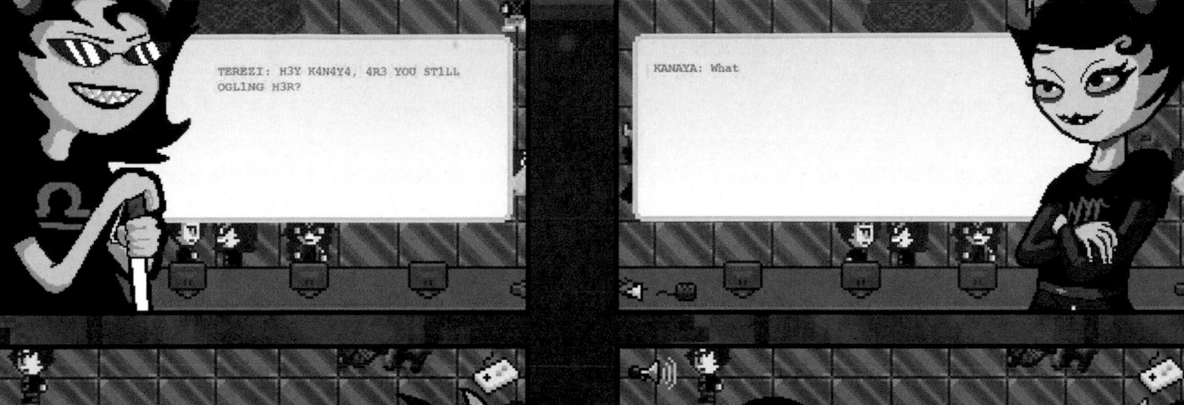
KANAYA: What

KANAYA: Is That What Im Doing

TEREZI: Y3S 1T 1S OBV1OUS

TEREZI: WHY TH3 1NF4TU4T1ON W1TH TH4T P4RT1CUL4R HUM4N

KANAYA: Hmm

KANAYA: I Guess I Find Her Sort Of
KANAYA: Intoxicating
TEREZI: OHHHHHHHHHHH??????? >8D
KANAYA: Intoxicatingly Underwhelming
TEREZI: >:?
> Talk to Kanaya.
> Be Future Kanaya.
> Cancel

Finally we can ferret out some new plot-relevant information from an obscure pocket of this game. We last saw Rose talking about the Green Sun upon revealing its existence, but we've heard nothing about a plan for using it in some way to defeat Jack Noir. This is some advance notice to watch out for a plan like that to start coming together. It's just a little tidbit to get us thinking. There's still lots of information missing, including: Jack is also the demon the trolls are hiding from, he's been Bec-ified, thus he draws his energy from the Green Sun, ergo it stands to reason that destroying the sun will weaken him. We have quite a ways to go to get up to speed on all that, unless you don't mind skipping down here to my notes where I casually and carelessly spoil you on literally everything, because I don't really see a good reason not to.

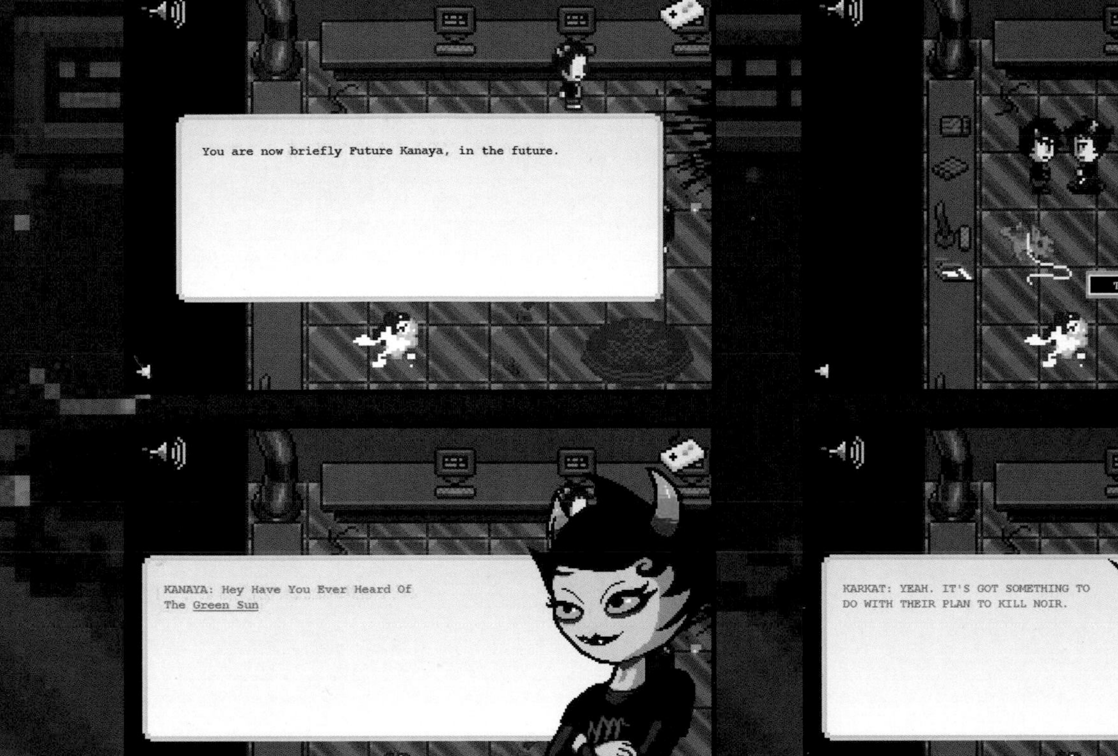
You are now briefly Future Kanaya, in the future.
Talk to Karkat.
KANAYA: Hey Have You Ever Heard Of The Green Sun
KARKAT: YEAH. IT'S GOT SOMETHING TO DO WITH THEIR PLAN TO KILL NOIR.

KANAYA: I See

KANAYA: Anything More Specific Than That

KARKAT: NOPE. I'VE GOT NO IDEA WHAT IT IS, WHAT IT DOES, WHAT ITS ROLE IN THE PLAN IS, OR IF IT'S GOT ANY CHANCE OF WORKING.

KARKAT: WE SHOULD PROBABLY WORRY ABOUT OUR OWN PROBLEMS.
VRISKA: Hey, if it isn't miss money8ags! How are you enjoying your fa8ulous wealth!
TEREZI: GOD, YOUR J34LOUSLY 1S R1D1CULOUS! NOBODY C4R3S 4BOUT STOCKP1L1NG M34N1NGL3SS TR34SUR3 OTH3R TH4N YOU. W1LL YOU GROW UP???

Talk to Vriska.
> Be Vriska.
> Cancel

VRISKA: If it was me, I would feel ashamed to get rich that way. 8y having a secret admirer just hand it to me like that, rather than earning it. That's just me though!

VRISKA: I guess you're right. I'm just giving you a hard time!

VRISKA: You know, like the good old days. Don't you miss our friendly rivalry sometimes?

TEREZI: H4H4H4, FR13NDLY?????

VRISKA: Sure! So to speak.

VRISKA: Anyway, just so you know, you're not the only one who can play a chumpy 8oy, and manipul8 him into doing what you want.

VRISKA: In fact, I'm not even going to use any powers! Just to prove it's no 8ig deal.

TEREZI: WH4T TH3 H3LL 4R3 YOU T4LK1NG 4BOUT

VRISKA: You'll see!!!!!!!! Oops, smell. Haha, 8n't it a 8ummer you never died????????

TEREZI: NO >:P

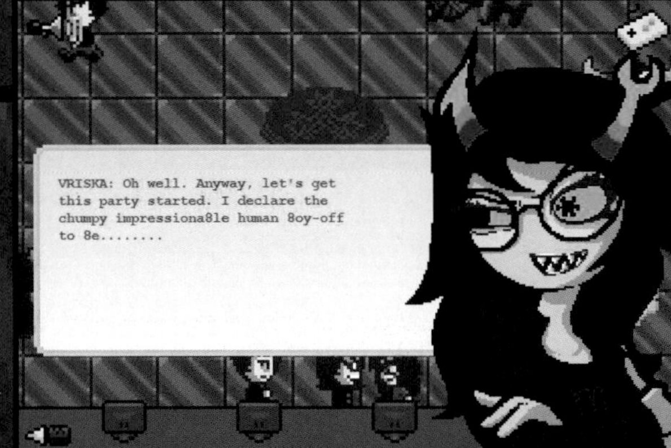
VRISKA: Oh well. Anyway, let's get this party started. I declare the chumpy impressiona8le human 8oy-off to 8e........

VRISKA: OOOOOOOON! :::;)

TEREZI: UGH, YOU 4R3 SO CR4ZY

A little glimpse into the background of how their boyfight proxy-rivalry kicked off. It seems like Terezi gets dragged into it reluctantly at first, and considers a lot of Vriska's goading to be childish, crazy, and obsessive. But at the end of the day, Terezi seems to get just as into the boy rivalry as Vriska does. This is probably how a lot of their competitions went in the past. It also speaks to the addictive quality that this unhealthy aspect of their relationship has, particularly for Terezi. She knows it's not good for her but can't seem to help getting roped back into the bullshit. After Vriska's death, Terezi's guilt-slash-withdrawal symptoms lead her to fill the addiction void with a trash clown. Which is a bit like being on some potent controlled substance, getting cut off, and getting hooked on the hard stuff to compensate. Shooting up in back alleys, turning tricks in exchange for more... Actually, in Gamrezi's case, those two ideas end up being more or less the same thing.

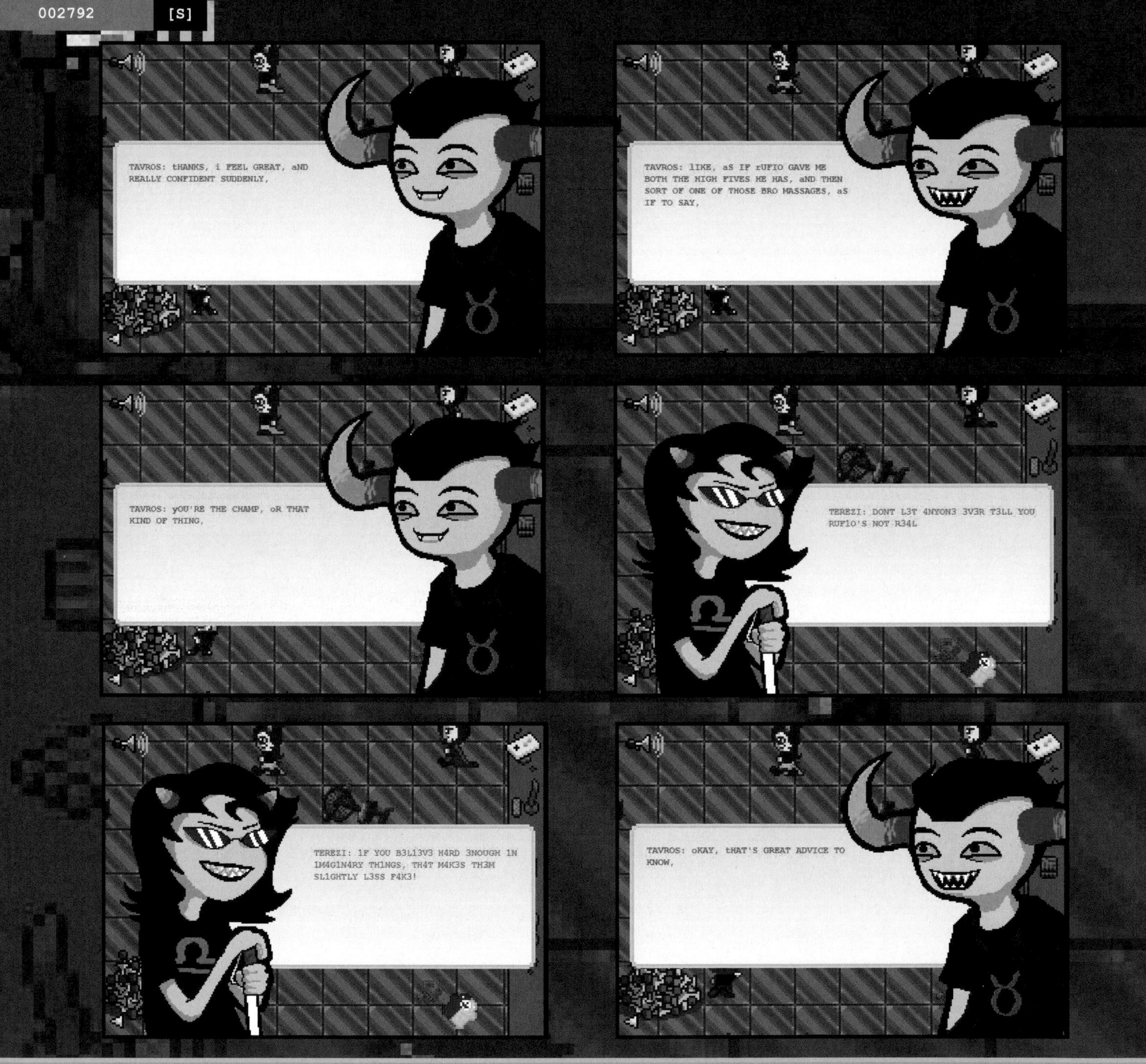

A fair question: Who's a worse influence on Tavros, Vriska or Terezi? Sure, Vriska paralyzes him in the first place, and pretty soon she will murder him in cold blood. But at least she keeps it real. For some reason Terezi insists on enabling his bullshit with a lot of misguided positivity and support. Just sickening, really. In due time, Terezi will pay a very steep karmic price for this crime, by having her Vriska privileges revoked.

Then Tavros fucks off to go fall down a whole bunch of stairs. We'll catch up with his point of view later. Mainly by watching him fall down some stairs.

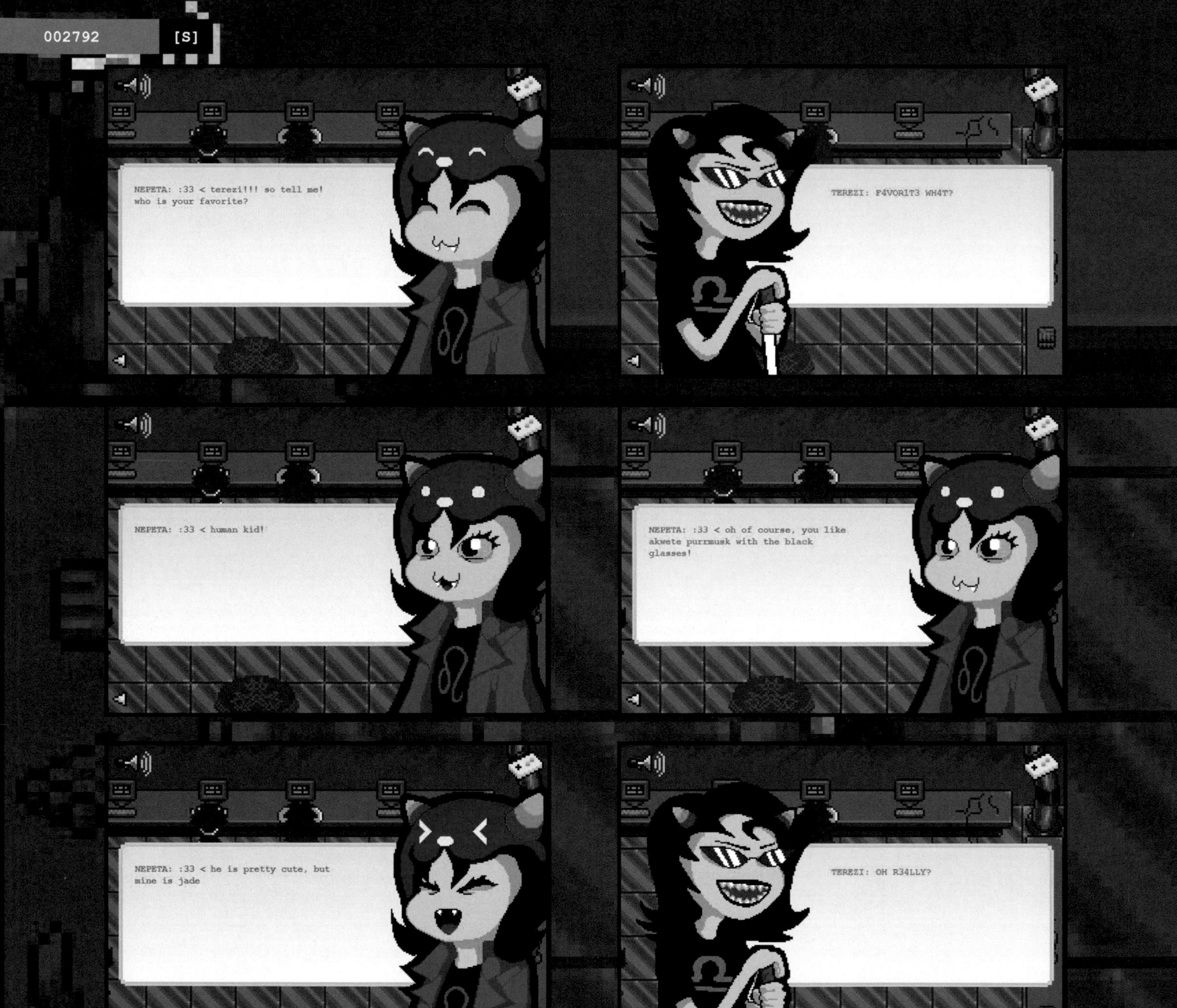

Nepeta almost immediately confirms to Terezi that she's been roleplaying with Dave somewhere on the timeline, by referencing his fursona, Akwete Purrmusk. This seems like a dumb, throwaway gag that will be meaningless forever, and it very nearly was. Until, at the last minute, the story dumps Davepeta in our laps. Nepeta literally fuses with another version of Dave to help him fully realize his fursona. A truly heartwarming end point for both their arcs.

Nepeta, maybe Jade just isn't into it? Maybe learn to take a fucking hint?? Sure, it seems like you two SHOULD get along, but what if that's just not how things always work? Don't be a rando. Just chill out. Mr. Purrmusk has shown a perfectly reliable willingness to tolerate your nonsense. Strider's roleplay fields have proven to be rich and fertile. Now stop wasting Jade's time, and go embrace your destiny.

FEFERI: Y-----------ES!!! I am sure of it.
TEREZI: UM, OK, 1F YOU S4Y SO F3F3R1!
Talk to Aradia.
> Cancel
ARADIA: Oh is that what feferi thinks

Feferi is right, the humans are the answer. But not because they actually have a good plan for solving all the problems. That never happens, in fact. The real reason is because they're the main characters. Leave it to one of the least important characters to have sort of a sixth sense when it comes to identifying the most important characters, even when no one else can.

ARADIA: thats nice
ARADIA: havent y0u underst00d anything ab0ut h0w parad0x space w0rks
ARADIA: 0f c0urse they are the s0luti0n
ARADIA: but they are als0 the pr0blem
ARADIA: every effect is als0 its 0wn cause
ARADIA: 0ur tw0 universes exist 0n 0pp0sing sides 0f a m0bius strip which is 0f c0urse n0thing but c0ntradicti0n

ARADIA: enj0y engineering the present c0nundrum as y0u try t0 s0lve it

ARADIA: im c0mpletely d0ne with this

TEREZI: GR34T T4LK1NG TO YOU 4R4D14, TH4T W4S 4 BL4ST4S USU4L

> Talk to Sollux.
> Cancel

SOLLUX: are you 2tiill 2pyiing on that iin2ufferable priick.

SOLLUX: 2eriiou2ly a dude giive2 a giirl a few buck2 and 2uddenly 2he cant keep her no2e off hiim, iit ii2 2o prediictable.

TEREZI: SHUT UP SOLLUX H3S COOL

TEREZI: 1 DONT G3T WHY YOU DONT L1K3 H1M, H3 R3M1NDS M3 OF YOU 4 B1T

SOLLUX: you thiink iim cool?

TEREZI: SOM3T1M3S!

SOLLUX: how often?

SOLLUX: don't 2ay half the tiime.

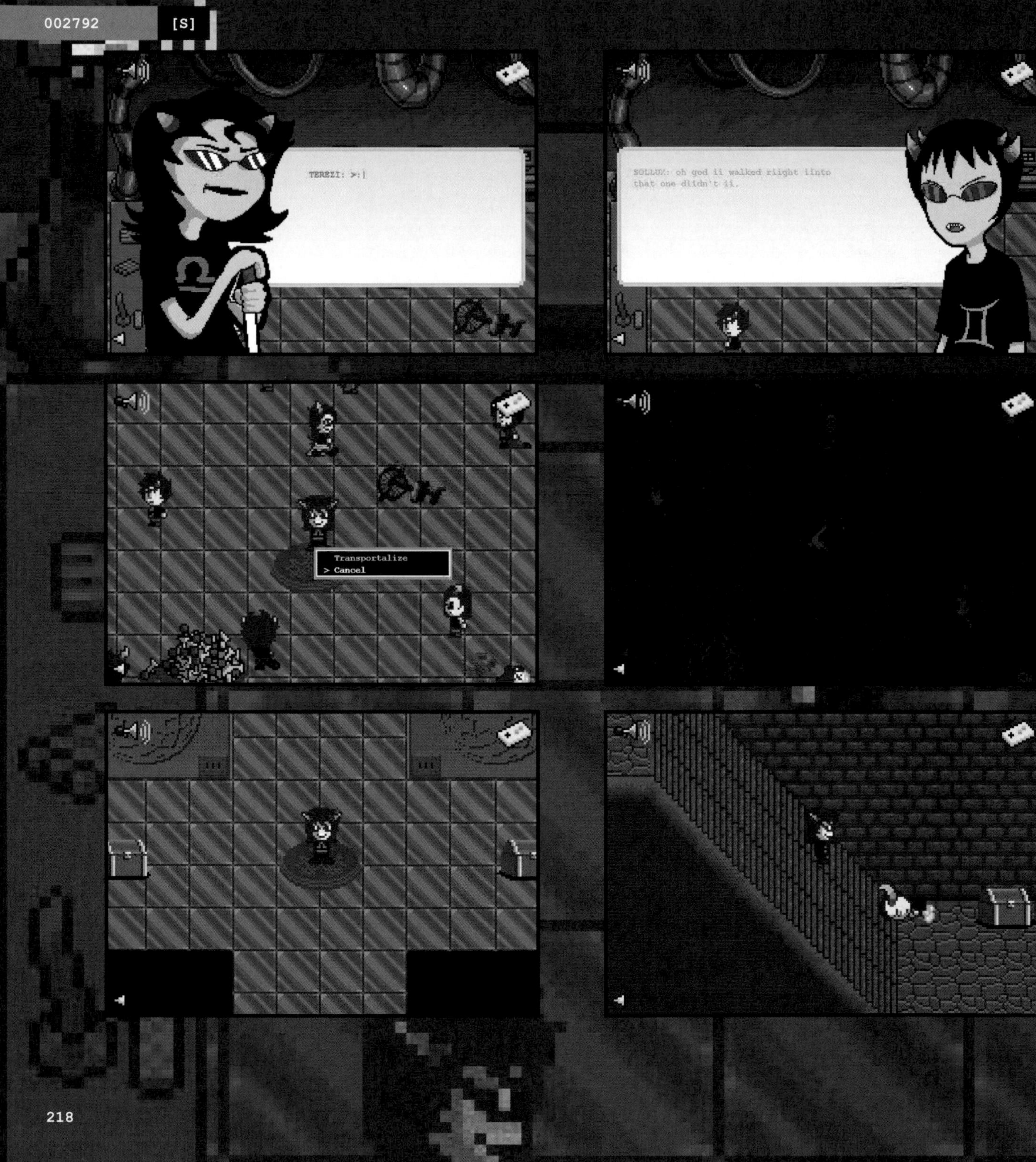
TEREZI: >:|
SOLLUX: oh god ii walked riight iinto that one diidn't ii.
Transportalize
> Cancel

I said that we'd catch up with Tavros and his struggle with stairs later, but I forgot that actually happens within the same game. So what this means is, there are even more moments of Tavros falling down the stairs to look forward to after this game is finished. Pretty exciting stuff.

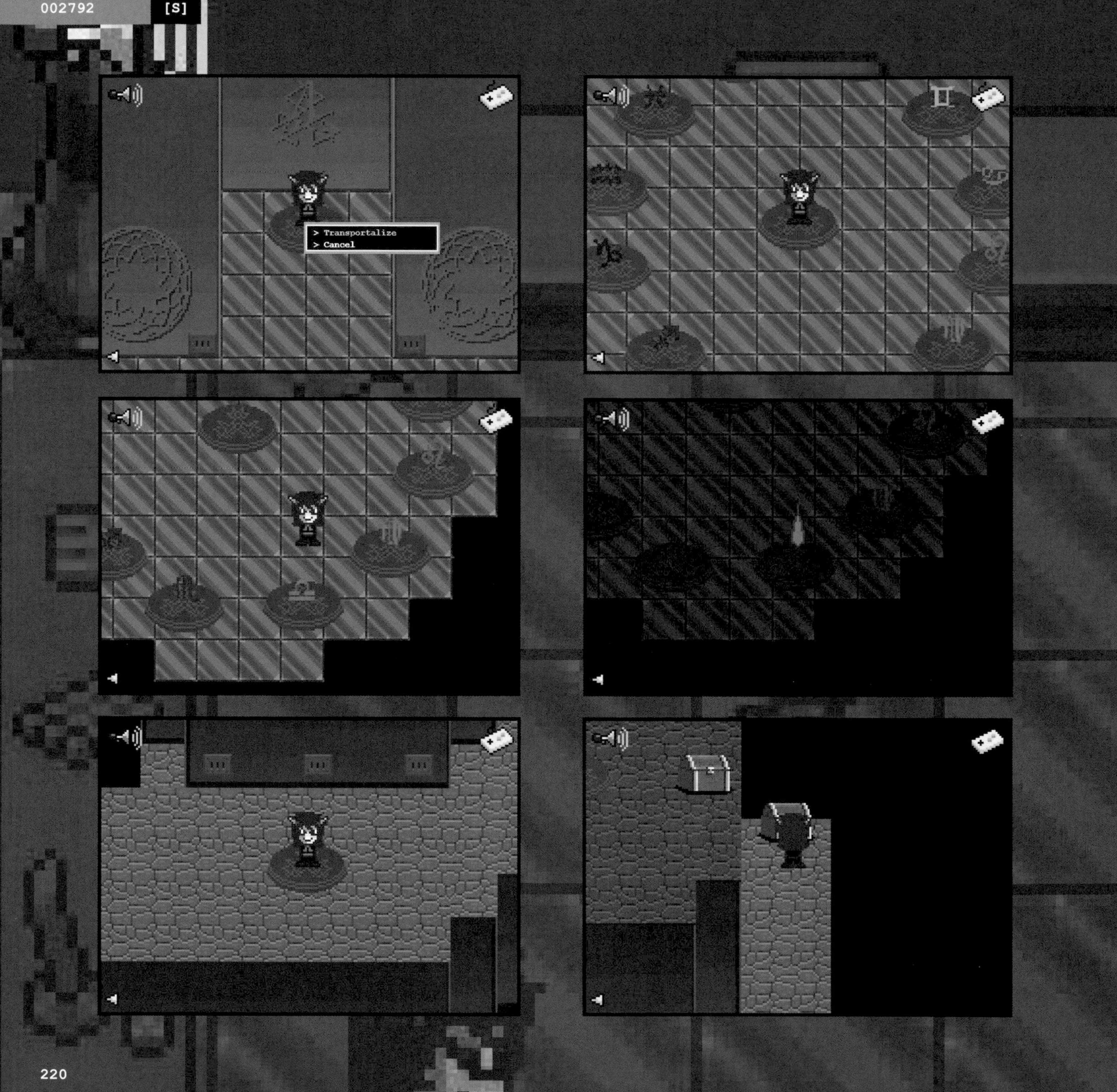

> Transportalize
> Cancel

[S]
002792
> Open Chest
> Cancel
You got SON OF LEMONSNOUT!
He smells no less sweet than the corrupt senator. And yet his lies... how they stink. The lemon never falls far from the tree!

The meteor has little puzzles to solve. Don't ask why. It's a game. And not one you're playing alone. They're playing it too. At some point Karkat actually did have to journey through this meteor as a *Sgrub* objective to create all their baby grubs in the first place, through ectobiology. So yeah, he probably had to do menial things like pushing clone jars on to special tiles to unlock doors, while hating every minute of it.

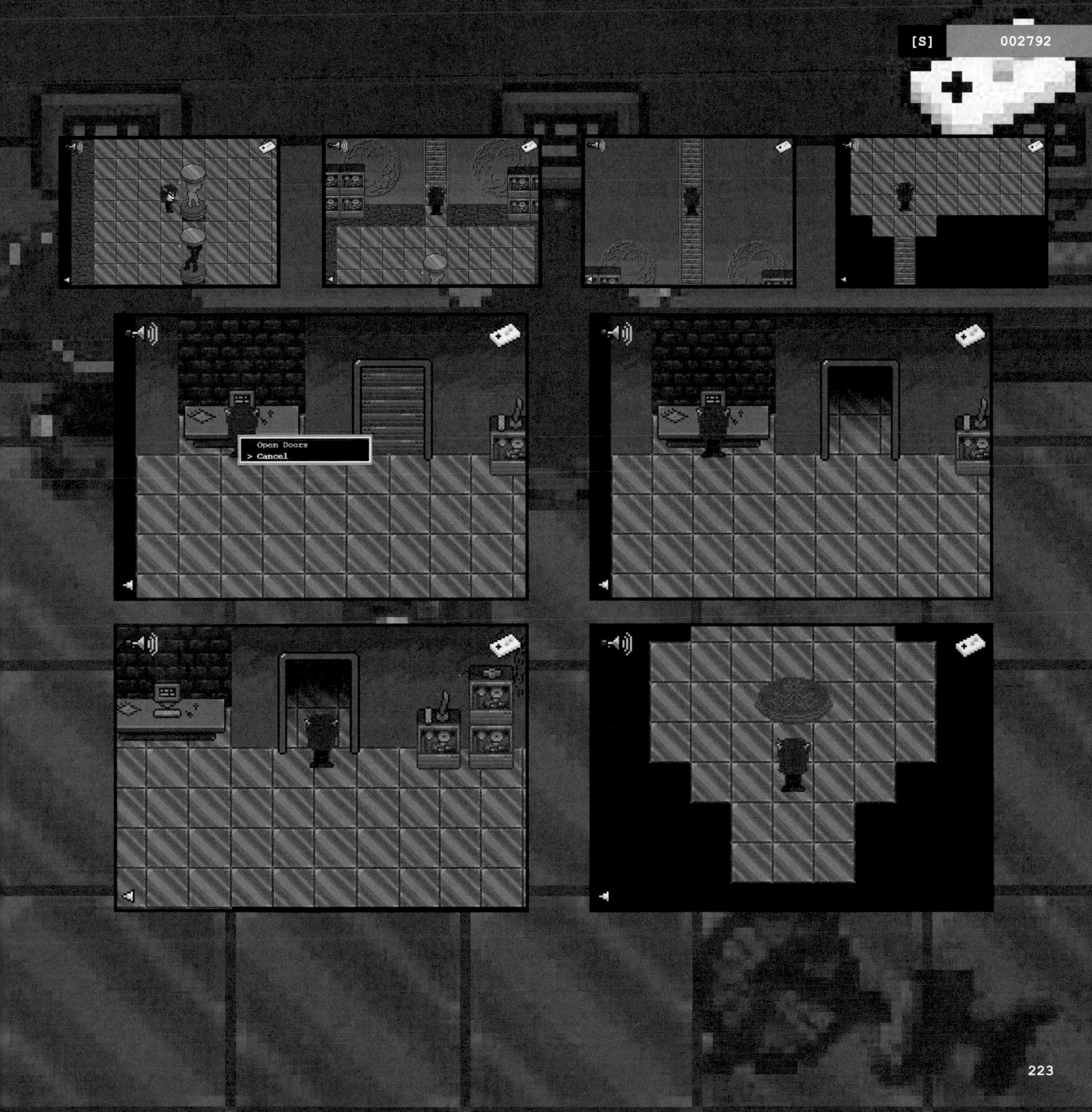
[S]
002792
Open Doors
> Cancel

> Transportalize
> Cancel

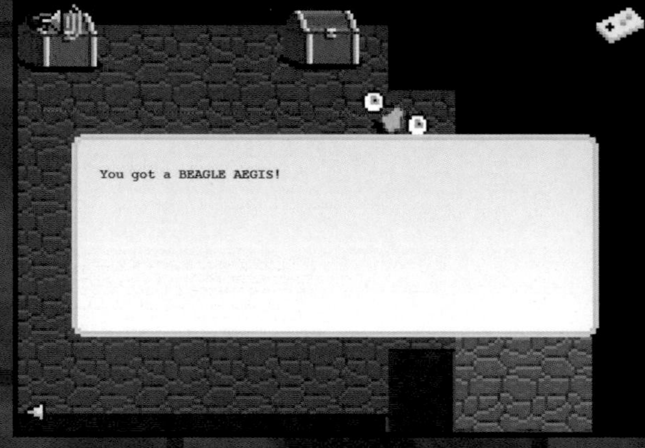
You got a BEAGLE AEGIS!

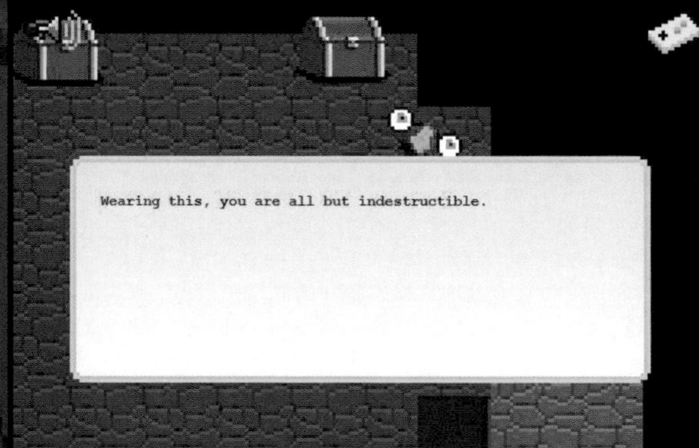
Wearing this, you are all but indestructible.

[S]
002792
You got a MUSIC BOX TIME MACHINE!
You got a FAIRY POSTER!
Yep, pretty much nothing that's not fake about fairies, that's for sure.
You got A BOONBUCK!

How trivial it seems now compared to your fortune of boonbonds. You chuck it into the chasm below.
Transportalize
> Cancel
You got A WILD CONSORT!

[S] 002792

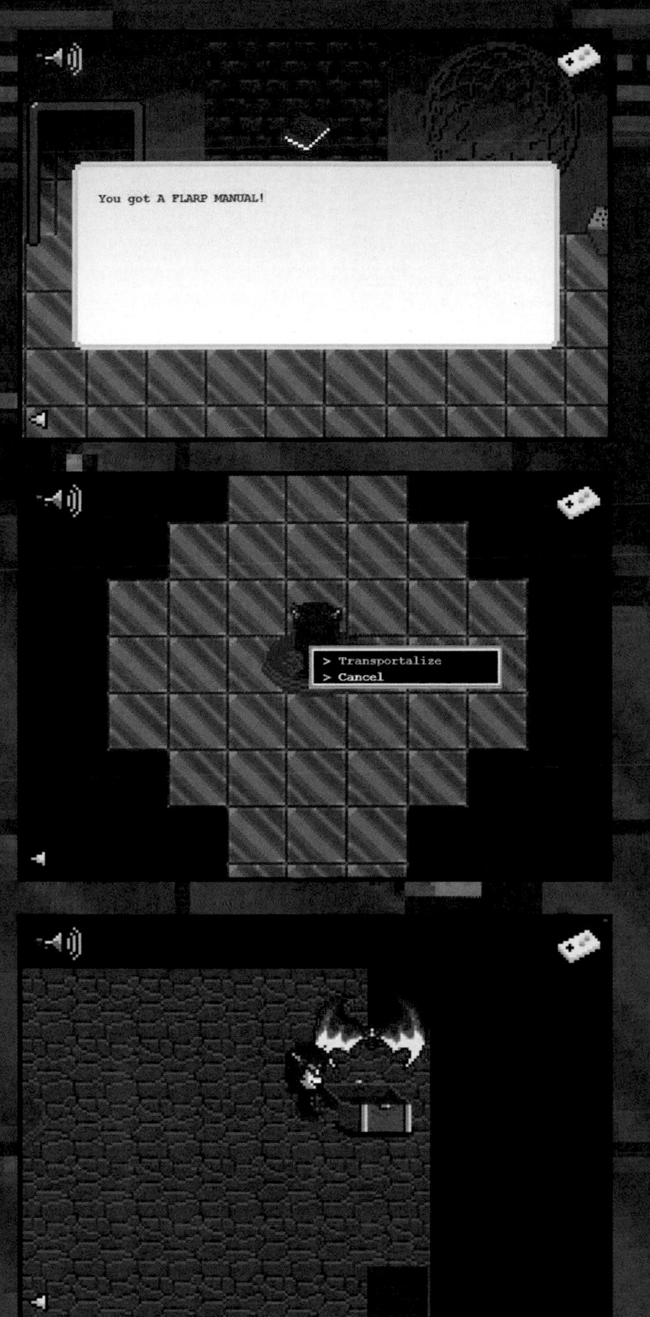
You got A FLARP MANUAL!
> Transportalize
> Cancel

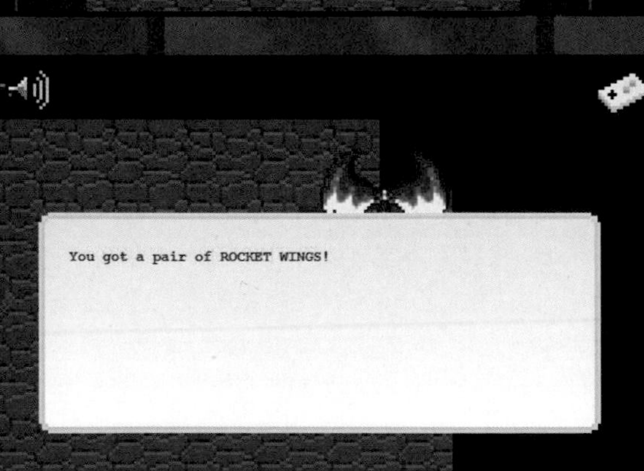
You got a pair of ROCKET WINGS!

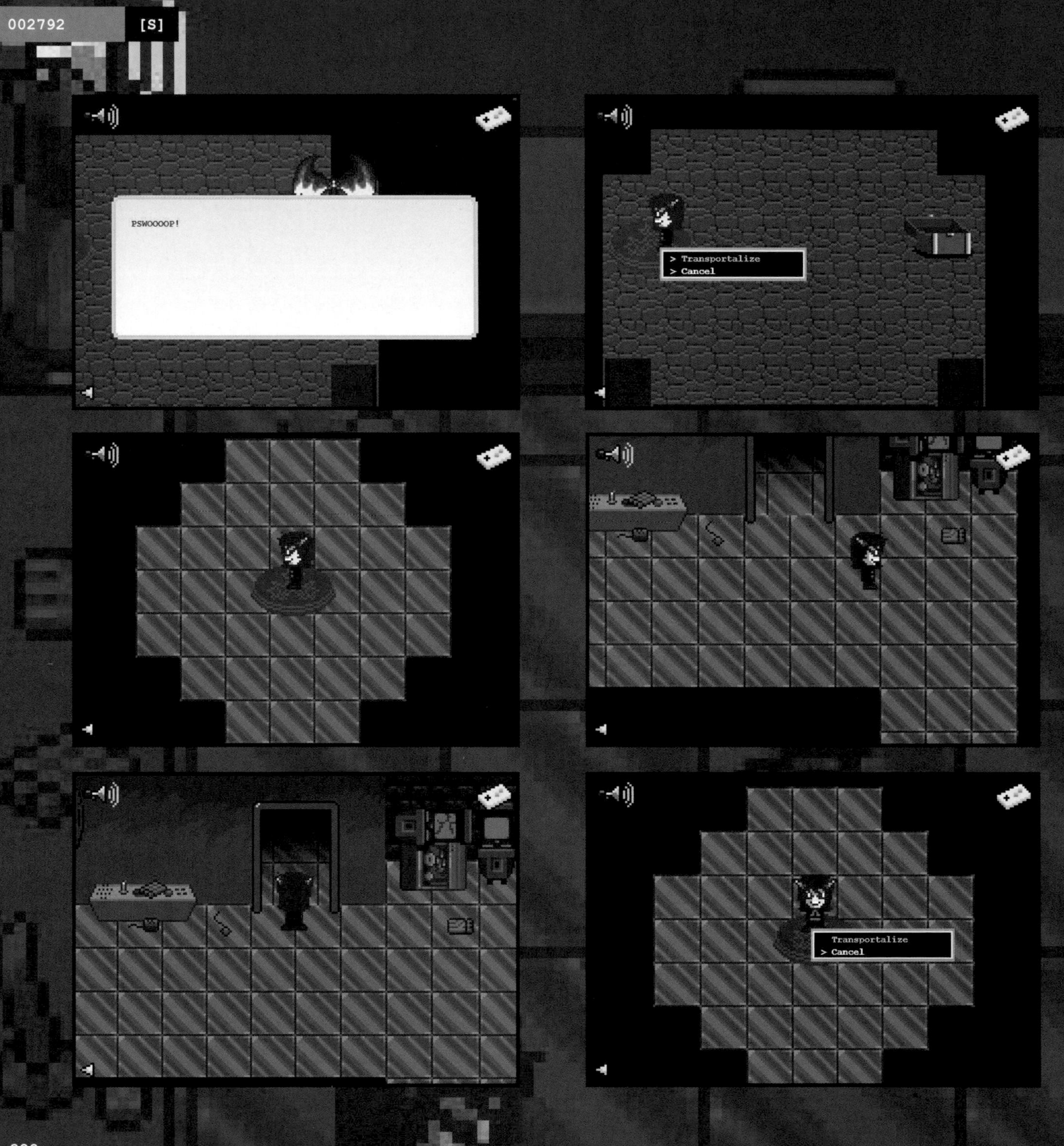
PSWOOOOP!
> Transportalize
> Cancel
Transportalize
> Cancel

You got a BRAINFORK!

For some reason you guys like to nab each others weapons and tuck them away in your own pivate chests. It's kind of silly. Seriously, what do you need this thing for??
You got the DEMONBANE RAGRIPPER!
Deadliest chainsaw in the universe.

[S]
002792
You got DEUCE CLUBS.
Least deadly pair of juggling clubs in the universe.
You got a GORGEOUS PIECE OF FINE ART.
Absolutely breathtaking.

You got THE ASSASSINATED CORPSE OF LIAISON PUMPKINSNUFFLE!
Some bastard got to one of your key witnesses! The plot thickens.

You got LIKE 13 BOONDOLLARS OR SOMETHING.
Whoop dee doo! You toss them into the abyss and make a wish.

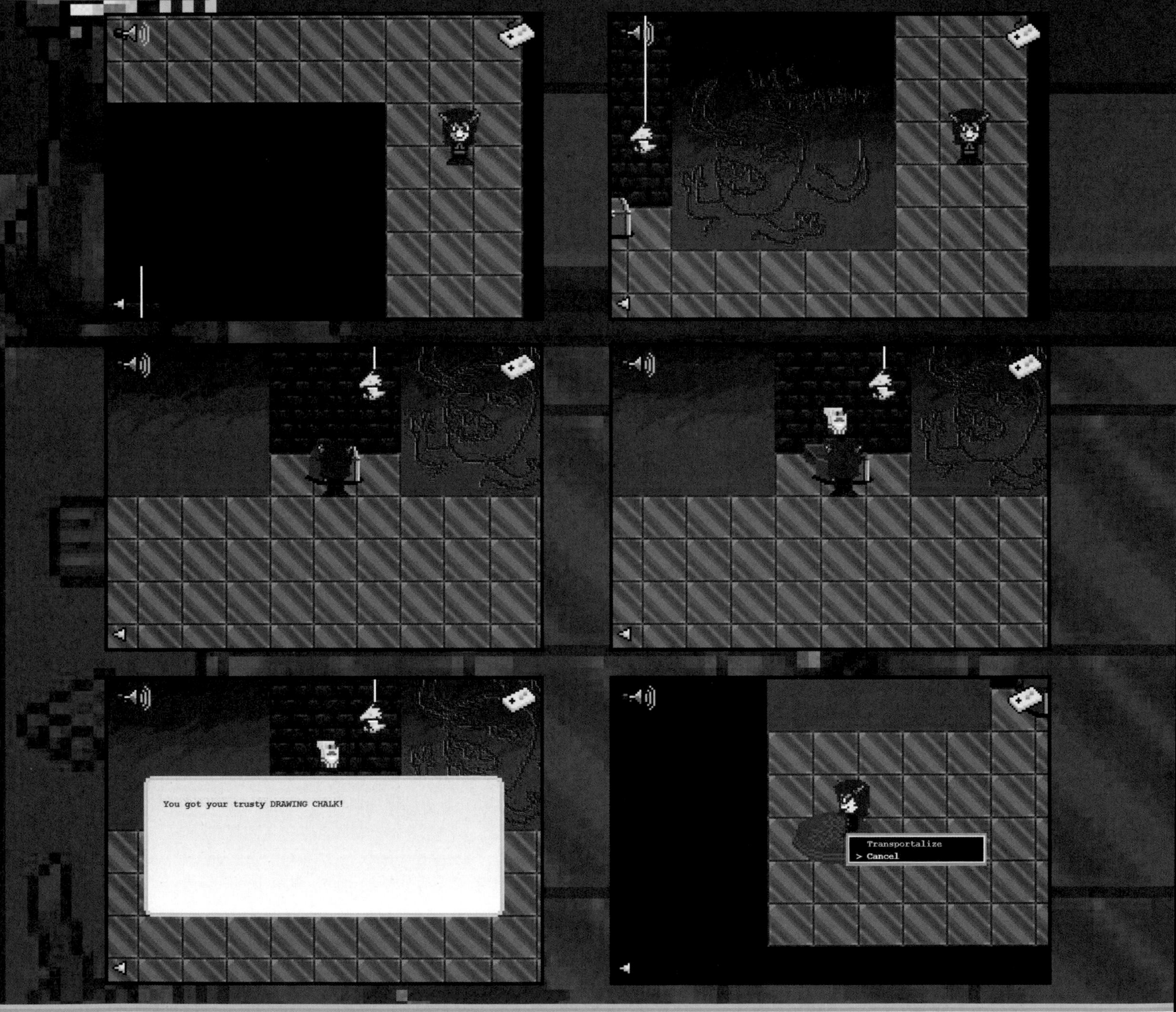
You got your trusty DRAWING CHALK!
Transportalize
> Cancel

That was a lot of consecutive pages without notes, involving a mostly uneventful transit through Terezi's private section of the map. Maybe this makes it seem like this game's map involves a gratuitous sprawl that mostly serves as a gameplay time sink, to flesh out the environmental color. But I think more is being established here in a fairly efficient way, giving us a good sense of the space and layout of this meteor setting, which will become one of the most significantly revisited places in the story. Here's a location in the meteor being established now, a place where Terezi makes chalk drawings on the wall. Later she adds to these drawings after befriending Dave. And much later, when Dave himself is on this meteor, they start drawing on the walls together, while the Mayor works on Can Town. Many locations you pass through in this game are revisited later as callbacks, and if you're on the ball, you'll remember them when you see them.

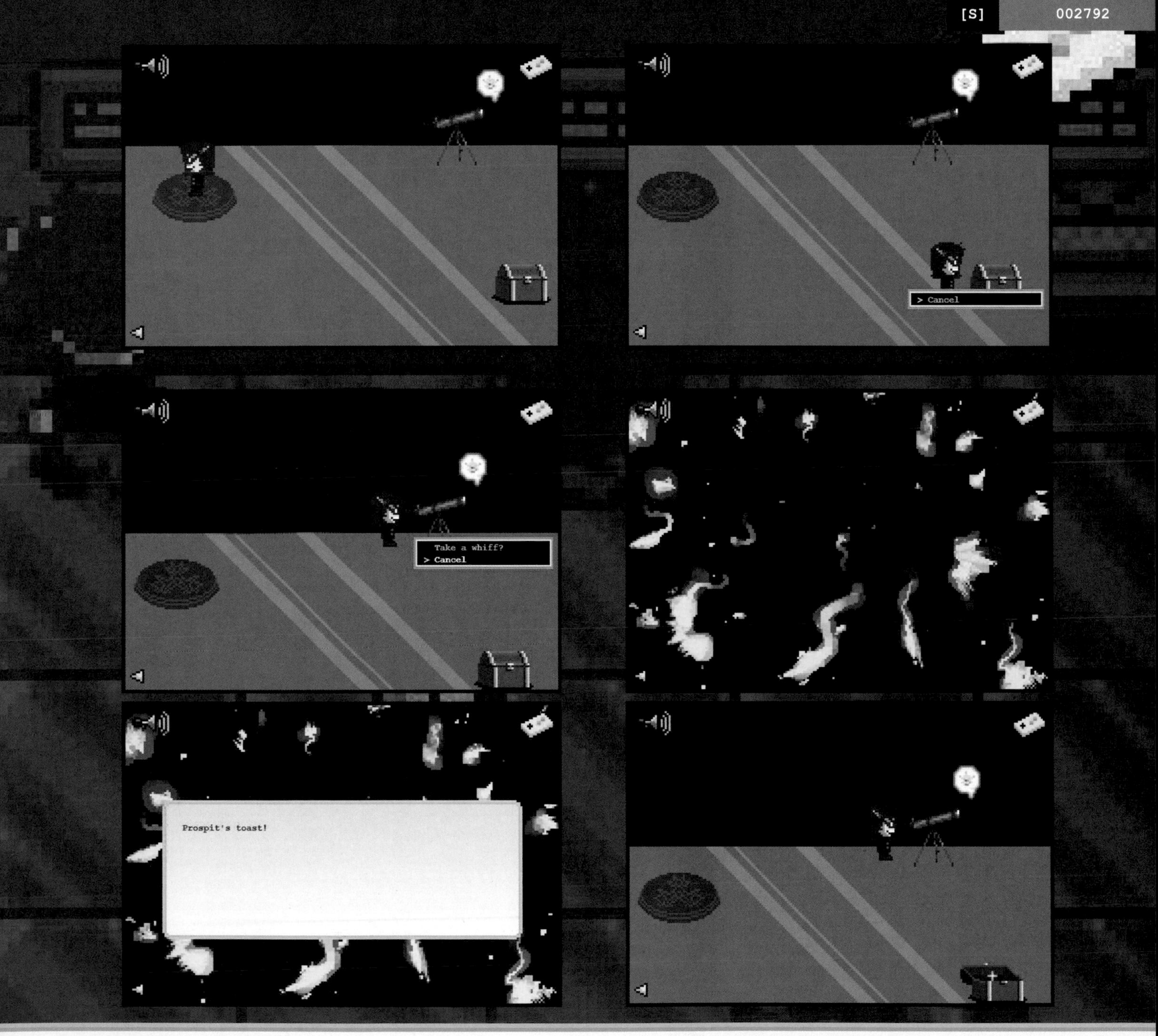

Here's how these timeline anchor points help us get our bearings. Terezi smells the remnants of Prospit, which recently blew up. So in a couple pages, when we time-skip ahead to her smelling the remains of Derse, we'll have a pretty good sense of where we are in the story.

> Examine chest.
> Cancel
There's nothing in here! Perhaps in the future you will think of something important to put in here.
Be Future Terezi?
> Yes.
> No.

The empty chest that you may fill in the future is just a time-hop transition trick, to bring us to...

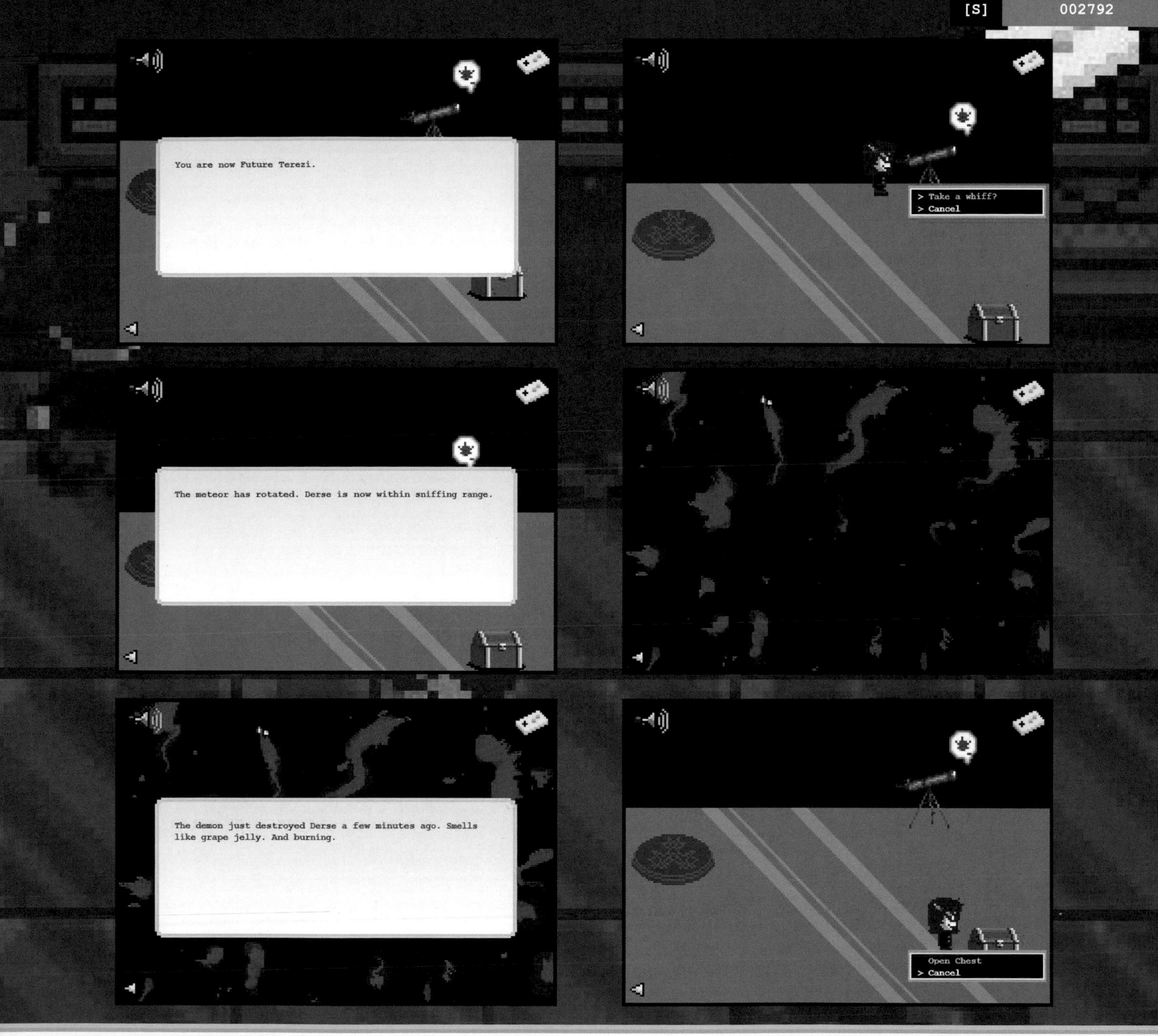

...the death of Derse, pinning us down about three hours in the future. A lot has happened in those three hours. Now, through the power of this flash-forward, we get to backtrack through Terezi's lair and get a sense of what the developments have been.

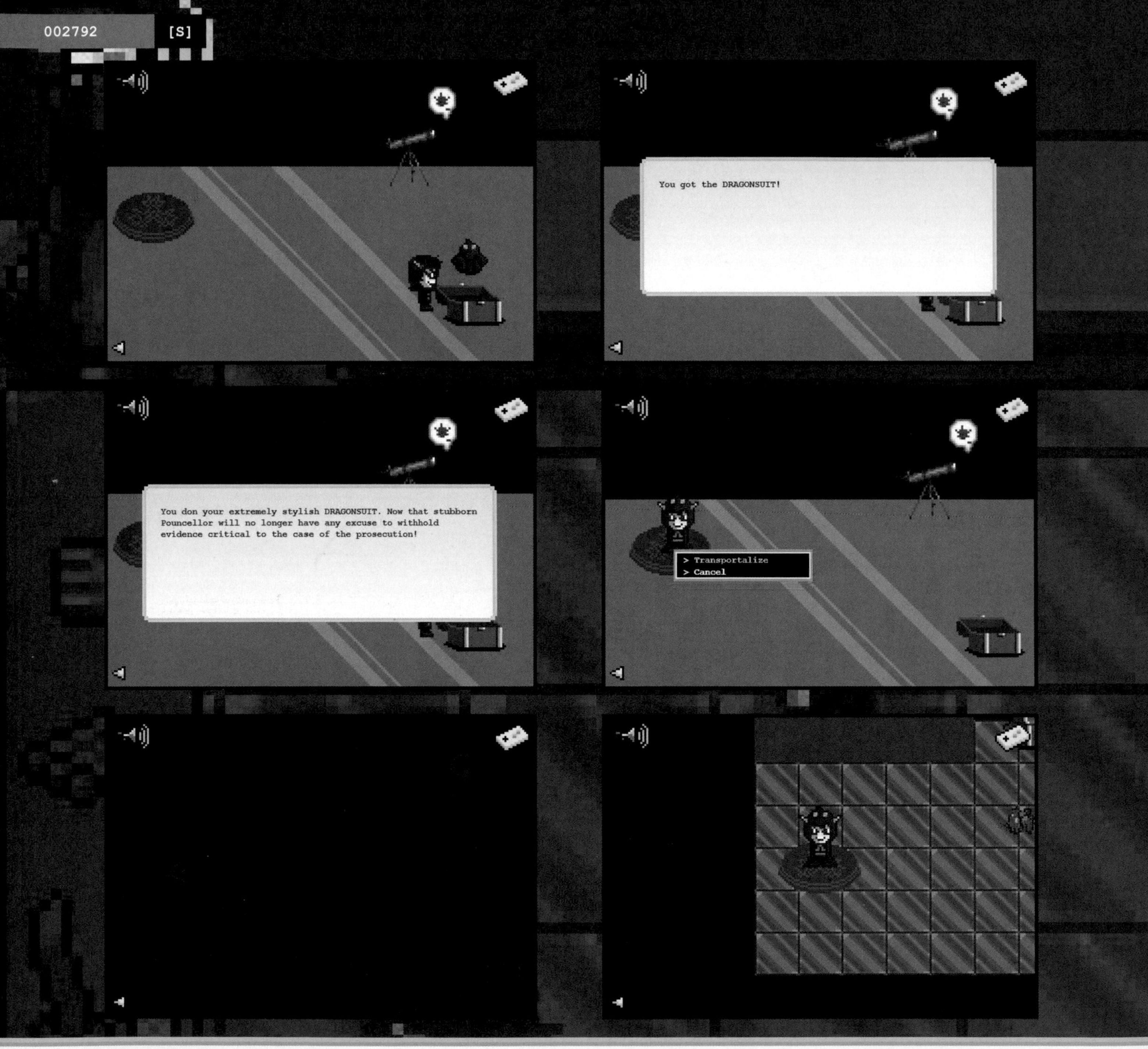

You got the DRAGONSUIT!
You don your extremely stylish DRAGONSUIT. Now that stubborn Pouncellor will no longer have any excuse to withhold evidence critical to the case of the prosecution!
> Transportalize
> Cancel

The empty chest transition device is also being used for a little wardrobe change, to help visually distinguish between the Terezi from this time period and the Terezi from the past we just got done controlling. If we ever see Dragon Suit Terezi in future panels, it can be used as another bit of guidance regarding where to put her on the timeline.

Three hours later, the full-blown Davening of Terezi is well underway. My feeling has always been that there are just certain types of people with specific personalities who were born to be diehard fans of *SBaHJ*. Terezi is clearly one of them.

The doors are jammed from overuse. That's what you get for hording so much useless bullshit in your private chests!
Transportalize
> Cancel

Talk to Nepeta.
> Cancel
TEREZI: *TH3 M1GHTY 4ND 4STOUND1NG DR4GONYYYD L3G1SL4C3R4TOR 3NT3RS TH3 3ST33M3D POUNC3LLORS OFF1C3 W1TH 4N URG3NT BUT FR13NDLY R3QU1S1T1ON PURS3D M4G1C4LLY 1N H3R M4J3ST1C SNOUT*
NEPETA: :33 < *the distinguished pouncellor nods in the most dignified and legal of manners at the dashing and well dressed legislacerator*
NEPETA: :33 < *she double checks a series of impurrtant legal clawses and rubber stamps them with wild abandon for the most judicial sort of approval pawsible*
NEPETA: :33 < this all looks to be in order! *she said*

Nepeta's hangin' out in the radial transporter array room for some reason. She's here to show you a cool secret. It's very exciting.

002792
[S]
NEPETA: :33 < please follow me! :33
NEPETA: :33 < *she also said*

This is kind of a standard RPG secret format. You look for vulnerabilities in the wall, and sometimes certain spots are permeable, which lead you to hidden rooms. But I don't think you were allowed to find this secret until Nepeta led the way, if I recall.

Earlier, Eridan made some reference to being more discreet with his pile of wands than Gamzee is with his pile of horns. Like it's shameful contraband that a guy should keep tucked away rather than letting it all hang out in the open like a shameless clown. So Nepeta's helped us stumble on Eridan's stash. Is nothing sacred???

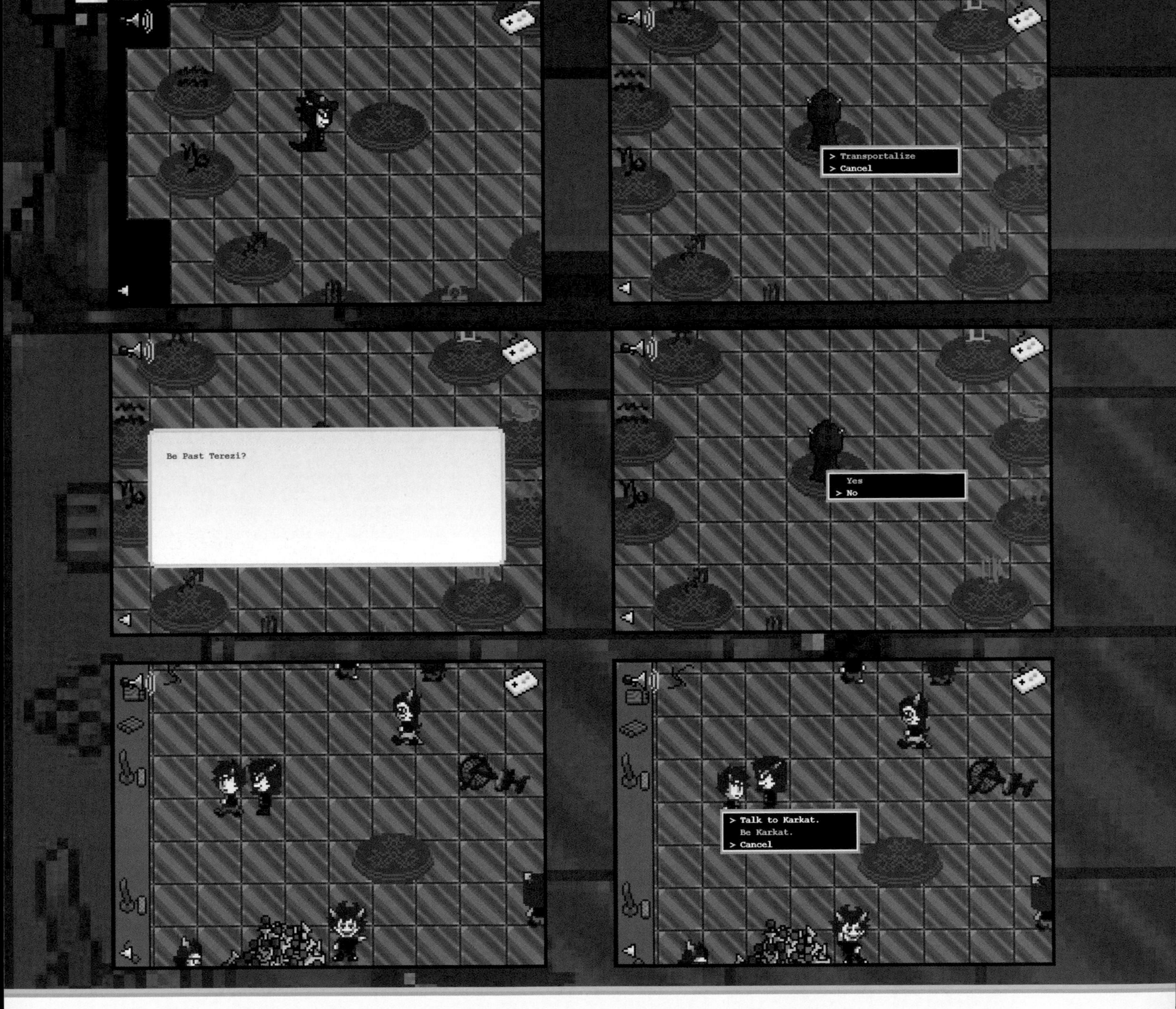

We switch back to Past Terezi before reentering the computer lab. Walking around and talking to people in the lab in the three hours in the future would expose too much info for now. We've had enough of a taste.

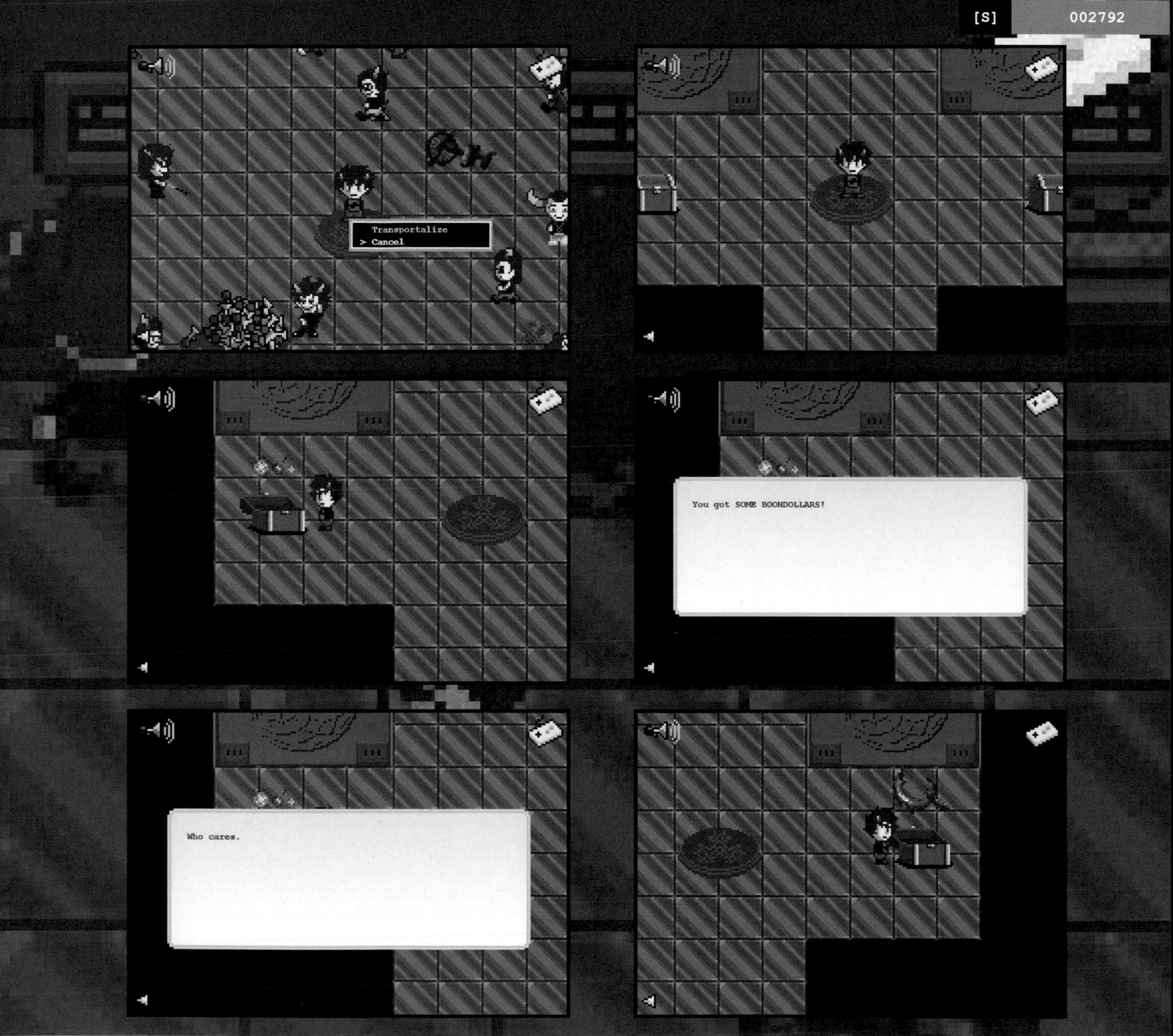

Now it's Karkat's turn. Again, while playing the game, you can do a lot of this in any order you want. This particular sequence is just how the material is being presented here in the book. Karkat seems like the best one to save for last. Ultimately, it's totally up to the player to decide when to move on and click the link to the next page. They can glean as much or as little from the game as they want, with no particular milestones to clear before being allowed to advance. Perhaps this is a double-edged sword, storytelling-wise. But there aren't many other ways to handle it in such a mixed-media environment.

002792

[S]

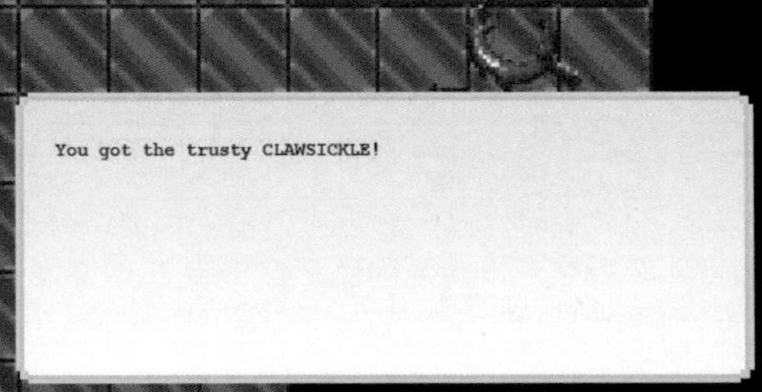
You got the trusty CLAWSICKLE!

Transportalize
> Cancel

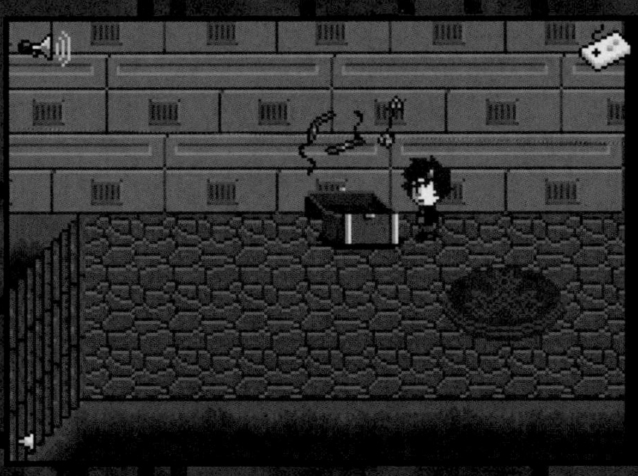

You got a BROKEN BOW AND ARROW!

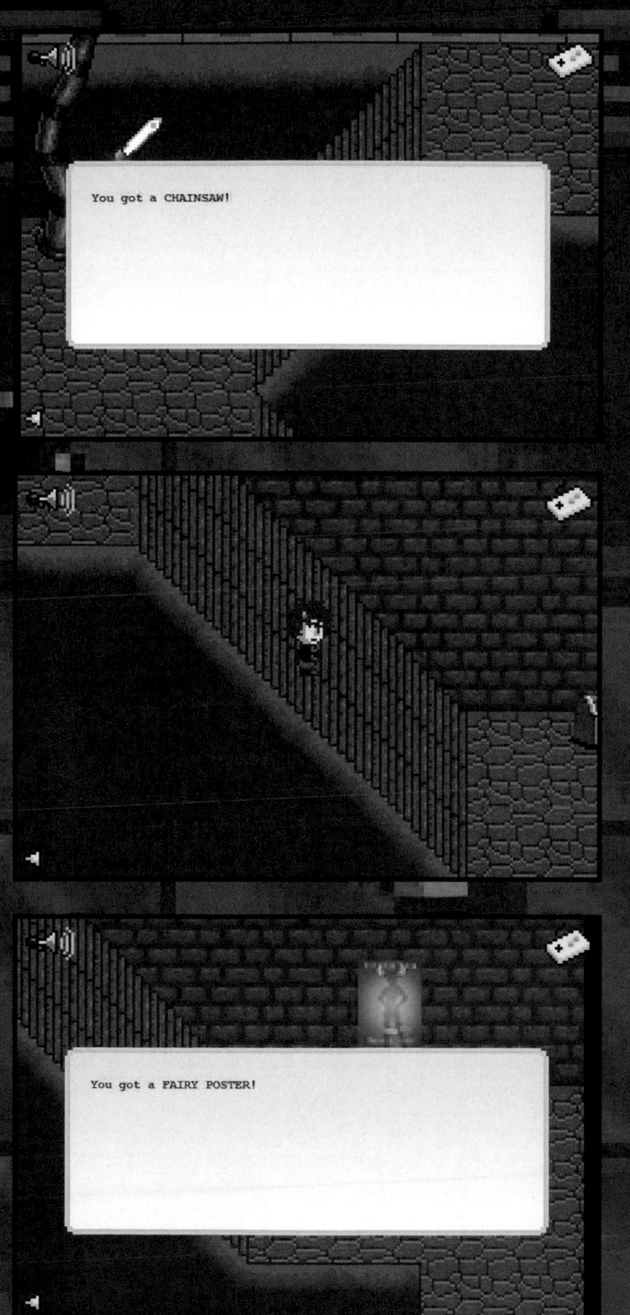
You got a CHAINSAW!
You got a FAIRY POSTER!

[S]
002792
Still some brown stains on it. Yuck.
Lovely, albeit imaginary.

002792

[S]

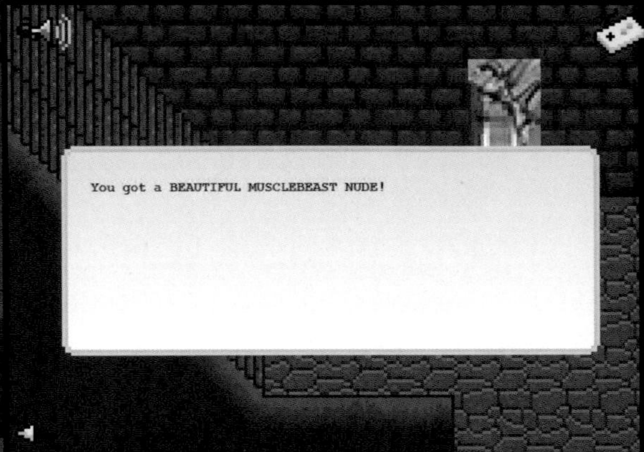
You got a BEAUTIFUL MUSCLEBEAST NUDE!

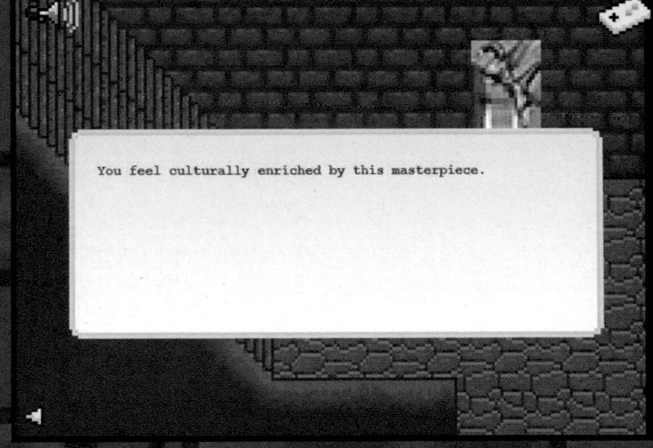
You feel culturally enriched by this masterpiece.

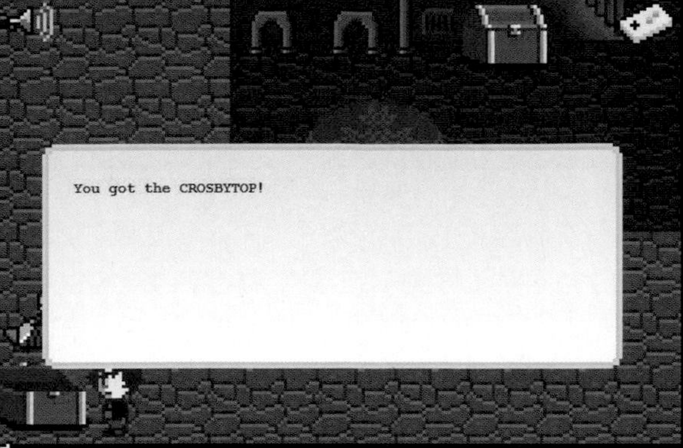
You got the CROSBYTOP!

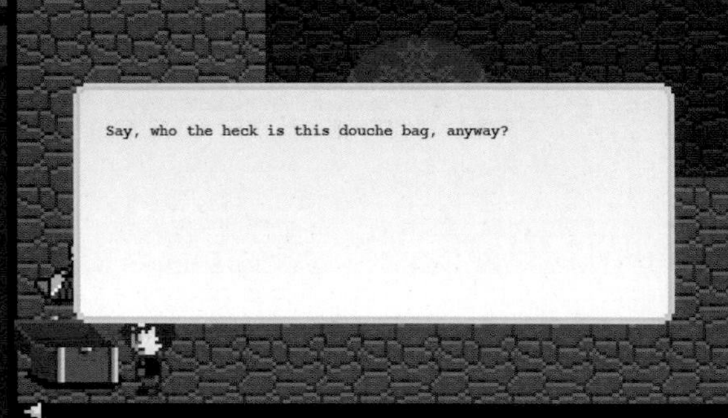
Say, who the heck is this douche bag, anyway?

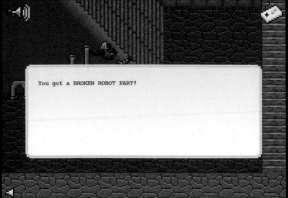

You got a BROKEN ROBOT PART!

Transportalize
> Cancel
You got SOME GLASSES OF FRESH MILK!
But... what is there to even get milk from around here?
Oh sweet jegus...

> Examine monstrosities.
> Cancel
Genetic abominations once so threatening now pose no challenge at all to players of your godly status. They are lucky to be asleep and behind glass. They are lucky to have your pity.

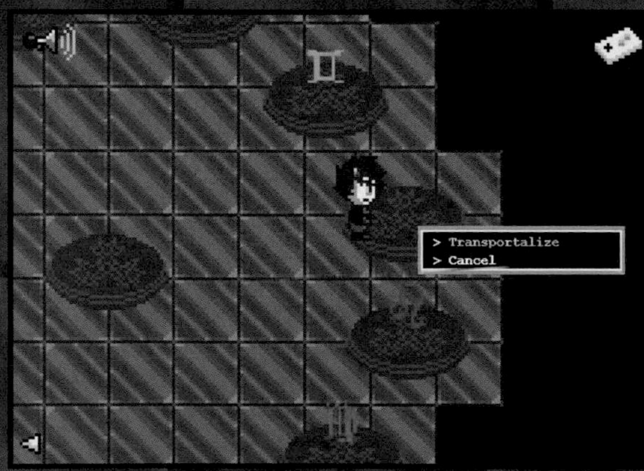
> Transportalize
> Cancel

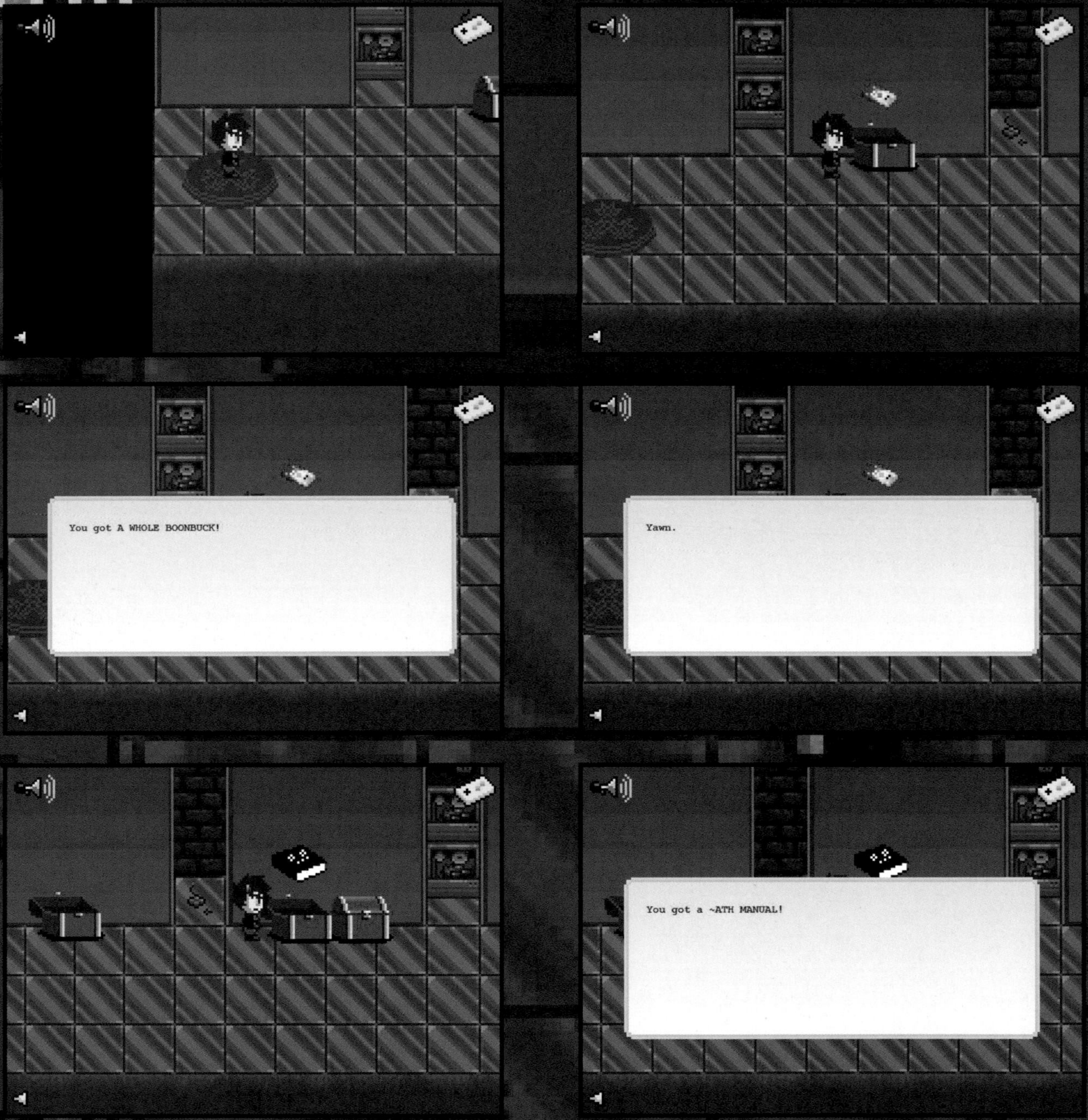

You got A WHOLE BOONBUCK!

Yawn.

It's so thick, you could kill someone with this thing.
And if you master what's inside, you just might kill everyone with it.
You got a TINKERBULL PLUSH!
R.I.P. little buddy. :'(

Recall that the Sassacre tome was touted as being thick enough to kill someone (or a cat, specifically), which foreshadowed the fact that it did literally kill someone (Nanna), and also literally did kill a cat specifically as well. We're getting a similar line here. It isn't *quite* used as a blunt instrument to kill someone exactly. But Doc Scratch does end up using it to put a pretty good beatdown on Spades Slick.

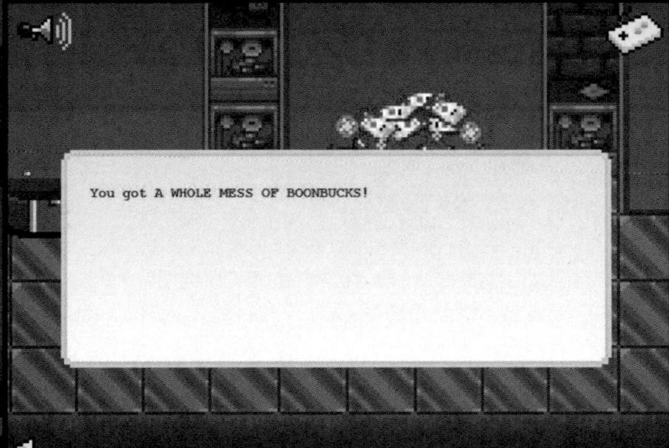
You got A WHOLE MESS OF BOONBUCKS!

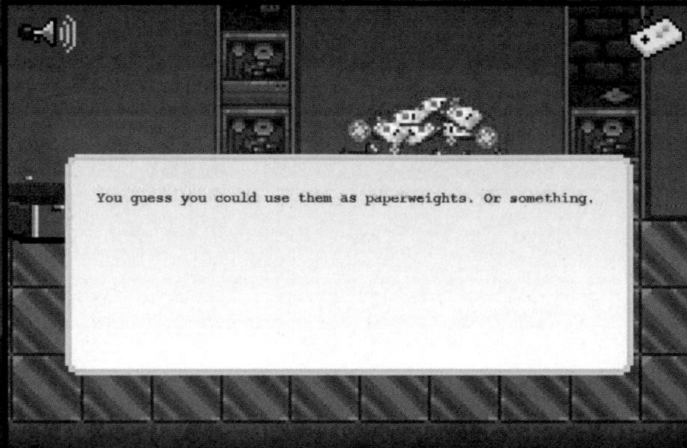
You guess you could use them as paperweights. Or something.

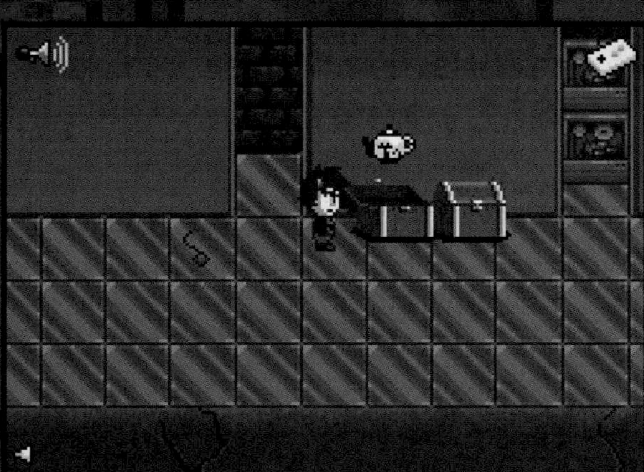

You got a TEAPOT!

You got a WICKED ELIXIR!
You chug the beverage immediately. Your vitals remain unchanged.

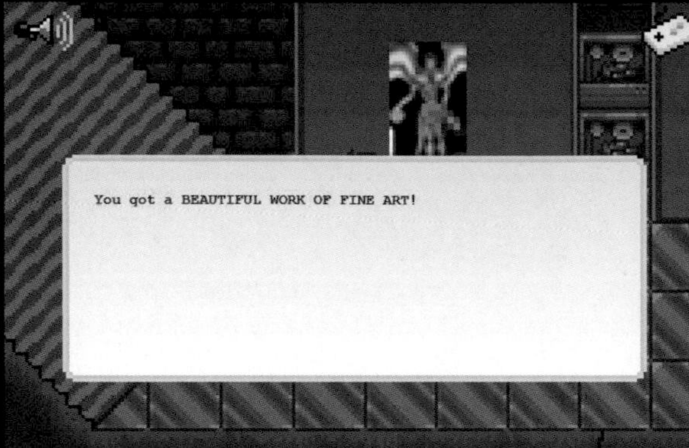
You got a BEAUTIFUL WORK OF FINE ART!

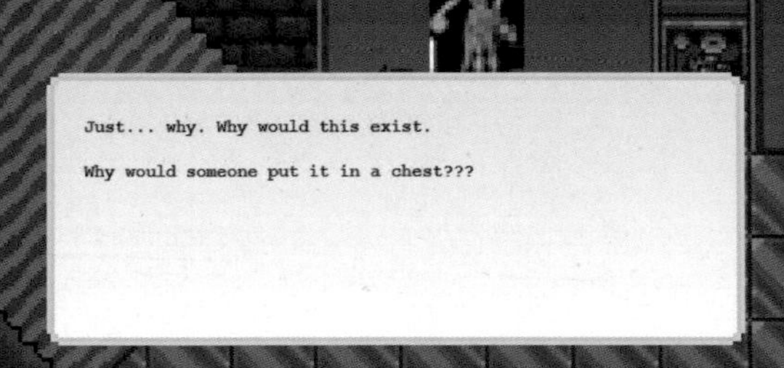
Just... why. Why would this exist.
Why would someone put it in a chest???

You got HOMES SMELL YA LATER!

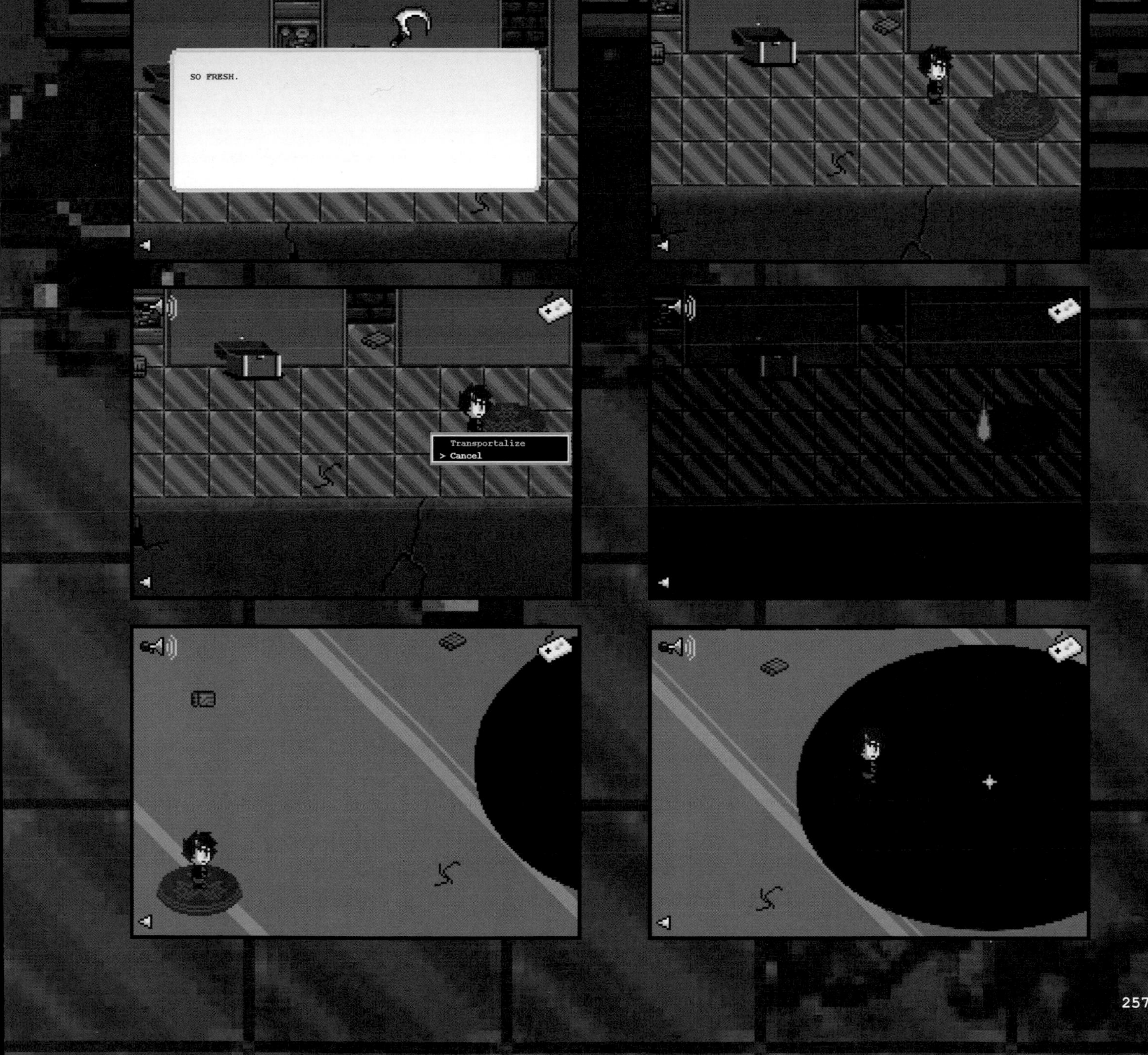
SO FRESH.
Transportalize
> Cancel

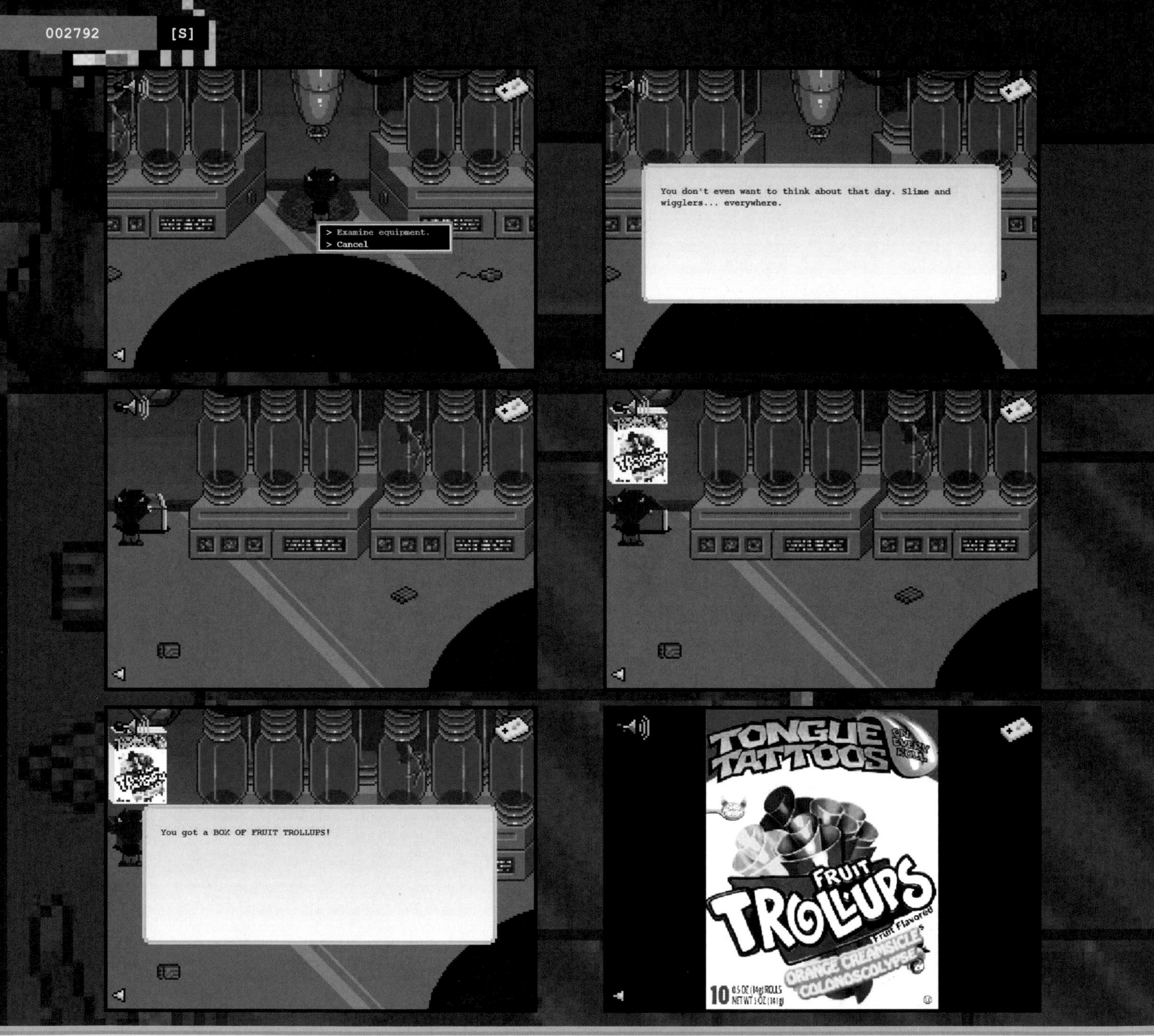

002792
[S]
> Examine equipment.
> Cancel
You don't even want to think about that day. Slime and wigglers... everywhere.
You got a BOX OF FRUIT TROLLUPS!
TONGUE TATTOOS
ON EVERY ROLL
FRUIT
TROLLUPS
Fruit Flavored
ORANGE CREAMSICLE
COLONOSCOLYPSE
10 0.5 OZ (14g) ROLLS
NET WT 5 OZ (141g)

Finally Karkat enters the same ectobiology lab he used to make paradox clones of himself and all his friends, just like John did. Also just like John did, Karkat appears to have created twice as many infants as might be expected. We know that John created their guardians as well, who are all true paradox clones (genetic copies of themselves, and themselves alone paradoxically, and therefore not related to each other). And then all their slime was mixed to create the kids, who are sibling pairs (Jake + Jane = John and Jade. Dirk + Roxy = Dave and Rose.) So this leads us to expect something similar happened here, especially now that we see two identical sets of twelve jars. Except, due to the way trolls breed, they don't have parent pairs, so their slime wasn't mixed that way. They're created through an "incestuous slurry," which implies all the slime is mixed together and results in each troll individually. It seems this process happened twice, once for the trolls we know, and then again for all their ancestors, who seem to be, if not exact copies, extremely close genetic copies of their descendants.

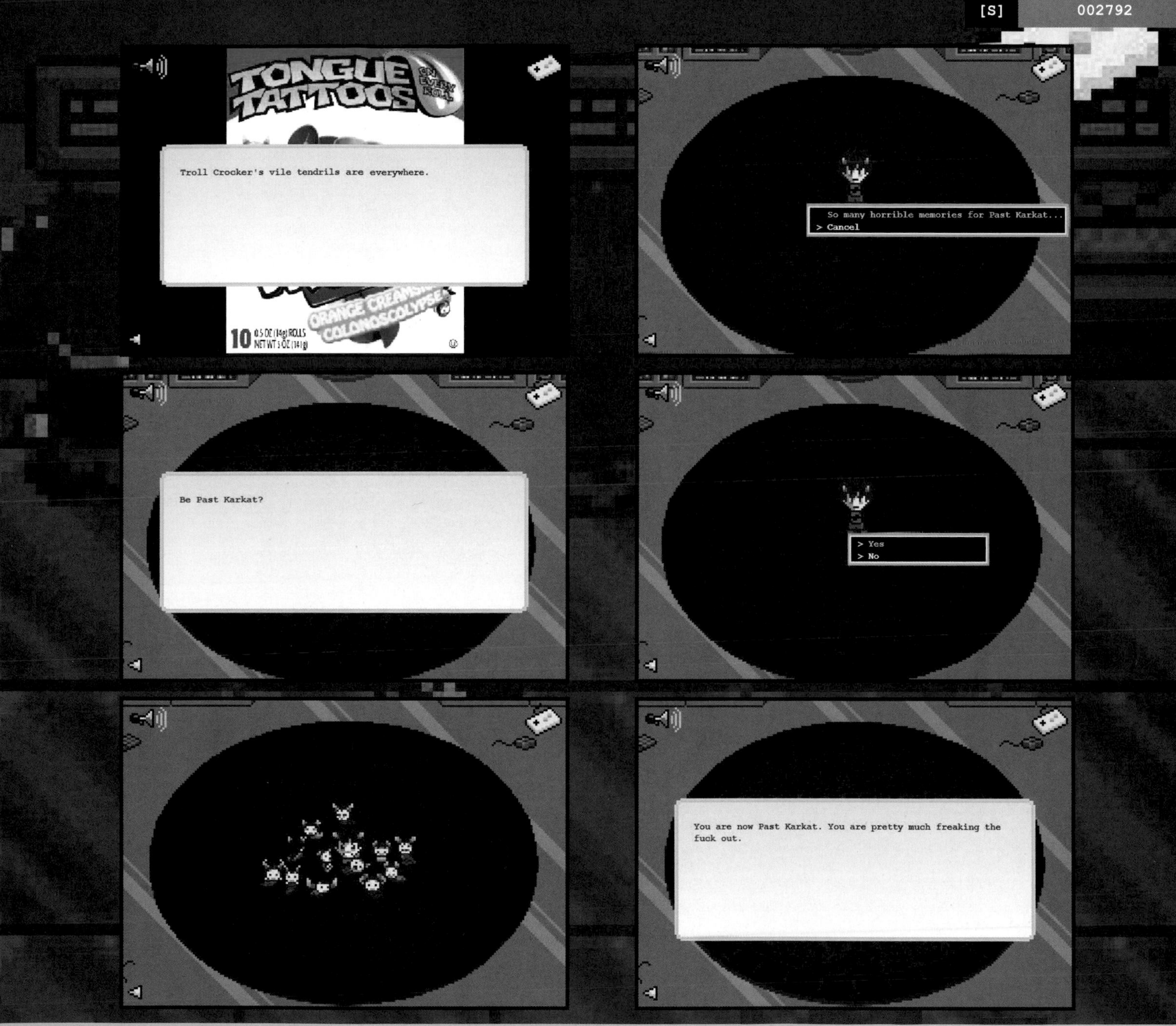

TONGUE TATTOOS
ON EVERY ROLL
ORANGE CREAMSICLE COLONOSCOLYPSE
10 0.5 OZ (14g) ROLLS NET WT 5 OZ (141g)
Troll Crocker's vile tendrils are everywhere.
So many horrible memories for Past Karkat...
> Cancel
Be Past Karkat?
> Yes
> No
You are now Past Karkat. You are pretty much freaking the fuck out.

We flash back to the moment he activated the cloning machine, and see him swarmed by freshly spawned grubs. Now the question is, are these his baby friends, or their ancestors? Which spawned first? It probably doesn't matter, since they're so similar. Whichever it was, the other group came next, but that's not shown here, because we're not diving into the ancestor stuff just yet at this point of the story. But that second array of 12 jars certainly starts putting the idea in our heads. It's probably the first concrete evidence that the ancestors are going to be a real thing in the story, rather than something vaguely alluded to as background lore during the Hivebent worldbuilding gauntlet. If you're perceptive, you stick this observation in your back pocket, and wait for the issue to come up again. And it does. Later in A5A2, when the dramatic arcs of all these trolls as a friend group start coming to a head, the introduction of all the ancestors as characters (see: Mindfang Diaries) mainly serves as a way of broadening those arcs to function as conclusions to these sort of long-running karmic destinies originally established by their legendary progenitors. Those backstories do a lot more than that too, including expanding on Alternian lore a little more, as well as establishing yet another roster of intensely beloved fan favorites with a few quick story strokes. Quick in page count, albeit kinda wordy (thanks, Aranea).

Aaaaaand that's the last page of the game. On this adorable note of ancestor-descendant ambiguity, let's move on. At the end of the day, it was only 150 pages or so, right? It's not like anybody else was gonna do something better with that paper.

Aw, there she is. All tuckered out.
You wonder what she is dreaming about? Surely something adorable.

Anyway, guess it's time to get down to business and save her life!
You prepare to initiate an uninterrupted sequence of life-saving events.

> John: Deploy... huh?

NANNASPRITE: HOO HOO HOO HOO HOO!

I guess it's time to go back to some material that actually advances the story? Sigh. *Must we*? Seriously, practically everything advances the story in some way. It's just that because it's a story about a game, we have these known benchmarks we're marching toward and then trying to pass. Like: John enters --> Rose enters --> Dave enters --> Jade enters. And so on. It's pretty regimented, and when some of these benchmarks feel elusive, it has a way of making it feel like story progress is being delayed. But that's only if you map story progress onto game progress in such a literal way. I cannot say it is unfair to *yearn* for the passing of these hurdles that the story imposes upon itself, and yet the story often finds ways of continuing to outfox itself, thus delaying them a bit further due to stupid shenanigans, or pranks, or... Oh, god damn it, Nanna. There you go, making a fool out of me by proving the very point I was in the process of making.

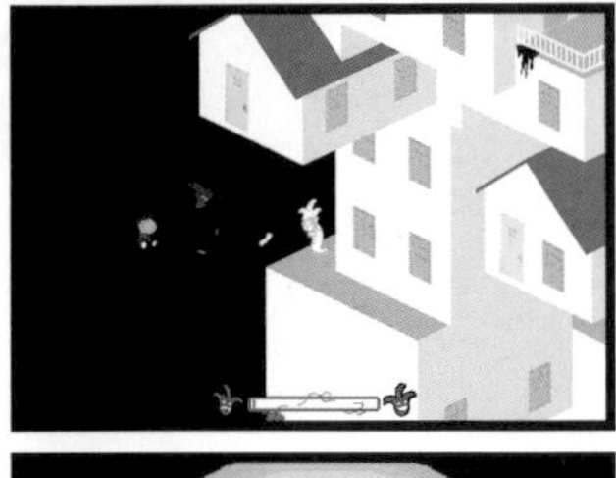
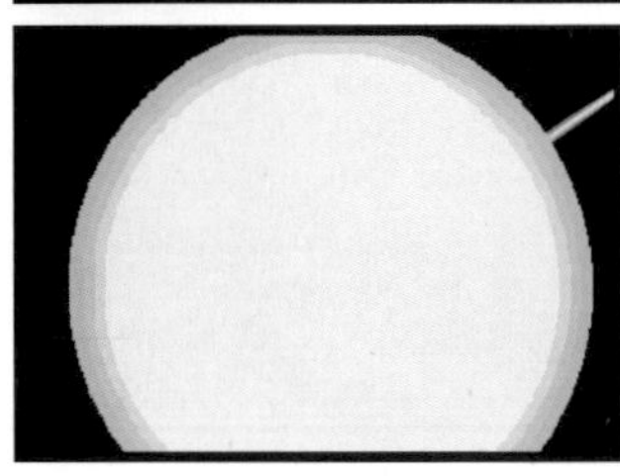
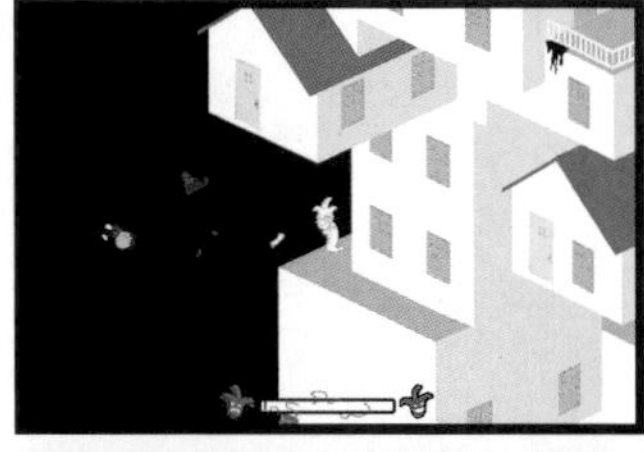
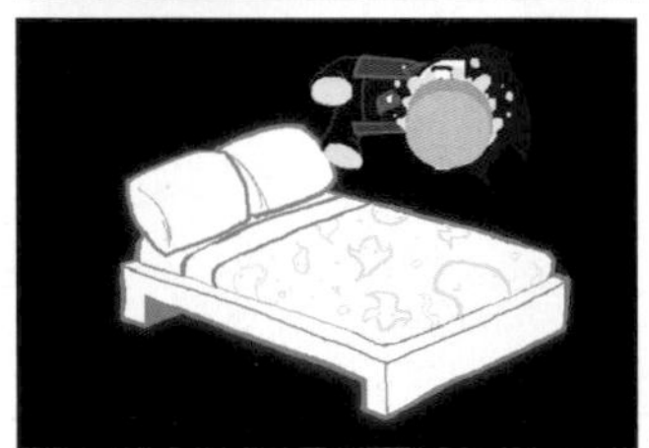

JOHN: nanna, what the heck!!!
NANNASPRITE: Hoo hoo hoo!
NANNASPRITE: John, you remind me so much of your father when he was your age. He was just as easily bested by this crafty old prankstress!
JOHN: really?
NANNASPRITE: Yes. It would be many years before he would take the gambit in an exchange with your nanna.
JOHN: but nanna, did you know he is not really my dad? and also, i am not technically your grandson.
JOHN: you are actually sort of my mother.
NANNASPRITE: Of course I knew this, John! I have known for many years.
NANNASPRITE: I have also known that in a sense, you are my father as well. You were the one to push all those buttons, after all!
JOHN: huh, oh yeah.
JOHN: don't you find it all a little strange?
NANNASPRITE: John, I am the ghost of an old lady

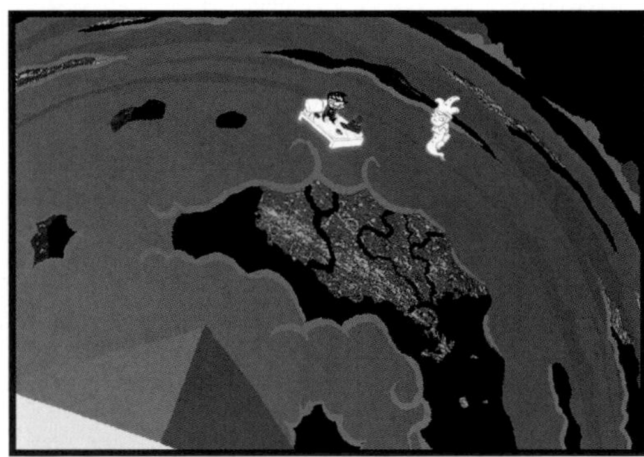

with one arm who is dressed like a clown. Why would that seem strange to me?
JOHN: heheh.
JOHN: so where have you been, nanna? i have been looking all over for you.
NANNASPRITE: I have been looking for you too, dear!

The prankster's gambit is back. I told you it would return. Hey, there's an oil splotch there too. Also, kindly grandmotherly rhetoric aside, can we maybe take a moment to ask...why the hell did Nanna DO this?? Is she just some sort of bitch? It seems innocent and all in good fun, but really, this is just plain fucking unnecessary. Once we get to know Jane better, in certain ways I think it starts to reveal there are facets to Nanna's character that cast some of her habits in a less charitable light. She was groomed to be the heiress of Betty Crocker, a.k.a. the Condesce, after all, in both this timeline and the post-scratch one. She broke free from Condy at a younger age to run her own joke shop but possibly still retained some dubious habits from that questionable upbringing. The full range of post-scratch Jane's arc reveals some dark thoughts and tendencies as well. Is it possible the simplest explanation is...deep down, she's just kind of a shithead?? It's more likely than you might think. Not to piss on anyone's good time if you like Jane or Nanna, though. At this point in the story, she easily exists in the sphere of "kindly, archetypical grandmother," who is a bit feisty but still only wishes to help. There is nothing wrong with taking this reading to exist as the sole truth of this character, at least in this particular incarnation of her existence. So we can probably just chill out with our Evil Nanna headcanons for a while.

JOHN: you have?
NANNASPRITE: Yes! It seems you have been rising through the rungs of your echeladder quite swiftly.
JOHN: yeah!
JOHN: now i am an ectobiolo...
JOHN: ectobiblio... shit!
JOHN: (oops! sorry.)
JOHN: ectobioblobabby sitter.
JOHN: damn it, you know what i mean.
NANNASPRITE: Yes, that is quite high. You have climbed so much faster than I did in my youth. I am so proud of you!
JOHN: thanks!
NANNASPRITE: You should have returned sooner! I could have given you this boon at a much lower rung.
JOHN: boon?
NANNASPRITE: Here, John. Take this.

JOHN: ok. what is it?
NANNASPRITE: You can use it to summon me wherever you go.
NANNASPRITE: Now we needn't endure those long spells without a good visit!
JOHN: oh cool, that is great!
NANNASPRITE: And now, the most important question of all.
NANNASPRITE: When was the last time you have eaten anything, young man??
JOHN: hmm, i guess it has been a good while!
JOHN: i've been snacking on gushers a whole lot. bluh...
JOHN: i never realized how terrible they were, actually.

See? Look, she's right back to redeeming herself, by granting boons and offering to cook a warm meal for her grandson. Everything is fine once more. Or in other words, the horrific cycle of abuse rages on.

NANNASPRITE: That is completely unacceptable.
NANNASPRITE: I will prepare you a healthy home cooked meal while you relax in your ghost bed and rescue your paradox sister.
JOHN: oh boy!
NANNASPRITE: What would you like? Name what your heart desires. I will use my spooky ghost powers to make it.
JOHN: wow, hmm...
NANNASPRITE: Why, John! Do you hear that sound?
JOHN: uh... no?
NANNASPRITE: It sounds as if your meal is nearly finished!
JOHN: really? already?
NANNASPRITE: BZZZZZ!

JOHN:naaaaaaaaaaaaaaaaaaaaaaaannnnnnnaaaaaaaaaaaaaaaa!!!!!
NANNASPRITE: HOOOOOOOOOOOOOOOOOOOOOOOOOHOOHOOHOOHOOHOOHOOHOO!

> Rose: Get hassled.

Wait...wait, no. She's gone right back to fucking with him. When is this wretched, prevaricating hag going to get her comeuppance? That's what I want to know.

These chumps just won't quit hounding you!

It's like they heard somebody over here was handing out asses, and they've known nothing but years of bitter ass famine.

> Rose: Answer Eridan.

-- caligulasAquarium [CA] began trolling tentacleTherapist [TT] --

CA: wwho are you tryin to convvince wwith this ludicrous poppycock
TT: ?
CA: magic is NOT REAL
CA: wwhatevver youre doin its not real its somethin else outright entirely
CA: its fancy and impressivve and all but its not the fuckin figmental storybook claptrap you wwanna make out like it is
CA: so howw about you get off your high skyhorse
TT: Why do you keep addressing me as if I'm some sort of spokesperson for the reality of magic?
TT: You can't needle me into a defensive posture on the subject. I just don't care.
CA: youre not usin magic just DEAL WW IT
TT: Fine. You win.
TT: These are science wands. I am a charlatan.
CA: ok i didnt say that
CA: i think you wwear the role pretty wwell wwhich is somethin i can appreciate
CA: theres a lot of showwmanship thats put in to comin off as a diabolical sort
TT: Thanks for the insinuation that I'm making an effort to project myself as a cartoon villain. What a compliment!
CA: wwell fine you dont havve to behavve vvillainous if youre bent up on actin against the

Oh, nice. Now *here* is what I will call a truly spicy meatball to discuss. The introduction of Hussnasty Mode. Also, looks like Eridan is chatting up Rose, as the previous game implied he would. But I think we can completely ignore that in favor of this art style topic, because it's more interesting, and also, Eridan sucks. I think shortly after I started rolling out weird drawings like this, someone asked me what I called the style, and I replied by naming it "Hussnasty Mode" myself, because well...it's a bit nasty, isn't it? Kind of raw, a little over-illustrated, and making use of a lot of jagged aliased pixel edges for a hatching-type effect. It was sort of the point to make it a little nasty, kind of aggressively incongruous with the other styles previously established. It is here that I will invoke a concept that I feel was incredibly important to the ongoing production of *Homestuck*, which I will call a "creative power move." But before I go off the deep end about all that, it's important to note that drawings like this are introduced in contrast with this simple RPG sprite mode, which was also established very recently as something that *Homestuck* was "allowed" to use as a stylistic presentation of characters and settings. That's partly the point here. That every time HS does something like this, it's widening its own umbrella in terms of what it's allowed to do stylistically, which includes dramatically simplifying and abstracting its forms. Which implicitly asks another question: Can HS "allow" itself to go in the other direction? To render characters with higher degrees of definition, regardless of congruity, and freely navigate this full artistic palette at any time, resulting in sharp stylistic contrast and a certain amount of visual thrashing? The answer to that question, almost immediately after it's asked in the form of dropping RPG-sprite Rose into a standard panel shot, is yes, HS can do that, and clearly it WILL do that. -->

grain a your nobility or somesuch
CA: i can play that role its not like i evver didnt get my gils dirty before
TT: Nobility? What are you talking about?
CA: wwell arent you
TT: No. What gave you that idea?
CA: the wway you
CA: ok
CA: i had a misconclusion about that so my fault
CA: obvviously you got rich blood so maybe when you crash landed you wwerent recognized for it by wwhatevver vvehicle upholds the class structure in human society
TT: That is exactly what happened. You figured it out.
CA: must of been fuckin brutal raisin up a commonblood wwhen you knew you wwere better than evverybody and its probably got you all messed up inside but maybe theres hope for you
CA: see i got a lot a experience bein nobility so ill let you knoww if you got a shot in hell at cuttin it pinkscarf
TT: ...
CA: fakemage pinkscarf howw does that sound
TT: You're a complete idiot.
CA: see this is good i think this could be a good thing
TT: What?
CA: this thing wwe got goin
CA: you obvviously hate me and i think i got it in me to get the dark propensities smolderin
CA: and wwere both obvviously dangerous elites in nature
CA: i think theres somethin there i mean look at howw you evven came into the wworld
TT: And how was that?
CA: killed a fuckin fuck ton of marine life accidental
CA: doin thats all i evver done practically the ocean wwas my killin cauldron
TT: Accidentally?
TT: Or on porpoise?
CA: hahahahaha see youre good wwith fish puns too i got so many a those you havve no idea
CA: i just think theres a fate thing here
CA: i mean i dont mean to strike you as too forwwardsuch but are you seein wwhere im goin wwith this
TT: Oh, right. Alien romance, I forgot.
TT: Pass.
CA: look i understand you dont understand that kind of thing in your culture i get that
CA: but maybe i could teach you to get it
TT: That's really sweet of you to offer.
CA: yeah and in return maybe you could teach me howw to bullshit magic like that
TT: You want to learn magic?
CA: yes teach me your secrets wwitch
TT: Sure. Let's begin.
TT: Consider this your first lesson in showmanship.

caligulasAquarium's [CA'S] computer exploded.

--> So having said that, let's see if I can wrestle this idea of a "creative power move" into the realm of comprehensibility. *Homestuck* is full of these moves. Sometimes they come off as really overt or aggressive, as this one somewhat does. There are a few others that probably qualify, like reprinting the entire troll romance spiel, Trickster Mode, and almost all of Caliborn's submissions. Perhaps the troll pirate erotica too? I'm sure we could name more examples if we put our heads together. There are more tame or friendly examples, such as, "Hey, guess what? Today HS gets to be a playable RPG game out of nowhere, and you didn't know it could do that." Anything that pushes the envelope, challenges people, keeps them on their toes and reminds them this is neither a safe nor static enterprise. People get very comfortable with art they enjoy, particularly if it's an ongoing, regularly delivered product that lets them settle into rhythms of expectation. It starts to feel like "theirs" in some ways. The favorable experience is taking place inside them, after all, so they feel like that experience belongs to them. Which is fair. Such is human nature, to start instinctively building a possessive relationship with the art we enjoy. But as much as it *feels* this way, it simply can never be entirely true. There is the way the reader wants the work to be, as dictated by the special feelings of fondness for what they're already familiar with, and there is the way the artist wants the work to be, as an expression of their ever-evolving vision, which can include anything. So any time I felt that certain people were getting overly comfortable with the way they assumed the story needed to be, whether it was the format, narrative structure, or art style, these little power moves were deployed as a means of "pushing back" against those forces. It's a way to make frequent statements on the media's versatility, but it also turned out to be a very effective innoculation against too many people getting those overly comfortable, presumptuous feelings about what this story "needs" to be in the first place. -->

> Rose: Answer Aradia.

-- apocalypseArisen [AA] began trolling tentacleTherapist [TT] --

AA: what d0 y0u think y0ure d0ing!
AA: just st0p
AA: st0p st0p st0p st0p st0p st0p
AA: maybe if i say st0p en0ugh s0mething else will happen instead 0f the thing that d0es
TT: Hi.
AA: y0u arent g0ing t0 st0p are y0u
TT: Do you want me to stop using magic too?
AA: n0 i d0nt care ab0ut that
AA: its y0ur quest t0 tear y0ur sessi0n apart
AA: i kn0w its exciting
AA: breaking stuff
AA: and n0t w0rrying ab0ut it
AA: but there are c0nsequences t0 hum0ring y0ur destructive impulses
AA: and c0nsequences t0 f0ll0wing
TT: ?
AA: what they say
TT: Who?
AA: y0u kn0w wh0
TT: You sound frustrated.
TT: Like you know you can't change my mind.
TT: I presume your future footage of me has already verified this?
AA: i d0nt even need t0 watch y0ur future acti0ns t0 kn0w this
AA: the kn0wing is the same as this elusive feeling 0f sickness thats been with me f0r years
AA: pr0bably since bef0re i died c0me t0 think 0f it
AA: it was always a big setup
TT: You died?
TT: Revived via dream self, I take it?
AA: n0
AA: i never had 0ne
AA: s0rt 0f a special case here
TT: Hmm.
AA: i just wish
AA: back when i was behaving recklessly
AA: i had s0me0ne t0 tell me t0 st0p listening
AA: even if i ended up ign0ring their advice
AA: it w0uld have been nice
TT: What did they tell you?
AA: i was assured i w0uld be saving my race
AA: which is maybe still true i d0nt kn0w

--> But such moves do come with trade-offs. Like jarring whiplash effects, or the risk of untethering the media from previously established rhythms of coherence (to whatever extent that coherence even really existed in the first place). In short, it can make things feel just a little bit Weird. But my take on that was always that it's okay, because that's explicitly what we've always been doing here: getting a bit weird with media, staying almost pathologically loose about everything, and making the best of the situation. The next fifteen book pages are where most of the dabbling with this style took place, using the story itself as a live canvas for messing around with it. I virtually never did any sketch testing of any sort outside of the comic. The comic itself always *was* the drafting process, in a totally transparent way, which was a policy that kept it rolling out FAST. Some of these drawings feel pretty out of control, a bit uncanny when juxtaposed with the other styles. But some seemed to strike a nicer balance, like the panel on the upper right, or the one where Rose talks to Jaspersprite in a few pages. If I used this style more, I probably would have gravitated toward whatever style variant felt most successful from this stretch of panel studies. But the fact is, I mostly discontinued it after this, with only a few exceptions here and there. The main reason was that, even with the more successful panels, it just felt like it added too much drawing time to the update process. The goal wasn't just to try new, crazy things, it was also to balance that with whatever sequential art methods could be done REALLY FAST, in a sustainable way. Slowing down to overly render a face with a lot of wild, aliased hatching wasn't really the best visual trade-off for the time investment, so it kind of dropped out of the comic's toolkit. -->

AA: but if it is then it will be the punchline t0 the vast j0ke
TT: Is that anything like the ultimate riddle?
AA: y0u really d0nt understand anything yet d0 y0u
AA: and yet y0u bug and fuss and meddle
AA: with things m0re danger0us than y0u can imagine
AA: what d0 y0u want with the s0urce 0f the first guardians
AA: what g00d d0 y0u really think c0uld c0me 0f it
TT: Do you know about it?
TT: The sun?
AA: y0u cant p0ssibly wield its energy 0r put it t0 c0nstructive use
TT: That isn't exactly my plan.
AA: y0u w0nt find it either
AA: its imp0ssible
TT: How do you know that?
TT: Could you please share your information with me?
AA: n0!
AA: y0u still havent gathered that y0ure the pr0blem
AA: im thr0ugh with c0nsci0usly c0ntributing t0 inevitable 0utc0mes
TT: Well,
TT: Aren't you doing that regardless? Right now?
AA: 0bvi0usly
AA: but im just talking
AA: maybe the things i say will indirectly trigger y0ur critical acti0ns
AA: maybe n0t wh0 kn0ws
AA: maybe!!!
AA: maybe if i behave in a manner s0 rand0m
AA: parad0x space w0nt kn0w h0w t0 handle it!
AA: blah BL00P blee BLUH!@#$%^&*()_+
AA: didnt see that 0ne c0ming did y0u pspace??? +?*rand(413^612)
AA: oh look and now i suddenly refuse to type zeroes in my sentences

AA: isnt that crazy! who thought that was even a possibility
AA: bslick never would have imagined THAT little vestibule of probability was tucked somewhere in his huge glistening blow sack
AA: ribbit ribbit ribbit
AA: WILL YOU LOOK AT THAT
AA: I JUST CONTROLLED THE RIBBITS AND I DID IT DELIBERATELY
TT: O_O
AA: hahaha!
AA: 0h w0w im sure y0u were just being faceti0us with that but y0u have n0 idea h0w funny that is right n0w
AA: y0u had n0 way 0f kn0wing thats a thing i d0 all the time but with zer0es
AA: this is great
AA: i think im 0n t0 s0mething here
AA: maybe if i dig deep en0ugh int0 my circuitry and rer0ute all 0f my reserve p0wer thr0ugh my quantum based rand0m number generat0r i can pr0duce behavi0r s0 c0mpletely 0ff the wall that parad0x space will have n0 ch0ice but t0 change everything!
TT: You have circuitry?
AA: maybe i will also rig my p0wer s0urce t0 the 0utc0me 0f the functi0n and rand0mly bl0w myself up!

--> I wonder if it comes across as a deliberate creative choice that Aradia's explosive, aggressive volley of random output ties directly in a metatextual way to the sharply vacillating visual presentations of the story itself? I don't know if that's scanning in an obvious way now, and TBH it was a long time ago, so I'm not sure to what extent I was hoping it would. Anyway, that's a *pretty* strange facial rendering that this graphic freestyling has resulted in. Stuff like this is plunging us about as deep into the uncanny part of the visual curve that the story ever allows us to go. Which is probably for the best, as is the fact that it pulls way back from this style pretty soon. But pushing it this far really hammers it home as a power move, because there's no way you can come away from this style sequence and conclude that the artist gives the slightest fuck about the various measures of formalism and consistency that you might wish he would abide by to optimize the reader experience. Creative power moves that essentially send the signal, "I just don't give a fuck about ____, and you can't make me," have a twofold consequence. First, it helps regulate the attitudes of those inclined to enforce such principles of formalism, by sort of preempting the inclination for such people to even regard it as a problem. Second, as an extension of that attitude-shaping effect, it forces people to focus on what the artist intends as the most important aspects of the work. Showing the visuals as this chaotic variable send the message that, "The specific visual presentations are not that important, and things exist on such a layer of abstraction that specific visuals may not convey anything that concrete at all, except a hypothetical expression of certain underlying platonic ideals functioning as the story's basic units." Which then forces you to focus on the elements which are noticeably NON-variable, like the nature of the dialogue, the focus on characterization and profile building, the examination of certain ideas and themes. All kinds of stuff that has no intersection with adherence to formalistic patterns that are designed to make readers more comfortable with their favorite serialized entertainment product. -->

AA: that w0uld be just
AA: really
AA: really
AA: really*rand(rand(rand(rand(rand(0M)*0M)*0M)*0M)*0M) where 0M = s0me number drawn quite at rand0m fr0m 0ne 0f y0ur absurd human hats
AA: !~M~0~D~N~A~R
AA: g00dbye r0se
AA: enj0y y0ur rampant indiscreti0ns
AA: talk t0 y0u later assuming i havent rand0mly bl0wn myself up!
TT: Wait, don't go!
TT: You were actually interesting.

--- apocalypseArisen [AA] ceased trolling tentacleTherapist [TT] --

> Aradia: Randomly explode.

You fail to randomly explode.

Of course you were just venting about all that. Why would you blow yourself up on account of that silly conversation? What rational reason could you possibly have to blow yourself up, or explode from any cause for that matter, now or at any point in the near future?

It just makes no sense.

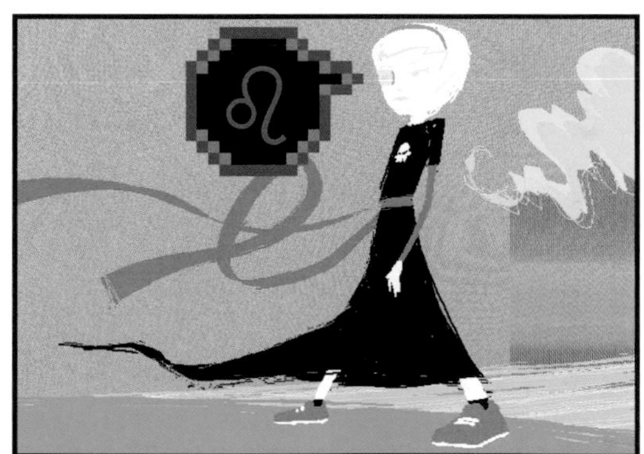

> Rose: Answer Nepeta.

--> We may conclude that, despite the extensive reasoning laid out here, the visual result of spontaneously dropping such an intense style into the comic out of nowhere could be regarded as "goofy as hell." I kinda buy that take. But there are still some things I like a lot about it. Like, if there was a comic done entirely in the art style used in righthand panel above, that could be a really fun thing to read. That high-energy, single-pixel-width scribblework in the cloud back there? Pretty good shit! But that's probably enough about Hussnasty Mode, both now and forever. We've got Nep on the line. Lots of cute BS ahoy.

-- arsenicCatnip [AC] **began trolling tentacleTherapist** [TT] **--**

AC: :33 < pst :oo
TT: Yes?
AC: :33 < heyyyyyyyyyy
TT: Why, what ever could you want?
AC: :33 < ummmmmmmmmm
TT: What could it be? I am completely confounded.
AC: :33 < sorry to bother you again!
AC: :33 < is
AC: :33 < um
TT: Is what?
AC: :33 < he available?
TT: Who?
TT: What is the name of this mystery fellow you seek?
AC: :33 < aaaaa youre just teasing me now!
AC: :33 < i f331 bad about bugging you about it
AC: :33 < but do you think you could purrhaps please spare your computer for just the most fl33ting of moments?
AC: :33 < i miss pounce a lot :((
AC: :33 < and talking to him reminds me of her
AC: :33 < sorry for the hassle
TT: It's ok. I understand.
TT: I think I have a more permanent solution.
TT: I mean purrmanent.
AC: :33 < yay! :OO

> Rose: Summon mystery fellow.

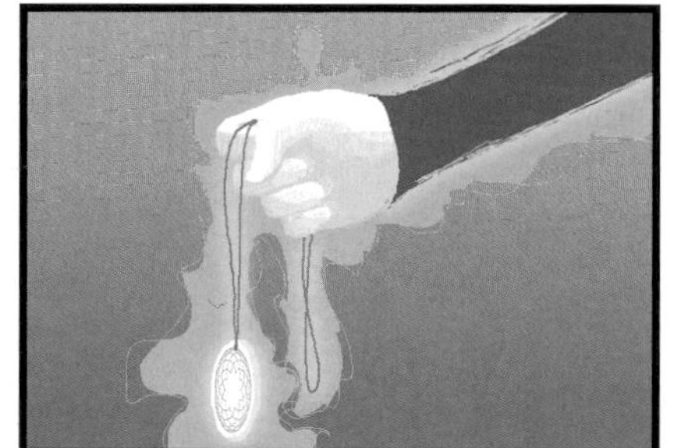

> Rose: Give Jaspersprite laptop.

You won't need it anymore. It served you well. You suppose there are a lot of things you've outgrown, now that you think about it.

I'm starting to pick up on something—I guess let's call it a running gag—that I don't remember doing. Maybe it was a subconsciously deployed running gag? The specter of "implied Nepeta conversations" is starting to haunt this half of the act. As I've mentioned before, her conversations aren't important enough to show directly. They're probably pretty funny, but there's a threshold of frivolity that a bunch of silly RP shit *just* fails to rise above, despite HS generally having no problem indulging in other kinds of frivolity. In other words, they're that pointless. So part of the gag here is, clearly Rose has talked to Nepeta. The subtext is that Nepeta may have even badgered her *so* frequently, asking if she could talk to Jaspers, that Rose plays it sarcastically, as if she can't imagine why Nepeta is bugging her again. Come to think of it, this is a clear precursor to the same running gag with Fefeta, which is dialed up to a greater extreme. She barely ever says a word in the comic, but everyone around her keeps implying that she won't shut up.

ROSE: Hi Jaspers.
JASPERSPRITE: Hi rose!
JASPERSPRITE: Purr purr purr.
ROSE: Jaspers, I am releasing you now.
ROSE: You are free to go do as you please.
JASPERSPRITE: Really rose ok if thats what you want i will go do that.
JASPERSPRITE: Oh rose!
JASPERSPRITE: Rose did you get to do any of the things that are important to your quest that i said?
JASPERSPRITE: Did you learn to play the rain rose?
ROSE: Not yet, Jaspers.
ROSE: It's a little complicated, but I believe I've embarked on another quest, one which surpasses the scope of the objectives local to this planet.
JASPERSPRITE: Meow what :3
ROSE: I'm saying there's something more important to accomplish now. Something more important than creating a universe.
JASPERSPRITE: Oh thats ok rose i wouldnt want you to feel obligated to do that.
JASPERSPRITE: I think that winning this game and getting the prize is up to you and your friends.
JASPERSPRITE: You get to decide whether or not you feel its right to do that and what kind of prize you want to make!
JASPERSPRITE: Its part of becoming who youre supposed to become i think.
JASPERSPRITE: But i really think you should consider going on the quest i said anyway!
ROSE: Why?
JASPERSPRITE: Because its not just an important thing to do to win the game.
JASPERSPRITE: I dont know i hope im not being too pushy rose its not my place to be im just your cat!
JASPERSPRITE: But the thing that made me how i am now seems to really want me to say this to you.
JASPERSPRITE: Your quest is really important for you to do.
JASPERSPRITE: Not really because thats how to get the prize.

JASPERSPRITE: But because its what you need to do for yourself!
ROSE: I see. I promise I will consider it seriously then.
JASPERSPRITE: Oh good!
JASPERSPRITE: I love you rose! I always have even when you were a little girl and i was an alive cat.
ROSE: Thanks, Jaspers, that's nice to hear.
ROSE: It's hard to remember, but I'm pretty sure I felt the same way back then.
JASPERSPRITE: It was fun getting to be your cat again rose even if it was just for a little while and also while being a princess ghost.
JASPERSPRITE: Bye rose!
ROSE: See you, Jaspers!
ROSE: If you see my mother in the course of your travels, tell her I said hello.
JASPERSPRITE: Ok I will do that! :3

> Dave: Get hassled.

Fortunately for all of us, Rose hands off the laptop to Jaspersprite so he can converse with Nepeta later, which allows us to read a more meaningful and emotional conversation right now instead. I remember a lot of people saying this conversation made them cry, and I don't remember as many people saying that about any other specific thing in the comic. I think it's just that we're getting down to something really basic and resonant here: the simple relationship between a girl and her cat, and the pure, uncomplicated love they have for each other. Too bad all of *Homestuck* couldn't be like this. Maybe then people wouldn't think I'm some sort of deranged asshole. Ah, what could have been. More plot-relatedly, Jaspers throws out some more stuff on Rose's quest for her to consider, and kind of nags her to do it. I've already talked a lot about Rose's peculiar upside-down arc. This is another one of those things that makes it feel like this quest is narratively what is demanded of her, which is the point. That it's supposed to feel that way to her, and has a strange sense of obligatory gravity surrounding it. Remember, this isn't really her beloved cat urging her to do this, it's more like the game speaking to her through her cat. Manipulative much??

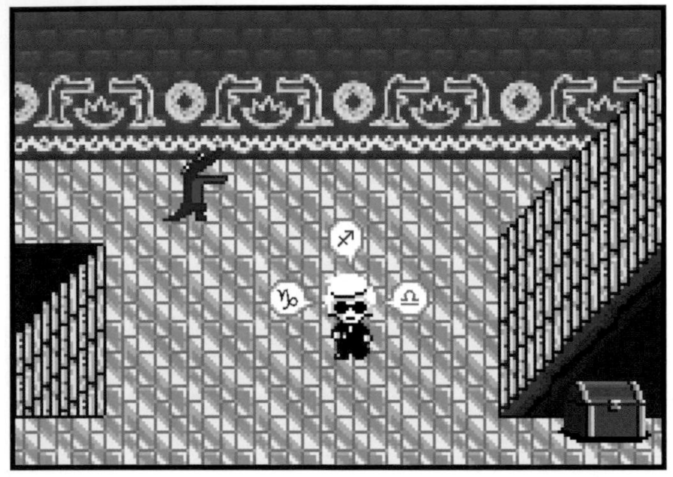

Chumps as far as the eye can see.

They are lining up for the sick fires. Your gaping furnace is hungry for coal, and they are poised to get goddamn shoveling.

> Dave: Answer Gamzee.

-- terminallyCapricious [TC] began trolling turntechGodhead [TG] --

TC: AlRiGhT My pInKeSt oF MoThErFuCkIn sTaR MoNkEyS
TC: ArE YoU ReAdY
TC: To gEt tHe hOrNs yOu dOnT HaVe
TC: CoNfIsCaTeD AlL LiKe tHe mOtHeRfUcKiN HoNkTrAbAnD ThEy aRe
TC: BeInG AlL IlLiCiT As tHe vAsT JoKe iTsElF
TC: AnD ThEn
TC: HaNdEd aT RiGhT BaCk tO YoU?
TG: what
TC: HaHa, SeE BrO, tHiS Is hOw i rOlL
TC: I SuPpLy tHe hOrNs tOwArD YoU, mEtApHoRiCaLlY SpEaKiNg
TC: SeE, lIkE
TC: ThAt's kInD Of a tRoLl mEtApHoR
TC: YoU GeTtInG YoUr hOrNs aLl hAnDeD To yOu, If yOu pEePs aNaToMiCaLlY WeRe sUcH To bE LiKe tHaT
TC: DoInG ThAt's tO MeAn lIkE YoU GoT MoThErFuCkIn sAsSeD OuT
TC: As iN TrOlLeD
TC: BuT BrO WhEn i tElL ThAt nOiSe aT YoU
TC: Im lIkE DoInG
TC: A DoUbLe mEtApHoR AlL ThE WaY

TC: AcRoSs sKaIa :o)
TC: BeCaUsE My hOrNs iM AlL AbOuT ArE ThEsE FuNnY HoNk hOrNs InStEaD oF hEaD hOrNs
TC: LiKe wHaT DoEs cLoWnS UsE
TC: AnD WhEn i'm aLl tO InViTe yOu tO GeT A LiTtLe mOtHeRfUcKiN SqUeEzE On
TC: It'lL Be a dOwNeD In, StRaIgHt fLaT, bOaRd sIdEd mIrAcLe iF YoU DoN'T GeT ScArEd sHiTtEnT ClOwNcArS
TC: ThAt's hOw wE PlAy tHe mOtHeRfUcKiN GaMe
TC: HoNk hOnK >:o)
TG: oh god thats right

It's funny how I just get done saying the Nepeta conversations are too useless to show, and then we have to plow through an entire conversation with this piece of shit and his barely legible alternating caps. I'm being disingenuous though, because we all know how important Gamzee is. At this stage, he's still a dark-horse villain, so it's easy to mistake this passage for a lot of pointless bullshit. But it's laying the groundwork for the radically game-changing Murderstuck arc coming up soon (not in this book though). I feel some obligation to keep reminding you of this now and then: LITERALLY NO ONE SAW THIS COMING. Not even one person, as far as I could tell. I spent every day scouring reactions online to all this. I guess the idea was too patently dumb? I feel like I use that to my advantage a lot. Like, "There's no way that will happen, it would be just too dumb." Sorry, suckers. Nothing is ever off the table.

TG: you were the best troll
TG: i remember now
TC: WhOa, I WaS?
TG: yeah
TG: i mean
TG: in the most ironic and hilarious ways possible
TG: but that really shouldnt even need to be said
TC: ShIt, I MuSt hAvE GoT To nOt rEmEmBeRiNg tHiS SoMeHoW
TG: it was months ago for me
TG: you did your bizarrely oblivious juggalo thing
TG: then bitched and moaned at me for ruining your religion or some horseshit
TG: like i guess a weird crisis in faith i dunno
TG: and then
TG: you kinda got over that i guess
TG: and we both proceeded to have one of the best rap-offs in the history of paradox space
TG: remember
TC: AwW MoThErFuCk, No :o(
TC: I MoSt sUrElY wOuLd gEt mY ReMeMbEr oN FoR A BiTcHtItS TiMe hAd lIkE ThAt
TC: My mInD'S NoT ThAt sHaRp nOw tHoUgH, iT'S BeEn aGeS SiNcE I HaD A GoOd pIe
TG: could be time shit
TG: you might not have had the conversation yet
TC: DoGg, I DoN'T KnOw tHaT Im aT A PlAcE To eVeN CoNtEmPlAtE FoR EnTeRtAiNiNg tHaT KiNd oF ThInG
TC: I DoN'T GeT TiMe
TC: I WaSn't tHe dUdE Of tImE
TC: I WaS ThE
TC: ThE MoThErFuCkIn
TC: BaRd oF
TC: FuCk
TC: I FoRgOt :o(
TG: do you remember if you watched any videos
TG: from earth
TG: that i might have sent
TC: nO
TG: dude i was telling you
TG: youve got to check this out
TG: trust me itll lift your spirits shit will all make sense to you finally
TG: youll finally figure out who you are and why you worship all this ridiculous clown bullshit
TC: Oh, MaN
TC: ThIs sOuNdS AmAzInG, i cAn't sEe hOw i wOuLdN'T Be aLl kIcKiNg tHe wIcKeD ShIt oUt Of sUcH KiNdS Of oPpOrTuNiTiEs
TG: and also why your planet has faygo for some baffling reason
TG: actually no nevermind it doesnt explain that
TG: that still makes no damn sense
TG: but like
TG: the thing youre looking for
TG: your dark clownish salvation or whatever the fuck
TG: your mirthful messiahs
TG: ahahahaha i cant even type that without lmao
TG: anyway theyre here dude
TG: check it out
TG: http://tinyurl.com/MoThErFuCkInMiRaClEs
TC: :oO

> Gamzee: Watch.

Up until his true aspect is revealed, Gamzee remains affectionately, or perhaps repugnantly, known as the Bard of Fuck. His true aspect, Rage, couldn't be revealed until the time was right, because it's pretty close to being a spoiler as to his true nature. Gamzee says his mind's not sharp because it's been ages since he had a pie (i.e. sopor slime). Which some readers took as implying that his withdrawal from this drug is what unleashed his violent tendencies. Hence murderous Gamzee often is fanonically referred to as "Sober Gamzee." And there is probably some truth to this, that without the sedative influence of the slime, he's naturally inclined toward violence. But I think the best explanation for Gamzee's turn is what Dave is about to do here: link him to a "Miracles" video by the Insane Clown Posse. For reasons I'll get into on the next page, I think this has a lot more to do with his transformation. Dave also boggles over why Alternia has Faygo and how that makes no sense. But we now know it makes perfect sense. It's not even remotely challenging to connect the dots. Faygo was imported to Earth by the Condesce, so as to foster her own home-grown, human-based cult of nasty clowns (ICP, and juggalos in general). She did the same thing with her own favorite soda, Tab.

This...

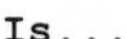

BlAsPhEmY

> Gamzee: ENGAGE HERO MODE.

This is what does it. WHY THOUGH??? /Dusts off my lectern and assumes professorial demeanor./ Gamzee is the "Juggalo Troll." If you already knew about ICP and juggalos, then his first conversation made it so glaringly obvious, it was almost impossible not to groan in recognition of this fact. The process of creating twelve trolls, each of whom embody satirical themes spoofing subcultures and various controversial internet profiles, was kind of a tall order, and it involved a bit of grasping at straws to fill out the group. The "Juggalo Troll" probably was the most egregious example of me saying, "Fuck it, we're just running with a really dumb idea here, and that's fine, because it's funny." So Gamzee's entire identity, and all characterization and points of lore surrounding him, including his absurd religion, is grounded in an especially stupid joke, even by *Homestuck* standards. So this is why being introduced to ICP finally makes him snap: it represents a collision between this satirical avatar, the fictional embodiment of this complete joke of an idea, and the fourth wall–breaking exposure to the very content he was designed to mock. On some level Gamzee understands that he's been forced to confront the fact that his entire existence is a joke. He was designed to ridicule that which he reveres. So he just fucking loses it and is never really the same guy again. It's almost a kind of dark, clowny enlightenment, an achievement of chaotic self-awareness. He quite effectively harnesses this grudge by getting revenge on the very story that created him for such humiliating satirical purposes. His method of revenge is linked to Caliborn's modus operandi (whom he comes to revere as the true godhead of his religious beliefs), which is to degrade and defile the story he inhabits. Gamzee's influence appears to be arbitrary, always occuring at the exact right (wrong) moment, to do the exact thing that will fuck things up in a totally incomprehensible way. He becomes an agent of plot chaos, of narrative entropy, and achieves a certain zen in the loathsome, capricious role he plays in the story. These tendencies are linked to his aspect, and could be seen as a certain mastery of it. Make no mistake: Gamzee sucks. He is, on a conventional layer, a "bad character." His personality is unpleasant, his actions are repellant, and his presence is always an affront to good taste and judgment. Yet, in my view, it's hard to avoid another conclusion that seems to contradict these awful truths about him: there are some potent themes and ideas governing his existence as a character, his actions, and the reasoning behind his dark turn.

This is completely pointless.

Technically, this is the panel where Gamzee turns, and never goes back to normal. It's a plot twist hiding in plain sight, disguised as a gag. Maybe if you are newer to the series, you will just refuse to believe me when I say this. But even at this point, there was *still* nobody at all who truly believed this guy was about to go nuts and kill people. You can camouflage a major story development in a lot of ways. The story throws hundreds of pounds of goofy spaghetti at the wall. It can be hard to pick up on what's supposed to be serious and what isn't. This scene just masquerades as another meaningless goof, and we quickly move away from the subject a page later. But the joke's on you if you never bought into Crazy Gamzee. This shit is real. Let's also maybe not lose sight of the fact that it's actually just plain funny that he starts murdering people? It's just a really funny thing to do with this useless idiot. Sometimes I would talk to a friend about *Homestuck* as I was making it, and would casually describe future events. Probably around this point, I just said something like, "Oh, yeah, in a couple hundred pages or so Gamzee is going to beat Nepeta to death with a juggling club." And she burst out laughing. It's totally ridiculous in the context of current story events. This guy isn't supposed to do anything important. But he announces his newfound role of influence in the story, as well as his murderous resentment for the story, by snuffing out the character who, up to that point, is the avatar for fandom enthusiasm—the one who adores the story and all things about it, the characters, relationships, etc. It is, yet again, kind of a rough-sketch concept for ideas that become more formalized through different avatars in Act 6. Caliborn, Gamzee's spiritual master, expresses the same malevolence for those ideas through his persecution and murder of Calliope.

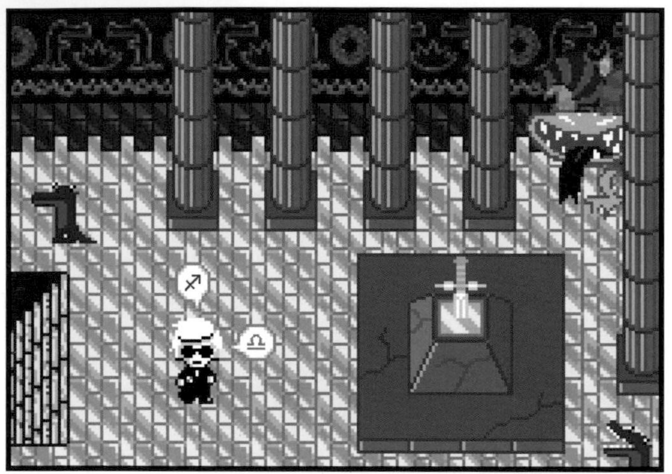

> Dave: Answer Equius.

-- centaursTesticle [CT] began trolling turntechGodhead [TG] --

CT: D --> I'm attempting to determine what it is that ranks humans in their class stru%ure
CT: D --> I'd assumed the color of your b100d would serve as the basis for placement in the hierarchy, as would be e%pected and natural, but I was mistaken
CT: D --> I was similarly in error believing the color of what you type corresponds with the color of your b100d
TG: it does bro
TG: my bloods red
CT: D --> Well, obviously
CT: D --> I understand that now, I'm not a f001
TG: on earth class is sorted out by who can drop the most delirious flow
CT: D --> I see
CT: D --> So, in other words, a sort of b100d letting ritual
CT: D --> To assess whose pulse is steadiest and thus whose flow is the most STRONG
TG: no
TG: well yeah
TG: verbal pulse
TG: rap battles
TG: the kings of wordtech ascend to godhood and look down on us patriarchally like urban watermarks in the sky
TG: this is like
TG: our religion man
TG: its fucking serious business its like what our whole culture revolves around
CT: D --> Really
CT: D --> So your social e%elons are dictated by the noble artform of the ancient slam poets
CT: D --> Or the Earth equivalent
TG: yeah well
TG: used to be dictated
TG: til the rapocalypse happened
TG: i still believe though
TG: in my heart so long as it keeps thumping the righteous beat

The ludicrous alternating tension between RPG Mode and Hussnasty Mode rages on. We even got a Hero Mode in the last panel (with the phrase "HERO MODE" printed in a repeating pattern in the background, in case you missed it). It's like an avant-garde community theater performance where one actor plays all the parts, which mainly just comes across as a single guy rolling and flailing around on the floor, screaming at himself. Ah, the complexities of the human condition. Man's inner struggle with his demons, with his mortality, with life itself. Beautiful. Hold on while I make my own struggling body pass out through a chokehold wrestling move, so I'll shut up for half a second, and talk about this great Dave/Equius conversation. This is a really good one, both for the quality of the ensuing rap-off, and the lore pertaining to Dave's quest sprinkled in here. It's another one of these presentations like when Rose was ripping apart the ruins to expose the Green Sun portion underneath, which was passively backgrounded as an idle point of curiosity, while the entertaining character interaction was foregrounded as the more relevant focus. I'd say Dave's quest lore here is treated as a *little* more important than that was, since the Dave-Equius relationship isn't actually as relevant as Rosemary's development, and this is pretty much the only time they ever talk. But it's still a good example of: foreground = fun, whimsical character driven banter; background = "important," interesting game lore and worldbuilding. Remember what I said about how the consistencies in art reveal what's important. This approach to storytelling is consistently embraced, even while the art style is overtly inconsistent.

TG: subwoofing out devotion every which way
TG: that he will come
TG: our savior
TG: was foretold hed come after meteors show up to drop it like its hot
TG: and hed gather up the ashes of our civilization and lift it like its heavy
TG: fuck im tearing up my ishades are gonna fry
CT: D --> I believe
CT: D --> That this is probably nonsense
CT: D --> I've already been hornswoggled repeatedly by your comrades, who I quite reasonably mistook for your superiors in b100dline
CT: D --> Your race makes a habit of deception, and I will not tolerate it
CT: D --> You will stop
CT: D --> I command that all verbal misdire%ion and hoofbeastplay will cease during my communications, is that understood
TG: hahahahaha
TG: douche
CT: D --> Did I say something entertaining
TG: if youre gonna spit that kind of bravado at me im just saying put it in rhyme
TG: lets hear what you got tooly mcsnoothole
CT: D --> I try to stay engaged with many aristocratic practices
CT: D --> But I'm not much of a poet
TG: come on
CT: D --> My poems are private
TG: whatever dude
TG: deprivatize them
CT: D --> If you're prepared to be particularly forceful about it
CT: D --> I may be suitably disgusted to comply
TG: just
TG: take whatevers in there
TG: that brorage lust youre feelin
TG: turn that bitch inside out like a broke ass millionaires pockets
CT: D --> Yes
CT: D --> Those are the sorts of assertive statements which could get me
CT: D --> Flowing
TG: alright
TG: weird but alright
TG: you sound wound up
TG: but my gears are airtight
TG: steer clear a the seer and the knight if youre scared of unfair fights
TG: youll drop like the staircase impaired, seein em spareds a fair fuckin rare sight
TG: for poor eyes like that millionaire whos pockets i mocked earlier
TG: hes paradoxically me but richer and surlier
TG: broke as his sword before his stock picks skyrocketed
TG: worth more than all the chests lockpicked and gold croc bricks and boonbucks i pickpocketed
TG: fillin folios with millions im milkin to pad out my pockets
TG: more chock full than sad trollian villains cloggin my blocklist
TG: so thoughtful to popul-
TG: -ate my slate with propositions to copulate to a spate of hemoerotic hotpix
TG: which i posit you got shit of that nature in spades
TG: as my shades got you locked in
TG: spyin a guy whos eyed more cocks and dicks than i got clocks and they got ticks
CT: D --> Just a thought. Let's mock a topic with less awfulness
CT: D --> If you'd use the e%cuse to be less culturally myopic, what are your views on abuse to the walking apocrypha
CT: D --> Would you choose if duly cued to put your bruising clop to a flock of naughty roboti%
TG: ahaha wow YES
TG: dont really understand that but yes
TG: ok hold that thought im gonna pull this fuckin sword out of the thing

> Dave: Pull sword out of thing.

Equius accuses Dave of "verbal misdire%ion and hoofbeastplay," but then he goes on to claim that he's not much of a poet. Which is a TOTAL LIE. His slam poetry is incredible. Also the conversation almost immediately veers in a homoerotic direction, due to Dave's frequent habit of using gay innuendo to own his targets, combined with Equius's habit of urgently insisting that others get assertive with him, making almost no effort to disguise the fetishistic nature of the demand. There are yaoi fires being stoked here in a completely plausible way. If Karkat had died, and Equius had survived instead, there's a decent chance things could have worked out a lot differently between these two.

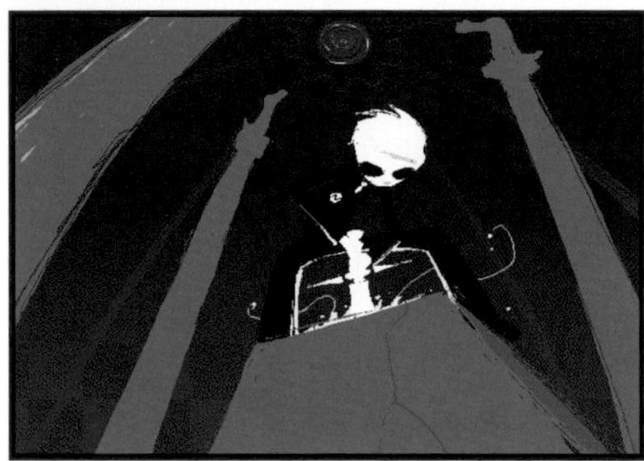

CT: D --> Perhaps it's that it's martial tacti%
that matter for status. Unless you redact this
CT: D --> I'd hazard in practice that it's a glass
of what's lactic that would impact this
CT: D --> Pragmatic to presume? A human metric for
grandness stands on fondness in honest
CT: D --> For wanton aplomb with strapping song
smithing, ripping sonnets of STRONGNESS
TG: yes
TG: still no clue what this shit means but keep
going
CT: D --> But perhaps
CT: D --> To divine class divides in unclassified
swine is butchering time
CT: D --> Your fauna I find requires too little
strength to savage in rhyme
CT: D --> I fear inferiors have monopolized my
highest priorities
CT: D --> Let's eschew crude inferiors, pursue
nude superiorities
CT: D --> Review z001ogical peculiarities, great
stalking enormities
CT: D --> Fle%ing in unison, baying at moons
within fraternal sororities
TG: holy shit
TG: what
CT: D --> Great musclebeasts tussle, bu%om in heft
CT: D --> With thunderous muscle, buttock to spec
TG: what the fuck

CT: D --> Connect blows to discover, how
invincible pecs are
CT: D --> Venture low to uncover, his inimitable
nectar
TG: oh god
TG: ok stop
CT: D --> Should song serve to placate one
CT: D --> And fortune holds he lactate some
CT: D --> STRONG hands tugging teat make great
ambrosia collectors
TG: hahaha
TG: jesus
TG: ok maybe youre actually the worst troll
TG: im thinking none of that was actually ironic
that was all pretty straightup wasnt it
CT: D --> What do you mean
CT: D --> Are you ordering me to conceal my poems
again
TG: nevermind
TG: god dammit
TG: fuckin piece of shit sword
TG: wont goddamn budge probably useless anyway
CT: D --> It 100ks to be a legendary weapon
TG: its a legendary piece of shit

CT: D --> Giving up on the treasure so easily
CT: D --> It strikes me as an artifact rooted in
universal lore of nobility

This almost feels like a slight role reversal from when Tavros trolled Dave. Tavros had no idea what he was getting himself into, got dunked on repeatedly, and ended up blocking Dave. Dave challenges Equius to a rap-off, is a little too cocky, and is completely unprepared for the fact that Equius likes to rap about huge, naked horse monsters, with loving descriptions of their anatomy and the process of milking their massive udders. But since Dave isn't a wimp like Tavros, this just earns Dave's respect, and they continue talking. Dave is satisfied enough that this guy is worth talking to about his quest lore. So, let's talk about that as well. -->

CT: D --> As valuable an asset as strength is
CT: D --> And as much as anyone with his wits is fond of being STRONG
CT: D --> Such weapons require finesse to operate
CT: D --> And surely in this case, to retrieve without damaging
CT: D --> Hence your no doubt frustrating restraint
TG: ok im kinda starting to wonder why youre bugging me now
TG: youre a fuckin creepy dude
CT: D --> E%cessive force will shatter such weapons
CT: D --> We both know this from e%perience
TG: what
CT: D --> The adult human who trained you
CT: D --> And taught you the ways of being STRONG
CT: D --> Remember
TG: you mean the guy who spent years beating my ass down with a puppet
TG: yeah i remember
CT: D --> Yes, and now, being learned in the ways of STRONGNESS
CT: D --> You like myself are unfortunately limited in the weaponry you may wield
CT: D --> Ironically the training which has ennobled you beyond others has made instruments of high b100d brittle in your hands
CT: D --> Hence the state of your favored weapon, hobbling your specibus
CT: D --> I know what this is like
TG: man
TG: im not that strong ok
TG: just cause i broke a cheap ass sword doesnt make me the fucking hulk
CT: D --> Oh
TG: what did you go around breaking a bunch of swords too
CT: D --> No
CT: D --> Bows
TG: how the fuck do you even wield a broken bow
TG: did you go around clubbing shit with the two halves
CT: D --> Yes
CT: D --> Sometimes

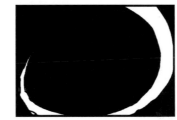

CT: D --> What are you doing
TG: whats it look like
CT: D --> Careful
CT: D --> About succumbing to these sorts of destructive
CT: D --> Urges
CT: D --> Addi%ion is a powerful thing
TG: so am i
TG: bow down before your new king bitch

--> The session always "knows" things about players. It knows Karkat has blood issues, so it gave him a planet full of bright red blood. It knows Dave has a thing about broken swords, which is tied up with his personal mythology related to the intersection between intense combat training for his destined role as a warrior, and deeply traumatizing abuse which causes him to resist the call to such heroism. He cites said abuse in the text above, in case there's any doubt this issue has been inseparably woven into the lore of his arc at an early stage. There's a lot to say about the broken sword as a symbol. I've probably already touched on it in earlier books. But what fucking good am I down here if I'm not willing to repeat myself? It's a complex symbol. First, there are two symbolic modes, an "Unbroken Sword" and a "Broken Sword," which have meaning in relation to each other. The simplest translation is that the unbroken sword is "The fully manifest, wholly embraced heroic arc. Suppressing reservations, answering the call, putting the tough training to use, despite the cost to oneself." Versus the broken sword, which is "The fractured heroic arc. An incomplete, broken self stemming from past trauma. A conflicted semi-refusal of the call, resulting in pursuit of combat and quest-fulfillment navigated through half-measure, wavering resolve, and compromised investment." Only one of these symbols can be fully embraced, and it means something to embrace one over the other. It becomes a statement Dave is making about himself, and the type of person he wants to be. But the statement has to be understood by him to be meaningful, and this understanding comes through his long-term inner reflections over his arc. The game also seems to provide frequent clues to help him understand these symbols and choices. It keeps offering up broken swords, or more specifically, a whole sword that can only be obtained by figuring out how to break it. -->

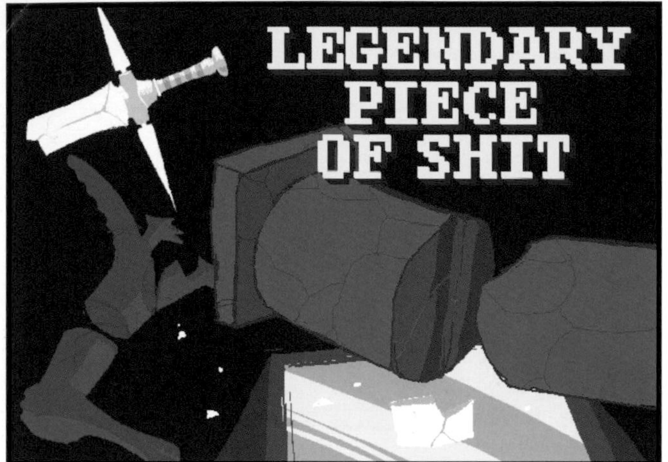

CT: D --> I think
CT: D --> I need
CT: D --> Something to dry myself off with

> Equius: Dry off.

> Dave: Take legendary POS.

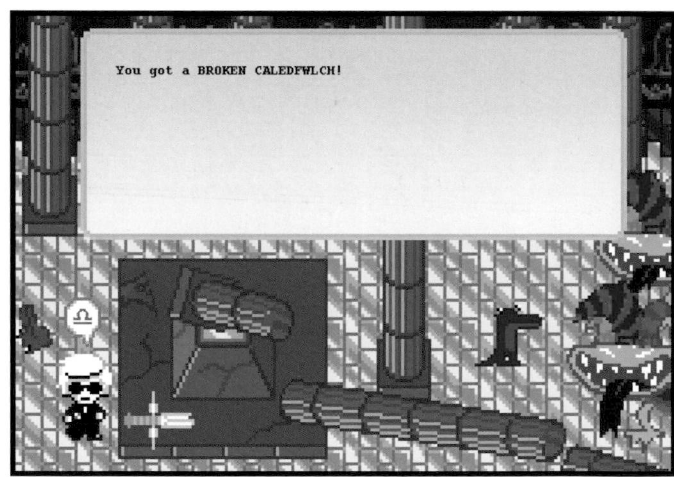

> Dave: Answer Terezi.

--> So here's a spin on the Arthurian legend (Caledfwlch is another name for Arthur's Excalibur) where the sword, instead of being removed through strength or the divine touch of a chosen one, must be broken to be freed. There's no other way, since this is how this game challenge was designed to be solved. It says, "This is a symbol for your heroic journey, and to some extent, who you are as a person. Now, what will you do with it?" In the long run, this sword-based *Sburb* quest does appear to have a formal endpoint, which is Dave using this sword to have his denizen forge the Royal Deringer, a much fancier mythical sword. And in forging that sword, he "heals" it, converting it to an unbroken sword symbol. Heroic arc, back on track, right? Except to wield *that* sword, Dave has to break it too, simply by touching it, as if his identity being linked to a broken sword is inescapable. There are ways of reading into what this means. Maybe it's that making yourself whole as a person isn't so simple? Maybe it's that Dave embracing the broken sword as his heroic talisman corresponds with his embracing who he is as person, flaws and all? Those things aren't going away, and they contribute to making him who he is. Similar to Rose's arc, which is more about embracing her imperfect sense of humanity rather than satisfying an external sense of obligation that includes the false promise of repairing the flaws of a damaged person through a path of shallow narrative regimentation. There are echoes of "two people who can't be fixed, and that's okay" in each other's arcs, but a lot of differences in the way their respective roads are paved to reach the destination. -->

-- gallowsCalibrator [GC] **began trolling turntechGodhead [TG] --**

GC: D4V3 GR34T N3WS!
GC: 1 FOUND 4 DR4W1NG T4BL3T
GC: DO YOU KNOW WH4T TH4T M34NS D4V3?
GC: DO YOU KNOW WH4T 1T M34NS W3 C4N G3T?
TG: please dont say this party started please dont say this party started
GC: TH1S
GC: P4RTY
GC: ST4RT3D!!!!! >8D
TG: god everything is about parties with you
GC: D4V3 TH3R3 1S NOTH1NG 3V3N CLOS3 TO B31NG B3TT3R TH4N P4RT13S, COM3 ON
TG: ok
TG: lets see some fine art then
GC: WHY 1T JUST SO H4PP3NS TH4T 1 H4V3 4 FR3SH M4ST3RP13C3 FOR YOU
GC: HOT OFF TH3 C4NV4S
GC: 4ND ON TO YOUR COMPUT3R GL4SS3S
GC: WH3R3 1T W1LL S1ZZL3 YOUR 3Y3B4LLS
GC: TSSSSSSSSSSSSSS http://tinyurl.com/D4V3XD4V3

--> Pausing Dave's arctalk to nod toward Terezi's elegant, deeply insightful artwork. Does she have some sense of instinctive empathy for Dave's plight? Is that partly what drives the attraction? Maybe she can smell his arc, as one which foists this struggle of self-acceptance, self-healing, self-love upon an absolutely crushingly cool, cool, coolkid. *SBaHJ* comics, and other creations of this nature, draw from a deep reservoir of highly perceptive apprehension of one's own condition, as well as others. What else to say about the matter of Dave's sword arc? Probably lots, but there's plenty more material in future books to obsess over down here. There's one other thing that springs to mind about the sword as a symbol, taking into consideration that a lot of these symbols are pretty multi-faceted and have ways of going through transformative evolutions as the story progresses. As a clue, look at the solution to this "sword in the stone" puzzle, and how unconventional it is relative to the original myth. It's reckless, destructive, a speedy end run around a situation that traditionally demands finesse or divine providence. So the broken sword doubly serves as a symbol for Dave's approach to this heroic journey, which isn't one he chose. (Rose blazed the trail of this destructive path, which then anchored the whole group to it via forces of predestination.) In other words, the solution to the sword puzzle was built to demand a hack. It's a microcosm for the solution to everything in this session, and the way the kids are destined to play it. Nobody is playing this thing totally straight.

002833

TG: ok that
TG: is every bit as shitty as all your other drawings
GC: SHUT UP!
GC: 1 4M ST1LL SORT OF G3TT1NG TH3 H4NG OF TH1S TH1NG
GC: 1 W1LL G3T B3TT3R >:P
TG: i like it though you dont gotta improve
TG: art skills are overrated
GC: TH4NKS D4V3
TG: its kind of weird though what the hell is actually going on here
TG: does this mean something
GC: Y3S
GC: 1T 1S TH3 COM1C R3PR3S3NT4T1ON OF TH3 N3XT L3G OF YOUR WOND3RFUL JOURN3Y
GC: YOU KNOW, TH3 ON3 TH4T 1 4M H3LP1NG YOU W1TH 3V3RY ST3P OF TH3 W4Y >:]
TG: yeah
TG: but
TG: why
GC: 1 4LR34DY 3XPL41N3D TH1S TO YOU D4V3
GC: TH3 COOLK1D H4S TO B3 TH3 B3ST, 4ND 1 H4V3 TO M4K3 H1M TH3 B3ST
TG: alright but
TG: i mean even if that made sense which it kind of doesnt
TG: karkat was saying how it was all a game and youre just flirtin and stuff
TG: and that we should quit it because he doesnt want you in my grill or me in yours or whatever
GC: OH, 1S TH4T WH4T H3 S41D???
GC: HMM 1 WOND3R 1F H3 COULD R33K OF J34LOUSY 4NY MOR3 PUNG3NTLY
TG: well yeah thats what i thought too
TG: and really if we got no other reason keep rolling with it at least theres that one
TG: to piss him off
GC: W3LL WH4T DO YOU TH1NK D4V3
GC: 4M 1 1N YOUR HUM4N GR1LL?
TG: im not saying i know for sure but it seems to me like
TG: my grill is your goddamn prison
TG: you are practically incarcerated in that fucker
TG: doing hard time on a bed of charcoal and lighterfluid
TG: privy to what i flame broil from below
TG: what im sayin is you got a front row seat to the brown side of my burger
TG: hows it smell btw
GC: 1T SM3LLS L1K3 D3L1C1OUS BURN1NG 4N1M4LS
TG: yeah i thought so
TG: so is that whats going on
GC: WH4T?
TG: is this some weird game involving flirtation and assassinations or whatever
GC: OH, 1 DONT KNOW
GC: M444444YB3...
GC: SH33SH!
GC: YOU 4ND H1M 4R3 4L1K3 1N SOM3 W4YS
GC: R34LLY BLUNT 4ND L1T3R4L M1ND3D
GC: 4ND QU1T3 FR4NKLY JUST 4 L1TTL3 B1T T4CTL3SS WH3N 1T COM3S TO M4N4G1NG TH3 L4D13S!
GC: H3 4LW4YS H4D TO KNOW 3X4CTLY WH4T TH3 D34L W4S 4ND 3X4CTLY WH4T MY MOT1V4T1ONS W3R3 4ND WH4T 3V3RYTH1NG M34NT 4ND BLUH BLUH BLUH
GC: 1T T4K3S TH3 FUN OUT OF 3V3RYTH1NG!
TG: thats pretty much the most insulting thing possible to say im anything like that raving gulf of shit
GC: W3LL OK 1M SORT OF 3X4GG3R4T1NG
GC: BUT R34LLY
GC: SOM3 S1M1L4R1T13S 4R3 TH3R3
GC: 1TS JUST YOUR 1SSU3S 4R3
GC: COOL3R >:]
GC: L3SS R1D1CULOUS 4ND TR4G1C
TG: issues
TG: what are you talking about
GC: W3LL, FOR 1NST4NC3
GC: K4RK4T W4S 4LW4YS TORM3NT3D BY H1S P4ST 4ND FUTUR3 S3LV3S
GC: 4ND TH31R M1ST4K3S
GC: L1T3R4LLY TORM3NT3D BY TH3M 1N TH3S3 4BSURD SCH1ZOPHR3N1C M3MOS
GC: 1T W4S 1D34L FU3L FOR H1S S3LF LO4TH1NG
GC: H3 B3C4M3 OBS3SS3D W1TH H1MS3LF 4S 4N 3LUS1V3 4DV3RS4RY
GC: R4TH3R TH4N JUST B31NG H1MS3LF 1N TH3 MOM3NT 4ND R34L1Z1NG WHO H3 W4S SUPPOS3D TO B3
GC: 4ND W4K1NG UP >:[
TG: wow ok what does that have to do with me
GC: NOTH1NG 1N 4 L1T3R4L S3NS3
GC: BUT 1 H4V3 OBS3RV3D YOU D4V3

Earlier I was pointing out how Daverezi had the air of someone (Terezi) finding a new person (Dave) to rebound with who seems fun and refreshing in the ways that contrasted with an aggravating ex. But then, after spending a little more time with Dave, she starts pointing out some similarities to Karkat, as if to note that maybe they aren't so dissimilar after all. Ain't that the way it is for some people, with their dating track record tracing a line through a whole bunch of guys who just end up being variations on the same basic type of guy. On the other hand, like she says here, she's sort of exaggerating these commonalities, perhaps to continue owning Dave, or maybe in a way, to own herself. There's a shadow consequence in pointing out the similarities between Dave and Karkat, which is beginning to pave the very long road that ends up in the heart of Davekat City. I'm not pretending that was "the plan" at this moment. God, what sort of bullshit artist do you take me for????? But establishing foundational similarities in their profiles, in the struggles they have with themselves, provides for a much stronger base compatibility, which makes the outcome more likely (and also welcome, to many). So what are their similarities? Terezi goes so far as to list some of them here. Could she actually be the first Davekat shipper ever, even as she actively courts Dave herself? Wow. I just blew my own mind, and yours. Let's consider Terezi an allegorical figure for the Daverezi shippers of this era, who would eventually turn out to be Davekat shippers, without having the slightest clue they were Davekat stans all along.

GC: YOU 4R3 4LW4YS G3TT1NG B41L3D OUT OF J4MS
GC: 4T F1RST BY YOUR BRO
GC: 4ND TH3N BY YOUR OWN FUTUR3 S3LV3S!
GC: 3V3N FUTUR3 D4V3SPR1T3 G3TS 1N ON TH3 4CT OF SHOW1NG UP POOR OLD PR3S3NT D4V3
GC: WH3N DO3S PR3S3NT D4V3 G3T TO ST3P OUT OF TH3 SH4DOW OF 4LL THOS3 FUTUR3 D4V3S??
GC: WH3N DO3S H3 G3T TO B3 TH3 H3RO, TH4T'S WH4T 1 W4NT TO KNOW >:D
TG: i dunno i guess maybe when i become future me
GC: H4H4H4H4H4H4
GC: TH4T 1S 3X4CTLY WH4T K4RK4T US3D TO S4Y
GC: 1T W4S 4LW4YS TH3 4NSW3R
TG: fuck who cares
TG: like i even give a shit about being a hero whatever that even means
TG: im not seeing the problem here future me is awesome he can bail me out if he wants
GC: Y3S, 3X4CTLY!
GC: B3C4US3 YOU 4R3 COOL 4BOUT YOUR PROBL3M
GC: 1NST34D OF 4CT1NG L1K3 4 S1LLY L1TTL3 PUP4
GC: BUT DONT WORRY, ON3 D4Y YOU W1LL G3T TO T4K3 YOUR TURN 4S H3RO!
GC: 4ND ON3 D4Y
GC: YOU W1LL T4K3 OFF THOS3 DUMB GL4SS3S 4ND L3T M3 G3T 4NOTH3R SN1FF 4T YOUR 3Y3S
TG: not gonna happen
GC: COM3 ON!
GC: 1 ONLY GOT ON3 L1TTL3 WH1FF 4T TH3M
GC: WH3N YOU W3R3 4 T1NY P1NK W1GGL3R W1TH 4RMS 4ND L3GS S1TT1NG 1N 4 CR4T3R ON TH4T S4D HORS3 YOU 4T3
GC: TH3Y W3R3 PR3TTY!
GC: 1T 1S SO S3LF1SH OF YOU TO K33P TH3M COV3R3D UP
GC: 4ND TH3 L4M3 S3CR3CY SURROUND1NG 1T 1S ONC3 4G41N R3M1ND1NG M3 OF 4 C3RT41N YOU KNOW WHO >:|
TG: hey look at this change of subject going down
TG: about this comic
TG: are you saying im about to fall asleep
GC: Y3S
TG: why
GC: 1 DO NOT KNOW
GC: M4YB3 YOU 4R3 R34LLY T1R3D!
GC: YOU DROP SUDD3NLY 4ND SW1FTLY, L1K3 4N 3X3CUT3D F3LON F4C1NG N4PPY JUST1C3
TG: i dont feel tired

TG: could be rose waking me up again
TG: bonkin me with yarn or some shit
GC: OH?
TG: can you see in my dreams
GC: NO >:[
TG: too bad
TG: last time i promised rose id take off my shades and look in the sky for some reason
TG: youre gonna miss a hell of a show
GC: BLUUUUUUUUUUUUUUUHHHHHHH >XO
GC: MOST 4WFUL COOLK1D!!!!!
TG: so i guess i have to summon davesprite too
GC: Y3S
TG: whys that
GC: WHY DO YOU TH1NK!
GC: TO B41L YOUR STUBBORN SP3CT4CL3D BUTT OUT OF TROUBL3 4G41N
TG: huh
TG: ok
GC: WH3N YOU 4R3 4SL33P, SOON 4 HORD3 OF V3RY POW3RFUL MONST3RS W1LL 3M3RG3 FROM TH3 RU1NS
GC: TO D3F3ND TH3 TR34SUR3 YOU H4V3 STOL3N
GC: OR D1D YOU TH1NK YOU W3R3 GO1NG TO W4LTZ OUT OF H3R3 W1TH TH4T COOL L3G3ND4RY SWORD 4ND F4C3 NO CONS3QU3NC3S?
TG: yeah kinda
TG: didnt think this useless horseshit was boss grade loot to be honest
GC: W3LL 1T 1S!
GC: NOW R3L34S3 M1ST3R OR4NG3 CR34MS1CL3S, ST4T
GC: 4ND H4V3 DR34MS 4S SW33T 4S H3 T4ST3S >:]

A Hussnasty portrait looms over this body of dialogue. Does that mean something psychologically intense is being discussed?? It probably just means that one was done of Rose, therefore one should be done of Dave as well to satisfy certain invisible demands of parallelism. That's all. There's been so much meta-talk of Dave "resisting the call" already, it's almost easy to forget it hasn't even really showed up much yet in the text of the comic. But we see it starting to creep into play here. And once it starts playing out, that sort of bullshit is so familiar to us, no matter how it's delivered in practice, that it sort of phones itself in. And Dave knows this too, as a savvy media consumer, which is partly why he finds it so embarrassing. We see this dynamic a lot in the future, this "like i even give a shit about being a hero" combined with "oh god i cant believe im doing the reluctant hero shtick im such a fucking cliche," which then turns into even more fodder for self-doubt and incrimination, in a ridiculous, hyper self-aware feedback loop. But for now, it's only just beginning, and it has not yet occurred to Dave that he's committing the sin of becoming a cliche.

TG: ok see ya

> Dave: Summon Davesprite.

DAVE: sup
DAVESPRITE: hey

DAVESPRITE: oh looks like you got caledfwlch
DAVESPRITE: you found that pretty fast
DAVE: is that how you pronounce that
DAVESPRITE: yeah i guess so
DAVESPRITE: i think its welsh
DAVE: what are welsh things doing in this game
DAVESPRITE: thats an awesome question
DAVE: fuck yeah it is
DAVE: is this thing as pointless as i think it is or do i need it for something
DAVESPRITE: tactically yeah its a downgrade since its what i used to make caledscratch which is obviously way better
DAVE: yeah thats what i figured
DAVESPRITE: caledscratch cycles the sword through its own timeline to points when its broken or nonbroken or old and rusted or recently forged etc
DAVESPRITE: and your snoop snowcone swords probably even better than that so yeah you got options

DAVE: fuck it ill just power through the rest of the game with the SORD.....
DAVESPRITE: hahahaha
DAVESPRITE: with unreal air as a mount fit for a true artifact knight

A Welsh element is in this game only because I used a Welsh variant on the name for Excalibur. That's basically why things from certain countries appear in this cosmic universe-creation engine steeped in ancient lore and myth. Because basically ALL things we know of come from various countries, which have long histories full of their own stories, and that's how we establish the underpinnings of our mythological knowledge base and entire frame of reference in the first place. Wow, this is an incredible point I'm making??? All things you know of come from one damn country or another. Someone should make me the fucking superprofessor of all Ivy League universities at once. *Sburb* is rife with lots of Greco-Roman elements (see next page), Gnostic elements, and so on. The names of things trace back to those mythic origins, and sometimes an alternate name like the Welsh variant for Excalibur is used so as not to be way too on the nose. Because if Dave learned from a crocodile something like "oh guess i need to go find excalibur... wait isnt that just the damn sword in the stone" then that kind of blows it, doesn't it? Another name for Excalibur, intriguingly enough, is Caliburn. Which, yes, you are absolutely guessing correctly that this word was the basis for naming Caliborn. Why was he named after a variation of Dave's magic sword? There's a good and very extensive explanation for that, I promise. By now you'd have to be utterly certifiable to doubt me on that. Just a complete lunatic. But now is not the time for that dissertation!!!!!! You're just gonna have to hold your horses for when the Best Boy is in the house.

DAVE: yeah
DAVE: goddamn jpeg hero
DAVE: right here
DAVESPRITE: did that shit ever land or what
DAVE: dude its long gone
DAVE: up in skaia now or something
DAVE: thrashing ill grinds on clouds
DAVESPRITE: fuck
DAVESPRITE: top priority make more
DAVESPRITE: thats an order from your celestial fuckin spirit guide
DAVE: yeah you got it
DAVE: so why wasnt this legendary pos in the sylladex you gave me
DAVE: did you chuck it after you alchemized it
DAVE: should i just chuck it too
DAVESPRITE: it was stolen
DAVESPRITE: by one of hephaestus's minions
DAVE: hes the denizen right
DAVESPRITE: yeah lord of the forge
DAVE: isnt that like a greek god
DAVE: or roman or whatever
DAVE: what is greco roman shit doing in here you know what never mind
DAVESPRITE: yeah pretty much
DAVESPRITE: anyway he gets pissed off you broke it
DAVESPRITE: and he wants it back
DAVESPRITE: to do something important with it though not really sure what
DAVESPRITE: hes a pretty ornery dude
DAVESPRITE: kept raving about how he was waiting for the forge to come
DAVESPRITE: which he needs to complete his work
DAVESPRITE: but in my timeline the forge would never come
DAVESPRITE: so he was extra pissed off
DAVE: whats the forge
DAVESPRITE: volcano
DAVE: huh
DAVE: you mean jades volcano
DAVESPRITE: yup
DAVE: so do you know this stuff cause youre from the future or cause youre a sprite
DAVESPRITE: both
DAVESPRITE: theres all sorts of stuff i suddenly knew about the game when i became this orange feathery asshole
DAVE: so now youre like
DAVE: a wise feathery asshole
DAVESPRITE: i am fuckin filthy with wisdom its sick
DAVESPRITE: i mostly know stuff about your personal quest
DAVESPRITE: what used to be my quest but i guess i got to deal with not being alpha dave no more
DAVE: yeah i guess
DAVESPRITE: shrug
DAVESPRITE: its all good
DAVESPRITE: anyway that sword
DAVESPRITE: its important to getting your shit figured out
DAVESPRITE: you were supposed to break it to get it out of the thing
DAVESPRITE: like another personal sort of mythological milestone you were supposed to clear
DAVE: really
DAVE: there was no other way to get it out
DAVE: thats kind of retarded
DAVESPRITE: well i dont know
DAVESPRITE: maybe if john was to try with his pure heart and shit it woulda popped out like a champagne cork and fuckin hero confetti woulda blasted him in the face
DAVESPRITE: but you
DAVESPRITE: we
DAVESPRITE: we had to break it
DAVE: ok
DAVESPRITE: theres a lot more i know about your quest
DAVESPRITE: all tangled up in ridiculous riddles and bullshit enigmas
DAVESPRITE: and maybe its all a moot point anyway in this timeline who knows
DAVESPRITE: but i think ill spare you all that crap
DAVESPRITE: cause its kind of boring
DAVESPRITE: and youll find out anyway
DAVE: yeah
DAVE: that sounds about like something id do if i were you
DAVE: which i am

Davesprite explains a bunch of facts about the sword quest which I already explained, but his wisdom doesn't include any of the Deep Meta that I just rolled out. So who's wise now, bird boy?! That's right, not you. It's me. Too bad I couldn't personally serve as Dave's spiritual guide. There is no limit to how cool he could have been.

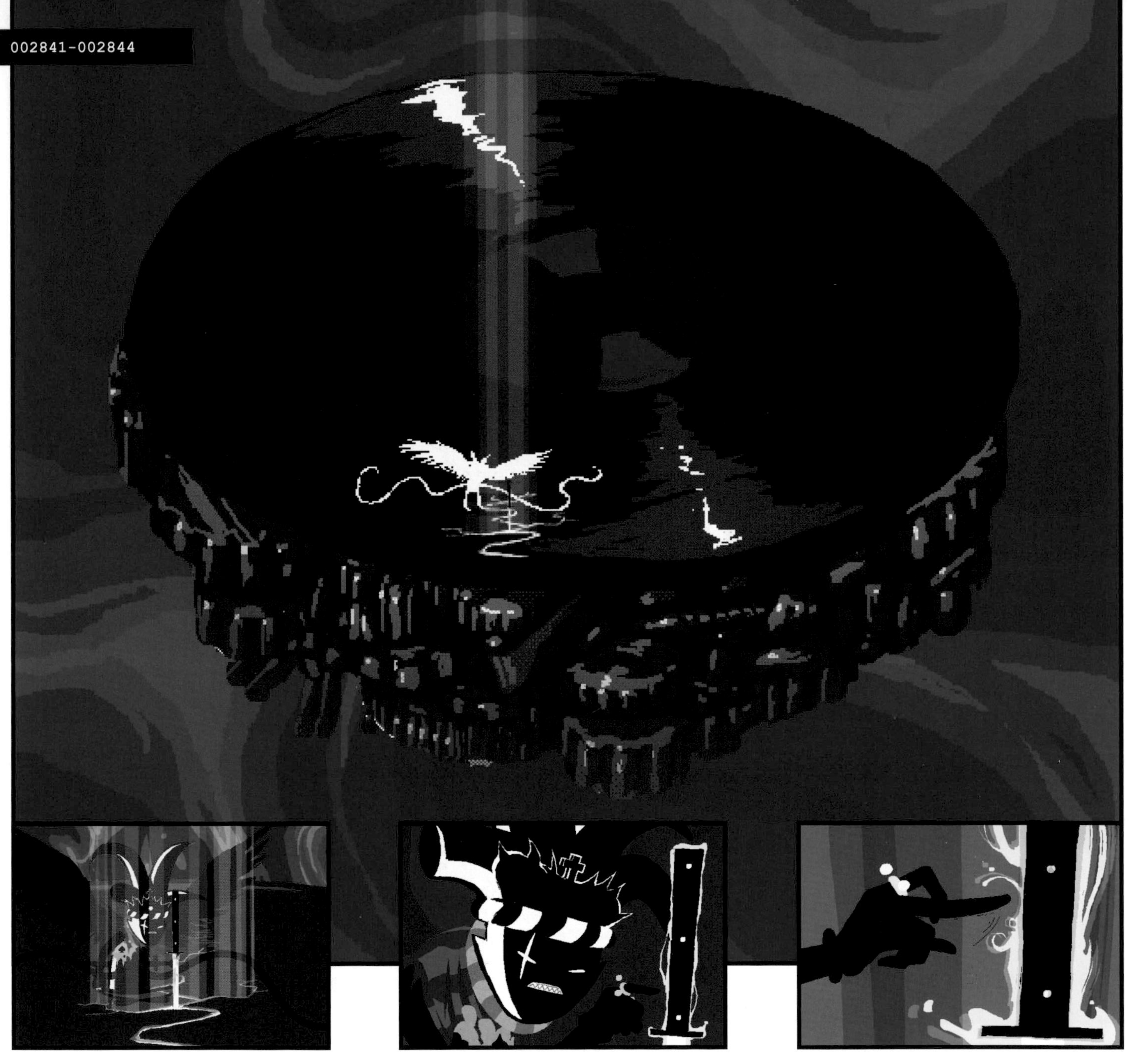

We last saw Bro and Jack dueling on this record platform, a.k.a. the Beat Mesa. That was during **[S] Descend**. Bro rather melodramatically stabbed his sword into this thing as sort of a hint to everybody about what needs to be done. Kind of a mini-scratch here, just to get the ball rolling. We didn't see where Bro went, though. Like Davesprite said, the guy's inscrutable. But Jack is clearly impressed. You can almost feel the man-crush percolating in his black, murderous soul as he inspects the mysterious energy enveloping this cool dude's rad anime sword. Clearly he has unfinished business with the man.

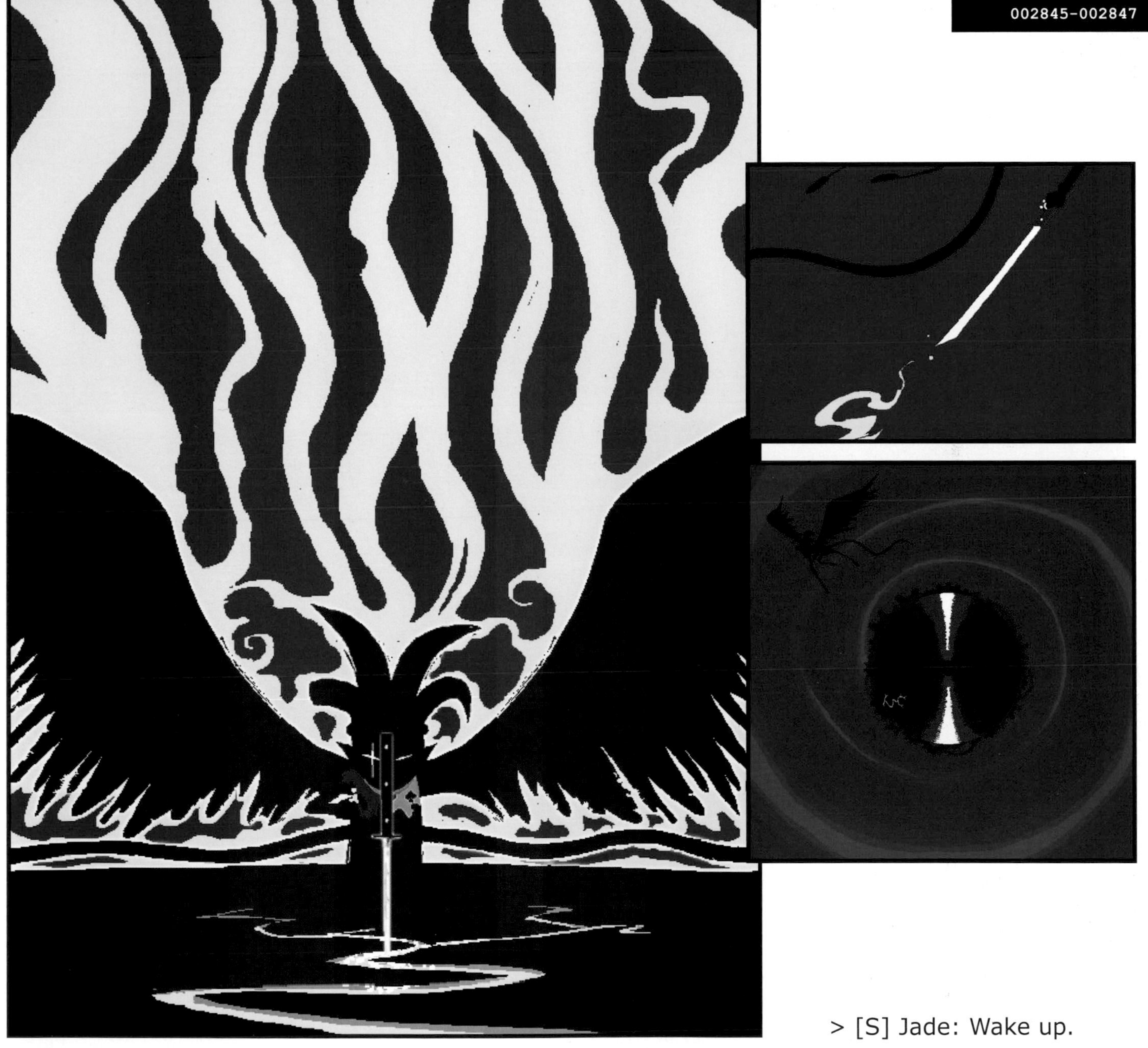

> [S] Jade: Wake up.

You know you've gotten into someone's head when, after you've finished dueling with him, you pull some sick move leaving your sword behind in the process, and the guy GOES TO THE BOTHER OF RETURNING YOUR SWORD, just so the two of you can finish your duel. Jack even has to go flying all over the damn place looking for Bro just to return the sword and resume the fight. "Hey, man. Yeah, you left this back there. I dunno if you MEANT to leave it stuck in that big record, or... So, you doing anything now? I mean, I'm not that busy, if you want to like, have another sword fight or... Oh, you ARE busy? So, what, like, tomorrow? Or...hey, that's cool. Look, it's not like I CARE. You think I CARE about having another stupid sword fight with you? Pff. Like I could even give a shit." ... "So, are we confirmed for tomorrow then? What time was that? I'm good whenever. Just...let me know, ok man?"

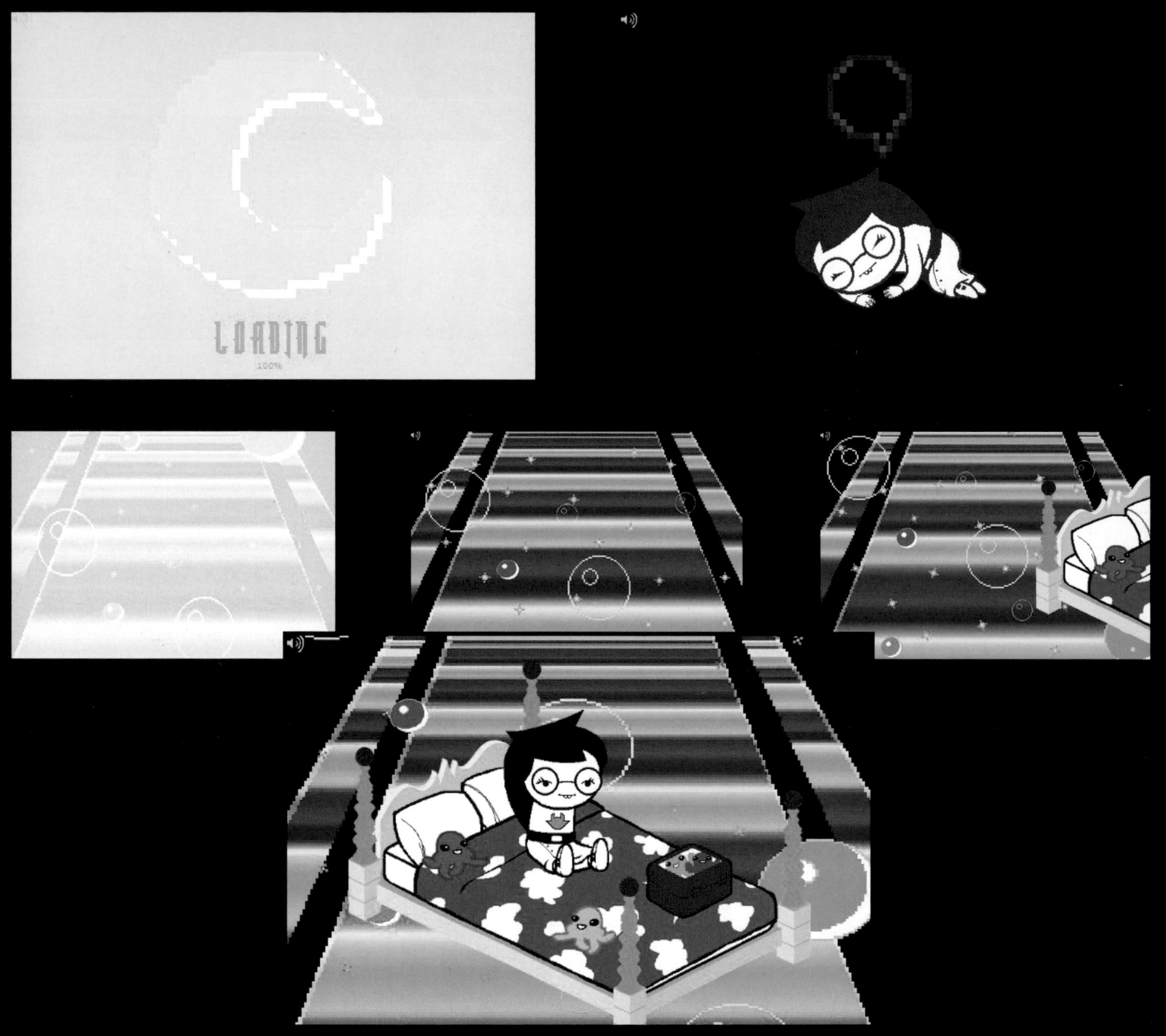

The book absolutely does not do justice to **[S] Jade: Wake up.** It's a much more "experiential" Flash than usual. Though nothing actually really "happens"? We get a glimpse at what it's like to have a Dark Nap, that is, to dream without a living dream self. I.e. the experience that Karkat was so upset about. It's a journey through madness. Kind of an audio-visual nightmare, with an obnoxiously escalating wall of noise. Probably a decent cinematic comparison would be when Willy Wonka took everybody through his weird tunnel of psychotic lunacy for some reason.

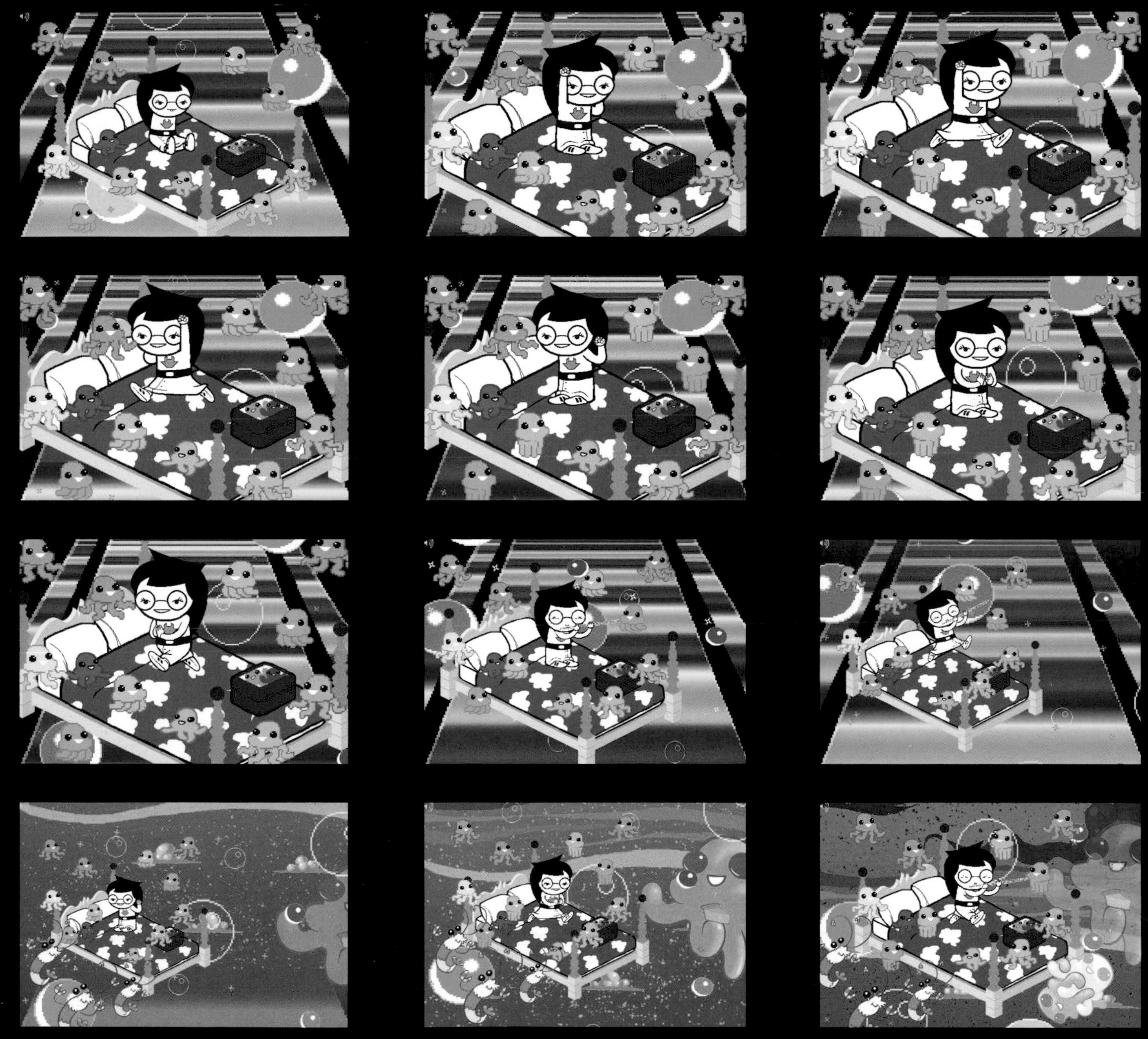

But as you can see, it all starts out pretty nice. Jade first imagines she sees a candy-coated version of this disturbing eldritch abyss. Literally: it's a Trickster facade. Squiddles canonically are known to be Trickster Horrorterrors. A perception of the beasts that is friendlier and more comprehensible to mortal minds. The illusion doesn't last long, though.

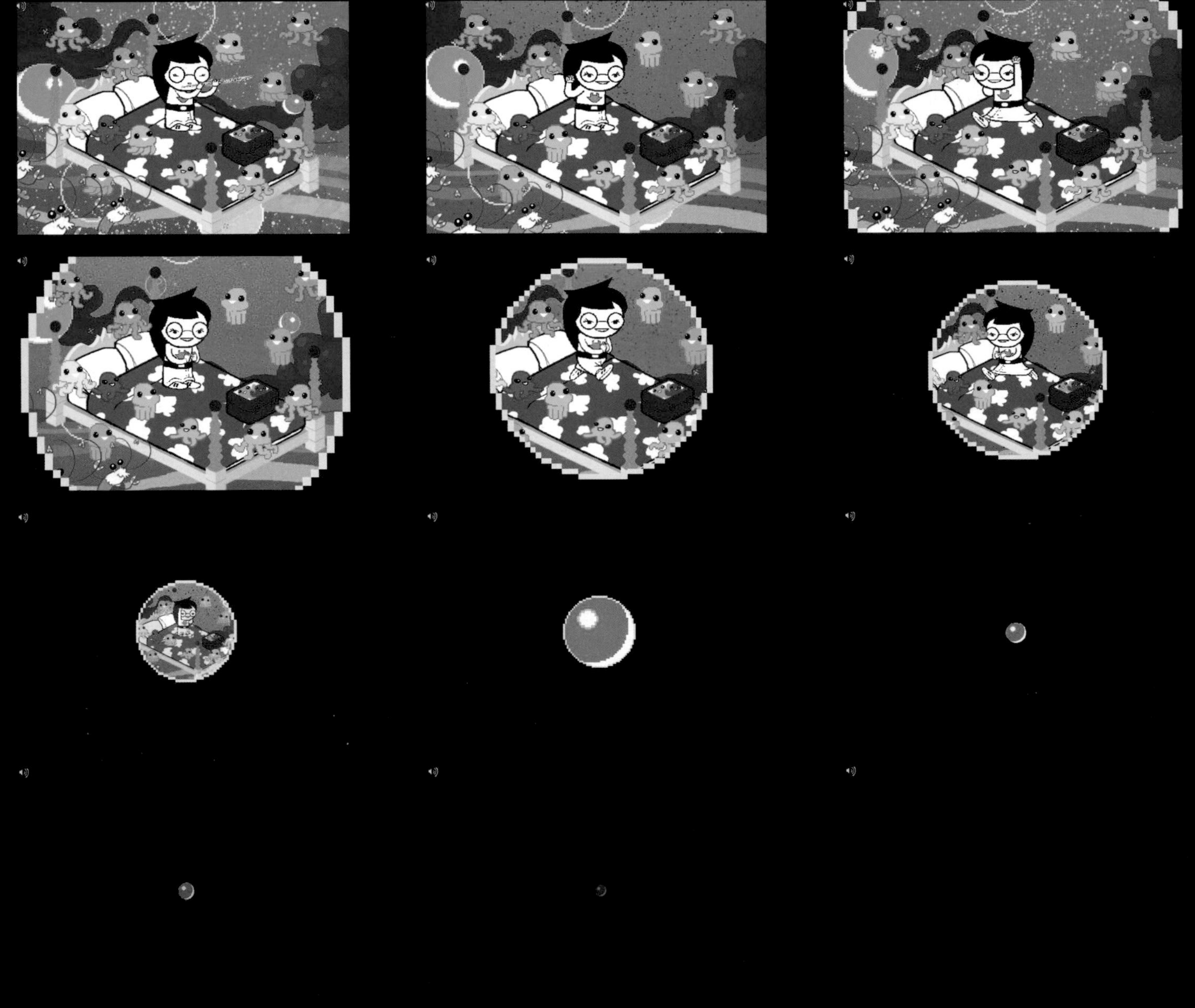

This is probably the first visual indication that the concept of dream bubbles exists. They don't usually look like this one, which is a low-fi pixel bubble in keeping with the fantasy it projects inside for Jade. Horrorterrors blow these bubbles, each of which serves as a little phantasmal oasis floating freely through the infinite, existentially unforgiving desert of the Furthest Ring. They stabilize a temporary realm of illusion for mortals to exist in without having to engage with the eldritch abominations just outside or the bleak expanse in which they live. So this is establishing the foundational basis for the afterlife in Paradox Space—not an eternal continuum like heaven or hell, but a purgatory of a more dubious nature, one that is actively maintained by vast, ancient monsters through a network of trillions of relatively small ephemeral bubbles. They pop, they get blown again, ghosts can drift freely from one to another. When we understand the broader cosmology of Paradox Space in this way, it starts to seem reasonable to begin thinking in terms of "bubble-based reality structures," which means that *Sburb* sessions freely floating through the abyss could also be seen as a kind of bubble. But a very special kind, which has the nucleus of Skaia in the middle, and thus is endowed with this all-knowing spark that can beget a stable, physical existence contained within a universe the players create inside of it. Do horrorterrors blow these bubbles too? IT IS UNCLEAR.

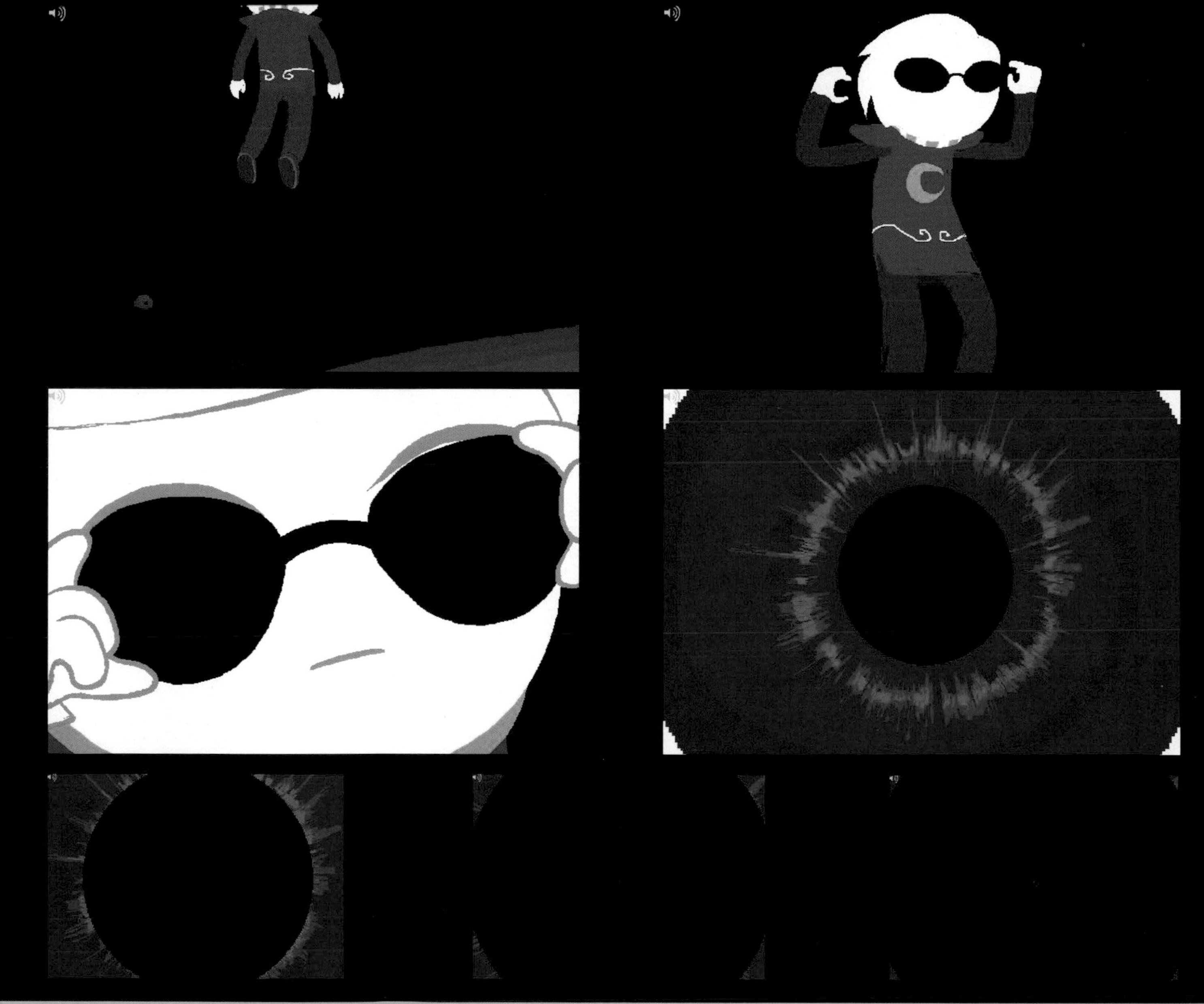

This animation, aside from accomplishing the worthy goal of totally freaking everyone out, also serves the purpose of acquainting everyone more closely with the existence of horrorterrors and their greater relevance to the cosmos and the story. Dave was recently urged to take his glasses off, and also to try listening to these beasts and see what they have to say to him. This is the "boon" which Derse dreamers have, and which Prospit dreamers don't. On Prospit, you have access to Skaia and all its cloud visions. On Derse, you have access to the grumblings of these distant monsters. Great consolation prize, huh? Skaia can inform Prospit kids what they need to do, and Jade enthusiastically embraces its counsel. But horrorterrors can somewhat play the same role, and provide mysterious instructions to both Rose and Dave that they have to parse. Their murmurings to Dave here carry a message of urgency, as he'll say later, and this starts laying the intel groundwork for the melodramatic suicide mission hatched later. Also, this shot confirms Dave's eye color pretty unambiguously, continuing a trend in the story where this very specific piece of info gets confirmed for each character, beginning with that strangely over-detailed portrait of Rose. For whatever odd visual thrashing that style added to the story, one thing it definitely established was the story's ability to focus with much greater granularity on the presentation of characters who for the most part are only "ideas" of people. Their abstracted presentation usually tends to communicate that "This is just an idea of a character, for whom many specific attributes are vague or variable." But by intensifying the presentation, and then highlighting it with one notable point of specificity, we can come away with some confidence that Rose's eyes are literally meant to be purple, rather than it just being another stylistic tick. Having established that, I think we can safely do the same for Dave here, even without the overly intensive rendering style.

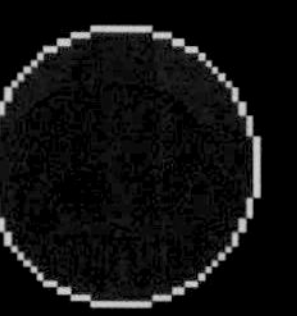

It's hard to even really describe what's going on with this page without the weird music that everything plays off of. Nothing is really going on with it? Hey, here's an idea, let's just ignore this page and move on. There's Feferi over there. She's worth talking about, right?

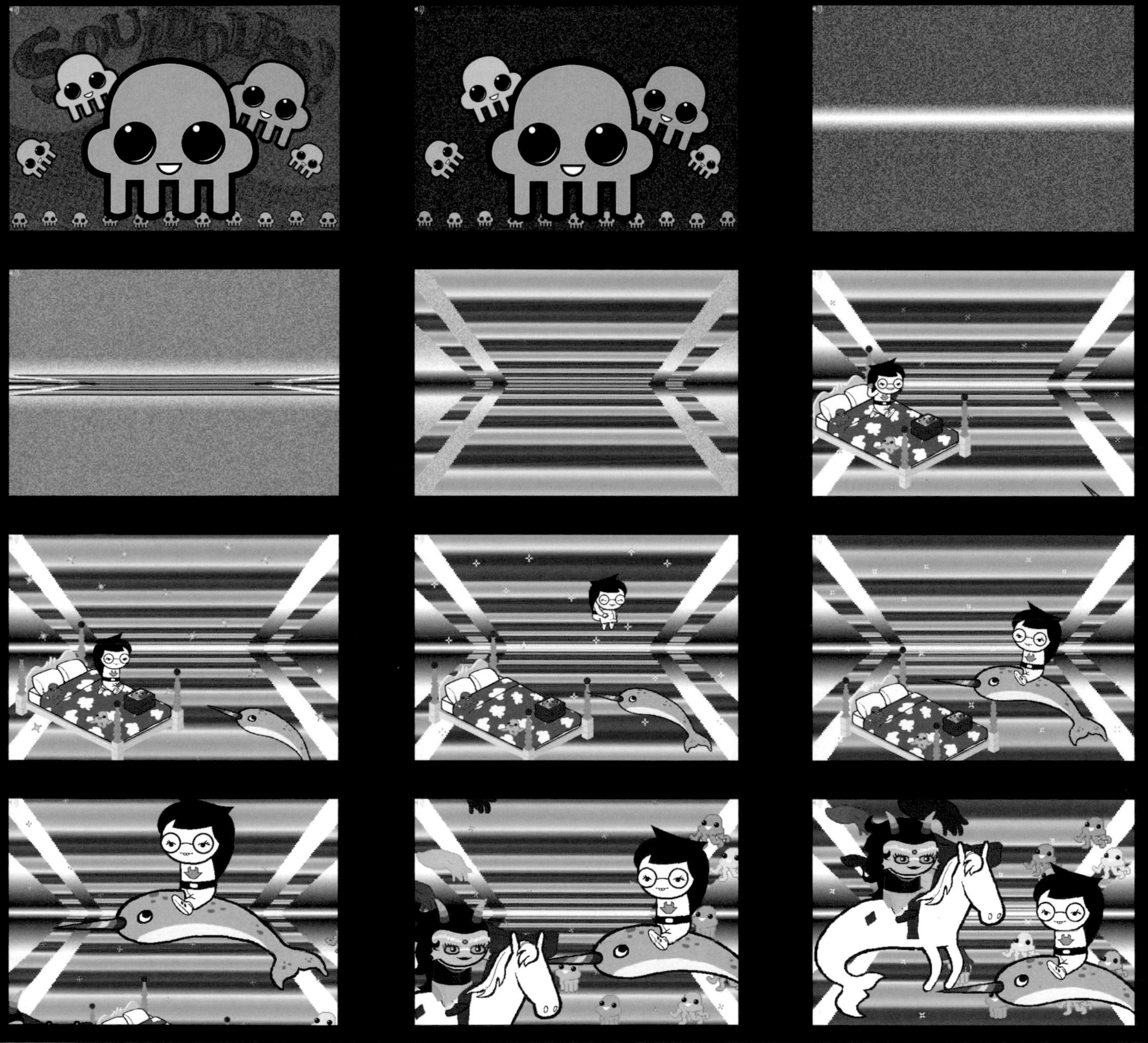

Remember that Feferi is presently grimnapping. "Presently" doesn't mean much, because the timelines are out of whack relative to each other, but "presently" from the STORY'S perspective usually does mean something. Remember the conversation Eridan just had with Rose, where she blew up his computer, and I ignored the conversation to talk about something else because he sucks and who cares about him? Well, I still stand by that decision, he sucks and who cares. But there was another purpose served by showing that conversation at that moment. "Eridan's computer explodes" is one of those key moments on the troll timeline we took note of during the recent RPG game. And linked to that moment is Feferi's dark nap. You could see her in the panel there near Eridan, sleeping on the horn pile, with a dark bubble over her. This reminds us that's what she's doing "now," just like Jade, and here they are, rendezvousing in this freaky dream bubble. Which, if there's one really important role Feferi plays, it's this: establishing "first contact" between trolls and humans through the dream realm, a.k.a. the afterlife. Feferi is quite chipper about it all and wants everyone to know there's nothing to worry about. That's pretty easy for *her* to say, though, since her mom is one of these monsters. But then, maybe that's how she knows they really aren't as bad as they seem.

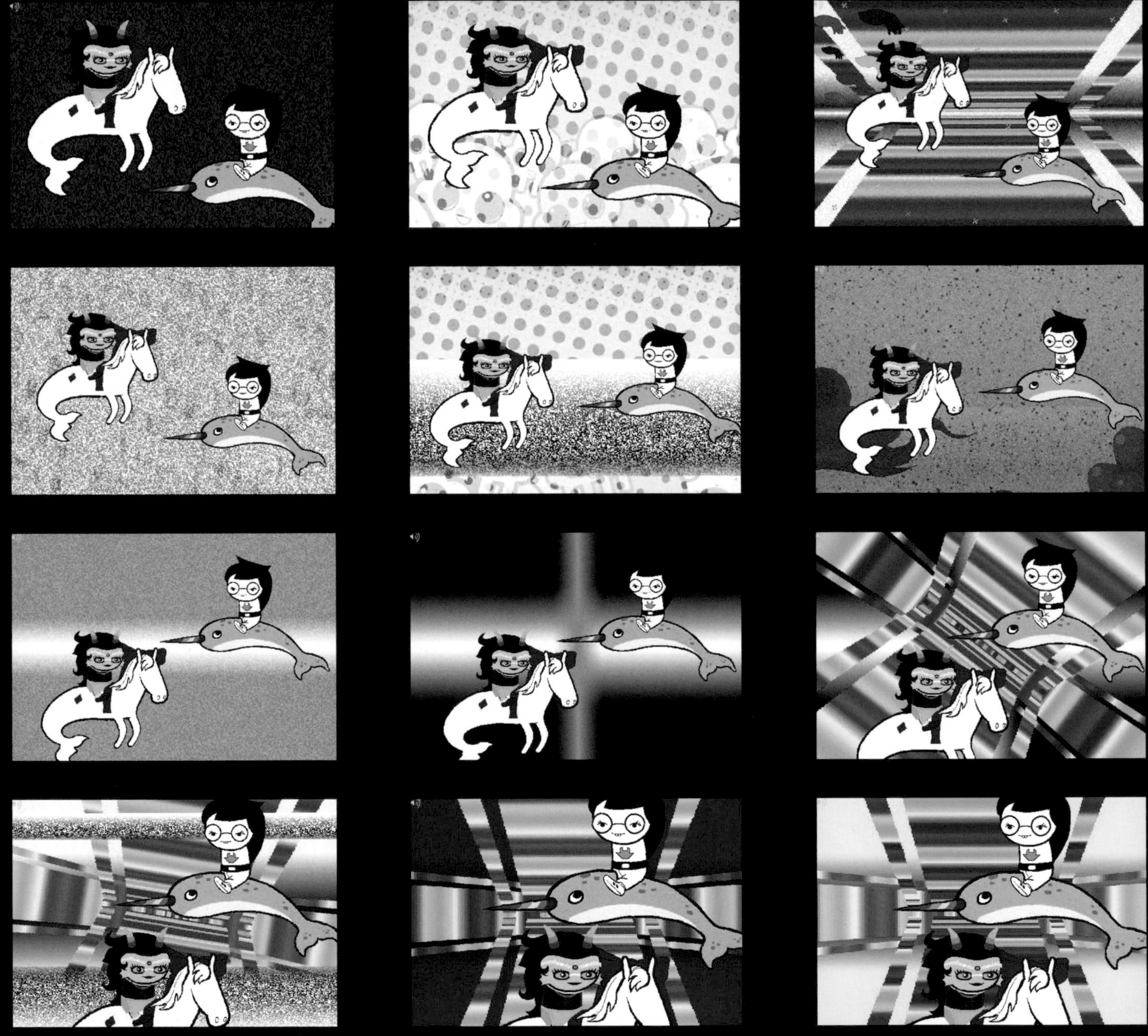

Okay, see, this thing with THIS page is, um...the really IMPORTANT point to make would be, uhhhhhhhhhhhhh. All right, you got me. There's nothing to say here. The thing about this animation is, for all the story-relevant things I've been saying about it, it's also just kind of a big shitpost.

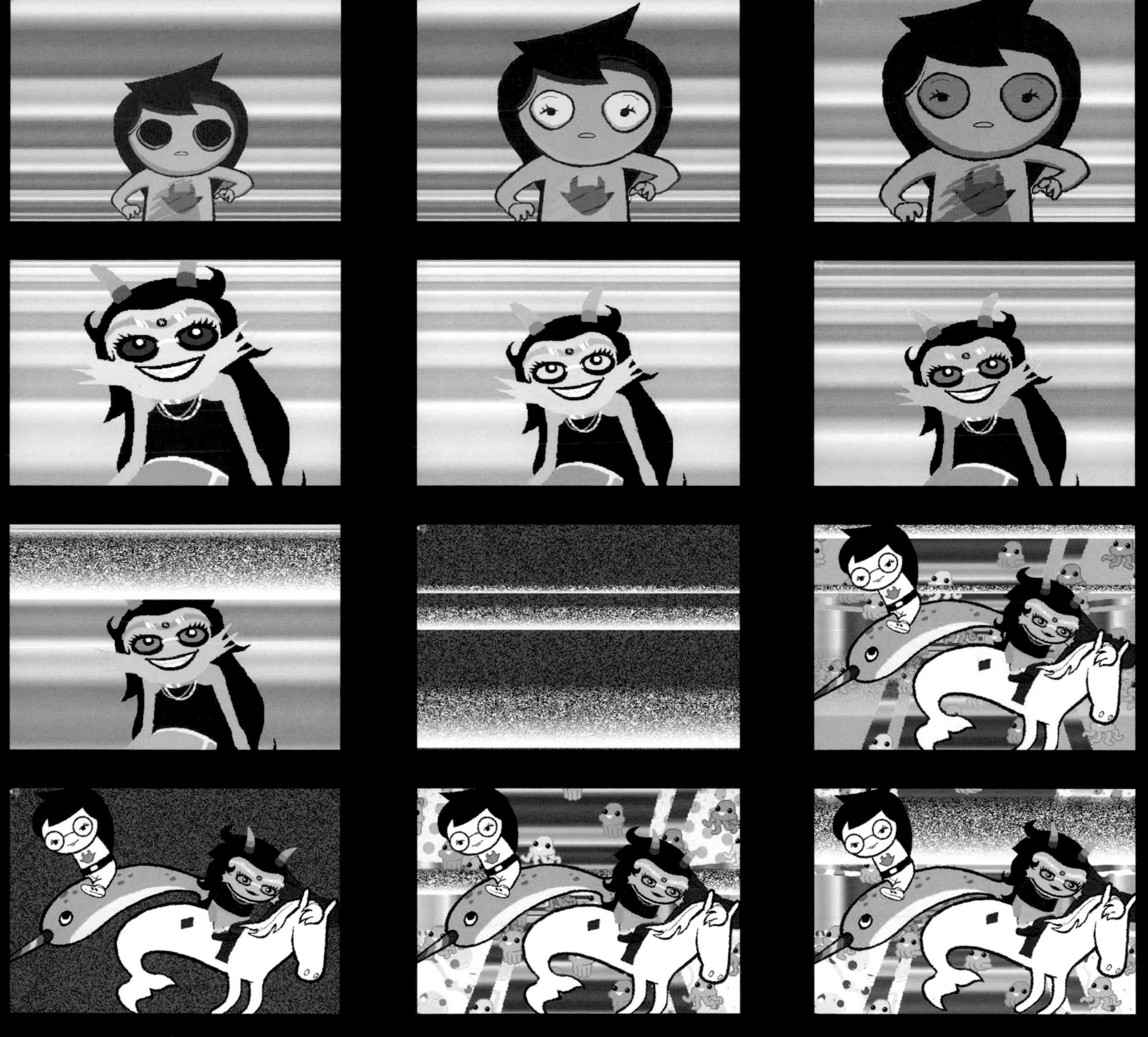

What's really going on is the bubble-based illusion is starting to unravel, and then insanity ensues. Jade is worried, Feferi isn't. She's just completely unflappable when it comes to this eldritch bullshit.

There's a moment in the song that makes it clear something is now very, very wrong. That's where we're at.

Probably the best way of looking at this in a non-abstract way is, this is the moment when Jade and Feferi's shared dream bubble pops. The illusion is over, and now their dream ghost projection-forms are hurtling freely through the abyss at great speed, before their phantom bodies (another weird concept in *Homestuck* that probably bears elaboration on, but much later) start to dissolve outside of the confining environment of the bubble that keeps them stable, causing them to wake up.

Then we go nighttime dumpster diving in the alley behind a bargain seafood restaurant. I mean, no we don't, this is all scary and serious and stuff. But there is sort of a running gag later where Dave and maybe some other people keep referring to these things humorously in terms of seafood analogies. But of course you don't eat these things, they eat YOU. Okay, that probably isn't true either. Although they do have huge, nasty mouths, as you can see. Which makes you wonder, what *do* they eat? What's even out there in the void? Smaller horrorterrors? That's probably it. There's likely just an entire diverse ecology of horrorterrors, with smaller ones very plentiful and larger ones more scarce, to keep the food chain balanced. Other than that, it's a complete free for all. I'm just literally making all this shit up right now, if it wasn't clear.

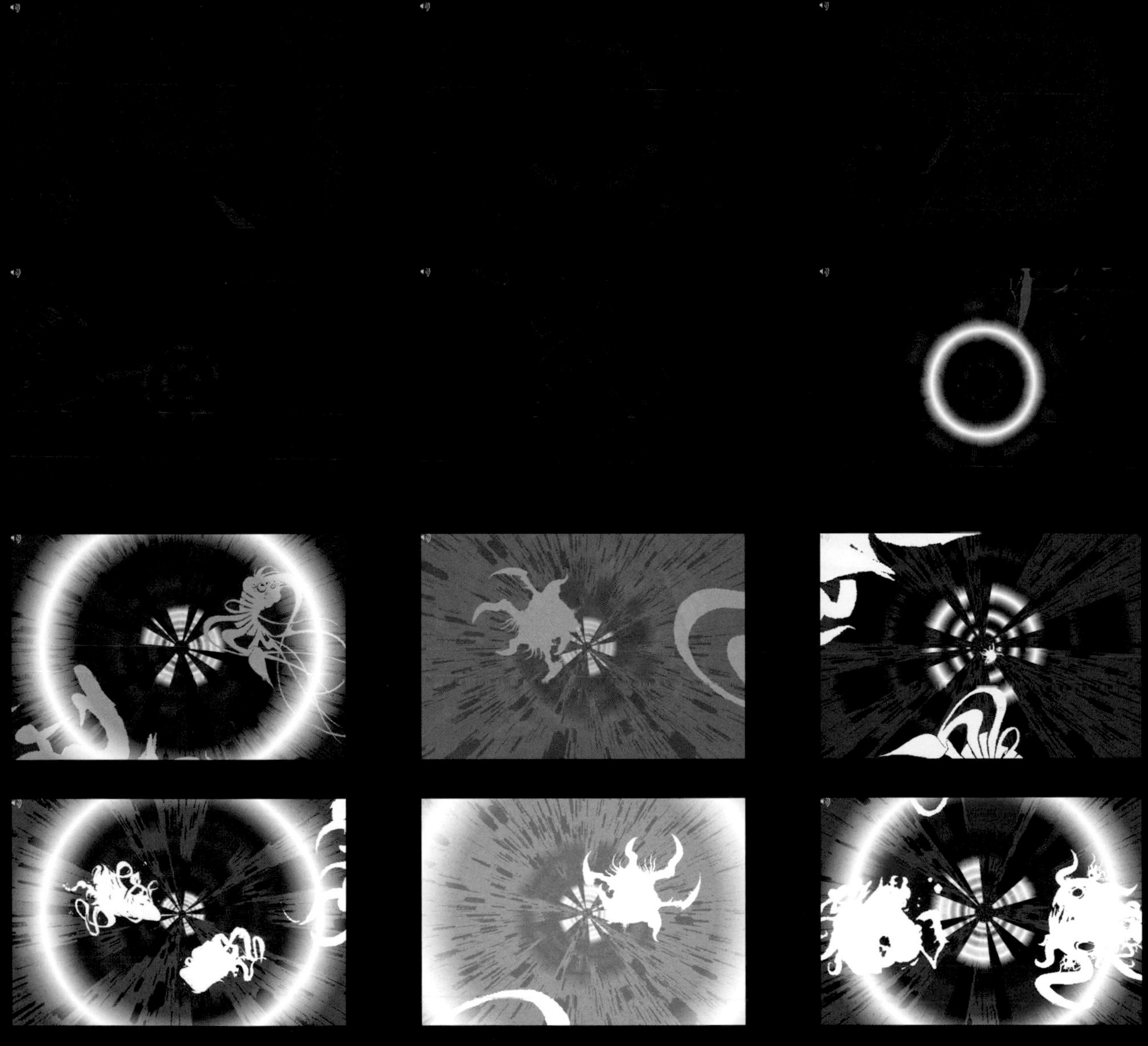

I said in an earlier book that these eldritch beasts were only imported into *Homestuck* because of their presence in *Problem Sleuth*, which used them in a much goofier way. It didn't really take their horrifying nature or the Lovecraftian tradition of them seriously at all. But the way HS starts blending them into its greater cosmology does seem to take them a little more seriously as literary devices from the horror genre. I never read any Lovecraft and don't really care about these creatures in respect to them being specific elements of his work. They were siphoned into the PS/HS lore from the wider pop-culture melange that has elevated the notion of an eldritch abomination into something transcending the original source material to become a more widely recognized fantasy trope. So this is the nature of their utility here, something touching on a more universal principle of alien horror which says that some alien life is so unfathomable and unsettling to us that even contemplating them is a gateway to madness. Neither good nor evil, their existence utterly eludes definition or judgment on mortal humanoid terms. They rule the infinite expanse of the Furthest Ring, where seemingly no other form of life exists except for them. And corporeal life as we understand it exists within this medium as a tiny subset of its total volume. It's implied, as I mentioned a few notes ago, that all comprehensible realities to us (such as dream bubble illusions, or *Sburb* sessions containing entire universes) actually are confined by little bubbles that these beasts whimsically blow, probably for no humanly comprehensible reason. This suggests that this godawful abyss and its gruesome inhabitants are the default reality. And the much more stable, relatable realms we enjoy, such as "a universe," are actually the rare exceptions: totally anomalous, dreamlike fields of experience that exist only briefly relative to the lifespan of these monsters, as the confining bubbles swell and pop.

This animation finally crescendos at the moment when you begin to think you can't take another goddamn second on Wonka's shitty boat. And then everything is okay. Except not really, because we float by one more awful monster, which has been wonderfully illustrated to make sure you realize, under particular rendering conditions, that these aren't all just a bunch of cartoon goofballs, but actually super-duper grotesque and scary entities.

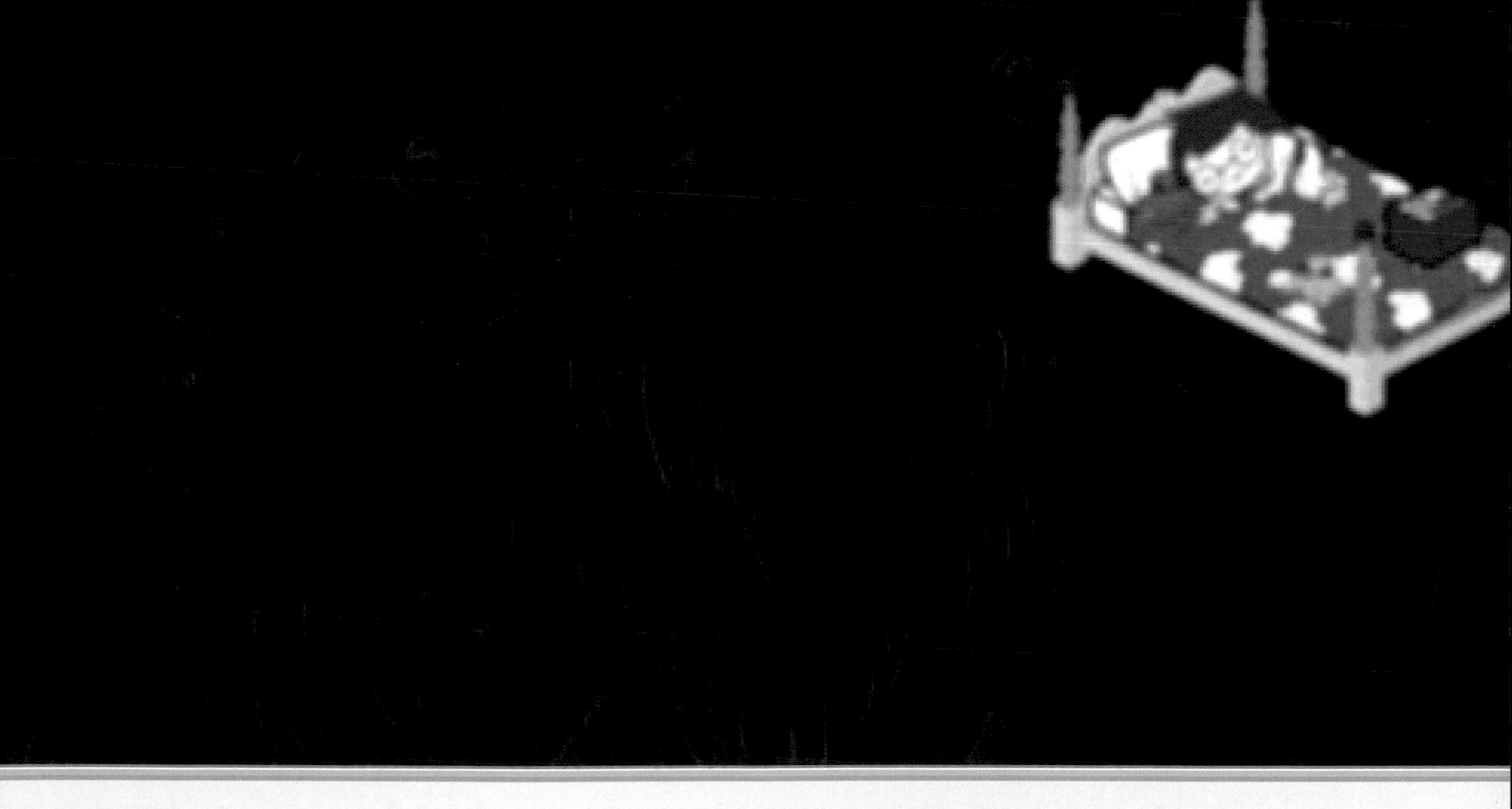

Good thing Jade's dream ghost projection-whatever is "sleeping" soundly through all this, otherwise she'd probably be really scared if she saw that thing. Except this rendering probably isn't literal? It might be a shot of what she's seeing through her mind's eye as she sleeps. In which case she is really scared right now. But it's fine, Feferi will reassure her and tell her all these space monsters are actually great. Some of her best friends are space monsters. Her MOM was a space monster. Don't be a bigot, Jade.

Jade finally wakes up. She went to sleep at some point in Act 4. It's tricky to pin down exactly when she fell asleep by casually skimming through the archive, but she's been asleep for well over 1,000 site pages. This is the nature of Jade's role in the story. She spends huge amounts of time being asleep, or compromised in some way, like being brainwashed. At one point, she even gets put to sleep *while* being brainwashed. But for now, she's finally awake and ready to play a more active role in the story. Her relevance starts snowballing from here and peaks during **[S] Cascade**, i.e. the midpoint of the story. I probably said this before, but the shape of her arc is a huge bell curve, rising slowly from the fog of her sleepy marginalization, peaking right in the middle, then gradually tapering back off as she starts getting compromised in different ways. Everyone's views on this may vary, but I always thought that for a story with a big ensemble cast, it was more interesting to have a wide variety of arcs of different shapes, sizes, focal points, themes, and peak moments, rather than somewhat artificially trying to make sure all the major players' arcs peak right around the same time at the very end. This aspect is a little bit underscored by what Jade does in **[S] Collide**. Her role there isn't about kicking ass, it's about having fun. And then, finally, about getting punched in the face for One Last Nap.

You suddenly understand jack shit.

Where are you? What just happened?

Oh great, now someone's bothering you. Boy are you not in the mood for getting trolled now.

> Jade: Answer.

cuttlefishCuller [CC] began trolling
gardenGnostic [GG]

CC: Glub glub. 38)
GG: what!!!!!
CC: S-E-E??
GG: see what!
GG: go away
CC: I told you!
CC: T)(ere is not)(ing to worry about at all.
GG: bluhhh what are you talking about....
GG: my head hurts
GG: just stop it, stop trolling me
GG: i hate you all!!!!!!!!!!!!!
CC:)(oly mackerel, looks like SOM-EON-E woke up on t)(e wrong side of t)(e absurd)(uman bed!
CC: C)(ill out, Jade. I am just following up on w)(at I told you earlier.
GG: about what!
GG: i dont remember talking to you at all
CC: About your dream! Your post-dreamdeat)(dreamself's dream.
CC: Errr. W)(ic)(is a term I just made up now. 38|
GG: my dream was horrible!!!
GG: i dont know what that was, i have never

dreamed anything like it
CC: Yes, I imagine not! You)(ave spent your w)(ole life dreaming about prospit, no?
GG: oh god....
GG: prospit :(
GG: is it really gone?
CC: Yes, Jade. It is time to face t)(e facts!
CC: Our moons are gone too. If we wis)(to sleep now, our dreams must take place in t)(e bubbles glubbed by t)(e gods w)(o live in t)(e Furt)(est Ring.

"Post-dreamdeath dreamself's dream" is a just a bullshit term Feferi makes up on the fly. It's all right, Fef, I was never sure which exact nomenclature to settle on when describing this dream ghost shit either. It's been a long time since we've checked in with Jade. She has a lot to catch up on here. Including the highly tragic destruction of Prospit, which was a beloved second home to her. Jade has always been a very cheerful, carefree kid up to this point. When she wakes up here, it seems to mark a new chapter in her life and a different evolution in her personality. One wherein she must finally confront "actual adversity."

CC: It is t)(e infinite space w)(ic)(divides all sessions, completely unnavigable and unfat)(omable, untouc)(ed by t)(e time or space of any universe in existence.
CC: Its lords are our slumberbuddies now. 38)
GG: uuuuuuuuugh D:
CC: Don't be ridiculous. T)(ey are not as dreadful as t)(ey look.
CC: In fact, t)(ey are quite)(elpful if you know)(ow to talk to t)(em!
CC: Don't you remember our dream? I was trying to s)(ow you t)(at t)(ere is not)(ing to fear.
CC: But t)(en... you kind of freaked out!)(umans are so M-ELODRAMATIC.
GG: oh......
GG: that was you?
CC:)(ELL YEA)(! 38D
GG: argh
GG: sorry but
GG: could you please
GG: not use all those stupid parentheses??????
GG: i can hardly read what you type and its giving me a migraine
CC: GLUUUUB oh fine.
CC: I will suspend my neato quirk just for you.
CC: I hereby renounce the royal mark of sea dweller supremacy in the interest of INT-ERSP-ECI-ES DIPLOMACY.
GG: what about the -E thing, can you stop that too? it is also annoying and stupid
CC: JEGUS JADE.
CC: Look! It is like a cool trident I throw sometimes.
CC: oooooo ---------------E
CC: How is that not awesome!
GG: meh :\
CC: Okay, you win. I have officially humbled myself before you. Entirely glubbing peasant-IFICATED for your pleasure.
CC: Shall I clip my fins for you as well, your majesty?
GG: hehehe
GG: ok, sorry for sounding bossy
GG: you seem pretty nice, and you sure do look exotic
GG: i kind of always thought you were all like
GG: a bunch of really obnoxious humans
CC: Well, thank you! On both counts, of being likened to something other than an obnoxious human, as well as on my exotic looks.
CC: For the record, you look pretty awesomely weird too.
CC: I introduced myself before, but since you do not remember, I will do so now. My name is Feferi, and I was going to be the Empress, but now I am not!
GG: hey feferi, i would like to remember......
GG: but everything is so foggy right now
GG: i remember prospit being attacked
GG: and
GG: falling.....
GG: aaaand
GG: i dunno :(
GG: do you know what happened?
CC: Hell if I know!
CC: In your pre-death dream at least. Oh, well you died obviously, so there's that.
GG: fffffff
GG: yeah, i gathered that! XC
CC: All I could see was what happened in your hive.
CC: You were asleep, and then your robot exploded.
CC: And then your lusus saved you! Kind of like mine saved me.
CC: Before she died. 38C
GG: ohhhhhhh!!!!!
GG: i do remember you!
GG: i remember you were talking to me about my lusus, and i had no idea what you were talking about
GG: and still sort of dont :\
GG: but you must mean bec
GG: also it was shortly before your friend sent me a weird message
GG: about how my robot was going to explode, and i should talk to him when it happens
GG: this was months ago
CC: Oh? Who was that?
GG: it was the most awful and angry one
GG: i am so sick of him, i really dont want to talk to that pathetic jerk ever
CC: Ah, Karkat. Of course.
GG: thats his name?
CC: Yes, he's our leader. Why did he want you to talk to him?
GG: hmmmm

Full disclosure: I just do not enjoy Feferi's quirk. I never have. The parentheses are annoying, and it's especially annoying how they get separated when they straddle a line break. Whenever someone contrives an excuse for her to stop using it (when she "gets real" with Eridan and drops it, or when Jade says it's giving her a headache), that's 100% me going, "Meh, I'm not feeling this quirk, time to drop it for a bit." Jade is me here. Thanks for asking her for me, Jade, I owe you one. Oh, you don't want to be punched in the face at the end of *Homestuck*? Let's not get fucking greedy here. Anyway, Jade reminds us about how Karkat used her dreambot exploding as a critical event for her to use as a reminder for Jade to message him. So now she's about to do that, cashing in that plot token. Very satisfying. As events get more convoluted, the characters all need to come up with different strategies for how to devise reminders and signals that will serve their communication purposes. Advanced reminders, unlike the simplistic, childlike reminders Jade wears on her fingers, which she is about to abandon for good in a few pages.

GG: thats right, it was about some kind of plan...
GG: which he said me from the future told him about?
GG: i thought it was total nonsense at the time
GG: but
GG: i guess he was telling the truth
GG: so maybe i should talk to him? i dont know
CC: Glubshrug.
CC: He's pretty harmless, really. You get used to his yelling.
CC: I do not even process it as yelling anymore. More like a lot of blubbering.
CC: More blubber spills out of that mouth than a gash in a poached whale.
GG: ewwwww
CC: Gluuuuuub, I just made myself hungry. 38O~
GG: ewwwwwwwwwwwww!
GG: fish aliens are weird
CC: Hey! We're the aristocracy. We've got a duty to be weird.
CC: Anyway, go talk to your shoutfriend I guess.
GG: ok feferi, it was nice talking to you
CC: And hey, if you want to take another nap sometime, let me know! They will be more than happy to glub us up another bubble.
GG: NOOOOOOOOOOOOOOOOOO
GG: i am never going to sleep again!
GG: never never never never never never
CC: PSH WE'LL SEE ABOUT THAT, MISS HORNLESS MCFINLESS.
CC: Why, if I'm not mistaken, you are looking a little drowsy right now. We may meet again sooner than you think. 38D
GG: yes, im so tired
GG: :(
GG: well, ok
GG: bye

gardenGnostic [GG] **ceased being trolled by cuttlefishCuller [CC]**

> Jade: Pester Karkat.

-- gardenGnostic [GG] **began pestering carcinoGeneticist** [CG] **--**

GG: ok, my robot exploded
GG: now what smart guy!
CG: HOLY SHIT, IT'S HARLEY
CG: COMMUNICATING WITH ME OUT OF NOWHERE OF HER OWN VOLITION
CG: HOLD THAT THOUGHT WHILE I GO INFORM MY DISGRACE OF A CLOWN FRIEND ABOUT THIS TRUE REAL LIFE MIRACLE, IT MIGHT LIFT HIS SPIRITS
CG: I HAVE TO SPREAD THE WICKED WORD LIKE I'M MASSAGING SHITTY SPARKLEDUST AROUND MY NETHER REGIONS TO ASSUAGE A VICIOUS RASH
CG: IT'S LIKE I'M SEASONING A FUCKING STEAK HERE.
GG: i knew i would regret this
GG: talking to you is so terrible
GG: its making my headache worse
CG: OH YEAH, BECAUSE TALKING TO YOU HAS JUST BEEN ABSOLUTE EUPHORIA.

CG: DON'T EVEN TALK TO ME ABOUT HEADACHES.
CG: RIGHT NOW THERE'S A LUMBERJACK SPLITTING WOOD ON MY THINK PAN.
CG: HE'S GOT THE FOREARMS OF A CHOLERBEAR, A MOUNTAIN OF LOGS, AND NOTHING BUT FUCKING TIME.

Tired: Fun-Loving Mary Sue Jade. Wired: Grumpy-Ass Bitch Jade. Who has arrived just in time to start completely dominating Karkat like the whiny little bottomboy he is. She does all her buddies the service of almost completely taking over Karkat's duties for practically the rest of the session. Maybe not consciously exactly, but he seems to latch on to her in lieu of bothering John after getting romantically rebuffed by him and making a fool of himself backwards through time. Jade is fresh meat for semi-amorous harassment, though he has to do a fair amount of repair work to get the ball rolling again after belligerently sliding into her DMs for years in the past, during the more reckless phases of his trolling binge. Jade's an easy mark for such a recovery though, since even though she's a grumpy bitch at the moment, she's still pretty nice and likes making friends. Final observation: the above panel I think is a pretty good hybrid style of all these flailing presentations over the last few pages. We went from Sprite Mode, to a Sprite-Hero Hybrid Mode, to some sort of Hussnasty Lite Mode, and now this one, which seems to blend them all in a decent way. This would be another one of these unusual art style candidates where I'd be inclined to say, if the whole thing were done in this style alone, that would result in a pretty solid piece of work.

GG: uuuugh shut uuuuup!
GG: will you just tell me what you wanted?
CG: I DON'T KNOW WHAT YOU'RE TALKING ABOUT.
CG: I DIDN'T TELL YOU TO CONTACT ME, NOT THAT I'M NOT TICKLED BY THE SURPRISE.
CG: LET'S CATCH UP. HOW IS EVERYTHING? HOW WAS YOUR DEATHNAP?? I CAN ONLY HOPE IT WAS AS REFRESHING AS MINE.
CG: WHAT'S THAT? HOW AM I? I'M GREAT, FEEL LIKE A MILLION BOONBANKS EVER SINCE MY LITTLE POWER SNOOZE.
CG: STILL PRETTY TIRED THOUGH. YOU LOOK A LITTLE DROWSY YOURSELF. BUT WE WON'T BE GOING BACK TO SLEEP ANY TIME SOON, WILL WE JADE?
CG: NO WAY. A PAIR OF FEISTY GOGETTERS LIKE YOU AND ME, WE DON'T HAVE TIME FOR DREAMS OF HORRORTERRORS FONDLING EVERY RECESS OF OUR NAKED PSYCHES, PLEASANT THOUGH THEY ARE.
CG: YOU HAVE A LOT OF IMPORTANT USELESS SCAMPERING AND GIGGLING TO DO. WHEREAS I HAVE A CRUCIAL DATE WITH A PNEUMATIC DRILL, TO BORE A HOLE IN THE CENTER OF MY FOREHEAD, DEEP INTO THE PLUMP ANGUISH BLADDER WHICH STORES MY ALIEN DISMAY FLUID. THAT'S A REAL THING WE HAVE, FYI.
CG: I WILL THEN PERFORM A LITTLE SOFT SHOE NUMBER IN THE PUDDLE OF FLUID THAT ACCUMULATES ON THE FLOOR, WHILE MAKING THE BIGGEST SMILE EVER ATTEMPTED BY SOMEONE NOT CLINICALLY RETARDED.
CG: I WILL DO THIS FOR YOUR AMUSEMENT, JADE. TO SAY THANKS FOR EVERYTHING.
GG: i cant believe i fell for this
GG: it was just a setup to troll me some more
GG: why do you go to such lengths to troll me? i just dont understand it
CG: TRY TO BE CULTURALLY SENSITIVE
CG: TROLLING IS AN ACTIVITY THAT SHARES A NAME WITH MY ENTIRE SPECIES
CG: DO I GET ON YOUR CASE FOR ALL THE TERRIBLE HUMANNING YOU DO?
GG: thats ridiculous, humanning isnt a word
GG: and if it was, it would be a nicer thing to do than trolling!
GG: you know what i mean, stop pretending you dont
CG: TELL ME JADE
CG: WHY ARE YOU SUCH A RACIST?
GG: aaaaaaa that is something a troll would say!
CG: YES, EXACTLY.
CG: I AM A TROLL. IT SEEMS WE ARE ON THE SAME PAGE.
GG: i mean you are being patronizing and disingenuous to get a rise out of me
GG: and that is really really shitty!!!!!!
GG: i am so tired of it, and i am done talking to you forever
GG: bye karkat, it was awful knowing you!
CG: WAIT
CG: OK LOOK
CG: I SERIOUSLY, HONESTLY DON'T KNOW WHAT YOU'RE TALKING ABOUT.
CG: YOU SAY YOUR ROBOT BLEW UP, AND THAT WAS SOME SORT OF SIGNAL TO MESSAGE ME?
GG: yes
GG: as if my day needed another reason to get worse
CG: YOU PROBABLY DIDN'T CONTACT THE RIGHT ME.
GG: what does that mean!
CG: I MEAN FUTURE ME IS PROBABLY THE ONE TO TALK TO ABOUT THIS.
CG: SINCE IT'S ALL NEWS TO ME.
GG: is this another prank
GG: you are seriously the worst at pranks
CG: I DON'T PLAY PRANKS, THAT'S JUVENILE NONSENSE.
CG: I DO TWO THINGS AND TWO THINGS ONLY, I DEVASTATE SORRY MOTHERFUCKERS, AND GET SHIT DONE AS AN AWESOME LEADER.
CG: IN THIS CASE, I AM ACCOMPLISHING THE LATTER.
CG: HERE, CLICK THIS AND WE WILL SOLVE THE MYSTERY TOGETHER.
CG:

GG: :|

> Karkat: Open memo.

When two kids formerly at each other's throats start working on becoming better friends, it helps for them to establish some stuff to bond over. Jade just bonded with Feferi over having a dead dream self and taking a very disturbing nap as a result. And now Jade and Karkat get to do the same thing, only it's probably a more effective bonding topic since, unlike Feferi, they both hated the experience. Or rather, this *should* be a good bonding topic, but here Karkat is, fucking blowing it with her again, because he just can't help himself. Of course, I don't really have to excoriate him for his thoughtless handling of the situation. He's about to give Future Karkat an opportunity to do that to himself. He is a Knight, after all. And one way he apparently decides to utilize his class is by white knighting on behalf of aggrieved damsels against his own earlier trolling efforts. Quite valorous, really.

CCG **RIGHT NOW opened memo on board FRUITY RUMPUS ASSHOLE FACTORY.**

CCG: HEY FUTURE ME, WHAT DO YOU THINK ABOUT THIS EXPLODED JADEBOT BUSINESS?
CCG: MUST BE SOMETHING REALLY MISSION CRITICAL, OR JADE WOULDN'T HAVE BOTHERED GETTING IN TOUCH WITH US, RIGHT?
CCG: SOMETHING IMPERATIVE TO OUR SURVIVAL NO DOUBT?
CCG: HEY DOUCHE BAG, ARE YOU THERE
??? gardenGnostic [?GG] **AT ?:?? responded to memo.**
?GG: oh jeez, why am i doing this
?GG: this is so stupid!
CCG: PIPE DOWN HARLEY, THIS PRACTICALLY DOESN'T EVEN CONCERN YOU AT THIS POINT
?GG: bluhhh youre so funny!!!!!
CCG: NOTHING TO SAY, FUTURE ME?
CCG: NOT EVEN A FEW PARTING WORDS OF SCORN FOR ME OR THE NARCOLEPTIC IDIOT?
CCG: IT'S BEEN A WHILE SINCE WE'VE SPARRED, HOW I'VE MISSED THE SWEET STING OF YOUR BARBS
?GG: are you enjoying yourself karkat?
CCG: HAHAHA YOU ARE SO DUMB YOU ACTUALLY THINK THIS IS A RUSE.
CCG: YOU'VE COME ALL THIS WAY AND YOU STILL DON'T GET THAT ALL THE SHIT WE'VE BEEN TELLING YOU ABOUT IS REAL.
CCG: WHY THE FUCK WOULD I BE PULLING A STUNT LIKE THIS, WHAT A WASTE OF TIME.
CCG: I REALLY AM TALKING TO FUTURE ME, HE'S JUST BEING AN EVASIVE TOOL.
?GG: well obviously i know some things youve said are true
?GG: its just hard to take everything at face value when youre always so nasty!
CCG: YOU KNOW, IT'S REALLY AMAZING HOW BEHIND THE TIMES YOU ARE.
CCG: IT'S ALMOST AS IF YOU'VE SLEPT THROUGH THIS WHOLE ADVENTURE
CCG: OH WAIT, THAT IS ESSENTIALLY TRUE.
CCG: IT WAS HILARIOUS WATCHING YOU GROW UP.
CCG: YOU THOUGHT YOU HAD ALL THE ANSWERS, FROLICKING ALL OVER YOUR ISLAND BEING INFURIATINGLY CHIPPER, BUILDING ROBO-BUNNIES LIKE A MORON AND ULTIMATELY RUINING EVERYTHING.
CCG: YOU WERE SO SURE YOUR DREAMS TOLD YOU EVERYTHING YOU NEEDED TO KNOW.

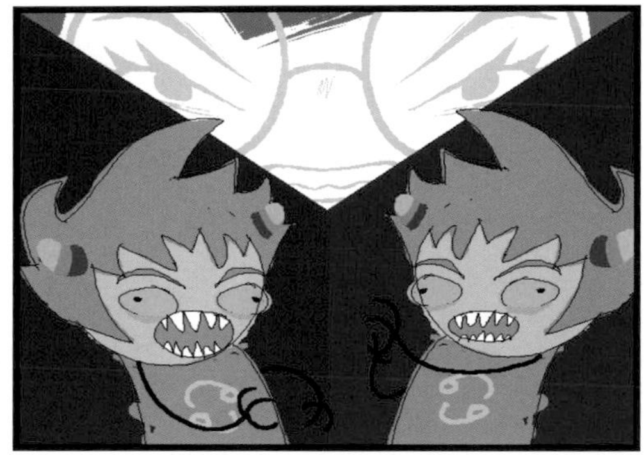

CCG: AND NOW LOOK AT YOU
CCG: YOU SUDDENLY UNDERSTAND JACK SHIT.
?GG: ok i understand that you are another group of players and you are in some sort of trouble.
?GG: but maybe if you had been nice to me instead of terrorizing me all those years i would have believed you
?GG: and we could have worked together to solve your problems as well as ours
?GG: it just makes me sad to think thats probably impossible now because you are so angry and stubborn!
CCG: DON'T TELL ME WHAT'S IMPOSSIBLE BECAUSE I'M ANGRY AND STUBBORN.
CCG: I FUCKING KNOW WHAT THOSE ASSETS MAKE POSSIBLE.
CCG: THEY MADE YOU POSSIBLE, GOT IT???
?GG: uh huh
CCG: DO YOU EVEN HAVE ANY IDEA HOW LUCKY YOU ARE TO BE GRACED BY MY DIVINE FURY?
CCG: TO HAVE THE PRIVILEGE OF GETTING TO BE STUDIED AND MOCKED BY ME FOR YOUR WHOLE PATHETIC MISERABLE LIFE?
CCG: DO YOU REALIZE I'M YOUR GOD? YES, YOUR LITERAL GOD, THAT'S RIGHT.
?GG: sure karkat, whatever you say!
CCG: AND I HAVE TAKEN TIME OUT OF MY BUSY GODLY SCHEDULE TO SCRUTINIZE YOUR POINTLESS EXISTENCE.
CCG: OUT OF THE COUNTLESS TRILLIONS OF LIFE FORMS I BROUGHT INTO REALITY THROUGH ANGRY GRUBFUCK POWER ALONE, I HAVE SELECTED YOU FOR EXAMINATION AND HARASSMENT.

Maybe the saddest thing about this spectacle is it takes an entire page of Karkat's bellyaching before his future self even bothers acknowledging his existence. Even though his future self is the one who arranged Jade and Karkat to connect this way in the first place, so as to send them on a path toward friendship. Future Karkat almost seems to deliberately give his past self enough conversational rope to hang himself with, buying enough time for Jade to say something that triggers Karkat so hard that he launches into one of his "I AM YOUR GOD!" tirades. Which by now we should know is a romantically coded message, because that's how he introduced himself to John before he proceeded to spadeflirt with him. Basically, Jade has barely been awake for a few minutes and she's already lunging headlong through the hormone-slicked slalom of interspecies romance. Welcome to the party, Harley.

CCG: PERSONALLY I THINK THAT WARRANTS A LITTLE GRATITUDE, AND JUST MAYBE, A BIT OF DEFERENCE.
CCG: A CURTSY, PERHAPS?
CCG: BUT YEAH GO AHEAD AND KEEP BLOWING ME OFF LIKE THE FLAKEY LITTLE TWERP YOU ARE.
FUTURE carcinoGeneticist [FCG] **3 HOURS FROM NOW responded to memo.**
FCG: HEY DON'T TALK TO HER LIKE THAT YOU UNCOUTH PIECE OF SHIT.
FCG: THIS IS REFLECTING POORLY ON BOTH OF US, IT'S GODDAMNED EMBARRASSING.
CCG: OH WOW, ANOTHER MIRACLE.
CCG: IT MUST BE PERIGEES EVE, BECAUSE GET A LOAD OF THIS HUGE BEHEMOTH LEAVING THAT JUST GOT DRAGGED IN.
CCG: JADE, OUR DUTY IS CLEAR. WE MUST DECK THIS TURD TO THE NINES.
FCG: OH MY GOD I CAN'T BELIEVE I ACTUALLY THOUGHT THAT WAS A CLEVER THING TO SAY. WHAT A DIPSHIT.
?GG: aaauugh what the hell!!!
FCG: JADE, I'M SORRY ABOUT PAST ME'S RETARDED BEHAVIOR.
FCG: I'M NOT GOING TO DRAG OUT A HUGE APOLOGY OR ANYTHING BECAUSE I ALREADY APOLOGIZED IN AN EARLIER CONVERSATION, OK. I'M JUST LETTING YOU KNOW.
CCG: GOD DAMMIT, ARE YOU SERIOUS?
CCG: I MEAN, AM I SERIOUS?????
CCG: WILL I BE SERIOUS ABOUT THIS SHIT. WILL I REALLY BACK DOWN LIKE A LIMP FRONDED STOOGE? PLEASE TELL ME YOU'RE JOKING.
FCG: PLEASE, JUST
FCG: SHUT UP
FCG: I CAN'T BELIEVE I EVER THOUGHT FUTURE ME WAS THE STUPID ONE
FCG: PAST ME IS THE DUMBEST BUCKET OF FESTERING DISCHARGE I EVER FELL ASS BACKWARDS INTO.
FCG: COME ON, YOU KNOW THIS TO BE TRUE. REMEMBER ALL THE PAST USSES WE USED TO TALK TO??
FCG: THEY WERE EVEN PASTER THAN YOU, AND THEREFORE DUMBER.
CCG: YEAH, I REMEMBER ALL THOSE DUMBSHIT PAST USSES, BUT THEY DON'T HOLD A FUCKING JACKASS CANDLE TO FUTURE USSES.
CCG: AND YOU'RE THE FUTUREST ME I EVER HAD THE CROTCH BLISTERING MISFORTUNE OF JAWING WITH, SO THE FUCKHEAD TROPHY GOES TO YOU.
CCG: I MEAN, MY GOD, WHY.
CCG: IS PROXIMITY TO THAT NASTY LOOKING SPACETIME RIP ON THE TIMELINE MESSING WITH YOUR HEAD?
CCG: IS THAT WHAT'S CAUSING YOU TO FEEL PITY FOR THIS IMBECILE?
FCG: LOOK, JADE'S NOT THAT BAD OK.
FCG: YOU JUST GOT TOO WORKED UP, AND YOU CAN'T SEE THAT.
FCG: AND NOW ALL THIS FROTHING PANDEMONIUM JUMPING OUT OF YOUR MOUTH IS JUST RIDICULOUS OVERCOMPENSATION FOR YOUR OWN SHORTCOMINGS AND MISTAKES, AND MASKING SOME FEELINGS YOU'RE NOT REALLY IN TOUCH WITH.
FCG: THIS IS ALL SO OBVIOUS, I'M FLUSHING LIKE A MOTHERFUCKER IN EMBARRASSMENT HAVING TO EXPLAIN IT TO YOU, AND EVEN WORSE, REMEMBERING HAVING IT EXPLAINED TO ME BY THE SMART ONE THREE HOURS AGO AND STILL ACTING LIKE A MOIST GLOBE EVEN AFTER BEING SO SOUNDLY SCHOOLFED.
CCG: I DON'T BELIEVE THIS. PLEASE TELL ME THIS IS A JOKE.
FCG: YOU SAID SO YOURSELF, WE DON'T JOKE AROUND. IT'S JUVENILE, REMEMBER.
CCG: I'M GOING TO VOMIT.
CCG: I'M MAKING A MENTAL NOTE TO SLAP MYSELF THREE HOURS FROM NOW, FOR BEING ENOUGH OF A SAP TO START DEVELOPING RED FEELINGS FOR A DUMB ANNOYING HUMAN, IF I'M READING BETWEEN THE LINES CORRECTLY.
FCG: I JUST SLAPPED MYSELF! I REMEMBERED MY LAME NOTE TO MYSELF FROM THREE HOURS AGO, AND THEN SLAPPED MYSELF SPECIFICALLY TO MOCK YOU.
FCG: IT STINGS TOO, YOU'LL FEEL IT IN A WHILE. AND THEN THE GHOST OF PAST ME WILL CRY.
FCG: PAST ME DOESN'T EVEN EXIST ANYMORE. HE'S A STUPID BAWLING WIGGLER PHANTOM. HE'S DEAD, NOT A REAL GUY ANYMORE, LIKE ME.
FCG: I'M THE REAL ONE. YOU'RE FAKE, A SHADOW OF A SAD MEMORY THAT PISSED ITS PANTS WHILE SCREAMING.
FCG: TIME TO DEAL WITH IT.
CCG **banned** FCG **from responding to memo.**
FCG **unbanned himself from responding to memo.**
FCG **banned** CCG **from responding to memo.**
CCG **unbanned himself from responding to memo.**

And just like that, the moment Future Karkat steps in, practically the entire page of dialogue turns to gray. Nobody can get a word in edgewise between these two. Their unrestrained auto-invective basically renders Karkat's neuroses totally apparent for Jade to marvel over. The consequences of this are hard to even fully keep track of. First, by defending Jade like this, Future Karkat is virtually making the case to his own past self to give her a chance, and to try to acknowledge that his aggression toward her is masking romantic attraction. If that wasn't nuts enough, the altercation doubles as an actual *confession* of this to Jade, which she now has to bear in mind as she goes forward befriending this guy. Like most other shouting matches Karkat has with himself, it's a complete free-for-all of self-owns and eyebrow-raising psychological revelations. And yet, in the totality of this clusterfuck, it's probably about as sufficient as anything else he could have done to get her to start giving the friendship a chance. How do you sidle out of something like this? You don't. This miserable basket case needs all the help he can get. Karkat trying to talk to someone while his future self is in the same conversation is almost as if you were talking to a friend or a crush, and you had a little demon on your shoulder who was shouting all your private thoughts out loud and then mocking you for every embarrassing thought you had. The frightening thing is, Karkat might be accidentally proving this method to be a fairly effective pick-up maneuver? Like, rather than negging the intended target, you have an utterly ruthless wingman at your side constantly negging you instead. Eventually, like Jade is about to do here, she just fucking snaps. Then once the ice is finally broken, it's all smooth sailing from there. Trust me on this.

?GG: i cant take this anymore!!!!!!!!
?GG: i dont even know what im reading here but its preposterous and ive had it!
?GG: i am just so angry, i cant believe i let you push me around all those years
?GG: you are completely out of your mind, i was too nice by just blocking you and typing frowny faces and stuff
?GG: i should have let you HAVE IT!!!!!!!!!!!!!!!!!!!!!
FCG: YES!!!!!
FCG: LET THIS FUCKER KNOW THE SCORE JADE. THIS IS HOW WE ROLL.
?GG: SHUT UP!!!!!!!
?GG: future karkat, if you really are future karkat......
?GG: where do you get off thinking you can just suddenly act like were pals because you said you apologized????
?GG: if you want to apologize then great i am all ears! but just mentioning it off hand and then yelling at yourself the same way you yell at me all the time as if i need a knight to come save me from yourself is so lame, not to mention completely insane
?GG: i cant even believe the things im typing here! this is so stupid, talking to two of you at once is the worst thing imaginable
?GG: you treat everyone horribly, even yourself, i cant even fathom how awful it is to be you
?GG: past karkat, youre acting like a bigger jerk than he is and i think you know that! why dont you take his advice and grow up
?GG: as if theres even a real difference between you two. three hours is hardly any time at all, you are the same person YOU FUCKING IDIOTS!!!!!!!!!
CCG: OH SHIT
FCG: YES, THAT WAS GREAT. WE BOTH HAD IT COMING, ESPECIALLY HIM. GREAT WORK JADE.
?GG: stop it!!!!
?GG: ugh, i dont know whats worse, jerk karkat or goofy sycophant karkat
?GG: i cant stand it, whether youre trying to be nice or just being a crazy asshole, you are just so weird!!!
?GG: im through humoring you, i dont even care about this stupid exploded robot mission, whatever that was
FCG: OH RIGHT, ABOUT THAT
FCG: YEAH WE NEED TO TALK
FCG: I MEAN WE HAVE ALREADY FROM MY PERSPECTIVE
FCG: BUT YOU'RE GOING TO BE REALLY BUSY SOON, BECAUSE YOU'RE ABOUT TO ENTER YOUR SESSION
FCG: SO DON'T WORRY ABOUT IT UNTIL YOU DO, THEN JUST HIT ME UP, WE'LL TALK ABOUT IT
?GG: hahaha, FAT CHANCE!!!!
FCG: LOOK I KNOW THINGS ARE WEIRD BETWEEN US RIGHT NOW AND YOU HAVE EVERY RIGHT TO BE MAD.
FCG: ESPECIALLY AT THAT LOSER.
FCG: BUT THINGS WILL CHANGE, IN TIME YOU'LL SEE I'M NOT QUITE SO AWFUL, OK?
??? turntechGodhead [?TG] AT ?:?? responded to memo.
?TG: ahahahahah oh god
?TG: dude i cant believe you were just getting on our case about hitting on the troll girls
?TG: and then literally the very next memo you are slobbering all over jade
?TG: thats just perfect hahahaha
CCG banned ?TG: from responding to memo.
FCG rebanned ?TG: from responding to memo.
?GG: dave wait dont go!
?GG: youve got to save me from this insanity :(
FCG: OH I SEE, NOW YOU COULD USE A KNIGHT, HOW VERY INTERESTING, HMMM.
FCG: GOD I CAN'T WAIT FOR YOU TO BE FUTURE YOU, SLIGHTLY LESS FUTURE YOU IS SUCH A GOD DAMN PILL
?GG: i cant wait for future you to future kiss my ass!
CCG: YEAH! THAT'S WHAT I'M TALKING ABOUT.
?GG: i also cant wait for past you to past drop dead and go to hell, PAST TENSE!!!!!!!!
?GG: when are those things going to happen?? or will have already past/future happened?????
?GG: i want to put another reminder on my finger so i know when its time to throw a party!!!!
FCG: HAHAHAHA, YOU HEAR THAT YOU OBSOLETE PILE OF GARBAGE? JADE JUST FLIPPED YOU OFF WITH A COLORFUL FINGER.

When Jade says she's "all ears," that's foreshadowing for when she has big dog ears later in the story. Ha ha, just joking, that isn't even remotely close to being true. Gotcha. Anyway, things really heat up quick here. Now that Karkat's unbelievably shitty strategy has broken the ice, they're letting loose all their bottled-up emotions. Who are they even kidding at this point? They might as well just be making out here. With the massively cross-pollinating collision between troll and human affairs resulting in stirrings of Vrisjohn, Daverezi, and Rosemary, you knew it was only a matter of time before someone latched on to Jade too. Jadekat is a highly respectable shipping endeavor. Clearly there's much to work with here. One could hardly be blamed for imagining it had a chance to make a deep run, perhaps even threaten endgame status. I mean, it *didn't*, but it totally could have, and there's nothing wrong with you sitting down in its cheering section. It also has some intriguing quadrangular dynamics with Daverezi, considering Davejade, Karezi, and Davekat are all powerhouse ships as well. Okay, I'm going to stop now, before someone puts me into the nerd catapult and launches me into the ocean.

CCG: MAN, SHE OBVIOUSLY HATES YOU MORE. SHE CALLED YOU A SYCOPHANT WHICH IS A HUNDRED TIMES MORE DESCRIPTIVELY WORSE THAN JUST BEING A RUN OF THE MILL SCUMBAG LIKE ME.
CCG: SHE IS TOTALLY ON TO YOU AND HOW DESPICABLE YOU'VE BECOME, CAN YOU BLAME HER FOR HATING US?
FCG: NO, I CAN BLAME YOU, YOU'RE THE ONE WITH NO MANNERS WHO'S ALL TWISTED UP INSIDE.
FCG: HOW'S THIS FOR A PACT, EVERYBODY.
FCG: PAST KARKAT ONLY TALKS TO PAST JADE FROM NOW ON, AND THE TWO OF THEM CAN BICKER LIKE SHITTY LITTLE CHILDREN FOR HOURS/YEARS RESPECTIVELY.
FCG: AND FUTURE KARKAT ONLY TALKS TO FUTURE JADE, AN ARRANGEMENT WHEREIN ONLY INTELLIGENT DISCOURSE TAKES PLACE BETWEEN TWO CIVILIZED, MATURE, GROWN ASSED ADULTS.
FCG: IS THAT TOO MUCH TO ASK??????
?GG: jesus will you just ban me already????
?GG: my head hurts so bad now i think im going to cry
FCG: MAYBE YOU SHOULD JUST BAN HER ALREADY AND END THIS TORMENT SINCE YOU DRAGGED HER INTO THIS.
CCG: FUCK THAT YOU BAN HER. YOU'RE THE ONE WHO SEEMS TO "CARE".
FCG: WILL YOU SHUT YOUR MOUTH, MAN THE FUCK UP, AND BAN THIS POOR GIRL ALREADY?
?GG: aaaaaaaaaaaaaaaaaaaaaaaaaaaaaaa XO
?GG: i will just ban myself!!!!
?GG: *JADE HARLEY BANNED HERSELF FROM RESPONDING TO THE GRUMPY SHIT HEAD MISERY ZONE, AND IS NEVER COMING BACK*
?GG: pchooooooooooooooooo
[?GG] ceased responding to memo.
FCG: OK, THERE. SHE'S GONE.
FCG: MAYBE NOW YOU GET IT.
FCG: HOW HIDEOUS EVERYONE THINKS YOU ARE, MAYBE YOU'LL FINALLY STOP FUCKING EVERYTHING UP.
CCG: HUH
FCG: WHAT
CCG: I THINK
CCG: I WAS PROBABLY WRONG ABOUT JADE
CCG: SHE'S A LITTLE LESS LAME THAN I THOUGHT
FCG: SHHHHSHHSHSHSHSH
FCG: SHE CAN STILL READ THIS YOU STUPID FUCK
FCG: NOW'S NOT THE TIME TO OPEN YOUR VEINS AND WRITE POEMS ABOUT YOUR FEELINGS
CCG: FUCK YOU, I'M JUST VOICING A HARMLESS OBSERVATION OK
CCG: IT'S NOT MY BUSINESS IF SOME LUNK HEAD IN THE FUTURE GETS CARRIED AWAY WITH WHATEVER LITTLE THOUGHTS I MAY OR MAY NOT NOW BE THINKING
FCG: I...
FCG: BUT
FCG: HOW COULD THAT EVEN BE A REAL THING I TYPED THREE HOURS AGO, HOW COULD I BE THIS STUPID.
FCG: WE ARE JUST THE DUMBEST FUCKERS WHO EVER LIVED AREN'T WE.
CCG: SPEAK FOR YOURSELF.
FCG: I DON'T EVEN HAVE THE ENERGY TO BAN US.
FCG: I'M JUST LEAVING.
[FCG] ceased responding to memo.
CCG: YEAH
[CCG] ceased responding to memo.

> Jade: Consult reminders.

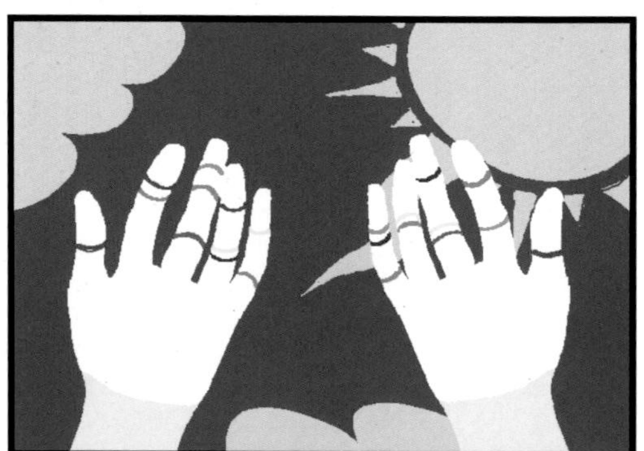

That was not a conversation you were hoping to wake up to. You feel more agitated and disoriented than ever.

You consult your reminders to get your bearings on what to do next.

But you can't remember what they mean at all. You have a feeling these are all useless now.

> Jade: Remove reminders.

The human session spans only about a day, but there are still signs that everyone is "growing up," at least in certain symbolic ways. Their guardians have moved on, their sprites are starting to go their separate ways too, and they're beginning to embrace a certain sense of adult responsibility for this journey with a bit of help from their new troll friends. Jade has just said goodbye to a certain childhood comfort: her life on Prospit, and her access to the all-knowing clouds of Skaia. She doesn't have a sprite to say goodbye to yet, because of course she's just getting started with the game herself. (Don't worry, she's about to get a doozy of a sprite very soon.) But ditching these colorful reminders on her fingers is definitely a big gesture that feels like it's closing the book on her childhood. No more cheating, hints, or spoilers. Those are for babies. In fact, she seems to start embracing this as a philosophy going forward, as she reprimands Karkat in future conversations for offering her "spoilers" by way of slipping out of chronological order with their respective chat connections. So she invents a fairly clever password system to keep things orderly.

You ditch the strings. All but one.

You don't remember what it was for, but it reminds you of something nonetheless. Something you can't believe you forgot about...

John!

He was falling in your dream. You tried to save him. You hope he is ok.

You look up at your house. Your cool satellite tower bedroom is gone.

What's that thing floating there?

> Jade: Head home.

Even her childhood bedroom is gone. No feelings are spared in this coming-of-age gauntlet. The room was full of just a bunch of silly, furry shit though. Maybe she should get over herself? Also, it's kind of funny that she keeps the blue string because it reminds her of something. And that thing is...John. She has been reminded by a blue piece of string that her best friend of many years, John Egbert, does in fact still exist somewhere. Man, no wonder she needed these things to keep track of her life. She'll forget ANYTHING.

Someone has connected as your server player.

You are pretty sure you know who it is.

> John: Be the someone who is Jade's server player.

You are suddenly John being the someone who is Jade's server player.

Since you have made short work of a delicious home cooked meal, you decide to bear down on this game. However, aromas from the ghost oven persist. What is that... lasagna? Wow, that smells great. Focus, Egbert, focus!

Since your paradox sister is still napping, you guess it couldn't hurt to set a few things up first.

> John: Deploy cruxtruder.

Rose, Dave, and now Jade sure seem to be showing signs of growing up. But not John. His nanna is still hovering around, cooking lasagna for him, while he subconsciously demonstrates his yearning for a father figure by continuing to display his dedication to the Cosbytop as a gaming platform despite the fact that, were it not for meteors destroying civilization, Bill Cosby would retroactively prove to be a bigtime rapist. John, maybe it's time to consider growing up and getting the fuck out of there? Hey, listen. It's not like I'm being *supervised* by anyone with good sense as I write these notes. There isn't a guy with a whistle standing behind me, going *PHWEET!* "No, stop. What you're saying there? Don't say that. There's absolutely no need to say the shit you're saying. Delete all that bullshit immediately, joke boy." Maybe I need a guy like that? Does anyone want to volunteer for the job? /Tumbleweeds rambunctiously bounce through the room./

This seems like the obvious place for this thing.

Be careful with that! Don't want to wake the doggy.

Jade's family sure is weird.

For such a huge house, things sure are cluttered in here. Got to make some space.

> John: Deploy totem lathe.

It stands to reason that John has never seen the interior of Jade's house. He has a pretty casual reaction to this ridiculous life she lives. But then again, his reaction to everything is casual. Except for revelations about fruit snacks, and reprising scenes from his favorite films. And now it's time for another episode of "someone recklessly mishandles the cherished belongings of a dear friend while setting up the *Sburb* equipment." You didn't really need these huge panels full of delicious vegetables, did you, Jade? No, of course not. Time to carelessly toss them outside from a great height rather than carefully putting them down in the living room or elsewhere. It's fine, she's going to start eating a lot more meat soon anyway.

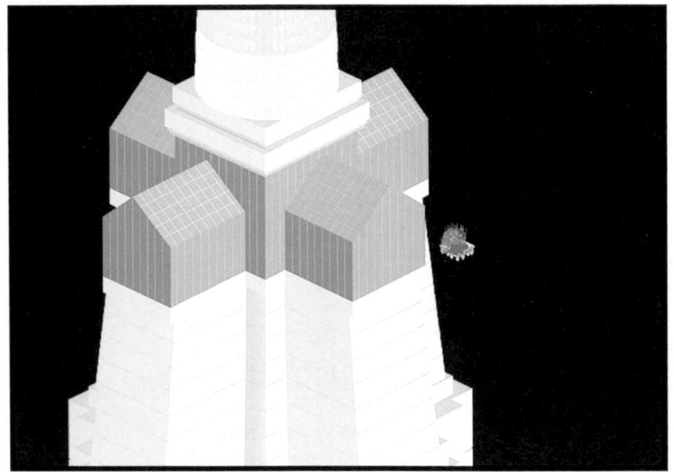

> John: Deploy alchemiter.

Jade can't catch a break today. Sandwiched between two screaming Karkats, with vegetable mayhem raining down on her from above due to John's buffoonery, she's under siege from stupid boys. Maybe Dave's about to burrow up from the ground under her feet and start blaring a trumpet at her obnoxiously, just to fully box her in.

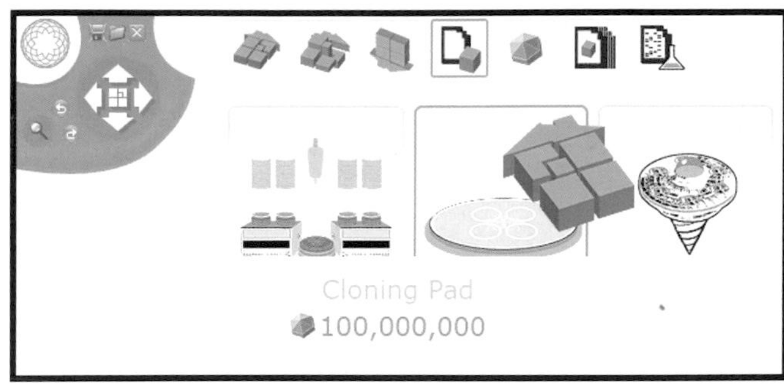

You suppose you could upgrade this thing right away, if Jade can spare some time to cooperate. You've got plenty of grist to spare.

There's a lot of new junk in the registry. You wonder what all this stuff is for.

It costs a fortune. You have a lot of grist, but not nearly that much.

> Jade: Go inside.

-- gardenGnostic [GG] began pestering ectoBiologist [EB] --

GG: john are you there???
EB: whoa, hey!
EB: you're awake!
GG: yes!
GG: im so relieved to talk to you and hear youre ok
GG: i mean.......
GG: are you ok john? your dream self i mean
EB: oh, yeah.
EB: i am pretty sure that i...
EB: he?
EB: am/is fine.
EB: i woke up on the battlefield which was on fire, and had flaming bits of prospit everywhere.
GG: :(
GG: yes, but that was not prospit. that was its moon which was severed by the crazy derse agent
EB: oh, you mean jack?

GG: i dunno!
EB: that is his name, karkat told me.
EB: i saw him there too.
EB: oh!!!!!
EB: i also got your present, and it saved my life!

John sees that new *Sburb* equipment is available in the interface. What unlocked the availability of these expensive items is the fact that Jade is about to enter the game, or specifically, that John has established the final player link with her. Jade is the Space player. As such, one of her responsibilities is to bring with her into the session that big volcano known as the Forge, which is a construct critical for the creation of a universe. All Space player–related activity pertains to universe creation, or, put in a more esoteric way, frog breeding. This is what Jade's supposed to be doing after she enters, figuring out the ins and outs of frog breeding. That is, their cloning process, which enables a player to mix and match genes until just the right tadpole has been made. But this is an idea we have no appreciation for yet, so we have no way of knowing that the items John is looking at in the upper righthand panel are for this purpose. We do see Jade get to work on this process later in the act, so we find out what the two devices on the left do. But the one on the right is kind of mysterious. It's actually the mechanism by which the tadpole is "loaded" into the planet's core, ready to be fired from the Forge into Skaia when the time is right. You put the tadpole into the bubble (note the doomsday dice cascader-like design), and the thing drills into the planet until it gets to the core. But the kids never needed to use it, because their tadpole serendipitously found another way to the core.

002868

GG: really?? :D
EB: yes, the bunny was so awesome, it was definitely the best bunny i got today.
EB: thank you so much, jade!
GG: <3
EB: when jack saw it, he flew the hell away. and then the bunny and i went on an adventure together.
EB: does the bunny have a name? i asked him but i don't think he can talk.
GG: i dont know! i did not give him one after applying the upgrades
GG: i gave her a girls name when i was very young, but now she is a different bunny, and also a boy i guess?
GG: its up to you john, he is your bunny
EB: oh, i did not even think of that.
EB: well if she grew up as a girl, then it's not right for me to suddenly make her a boy.
EB: hmm...
EB: you have no idea how tempted i am to name her casey again.
GG: hahahaha
GG: again?
EB: yes, i named a young salamander casey earlier, but then i left her at rose's house.
GG: you were at roses house??
EB: yes, but she was asleep.
EB: also, apparently i am supposed to marry rose. karkat said so.
GG: what!!!!
EB: it is true, it is a fact from an alien.
GG: ugh he is so weird
GG: you shouldnt listen to him!
EB: heheh, i did not take him that seriously.
EB: but karkat is cool, he is angry and funny.
GG: D:
GG: he is angry and a huge pain in the ass
GG: have you ever talked to two of him at once????
EB: haha, no!
GG: dont ever do it! you will get a headache
EB: that sounds kind of awesome.
GG: nooooooooo, think again
EB: i've got it.
EB: i will name her liv tyler.
GG: ????
EB: the bunny.
GG: :|
GG: you mean from armageddon?
EB: yeah!
GG: john that is so stupid
GG: but also kind of cute i guess
GG: ok then the bunny will be named after your silly movie star fantasy crush
EB: it's too bad i can't marry liv instead of rose.
EB: the girl i mean, not the bunny.
EB: but i guess she is probably dead now, along with all the other glamorous movie stars who come out to shine on the silver screen.
EB: that's pretty sad.
GG: yeah......
GG: that reminds me john
GG: have you looked in the lab yet?
EB: the lab?
GG: the big room in the sphere at the top of the tower
EB: oh, no. why?
GG: could you do me a favor and not look in there?
EB: ok. why, is there a secret in there?
GG: its nothing that secret or personal or anything....
GG: it is just something kind of sad and weird for you to see
EB: what is it?
GG: it is my dead dream self
GG: it has been there for years, i always knew i would die but i did not realize it would go like this....
EB: oh...
EB: errr...
GG: what?
EB: i have sort of already seen... that.
EB: not in the lab, but on the battlefield.
GG: oh no!!!!!
GG: im sorry john :(

As much as we all loved Hivebent, it still had this massive delaying effect at a point in the story immediately following a critical crescendo of super exciting plot stuff. We had to plow through Hivebent for hundreds of pages, and then through quite a lot of A5A2, before finally returning to some really basic stuff from **[S] Descend** that felt like a big deal at the time. Specifically, "Hey, remember how Jade sacrificed her dream self to save John, and how her robot bunny present saved his life, and all that other stuff??" It feels like that all happened ages ago. Now they finally catch up about it, but so much has happened between now and then that the accumulated intrigue has kind of started to have a muting effect on the intensity surrounding the events of **Descend**. There's a lot more going on now, and them touching on the topic of Prospit's destruction, Jade's dream death, and a heroic bunny rescue all seem like pretty casual points of conversation that can freely mingle with other banter, like how multiple Karkats have been macking on Jade lately. This is a pattern that plays out a lot in HS, probably unavoidably due to its scale, the size of the cast, and how many plot threads are being handled at once. Sometimes series of brewing events all coalesce and galvanize through some intense, dramatic, single event, as in **Descend**, **[S] Make her pay**, or the mother of them all, **[S] Cascade**. -->

EB: it's ok.
EB: i was so confused and sad when i saw you lying there...
EB: i'd rather not talk about it i guess.
GG: i understand
EB: but, i wonder...
EB: if your dream self died...
EB: then what were you just dreaming about now?
GG: ummmmmmm
GG: i think i would rather not talk about that either
EB: ok, that's cool.
EB: oh, also...
EB: i found your ring.
GG: you did????
EB: yes...
EB: but then i woke up, and didn't have it anymore.
EB: so i am not sure where it is now.
GG: oh nooooooo
GG: john that ring is really important, it belongs to the white queen!
EB: oh, whoa.
GG: when you go to sleep again, you should try to find it and keep it safe!
EB: ok, i will do that.
EB: hey jade, we have a lot to catch up on, but how about later?
EB: we have to hurry, remember there is a big meteor heading for you right now?
GG: yes i have seen it, it is so huge ._.
GG: how much time do you suppose we have?
EB: i will find out now!

--> But then those plot points are taken off the burner and put aside on the counter to cool, often for quite some time. This lets the story drift back to the casual, silly stuff, which can be seen as HS kind of gravitationally reverting to its most fundamental nature: ridiculous kids BS'ing with each other about stupid shit. But it was also a necessary thing to do from a creative production standpoint: I couldn't always focus just on the intense stuff and keep relentlessly following through on it while it was piping hot, because that was not a sustainable proposition in terms of effort (a thing the kids at home never really understood, while feeling inclined to grouse about pacing issues). So this gradual "cooling effect" of hot plot points actually became deeply interwoven with the story construction and how that flowed. The hot material is always revisited though—rarely is anything *totally* dropped—but when it comes back into play it definitely has a different effect for having spent several hundred (or even thousand) pages sitting on the windowsill to cool. That cooled-off material becomes a different kind of ingredient than it once was while it was red-hot, as if the recipe called for it to be set aside to cool, to change its nature, its feel, and the way it tastes. And meanwhile many other exotic ingredients have been prepared. So when the cooled-off ingredient is reintroduced, now it just feels like all the other ingredients coming together to make something new, rather than still feeling like "the most important thing going on," as it once did. So then this amalgamation of new ingredients together with old, previously amalgamated ingredients, forms a new recipe, waiting for its turn to get thrown into the oven so everything can approach another critical galvanization as before. Rinse and repeat, until HS finally and miraculously ends.

> John: Open cruxtruder.

Speaking of revisiting the hot stuff, Jack finally catches up with his new ninja bro-crush, tosses him his sword, and silently expresses an interest in "throwing down" here in this new dramatic setting. As Dirk stands there nonchalantly with his back turned, holding his cool rocket board, you can almost hear him say "What took you so long?"

EB: oh fuck!

Trying to parse what's happening in some of the animated GIFs rendered into static sequences in these books is probably not the easiest thing in the world, huh? What's going on here is: John uses a globe to open the cruxtruder, but the globe bank-shots toward Jade, and Bec steps in to protect her by mask-wiping the thing into space. Then Bec hops outside so we get another look at how big that meteor is, and also, how "almost here" it is. It's really, really "almost here." And big.

EB: ok, we have 10 minutes and 25 seconds.
GG: hmmmm i wonder what the significance of that number is
EB: why would it be significant?
EB: numbers don't always need to have significance!
GG: but they usually do!
EB: ok, well the number is now less than it was, and therefore less significant.
EB: and by less, i mean more! you had better hurry upstairs and make your special item.
GG: yes, youre right
EB: hey, what do you think we should prototype this fussy little orb with?
EB: heheheh, it seems like so long ago that rose fed mine a clown.
EB: we were just messing around, we didn't even know what we were doing.
GG: i dont know...
GG: there are so many possibilities
EB: yeah...
EB: it's almost like your grandpa put all this crap here knowing we'd have to make that decision.
GG: hmmmmmm!
GG: yes, it sure seems that way
EB: he seems like he was an awesome guy, i would have liked to have the chance to talk to him.
GG: well
GG: maybe you will get that chance john
EB: oh?
GG: yes, as a matter of fact i am sure we will both get that chance!
GG: i once dreamt that we would
EB: huh...
EB: wait, are you saying we will prototype him?
EB: like i did with nanna, to bring her ghost back to life?
EB: as...
EB: another ghost?
GG: sure, why not!
EB: i guess that makes a lot of sense, actually.
GG: that is what i believe this game is for in part

GG: you got to bring back your nanna, rose brought back her cat, i can bring back grandpa, and dave...
GG: dave got to bring back a dead bird because of course he is too cool to have any dead family members
EB: yeah, also he brought back himself from the future.
EB: who... wasn't dead, but was going to die maybe? i dunno.
EB: specifically to save my life, as well as

In fact, John comes right out and says exactly how "almost here" the meteor is for us, so we have a very concrete appreciation for the stakes. Thanks, John. Oh, and Jade? 1025 obviously is 413 + 612. I thought you were supposed to be a science genius or whatever? Some genius. The kids get a little meta about all the crap strewn around her house, as if Grandpa knew this was a choice Jade would have to make and so gave her a lot of options. Which of course is what I was actually doing, by putting all that stuff in here. Jake is inappropriately stealing my credit for advance planning and cleverness, which he does not deserve. The purpose of the objects was to supply Jade with a lot of prototyping options, but more accurately, it was to supply readers with a lot of fuel for speculation, doubling as excessive misdirection for what was really going to end up in that kernel: a whole spriteload of magic dog.

yours, i think.
GG: wait, he did????
EB: yes.
GG: that is
GG: soooo coooooool :O
EB: it's pretty neat, i guess.
GG: i almost completely forgot i was his server player!!!!!
GG: i hope hes not in trouble, i should check on him
GG: we probably have so much to catch up on
EB: i just messaged him, he is not answering.
GG: i dont see him in his house either :(
EB: ehhh, he's fine, he has been doing a lot of time traveling.
EB: i talked to him from the future, so he must be ok now to make it that far.
GG: oh, ok...
GG: jeez, i feel so out of the loop :(
EB: yes, that is why we need to get you in the loop!
EB: the loop being the game. hurry upstairs! your transporty pad thingies take you straight up, right?
GG: yes! ok here i go
EB: oh, wait!!!
GG: what!
EB: what do we do about prototyping?
EB: we shouldn't put your grandpa in yet, unless we want lots of imps and ogres and stuff that look like your grandpa.
GG: augh, noooooooooooooooo
EB: we could put in something really lame, to make all the monsters weaker!
EB: or at the very least, more ridiculous looking.
EB: like one of these weird pictures of blue ladies lying around.
EB: what's the deal with those, anyway?
GG: oh god, dont get me started :|
GG: he was a strange and silly man
EB: i guess we could just put nothing in and see what happens.
GG: hmmmmmmm, perhaps
GG: is that allowed?
EB: i don't see why not.
EB: maybe i will ask rose, because she suddenly understands everything for some reason.
GG: yes, thats a good idea
EB: we have ten minutes to think about it.
EB: whoops! i mean a lot less than ten minutes!
EB: hurry upstairs, go go go!!!

John, there's not much of a mystery here: Jake was just unusually horny for blue women. And now you yourself are blundering right into one such woman's web. No wonder you and he are related. Back to the prototyping issue. The more you review the banter surrounding this topic and all the factors piling up, the more it starts to feel like the Becsprite outcome was fairly predictable, or at least within guessable territory. The kids speculate about putting in something lame or ridiculous to make the monsters weaker, which, narratively speaking, smacks of a plan that isn't going to work. So if you use that as a clue to get on the story's wavelength, you'd be led to think, "What could possibly go wrong here that would accomplish the opposite effect?" And there aren't many good answers to that. Knights, mummies...none of this crap realistically is going to make Jack *that* much stronger than he already is. Bec is the only thing around here with that kind of power. Probably the only deterrent to guessing this will happen is that Bec has been established to be SO powerful that his prototyping would escalate the stakes so radically, it almost doesn't feel plausible. How do you beat Jack if he's omnipotent, can teleport anywhere, and is basically indestructible? But then, that's also what makes **[S] Jade: Enter** such an intense development. It also makes everything kind of fit: why the kids blew it and made their session unwinnable, as the trolls have been warning them since the start. It connects a few other dots too. Even so, I don't remember many people predicting the idea with much confidence. Some guessed it as a possibility, but nobody thought it was a slam dunk. Part of that is probably due to HS establishing itself as a thing that makes a fool out of you if you start feeling too confident you know where it's going. If not for that quality, probably a lot more people would be like, oh yeah, that dog's going in that thing, NO DOUBT. People would smell it coming just due to their natural narrative spidey senses. This is actually what you're competing with when you write a story. Everyone's like a weird savant when it comes to sussing out narrative payoffs, because we all consume such an outrageous amount of shit and therefore know all the tricks. So you really have to pull out all the stops if you want to consistently bamboozle people.

> Jade: Proceed to stairwell.

Davesprite got the message: "Show up by the oil falls if you want an ass kicking." On the previous page, Bro reaches for his puppet, cool as can be. Like, "Oh, you brought my sword back? That's nice of you. But this puppet here is my true weapon." It's a multi-faceted weapon: a floppy bludgeoning tool, a weapon to train a young warrior with as a little mock-sparring partner, a weapon of psychological torment to harden his protégé against his enemies, and perhaps to subconsciously remind him of who his ultimate foe is, by flailing the vessel for his dark soul in his face. "Puppet as a weapon" extends well beyond Bro's use of Cal. Doc, who is essentially a glorified puppet, describes himself as his master's weapon. There's a deeper meaning to this as well, which is probably best covered when Doc returns to prominence. Caliborn, whose soul resides in Cal, also has a name based on a weapon. Excalibur, or Dave's Caledfwlch, which was a point I was hovering around earlier. There's a lot to get into there as well, but again, let's not be rude, and instead wait until he's actually around. The idea that Caliborn's name has anything to do with Dave's weapon seems like such a screwball fact, but you can start to see the vague contours of governing logic there once you delve into the "puppets = weapons" motif which rears its head now and then.

EB: what is this thing, anyway??
EB: and why is it blocking your transporter?
GG: it is some sort of terrible creature my grandpa hunted
GG: he called it the typheus minion
GG: i always hated it!
EB: typheus?
EB: like the web browser?
GG: i guess so
GG: it is probably a coincidence though
EB: hmm, i don't know...
EB: if you think numbers always mean something, why wouldn't browser names?
GG: yeah maybe.....
GG: i guess it would make sense for someone to name a really awful web browser after such a hideous monster
EB: wow, you sure do hate that thing!
GG: well sorry, i just found it sort of a weird and creepy thing to grow up with!
EB: i think it is pretty cool.
EB: and he is actually sort of cute to be honest, :p
GG: :p!!!!!!
EB: oh, and screw you, typheus is an awesome browser!
EB: it is old school.
GG: joooohhhhhn, it is so crappy
EB: typheus is the best and that's really all there is to say on the matter.
GG: YEAH RIGHT
GG: now is obviously not the best time to have the argument about whose browser is better....
GG: but really john you should upgrade to echidna, its so much nicer
GG: after you upgrade your clunky old computer of course :P
GG: maybe when i am in the game, i can give you one of mine!

EB: oh please.
EB: i will have you know, miss fancy computer dork...
EB: that i DID upgrade my computer.
GG: oh???
EB: yes, you are talking to the proud owner of a brand new BILL COSBY COMPUTER, ok?
GG: :O
EB: it is a stylish laptop in the shape of none other than bill cosby, the comedy LEGEND himself.
GG: omg
EB: he is looking a little sly, and fatherly, and he is wearing a sweater, and he is bill cosby.
EB: i made it with my alchemiter.
GG: john that is incredible
GG: i cant wait to make stuff like that!!!!!!
GG: except...
GG: all my awesome stuff exploded with my room :(
EB: then you will just have to make lots of NEW awesome stuff!
GG: yay!!!
EB: ok hold that thought, im going to yank this stupid monster off of the thing.

> John: Yank monster off of thing.

Come on, John, obviously Typheus is your denizen. Try to read between the lines and start making a few leaps in logic. John and Jade have a little spat here over browser preference. Maybe this idea is outdated? I don't think anybody really gives a fuck about which browser to use anymore. Also most people just use their phones to Do Internet anyway, and browsers aren't much of a thing on those. There was an era where this was real shit though. Kids these days gotta believe me on this. Like, Explorer vs. Firefox vs. Netscape vs. Safari vs. Chrome vs. Opera... Man, remember Opera? Ridiculous. Then they start talking about... Oh no. They're talking about Cosby again. And John just said he's looking a little sly. Jesus, John. Why did so much Cosby bullshit metastasize through this part of the story? Maybe I should have had John go back and retcon all the Cosby references out of HS.

EB: augh!!!!!!!!!!!
EB: i am making such a fucking mess in here.

> Jade: Go upstairs.

Another sequence that works much better as a GIF. John drops Typheus, and all the Grandpa crap goes flying and gets completely jumbled. Note how this bit of slapstick is actually just a huge prototyping tease. Look at how close Grandpa's head is to the kernelsprite. And the blue lady portrait, just teetering on the brink. And a blue lady doll, which now seems kind of conspicuous. John ultimately does opt to use it for prototyping, for some reason. Probably due to his brewing fixation on Vriska. And he very nearly succeeds in "upgrading" Jack with this harmless, silly doll. Until the meddling blue spiderlady herself intervenes and makes something very bad happen instead. You see, she wanted to be "important," etc. etc.

GG: what is the problem!!!!
EB: oh, nothing.
EB: i am just dropping monsters all over the place, that is all.
EB: are you upstairs?
GG: yes
EB: ok, good.
EB: i left the cruxite by the lathe, as well as the punched card with the green thingy on it.
EB: you should have plenty of time to make it. no drama here!
GG: nice!
GG: how much time?
EB: a little more than 6 minutes.
EB: in the meantime, i will try to contact rose and get this prototyping nonsense sorted out.
EB: it's so confusing...
EB: in my foolishness, i came very close to prototyping your grandpa.
GG: D:
GG: john, try to be more careful!

EB: we very nearly had to face our grandfatherly paradox-dad as a last boss.
EB: that would probably be the worst case scenario.
GG: um.....
GG: what?

Oh, Jade still hasn't gotten the memo, I guess: her grandpa is her dad. Hence the confusion in her last line up there. But we'll leave it at that, because it's funny, and also, the last thing we need is another gratuitous Egbertian explanation roughly along the lines of "BY THE WAY! WE'RE ALL RELATED IT TURNS OUT, WHICH MEANS EVERYTHING IS ONE BIG INCEST TRAP NOW!" Actually, maybe that would have been a good line, now that I think of it. Oh, it looks like my life coach has just opened another bottle of scotch.

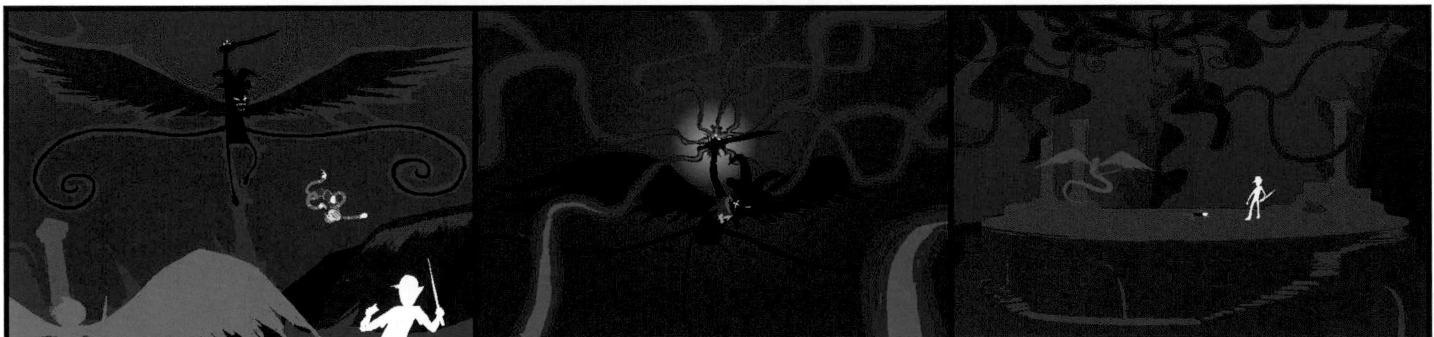

I dunno what to say about this scene, other than it's all pretty cool. Good drawings, sharp action, it's all happening, man. However, I will say this battle has finally brought to the fore an ominously lurking question, at least for those of us who are obsessed with whatever there is that can possibly go wrong and like to ask lots of questions to that effect. Which is...isn't a fantastical planet literally covered in oil KIND OF a big fire hazard?

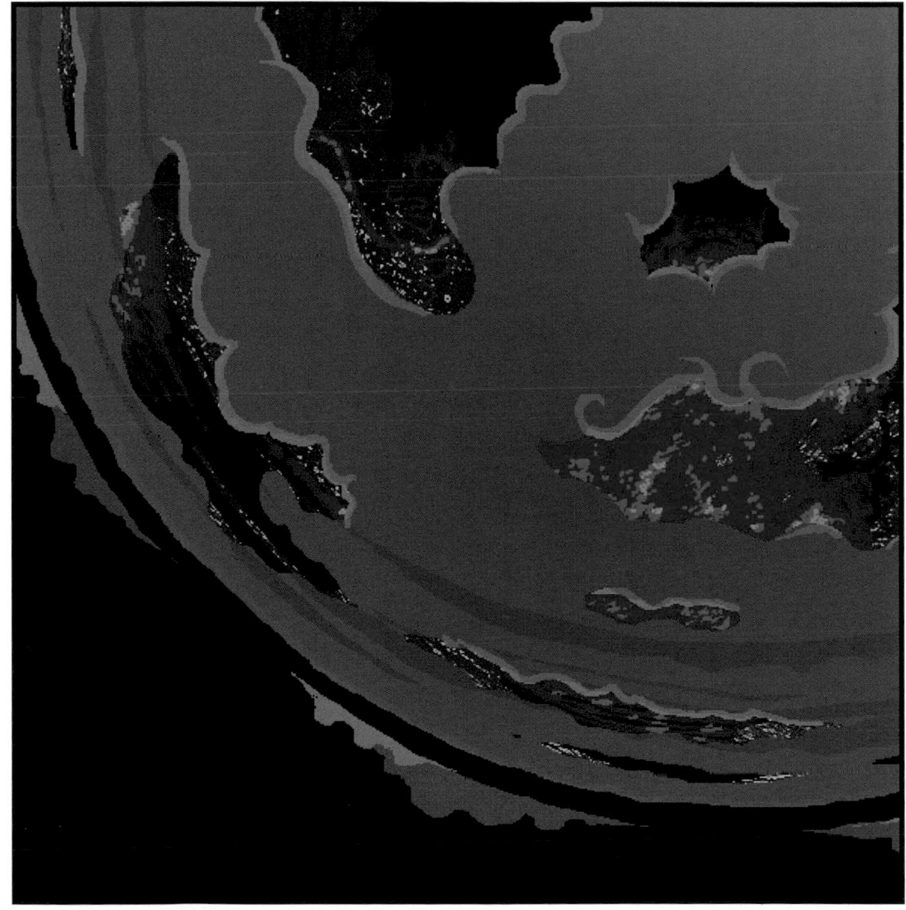

More sick panels. Didn't Saddam Hussein basically do the same thing during the Gulf War? This sounds like stray trivia, but it's actually an important point of characterization. Because now we have formally confirmed that Jack Noir is at least as bad as Saddam Hussein.

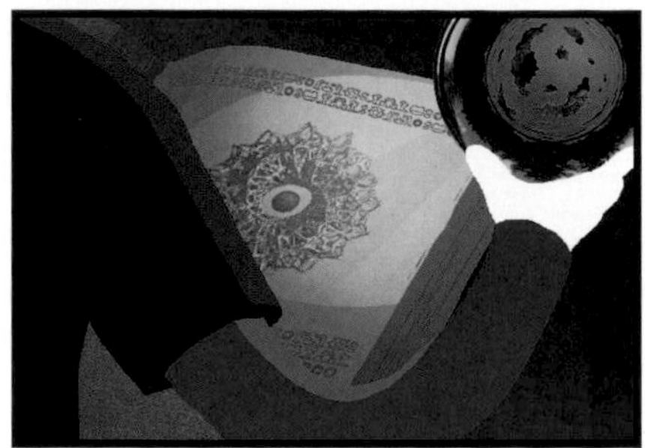

> Rose: Answer John.

-- tentacleTherapist [TT] began pestering ectoBiologist [EB] --

EB: rose, i have a question, and i am in a hurry!
EB: so hurry up and answer!!!
TT: Did you know your planet was on fire?
EB: oh.
EB: it is?
TT: Yes. It makes a good light for reading, actually.
EB: ok, haha, that's a confusing thing you said, but that topic will have to wait!
EB: jade is minutes away from entering, and i need to decide what to do with this kernel sprite.
EB: i really don't want to mess up and do something stupid.
EB: i was thinking about not prototyping at all, to not give the monsters any new powers.
EB: what do you think, rose?
EB: i thought i'd ask since you seem to know all the mysteries.
TT: Yes, I do seem to be shadowed by each mystery and its somber cortege of riddles, don't I?
EB: yes.
EB: that is exactly what i was going to say.
TT: First of all, I should preface this conversation by saying I know exactly what you and Jade are going to do.

EB: um...
EB: ok?
TT: The more of our future I've been allowed to see, the more I'm presented with a challenge I'm not very comfortable with.
TT: The trolls have tipped us off about what's to come without any regard for the consequences, as appears to be their nature.
TT: But maybe that's why it's worked for them.
TT: Maybe their indiscretion mingles with the cosmic noise that is the fabric of temporal uncertainty.
EB: bluhhhhhh...
EB: rose, tick tick tick!!!

This obscure tome gives us a brief glimpse of the Battlefield's final form. It transforms from its current state, a sphere, into this Sphere Plus, once Jade enters and completes the chain. The idea is that it keeps ramping up in geometric complexity with each player entry, from plane, to cube, to planet-like sphere with mountains and such, to this thing that entails spatial dimensions going haywire in its orbit. What did the Battlefield look like after twelve entries in the troll session? That's anyone's guess, but I wasn't about to tie my brain into a knot trying drawing that out for you. Picture it how you will. Also, I guess turtles can grow beards? Sure, why not.

TT: Sorry, John.
TT: I'm just nervous about it.
TT: About whether telling you what you definitely will or won't do will alter a predetermined outcome.
TT: The result would be a splintered timeline, and we would all be sentenced to eventual oblivion.
TT: I'm presently optimistic this has not happened yet, and this is still the alpha timeline. I'd like to keep it that way.
EB: oh, wow.
EB: you mean like when i died in another dimension, because terezi hornswoggled me?
TT: Yes, sort of.
TT: It isn't much fun, John.
EB: what's not?
TT: Living for months in an offshoot reality, waiting for the curtain to drop.
EB: oh, ok, i see.
EB: well, uh...
EB: is there anything you can tell me?
TT: Hmm.
TT: I guess I can permit myself to tell you this, somewhat definitively.
EB: what?
TT: Failing to prototype the kernel is the absolute worst thing that you could possibly do.
TT: Like, ever.
EB: oh no!
TT: We would come into possession of all the disasters.
TT: Exhaustive possession. Monopolization, in fact.
EB: then i guess i will not do that.
EB: why is it so bad?
TT: Because the battlefield will not be able to heal, and then transform.
TT: It will not reach the stage which allows it to become ready to receive our universe.
EB: but...
EB: i thought you said it wasn't going to be able to make a universe anyway?
EB: wasn't it barren or something?
TT: Yes.
EB: so why is it important?
TT: Because if it does not reach this stage, we will not be able to recover the treasure hidden in its core.
TT: Which is to say,
TT: You will not be able to recover it.
TT: When you go to sleep again.
EB: OHHHHHH.
EB: why didn't you say so, of course the answer is treasure.
TT: Yes. This is the treasure that will give us hope.
TT: But only if it comes into being in the first place.
EB: what is the treasure exactly?
TT: John, what is that sound?
EB: what sound?
TT: It seems to be a ticking noise.
EB: aaaahh!
EB: yeah, i've got to go. we can chat about treasure later.
EB: anyway, i will sort out this prototyping silliness myself.
EB: thanks rose!

-- ectoBiologist [EB] ceased pestering tentacleTherapist [TT] --

> Jade: Examine punched card.

Rose is tucked away in some completely unknown, unmapped library, probably somewhere deep in some pink turtle ruins. Off-screen, she's continued down the path we've been led to assume she would, which is pulling her deeper into studies of the occult, investigating the more arcane secrets of *Sburb*, which seems to be sending her further away from the type of journey her friends can relate to. Her increasing levels of knowledge not only cause her to come across less like the "old Rose" they all know, but also seems to make her more cautious and paranoid. She's less inclined to freely share information, where before she was dumping any thought that popped into her head into the FAQ. It's for everyone's own good of course—she doesn't want to create a doomed timeline. Still, it seems like a departure for her, a venture down a troubling road others can't follow or understand. Down a...grim road, if you will. A dark road. The road is both grim and dark, is what I'm saying. Rose notes the importance of the Battlefield's final form, but tellingly, she sees that importance as deriving not from its fully realized creative potential, but from the destructive potential that can be mined from it. There's only one thing Rose really wants: the huge bomb hidden in its core. A bomb that is super important to the highly emo plan which has been percolating in her troubled teen brain ever since she started smashing everything to pieces.

What the heck is this?

> Jade: Carve totem.

> Jade: Pester Dave.

-- gardenGnostic [GG] began pestering turntechGodhead [TG] --

GG: dave!
GG: are you busy?
GG: i dont have much time!
GG: i am about to make my entry item, and its a little confusing
GG: i think the more players we add, the trickier they are to... um......
GG: activate!
GG: like yours was
GG: i figured we could brainstorm about it, while john fusses with the kernel
GG: hellooooooo?
TG: nak nak nak
GG: :o
TG: nak nak nak nak nak nak
GG: :\
GG: whaaat....?
TG: nakka nakka nak

GG: dammit dave!!!!!!
GG: this is really urgent!
TG: MY GLASSES ARE TALKING TO ME MY GLASSES ARE TALKING TO ME
TG: naknaknaknaknaknaknaknaknaknaknaknak
GG: ._.

Top-shelf gag here, Dave's shades getting hijacked by a nakadile. It's best that I tell you which things are funny. I bet you appreciate it. I'm going to keep making some self-evident points here, hang on. Dave is asleep, which means Jade can't talk to him. It would be nice if they could catch up, just like she and John did, and I bet they would like that, but this brings up a challenging aspect in managing this big ensemble. The dialogue is all very banter-driven, and there are a lot of characters, which means there's a mathematically very wide range of pairings to consider for such banter, even if you limit it to only the most relevant pairings. It was always an option for me to just...ignore the potential for banter, by not showing it. For example, the Rose/Jade chats never got much play, and I think that was largely due to these bandwidth issues. As a result, they're a lot more likely to talk to/about the boys than each other, which wasn't a thing that was "designed" about their relationship. It just resulted organically from the factors I'm describing here. (The Jade/Rose ship name is Bye-Bye Bechdel, FYI.) Aside from just ignoring certain conversational matchups, it actually helped the writing process a bit to have these little devices that blocked certain conversational possibilities, and so narrowed the potentially wide range. Usually that device is "person is asleep, or otherwise indisposed." Like Jade is for much of the early acts, which actually does free the characterization bandwidth a bit while establishing some fundamental things about the other characters. Here, she's just finished catching up with John, plus weathering an icebreaker fracas with the Karkats. I think it would be goofy pacing to then have her really hash it out with Dave. That's something that can, and does, wait until later. So Dave being asleep turns out to be narratively convenient, and was partly designed to be so. The sleeper is awake, the waker is asleep... How the turn tables...

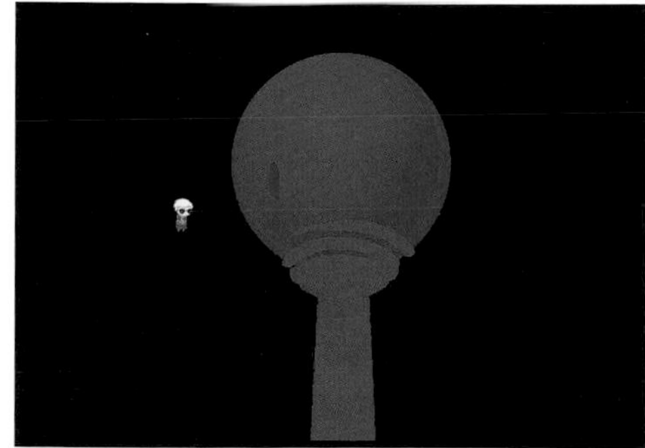

> Dave: Visit paradox sister.

> Rose: View John.

Speaking of wakers and sleepers, both Rose and Dave watch each other sleep, in a way. Rose creeps on him through her sweet crystal ball (i.e. the exact asset for the dream bubbles later), while Dave creeps on her in her moon room. But them hanging out as dream selves is kind of old hat by now. What's new is the ominous, dark aura surrounding Rose. Obviously this is because she is descending into the the fabled blackdeath trance of the woegothics, as she says to John in a few pages during a sort of self-effacing roast on this subject. It's all a big fucking joke. Until it isn't. (And even then, it still is.) A note on Dave: any time we get the rare privilege of seeing him without his shades, it mainly serves to remind us how off the charts his eyebrow game is. They're really something.

> John: Wake up.

Wait, what happened? Where are you?
Hey is that your...

NO BILL NOOOOOOOOOOOOOOOOOOO

How many times must you say goodbye??

NO NANNA NOOOOOOOOOOOOOOOOOOO

Well, at least you are pretty sure she doesn't live in there. She is probably still back at your house, baking or something.

> John: Pester Jade.

There is no way to interpret this moment as anything other than an incredibly astute foreshadowing of what happened to Cosby's career and legacy later. He's literally being tarnished here, and is about to disappear into the thick sludge of scandal forever. Just as well.

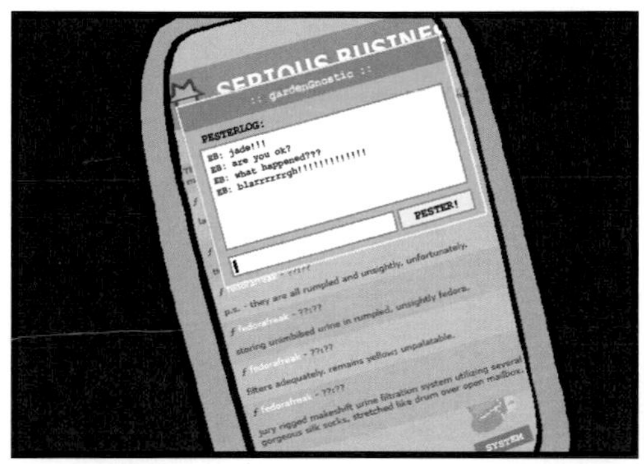

There is no answer.

YOU ARE JUST SO FRUSTRATED wait why the hell would you do that, what was the point.

> John: Equip goggles.

In spite of being an idiot, you still have a viable remaining communication device.

And as fortune would have it, someone is communicating with you now. This girl better have some damn answers!!!

> John: Answer Rose.

This is a little reminiscent of those times John kept launching stuff from his sylladex out of windows and whatnot due to his bungling shenanigans. He has come a very long way. Rather than doing incredibly stupid counterproductive things by accident, he's graduated to doing incredibly stupid counterproductive things on purpose.

-- tentacleTherapist [TT] began pestering ectoBiologist [EB] --

TT: John.
EB: blaaauuuuuuuuugh, what happened!!!!!
TT: You were sleeping.
EB: yes, i know!
EB: on the corner of my ghost bed!
EB: in the middle of an oil ocean!
EB: for some reason!!!
TT: Why were you sleeping?
TT: Everywhere I look, I see boys taking naps.
EB: um...
EB: i have no idea.
EB: i don't remember what happened, i was in the middle of helping jade...
EB: and then...
EB: i guess my bed crashed?
EB: and i got knocked out i guess.
EB: i was dreaming.
EB: i couldn't have been out for that long, because my dream was really short.
TT: You weren't.
TT: Ten minutes, I'd say.
TT: What were you dreaming about?
EB: i was on the battlefield again.
EB: but i did not have time to seek the treasure!
TT: I wouldn't imagine so.
EB: but...
EB: i did see a black guy wrapped up in my ghosty bed sheets.
EB: he was acting very suspicious.
TT: A black guy?
EB: oh...
EB: i do not mean like, an african american or anything.
EB: like bill cosby.
TT: Thanks for clearing that up.
EB: r.i.p. bill. :(
EB: this fellow had a hard black shell, like all the dead guys do.
EB: i followed him for a bit...
EB: and then some sorta ruckus transpired, and i woke up.
EB: and now jade won't answer!
EB: do you know if she's ok?
TT: She's fine.
TT: But you're not.
EB: i'm not?
TT: Remember how I said your planet was on fire?
EB: oh yeah...
EB: that didn't by any chance stop being a thing that was true, did it?
TT: It did not.
TT: Do you see that pinkish hue behind you, bleeding over the horizon?
EB: fuck!!!
EB: rose, this is all oil! it'll all just explode any second, won't it???
TT: I don't think the fire's rate of propagation is quite as fast as you're imagining.
TT: But the danger is still significant.
TT: Especially considering that your bed is sinking.
EB: fuuuuuuuuuuuck!!!!!!!
TT: Relax.
TT: Look to your right.

> John: Look to your right.

It's important to note that we didn't actually see John fall asleep, and we last saw him wide-awake, helping Jade like he says here. Then he was asleep for ten minutes, and now he's awake again. So this is a little hitch forward in time, with some missing action behind it. We don't know what happened, why he fell asleep, or what the ramifications of that are. We're getting set up to fill in those blanks with **[S] Jade: Enter**, which starts in a few pages. John falling asleep is what triggers Jade's prototyping mishap, but ten minutes apparently isn't *quite* enough time for Jade to enter the session and for the prototyping to result in the dire consequences it will have on Jack. (The main indication John will have of this event is when the fire turns green.) So surely there isn't much time between now and when that happens. But it's enough time for John and Rose to squeeze in this conversation, where he dutifully cautions his friend about the perils of grimdarkness.

TT: This will at least buy you some time.
TT: If you stay calm, and we work together, we can get you out of this.
TT: I'm practically an expert at escaping fires by now.
EB: ok, thank you rose.
EB: hey, how do you know these things anyway?
EB: can you see me somehow?
TT: Yes.
TT: I have a crystal ball.
EB: oh man, really?
TT: Yes.
EB: like a magic one?
TT: I think so.
EB: can it show you the future?
EB: is that how you know what's going to happen?
TT: No, it can only show me various locations in the present moment, as far as I can tell.
TT: My perception of the future has been informed by other sources.
EB: like what?
TT: Informants.
EB: durrrrr.
TT: Whispering gods, memories sifted from dreams, cryptic readings from unearthed talismans, conclusions drawn from riddles deciphered - every gambit you'd expect a quest to extend to an emerging seer.
TT: Just as I presume an heir would be supplied with what's needed for his maturation, assuming he's looking for it.
EB: oh... yeah.
EB: point taken. i guess i should be looking, huh?
TT: You should probably be doing what you're doing.
EB: okay, so...
EB: with what you've learned from your dreams and gods and magic and stuff...
EB: do you have it all mapped out now? do you know everything?
TT: I didn't know why you were asleep, did I?
EB: yeah, but...
EB: neither did i!
TT: I have more pedestrian sources too, you know.
TT: Sometimes trolls blither tidbits about the future, and I can't help but take note of it.
TT: Just as they do with you.

TT: You also have access to the oracle clouds in Skaia, whereas I do not.
EB: oh yeah.
TT: Knowing the future is no remarkable feat here.
TT: It appears to be a fact of life.
TT: I'm not all that special, John.
EB: ok, buuuuuut...
EB: i guess that's not all i'm talking about.
EB: you seem a little different.
EB: kind of, um... spooky?
TT: Really?
EB: i just mean that before, it felt like we were in this adventure together, figuring stuff out as we went along.
EB: and now you have all the answers! because of magic, and other mysterious reasons!
EB: and you want to use your powers to break the game, and i still don't really understand why, and...
EB: bluh.
TT: I'm not actually trying to caricaturize a grim sorcerer.
TT: There's still a perfectly intact piece of my mind which realizes how ridiculous it is to be flying across rainbow oceans with a couple of magic wands and a salamander in a little cowl.
TT: And it wasn't without swallowing a little embarrassment that I revealed I was using a crystal ball just now.
TT: It's all pretty absurd.
TT: And yet,
TT: It's been fun, and above all, practical.
TT: For solving our problems.

There was a stretch of time when some readers were legitimately worried that Rose was in the process of "going grimdark." (This was well before she literally did that, and before the phrase ever appeared in the comic. They're the ones who pushed that phrase into the comic's lexicon, much like they did with Trickster Mode.) It just seemed like a funny thing to me for readers to "worry" about. I'm not sure whether it was actual concern for this fictional character's well-being, or more of a variation on the fandom staple, "This character is going through some changes and drifting away from the profile I know and love, and I don't like it!" Either way, it was sort of funny, and within that context their conversation here reads as a little response to that. Like John is the "concerned" guy, and Rose is telling him not to worry. She comes across as pretty reasonable about it, actually. So I guess the REAL punchline is, despite these highly rational reassurances, later she just bellyflops into the deep end of the goth pool and fully "goes grimdark" as an actual serious plot point. Which reads as much more of a takedown of this ridiculous fanon-imposed idea than this brief conversation does. If nothing else, it sure does COMMIT to lampooning the idea, via a totally serious and deadpan integration into the story. Which sure seems to happen a lot in this comic.

EB: ok, yeah, you're right.
EB: i guess i just started worryin'...
EB: that you are getting away from us!
EB: because you know everything, and you're magic, and you have a crystal ball, and a salamander, and you are basically a wizard.
EB: and that's cool, and it sure does sound fun...
EB: but i kinda think it was more fun when you just did things like read books, and tell jokes.
TT: I still read books and tell jokes.
EB: BA-DUM PSHHH!
TT: John,
TT: That was mean.
EB: sorry. :(

EB: well, if you do not have any objection...
EB: maybe later, i will drop by your planet again and rescue you, thus breaking the spooky spell put on you by your nefarious, shadowy masters.
TT: Swoon!
EB: that way you will stop being so grimdark and ominous, and basically completely off the deep end in every way, as is now painfully obvious to anyone with a brain.
TT: I will do by best to occupy myself as benignly and unmagically as possible until you show up.
EB: yes.
EB: please write some happy stories in your journal, about lively horses, and conspicuously not about wizards, or sadness.
TT: ... "Happy?"
TT: What is this strange, unsad emotion of which you speak?
EB: yes, this is good.
EB: you see rose, these are jokes.
EB: this are what they look like, do not be alarmed.
TT: Jokes?
TT: Are those the things people say when they want unusual noises to come out of the pliable crescent-shaped holes sometimes found in people's faces?
EB: laughs, rose. laaaughs.
EB: also, those crescenty looking holes where laughs come out of?
EB: those are smiles!
EB: observe... :D
TT: I need to make a note of this.
TT: Excuse me while I open this tome bound in the tanned, writhing flesh of a tortured hellscholar. The screaming will subside shortly.
EB: ok, i will wait patiently.
TT: Continue to not be alarmed as I record your advice with runes stroked in the black tears bled from the corruption-weary eyes of fifty thousand imaginary occultists.
TT: And then brace yourself for the fabled blackdeath trance of the woegothics I will slip into, while quaking in the bloodeldritch throes of the broodfester tongues.
EB: no, rose!
EB: that sort of nonsense is exactly what is out of the question!
EB: i see things are more urgent than i realized.
EB: i will have to venture there straightaway, and slap you right out of that silly old trance!
TT: One is not easily shaken from the broodfester tongues, John.
TT: They are stubborn throes.

Frankly, John is coming off as a bit of an asshole here. They've only been at this, what? A few hours? The better part of a day at most. And he's pointing to some of Rose's habits as evidence that she's fundamentally changing in temperament? "You used to tell jokes and read books. But Rose, it's been HOURS since I heard you say a joke, or talk about a book you like!" Dude, you've been sleeping a lot and getting harrassed by trolls all day. You barely know anything about what she's going through, and it's only been a few hours. Did you know that people can go a few hours acting a little differently than they usually do? It's called being in a "mood." But it's understandable that John sounds a little dumb here, since he's partly serving as a mouthpiece for a dumb fandom-subset attitude, which is always a surefire way to give one of your characters a temporary lobotomy. On rereading this, John's end of this conversation really strikes me as "Dumb Dude Tries Talking To A Girl Online" sort of material. Maybe he's suddenly a little nervous because now it's in the back of his head that he's "supposed to marry her"? That's a possibility. Anyway, Rose then starts saying a bunch of funny stuff which basically amounts to roasting John for his irritating remarks which border on concern-trolling. And he deserves a good roast. (Even though he turns out to be right about his grimdarkness concerns, but never mind that.)

EB: oh.
EB: well shit.
TT: Besides, you can't come to my planet right away.
TT: You will need to recover the treasure first, because it must be delivered to me.
EB: oh yeah.

EB: what is this treasure, anyway?
EB: and how's it gonna save us!
TT: You'd probably be disappointed if I described it.
EB: tell me anyway!
TT: Ok.
TT: It's called **The Tumor**.
EB: ...
EB: you're right, that is the shittiest sounding treasure i have ever heard.
EB: so what is this tumor supposed to do?
EB: and what is the significance of...
EB: removing it, i guess?
EB: does that mean im curing the battlefield or something?
EB: like the planet's doctor?
EB: hello?????
EB: rose?????????????
TT: Sorry.
TT: I was preoccupied.
EB: by what?
TT: Oh, let's say,
TT: Troll stuff.
TT: You know how it is.
EB: ????????????????????????????????
TT: Incidentally, looks like you will have your own troll stuff to attend to shortly.
EB: i will?
TT: Yes.
TT: Involving the one who hates you, and the one who likes you.
EB: um...
EB: which ones are those?
TT: You don't have a guess?
EB: uh... karkat and vriska?
EB: oh god, i was right. there they are now.
EB: how did you know?
TT: I have to go, John.
TT: Talk to your trolls.
TT: We'll catch up shortly.
EB: wait!!!
EB: there's stuff you didn't tell me!
EB: what happened with jade? did i mess anything up with the prototyping??
EB: aaaugh, why can't i remember!!!!!
EB: don't go yet rose, tell me!
EB: rose???????
-- tentacleTherapist [TT] ceased pestering ectoBiologist [EB] --
EB: BLUH BLUH
EB: HUGE WITCH

> John: Answer the one who hates you.

The Tumor is another mysterious concept tossed out for us to puzzle over, one that is apparently so special, it gets its own text color. The fact that the Green Sun fits this description as well may suggest to us that these two cosmic bodies may have a date with one another. But we'll just have to see about that. John seems to deduce that removing the Tumor from the Battlefield will result in "curing" it of a cancerous ailment. And he's not wrong about that. Their session has a really big defect, and the Tumor is a very literal, explosive embodiment of this fact. Much later we see the Alpha trolls had a sort of mini-tumor in their session too, suggesting this is just something certain sessions have. Doomed sessions have a way of building these tumors in as a means of providing a sort of self-imposed cleanup service for Paradox Space. But this topic can probably wait for when we actually see the thing in action. John describes himself as the planet's "doctor," which seemingly references the name of the song that accompanied the animation that first revealed LOWAS. The name of the song didn't have anything to do with this idea at the time (I didn't even name the song), but I did sort of retro-fit its name to suit the story purpose. The theme of "planet healing" runs throughout all the lands. The need to clean up a planet covered in oil, a planet of polluted oceans, a planet of clockwork gummed up by sticky amber, a wintry planet affected by nuclear fallout. And now, finally, a planet in the middle of all of them that has a literal tumor which will destroy everything if not removed. The Tumor is a signifier that this null session is terminal, doomed from the start, thus rendering the other cleanup jobs posing as "personal quests" as moot. But ordinarily they show what *Sburb* has to offer: "fix" your planets to complete the cosmic quest, and "fix" yourself to complete your personal quest. But as I've been getting at a lot down here, things just ain't that simple. Personal growth via outward, institutionally regimented means is a path of false promise. And from this vantage, it begins to make sense on a thematic basis why the session was "doomed from the start." The Tumor in the heart of the Battlefield is, in a way, the game acknowledging this dark truth about itself.

002925

-- carcinoGeneticist [CG] began trolling ectoBiologist [EB] --

CG: IT'S ME AGAIN, ASSHOLE
CG: THE ONE WHO HATES YOU, REMEMBER?
CG: OR SHOULD I SAY FUTURE-REMEMBER???
EB: karkat!!!!!!!!!!
CG: AGAIN WITH KNOWING MY NAME
CG: IT'S REALLY FUCKING UNSETTLING WHEN YOU DO THAT.
CG: I WONDER HOW FAR BACK YOU KNOW IT
CG: I'M GOING TO HAVE TO MAKE A SPECIAL POINT OF NOT BEING THE ONE TO TELL YOU, I DON'T WANT TO GIVE YOU THE SATISFACTION.
EB: hey, shut up a second!
EB: i need you to be nice for a change and do me a favor...
EB: have you talked to jade recently?
EB: can you tell me what happened to her??
CG: WHO THE FUCK IS JADE.
EB: uh...
EB: hmm.
CG: JOHN, THE FACT THAT YOU ALWAYS SEEM TO THINK I CAN READ YOUR MIND JUST UNDERSCORES WHAT A HARROWING GODDAMN IDIOT YOU ARE.
EB: jade is the girl who i am pretty sure just entered our session.
EB: she is my client player.
CG: OH, YOU MEAN THE ONE WHO FUCKS EVERYTHING UP.
EB: um, yeah... i thought you knew that? you talked to her a bunch of times, apparently.
CG: WHY THE FUCK WOULD I KNOW THAT.
CG: THIS IS ONLY THE SECOND TIME I HAVE EVER TALKED TO A HUMAN.
CG: AND THE FIRST TIME, MUCH TO MY MIGRAINE COMPOUNDING REGRET, WAS WITH YOU.
EB: oh!
EB: ok, i see what is going on here.
EB: we are finally getting to our first couple of conversations. cool!
CG: NO, NOT "COOL".
CG: WHAT IS GOING ON HERE IS VERY MUCH ANTITHETICAL TO YOUR PRIMITIVE HUMAN NOTION OF "EARTH COOL".
CG: YOU SEE, IN OUR FIRST CONVERSATION, WE DIDN'T EXACTLY GET OFF ON THE RIGHT FOOT.
CG: IT IS A FOOT WHICH SHOULD HAVE REEKED OF YOUR VERBAL RUINATION.
CG: BUT INSTEAD IT SMELLED LIKE
CG: WELL, LET'S NOT GET INTO THAT.
CG: I AM HERE TO DO WHAT YOU AND YOUR PATHETIC CADRE OF CO-HUMANS FAILED TO DO, WHICH IS SET THE RECORD STRAIGHT.
CG: I AM HERE TO UTTERLY ANNIHILATE YOUR SHIT.
CG: I WILL STAY ON MESSAGE THIS TIME. I WILL NOT BE DETERRED BY YOUR GOOFY MANNERISMS AND YOUR ABSURD PENCHANT FOR REVELING IN SELF ABUSE.
CG: WE WILL GET OFF ON A FRESH FOOT, AND BY FRESH I MEAN MOST FOUL INDEED.
CG: ITS TOES ARE WIGGLING UNDER YOUR HIDEOUS PINK NOSTRILS. NOW BREATHE DEEP YOUR MISFORTUNE, YOU SAD LITTLE CLOWN.
CG: THIS IS THE END OF YOU. THAT AROMA YOU DETECT WAFTS FROM THE BOUQUET PERCHED ON YOUR CORPSE BOX.
CG: NOBODY CRIES, EXCEPT YOUR SHITTY GHOST. HEAVY SOBS FROM A SPECTER OF UNQUALIFIED FAILURE.
CG: IT IS A SYMPHONY TO MY ANGRY EARS.
EB: so... the smell is from a foot... but also from funeral flowers?
EB: this metaphor is confusing.
CG: STFU
CG: I'M ONLY GETTING STARTED.
EB: yeah, i know!
EB: this is all that big time trolling i was looking forward to.
EB: and it's pretty good so far, and ordinarily i would be excited to hear more...

The second Karkat conversation, from his POV this time. One side effect of his "backward conversation" gag is it doubles as a useful countdown stitched into the narrative. We saw his first conversation at the beginning of A5A2, in a bold flash-forward. Now, here's his second. So we're sort of boxing in the remaining events between them, and letting it be known that we're close to catching up with some key events we've been anticipating. There aren't that many items left to check off. We still need to find out how John gets those nice blue pajamas. We need to learn about how the plan comes together that leads John to say "see you soon." That first shot of John sitting there, cheerfully talking to Karkat in his blue jammies, I think carried that somewhat overwhelming feeling you get when you see something a little too far in the future to be understandable. You wonder, "How will we even GET here?" But enough pieces have fallen into place in this act so far that you can kind of start to visualize the path. But there's still one huge piece missing, which is coming up two pages from now. It finally addresses the issue of "how the kids fucked everything up," which Karkat has been hysterically banging away on since he first appeared in Act 4.

CG: YOU SEE WHAT I MEAN???
CG: YOU ARE ACTUALLY ENJOYING THIS, WHAT A SICK FUCK.
EB: but i really am concerned about what happened with jade!
EB: my request for a favor still stands, even though this is early you, and you still think you hate me.
CG: DON'T QUESTION THE SINCERITY OF MY HATE, JUST DON'T EVEN FUCKING GO THERE.
EB: ok, fine! you hate me sooooo much, like, for real.
EB: can you just tell me what's up with jade?
EB: can you see her?
CG: YEAH I SEE HER
CG: IT'S MAKING ME MAD SEEING HER
EB: can you tell me what happened? what did she do that was so bad?
CG: HAHAHAHAHAHA
CG: HERE I AM TALKING TO YOU MOMENTS AFTER YOU DID THE TERRIBLE THING, AND YOU STILL DON'T EVEN KNOW WHAT YOU DID!
CG: INCREDIBLE, YOU TRULY ARE DUMBER THAN I THOUGHT.
EB: ok!!! i'm an idiot! can you just tell me anyway????
EB: whoa...
CG: WHAT
EB: the ground is shaking...
EB: what's going on?
CG: I'LL TELL YOU WHAT'S GOING ON.
CG: WHAT YOU FUCKING DID IS WHAT'S GOING ON.
EB: so tell me what i fucking did!!!
CG: OH, YOU WANT TO KNOW WHAT YOU FUCKING DID?
EB: yes!
EB: please, no more stalling or "i already told you's" or any other maddening nonsense!
EB: just...
EB: TELL ME!
CG: VERY WELL, JOHN HUMAN EGBERT.
CG: I WILL TELL YOU WHAT YOU DID
CG: READY FOR ME TO TELL YOU WHAT YOU DID?
CG: HERE'S ME, TELLING YOU WHAT YOU DID
CG: OK, HERE GOES
CG: WHAT YOU DID IS AS FOLLOWS
CG: AS SUCH
CG: AND THUSLY
EB: :|

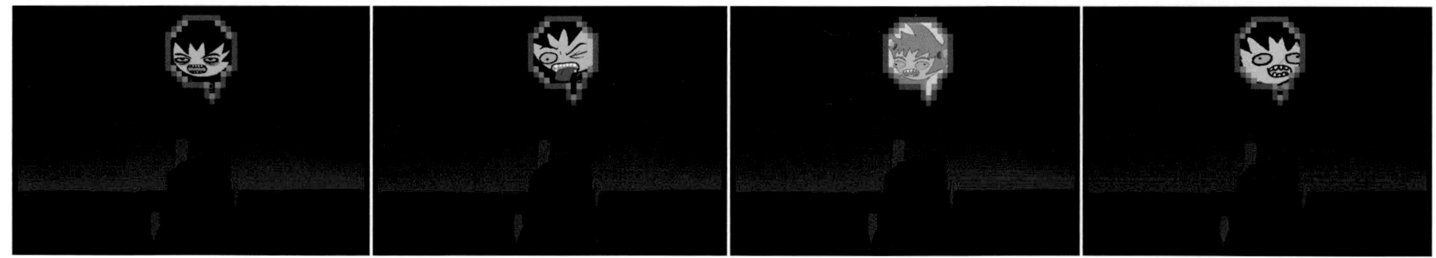

He then proceeded to tell you what you did, as such.

And we then proceeded to watch.

Thusly.

> [S] Jade: Enter.

And speaking of hype, the remainder of this conversation just tees up the Big Question for us in a really overblown way. It's not that often that the pages before a major animation go to any lengths to say "GET READY FOR SOME *SHIT* FOLKS!!!" Usually some casual stuff is rolling along, then these episodes kind of ambush you. An exception is made here. Why dance around it anymore? For quite some time, the comic's been making such a big deal out of several plot tokens about to be cashed in at this moment: Jade finally entering to complete the chain, the huge screw-up that kills the kids' chances of winning, and the resulting ruin of the troll session too somehow. So did this animation live up to the silly amounts of hype the comic itself theatrically pumped up for the moment? If you really want to know, ask one of the wise, battle-hardened Homestuck Elders. Those who were there at the time. Surely they have stories to tell.

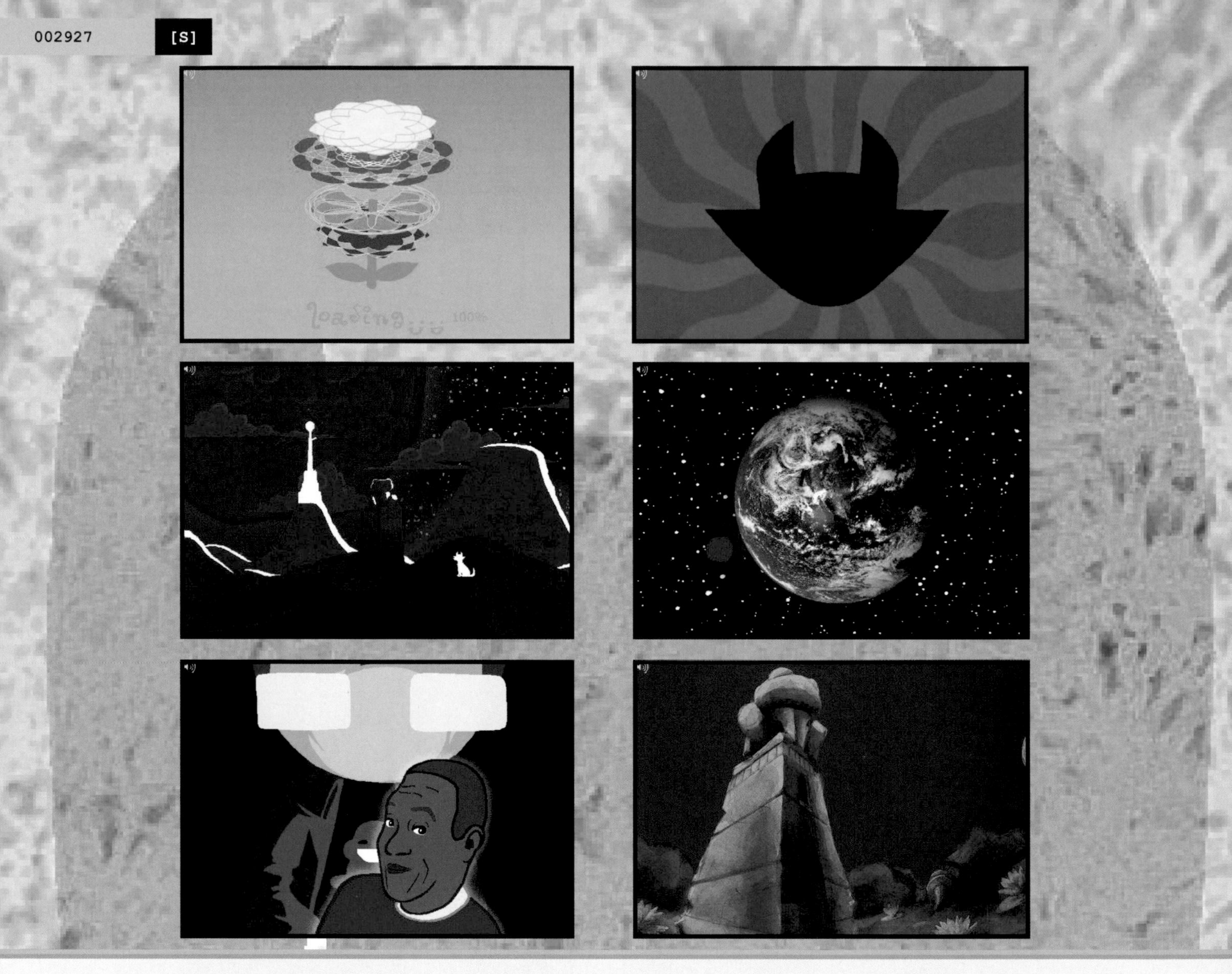

[S] Jade: Enter is a high-energy Flash. **[S] Descend** was the last one the fit that description, but this one probably has a higher intensity and stakes-raising gravitas. Maybe the most high-energy page in the story, by those standards? **[S] Cascade** and **[S] Collide** are up there, but they're both long enough that the intensity is a bit diffused across their fifteen-plus minutes. **[S] Caliborn: Enter** and **[S] GAME OVER** both compete. This is a nerdy thing I'm doing, rating my own shit by arbitrary metrics, isn't it. But there's no way you're not a huge nerd, otherwise you wouldn't even be reading this note. So let's be careful about what we throw in glass houses. Speaking of which, in a few pages Jade is about to get thrown through the wall of her own glass house.

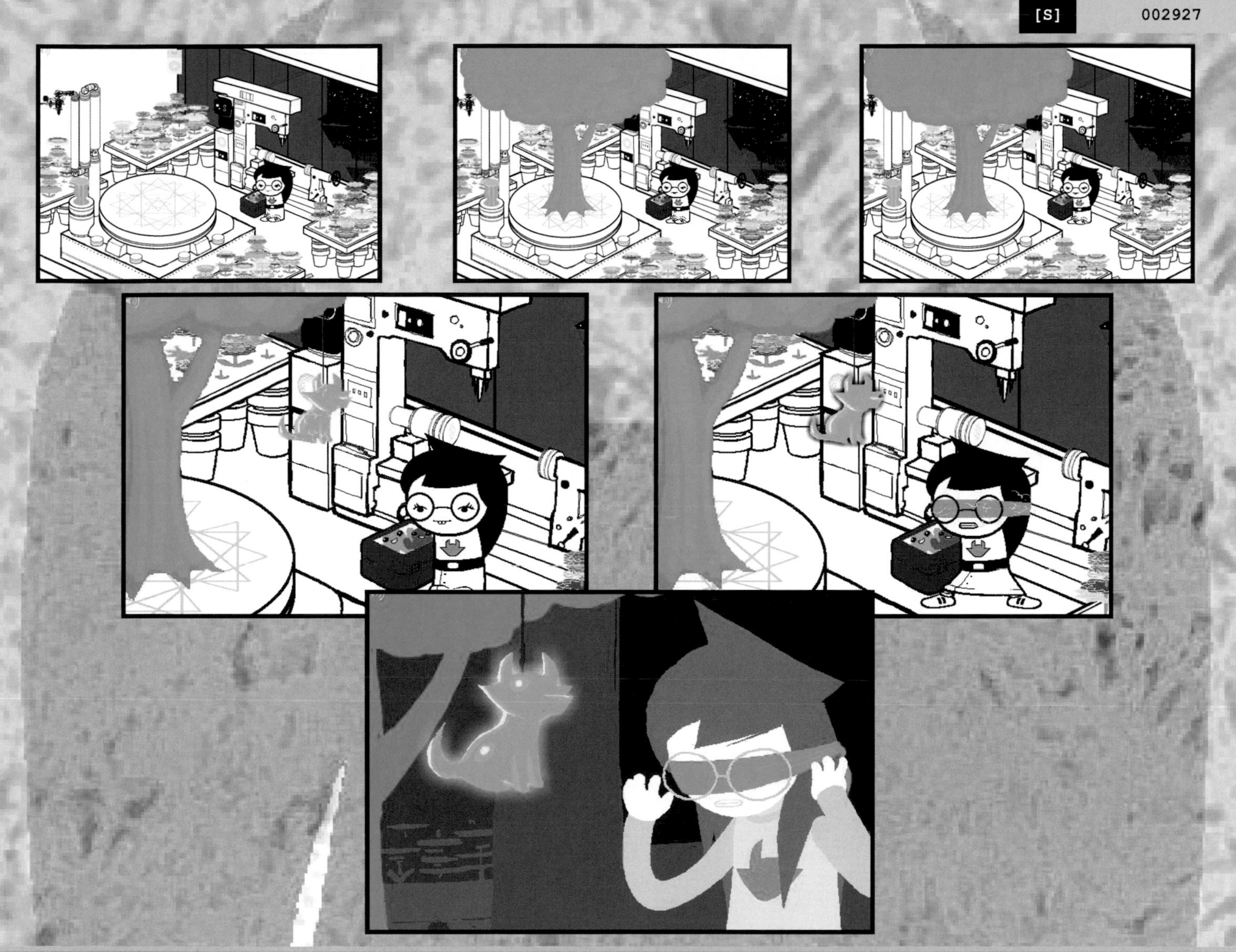

The "entry item challenge" is established right away here. Each of these challenges escalates in obscurity with every new player who enters, becoming more esoteric and less clear with what exactly the player is supposed to do to solve it. First, Jade is shown the piñata, so she knows it's there. Then she's magically blindfolded. No way she's getting that thing off until she's in the game, or dead. So she can deduce what to do: smash the thing open, obviously. Except it's not that simple. She'll try that soon and it won't work. She's gotta shoot it, while blind. Which is hard! So now we know everything about all four entry-item challenges. There's plenty to say about all of them. Should I make this another long post? Yeah, why not, what do we have to lose at this point. Look, I'm even going to include a line break. You can't stop me. No one can.

I talked about this way back, maybe even in an earlier book? Well, here I go again, so hold on to your ass. There are four entry items: Apple of knowledge, Bottle of wine, Crow's egg, Dog piñata. A, B, C, D. All of them are related to new life or new beginnings. You bite the apple, you fall from grace, enter a new world, begin this wild journey. You smash a bottle to christen a ship. An egg hatches, creating new life. You break a piñata to celebrate a birthday. Each involves breaking or puncturing something. Each involves a form of sustenance, or something to consume (piñatas have candy inside). Two are vessels for the substance (bottle, piñata), two are the food items themselves (apple, egg), and one arguably counts as both (egg). Two of them drop from the same basic tree template (apple, piñata). They ramp up in complexity. John's is a simple test: bite the forbidden fruit. Not much to it. A single unit of departure, almost conceptually elemental, like an apple, as Rose goes on about later. The challenges get trickier. Rose has to break a bottle. Easy enough idea, but things go wrong, and she has to take a blind leap to get it done. A sacrificial gesture, and one of faith in a friend (Jaspers). Dave's is even more obscure. A simple test of patience, but one that's not clear. He isn't told what to do and just has to wait. Non-action is the key, and in a way it's another gesture of faith under dire circumstances. Finally, Jade's challenge incorporates a lot of these elements. It's another "blind faith" situation. She has to take a shot in the dark. There's a sacrificial gesture, but instead of risking herself (like Rose), Jade must symbolically sacrifice her friend via effigy and cannot complete the sacrifice without help from that friend. (Bec must redirect the bullet. There's no way this works if he doesn't.) It is also a signifier that the pet she knew as a friend her whole life is about to, in a way, become her enemy. Like a good dog gone bad, who now must be put down.

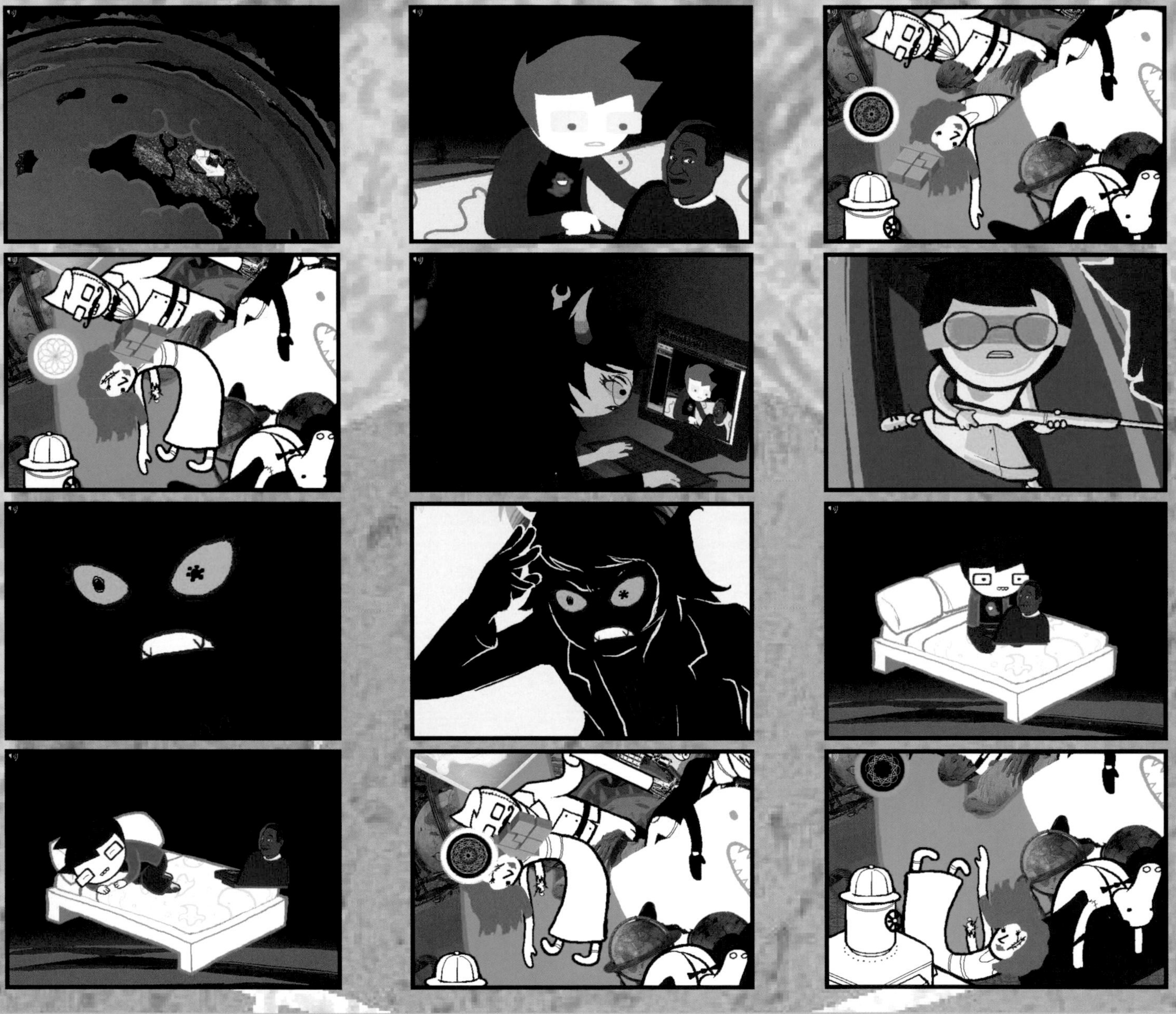

The mystery of how John falls asleep and shipwrecks his bed in the oil is quickly addressed here. First, note how before he grabs the blue lady doll, he actually maims it a bit. He rips its eye. That way, Jack will have two damaged eyes, and theoretically should be totally blind. Meaning they'd have to face a blind adversary with a fabulous blue mane of hair. But of course we know that doesn't happen. John falls asleep and drops the doll at the last minute. Why? Vriska. It's like that joke in *The Simpsons*—any time you're wondering why something happened, just assume a wizard did it. Except in *Homestuck* the wizard is Vriska. Why does she do this? She wants to be important so desperately, she's willing to insert herself into the narrative even if it's for bad reasons. She wants to be the one directly responsible for the creation of the "ultimate end boss." Which is pretty dickish of her, I suppose. But when you think about it, there's something kind of pathetic about it. Because it's not really even her idea: the fact that she knows it *happened* is what gives her the idea. She knows Bec Noir is what made the session unwinnable, and by browsing Trollian, she could see the event that leads to his creation, which is John falling asleep at exactly the wrong moment. But when Vriska saw it happen on the screen, she had no way of knowing his nap was because of her. Until she decides to become responsible for it, thereby making it true in the first place. So she's not even the original author of her own diabolical self-insert intervention. This was established earlier as something she does, given her nature as a thief. She takes credit for other people's stuff, like Equius's robot that she was going to regift to Aradia. Vriska slaps her name on things and claims them for her own. In this case, she even slaps her name on the IDEA of slapping her name on the origin of Bec Noir. Neither thing really originated from her in a meaningful way.

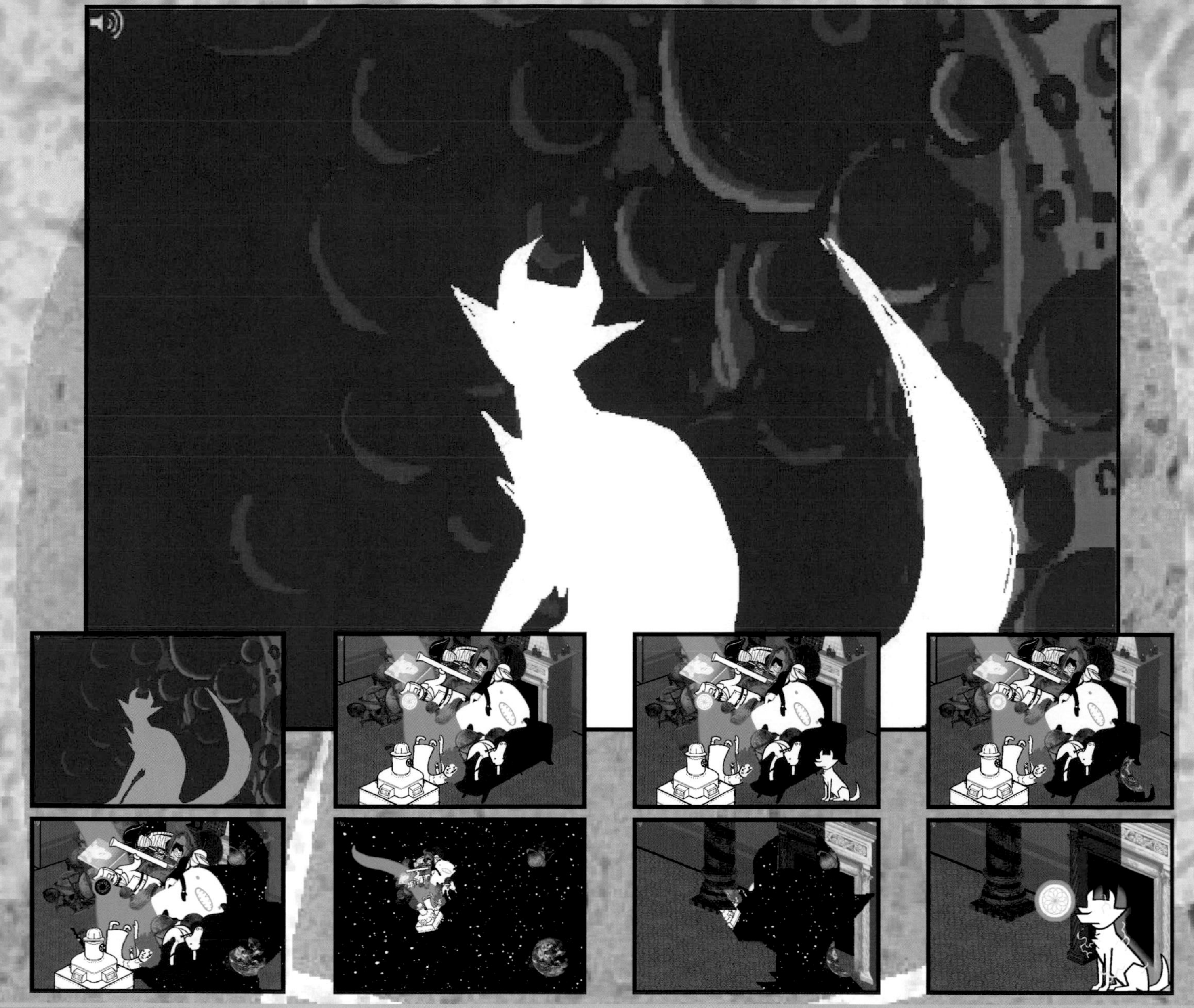

Bec considers how to handle the crisis and defend his master's life. First, he gets all the trash out of the living room, which is both a nice decluttering measure (so all that crap is gone and I don't have to think about it anymore) and a signal closing of the possibility that anything from that pile is going to end up in the kernel. There is a good question here, which I don't think ever gets a totally clear answer, outside of a series of factors you can make some deductions from. Which is: why does Bec actually do this? Prototype himself, I mean. If the goal is to eliminate the meteor threat, he already has the power to do that easily, by teleporting it somewhere else. Is it mere doggy whim? An instinctive, ominous desire to increase his power? An inbuilt impulse to cooperate with predestined events critical to this session? Is he under some sort of influence? Is it TAVROS??? (Later Tavros is demonstrated to have the ability to control Bec. This is how he ends up getting Grandpa killed.) One argument against that possibility is that Tavros is fundamentally allergic to doing anything extreme or important. He's kind of the anti-Vriska. "Taking credit" for the rise of Becsprite in this manner is something Vriska would do (in fact, she just did). Alternatively, since she just showed the willingness to do this, you could also speculate that she controlled Tavros to control Bec to do this. But that's REALLY going down a rabbit hole of conspiracy. -->

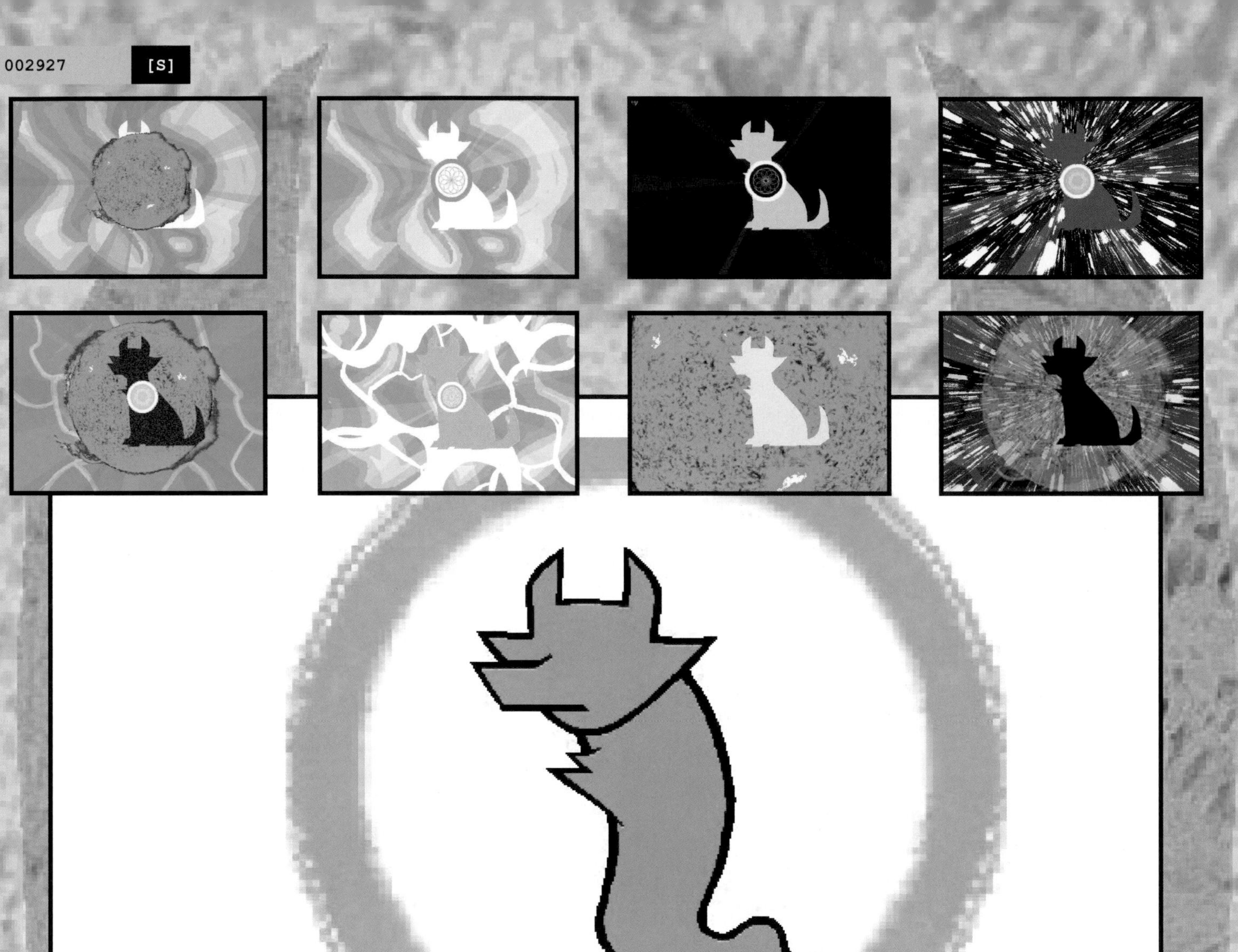

--> I could just tell you what my opinion is. You may do as you will with it, if you decide I am a credible source on this subject. I think it's more interesting to consider behaviors like this as instinctive features of a First Guardian. We always got kind of a creepy vibe from Bec. He's technically defending Jade, but there's something ominously ulterior about his presence. If there are any beings who would be uniquely encoded to instinctively commit whatever self-fulfilling deeds are critical to *Sburb*'s agenda, it would be a First Guardian. We've seen how Doc Scratch has no compunction about doing the same, but he does so by bringing his powerful intellect to bear on the task, rather than the way a dog would handle it, through powerful instinct. There are many necessary features of blowing up the meteor like this. The Bec-head exile station must be seeded in many parts all over the planet. The destruction of Earth, a shame though it is, is still critical to everything. If he simply teleports the meteor away, there's no impact of this size to wipe everything else out. Yet he can't let it strike the house. So this seems to be the best compromise. Oh, also let's not forget that the existence of Bec Noir is critical to the ultimate dysfunction of this session. Maybe that's why Bec is a little creepy. He's only innocently following his instincts, but his instincts demand that he help bring about some very dark outcomes.

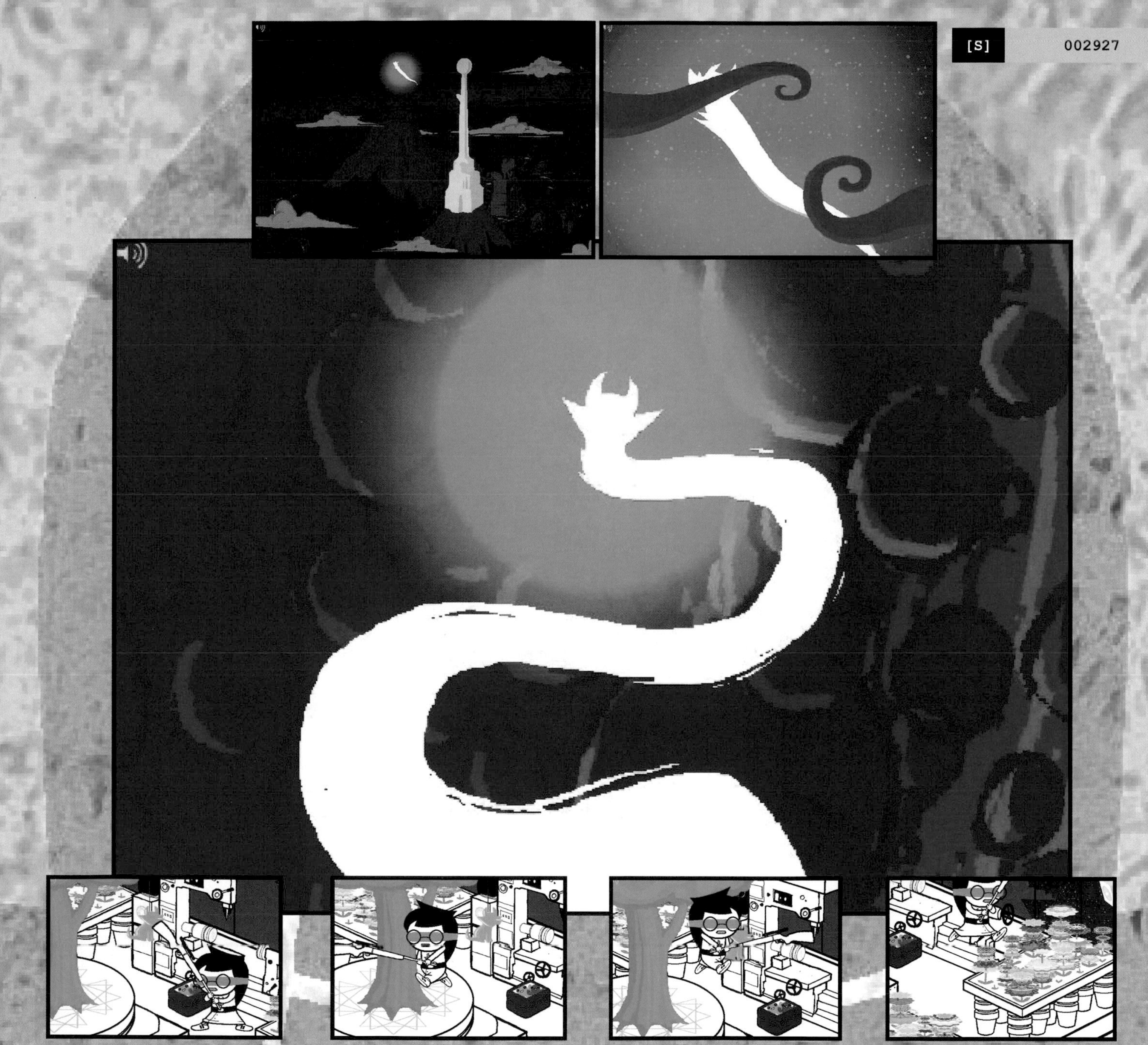

> Becsprite: Engage snake mode. That's one long, magic dog. Yeah I dunno what's going on with that either. It looks cool? There are some extremely mild hints of the tadpole's journey up to Skaia. Jade also flails around down there with her rifle, still assuming you have to bash the piñata like normal. It's a little reminiscent of when she was running around her greenhouse with a bag of fertilizer, goofing off. I hope you're learning a valuable lesson here, which is that things are often reminiscent of other things. If they weren't, then every discreet concept you could think of would be perfectly unique, have no relation to any other concept, and we'd be adrift in a sea of totally inert, noncombinative principles, which *frankly* sounds like total madness. Heh, here I am on my high horse about certain topics again. It's usually at this point in the spiel that my grandkids mix a powerful sedative into my applesauce and put a padlock on the door to my nursing home.

This entry challenge is kind of brutal. When you do the obvious thing you're supposed to do with this piñata, it punishes you with a huge explosion that launches you out of your highrise greenhouse. You know, if you happen to have one of those. A few notes ago I talked about this challenge as a symbolic gesture of having to put down a good dog gone bad. Some notes of *Old Yeller* here, which is a tale about a kid who has to shoot his dangerous dog as sort of a symbolic coming-of-age gesture. Except since Bec is omnipotent and basically indestructible, he can't actually be put down. The sacrificial gesture can only be conveyed through effigy. There's been a lot of foreshadowing about this, like Dave referring to Bec as a devilbeast and saying he'd take him out behind the shed and shoot him (probably jokingly, but who knows really). Jade's strife with Bec is presented as kind of a playful iteration of this idea, where she's playing "fetch" with bullets, but in doing so, is effectively shooting him in the head and letting his crazy powers outmaneuver the bullet across time and space. The challenge here is sort of a final callback to these ideas, putting the concept of a symbolic sacrifice of a deadly animal in a more serious and high-stakes context. Bec is a good dog, a best friend, a vigilant guardian, but there are ominous signs he's very dangerous too, a beast who potentially is at risk of biting the hand that feeds him. This explosive trap set by the piñata, innocently inviting Jade to do the obvious thing but severely punishing her for it, is a little facet of this symbolic challenge: the lurking threat of a seemingly good dog lashing out. And the "bite" is commensurate with the dog's ridiculously overpowered status.

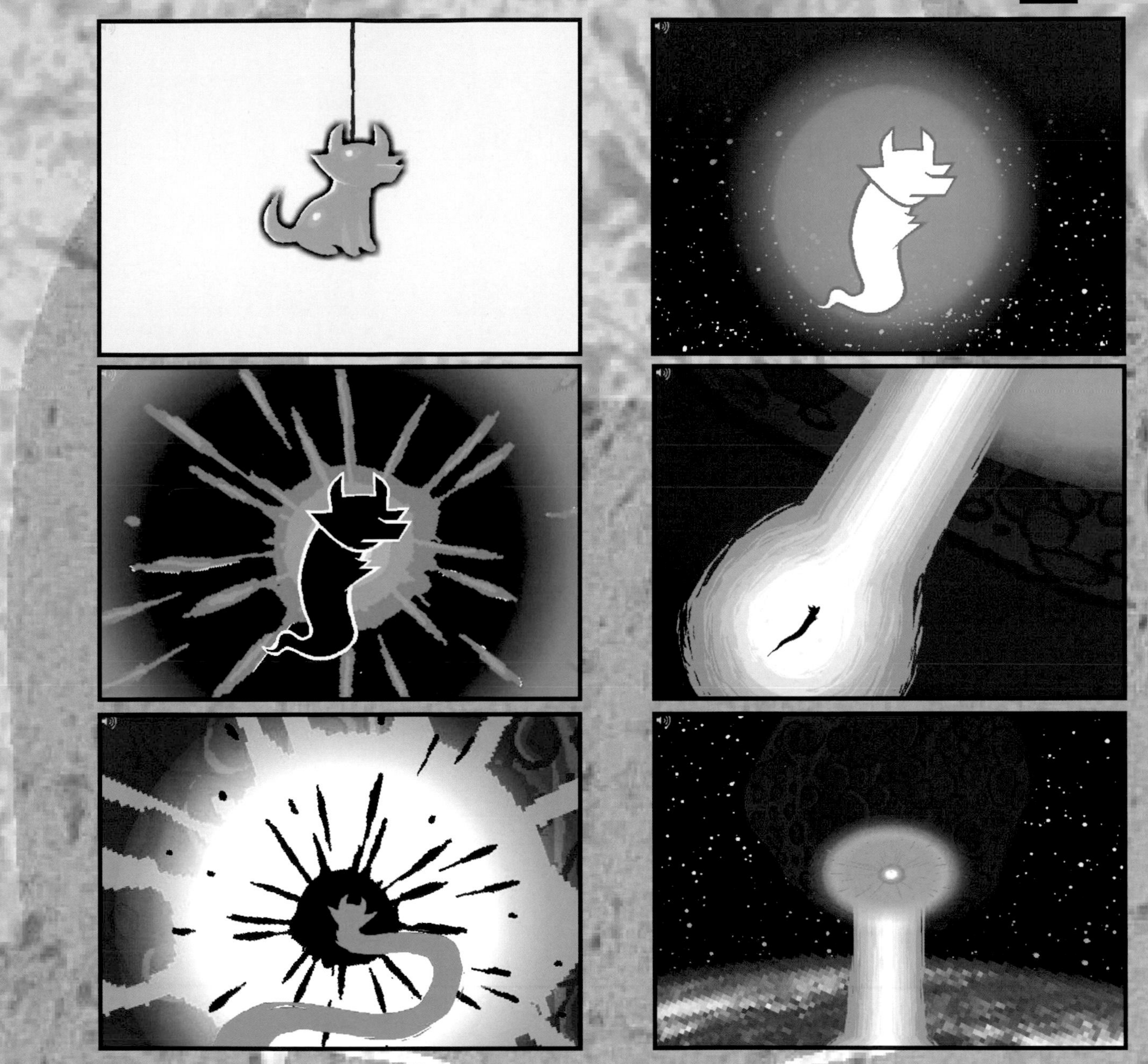

So... Bec can do this? Yeah, looks like he can do this. At least, *now* he can. Could he shoot huge lasers before he prototyped himself? It doesn't actually seem like that was in his power set during his prior strife sequences. He could teleport anywhere, resize stuff, move at warp speed, crackle with electricity and green fire. Sprites, however, have been previously established as laser-blasting entities—Nanna can do it, and we saw Calsprite do it. So this seems like a pretty decent answer as to why Bec wanted to prototype himself, at least in terms of immediate abilities gained. It was the only way to blast the meteor into a million pieces before it enters the atmosphere. Blowing it up is a very important need, according to his instincts.

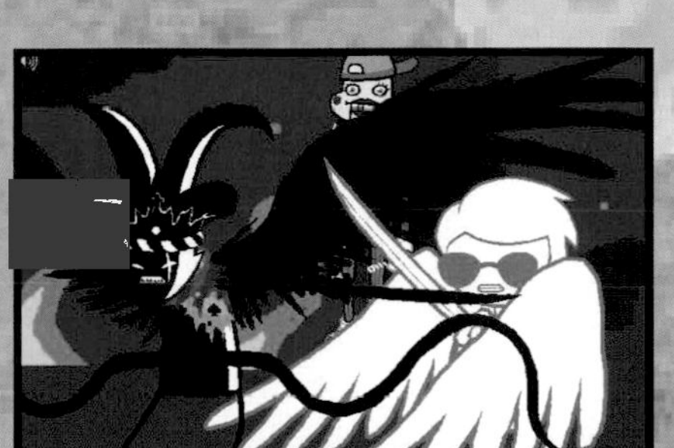

Getting the Bro/Davesprite/Jack fight into the mix here was important not just because it was Cool, but aslo because now that we just saw Bec prototype himself, this is kind of a bigtime Oh Shit moment for the consequences that's about to have on this battle. Bro and Davesprite are holding their own pretty well for now, but these rad dudes are about to have serious problem on their hands. Good thing Bro decided to draw Jack into fighting him at the precise location of his future tomb. Saves everyone a lot of trouble.

Jade's falling from her tower, doesn't have much time, and takes literally the only action available to her, which also happens to be the correct action. Which is to take a random blind shot with her rifle and hope the bullet somehow winds up hitting the piñata. Luckily for her, shooting in practically any direction would have gotten the job done, since now that Bec is a sprite, he understands how to cooperate with the game logic to assist his player. He redirects the bullet, just like we saw him do on his strife page. Somewhat morbidly, I guess, this also involves him assisting with the completion of his own ritual sacrifice via effigy, by taking a bullet through his own head first, warping space, and allowing the bullet to pass through his effigy's head. Truly a good dog, a best friend, and loyal to a fault. Kind of like if Old Yeller brought Travis the gun, loaded it, used his mouth to aim it for him, put his paw on the kid's finger to fire the gun, and then ran in front of the bullet. So tragic.

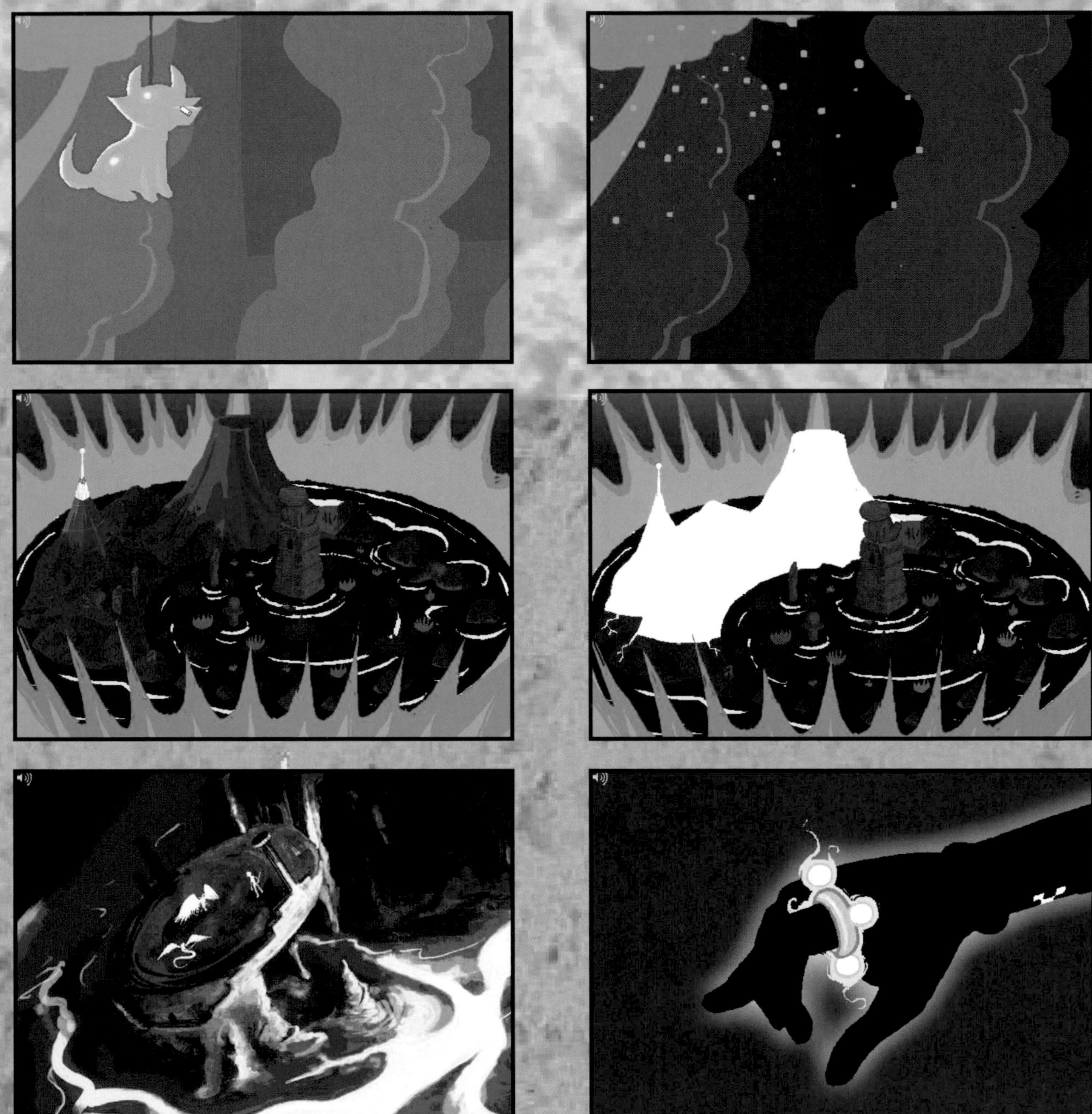

As has already been implied (by the glimpse at Kanaya's land, which included the volcano next to her hive), the Forge is swept into the session along with the Space player's house. That whole patch of land is treated as a sort of unit. Actually, this information was provided way back at the end of Act 2 (in **[S] WV: Ascend**) when we saw WV fly to the site of the frog ruins on post-apocalyptic Earth, and there was the huge depression in the ground where both Jade's house and the volcano would have been. Now we finally see that gash in the land being created. The session won't let the Space player enter without her huge, lava-propelled, tadpole-firing gun, will it? Unless the session is impotent (i.e. a void session), in which case it's more than happy to leave Jake's volcano behind. But then, he's not a Space player. He's a Hope boy. Those guys seem more about diminishing the likelihood of procreation than improving it. (Remember what Eridan did with the matriorb?) So it makes perfect sense that Jake is responsible for his session's impotence, and not just because he's a loser. But that doesn't exactly help, either.

This is a very similar sequence to Jack's first dramatic transformation in **[S] Jack: Ascend**, with the same pose and all. Except instead of becoming more ridiculous, this time he becomes more terrifyingly badass. Oh, wait. No, he's...he's growing a dog snout. Okay, I take that back, he's getting ridiculous again. Still, I think it's safe to say this version of him is more intimidating than Clownjack, especially since we know of Bec's capabilities. When designing him, I had a few options. I could just keep piling more shit on him, make his design an even more garish, cluttered aggregation of prototyped elements, which I think was the expectation established by the mods we saw in the troll session. But instead I kind of simplified the design, collapsed the clown hat, hid the tentacles (he keeps them "phased out" and can bring them back when he wants), and streamlined his silhouette overall. This makes the design stronger, and perhaps just as importantly, much easier to draw. You can never rule that out as a factor in the way characters are designed.

Have we talked about the specific relationship between Bro and Davesprite? This is probably the last chance, since Bro is about to die a Warrior's Death, and Davesprite is about to fly the coop and go unseen for a long time, making us think he might have died, like an inconsiderate bastard. We never see any interaction between Bro and Davesprite except for this stoic alliance they form to fight Jack, probably while exchanging a series of curt nods and glances now and then. This is the bonding moment they have, possibly of a reconciliatory nature on some level, where they are unified in combat, putting aside their differences to take on a powerful adversary. Contrast this with Dave's bonding moment with Dirk at the end, which is much more substantive, an emotional deep dive rather than this symbolic appearance of solidarity. Even though they're basically the same person, and are two facets of one bigger character profile, there are a lot of ways in which Dave and Davesprite diverge. Dave, as the supposedly "real" version we keep the spotlight on, has the luxury of pursuing the full scope of his longform emotional arc, or the "broken sword" path. He gets to be the more emotionally complex guy and sift through the traumas of his past with Dirk himself, a more humanized iteration of Bro. Whereas Davesprite, as a sort of self-aware runner-up splinter of Dave himself, is relegated to a shallower and lonelier hero's journey, or an "unbroken sword" path (note that his sprite form endows him with a whole sword permanently). So what choice does he have but to embrace the superficial qualities of the hero's journey, the kind which (in the context of Dave's arc) requires that you push your feelings down, suppress your traumas and all the things that make you what you are, man up and be a cool sword-wielding hero, just like they're doing here. This is all he gets, the stoic, voiceless facade of Dirk, the abusive guy who made his childhood miserable. But none of that matters now. All that matters is The Fight. Of course, Davesprite's arc extends quite a bit beyond this moment as well, but starting to understand his journey in these terms sheds more light on him as an individual rather than just viewing him as Other Dave. There's a lot more he has to cope with later, as a superfluous doppelganger of a more important person, who just seems to linger on without purpose, and has to live the more shallow version of Dave's arc. The ultimate endpoint of Davesprite's journey can be seen as a final release from these existential burdens, both for him specifically, but also for Dave himself as a more "generalized concept" of a person.

/Slams hard on the brakes of the Davesprite meta, sending the vehicle screeching and swerving off the road./ Hey, look! A really important revelation, ensconced in an already manic, overloaded animation. This is a big deal. Not only are we finding out that Bec is the fourth prototyping, pushing Jack to ludicrous heights of invulnerability, we're also filling a glaring hole in the troll side of the story: the identity of the indestructible demon, and how he got there. We were mostly led to believe the demon was Lord English, via red herring language that coded Jack in all the same ways English was coded. There was also no reason to expect it was Jack, since "indestructible demon" didn't describe him accurately at the time. But now it clearly does. As for how he got there, well, he just appeared on the frog platform, freaked out all the trolls, and Aradia with some quick thinking got them all the hell out of there. That's a good enough explanation for now. Of course, we don't yet know *how* he zapped to that frog platform, where he came from, or what led to those events. We need to wait for **[S] Cascade** to finally plug that gap.

002927 [S]

SOMEONE needed to clean up all these doomed Aradiabots. Jack volunteers for the job. It would be confusing if there were this many of them sticking around forever. Of course, they all must have known this was their endpoint. And yet they all waited for him to show up anyway. They welcomed their demise, since it was always unavoidable. I guess that's what doomed means? Whew, edgy stuff. Meanwhile, Karkat's dream self finally wakes up, just in time to see his stab buddy one more time, and then die.

Jack's Bloody Hand is a new mystery. That's what we do here—we answer some important questions while introducing a few more. "What's the deal with the bloody hand" is an obvious question that lingers for the rest of the act. In addition to just being another little rolling mystery, it also nicely doubles as a distinguishing mark between Jack in the human session and this future Jack who travels to the troll session. So now whenever we see bloody-handed Jack without much surrounding context, we automatically know it's the one in the troll session. As for where the blood came from, that's another answer that **[S] Cascade** provides, and is super, duper, super, super sad.

Here's a nice transition trick. Jack mask-zooms into a starfield out in space, and the starfield gradually transitions into gently falling snow, as the background shifts to the mysterious wintry fog of whatever Jade's land is. It a teasing reminder to us that, oh yeah, despite all this dramatic shit, Jade actually *did* enter her land, which is a major milestone of progress and something to look forward to. Her successful entry challenge wraps up with a little callback. She's falling from her tower yet again, just like she did in **[S] Descend** when her robot blew up her bedroom and she fell while sleeping. Now she's falling again, but wide-awake this time, and she seems pretty pleased about it?

CG: YOU MADE AN UNBEATABLE BOSS IS WHAT YOU DID.

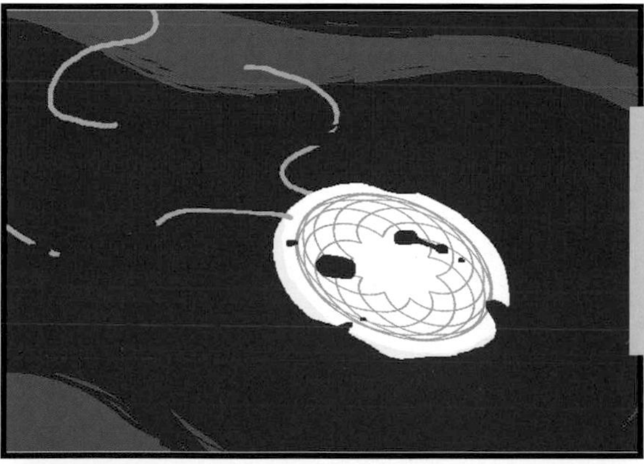

CG: THE IDIOT YOU CALL THE JADE HUMAN WENT AHEAD AND PROTOTYPED HER FREAK OF A LUSUS, WHILE YOU DECIDED TO TAKE A NAP FOR SOME REASON RATHER THAN DOING WHAT A LEADER IS SUPPOSED TO DO AND STOP HER FROM BEING SO FUCKING RETARDED.

CG: YOUR VERSION OF JACK, WHO YOU WERE SOMEHOW DUMB ENOUGH TO ENTRUST WITH THE QUEEN'S RING, BECAME ESSENTIALLY INDESTRUCTIBLE.
CG: HE THEN WENT ON A RAMPAGE THROUGH YOUR POINTLESS SESSION, WHICH HILARIOUSLY, WAS ALREADY A LOST CAUSE EVEN BEFORE THIS HAPPENED!
CG: I AM JUST BESIDE MYSELF WITH THE SPECTACULAR BREADTH OF YOUR FAILURE.

We didn't even need to see the rest of the battle. Bro's just fuckin' dead. Of course he is. In a way, trivializing his death by making it happen off-screen is actually a more effective way of demonstrating the extreme power imbalance resulting from Jack's transformation. The contest between them became so lopsided, it wasn't even worth showing.

CG: AND IF THIS WASN'T BAD ENOUGH
CG: YOUR "SOLUTION" LATER WOULD BE TO OPEN A RIFT IN SOME GLORIOUS GESTURE OF MEANINGLESS SUICIDE.

CG: AND I HAVE NO IDEA HOW
CG: BUT THE RIFT YOU OPENED ENABLED HIM TO ENTER OUR SESSION, JUST AS WE WERE ABOUT TO CLAIM OUR PRIZE.

CG: AND NOW WE'RE THE ONES WHO HAVE TO FUCKING DEAL WITH HIM!
CG: SO THANKS A LOT, SHIT HEAD.

Meanwhile, Karkat continues his rant, wherein he infodumps all these astounding revelations we just saw in a very straightforward way, which he could have done literally at any time earlier, thus blowing the surprise for us all. The reason he didn't is because he already did, right here. This is his second conversation with John. It makes complete sense that he would dump this all out there in a totally straightforward way, almost immediately upon contacting John. Why wouldn't he? Karkat doesn't give a fuck about dramatic irony, or protecting you from spoilers. Once again, we see the advantages of his backwards conversation from the standpoint of guarding the narrative from exposing things readers shouldn't know yet without making the characters seem exceedingly irrational. Thank GOD for Karkat's stupid blundering, it really bailed me out of some storytelling logic puzzles. Also note the totally sick transmutation of the oil fire from red to green, dramatically signifying the horrific rise of Bec Noir. I'm not sure why this happens? I mean, on a technical level. I guess Green Sun fire is a special kind of fire that..."infects" normal fire and spreads like kind of a fire-based plague? That sounds cool, let's run with that.

EB: jade prototyped a lusus?
EB: what's that?
CG: OH
CG: OK, MY BAD, I FORGOT I WAS TALKING TO A MEMBER OF A GENERICALLY BIZARRE ALIEN SPECIES.
CG: I GUESS SOME HUMANS HAVE A LUSUS, WHILE OTHERS DON'T? WHATEVER.
CG: HER LUSUS IS THE CREATURE WHICH SERVES AS HER CUSTODIAN.
EB: oh, you mean her dog!
CG: I GUESS
EB: so, she prototyped becquerel?
EB: why is that so bad?
CG: JOHN, DO YOU EVEN KNOW ANYTHING ABOUT YOUR FRIENDS?
CG: IS THIS HOW HUMAN FRIENDSHIP WORKS? YOU JUST DON'T KNOW SHIT ABOUT EACH OTHER?
CG: HER LUSUS EXHIBITS THE PROPERTIES OF A LEGENDARY ENTITY CALLED A FIRST GUARDIAN.
CG: IT IS AN ABSOLUTE MONSTROSITY.
EB: what properties?
CG: OK, FOR STARTERS, NOTICE HOW THE FURIOUS WALL OF FIRE CURRENTLY RUSHING TOWARD YOU IS TURNING GREEN?
EB: uh oh...
CG: YEAH
CG: THOSE FUCKING PROPERTIES.
CG: BUT IT'S A LOT MORE THAN THAT.
CG: AS THE DEFENDERS OF THEIR PLANETS, THEY'RE VIRTUALLY OMNIPOTENT.
CG: PROTOTYPING ONE IS ABSOLUTELY UNCONSCIONABLE.
CG: THE RESULT IS A BOSS A HELL OF A LOT WORSE THAN WHAT WE HAD TO FIGHT, AND WE PROTOTYPED TWELVE TIMES RATHER THAN A MEASLY FOUR.
CG: AND ONE OF OUR PROTOTYPINGS INCLUDED AN OUTER FUCKING GOD THE SIZE OF A CITY!
CG: I HOPE THIS PUTS IN PERSPECTIVE HOW TERRIBLE YOU ARE.
EB: huh...
EB: yeah, it kind of does.
EB: i'm sorry karkat, i didn't realize we screwed up so bad.

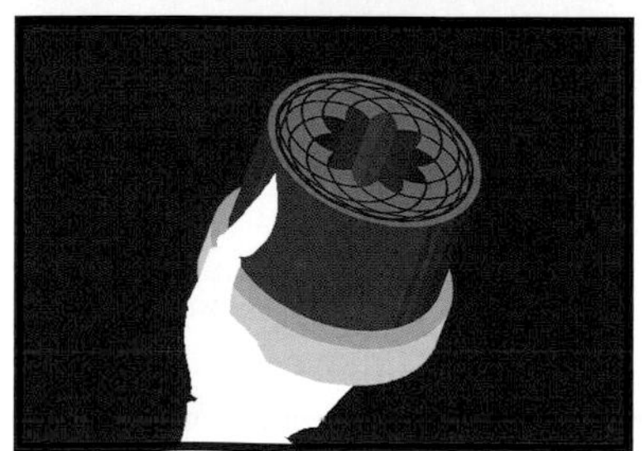

John and Karkat's conversation continues while we somewhat incongruously pop in to see what the White Queen is up to. She brought a special key of some kind, because she came *highly* prepared to do whatever the hell it is she's doing here in exile land. Here's another thing where I just come out and say exactly what happens later, because nothing insightful or meaningful can be said unless all of that is totally spelled out here in advance, and it's time for you to just DEAL WITH THAT. Oh, you don't care about spoilers, and obviously haven't cared for many hundreds of book pages already? Great. The Queen's plan here is really simple: she knows about the horrible threat Bec Noir poses. She's had access to Skaian clouds for a long time, and thus knows many things while still not knowing others. (Such as whether or not this plan actually works. All she seems to know is it's worth a shot.) Her goal is to destroy all of the exile stations, which serve as portals back into the human session. This will lock Jack in the session (at least, by destroying *most* entry points...but she seems to forget about one very important one in the frog ruins). She's containing the damage by burning the bridges. This key switches the final Bec-head station from "broken and scattered everywhere" to "solid," reassembling it right here. She does this so she can destroy it. Why reassemble it just to blow it up? Why not just leave it like that? Because bombing it is the only way it stays disassembled for good, in case some crafty son of a bitch like DD might have gotten a duplicate key or could hack this keyhole. Point is, it's better to be thorough, and this way we get to see the fourth station, which is pretty cool. Like all exile stations, it's modeled after the entry item of the player whose house formerly occupied the station's landing site. In this case, there was no single landing site, since Becsprite blew the huge meteor carrying it to a million bits. But the most important piece landed here: the piece with the keyhole that activates its homing beacon for reassembly purposes.

CG: ALRIGHT WELL
CG: I WASN'T EXPECTING YOU TO MAN UP AND APOLOGIZE FOR IT, SO OK I'LL GIVE YOU CREDIT FOR THAT.
CG: BUT IT'S NOT STOPPING ME FROM DETESTING YOU AND IT SURE AS FUCK ISN'T GOING TO DERAIL THIS RUNAWAY HATE TRAIN, JUST SO YOU KNOW.
EB: oh, yeah, i know.
EB: you're really gonna tear me apart!
EB: i just feel kind of bad i fell asleep, i don't know what came over me.
EB: maybe i ate too much lasagna.
CG: HEY, INOPPORTUNE NAPS HAPPEN IN THIS GAME.
CG: EXCEPT TO ME, BEING THE STALWART MODEL OF LEADERSHIP I AM.
CG: I MANAGED TO STAY AWAKE FOR SEVERAL WEEKS STRAIGHT, I DIDN'T WANT TO LET MY GUARD DOWN FOR A SECOND.
CG: BUT THEN

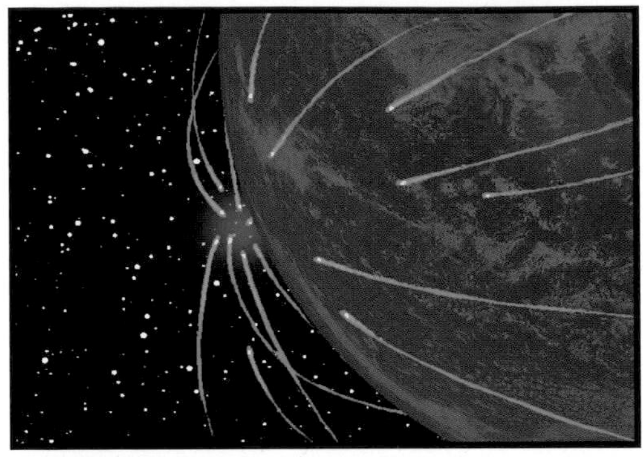

CG: AFTER IT WAS ALL OVER, AND WE RETREATED IN FAILURE
CG: I FOOLISHLY DID.
CG: AND THAT'S WHEN I SAW HIM.

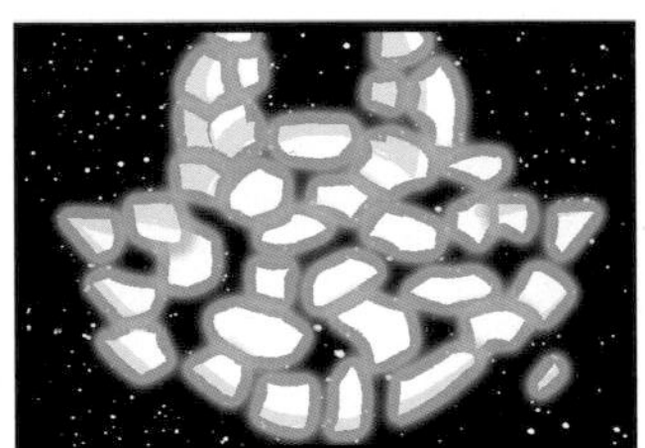

EB: who?
CG: JACK.
CG: I DIDN'T RECOGNIZE HIM WHEN HE FIRST APPEARED.
CG: BUT ON PROSPIT, I SAW HIM UP CLOSE, WITHOUT ALL THAT RIDICULOUS GREEN SHIT OBSCURING HIM.
CG: I COULD HARDLY BELIEVE IT WAS REALLY HIM BY THE WAY HE LOOKED, BUT I JUST KNEW.
CG: HE WAS WEARING A RING I DIDN'T RECOGNIZE, CERTAINLY NOT ONE BELONGING TO OUR QUEENS.
CG: WE DESTROYED THOSE.
CG: HE WORE IT ON HIS ONE HAND, WHICH WAS COVERED IN OUR MUTANT BLOOD.
CG: AND THEN
CG: JUST LIKE THAT
CG: HE KILLED ME
CG: AND I GUESS
CG: EVEN THOUGH IT WAS PROBABLY JUST HIS WAY OF SAYING HI
CG: I STILL FELT KIND OF BETRAYED.
EB: betrayed?
CG: YES JOHN. BETRAYED.
EB: um, ok.

As I just said: Bec blew up the huge meteor, which contained the Bec-head station, and therefore the pieces of the station were scattered all over the world. Also note that the station being blown to bits was factored into its design schematics and functionality. As a large vessel, it "knows" it's going to be scattered into pieces and so has two modes: broken and whole. And a user can toggle between the two modes using a key, as the queen just did. This is true of the egg station as well, which also has two modes: halved and whole. The queen used the same key to switch the egg station to whole and journey here with it. Note that the egg found in two halves also had to do with the fate of its carrying meteor, which was split in half by Bro. Also note that the fate of the station corresponds with what happens to the entry item. Dave's egg hatched, splitting in two pieces. The Bec piñata was also shot, busting it into many small pieces, just like Bec did with the meteor. So maybe we can extrapolate here about WV's cork station. It was fired from a much larger bottle station, buried deep in the sand, but we never saw the full bottle. We know that Rose's entry item was also a bottle, which she had to grab by the neck and smash against something. So does this mean the buried bottle station was actually broken, under the sand? The evidence here seems overwhelming.

CG: WHEN I WOKE UP, EVERYONE HERE WAS BUZZING ABOUT THESE ALIENS CALLED HUMANS.
CG: SO NATURALLY I'M LIKE WHO GIVES A SHIT, RIGHT?
CG: WELL, WRONG.
CG: I PRETTY QUICKLY DETERMINED THAT HE WAS FROM YOUR SESSION, NOT OURS.
CG: SO HE WASN'T REALLY "MY JACK"
CG: AND I WAS SORT OF RELIEVED
CG: RELIEVED BUT ALSO ENRAGED
CG: I'M SURE YOU KNOW THE FEELING.
EB: er...
EB: not really.

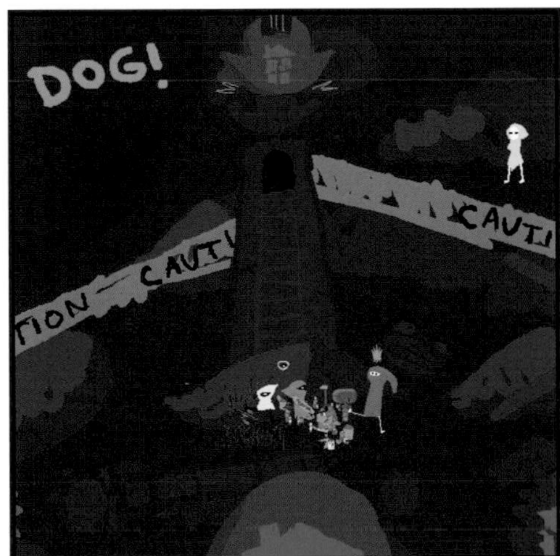

CG: ANYWAY, THAT'S WHAT HAPPENED, AND THAT'S WHY YOU ARE SUCH A DISGRACE.
CG: THIS IS PROBABLY THE LAST TIME I WILL EVER EXPLAIN ALL THIS STUFF TO YOU, BECAUSE I CAN'T IMAGINE IT WILL HELP MY HEADACHE MUCH TO REPEAT MYSELF.
CG: I BET IT'LL BE PRETTY FRUSTRATING FOR YOU IN THE PAST!
EB: i suppose it was...
EB: but meh, it is all water under the bridge.
EB: which is where trolls and their shenanigans belong!
CG: HA HA! I'M LAUGHING MY ASS OFF AT YOUR FUNNY FUCKING JOKE.
CG: I HOPE THIS IS THE CALIBER OF HUMOR I CAN EXPECT FROM YOU IN THE FUTURE-PAST, EGBERT.
CG: IT'LL BE A REAL TREAT TROLLING YOU WITH MORE OF THOSE NUB SLAPPERS TO LOOK FORWARD TO!
EB: oh, there will be lots of great material. just wait until i start handing out rabbits, you will love that.
CG: WOW, WHAT A CRYPTIC STATEMENT.
CG: CHECK THIS OUT, I DON'T GIVE A FUCK.
CG: ANYWAY, GUESS I'LL GET GOING AND LET YOU DIE IN YOUR FIRE, WHICH YOU REALLY SHOULD, BUT YOU'RE OBVIOUSLY NOT GOING TO FOR SOME REASON.
CG: I'VE GOT TO REWIND THE TAPE ON THIS CLUSTERFUCK AND FIGURE OUT WHAT WENT WRONG.
EB: yeah, i should get going too.
EB: my friend is pestering me, and i doubt she likes to be kept waiting.
EB: (she is sort of the bossy type!)
CG: WHY WOULD I CARE ABOUT YOUR DUMB HUMAN FRIEND AND HER PETULANT, MEANINGLESS DEMANDS.
CG: WHAT COULD THAT POSSIBLY HAVE TO DO WITH ME.
EB: ummm...
EB: yeah, you're right, it is probably of no significance to you whatsoever.
EB: (hehehehe)
CG: A;SLDKJFSDLKFJS;LDJFLK;J
CG: HERE, JOHN HUMAN DIPSHIT.
CG: HAVE A SECOND AND PENULTIMATE FUCK YOU:
CG: "FUCK"
CG: "YOU"

The final station plops right on top of the beheaded frog statue. There sure seems to be some heady symbolism here. Wow, what a great pun I just made. The frog temple is a hallowed Prospitian site of worship. Frogs, which embody the new universe Prospitians help the kids create, are sacred to them, just as they are reviled by Dersites, who are designated as the opposition force to the creative challenge within *Sburb*. The statue was "conveniently" beheaded much earlier to make way for the reappearance of this station, timed exactly with the rise of Bec Noir. The frog head reads as an old god or figure of worship being overthrown and replaced by a new, wrathful god, a grim false idol asserting dominance over the former kingdom of the genesis frog. In other words, this is Bec Noir's universe now. He hasn't arrived yet, but it's only a matter of time, and the realm is now his to do whatever he wants with. As a Dersite, what he wants unfortunately is to kill any frog he sees, especially one as important as this. And killing the frog means destroying the entire universe contained within it, which he has seemingly just achieved enough power to accomplish. The threat Bec Noir poses to the universe is not totally clear, since the story hasn't really connected those dots for us yet. But you can see how there was a long breadcrumb trail setting all this up, mostly through symbolism of frog desecration. The total destruction of universes has been a dire possibility looming in the background noise of the story since the beginning.

CG: MAY IT MARK THE SECOND OF MANY TO COME, AND THE MAGNIFICENT DENOUEMENT TO MANY RECEIVED.
CG: TOGETHER WE JUST TUGGED AT THE BOW TO UNRAVEL A PRESENT FULL OF GO FUCK YOURSELF.
CG: HAPPY WRIGGLING DAY YOU UGLY PILE OF TRASH.

-- carcinoGeneticist [CG] ceased trolling ectoBiologist [EB] --

> WV: Examine fourth station.

There is something familiar about this.

> WV: Examine pumpkin.

You feel as though there is something you've forgotten. Something concealed in long slumbering memories.

> WV: Examine ring.

AR has known the score for a long time. Ever since he first reacted to the Bec pumpkin with fear and deference, we knew he knew something was up. He knew about Bec, because he was there when DD made him. What about Bec Noir though? Not much reason to think AR knew about him. But don't worry, Noir will introduce himself soon enough, with his customary greeting. Meanwhile, something is jogging WV's memory here. Man, these guys really are a bit slow sometimes. They keep forgetting things, get reminded by something, and we get to see another flashback that helps us learn more. So I guess we should be thankful? Really, it's just a by-product of the fact that exiles live so long. If you did all this stuff, but then spent several boring centuries wandering through a desert, you'd probably forget a bunch of it too. You might need some potent recurring symbols to jog your memory.

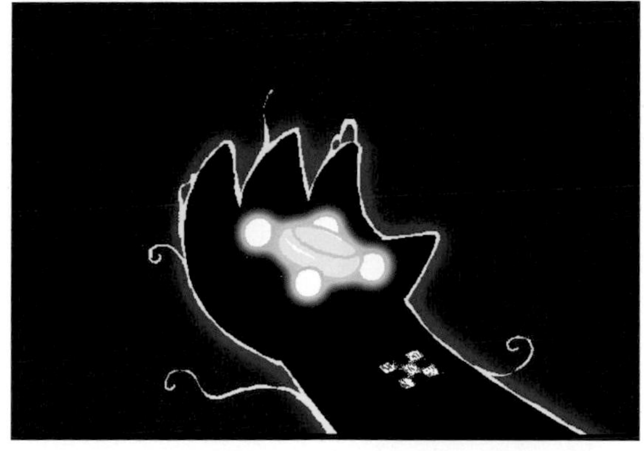

You have not inspected your treasure in years. You have spent ages guarding it without understanding its purpose.

Its only purpose you have understood has been to remind you of things you have taken care to forget. But now...

You think it is time to remember.

> WV: Remember.

Of course! The boy on the screen!

He must be the same one. You do not know how it is possible. But you are sure it is him.

John is the boy you saw that day.

John is the windy one.

WV's sudden big recollection is just that he met John on the Battlefield and had a whole slew of adventures with him. And not just the Prospit-clothed dream John. WV calls him the "windy one," which implies that WV has had some exposure to John's wind powers. This is a new mystery for us to track. Sounds like John will end up back on the Battlefield at some point, connect with WV, and do a bunch of windy stuff. WHAT IS GOING TO HAPPEN???

> WV?: Defend treasure.

Egad, a thief approaches!!! This pajama'd rogue surely seeks to put his mitts on your newfound glowy treasure.

He is definitely a thief. You have an eye for these types. He is either a master thief himself, or at the very least, an apprentice of one.

All things related to these magic rings have really blatant, totally undisguised, homage-like connections to elements of *The Lord of the Rings*. Like chucking the rings into a magic volcano to destroy them. Or a ring getting chopped off a gnarly royal finger with a broken sword. There are a lot of these nods, and they're blatantly unsubtle. WV here is a little Gollumy in his protection of his precious ring, which he too found in a river. There's really nothing more to be said about all of this except for, "Here is some stuff that is deliberately and consistently similar to a thing you know about." I exist down here if for no other reason than to repeatedly hammer you with totally obvious shit.

P.S.: That last line is basically WV going, oh yeah, this dude looks like a chump who's DEFINITELY getting played by Vriska.

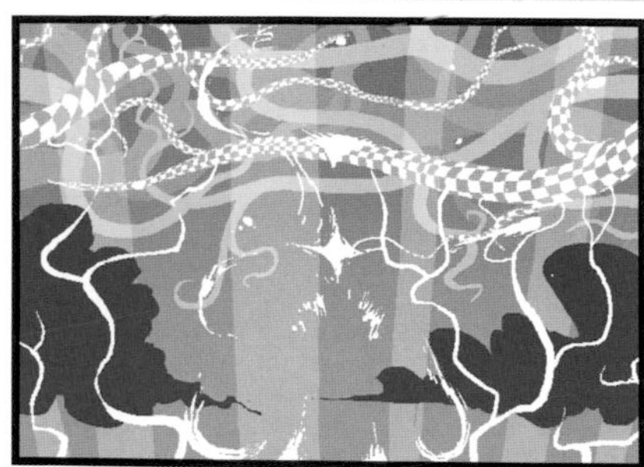

> John: Wake up again.

> WV: Command the thief's apprentice.

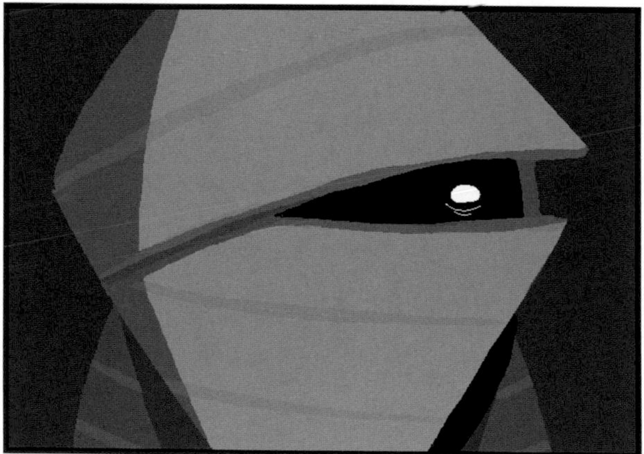

There is so much left for him to do.

> sir john, i have politely returned.

The moment WV remembers meeting John, he runs back into the station to check him out on the monitor again. Conveniently, John is cued up at the exact point in the story that we are caught up to. There are no Trollian-style hijinks with these station monitors. They progress linearly, almost like a live stream of the session piping directly into the station. Which means the passage of time we witness for the exiles maps directly onto the passage of time for our heroes in the session. Hence, from the POV of a station monitor, we have a fairly concrete approximation of "now" from a storytelling perspective, which is a useful device when it comes to a story that hops madly all over its own timeline. I INSIST THAT THIS IS INTERESTING. So I'll keep on it for a bit. Time is an extremely fungible resource inside the *Homestuck* narrative. We go backwards, forwards, hop to different timelines and entirely different fields like the troll session, where that timeline is untethered from the human universe and session. So basically, it's a mess. But there is another kind of meta-timeline existing outside the story: the timeline for the reader, which ties to the pace of story progression and what "present moment" is being focused on through the viewport of the website. The present moment can include any juxtaposition of several events that are taking place at different points in time, or different universes and sessions. Thus two things that *don't* happen at the same time inside the story (like what we're watching here) *do* appear to happen at the same time *outside* of the story. This is the nature of "circumstantial simultaneity," which Doc Scratch gets into a bit later. Remember how the exile station monitor was originally introduced as sort of a meta-viewport for the story from within the story. Story commands could still be entered, directing the character to do things, except those commands were now being entered by...another character in the story. So that means these station viewports, any time we see them, are pretty reliable windows into whatever we might call "the present moment" from the perspective outside the story. In this case, it's very close to "now" for us. Just a little before **[S] Jade: Enter**.

Yes, and it seems you have remembered your human etiquette as well.

John is busy at the moment. He is talking to his friend.

> oh dear. the purple text human again?

Yes. Her.

> what about the green text human, that one was nicer.

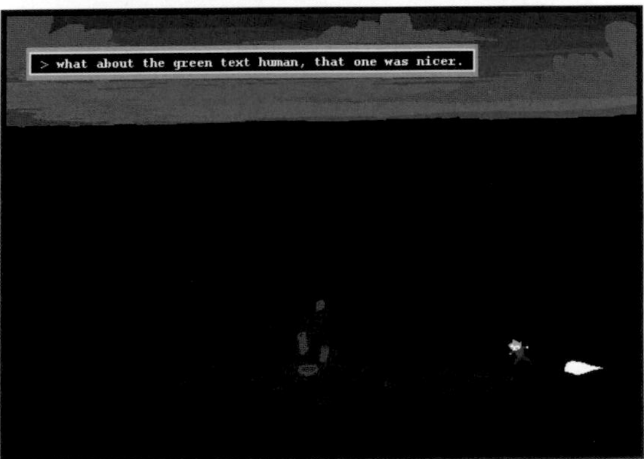

John is asking about her. But to no avail. She is currently preoccupied.

> drat. please continue to solicit her graciously, good john.

It's nice to see that WV has retained his good manners. The narrative text acknowledges this and reacts to his questions. There are some unusual moments in the story where I appear to be almost directly conversing with my own characters—these exile, command-prompt moments, which are more subtle, and the easter-egg, self-insert moments in the Meenahbound RPG games, which are a bit more overt. And finally, all roads lead to what's far and away the most egregious example of this: my contentious relationship with Caliborn through his own diabolical meta-terminal. Which is great, so that's how you know all this bullshit is worth it in the end. I never gave Caliborn a tome on human etiquette though, which is a shame. Instead I forced him to bone up on drawing manga. I guess that ended up being a pretty good investment anyway.

He will.

> why are you on a small rock? are you in peril, sir?

Why yes, he is in peril. He was stranded there on account of a nap instigated by the one he apprentices under.

> the master thief! is that who you are talking to now, john?

No, now he's talking to the Knight.

> i don't like the gray text knight. it is an unpleasant human

> WV: Give the unpleasant human the Human Etiquette book.

He is not a human.

> john, stop talking to the gray text not human immediately.

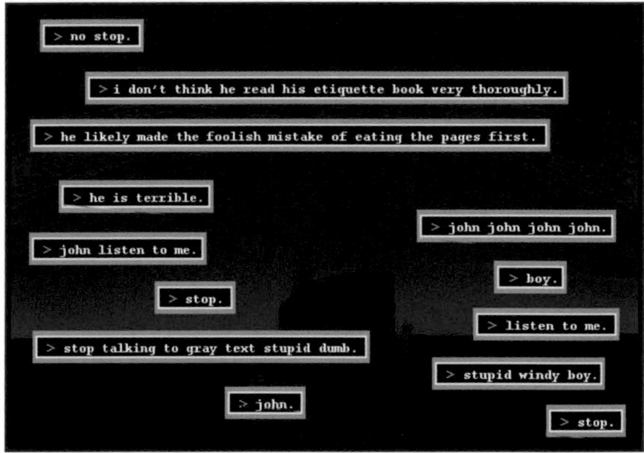

John is too engrossed in the conversation to entertain your wishes.

> stop stop stop stop stop stop.

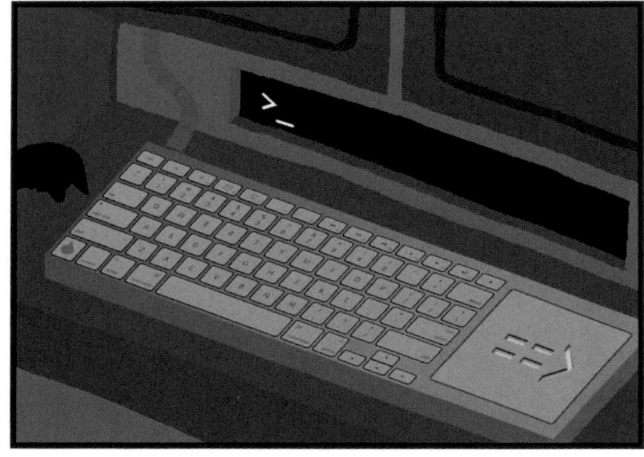

The matter he is discussing is quite urgent. Perhaps he'll humor you another time.

Ah, so that's your plan, is it?

Yelling will get you nowhere. Don't you remember?

> WV: Push it.

Nice to see that WV has the same thought I had, which is that Karkat could really stand to brush up on his human etiquette. This sequence reveals that while we were reading this scene a little while ago, WV was actually at the command prompt pulling John's strings somewhat, and if not directly controlling him, at least probably making him feel agitated. Which from earlier WV commands, appears to be all he's really able to do.

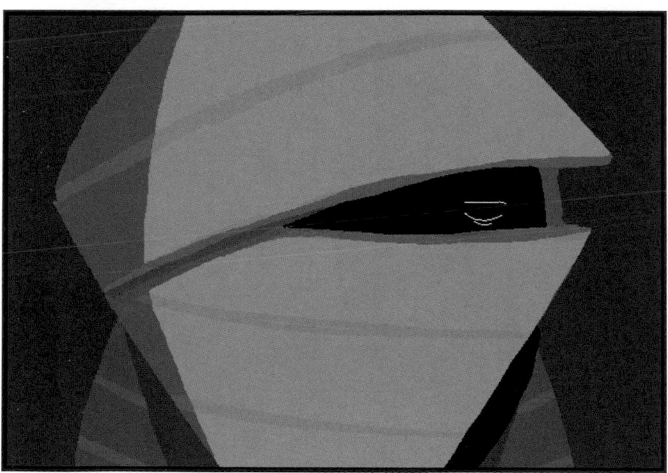

You see what happens when you forget your manners?

WV begins to realize that when John is engrossed in conversation, being polite doesn't really pay off when it comes to getting his attention. So WV hits capslock again to raise his voice, but apparently there's a hidden punishment for this. The hole blasted in the side of the station gets sealed up, almost like an emergency airlock in case of a hull breach in space. Now he's trapped in here. WHY? What a ridiculous question. It's totally reasonable that the tab button would open a hidden compartment containing Tab soda, and it's also totally reasonable that deactivating capslock, and then activating it again much later, would be the hidden mechanism for the manual override on the emergency airlock seal. Okay, you got me, maybe this is stupid? Yes, it is. But it's a great precursor to the contentious Caliborn/Author debacle. WV's experience with these station terminal shenanigans establishes a good precedent for the fact that when you mess around with the author via these peculiar meta-machines, there are all sort of arcane, ludicrous punishment-traps around every corner. None of them make much sense, and all of them can come out of totally thin air, without having much logical basis. It is my sole right as a vengeful author-god to enforces such penalties.

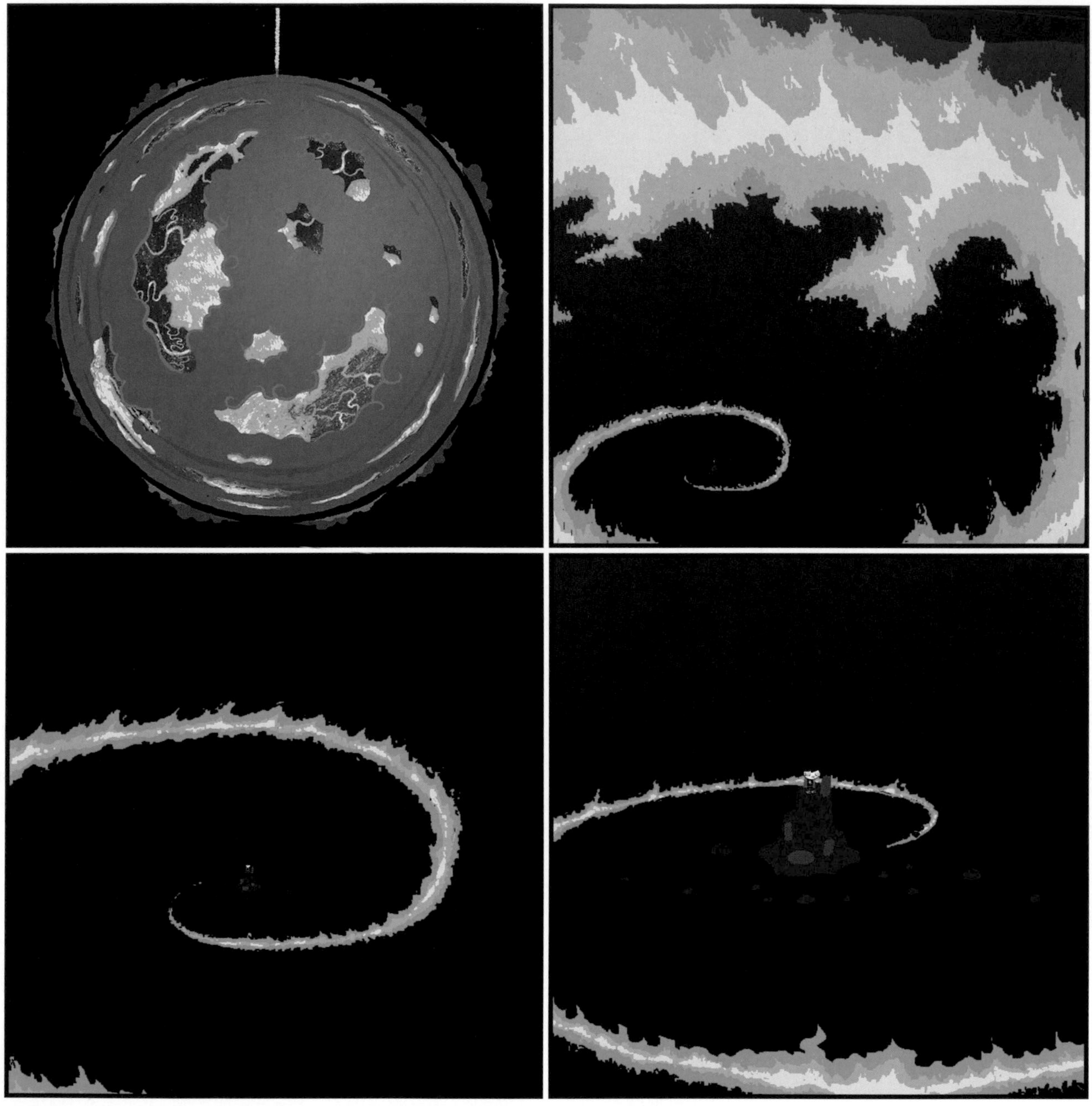

Nice panels, sweet art, yada yada... Don't forget to notice things, though. "Things," you ask? Yes, things. Every single fucking thing. You should always be snapshotting every visual in *Homestuck* you see with your photographic memory, and filing it away for future recall purposes. Any visual can become a single esoteric word in a huge visual vocabulary. This "word" here establishes an idea. A great body of green flame projects a swirling arm of fire, spiraling toward a focal point against a black canvas. Just like in Act 7, when a black hole consumes the Green Sun.

> Apprentice: Answer thief.

-- arachnidsGrip [AG] began trolling ectoBiologist [EB] --

AG: Pssssssst.
AG: Hey 8rave leader.
AG: John!
AG: Stop ignoring me. My messages should receive top priority.
AG: Who are you talking to? I don't appreciate 8eing snu88ed like this. How ungr8ful can you get!
AG: Maaaaaaaan.
AG: Come oooooooon........
EB: hey vriska, sorry to keep you waiting!
AG: W8ting?
AG: Oh! I guess so. I hardly even noticed! I am like this really huge deal, and have a lot of stuff to keep me 8usy, remem8er?
EB: yeah, i know.
EB: um, sorry to cut this short, but this isn't really the best time to chat!
EB: i am in the middle of an ocean of oil that is ablaze with a lot of green fire.
EB: i need to figure out a way to escape!
EB: unfortunately, i fell asleep for some reason, and my bed landed here.
EB: i can't believe i was so stupid.
AG: Don't 8eat yourself up a8out it!
AG: I was the one who put you to sleep.
EB: you were?
AG: Yeah!

EB: um...
EB: you can do that?
AG: Yes, that seems to 8e the limit to what I can do to your primitive species.
AG: I guess our 8rains don't really work the same way? Who knows!
EB: hmm.
EB: what do you mean, "limit"?
EB: are you saying you can usually do more than that?
AG: Duh! So much more, John. I have a lot of gr8 powers.
AG: When we have more time, I will tell you all a8out them.
EB: ok, that is pretty cool i guess...

Vriska spends seven lines nagging John for attention, and then when he answers acts like she didn't notice he left her hanging. As if he could't just scroll up and read her whining. And of course she knows that. Is she being facetious? Ironic? Who even really knows. She's the sort of person who can flagrantly alter the self-evident truth about something anyone else can plainly observe, and then truly believe the rebranding of reality that she retroactively imposes through sheer force of will. Which includes her own statements and actions. It also includes certain story developments, like "becoming responsible" for the rise of Bec Noir. She's even admitting to it right here. She's proud of it! That was the whole point, after all, to get credit for it. If nobody knew she did it, least of all her nerd crush here, what would even be the point?

EB: but...
EB: why???
EB: why would you put me to sleep and put me in this predicament?
AG: John, soon you will understand that you are meant to rise to gr8tness.
AG: This can't possi8ly happen unless you are challenged.
AG: There will 8e times when your limits are tested. This is one of those times!
AG: I know this 8ecause I can see your future right here in front of me. You should trust me!
EB: ok, but...
EB: i kind of get that, but it's also kind of odd...
EB: if you're seeing my future, and you know those things are the outcome, then why are you going back and...
EB: i guess, involving yourself with these events? see what i mean?
AG: Oh John, this should 8e so o8vious to you 8y now.
AG: You are going to 8ecome a gr8 hero, that much is sure.
AG: 8ut I want to 8e the one responsi8le for it!
AG: And now I am pretty much guaranteed to 8e.
AG: ::::)
EB: ok, that...
EB: SORT OF makes sense, i guess.
EB: but it's kind of hurting my head to think about!
AG: You don't have to think! Just leave the thinking to me.
AG: All you have to do is dig deep down, find your hero powers, and get yourself out of this jam.
AG: You can do it, John. 8e the hero!
AG: Just like in one of your movies a8out sweaty, rugged adult human males.
EB: ah HA!
EB: so you did watch that video I sent.
EB: what did you think?
AG: It was ok.
AG: I admit it was a little 8etter than I expected.
EB: yesssssss, i knew it!
AG: 8ut who cares! Let's not get sidetracked 8y films a8out wounded, muscular renegades.

AG: 8y the way, John, have you ever considered growing your hair out?
AG: I 8et it would look fa8ulous.
EB: no, it would look so stupid!
AG: I don't know a8out that!
AG: I have an eye for fashion. 8 of them, in fact!
EB: i thought you didn't want to get sidetracked!!!
AG: Oh yeah. Whoops. ::::\
EB: anyway, putting me to sleep and landing me in hot water is one thing...
EB: but you sort of indirectly caused a MUCH BIGGER problem!
EB: before i fell asleep, i was about to prototype something really ridiculous to make jack weaker.
EB: i am pretty sure that it would have made jack lose both eyes, both arms, and give him silly blue hair, and possibly also make him be a girl?
EB: he probably would have been pretty easy to beat!!!
EB: but instead, it was prototyped by jade's first guardian dog lusus.
EB: and now he is unstoppable!
EB: and he becomes the one who is stirrin' up all that trouble in your session too!
EB: i mean, it sounds like your intentions were good, but you probably didn't realize to what extent you were messing everything up!
AG: Don't 8e a8surd, John.
AG: Of course I realized that would happen.
AG: It was pretty much the whole point, you goof!
EB: what????????

Vriska's also revealing that she's begun giving John the Tavros treatment: "testing" him and putting him in horrible situations to see if he can thrive, grow stronger, and be truly worthy of her romantic attention. Tavros was a complete flop, but she has much higher hopes for John. Of course, she's cheating—she can see John's future and knows he responds well to the challenges. But maybe that's how it is sometimes. You're repeatedly disappointed by your ex, and you want so badly for this new guy you're really into not to repeat any of those shortcomings. So you kinda give him a cheat sheet. Let him know what bad lame weak losers do, and since YOU'RE not a bad lame weak loser, YOU won't do those same things and let me down, WILL you, John? No way. Look, here's a challenge to prove your worth. She's got a preeetty good feeling John won't disappoint her... ::::;) (Double-checks in his future to make sure... Okay, whew, good.)

EB: vriska, why would you do that!
AG: Jegus, calm down.
EB: but!
EB: no!
EB: why should i calm down when you just said you deliberately sabotaged all of us?
AG: Relaaaaaaaax.
AG: Listen, John.
AG: Regardless of what I did, he is already here.
AG: I know this consequence will 8e hard for you to accept, 8ut whenever you feel angry or confused a8out it, just repeat this to yourself.
AG: It should 8ecome your mantra!
AG: He is already here.
AG: Say it, John!
EB: but what does that mean!
AG: It means what it sounds like! He's already here!!!!!!!!
AG: Here in our session, trying to hunt us down! Man, this should 8e elementary to you 8y now.
AG: No matter what you or I or any of us did, Jack's here now. That's the reality!
AG: And if I didn't stop you, it wouldn't have changed the reality for us here. We'd still 8e hiding on this rock, and he'd still 8e out there, sniffing around for us.
AG: He wouldn't just disappear! That's not how this time stuff works.
AG: All that REALLY would have happened is I would have allowed you to do something you weren't supposed to do!
AG: You would have prototyped with your pretty 8lue doll, 8ecause of course deep down you know you are o8sessed with me.
AG: And then you and all your friends would exist in a splintered timeline. And you wouldn't even 8e a8le to talk to me anymore! ::::(
AG: And then you'd 8e doooooooomed.
AG: I mean, more doomed than you are already. ::::;)
AG: Trust me, I am really smart. I have this all figured out.
EB: i don't know if that makes sense!
EB: i mean, it kind of does...
EB: but something doesn't really add up about it.
EB: if you knew he was going to be created regardless of what anyone did...

EB: why did you decide to involve yourself that way?
EB: like the way you are involving yourself with me becoming a hero or whatever?
AG: You just answered your own question!
AG: I did it 8ecause I wanted to 8e the one responsi8le for cre8ting him.
EB: augh!
EB: BUT WHYYYYYYYY!
AG: 8ecause, John.
AG: It only makes sense that I would be the one to cre8te him.
AG: Since I am also going to 8e the one to kill him.
EB: that is the dumbest thing i have ever heard.
AG: Don't 8e that way.
AG: Just 8ecause you have your whole reckoning ahead of you to kill Jack, and somehow fail, doesn't mean you have to 8e 8itter a8out it.
EB: i am not bitter! i just think your plan is dumb.
EB: if he is as strong as karkat says, he will probably kill you!
AG: Karkat doesn't know nothing a8out anything.
AG: He never really appreci8ted how powerful I 8ecame. No8ody did! I am easily the strongest troll 8y far.
AG: I am also extremely lucky! That is one of my powers, John. 8eing super lucky, and making my foes super UNlucky. ::::)
EB: er...
EB: is luck actually a real thing?

There are a couple of aftershocks from the Hussnasty Saga. The panel above, sort of like the Shocked Kanaya meme panel, becomes a recurring visual too. And like the Kanaya one, this one gets coded with the type of content associated with it, which is roughly "the depicted troll revels in a diabolical monologue about their clever schemes," or something to that effect. Vriska drops the hubris-bomb here that she's mainly doing all this so she can beat Jack herself. Terezi, under her own portrait in this style, lays it on thick with Dave about themes pertaining to luck and matters of the mind. Kanaya Gets Real with Rose about some heavy stuff. Tavros tries to go on his own Vriska-like rant with Jade, but comes off as just lame and obtrusive. And Karkat's version is mostly a big goof. I kind of like the idea of using these intensive, overbearing renders when the character is being intensive and overbearing in their discourse. And yet, whenever I see these panels, I can't help but wish I made the skin stylistically much darker, so that the light shining on the face actually reads as colored illumination rather than just kind of a reduced-opacity layer tint. So it turns out "doing art" sucks, actually??

AG: Yes, and I've got all of it. I am completely untoucha8le.
EB: you sound pretty cocky! you should be careful about that, that is totally how people have bigtime downfalls.
EB: especially when they act kind of nefarious!!!
AG: Nope, I don't have to 8e careful! Too lucky for caution to matter anymore. Them's the 8r8ks!
AG: 8ut don't worry, once all is said and done in your session, and 8y some incredi8ly lucky 8r8k of your own you manage to survive the scratch, we might actually get the chance to meet.
AG: And if so, assuming I haven't gotten too 8ored w8ting around and mopped the floor with Jack already, may8e we can take him down together!
EB: wow, uh...
EB: i am not sure who would make me more nervous, you or jack.
AG: John, that's something a loser would say, come on.
AG: You should have no reason to 8e scared of me.
AG: 8y the time I am through with you, you should 8e even stronger than me.
AG: This is the way it ought to 8e, I think. ::::D
EB: you really think we will meet?
AG: It is a distinct possi8ility.
EB: so...
EB: um, if we meet...
EB: are you going to...
EB: uh.
AG: What?
EB: like,
EB: when you see me,
AG: John, what the hell are you trying to say?
EB: karkat said that...
EB: you might...
AG: Whaaaaaaaat????????
EB: oh jeez, i dunno.
EB: never mind.
AG: You shouldn't listen to anything that loudmouth says.
AG: He had his shot 8eing in charge, and failed misera8ly.
AG: It's my turn now. Scratch that.
AG: OUR turn.
EB: bluhhhhhhhh.
EB: if you say so.
AG: Now quit whining and get yourself out of this mess.
AG: Dig deep down inside that pink, nerdy little torso of yours, find your awesome hero mojo, and do what you're a8out to do.
AG: I will talk to you again after you figure it out.
AG: 8yyyyyyyye! <3
EB: wait!

-- arachnidsGrip [AG] ceased trolling ectoBiologist [EB] --

EB: what am i about to doooooooo!
EB: o.
EB: there, that was a 9th o. you don't even deserve 8!!!!!!!!
EB: whoops...

> JOHN, I APOLOGIZE IN A MANNERLY WAY FOR MY BIG LETTERS.

Come on. You can't both yell and try to be polite at the same time. It's one or the other.

> BUT I MUST URGE YOU TO ADDRESS THIS DANGER.

John is *Homestuck*'s formal protagonist, and also its go-to straight man, which means he's most likely to respond with "That's whack!" to any given person's crazy nonsense. So of course he jumps all over Vriska's scheme as the classic cocky plan that leads to a tragic downfall. It's just complete and total horseshit, and nobody ever pretends it isn't. Not even the story, really. Then, once Vriska is drunk on her self-indulgent unveiling of her MASTER PLAN, the conversation skids back into this uncomfortable romance that she's forcibly conjuring in plain sight, and which John's been nervously contemplating because for some reason he always finds Karkat's unhinged romantic prognostication to be oddly persuasive. It's punctuated by that glaring "<3" she adds at the end. Do I hear wedding bells? Wait, no. Those are the bells that ring when something sucks. There's no time for John to find any of this offputting, though, because WV starts yelling at him.

The danger currently has John's full attention. What would you like him to do?

> WHY DON'T YOU DO THE WINDY THING?

John has no idea what the windy thing is. Maybe you could be more descriptive?

> BOY, YOU'RE BEING VERY STUPID.

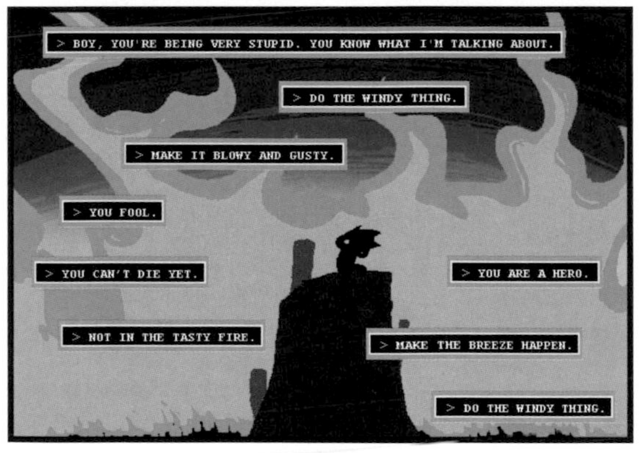

He really has no idea.

Better hurry! He's in big trouble here.

> DO THE WINDY THING DO THE WINDY THING DO THE WINDY THING

Amusingly enough, WV's brash bellowing is actually the thing that prompts John to dig deep down and unleash his powers to solve this problem. Which sort of undercuts Vriska's claim that she's the one responsible for his rise as a great hero. Just more stolen credit, which she'd have no problem with taking if she were aware of it. WV soldiers on, as the unsung hero he is.

John suddenly does the windy thing.

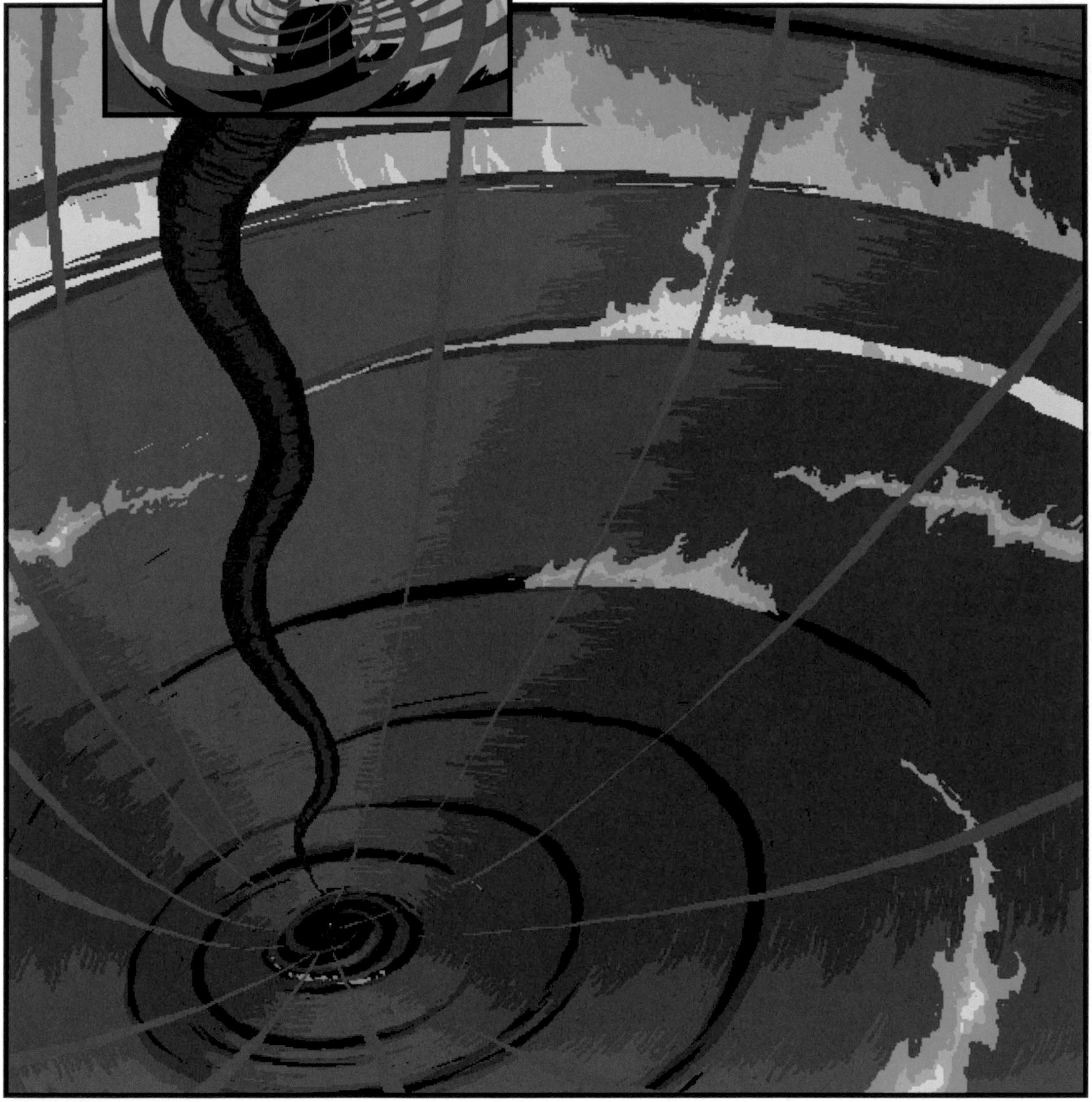

"The windy thing" is a ridiculous phrase for a special power. But it kind of stuck informally as the description for any time John does stuff with wind, and later the same construct gets used to describe powers of the other aspects, like the timey thing, mindy thing, etc. I don't remember how often this phrase comes up for other aspects in canon, but fandom really jumped on it. WV inspired John's greater sense of communion with his aspect, resulting probably from some combination of external urgency and internal brain-yelling. This is actually a more impressive feat than whatever hacky garbage Vriska is trying to pull off, since she has the luxury of looking a few minutes ahead on Trollian, seeing what John does, and deciding, "I want that to be meeeeeeee!" WV can't see the future, so his badgering comes off as a more sincere attempt to help John. The only thing WV's going off of is his distant memory from the Battlefield that John is, in fact, capable of doing some sort of windy thing.

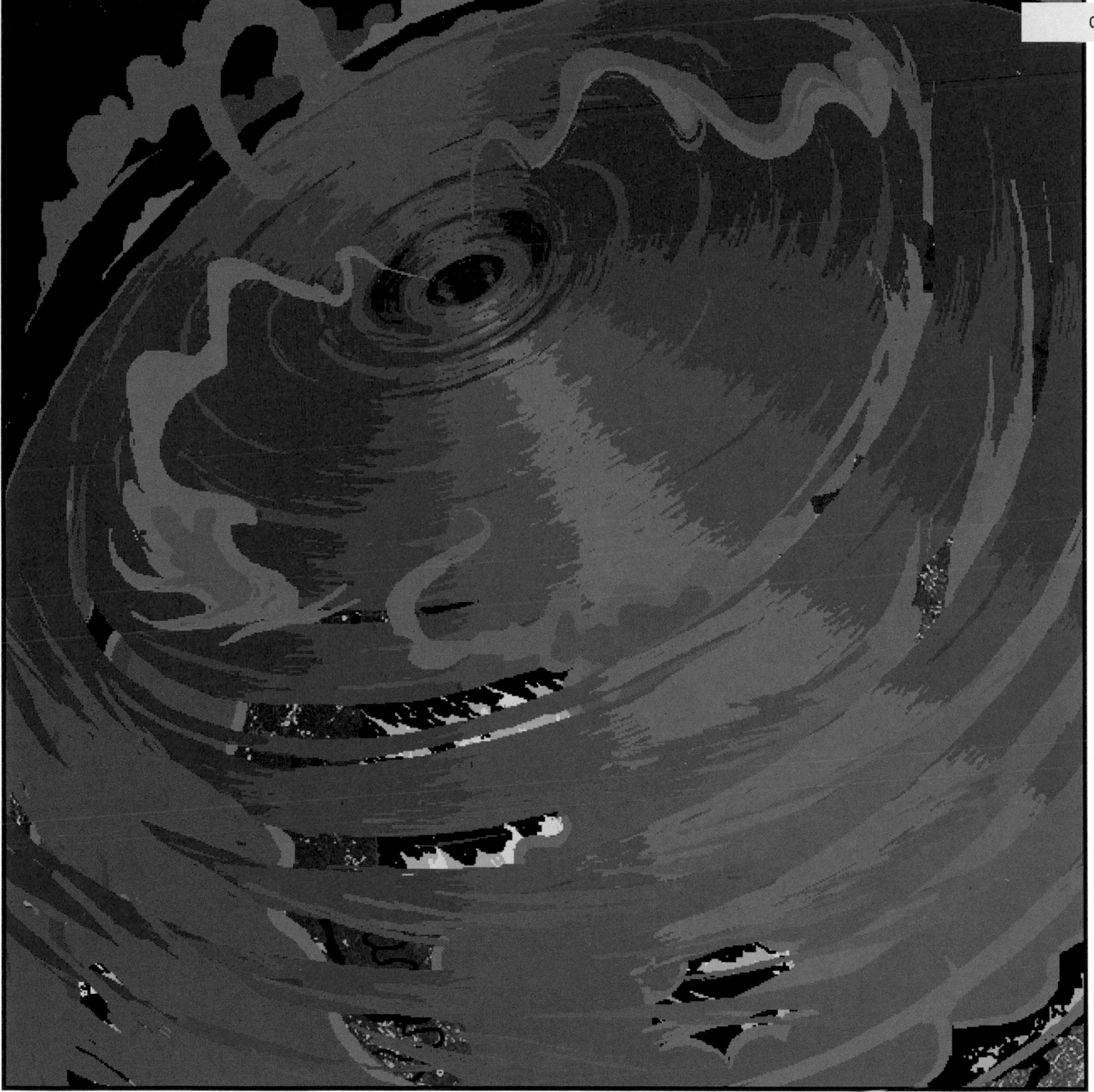

This is probably the first real indication that John is capable of doing cool and formidable shit, instead of just being a useless dork with silly hammers who likes movies and flounders around. Is it enough to pose a threat to Bec Noir? Well, it's enough to put out a lot of green fire. But as sick as this is, John won't cut it until he's god tier at least. Even then...eh, he's still gonna need some help. It's better to look at any given god tier kid as a good piece in a diversified party of heroes, who all play a useful role in a bigger fight, as finally seen in **[S] Collide**. At this point, you couldn't be blamed for presuming Bec Noir to be the ultimate threat who the heroes are all prepping to take down in the end, but the truth is, he's just one of many imposing villainous figures by the time we get there. The story just isn't built to have that kind of traditional, villainous focal point in the long run. Hell, even the "supreme villain" isn't really the villainous focal point. More like an elusive parody of one. A more symbolic Figure of Menace, or a demonic avatar for the dire preconditions of adversity built into Paradox Space. We heard Vriska a few pages ago invoke his catch phrase, but in reference to Jack rather than English: "He is already here." It's true. The threat, whether it's Jack or LE, already exists, regardless of whether you try to bring him about or instead preempt his existence. Any "supreme villain" in this story will be intrinsically stitched into the fabric of cyclical reality. You can't stop them from coming into being, and you can't make them dead until they're good and ready to go, as authorized by Paradox Space. As such, the emphasis in the story never really is "How to stop the villains," even though the heroes presume it must be due to consuming all the same media we do. The emphasis is on Other Things, existing in a state of tension with traditional adversities in the backdrop. And if you have become a scholar of these book notes—which, sadly, you obviously have—then you must know all about what those Other Things are by now.

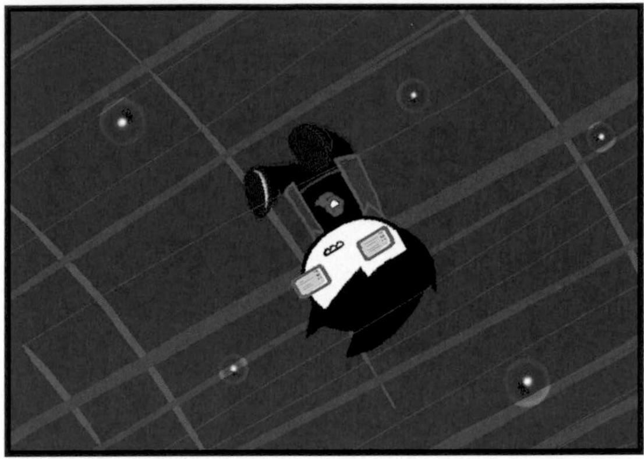

-- arachnidsGrip [AG] began trolling ectoBiologist [EB] --

AG: Fly, Pupa!!!!!!!!
AG: Flyyyyyyyyy!
AG: Hahahahahahahaha!
EB: oh, hey.
EB: who's pupa?
AG: No8ody, just some loser.
AG: Look at that, you did it!
EB: did what?
EB: you mean, this windy thing here?

> Dave: Snoop.

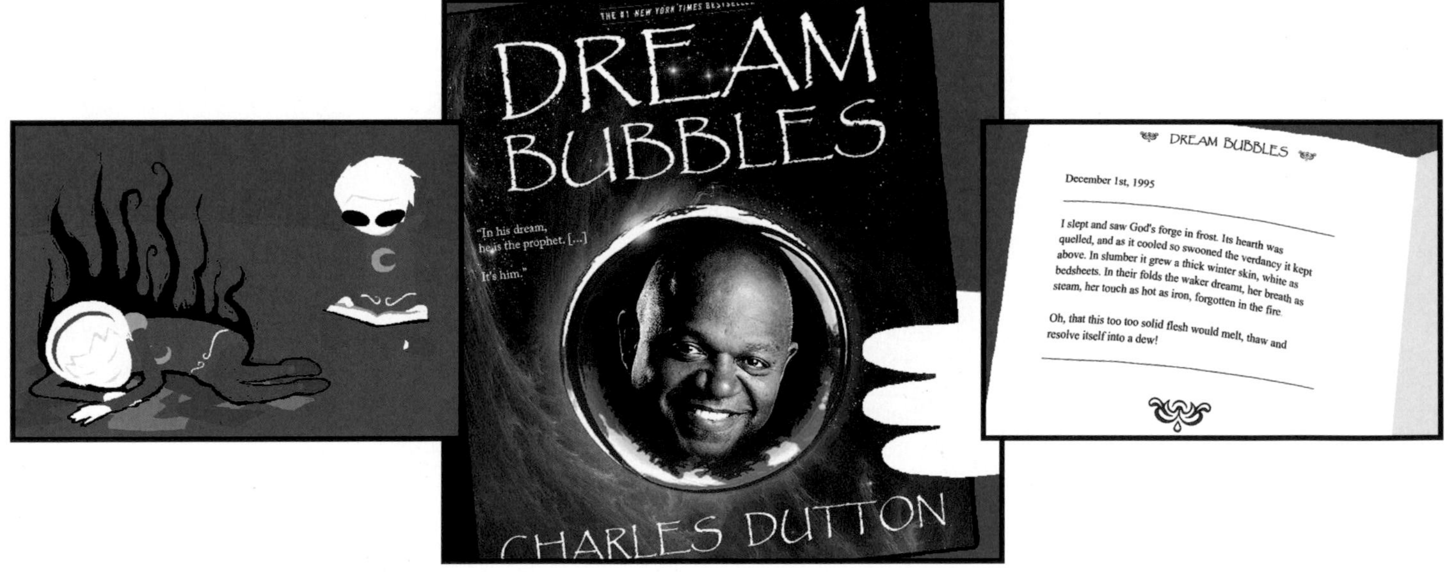

> [S] ==>

Pretty deep cut here, Vriska dragging her old "Fly, Pupa" burn into John's moment of triumph. Maybe she's repurposing her old jab at Tavros to be more legitimately congratulatory toward her brand-new boyfriend, known as Better Tavros? Whatever, who cares what this crazy person meant. In another story, you could imagine John's big, windy display as foreshadowing for when he finally, triumphantly uses this ability to defeat a terrible endboss, like Jack or LE. Like maybe John makes a huge WIND FIST and crushes LE to death, and we're like, WOW, and throw a big party and cry a lot. Too bad I just debunked that. John still get to use this rad new power in a lot of important ways, but they tend to be more procedural and plot-advancing rather than tactical. For example, he summons a huge Wind Drill to carve the Tumor out of the Battlefield (and the hole nicely doubles as an entry point for the tadpole much later). And finally, the supreme validation of John as the best Windy Boy is when he uses his power in a way that's visually reminiscent of first time he uses it, on the previous page. That's at the final completion of his quest, after blowing all the clouds away, fully realizing his retcon powers, freeing himself from the confines of the story and transporting LOWAS to the blankspace, thus releasing the fireflies just as the salamanders foretold. An offbeat metaspin on the type of personal quest we might have originally imagined when first exploring LOWAS. So the point I'm getting at here is, when we see John's potential here with all this cool wind blowing around, it really is the beginning of a lengthy arc related to the development of this ability, and the final implementation of it to do something narratively critical. It's just that the full ascendancy of this potential doesn't play out in combat. It's about freeing himself, and everyone else, from the cyclical, fatalistic prison of the story, wherein they find themselves surrounded by unbeatable foes who all tend to be "already here."

"I slept and saw God's forge in frost. Its hearth was quelled, and as it cooled so swooned the verdancy it kept above. In slumber it grew a thick winter skin, white as bedsheets. In their folds the waker dreamt, her breath as steam, her touch as hot as iron, forgotten in the fire.

Oh, that this too too solid flesh would melt, thaw and resolve itself into a dew!"

-Acclaimed actor and sleeping prophet, Charles Dutton

Charles Dutton had a respectable acting career, and I'm sure he said many memorable things, to whoever might have been listening. But he didn't say this. Shocking, I know. What's with all these misattributed quotes? Did I explain this? We've just covered a big stretch of story which, thanks to Vriska, has been heavy with notes about crassly misappropriating certain kinds of content—words, deeds, entire story events—and slapping someone else's name on those things to retroactively reassign credit and reshape the way the content is perceived. Almost a cyclical contamination of the content, an attempt to confuse and misdirect by repurposing what is already known. Combine this element with the misquotes that go back to Act 1, as well as some other things like the tendency to rename pets, and it seems to me we have the basic constituents of what you might call a "theme." What is the nature of the theme? What does it mean? Do I need to tell you everything?? Maybe it's time for you to put that noggin of yours to work and come up with some of your own answers. I already know what it means. My boy Dutton over there knows what it means. Look at him. He's tickled as fuck that you can't figure it out. Laughing his ass off at your ignorance. Good, I'm glad you feel ashamed, it's character-building. What I *will* say is, the latter part of the quote, about solid flesh and dew, that's Shakespeare. The rest of it I just made up. You can kind of tell, right? None of the other poetic excerpts had original material woven into the misquoted text, but Jade always was the pattern breaker of the group. Customizing the false quote with specifics relevant to this moment—the forge, winter skin, bedsheets (Jade's on a bed in this Flash), irons in the fire—makes it better suited to her land intro. It's also sort of retro-fitted to the Shakespeare line, expanding on the idea that a blanket of snow is like a layer of flesh, which can melt upon the introduction of a heat source. Like the first human to appear in a frozen wasteland, or the dormant volcano she brought with her, which she has the ability to stoke. There's...a lot going on here??? The point is, then I slapped Dutton's name on it for some insane reason, and called it a day.

LAND OF FROST AND FROGS

Another land intro, more scenery porn and haunting music. I don't usually subscribe to the idea that these books absolutely murder the souls of the animations by making them static, but these environmental pieces really do feel vacant without the music. There was some magic in getting to know these places for the first time in the Flash format, and I think this was one that really sold that feeling in particular. The "Frogs" in the LOFAF title remained garbled right up until this moment, to keep you guessing. Finally the time is right to show it. Is it a stunning reveal? Not really. But censoring it until now lets us know it's a significant bit of information, and the moment it's revealed kind of signals something about the mystery word. That signal is something like, "Hey, it's time for us to start getting serious about frogs and meditate upon their deeply significant cosmological role in the story." The Space player is all about creating space, i.e. the universe itself, which is one big frog, so she's all about frogs, breeding them and then deploying one special frog into Skaia via the Forge. We've finally crossed that threshold, and so has Jade. It's frogtime.

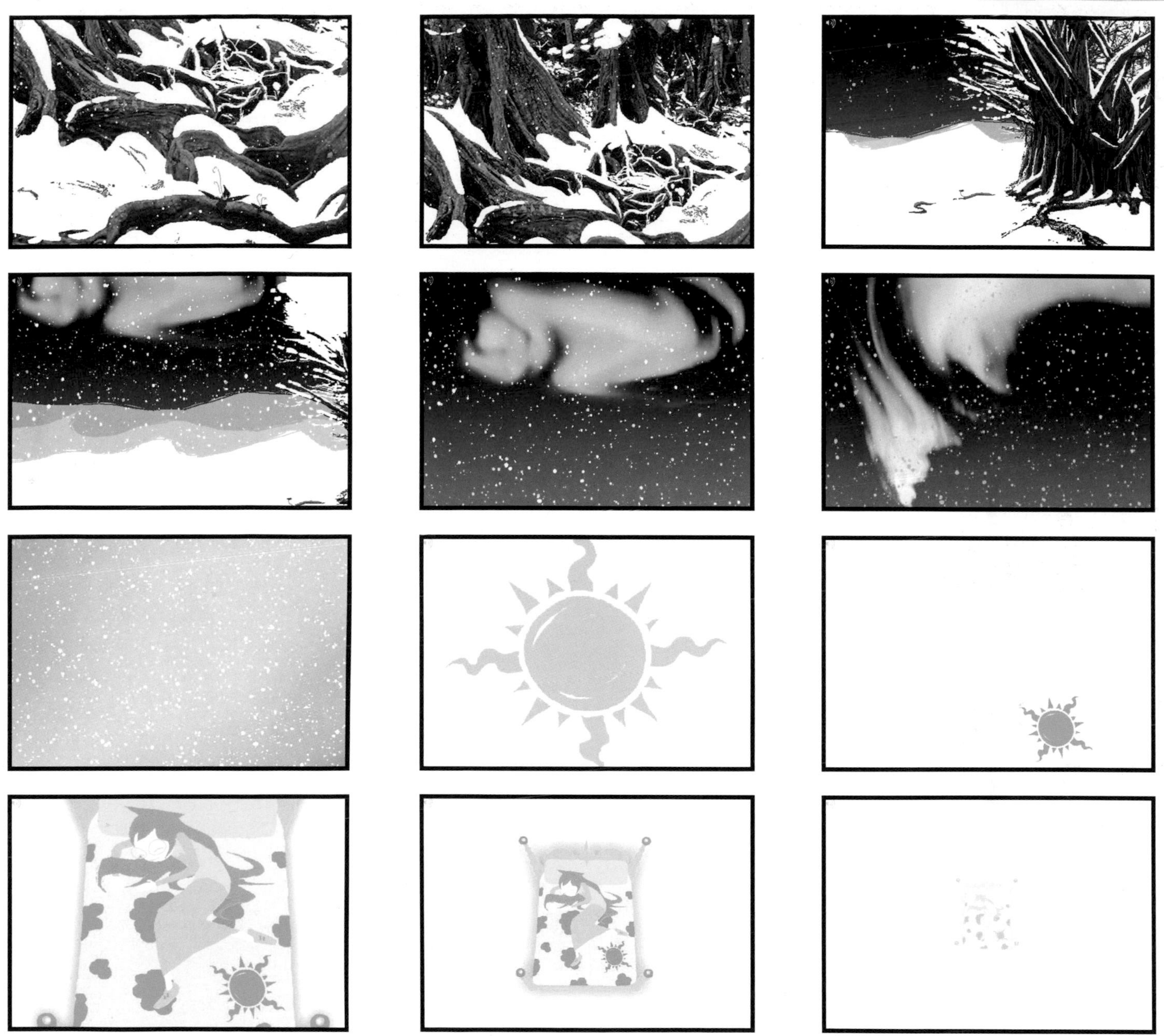

The "pollutant" of Jade's land is thick snow cover, brought about by something in the general department of nuclear fallout. Her bedsheet pattern has stylistically flipped to green, with the recurring sun icon conspicuously assuming this hue, in direct reference to—brace yourselves– The Green Sun. I know, the symbology is getting pretty hard to interpret, but hang in there. Much like Bec's head on top of the frog ruins reminds us of Bec Noir's sudden domination over these realms, flipping the familiar sun sigil to green also signals that the Green Sun and its infinite energy supply are fully presiding over events now as well. It has the whole session, and this planet in particular, on lock. The green Bec-powers have always been associated with a sort of radioactive energy, so that would seem to be the impetus for this wintry nuclear fallout that's enveloped this planet, which is otherwise covered with banyan trees and frozen lakes full of frogs in icy stasis. LOFAF is the planet that goes through the most dramatic change when its ecological problems are solved. It quickly transforms into a tropical, swampy planet rife with all kinds of amphibious life ready to be harvested for cosmic breeding duties. It also seems to be the most trivial cleanup challenge, since all you have to do to get rid of the snow is light the Forge, making the planet warm enough so the snow melts. Jade does not appear to have much trouble doing exactly that later in this act. But it probably doesn't hurt that she gets some help from another Space player who already did it.

> Jade: Answer.

cuttlefishCuller [CC] began trolling gardenGnostic [GG]

CC: Glub glub glub glub glub!
GG: oh.............
GG: nooooooooooooooooooooooooooooooo
CC:)(ey, take it easy!
CC: I'm not)(ere to give you a)(ard time like my buddies)(ave been.
GG: but youre a troll
GG: and thats what trolls do!
GG: even when they say they wont
GG: sometimes especially!!!!!!
CC: Ok t)(en, you can be t)(e judge of t)(at. I won't be long!
CC: I've just come to say a couple t)(ings.
CC: FIRST!
CC: None of t)(is is really your fault!
CC: T)(is is swimmingly obvious to everyone)(ere w)(o takes a glubbing moment to t)(ink about it rationally.
CC: W)(ic)(isn't many of us! But still.
GG: ok.....
GG: even though i still have no idea what youre talking about
CC: I mean, your lusus jumped rig)(t in t)(ere to save you!
CC: Just like mine did.
CC: Well ok, mine was dead at t)(e time. 38(
CC: And s)(e just kind of...
CC: F-ELL IN!

CC: Kinda drifted down like fis)(food, and POW, GL'BGOLYBSPRIT-E.
CC:)(e)(e)(e)(e)(e)(e)(. S)(e was so funny.
GG: whats a lusus!!!!!
CC: It's a big ol' monster custodian you grow up wit)(!
CC: S)(-E-ES)(,)(ow freaking retarded do you)(ave to be not to know somet)(ing like t)(at?
CC: I'm joking, of course. 38)
GG: :\
CC: I wanted to glub somet)(ing -ELS-E to you well before you started playing.
CC: Just to get t)(e idea in your)(ead!
CC: I am Feferi, by t)(e way. Abdicated empress to be!
GG: ok feferi. what is it?

And then, right away, we go backwards in time. Why get right down to business with Jade's land exploration when we can mess around some more and flash back to Feferi's first interaction with Jade? Nice point you made there, and I promise I feel very owned by it. But cool your jets, wise guy. We're doing a transitional trick here, and we'll get to Jade's land in a couple of pages, all right?? This seems like a flashback, but really it's the first good example of a dream bubble in action. The heart of Act 6, a.k.a. the Badlands of Homestuck, are rife with these things as a primary setting for story action. This scene introduces us to how dream bubbles work, without actually letting us know it's taking place inside of one (although we can start to infer this as the chat goes on). The full demonstration of dream bubble mechanics comes later, so for now this just reads as a run-of-the-mill, "jump scare" dream sequence we see all the time in media. A dream bubble sequence always starts with an innocent-looking flashback, which the story has made clear by now it will deploy at any time, for any reason. So from now on, you really have to be on your toes. When a flashback starts, you have to wonder whether it's a "real" flashback or the beginning of a dream bubble sequence. Dream bubbles always first assume the appearance of someone's memory, whether they're dreaming or dead. All environments inside of bubbles are made of nothing but memories. The environment starts to become malleable, sort of like a memory-collage, either once the dreamer gains awareness they've already done all this before, thus realizing they're asleep or dead, or once other dreamers or ghosts show up to start mixing their memories into the bubble as well. This makes for some pretty interesting settings later on, at least visually speaking.

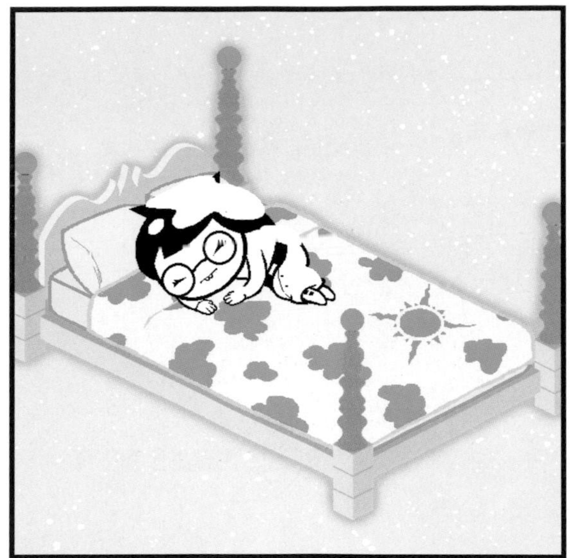

You have got to stop falling asleep.

> Jade: Get out of bed.

You de-bed.

The snow is quite deep.

> Jade: Pester John.

This is the second time Bec saves falling Jade by catching her with her own bed. This time, instead of mask-zapping the bed to break her fall, he's levitating it, which appears to be a new power resulting from his spritehood. Getting overpowered much, Bec?? Looks like it. That's fine, though, because in due time Jade will fuse herself with Becsprite, and then SHE will be the one who is overpowered. Thus fully realizing her destiny as both a furry and a Mary Sue.

You would like to report to John, but it seems you have misplaced your laptop!

That's right. It was in the atrium when you got slapped with that stupid blindfold and all hell broke loose.

You hope it's ok! It was your favorite computer, AND your favorite lunchbox.

> Jade: Climb.

Huh?

> Jade: Turn around.

You don't see anything.

Someone out there is messing with you. Good thing grandpa taught you never to leave home without your rifle, even by accident.

> [S] Jade: STRIFE!!!!!!!!!!!!

We're in Callback City again. We're always in Callback City. These panel layouts are the same as when Jade was first getting rather impishly stalked by Bec on her island. And now she finds herself getting rather Bec-ishly stalked by an imp. The poetic justice of it all is devastating.

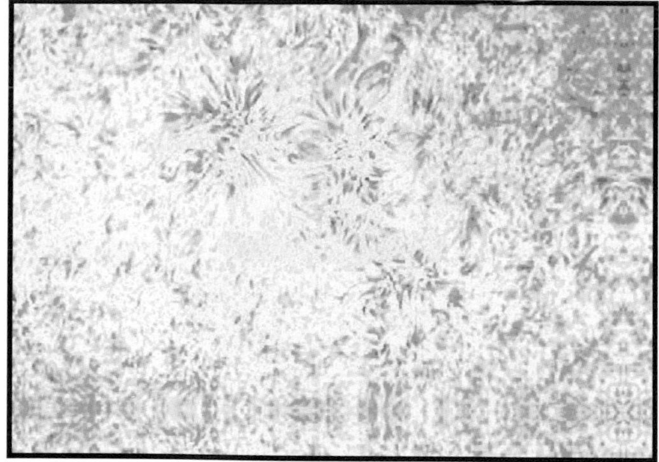

It's been quite some time since we did a full-fledged strife page, with music and everything. You may recall there was a phoned-in one in Hivebent, with Karkat flailing his sickle at his crabdad in a single GIF. You have to go way back into Act 4 to find another legitimate one. They sort of fell out of favor as a format, since it was mostly a waste of creative man-hours for very little story-advancing return. The strifes always were just flavor pieces to help prop up the feeling that the story is also a game you can semi-play. But as the narrative intensity and complexity kick into higher gear, the story leans toward other devices to achieve this effect, while still pushing things forward, like the RPG mini-games. But *Homestuck* has a way of always coming back to earlier formats and ideas as if to say, "Don't forget, this is still a thing we can do." This strife also does double-duty as a reminder that, due to the Bec debacle, not only do the players now have to deal with Bec Noir skulking around the session, but all the lesser enemies got an insane power boost too. Just this one shot of a uranium imp in Bec Mode allows us to extrapolate the effect across a full session of enemies, and so realize how untenable it probably is now for the players to accomplish even basic things.

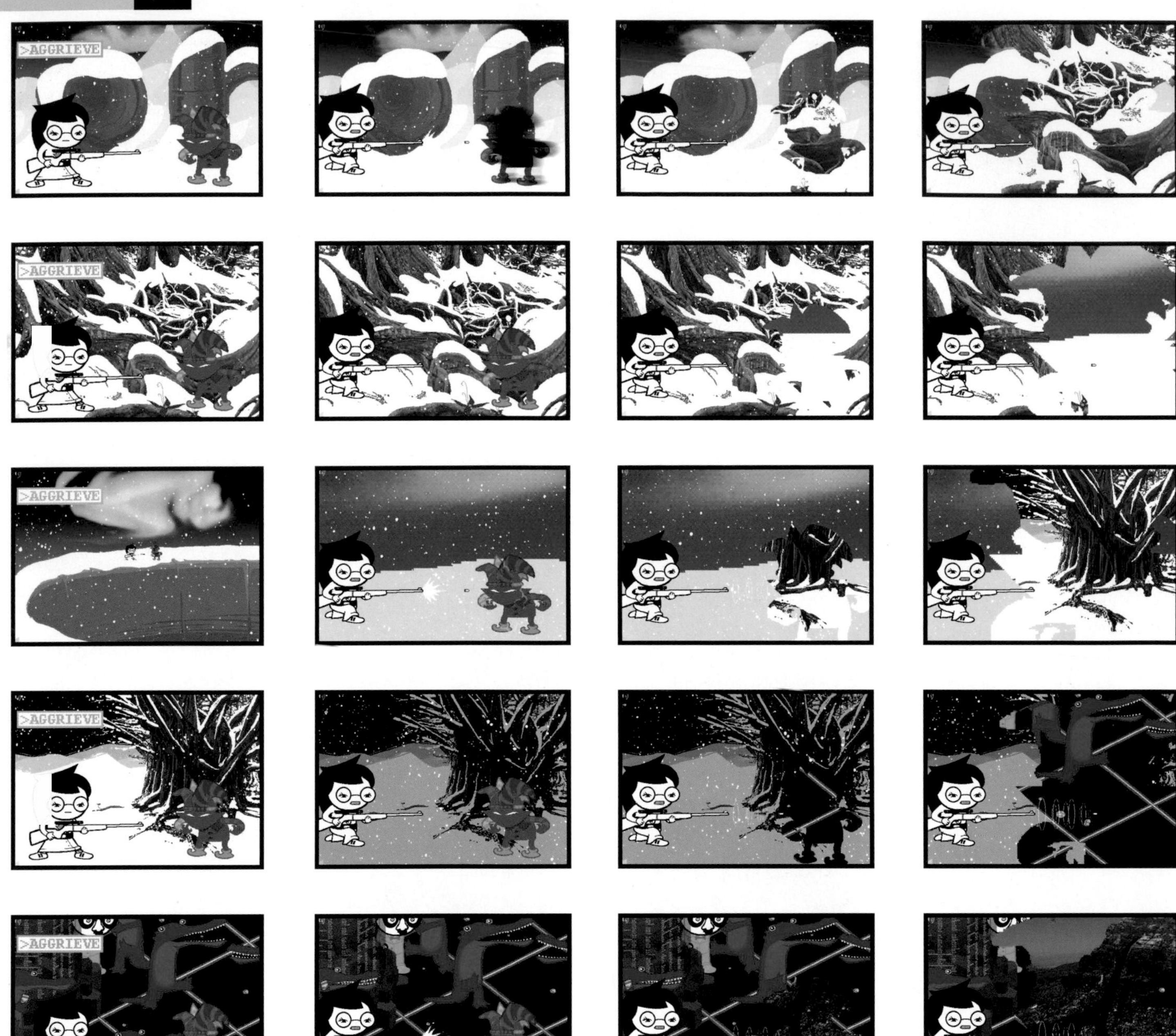

Other than that, there's not much to say about this strife. It's kind of a gag, a reprisal of Jade's original fight with Bec, but we're also getting a little teleportation tour of all known locations throughout the session, plus some we haven't seen before.

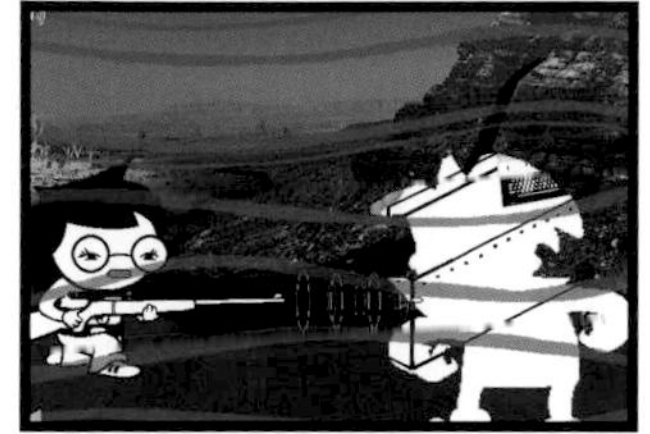

But just because this strife page is basically useless, it doesn't mean we can't do a few small useful things along the way. Jade swings by Dave's golden ruins and fires a shot that wakes him up. So, cool, he's awake, which means that soon Dave and Jade finally will be able to talk and catch up on stuff. In fact, he's got a great reason to get in touch with her, since he just saw her randomly appear in his land with an imp, fire a gun, and disappear again.

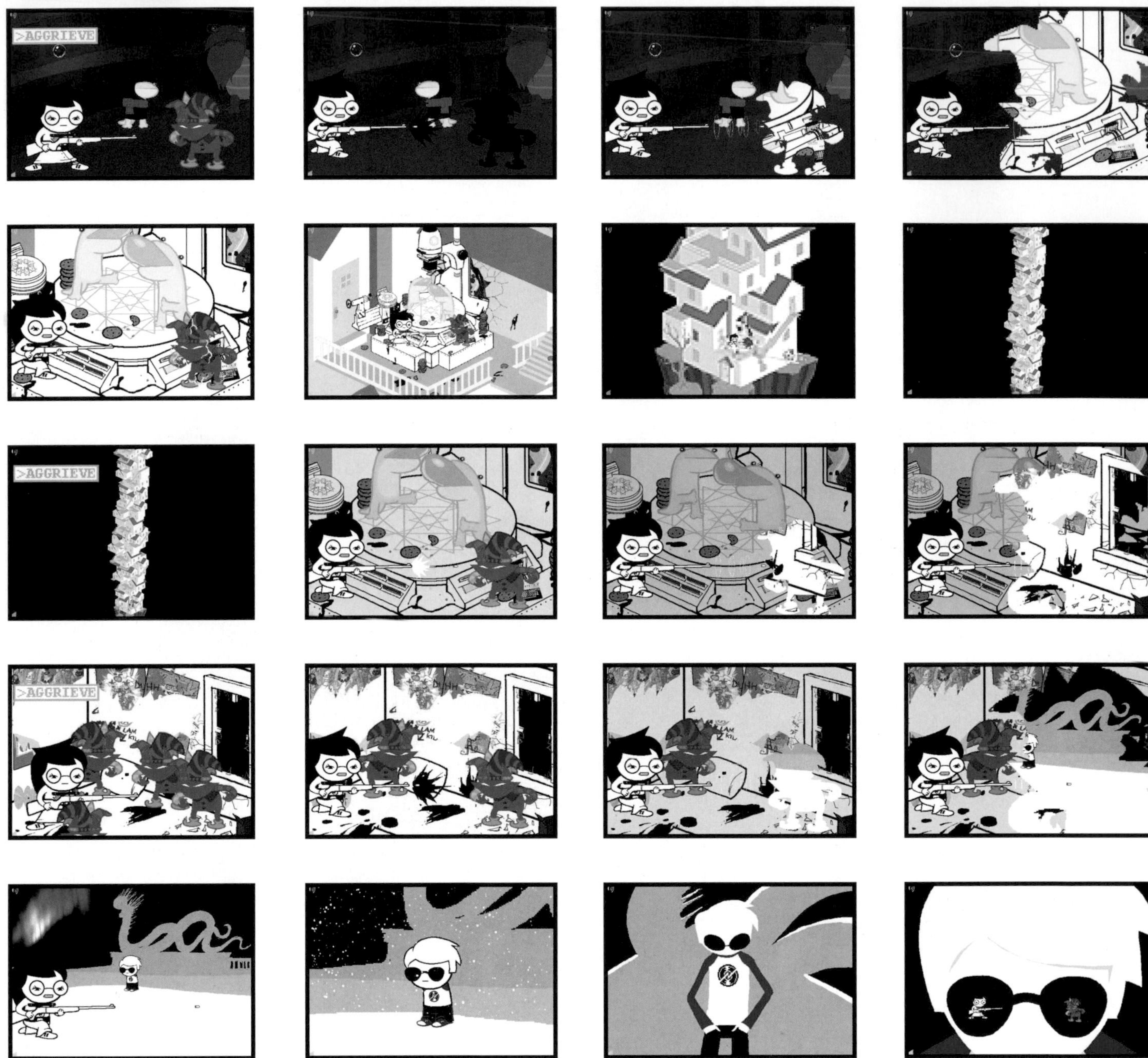

Here's another useful datapoint in a panorama of nonsense: a glimpse of a huge statue of Jade's denizen, Echidna. If you were following along back in the day and were ass-deep in *Homestuck* lore, the moment you saw that statue, you'd have known it was Echidna. Why? Because it was previously established that the kids' browsers all had the same names as their denizens. We've already seen the little two-tailed snake icon on Jade's desktop. And here's a huge snake beast with two tails. We also know that the wands the bunny was wielding are the Quills of Echidna. And those needley things on the denizen's back sure look like quills. There's also a Future Dave strolling around, ridiculously underdressed for the weather. What's he doing out there? Do we ever find out? I don't remember at the moment. I think his presence here is mostly about letting us know Future Dave really gets around. He's got a lot more time to spare than everyone else.

Bec decides that's enough of this foolishness. What do you do with Bec-powered things? How do you beat them? You just don't. The only thing that can take down a Bec-powered thing is another Bec-powered thing. This is helpful to know. And seeing this principle in action here, I guess it shouldn't have been that surprising to find out how Bec Noir ends up being stalemated for most of the story, and then finally defeated. Yes, that's right. I am now spoiling the hell out of a hugely important thing that happens in **[S] Cascade**. A Bec imp appears, stops Jack dead in his tracks, and chases him across the Furthest Ring for several years.

Good dog.

Best friend.

> Jade: Level up!

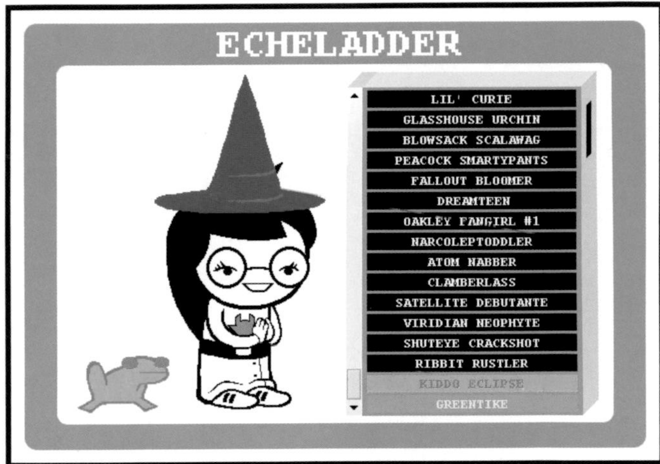

You finally hop off the lowly GREENTIKE rung and secure your position on the somewhat respectable KIDDO ECLIPSE rung.

You have a lot of climbing ahead of you.

> Jade: Thank best friend.

JADE: thanks bec, good boy!
JADE: soooooo...
JADE: can you talk now?
JADE: what do you have to say?

The echeladder is another thing that hasn't gotten much play in a long time. It's nice to see it back, because you definitely think it's one of the best pseudo-systems in the story. We didn't see it at all in Hivebent. In fact, in the long term it seems to only be used for the John/Jade/Jane/Jake side of the family tree. At least, in terms of what the reader is exposed to. Why is that? I won't answer that question, sorry. Instead, check it out, instead of a feather Jade gets a frog which varies with each rung. Cause she's a Witch, get it? Whereas John is an Heir. Though I guess Heirs aren't really known for wearing feathered caps? It makes sense for a Page though, which is why Jake also has a feathered cap for his rung climbing. Maybe it's just that Heir is kind of a lame class, just like Page, so they both get the dorky Robin Hood hat. But then Jane has a fedora with a press ticket in it? Now I'm confused. Maybe these things don't perfectly correlate to class at all and can just be whatever the fuck I wanted them to be? Guys, it's not like any of this shit is even real. Jade isn't literally wearing a green witch hat up there, it's just a funny visualization. Wow, I just discovered a great escape hatch for explaining any remote logical inconsistency in this story. Ha ha, you're actually trying to make *sense* of all this bullshit? Lol, nice try.

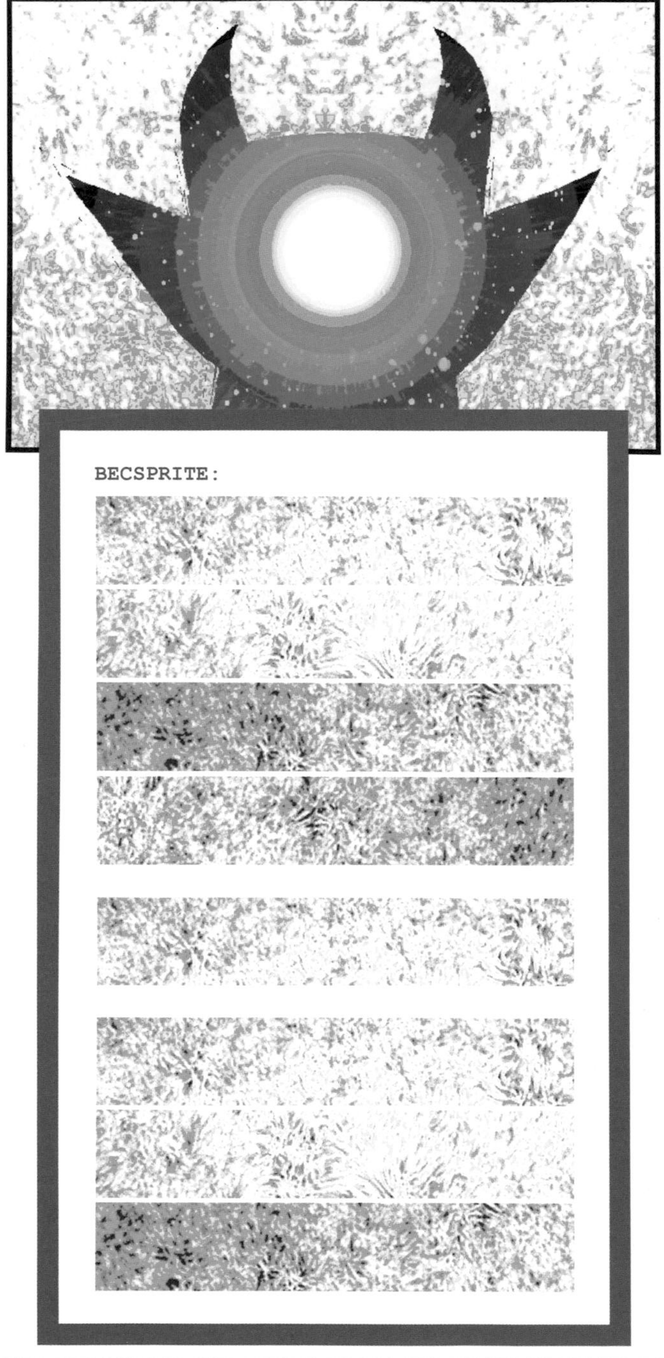

I regret that these graphics are not animated, because the intended effect here was definitely to give you a seizure. No offense to those of you who actually are prone to seizures. But come on, by this point you all must know that the entire website is a nonstop parade of hellish seizure traps. Now that they're all books which you can safely read, maybe you can finally stop regarding me as Satan?? Thanks. Normally, any sprite can talk, even ones prototyped with pets. Jaspersprite can, so it stands to reason Becsprite can too, right? But no, that doesn't feel right. Bec is too ominous to talk. He's the consummate silent guardian. Ludicrously powerful, unwaveringly loyal, but still giving you an uneasy feeling even as he defends you. So I didn't want him to be like "oh hey jade, it is i, becquerel, who can finally talk now." He just visually shrieks some unfathomable fields of green fire under the spritelog cut. I'm guessing you aren't well versed in translating rapidly flickering green-fire GIFs into English, but I like to think it's pretty obvious what Bec is saying here anyway. He's giving Jade some information that's absolutely critical for her quest, and wondering if she's ever heard of the legendary Updog.

You think you will try to keep conversations with Becsprite to a minimum from now on.

> Greetings.

You have extraordinarily bad timing. Her guardian will not be pleased with your intrusion.

> Don't I know you?

Hello.

Yes, you do.

You might want to step away from the computer.

I guess it's at this point I should express regret for describing this "Shocked Kanaya" panel format as one that consistently communicates a sense of stunned romantic attraction for whatever they're looking at. Because if I didn't, then I would have to admit that the idea being conveyed here suggests that Jade has just developed a crush on her overpowered nuclear dog. Which would be horrible if that's what I was saying. Just awful. Hold on, my beleaguered life coach just popped in again, no doubt to make another fruitless attempt to steer me away from bad decisions. Wait, no, that's not my life coach. It's my priest. He's carrying an entire bucket of holy water, and...yeah, I'm completely soaked now. He just turned around and left, without saying a single word. Thank you, Father.

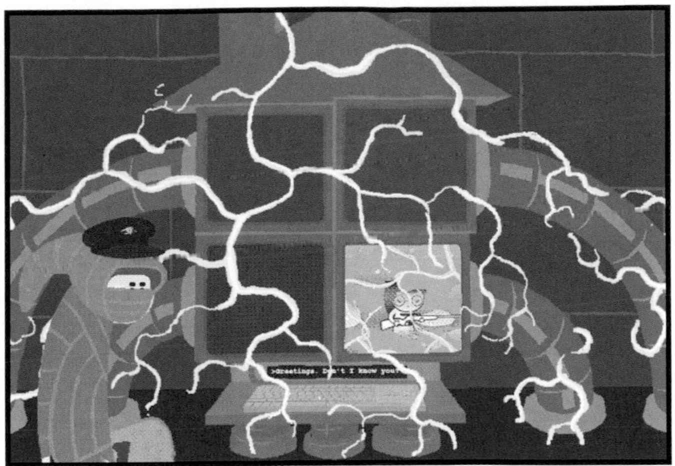

> PM: Rule.

You have no idea how to rule. What orders could there possibly be to give anyway?

All you want to do is deliver mail. You do not want to be the stupid queen. And you do not want to wear this stupid mailbox crown.

THIS IS STUPID.

> WQ: Approach queen.

We're finally coming back to something introduced in Act 3, when we got the tiniest glimpse of Jade's land as well as this specific event. Which indicates how early some of these ideas were established, way back when basic story pieces were still being put into place. In Act 3, we didn't have much to go on yet—was that snow? Volcanic ash? In fact, we hadn't even met Bec, so it was hard to discern what was going on with this green energy. When Jade strifed with Bec about a hundred pages later, at that point we could deduce this explosion had something to do with him. The main missing piece of info at that point was Bec's prototyping, and the fact that as a sprite, he sensed PM's console interaction and reacted by "protecting" Jade from this obtrusive mail lady. The timeless rivalry between dogs and mail carriers is one of the understated gags going on here. Hold the phone, there's more hot trivia. Remember in an earlier note I was talking about how damage to the player's entry item seems to manifest as damage to the corresponding station? Bec blew up the huge meteor, scattering its pieces all over the world, and the piñata similarly was busted into a lot of pieces, so the Bec-head station came in a bunch of broken pieces too. The egg cracked in half, and Bro split the egg meteor in half, so the egg station came in two halves. I speculated that because Rose broke her bottle entry item, the bottle station may be broken under all the sand. So what about the apple? John bit the apple, but there didn't seem to be any sign of a bite mark or puncture...until now. Good thing that Becsprite was alert to this minor inconsistency and kindly helped make the correction.

Your new ruler seems upset. You understand it is not easy being in a position of authority.

You politely inform her that as the queen she is under no obligation to wear a crown. It is her decision.

She should understand that a queen is the sum of her decisions, not her fashion accessories. And no queen makes decisions alone. All wise rulers surround themselves with trusted advisors.

The new queen should understand she has friends to help her.

> PM: Appoint royal advisor.

You make your first decision as the new Prospitian Monarch.

Closing that terminal explosion loophole is a good excuse to transition back to PM and check in on what she's up to now. This whole "PM becomes the honorary queen" tangential plotline is mainly for the purpose of taking a few steps here and there to elevate PM as a more important exile than the others, at least in terms of being the one to traverse a long-term heroic arc. I remember that when this was all happening, there was some wild overestimation of the relevance of the exile subplot. Some readers seemed to think that the exiles were this crucial cast of side characters who were brutally discarded when **[S] Cascade** came around, therefore wasting the narrative engagement with them in the first place. That's really not what was going on. All this action happening in the margins of the story is largely dedicated to priming PM for her heroic ascension, to stalemate the Noir threat for a good while so that other arcs could be developed, and then to finally take him down. It's probably hard to discern while the story is still building up to that, but all the exiles are really just playing supporting roles around her: WQ is the wise mentor figure who elevates her by royal mandate, and WV and AR are the goofy, comic-relief sidekicks and/or romantic interests (?). They all get cut down, which not only serves to collapse this plotline and help simplify an ever-broadening story, but also functions as an utterly standard narrative device wherein the hero is righteously motivated to action through the deaths of those close to her. -->

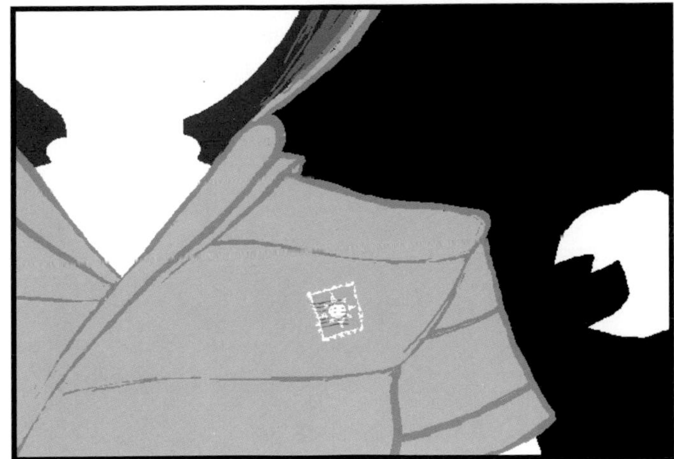

The Questant receives the new ROYAL INSIGNIA.

> Jade: Return.

You return to the GRAND FOYER. It's a bit less cluttered than you remember it being.

--> Which is an idea sometimes referred to as "fridging" characters. But I don't need to tell a media genius like you about tropes, do I. Fridging a character is commonly used to refer to a situation when a female character is killed to heroically motivate a male character, a plot device that involves a kind of sexist erasure. That's obviously not what's going on here, since the tragic cullings revolve around and motivate my indisputably fabulous feminist icon, the Peregrine Mendicant. To be honest, the only reason I'm talking about this subject at all here is, it made me remember that in Act 6 (i.e. the Hell Act), a variety of murdered people are literally stored in a refrigerator on several occasions. Obviously this is because Gamzee put them there. And then later he wound up in there himself. What statement am I making by invoking this trope in this baffling manner? We really shouldn't be talking about Act 6 shit too much before those books happen. It's too cursed. All you need to know is that Gamzee is my wildcard tool, which I can pull off the shelf any time I feel the need to do something totally inexplicable, inadvisable, and in atrocious taste. The list of things includes talking about Gamzee at all, for any reason, in these author notes. It should relieve you to know this, just as it should relieve you to know that my personal priest is praying hard for me in his church every single day.

JADE: what happened in here?
JADE: where is everything? all the globes and houseguests...
JADE: and the cruxtruder???
JADE: and grandpa???????????
JADE: bec, what did you do!
JADE: has someone been a bad dog??
JADE: wait never mind, please dont answer that!!!!
JADE: @_@

> Jade: Go upstairs.

You return to find your beautiful atrium in ruins. And to make things worse, your alchemiter and totem lathe were destroyed as well.

On the bright side, it looks like your LUNCHTOP was undamaged.

> Jade: Retrieve lunchtop.

You have been dying to get back to your computer so you can touch base with John again. He has probably been going crazy wondering about you.

But it seems someone else is messaging you right now.

> Jade: Answer Dave.

Jade, I threw out all of your shit because I got sick of it. It was too much, and I needed to make room for the alchemiter I'm about to put on the floor there in a few pages.

-- turntechGodhead [TG] began pestering gardenGnostic [GG] --

TG: hey
TG: welcome to the medium finally i guess
GG: hey!!!!!
GG: last time i talked to you i was asking for help and you were just nakking at me
GG: what was up with that bro???
TG: ok i dont know what youre talking about it was probably just some horrorterror chirping at you during one of your nap bubble mindfucks
TG: its not the point i just wanted to say
TG: i just saw you
GG: you did?
TG: yeah
TG: you appeared for a second
TG: shooting at an imp
TG: then you disappeared
GG: ohhhhhhh
GG: yes, i did get around during that battle didnt i?
GG: it was really intense!!!
GG: those stupid things are impossible to kill :(
TG: no you can kill them
TG: youll get better dont worry
GG: in the heat of the fray i didnt notice you!
GG: where were you?
TG: three places
TG: i remember seeing you twice before in different locations
TG: but at the moment im standing in the middle of this snowy goddamn field freezing my shit off
TG: just wanted to see if you were cool
GG: yeah im fine, thanks for asking!
GG: what do you mean you remember seeing me?
GG: was i jumping through time or something?
TG: no i was
TG: this is future me
TG: one of the future mes that is
GG: youre from the future?
TG: yeah jade thats what future me means
GG: :p
GG: john told me you have been doing some time traveling
TG: yeah
GG: that is.....

GG: really really awesome!
TG: its ok
TG: hey its pretty fucking cold
GG: i knoooooow
GG: it is a really neat place but its freeeeezing :o
TG: so im gonna go some place warm be back in a while later
-- turntechGodhead [TG] ceased pestering gardenGnostic [GG] --
GG: wait!
GG: dave!!
GG: uuugh stupid lousy cool dudes
-- turntechGodhead [TG] began pestering gardenGnostic [GG] --
TG: ok im back
TG: an hour later
GG: an hour?
TG: an hour for me
TG: a second for you
TG: i ran around for an hour got my ass some place warm
TG: went back in time
TG: picked up where we left off
GG: :O
GG: i can not believe how cool that is
GG: this is me believing neither that, nor its coolness :O
TG: yeah
TG: i guess im sorta used to it by now i dont think of hours going by the same way anymore
TG: i mean

I guess I was wrong a few pages ago. When Jade fired her gun and woke up sleeping Dave, that wasn't what prompted him to message her. He waited until he became a future version of himself, the one standing in the snow, before finally contacting her. I should have remembered this, because it's a pretty Dave way of handling the situation, like "oh jade randomly appeared and fired a gun waking me up? thats cool ill just wait many hours and do a bunch of time traveling before getting around to messaging her about it." Then Jade gets kind of carried away about how awesome it is Dave can time travel, when he uses the ability to log off for an hour, go back in time, and pick up the conversation without missing a beat. Except it's not *that* cool, since she's already had a bunch of similar conversations with the trolls, who've been doing the same thing by hopping around the Trollian timeline. She's probably only wilding out about it because at this point in the story, she's still a shameless Davejade shipper. Karkat should take a few pointers from Dave here. Instead of dragging multiple versions of himself into the conversation and screaming at them in front of Jade about how they have a crush on her, he should try Dave's strategy, which apparently involves being such a stupid lousy cool dude that that he doesn't even bother messaging her when she randomly appears during his nap and wakes him up with gunfire.

TG: they are my hours but not everyone elses theyre kind of like private hours all to myself
TG: while everyone else is sort of in slow motion stuck in the thick of the alpha
GG: hmmmm...
GG: i dont know if i get that but ok!
TG: well yeah
TG: my thing is time yours is space
TG: pretty different things
TG: you GET things about space i dont
TG: or you will
GG: i will?
TG: yup
GG: ok........
GG: but anyway youre right, its coooold!!!!!!
GG: i have to go back inside
GG: i wish i had winter clothes
GG: and if i did, i ALSO wish that my wardrobifier didnt blow up with all of my beautiful clothes inside it :C
GG: im so horribly unprepared for this.... i have never even seen snow before, can you believe that!!!
TG: pretty believable since you lived on guam or wherever the fuck
TG: and also inside an active volcano
GG: derp yes dave that is so where i lived
GG: that is as biographically accurate as it gets about me!
TG: well ive never seen it either now that i think about it
GG: no???
TG: no
GG: isnt it great?????
TG: nah
TG: lavas better
GG: lava is NOT better than snow :|
TG: yeah it is lava and skeletal skyscrapers all melting and shit how is that not way cooler than
TG: snow and
TG: like
TG: more snow
GG: you cant play in lava, its no fun
GG: you can only die in lava
TG: snows a big chilly carpet of nobody gives a shit
TG: like old man winter spread around his nasty mayonnaise and turned the landscape into his personal asshole sandwich
GG: eww dave no
TG: when i look around all i see is the miles of unharnessed snowmen im just too damn cool to build
GG: no this is so lame
GG: i am hearing an insane and stupid guy say stupid idiot things while wearing dumb sunglasses for lame morons!
TG: whoa jade with the fucking haymaker
TG: i need to go look for my teeth on the canvas as soon as shit stops spinning and there stops being like ten of you
GG: heheheh
GG: why dont we play in the snow later
GG: as soon as you get some....................................
TG: time
GG: ....
TG: time
GG: ....
TG: time then shades
GG: ....
TG: time
GG: ....
TG: time/shades lets go
GG: ....
GG: ....
GG: ...
TG: oh my fucking god
GG: ..
GG: .
GG: time 8)
TG: im not gonna play in the snow
TG: maybe you missed those credentials i flashed which clearly stated me being too cool for that
TG: like federally too cool
TG: my coolness is named after a dead president plus his middle initial to make it sound extra legit
GG: i know youre joking around, you are not too cool at all, you dont even think that
TG: ok
GG: brrrrrr
TG: i thought you were going inside
GG: i forgot :\
TG: well at least make some damn clothes
TG: something warmer why dont you alchemize some shit

Dave makes a joke about Jade being from Guam or wherever, but the exact coordinates are (-0.955766 -174.759521), or per the *Homestuck* wiki, 150 miles southeast of Baker Island and 50 miles north of Winslow Reef. This is actually a long way from Guam. About the span of the U.S., from one point in the Pacific to another. I probably made this joke because I used to live in Guam. Which sounds like a joke, but it isn't. I doubt anybody knows this fact about me. Most people don't know things about my life, because my life makes no sense whatsoever. It's hard to track, because I've moved well over fifty times, and there's a lot of disinformation that has accumulated throughout the known lore. The time I lived in Guam isn't disinformation though. It's undisinformation. Sometimes you need to mix a striking piece of truth in with an array of bland falsehoods to keep people wondering. One more thing about Jade's island location: I originally chose those coordinates because I saw something very mysterious there on Google Maps back in 2009. But on looking again, I don't see it anymore. Was it scrubbed from the system?! Nice try, government. Looks like you forgot who you were dealing with for a second.

GG: i cant!!!
GG: all that stuff blew up
TG: blew up
GG: its a long story that involves a pinata and a gun and a very naughty doggie
TG: i completely understand everything about that practically entirely
GG: so anyway, that reminds me ive got to talk to john!
GG: ive got to get him to make me some new gizmos...
GG: assuming thats even possible
TG: no dont bother john

TG: hes on like his fuckin
TG: wind mission or whatever
TG: getting all his ridiculous magic cyclone powers on and realizing his huge blowy destiny
TG: as the chump of shoosh
GG: john has magic cyclone powers?
TG: almost
GG: whoa....
GG: you guys are all so much better than me, i feel sooooo lame
TG: we all start out somewhere
TG: remember how i was scrambling up that tower to get that egg like an idiot
TG: what the hell was i doing
TG: i was like goddamn pooh bear in a tree reaching up his fat fuckin pooh paw for some mother fuckin honey
GG: heehee
TG: so even though im awesome now at one point i was plausibly likened to an autistic stuffed animal
TG: and you even knew what to do
TG: you told me how it worked all christopher robinning my ignorant ass about that egg
TG: but i was all like IM A LITTLE BLACK RAIN CLOUD BITCH WATCH ME CLIMB
TG: so maybe youre startin out with more sense than me
GG: maaaybe
GG: :)
TG: in any case egbert lost his computer and game disc
TG: so he cant do anything for you anyways
GG: oh no
GG: did he lose it in a magic cyclone?
TG: probably some shit like thats what happened
TG: but youre not completely screwed
TG: we just have to think outside the box here
GG: we do?
TG: yeah honestly i figured wed have to do something like this
TG: so i guess here we are doing it
GG: doing what??
TG: well youre my server player remember
GG: yes
TG: i need you to deploy something first
TG: in my apartment
TG: in a few hours ill go back there and we can continue this
GG: oh jeez, a few hours????
-- turntechGodhead [TG] ceased pestering gardenGnostic [GG] --
-- turntechGodhead [TG] began pestering gardenGnostic [GG] --
TG: yeah
TG: as in a few seconds
TG: im back at my place now
GG: fastest hours :o
TG: yeah
TG: now
TG: deploy the intellibeam laserstation
GG: but that costs so much grist!!!
TG: no it costs practically nothing
TG: check out how much ive got
GG: omg...

> Jade: Deploy laserstation.

While Dave admires this iguana statue in some unremarkable ruins at a random location on Jade's planet, many of you I'm sure will be pleased to realize that Dave apparently maintains an autistic Winnie the Pooh headcanon. Jade does not remark on this, however, which quite frankly betrays an absolutely repugnant lack of appreciation for Dave's inclusivity. Maybe he should call her out about it on one of his blogs. Hang on, I'm getting word that my life coach is calling my priest, and asking what my new address is. He lost track of me since I've moved about four times since his last visit. My priest is currently too drunk to remember the fake new address I gave him. Everything is going according to plan.

GG: what does this thing do?
TG: its mostly pretty stupid and useless
TG: but itll come in handy here
TG: it reads captcha codes
GG: on the back of cards?
TG: yeah
GG: but
GG: we can already read those!
TG: some are too garbled and complicated
TG: the human eye cant decipher them
TG: needs sophisticated scanning technology
TG: and artificial intelligence to figure it out
GG: hmm
GG: but isnt the whole point of captchas that only humans can read them?
GG: and not robots???
TG: yeah well
TG: thats why this is so dumb

> Dave: Eject disc.

TG: i guess some captchas are so incomprehensible cause the game thinks it would be too cheap to let you duplicate them
TG: like an anti piracy measure
TG: so the solution to the anti piracy measure is to override the anti spam measure
GG: anti spam?
TG: well yeah thats what captchas are for
TG: and theyre on the back of cards for a really good reason
TG: cause god knows the last thing youd want was some web bot being able to figure out the code for like
TG: a potted plant
TG: that would be fucking mayhem
GG: yeah obviously!
TG: but in order to effectively cheat here weve got to open pandoras spam box
TG: and release the laserstation into the world with its leering intellibeam
TG: now no captcha is safe youll have bots signing up for email accounts and duplicating potted plants and shit

GG: oh nooo
TG: basically robots are in control now
TG: which is good news and bad news
TG: the bad news is theyre all pornbots and theyve got LOADS of provocative material theyre just dying to share with us

Honestly, the "intellibeam laserstation" is a sleeper candidate for one of the funniest ideas in *Homestuck*. Jade's observation basically underscores why. I think there's some inherent absurdity to the idea of captchas in the first place, which probably is why I thought it was a funny idea to include them as part of a ridiculous inventory system. Even in the old days of the internet, there was this understanding that there are certain things you don't want robots to be able to do, particularly things that could lead to exploits and vulnerabilities. So to combat that, we came up with this concept that there are tasks which a human can perform but a robot can't. And simply by stating that premise, we're already off to the races of absurdity, because it's just asking for trouble to assume that the execution of a task you've designed for a human can never be matched or exceeded by a robot. It's probably always going to be a matter of time before advancing technology makes a fool out of you. So naturally an arms race starts developing between increasingly complex captchas made to outfox AI, and the advancing sophistication of AI itself. -->

GG: whats the good news?
TG: thats also the good news
GG: dave i still dont know what youre actually doing here
TG: whats it look like
TG: im duplicating my server disc

> Dave: Scan.

GG: oh....
GG: to give it to john?
TG: nah i told you were not bothering john
TG: hes got shit to do
TG: ill just install it
GG: but...
GG: you are already roses server player!
GG: and john is mine!
GG: not to mention im yours!!!
GG: can you really be a server player to your own server player?
TG: dont see why not
TG: we have to get creative here
TG: this games already so far off the rails what else is there to do but improvise
GG: but i guess
GG: i thought that john sort of.....
GG: HAD to be my server? you know?
TG: well he was

TG: he got you in didnt he
TG: but now hes not
TG: been a change of plans
TG: time to roll with it

> Dave: Read code.

--> Inevitably, it's going to result in captchas that are too cryptic for humans to solve, because they're so well guarded against increasingly clever robots. Until finally they become so unfathomable that you've entirely reversed the premise of captchas by making them something that only robots can solve, and not humans, which utterly nullifies the point of their existence. Or maybe worse, they lock humans out of those tasks which only they were meant to understand or perform. It's the inevitable end of the road to an initially good idea, and carries the feeling of a technological punchline once we get there. When you write science fiction of an absurd nature, everything is always a big, funny joke until suddenly it's real. In the future, people will probably wonder why I even thought this was funny. Like, of COURSE robots can crack captchas we don't understand—they're smarter than us, dummy.

GG: well youre from the future right?
GG: dont you know already if itll work?
TG: yeah more or less
TG: i never really studied how it went down all that closely
TG: i just figured when the time came to sort it out the right thing to do would be obvious
TG: like it is now
TG: managing the loops is a balance of careful planning and just rolling with your in the moment decisions
TG: and trusting they were the ones you were always supposed to make
TG: by now im pretty used to having my intuition woven into the fabric of the alpha timeline
GG: pretty smooth dave
TG: yeah i know
GG: shades for everybody
GG: 8) 8)

> Dave: Duplicate disc.

TG: thisll be the disc i use for your connection
TG: while the original will stay bound to roses connection
GG: so you will be the server for BOTH us ladies???
GG: you just keep getting smoother, i cant handle all this smoothness
TG: well technically
TG: i will be your server
TG: and past me will stay as roses server
TG: which is to say present me will
TG: the one in the black suit
GG: ohh...
GG: i guess that makes sense
TG: he can keep managing her for a while
TG: until she sorta checks out soon and becomes totally useless
TG: then he can start hopping around time like i did
TG: make a ton of money and stuff
TG: eventually become me
TG: and become your server player
GG: ok i think i understand that!
TG: yeah see its not hard to get the hang of
TG: in the meantime ill kind of loiter around this timeframe to help you out for a while
GG: yessss thanks dave <3
GG: um
GG: what do you mean rose will check out? :\

The fact that Future Dave steps in, duplicates a disc, and functions as Jade's server player in addition to Rose's is kind of a curveball in terms of expected session structure. By now we know we're allowed to play fast and loose with the rules the story has established for the game. The story in a generalized way is always broadcasting the formal rules of *Sburb* and how it's "supposed" to go, whereas the narrative itself is often deviating from these rules in surprising ways. If *Homestuck* were a real game, it would make sense for its rule structure to be strictly followed in order to promote stability and playability. But since it's a story *about* a game, the deviations are what make it more interesting, in a way that it couldn't be if it were just a paint-by-numbers type of illustrated portrayal of a game idea. The deviations from a formal *Sburb* playthrough become the striking beats of narrative and arise from exhibitions of character choices and agency. They are the fuel for the surprises, the volatility and unpredictability of how things play out in practice rather than in theory. In a really simplistic way, you can look at most narratives as a cyclical procession of this basic idea: Expectations --> Deviations --> Expectations --> Deviations... It just happens that in *Homestuck*, the material for this repeating cycle is mostly the rules and structure of a game, and then later, expanding that cycle to include the rules and structure of *Homestuck*'s narrative itself. But the fact that a story about a game almost *needs* to involve deviations from its own self-imposed rules in order to generate interesting material from a narrative standpoint tells you a lot about why *Homestuck* is the way it is. The "broken session" they're always struggling against is stitched into its story DNA as something that you could see as inevitable from the beginning. Structural dysfunction was always hiding in the marble, waiting to be chiseled out, because otherwise you're left with a more static narrative environment that provides less opportunities for satisfying these little expectation/deviation cycles. -->

TG: dont worry about it just some more future stuff
TG: now i need you to go downstairs
GG: uhhhh ok

> Jade: Go downstairs.

TG: im just going to cut right to the chase and upgrade your alchemiter so you can avoid a lot of bullshit
TG: ill give you some codes and you can punch cards and slip em into jumper blocks
TG: which are really the exact same codes you first gave me when we upgraded my alchemiter
TG: which seems like a hella long time ago
GG: it does doesnt it
TG: yeah but it kind of literally is for me
GG: how long?
TG: few days i guess
GG: ok thats not THAT long :p
TG: whatever

> Dave: Deploy and upgrade.

GG: yaaaaaaaaaaaay!

> Jade: OH GOD HURRY UP AND ALCHEMIZE STUFF GO GO GO.

--> So Dave suddenly grabbing the intellibeam and lifehacking a new disc to disrupt the server order, when we didn't know this was a possibility, seems like a good moment to stop and reflect on this idea, the distillation of which is: the perpetual "broken game" conceit is actually endemic to *Homestuck* as a creative premise and in the way that premise was executed improvisationally in front of an online audience. "Here's a game, and everything goes the way it should," is very different from "Here's a game, and things go wrong all the time." The former is potentially listless and rigid when pursued through an improvisational medium. The latter allows the story to take shape in vibrant, unpredictable ways. And since it organically takes the shape of a story about a broken, dysfunctional, hostile environment for these kids to explore, practically every theme and conceit follows from these circumstances as well. They embrace a pattern of hacking, shortcuts, destroying guardrails, and rebelling from the imposed rigidity of a game rigged against them. These rebellious tactics keep picking up steam, especially as the roster expands and other characters like Vriska influence events and push those tactics even further. The players' personal quests seem laced with the idea of cracking a system or deviating from formula: breaking a sword to remove it from a stone, or making oil vanish by superseding narrative boundaries. This connects to the basic question of whether to embrace the regimentation of a heroic path conveniently laid out for you (the expectation), or to reject it as the shallow and rigid confinement of personal destiny (the deviation). These issues are expressed through the fundamental language of platonic idealism: perfect ideas of things, and then specific, imperfect instances of those ideas, or varied permutations, evolutions, or hacks of those ideas through alchemy. The way *Sburb* "should" go is an ideal (expectation), but the disastrous, chaotic way it actually goes is an imperfect instance (deviation). An "idea" of a person, such as Rose, along with her regimented heroic quest for growth, and all the great things she might imagine herself to become if she followed it, is an ideal (expectation). The messy, flawed, yet more genuinely human individual she does become resulting from her errant choices and rejection of formalism, is an imperfect instance of an ideal (deviation). What's the bottom line here? This is a lot. I know it's a lot. *Homestuck* is, in fact, a lot. I feel like I should better synthesize this somehow before I blow this popsicle stand. Check it out, here comes another rare line break down here in the laugh basement:

Homestuck, as an examination of all forms of creative practice, whether cosmic or artistic, isolates the tension between perfect, celebrated idealization and specific, flawed instantiation. The purity of the ideal is what's initially sought, but the imperfection of the specific is what has true value. Conflict and suffering arise from the guilt and stress associated with overvaluing the former. Deliverance and humanity come from recognizing and embracing the latter.

Hey, calm down! Just because it's snowing outside doesn't mean it's Christmas just yet.

There are still plenty of things to do before we bother with that sort of nonsense. Take a deep breath, put the cards down, and relax.

> Dave: Wake up.

You already woke up when Jade fired her rifle a foot and a half from your eardrum, and then disappeared.

This idiot here is nakking it up with your ISHADES. Someone is pestering you directly into his brainless reptilian face.

> Dave: Retrieve shades.

STEP OFF.

...

You decide he can keep the SORD..... though.

> Dave: Answer Rose.

The narrative says it's not Christmas yet. This is true. When this page was first posted online, it was still a couple weeks before Christmas. I saved Jade's sweet alchemy binge for Christmas Day. That won't happen in this book. So even if you literally got this book as a Christmas present, it still won't be Christmas for you until the next book comes out. Sorry.

-- tentacleTherapist [TT] began pestering turntechGodhead [TG] --

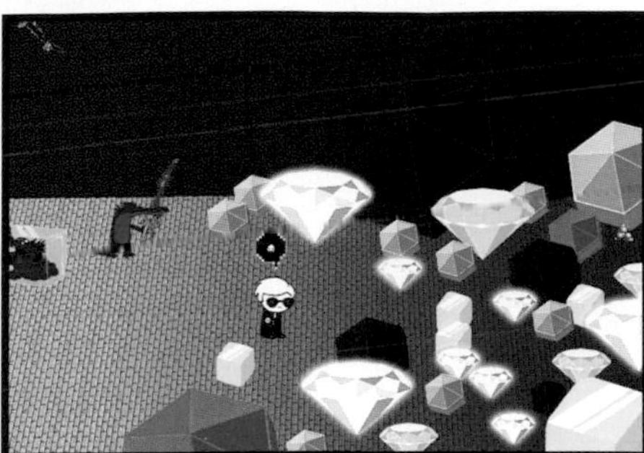

TT: Hi there.
TG: nak nak nak
TT: Don't mind me.
TT: I'm just waiting for that guy on the pile of sharp objects to wake up.
TG: THE GLASSES ARE TALKING AGAIN
TG: naknaknaknaknaknaknaknaknaknaknaknaknaknak
TT: If you don't stop nakking, I will turn you into a thorn bush.
TG: :V
TG: :(
TG: hey
TG: what just happened

TT: You fell asleep.
TT: Orange Bird Dave killed some monsters and flew away.
TT: Jade fired a bullet at an imp and vanished.
TT: And you woke up.
TG: oh yeah
TG: so shes here then
TT: Yes.
TG: is she ok what was going on there
TT: Yes, she's fine.
TG: i guess i should catch up with her
TT: You already are.
TG: i am
TT: Future you is.
TG: oh ok time travels involved
TG: thats all you needed to say everythings cool and under control then
TT: How was the nap?
TG: weird
TG: and kind of boring
TG: i was in your dream room for a while spying on you
TG: being all creepy and dream duplicitous and shit
TT: It's ok.
TT: I was being similarly wake duplicitous.
TG: whats with your book collection
TG: or
TG: dream book collection
TG: all your books are bizarre and terrible
TT: No, my books are great.
TT: I can recommend some good titles for the next time you're asleep.
TG: nah
TG: but yeah i understand defending your collection i guess if you were in my dream room and talking shit about my awesome dream portraits of dream stiller and dream snoop or whatever wed have to have a fucking talk
TT: Did you do anything on the moon besides rifle through my belongings?
TT: Such as remove your shades and turn your gaze Ringward, by any chance?
TG: oh
TG: yeah
TG: i did
TT: What did you see?
TG: horrible things
TT: Horribleterrible?
TG: yeah
TG: it was like
TG: peering through the dark portal of an eldritch red lobster

Dave's glasses clearly detect voice and translate the speech to text that's then posted onto Pesterchum. That's the only possible way these hands-free devices the kids have make sense, although there are some logical anomalies that call this into question. Like the emoticons there. How is the crocodile "typing" those? He's obviously nakking away, which is his verbal expression of choice. Then Rose chimes in, and in great alarm, he makes an outburst in English, and then continues nakking furiously. But...does he actually hear the glasses talking to him? Or is he just reading Rose's text on the small screens inside the shades? Since he describes it as the glasses "talking to him," it makes it seem like Rose's text is being converted to an audible format rather than just being displayed on the little screens inside the shades. Are the shades voice-to-text, and ALSO text-to-voice? How do the shades know when a crocodile frowns, or makes a :V expression? Are crocodiles even CAPABLE of frowning?? I feel like I'm going insane.

TG: and scoping out its all you can eat seafood buffet
TG: and
TG: when i saw them
TG: their voices became clearer
TT: What were they saying?
TG: i couldnt really focus on anything specific
TG: but
TG: in totality
TG: im pretty sure it was
TG: like
TT: ?
TG: a plea for help

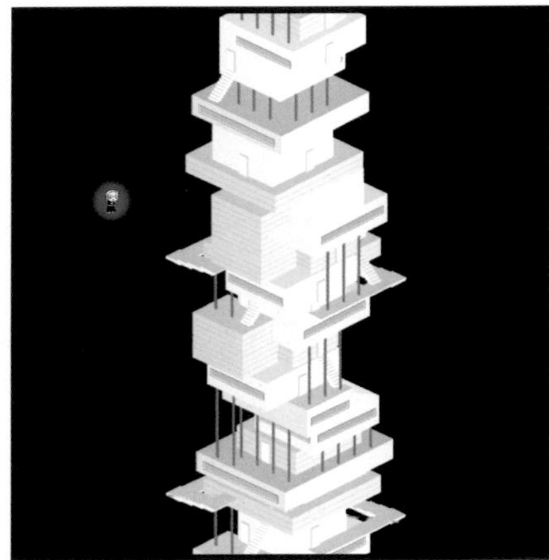

TT: That's good.
TG: no it was disturbing
TG: so i slapped my shades back on
TG: went and perved up some sleeping girls room to take my mind of it
TT: It means they're reaching out to you.
TG: oh god why would i want that
TG: im not about to get molested by calamari with fucking teeth
TG: use your powers and like
TG: stroke a mummys paw or some horseshit and open a dark channel
TG: tell them to keep their lecherous flagella to themselves
TT: You're going to have to help them.
TT: Even if you don't like them.
TT: They're being massacred.
TT: Presently, already, and still to come.
TG: whats that mean
TT: It means time doesn't work rationally out there.
TT: Nor does space.
TT: But that doesn't change the reality of the threat.
TG: who cares if theyre getting killed
TG: theyre hideous and obnoxious
TT: You're underestimating the nature of the threat.
TT: At this point, the threat isn't to our session, or any given universe.
TT: It's to the perpetuation of reality itself.
TT: You wouldn't be saving them, per se.
TT: You'd be saving everything.
TG: oh ok cool

TT: They've revealed some of their secrets to me already, and given me a few errands to run.
TT: This is why you might have observed some unusual behavior from me.
TG: oh shit youre kidding
TG: no really are you serious i didnt even notice
TG: fuck mind = blown
TT: Once these convulsions of explosive laughter subside and finish rocking my very foundation,

Here Rose is playing the role of Dave's therapist, as she surely often has, while exploring the topic of tentacled creatures. A Tentacle Therapist, if you will. I'm declaring her arc officially complete, as of this moment. The rest is gravy. A thick, ominous, seafood bisque–like gravy, as one might find in an eldritch Red Lobster. So thick it successfully obscures whatever someone might be trying to distract you from. Such as commenting on the fact that, despite knowing they're siblings for some time already, Dave continues blundering around Freudian language during heart-to-heart conversations with his sister and never really stops doing so throughout the entire story. During my last confessional, my priest made me promise I would never bring this up again. I think I'm the only parishioner who he makes swear a vow of confidentiality in the confession booth, rather than the other way around.

TT: I might point out that you haven't really been as astute as you're implying.
TT: You've deliberately fogged your vision your entire life with ironic eyewear while awake, and while asleep, though perfectly alert, you've chosen to ignore your surroundings.
TT: But now that you've seen them, you have a choice to make.
TG: ok
TT: They will only tell me so much.
TT: They would like an audience with the prince of the moon as well.
TT: We are like the emissaries to what lies beyond this small bubble in their unfathomable dark foam.
TT: Derse skirts its edge, and during the lunar eclipse, we graze it, and that's when their intent for us becomes clear.
TT: I'm doing my part, but they have a mission for you as well.
TG: what am i supposed to do
TT: Listen to them.
TT: My understanding is,
TT: They will teach you how to navigate the unnavigable.
TT: The result should be a map.
TG: like
TG: a treasure map
TT: No.
TT: Something a little more astronomical.
TT: Like a star chart with no stars.
TT: Hence the challenge.
TG: why
TT: To plot a course through the Furthest Ring.
TG: plot a course to what

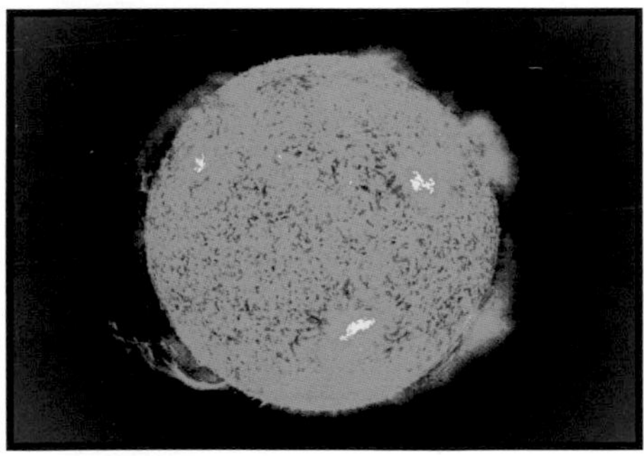

TT: The power source of the first guardians.
TG: oh right the green sun ok
TG: wait sorry
TG: i mean the Green Sun my bad
TT: Yes, that's much better.
TG: whats the deal with this thing
TG: i mean aside from giving jades dog his devil powers
TG: and by extension i guess jack
TT: What's the deal with it?
TG: yeah
TT: I don't know that there is a deal with it.
TT: Beyond the deal you just described.
TT: It is what it sounds like.
TT: A huge sun out in the literal middle of nowhere, and it is bright green.
TT: It is simply,
TT: The Green Sun .
TG: how big
TG: i need a sense of scale here
TG: is it like the size of our sun
TG: or bigger
TG: or is it only as big as like
TG: planet fucking jupiter
TT: It is nearly twice the mass of our universe.
TG: ok thats pretty fucking big
TG: see how important that contextualization was now i know how fucking impressed i should be
TG: i mean hopy shit thats huge
TT: Happy I could help.
TG: so ok i make a map to this thing
TG: with the help of a million rambunctious gross tentacle mutants
TG: and then i guess we go there for some reason
TT: Yes.
TG: why do we need a map
TG: cant they just
TG: tell us what direction its in
TG: point a spaceship that way
TG: blast off to adventure
TT: No.
TT: The geometry of the Furthest Ring is too complex.
TT: Remember, its spacetime is labyrinthine.
TT: In fact, it's not really accurate to call it spacetime at all.
TT: Since it is outside the domain of any created

Splintering Dave into two Daves, a Present Dave (black suit) and a Future Dave (red sleeves) was a pretty strong move, actually. It compartmentalizes the two Daves into one who's on Rose duty, and another who's on Jade duty, which involves dealing with two completely different types of conversations and probing different facets of his personality. Rose throws the heavy stuff at him, whereas Jade represents a reprieve and keeps it light. But then, this was Rose's idea, wasn't it? He woke up, remembered Jade passing through, and Rose said, oh yeah don't bother with her, Future Dave will get around to that. This meant Rose could hog Present Dave all to herself and harangue him about troubling matters pertaining to their obligation to save a bunch of repulsive, uncaring space monsters, the metaphysical burdens of plotting a course through infinite featureless void, and some discourse about a sun twice the mass of a universe. A nice play by Rose, but also a nice play by me, because we can really bear down on this quality infodump. This is all pretty important, so stop getting distracted by my allusions to incest, or my bizarre insistence on talking about my priest, okay? What really coalesces in this conversation are all the important pieces that combine to form The Point of Act 5, or the actual "plot," as you might call it. A plan which will involve delivering a huge bomb to the Green Sun, and all the things that couldn't possibly go wrong with that.

universe, where those properties have become instantiated and stabilized.
TG: i can kind of get that time is messed up there
TG: with like loops and causality paradoxes and shit like that
TG: being the knight of time here
TG: not really sure why navigating the space would be a problem though
TG: space isnt my thing remember
TG: what is it like
TG: full of wormholes or something
TT: It depends.
TT: The greater the distance you travel through it, the less reliably time flows.
TT: And the more time you spend in it, the less reliably space behaves.
TT: Time and space aren't as different as you might think.
TG: i thought you werent supposed to know shit about either
TG: seeing as youre the seer whatever that means
TT: I think it means I'm supposed to know shit about the big picture.
TT: Which includes tidbits like that.
TT: But the insides of my shoes stay free from the grit of the minutia.
TG: fair enough
TG: so i take my map and fly to this thing
TT: No, I do.
TG: ok you fly to it
TG: then what
TT: That depends on if John is successful.

TG: you mean with the quest youre sending him on
TT: Yes.
TG: is there anything you do thats not sending dudes on quests
TT: Nothing whatsoever.
TG: so hes got to get the cancer out of skaia right
TT: Yes, The Tumor.
TG: yeah
TG: so whats The Tumor do
TG: i mean the tumor
TG: jesus can we stop with the fancy colored text bullshit
TT: I guess so.
TT: I thought it was more fun that way.
TG: well ok you can keep doing it then
TT: Thanks.
TT: <black>The Tumor</black> is quite a large growth at the center of the battlefield.
TT: He won't be able to remove it without fully realizing his abilities.
TG: ok cool what is it
TT: Can you promise you won't tell him?
TT: It would probably make him more nervous than he needs to be if he knew.
TG: ok i wont say anything
TG: just tell me
TT: It's a bomb.

Here we find some things out. Things we were earmarking for finding out, forgot about, and then remembered, like "What does the Tumor do?" Had that all earmarked for finding out and everything. And now it's found out. It's probably a little harder to appreciate these incremental nuggets in these books if you read along with these notes, because of course I just fucking ruin everything down here. The moment we first heard about the Tumor I was like: HEY! THAT'S A BOMB. It's a big, fat bomb. Did I mention? Huuuuge bomb. That's what the Tumor is, guys. Rather large thing that goes "boom." So when Rose says that here, it loses just a bit of the punch it once had. Whatever. Try not to act like you're not totally used to me ruining stuff by now, including your life. I will feel insulted. Also, I remember some people thinking those <black> </black> tags were a formatting error. No, it's just a joke. A really subtle joke perpetrated by Rose. How is that even a joke, you ask? I don't even know if I can say. Sometimes, if you need certain types of jokes explained to you, it means you're probably never gonna get them no matter what. Some people have really weird, ultra-deadpan senses of humor that border on feeling alien. Rose is a bit like that. And there are many types of people who could have no possible way of knowing that half the deadpan jokes they make are even jokes at all. Jade's probably one of those people. Is *that* why they hardly talk? Good thing they're both passionately fixated on the same two idiot boys, or they probably would never have bothered with each other at all.

TT: It is set to detonate precisely when the reckoning ends.
TT: This is how long we have to put this plan into motion.
TG: what the hell is a bomb doing in there
TT: It could be a feature of any session not meant to bear fruit.
TT: A means to wipe out a null session rather than leaving it lingering in paradox space for eternity.
TT: Or it could be a mutation specific to our session.
TT: I really don't know.
TG: first time for everything i guess
TG: seriously whered you get all this info
TG: did you get it all from the gods
TG: are these just a bunch of orders youre following
TT: Not exactly.
TT: They've urged me in certain directions and guided my exploration.
TT: I've obtained some answers from them, but ultimately, this idea is mine.
TT: Plus, I have other sources.
TT: One in particular has been quite illuminating.
TG: what
TT: I've been referring to him as an informant, when people ask.
TT: Which isn't often.
TG: what you mean a troll
TT: No.
TT: It's a man who exists in another universe.
TT: He wants to die.
TG: sounds like a really credible dude sign me up for trusting everything he says
TT: Only as credible as the omniscient tend to be.
TG: oh so he knows everything
TT: Yeah, I think that's what omniscient means.
TT: But maybe I'll ask him about that, since he's the omniscient one.
TG: even if he is omniscient which he probably isnt what if hes just lying
TT: He says he doesn't lie.
TT: For some reason, I believe him about that.
TT: He's a convincing fellow.
TG: whys he want to die
TT: He no longer has a purpose now that he's done everything required to summon his master.
TT: As a first guardian, he's completely indestructible.
TT: Well, almost completely.
TG: wait
TG: what
TT: His power is derived from the same source as Earth's guardian.
TT: And conveniently, that of our nemesis as well.
TG: ok i get it now
TT: When John delivers the tumor,
TT: And I do mean **The Tumor**,
TT: I and I alone will navigate the Furthest Ring.
TT: And I will destroy the sun.
TT: By which I do mean the GREEN MOTHER FUCKING SUN.
TT: And in case it wasn't clear,
TT: I won't be coming back.

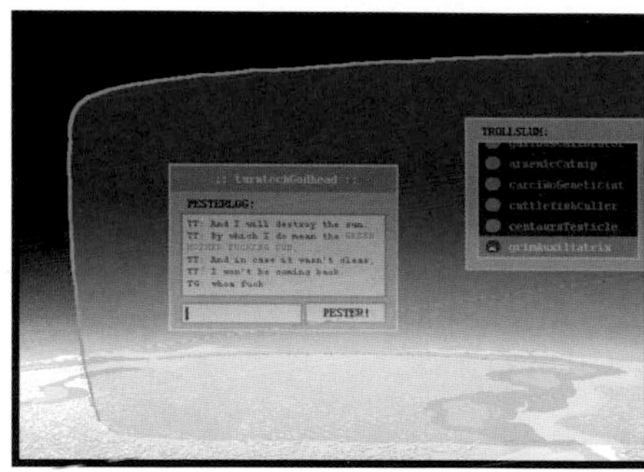

TG: whoa fuck
TG: a suicide mission are you serious
TG: no bullshit thats not happening
TG: hey look suddenly everything we just talked about was useless because its time to make a plan that doesnt fucking suck
TT: Let's not be so dramatic.
TT: I was talking about my dream self.
TT: She's the one who won't be returning.
TG: oh
TG: haha yeah thats fine i guess
TG: those fuckers are all kinds of mad expendable

Rose also lets on that Doc Scratch has been feeding her intel. She doesn't directly reference him, but we'd have to be total boneheads not to figure out that's who she's talking about. Unlike Doc, who is the opposite of a bonehead. His head is a cue ball, and therefore, he is omniscient. The fact that he's involved should immediately make us nervous, because we've already seen enough to understand that he, like me, completely ruins everything. It's also alarming to learn he's messing with Rose in the same conversation where she announces an audacious suicide plan to destroy the Green Sun. But don't worry, it's only a fake suicide, whew. Actually, it turns out to be real, but she doesn't know that, because he doesn't tell her. Lies of omission is how he rolls, especially when it comes to withholding info that could prevent people from getting hurt or killed. I'm sure she thinks her suicide plan is totally reasonable and will pan out the way she assumes. And maybe it even could be reasonable. There's just one problem: she hasn't factored her imminent grimdarkness into her emo plans. Going grimdark and blundering around gothically turns out to be the perfect way to transform your fake emo suicide plan into a real emo suicide plan.

TG: way to leave me hanging there
TG: for someone whos saying lets cool it on the drama the whole i wont be coming back thing is a pretty theatrical bombshell
TG: for future reference
TT: That's true.
TT: Your outburst was pretty sweet though.
TG: yeah i know
TG: so when do i do my thing
TG: make this map
TG: which i guess is just like
TG: a solid black piece of paper
TG: this is going to be fucking stupid isnt it
TT: If there's one thing you have more than any of us, it's time.
TT: So, whenever you like.
TT: As long as conventionally speaking, it's quite soon.
TG: alright
TG: so
TG: dog it as long as possible
TG: then travel back to about now and go to sleep
TT: Sure.
TT: And if you have trouble going to sleep, maybe you can ask your patron troll to trick the telepathic one into putting you to sleep again.
TG: what
TT: Each of us seems to have a troll infatuated with helping us. Haven't you noticed?
TG: no
TT: What about the psychopath who's currently helping you?
TG: oh yeah terezi
TG: no shes cool
TT: Isn't that camaraderie blossoming into some sort of interspecies whatever?
TG: its blossoming into an interspecies partnership in incredibly shitty cartooning
TG: what do you mean get her to trick someone into putting me asleep again
TG: when did that happen
TT: Just now.
TG: who did that
TT: That would be John's patron troll.
TG: god
TG: fuckin trolls
TG: too many of them who can even keep track of this shit
TG: which ones yours
TG: is it the absurd juggalo one that would be hilarious
TT: There's a juggalo one?
TG: yeah see what i mean
TT: She's contacting me now actually.
TG: oh ok
TG: well im suddenly not interested so go talk to your fairy god troll
TG: ill be over here paving the way for your elaborate dream suicide
TG: when i feel like getting around to it i mean
TT: Thanks.
TG: later

-- turntechGodhead [TG] ceased pestering tentacleTherapist [TT] --

> Rose: Answer fairy god troll.

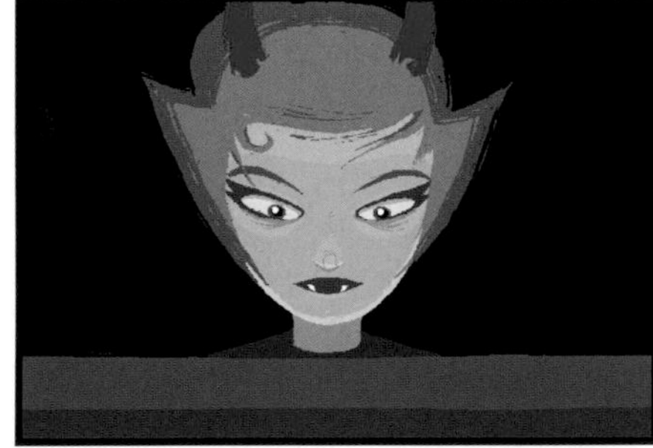

The fact that Rose doesn't seem to know who Gamzee is probably qualifies as some of the sickest shade I could have thrown at him at this moment. Rest in pieces, you sack of shit. :o) The idea of a patron troll is also brought up by Rose. This was a phrase used by fandom at the time which I appropriated into canon, to describe something going on that I've already been talking about here. But I haven't been using the phrase "patron troll" until now. I've been touching on it through the parlance of shipping, because that's probably the best way of dropping the pretense that these patron trolls latching on to humans has to do with anything other than awkward romantic posturing. A patron troll is one who shows overbearing, poorly disguised romantic interest in their human target, and expresses this through the form of intensively meddling with said human any chance they get. Hence why earlier I described this detailed recurring portrait format as a visual cue associated with this behavior. You don't get a portrait like this unless you are currently getting HELLA up in someone's grill about some heavy and personal shit. Therefore, we may conclude that any time we see a portrait like this, it is formal confirmation that this is the patron troll of whoever they're talking to. Jade's patron troll appears to have some ambiguity though, since both Karkat and Tavros are depicted with such a portrait, and both trolls end up attempting to fit the description. But make no mistake, Tavros is the pretender here. I'll get to that in a few pages.

-- grimAuxiliatrix [GA] began trolling tentacleTherapist [TT] --

GA: Since The Gap Between Your Present Moment And The Implementation Of Your Mystifying Self Destruction Continues To Narrow
GA: This Will Be The Last Conversation In Which I Attempt To Talk You Out Of It Nicely
TT: I explained this.
TT: The intent isn't true self sacrifice.
GA: First Of All Youre Underestimating The Gravity Of A Dream Death
GA: Its A Pretty Serious Thing Okay
GA: And Dream Selves Are Important To A Person In Ways That Arent Always Obvious
GA: I Think Youre Being Frivolous But Thats Not Really The Sentiment Reinforcing The Exoskeleton Of My Argument
GA: Soon You Will Be Blacked Out Of Trollians Viewport
GA: And I Have No Explanation For This
GA: And Neither Do You
GA: So Ill Just Assume The Worst And You Should Too
TT: Are you sure it's not because I'm sleeping?
GA: Ive Seen You Sleep Before
GA: You Are Just
GA: Asleep
GA: On Screen
GA: Peaceful And Harmless And Posing No Threat To Anyone
GA: Unless I Guess You Are Up To Mischief In Your Dreams Which I Cannot Rule Out
GA: Actually Thats Probably What You Do In Your Sleep What Was I Thinking
TT: Shh...
GA: Uh
GA: What
TT: Blah blah blah!
GA: Right Sorry
GA: Im Saying This Is A Special Case
GA: It Is Foreboding And Disconcerting And You Are Being Reckless
TT: You're right, I can't explain why I go dark on your monitor.
TT: But I'm confident in my plan. I have it under control.
GA: Your Hubris Is Really Astonishing
GA: Easily Twice The Mass Of A Universe I Think
GA: That It Hasnt Collapsed Upon Itself Into A Tiny Lavender Singularity Is The Most Striking Marvel Paradox Space Has Coughed Up Yet
TT: Maybe it did?
TT: Maybe that's what went wrong.
TT: We figured it out!
GA: No Please Stop
GA: Humor Wont Deflect My Really Big And Important Tirade Okay
GA: You Are Investing Too Much Confidence In Evil Gods Who Oppose Skaia And Your True Purpose And
GA: I Cant Abide That
GA: And
GA: As Difficult As This Is For Me To Confess
GA: I Think Your Plan Is Very Dangerous
GA: And So Are You
TT: Oh?
GA: Yes
GA: And
GA: Im Afraid I Am Going To Have To Devote All My Efforts To Stopping You
TT: I'm sorry to hear that, Kanaya.
TT: What did you have in mind for this new and exciting adversarial phase of our relationship?
GA: Im So Glad You Asked
GA: You See
GA: I Have Been Training A Powerful Wizard
TT: !

They only met today, but Kanaya and Rose already act a bit like a married couple. They seem to have spoken enough already that they've achieved a comfortable familiarity with each other's patterns. Rose interjects a brief, rather uncharacteristic "Shh" and "Blah blah blah" that seem to playfully reprimand Kanaya's habit of babbling on at length in an overly worried way. Which suggests this is a habit Rose has noticed and commented on enough already to reduce further commentary to a lighthearted shorthand. You get the sense that there's more going on here than with other patron troll relationships, something of greater substance between the two, because Rose doesn't really talk to other people this way. That's part of how character development works: firmly establishing someone's voice, patterns, and habits, then watching how they deviate from those under specific circumstances. *Homestuck* goes a little nuts with that idea through splinters, doomed selves, fusions, etc. This isn't even a splinter though, it's as basic as can be. A facet of Rose's personality that emerges when talking to a particular person. Maybe that's just another kind of splinter, in a way? The idea of splinters was always meant to capture the idea that a person is a great composite of inner multitudes, regardless of whether the faceting is metaphysical or mundane. Either way, Kanaya's very earnest, motherly badgering seems to bring out a side of Rose's personality that we haven't gotten to see much. What else is there to say about this... It's cute? I could go on doing all sorts of analytical backflips down here, but maybe at the end of the day there's just a bunch of cute shit taking place between these two, and that's all there is to say on the matter.

GA: Yes Your Shout Pole Is Like A Tower Broadcasting Your Fear Across The Ring And You Are Right To Be Afraid
GA: I Have Commissioned None Other Than The Legendary Prince Of Hope And I Am Teaching Him The Ways Of White Sorcery
GA: I Have Observed Your Methods And You Will Come To The Most Unwelcome Realization That All Of Your Guile And Cunning Has Finally Backfired
GA: This Noble Magician Of Pure Light Will Serve As The Counterpoint To Your Arcane Debauchery
GA: He Will Hunt You Down And Goodness And Hope Will Prevail
TT: Is it too late to throw myself at your mercy?
GA: Yes Its Much Too Late For That

TT: I see.
TT: Then clearly I will have to prepare for this soul sundering duel, whilst making my own funeral arrangements.
GA: Oh Yes I Do Believe Securing A Corpse Box Would Be Prudent
GA: Fitted To Dimensions Suited To Your Myriad Of Unassembled Leaky Body Parts In Aggregate
TT: What will herald the arrival of this swift and righteous thaumaturge?
TT: Will I be blinded by the fearsome lashes of light ribboning from the incandescent coastline of his beauteous aura?
TT: Should I borrow my friend's sunglasses?
GA: Yes Definitely
GA: Definitely Do That
GA: Wait I Hope That Wasnt Too Emphatic
GA: Maybe At This Point I Should Clarify This Is All A Big Joke
TT: Yeah.
TT: I was getting that.
TT: You don't always have to tip your hand, Kanaya. You were doing well.
GA: I Was
TT: Mm-hm.
GA: Okay Great
GA: I Think What I Find Most Challenging About Human Insincerity Based Humor Is The Degree Of Commitment To The Fantasy Which Is Apparently Requisite
TT: We take it very seriously.
GA: I Mean To Say
GA: The Gesture Of Hostility In This Case Was The Joke
GA: I Did In Fact "Train" This Character
GA: I Made Him A Wand To Shut Him Up
TT: Wait, you did? Really?
GA: He Wouldnt Stop Harassing Me For Your "Secrets"
TT: That's incredible. Well done.
GA: Hes The One With The Royalty Complex And Speaks With All The Extra Vees And Doubleyous
TT: Oh, I knew exactly who you were talking about from the start.
GA: Okay
TT: I must say, this little project pleases me.
TT: Do keep me apprised of all further developments.
GA: Okay I Will
TT: At least until my looming grimdarkdeath steals me away.
GA: Uh
GA: Yeah That
GA: Is Still Something That I Dont Really Want To Joke About
GA: I Hope That Came Across As A Sincere Statement

> Jade: Answer fairy god troll.

Here we have a story as old as time: a motherly lesbian apprentices a disgruntled fuckboy in the arts of white magic to take down her grimdark girlfriend, as a joke to impress said girlfriend, only to have the fuckboy turn on his lesbian master, blast a hole in her chest with his wand, and later get slaughtered with a chainsaw when the lesbian resurrects as a cool vampire. And ironically, she doesn't even get any points from her girlfriend for doing all that, because she wasn't around to see it. At least her "ex" is pretty impressed.

-- adiosToreador [AT] began trolling gardenGnostic [GG] --

AT: hEEEY, jADE,
GG: oh hi!
GG: i remember you, you talked to me a lot in my dreams
AT: yEAH, bUT NOW i'M TALKING TO YOU BEING AWAKE,
AT: bECAUSE,
AT: yOUR ROBOT CAN'T TYPE,
AT: bECAUSE IT HAD AN EXPLOSION,
GG: yup!
GG: thats because my dream self died
GG: pretty catastrophically!
AT: aW, nO, i'M DEFINITELY PRETTY SORRY TO HEAR THAT,
GG: thanks, but i think im ok
GG: i felt pretty shaken up at first though
AT: yES, i DID TOO,
AT: i SPENT SO LONG SLEEPING AND DREAMING AND PLAYING ON PROSPIT,
AT: tHAT BEING AWAKE WAS MADE TO FEEL WEIRD, aND i DIDN'T LIKE IT FOR A WHILE,
GG: yeah i have done a lot of sleeping myself :)
AT: oH, yES, i KNOW, bUT,
AT: i SAW YOU, yOU WERE AWAKE A LOT TOO,
AT: aFTER A CERTAIN MOMENT, i SPENT JUST ABOUT EVERY WAKING HOUR BEING ASLEEP,
GG: wow why did you sleep so much???
AT: iT WAS JUST A BETTER WAY TO BE, mORE PEACEFUL AND FUN AND,
AT: i GUESS,
AT: tHERE WAS SOMETHING THAT HAPPENED THAT WAS INCREDIBLY TERRIBLE,
AT: aND SAD,
AT: aND MADE ME FEEL TERRIBLE AND SAD AND SLEEPY, sO i SLEPT, a LOT,
GG: oh no what happened that was so terrible?
AT: i'D PREFER,
AT: tHAT THE THING i WANT TO TALK TO YOU ABOUT NOT TURN INTO THAT TOPIC,
GG: ok sorry for prying!
GG: what did you want to talk about?
AT: i WANTED TO ASK YOU PERMISSION,
AT: i WOULD HAVE ASKED PERMISSION THE FIRST TIME,
AT: bUT AT THE TIME YOU WERE NOT ABLE TO GIVE IT, oR TALK OR ANYTHING,
GG: permission for what?
AT: tO COMMUNE WITH YOUR LUSUS,
GG: with bec?
GG: uh....
GG: what do you mean by commune?
GG: and
GG: what do you mean the first time!
GG: you did it before?
AT: yEAH,
AT: iT MEANS TO TALK TO HIM, aND, sUGGEST HE DO SOMETHING WHICH IS GOOD,
AT: fOR HIM, aND ALSO FOR PEOPLE HE LIKES,
GG: ohhh
GG: like a psychic power??
AT: yES,
GG: pretty sweet!
GG: when did you do it before?
AT: oH, vERY RECENTLY, pERSONALLY SPEAKING,

Looks like Tavros has graciously decided to embarrass himself one last time before the end of this book. Thank god, I was starting to worry you might finish the book without having it seared into your brain what a loser he is. This should tide you over until whatever he does to stink up the next book. Which is die pathetically, iirc. There isn't much he doesn't do pathetically. The thing he's doing pathetically here is not wanting to talk about whatever traumatic experience happened in his session that makes him want to sleep most of the time. Which I believe is in reference to failing to kill Vriska in her quest cocoon while she was bleeding to death. Which is also pathetic. Tavros's entire existence is a series of pathetic reactions to pathetic things he did, and then handling those pathetic reactions in a pathetic way, which leads to even more pathetic actions. Couldn't kill Vriska? Pathetic. Doesn't want to talk about it? Pathetic. Uses it as an excuse to relate to Jade while pathetically cruising her in an icky and sycophantic way? Pathetic. Trying to steal Vriska's style by communing with Bec and influencing the session? Pathetic. The dumb thing he's about to admit he did to "help" Jade as a child? Well, you'll see...

AT: bUT FOR YOU IT WAS VERY LONG AGO,

AT: aND, iT WAS A REALLY GOOD EXAMPLE i THINK,
AT: oF EXACTLY WHY WIGGLERS SHOULD NOT BE ALLOWED TO DUAL WIELD FLINTLOCK PISTOLS,
GG: hehe what?

AT: sO, i DID THE LIBERTY OF COMMUNING WITH YOUR LUSUS,
AT: wHICH i HOPE WASN'T OUT OF LINE,
AT: bUT LIKE i SAID, yOU WERE UNAVAILABLE,
AT: uHHH,
AT: bY WHICH i MEAN, uNAVAILABLY SMALL,

On the other hand, I guess Tavros did technically save Jade's life? Huh. Maybe Tavros is actually great, and Jade is just being an ungrateful bitch yet again. Wait. Hold on, I'm doing some more calculations...and, nope. My anti-Tavros instincts were right. They're always right. The thing is, Bec obviously wasn't going to let Jade shoot herself in the first place. Of course he wasn't. He blew up a huge meteor and wrecked the entire planet just to save her. He didn't need this intervention. Tavros, like Vriska, just took credit for something that was inevitable. But when Vriska does it, she manages to elevate her status as a diabolical personality. When Tavros does it, he just elevates his status as a pathetic weenie. The only thing he really accomplished here was killing Jade's grandpa. There's no way Bec would've ever done that without Tavros's interference. So, great going, Tavros, everything you did sucked.

AT: sO THEN i COMMUNED HIM TO USE HIS AMAZING POWERS, tO,
AT: iNTERVENE,
AT: aND REROUTE THE PROJECTILE AWAY FROM THE PATH THAT WOULD HAVE HARMED YOU,
AT: aND ALSO,
AT: aS A WONDERFUL BONUS AND COINCIDENCE,
AT: iT HAPPENED THERE WAS A FELON ON YOUR PROPERTY,

AT: iT WAS i THINK SURELY AN AGING ROGUE WHO WAS VERY MUCH KEEN ON INTRUDING BETWEEN YOUR REALLY NICE LOOKING FAMILY,
AT: aND AS FORTUNE WOULD HAVE IT,
AT: tHE SMALL MISSILE WAS REDIRECTED INTO THE SENIOR INTERLOPER'S CHEST,
AT: aND HE DIED,
AT: }:)

The only thing good about Jake's death, which Tavros brings about by accident, is that it completes the loop of poetic justice wherein Jake is killed by the very flintlock he came down to Earth with as a baby and used to murder Mark Twain. We also get a nice vignette of Jake's idiotic day-to-day habits as an old man, where he apparently makes a practice of taking this blue-haired doll on nice dates. After all the philandering he's done over his life, he probably figures this is a refreshingly uncomplicated way to court women. The more we learn about Grandpa, and then the more we learn about young Jake, the more it all starts to make sense. In Act 6, Jake seems to have the trajectory of a loner. Whether this is due to an actual preference for solitude or to him constantly fucking things up and alienating people in his life, is up to you to decide. One more thing about the flintlock: all the Alpha Kid personal items they travel to Earth with seem to be related to death, either something that dies on the way down or is later used to kill with. The pony and kitten both die. The joke book kills Nanna, then later kills a cat. The flintlocks kill Sassacre, then Grandpa. The bunnies are used to create Liv Tyler, who's an instrument of death and dies later. Lil Cal is Bro's weapon, and is a vessel for...well, you know. The only thing that doesn't seem to fit is Jane's hat. Sorry, I know I'm generally decent at pulling explanations out of thin air, but I don't think even I can make that work. Wait, the hat belonged to John's dad, and his dad died. Whew, I think we nailed it. *Homestuck* wasn't flawless for a very brief moment there, but now it's back to being flawless thanks to my quick thinking.

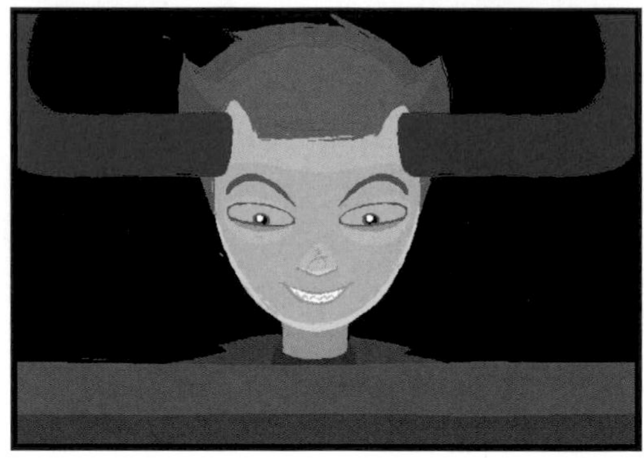

GG: omg......
GG: that wasnt a senior interloper, im pretty sure youre talking about my grandpa!!!
AT: oH,
GG: and if im interpreting correctly....
GG: youre saying you used bec to make me shoot him???
GG: augh thats so awful!
AT: uHH,
AT: wHAT'S,
AT: a GRANDPA,
GG: oh boy
GG: ok it is basically an old man, who serves the same role as i guess a lusus does on your planet?
GG: he was like my dad, he took care of me!
AT: wHOA,
AT: tHAT IS A REALLY WEIRD CULTURAL THING, i GUESS,
GG: sigh...
AT: sORRY THEN,
AT: aBOUT,
AT: mY CULTURAL IGNORANCE,
GG: well im not blaming you or anything
GG: it sounds like you were just trying to help
GG: and you did save my life
GG: but......
GG: i mean jeeeez
GG: talk about a misunderstanding
AT: wELL,
AT: nOW i FEEL VERY STUPID,
AT: bUT,
AT: i DON'T THINK i WILL GIVE INTO BAD SELF ESTEEM THIS TIME ABOUT THIS,
AT: iT'S IMPORTANT TO STAY CONFIDENT ABOUT STUFF, DON'T YOU AGREE,
GG: uh
GG: sure?
AT: aND i THINK THIS IS A GOOD OPPORTUNITY FOR US TO BOND, aND BECOME CLOSER IN AN EMOTIONAL WAY,
AT: pROBABLY,
GG: .... it is?
AT: oH YES, sEE THE FUNNY THING IS, i ALSO KILLED MY LUSUS BY ACCIDENT,
AT: i MEAN, mY LUSUS THAT WAS A LITTLE FAIRY BULL, nOT AN OLD MAN WITH A HUGE GUN,
GG: oh nooo
GG: how did that happen?
AT: i MURDERED HIM INAPPROPRIATELY WITH A FOUR WHEEL DEVICE,
GG: :|
GG: ummm what kind of device?
AT: lIKE, tHE KIND BASICALLY FOR CRIPPLES TO SIT IN, aND ROLL AROUND,
GG: oh you mean a wheelchair!
AT: i GUESS, tHAT'S A WAY TO CALL IT,
GG: how...
GG: did that happen?
AT: wELL,
AT: i WAS SITTING IN IT, bEING CRIPPLED LIKE USUAL,
AT: aND HE GOT UNDER THE WHEEL IN HIS NAP,
GG: D:
GG: im so sorry
GG: um also
GG: i didnt realize you were paralyzed
GG: not that im saying sorry for that! that would be rude i think
GG: i am just saying sorry for your loss
AT: oH, iT'S OKAY, oN BOTH THINGS,
AT: hE CAME BACK TO LIFE FOR A WHILE, aND COULD TALK, AND THAT WAS FUN,
AT: aND ALSO,
AT: i'M NOT PARALYZED ANYMORE, }:)
GG: oh?
AT: nO, i HAVE ROBOT LEGS, aND i FEEL GREAT, aND i CAN WALK,

There's the patron troll portrait I warned you Tavros would get but doesn't really deserve. He's trying so hard to be Jade's patron troll, and it just isn't working. Sadly, he doesn't even have enough depth as a person to be intensively, amorously meddlesome toward anyone, or to turn the screws on Jade's psyche in any meaningful way. Except for this cheap trick where he comes out and goes, lol remember when ur grandpa died? That was me. }:) It's bad, it's utterly inorganic, it smacks of desperation, and is nothing more than an annoying problem for Jade to deal with, just another tangle of obnoxiously brittle boyfeelings for her to tiptoe around. Look how nice she's being. He doesn't deserve this. It must be exhausting for her, especially with all the other ludicrous boy duties she has to keep up with. John, Dave, two Karkats... Karkat is a much more legitimate candidate to be her patron troll, and he gets one of these portraits later (two actually, if you count the shitty gag one). Which makes this one kind of a red-herring patron troll portrait. It's kind of a psycheout? Not that it even technically matters who's the patron troll of whom, but people actually did track this stuff as if it were direly important. Karkat is an infinitely superior patron troll for Jade, because clearly he is capable of getting her to actually care enough about whatever horseshit he's lathered up about, and he has the capacity to behave as the psychologically challenging foil for her that one must be in order to qualify as a patron troll, according to me, and the long list of fake rules I have about literally everything.

GG: wow nice!
AT: oH YES, iT IS TRULY NICE,
AT: i AM A NEW AND DIFFERENT GUY, mOSTLY,
AT: bEING NOT PHYSICALLY HANDICAPPED IS MOST CERTAINLY THE KEY TO HAVING HIGH SELF ESTEEM,
GG: um
GG: that.....
GG: i dont know if i agree with that!
AT: oH ABSOLUTELY, tAKE IT FROM ME AS WHAT FACT IS TRUE,
AT: aND NOW, i FEEL EMBOLDENED TO DO BOLD THINGS THAT HEROES SHOULD DO,
AT: lIKE, sAVE THE LIFE OF A PRETTY GIRL, AND KILL THE FIENDISH OLD MAN, wHO,
AT: wHOOPS, wASN'T FIENDISH, aND YOU LOVED HIM, sORRY,
GG: well
GG: thats good i guess
GG: i just wish...
GG: maybe you'd told me what happened when i was younger?
GG: i spent years wondering about it!
GG: when i was REALLY young, i was sure the doll sitting across from him did it
GG: and for a long time i was terrified of the evil blue girl!!!
GG: she sort of haunted my childhood and i had trouble sleeping for a long time
GG: but of course i got older and realized that was silly, but then i just speculated that maybe it was suicide
GG: which was just a really sad thing to think about!!!
AT: wOW, yEAH,
AT: i,
AT: tOTALLY BLEW THAT THEN,
AT: i GUESS i COULD STILL TELL YOU ABOUT IT IN YOUR PAST,
GG: buuuut...
GG: even if you do, i dont remember you doing so!
AT: oH,
AT: tHEN i GUESS I WON'T,
GG: er
GG: ok :\
AT: bUT YEAH, iRREGARDLESS,
AT: tHIS IS LIKELY TO BE EXACTLY THE KIND OF THING NOT TO STAND IN THE WAY ABOUT GOOD FEELINGS ABOUT MYSELF,
GG: ....
AT: i MEAN, i SAW THAT YOUR LUSUS SAVED YOU ANYWAY, iN ADVANCE,
AT: aND,
AT: i JUST WANTED,
AT: tO MAKE IT POSSIBLE SO THAT i WAS THE ONE INVOLVED WITH BEING THE HERO THERE,
AT: tO SAVE YOU,
AT: lIKE, tO PUT MYSELF IN YOUR STORY, iN A BRAVE CAPACITY, bECAUSE,
AT: tHAT'S WHAT FEELING GOOD AND POSITIVE ABOUT YOURSELF IS ALL ABOUT,

GG: woooooow...
GG: you sound really confused to me!
AT: aBSOLUTELY, i AM CONFUSED LIKE A FOX,
AT: tHE KIND THAT HAS HIGH SELF ESTEEM,
GG: heheheh
GG: youre incredibly silly
GG: i cant really tell to what extent youre joking around here!
AT: i UNDERSTAND THAT, aND JOKES HAPPEN, yES,
AT: bUT FEELING GREAT ABOUT YOURSELF IS NOT A JOKING ISSUE,
AT: iT IS HEAVY DUTY BUSINESS, aND NEEDS TO BE GIVEN ALL THE SERIOUSNESS THAT SAD THINGS GET,
AT: i'VE LEARNED THAT, fROM MY FRIENDS, AND ALSO, FROM RUFIO,
GG: rufio?

Jade's face says it all. That's the face I was making any time I was drawing or writing Tavros. Jade also lets on about her fear of the "blue girl," which implies that Vriska in some way may have been haunting her childhood. Which is true, of course, as you will see in a few pages through the magic of retroactivity and Vriska's penchant for vainglorious rebranding of canon events in her own image. The bottom line is, when Vriska does it, it's cool, and when Tavros does it, we all want to barf.

AT: yES, hE'S A FAKE,
GG: what do you mean fake?
AT: a FAKE GUY i MADE UP IMAGINARILY,
AT: hE NEVER STOPS BEING A THING THAT'S NOT REAL,
GG: ohh like an imaginary friend....
GG: heh, ok
AT: i'M PRETENDING THAT BEING FULLY HONEST ABOUT RUFIO'S FAKENESS, AND,
AT: bEING UP FRONT ABOUT HIS GENERAL FRAUDULENCE, tHAT IT WILL ONLY GIVE ME EXTRA CONFIDENCE,
AT: i'M PRETENDING THAT AS HARD AS i CAN, iN THE MOST CONFIDENT WAY,
AT: wHICH MAKES IT PARTIALLY MORE TRUE,
GG: that
GG: sure is a philosophy you have there!
AT: yES, bEING CONFIDENT IS ALWAYS ABOUT SAYING AND DOING THE THINGS YOU FEEL,
AT: eVEN IF THE AFRAID PART OF YOU SAYS, nO, pLEASE DON'T DO THAT,
AT: lIKE, uHHHHHHH,
AT: hERE IS A THING i'M AFRAID TO SAY TO YOU, jADE,
AT: bUT,
AT: i'M TOO CONFIDENT NOW TO LET MY AFRAIDNESS MAKE ME FEEL TERRIBLE,
GG: oh??
GG: well, what is it?
AT: rEMEMBER, i TALKED TO YOU A LOT WHEN YOU WERE SLEEPING,
GG: yes
AT: uHH, aND,
AT: wE TALKED ABOUT LOTS OF THINGS, aND WE HAD SOME THINGS IN COMMON, aND IT WAS NICE,
GG: sure!
AT: aND i THINK CONSEQUENTLY, tHE EMOTIONAL RESULT IS PROBABLY,
AT: tHAT MAYBE i HAVE SOME POSSIBLE RED FEELINGS FOR YOU,
GG: red feelings?
GG: you mean
GG: whoooooaaaaaa
GG: wait
GG: really? :o
AT: wOW, tHAT SURE WAS A HARD THING TO SAY AND MADE ME INCREDIBLY NERVOUS,
AT: bUT i SAID IT BECAUSE OF MY REMARKABLE LEG-POWERED SELF CONFIDENCE,
AT: aND NOW i THINK ALL THAT'S LEFT IS DEFINITELY YOUR RECIPROCATION ABOUT THAT, pROBABLY,
GG: um.................
GG: well
GG: i dont think i can reciprocate!
AT: uH OH,
GG: i mean
GG: youre nice
GG: but i dont really know you...
GG: i dont even know your name!
AT: oH GOSH, hOW STUPID CAN i BE,
AT: i FORGOT TO SAY,
AT: i'M TAVROS,
GG: ok tavros
GG: i dont know if youve fully thought about this!
GG: you dont actually know me very well either
AT: oH YES, i SURELY DO,
AT: bECAUSE WE HAD A NUMBER OF SPIRITED CONVERSATIONS, wHEREIN YOU WERE VERY NICE AND PLEASED TO SPEAK WITH ME,
AT: dID,
AT: i MISINTERPRET THAT, wAS IT NOT ACTUALLY NICENESS,
GG: well no
GG: i was being nice
GG: because
GG: i like to be nice to people when i can, and when they are nice to me
GG: but......
GG: things are a little more complicated than that, you cant know someone just by a few conversations!
GG: i mean, i only talked to you when i was asleep! i am kind of different when im dreaming...
GG: i forget things, and at times im not totally sure whats real
GG: dont you remember thats what its like to dream on prospit?
AT: uH,
AT: kIND OF,
GG: sorry, i feel bad about having to disappoint you...
GG: but i dont know what else to say
AT: bUT WHAT ABOUT,
AT: mY ATTRACTIVE BRAVADO,
AT: aND IGNORING MY INSTINCTUAL COWARDICE HARD ENOUGH TO SAY THAT i LIKE YOU,
AT: iSN'T THAT,
AT: sUPPOSED TO BE VERY ATTRACTIVE, aND ENCOURAGE

If you're one of these people still somehow stanning for Tavros, please. For the love of Jesus, just stop. Learn to respect yourself. Maybe call your friends and organize an intervention. When they ask who it's for, just say it's a surprise and they'll find out later. Then you hide in the room while they all come in, like it's a surprise party. And you jump out, wearing your Tavros horns, and your Taurus shirt, and yell, SURPRISE! It's me. I'm the piece of shit. Then throw yourself at the mercy of these people. Never let go of them, for they are true friends. After the intervention, try to get the Pope on the line to canonize them, for they are true saints just because they're willing to be in the same room with you, let alone call you a friend. Actually, come to think of it, this exact scenario is how I met my priest and my life coach.

THE MAJOR HAVING OF FLUSHED FEELINGS IN OTHERS,
AT: i GUESS WHAT i MEAN IS, wHAT ABOUT ALL MY CONFIDENCE,
AT: wHAT DO YOU THINK ABOUT THAT,
GG: jeeeeeez, um...
GG: tavros i am really flattered you like me and all
GG: and that sure is confident of you to say so! and thats great buuuut...
GG: i guess confidence is one thing but there is such a thing as being toooo forward i guess?
AT: wOW,
AT: oK,
GG: i aaaalso think...
GG: and really this is just polite friendly advice!
GG: that if youre really confident you dont always have to say it all the time
GG: it...
GG: oh man im sorry to say
GG: it just comes of as a little insecure and off putting and kind of defeats the purpose!
GG: and all things considered i think we should just stay friends
GG: or really........
GG: continue building a friendship in the first place, since like i said we dont actually know each other that well!
AT: yEAH,
AT: uUUUUUUHHH,
GG: sorry :C
AT: nO, nO, iF i'M BEING REALISTIC i THINK THAT'S WHAT'S REASONABLE TO SAY TO ME,
AT: aND i'LL WORK ON TONING DOWN MY SELF RESPECT A LITTLE,
GG: aaaah no! you should have self respect
GG: just...
GG: oh boy this is frustrating
GG: can we talk about this later?
GG: i have some things to do!
GG: why dont we get back to the original point
GG: why do you want to commune with bec again?
AT: yES, oF COURSE,
AT: i WANTED TO GET APPROVAL FROM YOU, tO COMMUNE HIM AGAIN,
AT: nOW THAT HE'S A SPRITE,
AT: tO PERPETRATE ONE OF MY HEROIC IDEAS AGAIN,
GG: uh-ohhh

GG: what is your idea this time?
AT: i WILL SUGGEST TO HIM THAT HE ATTACK YOUR ADVERSARY,
AT: aS WELL AS OURS,
AT: aND MAYBE BEAT HIM, tO SOLVE EVERYBODY'S PROBLEMS,
GG: wow, i dunno about that!
AT: bUT i HAVE GREAT SKILL IN COMMANDING BEASTS TO GLORY IN BATTLE,
AT: aND YOURS IS SURELY THE STRONGEST BEAST I'VE SEEN!
GG: but hes my best friend!!!
GG: and you have already managed to get one of my family members killed
AT: bUT ACCORDING TO MY SELF CONFIDENCE, i THINK i'M PRETTY SURE i CAN USE HIS POWER TO BE SUCCESSFUL,
AT: wHOOPS, PRETEND i DIDN'T MENTION MY SELF CONFIDENCE, oR SAY ANYTHING OFF PUTTING,
GG: but all of our adversaries have inherited his powers!
GG: i would imagine the strongest guy would have all of his powers, and then some!!!
GG: i am really not comfortable with this
AT: oH,
GG: you said you are asking me permission first and i appreciate that
GG: but if you are asking im afraid my answer is no!
AT: oKAY, i RESPECT THAT,
AT: bUT, i WONDER,
GG: what?
AT: i WONDER IF A TRULY SELF CONFIDENT GUY, wITH

Speaking of saints, Jade is handling this like a champ. You've got to hand it to her. Rose would have logged off at the first whiff of a lecherous "uHHHHH." That's one reason why Rose is better than Jade. She doesn't let atrocious boys mess with her. She blows their computers up and goes back to chatting up the cool girls. I guess some girls need to work the cesspit of intolerable boys. This seems to be one of Jade's burdens, really. Maybe I'm being too hard on her. She's taking a big one for the team here. As she comes of age she seems to be one of these people who is particularly ensnared in the brutal vice grip known as the abomination of heterosexuality. As a youth it makes you put up with some completely insane and unpleasant things no rational person would subject themselves to, like endure a full conversation with Tavros, or navigate hormonally charged relations between several versions of Karkat, while nurturing a crush on multiple versions of Dave at once. Maybe I haven't been giving Jade enough credit all along. Maybe she's always been the hero *Homestuck* needs but doesn't deserve.

THE BEST SELF ESTEEM THERE IS, wOULD EVEN NEED TO ASK,
AT: mAYBE THE BEST GUY WOULD JUST KNOW HE WOULD BE SUCCESSFUL, aND WOULD DO IT ANYWAY BECAUSE IT IS FOR YOUR OWN GOOD, aND EVERYONE ELSE'S,
GG: no way!
GG: that would be smug and arrogant and would make you a bully!!!
GG: later if my friends and i want to ask bec for help and decide thats our best hope, then thats our business
GG: until then, just please stop meddling!!!!!!
AT: wOW, oK,
AT: yOU'RE RIGHT ABOUT ALL THAT, i'LL RESPECT YOUR WISHES,
AT: oR,
AT: wILL i? }:)
GG: noooooooooo dont dont dont dont dont
GG: im serious
GG: uuuuggghh i think my headache is coming back
AT: i WAS jUST,
AT: mAKING A JOKE,
AT: sORRY, }:(
AT: i GUESS US BECOMING A FRIENDSHIP DOESN'T HAVE TO HAPPEN NOW,
GG: no...
GG: its fine
GG: i just really dont want you to do that ok?
AT: yEAH,
GG: i have to go now
GG: bye tavros

-- gardenGnostic [GG] ceased being trolled by adiosToreador [AT] --

arachnidsGrip [AG] began trolling adiosToreador [AT]

AG: Aaaaaaaahahahahahahahaha!
AG: HAHAHAHAHAHAHAHA!!!!!!!!
AG: Oh my god, I cannot 8elieve how hilariously pathetic that whole exchange was.
AG: Even 8y your wretched standards, Toreadork!
AG: Hahahahahahahaha, oh god I can't 8reathe!!!!!!!!
AG: A8solutely priceless. XXXXD
AT: hEY, vRISKA,
AT: tHAT WAS SUPPOSED TO BE A PRIVATE CORRESPONDENCE, oF A PERSONAL NATURE,
AT: hOW COULD YOU EVEN BE READING THAT,
AG: Pff. Tavros, sometimes your stupidity surprises even me.
AG: Next time you decide to open your heart to an alien girl........

AG: Make sure her chat client isn't 8eing holographically projected for all to see, ok?

> Thief: Tear into Page.

Speaking of heroes we need but don't deserve, Vriska jumps in to save us from this abomination of a conversation. Since Vriska is taking over for me on the Tavros roasting front, I can probably take five. Maybe go make a sandwich.

AT: uH,
AT: wHOOOPS,
AG: It was so em8arrassing just reading that Tavros. I'm em8arrassed!
AG: I am actually feeling genuine em8arrassment. Your o8scene incompetence is actually polluting my otherwise pristine composure. Nice going!
AT: sO,
AT: i DON'T CARE,
AG: Jade let you down too easy. She's too nice! Someone's got to tear into you for that appalling display, and once again, guess who's shoulders that falls on?
AG: That's right. Vriska's, as usual.
AT: i THINK SHE HAS THE RIGHT AMOUNT OF NICENESS, pERSONALLY,
AT: aN AMOUNT THAT IS SOME, iNSTEAD OF,
AT: nONE,
AG: Hey, I'm nice when it matters, and where it doesn't strangul8te the critical development of people I give a shit a8out, ok?
AG: Really I don't know what you see in her. She is completely useless, like you.
AG: W8, of course!!!!!!!! It makes perfect sense. You and she represent the ideal matespritship, how could I have 8een so 8lind!
AG: Two perfectly pointless gru8s in a bucket.
AT: nO, i HAVE TOO MUCH SELF CONFIDENCE NOW TO BE UPSET BY YOUR SCANDALOUS IMAGERY,
AT: i DON'T THINK SHE IS USELESS,
AT: aND i DON'T THINK i AM EITHER,
AT: bECAUSE OF NEW SELF ESTEEMS OBTAINED, rEMEMBER,
AG: Oh will you please stop going on a8out your fucking self esteem.
AG: I will say this much a8out her, she was right a8out that. How insuffera8le can you get, prattling on and on a8out how confident you are.
AG: Tavros, you give confidence a 8ad name. I gave you all the chances in the world to earn it, to earn REAL confidence, and you failed.
AG: You couldn't even do the one little thing I asked you to! The one thing that would have made you man up once and for all.
AG: So instead you flew away and cried, and decided to sleep away your sorrow for the rest of the adventure.
AG: Do you have any idea how sick that made me? Everything a8out you makes me sick.
AG: When you talk a8out your self confidence, I throw up a little. You don't know what confidence is. Ro8o-legs don't give you confidence, that 8n't no more true than saying my ro8o-arm gave me mine. See what I mean?
AG: Your confidence is faker than even the great Rufio himself, Lord of the Unreal. It's pure fiction, a false fakey fraudy con jo8 from a wimpy loser charlatan 8ullshit artist.
AG: It's shallow and nause8ting, just like you. Do us all a favor and SHUT UP a8out it.
AT: oK, i THINK,
AT: tHIS IS ACTUALLY MAKING ME PRETTY MAD,
AG: Yeah right!!!!!!!!
AG: I'll 8elieve that when I see it, chump.
AT: i DON'T WANT YOU TO MOCK ME ANYMORE,
AT: i DON'T KNOW IF MY CONFIDENCE IS REAL, oR WHAT,
AT: bUT i WOULD LIKE YOU TO STOP SAYING STUFF LIKE THAT TO ME,
AT: aND TO STOP SAYING BAD THINGS ABOUT MY FRIEND JADE, tOO,
AG: Jade is an idiot.
AG: A useless, 8oring no8ody. What has she done for her party other than fuck up every step of the way? What does she ever do 8ut take naps and get in trou8le?
AG: She's awful, and you deserve each other. Oh w8, except she h8tes you!!!!!!!! Ahahahahahahahaha. Even the 8oring pointless girl h8s you, talk a8out a guy who can't get a 8r8k.

/Yells from the other room while grabbing some things out of the fridge./ Vriska is knocking it out of the park here! /Unscrews an ancient jar of mayonnaise, gives it a smell. Recoils, tosses it in the trash./ I have nothing to add to this!

AG: Though I guess she's not compleeeeeeeetely useless. ::::)
AT: wHAT DO YOU MEAN BY THAT,
AG: Ok, Tavros, I gave her credit for something, so I'll give you credit for something too.
AG: Your plan to control her lusus really wasn't a 8ad idea!
AG: And using your a8ility to "save her life" (lol) was a pretty good way to test how effective your powers are across sessions.
AG: Pretty good way to practice, to know where you stand!
AG: Practicing your a8ilities is important, so when it comes down to using them for something that really matters, you know you're ready for prime time.
AG: I know this first hand.
AG: I got lots and lots and LOTS of practice with your little guinea pig friend. ::::D
AG: So really, turns out she wasn't so useless at all! Far from it.
AT: wHOA, wHAT,
AT: aRE YOU SAYING YOU DID TO HER,
AG: Not really the point!
AG: The point is I'm trying to pay you a compliment.
AG: At this point, you are so sad and disgusting, you should treat anything nice anyone has to say a8out you like a chest full of shimmering 8oon8ucks.
AT: oKAAAY, gOD,
AT: wHAT,
AG: Like I said! Your plan was solid.
AG: Controlling the guardian to go after Jack was a fine idea. Sure would stir some shit up! 8etter than 8eing an insignificant stuttering piece of trash all the time, I say.
AG: And you were definitely on to something a8out doing it "irregardless" (lol) of her wishes.
AG: 8ecause it's for her own good! That's what winners do. They do what is right for someone they care a8out even if the other person does nothing 8ut 8itch and moan and act ungr8ful a8out it. 8etter you learned 18 than never.
AG: In fact, I would go as far as saying that if you went ahead with her plan against her wishes, it MIGHT just earn you a smidgen of respect from me.
AG: We'll see.
AG: There's really just one catch.
AT: oH,
AT: wHAT'S THAT,

AG: The catch is it's not going to work!
AT: wHAT ISN'T,
AG: Are you even listening to me? Man, clear the Rufio wax out of your ears.
AG: You couldn't sic the guardian on Noir even if you were inclined. Not even if I were to MAKE you inclined! :::;)
AT: uHH,
AT: wHY,
AG: 8ecause you are dealing with a pro here. I already thought of that.
AG: I thought of everything!

Here's where Vriska boldly claims she's actually behind almost everything in *Homestuck*. Apparently all of Jade's narcolepsy was just Vriska practicing her powers on a test human. And Vriska influenced agents to create Bec, or "nudged" them to do what they wanted to do anyway. In other words, more retroactive rebranding to slap her name on a thing that probably was going to happen anyway. More fantastic work by *Homestuck*'s one true superstar. Jade probably wasn't going to be falling asleep all the time without Vriska's "experimentation" though, so she probably has legitimate claim to being the original author of Jade's narcolepsy. I remember some people (i.e. losers) were grousing about this reveal a little bit, and that the story kept on revealing things that Vriska was responsible for all along. As if that wasn't totally great. My only regret is not making Vriska directly responsible for even more shit. I think some readers thought this reveal reframed an interesting character trait of someone they liked (Jade) and made it feel less special, more artificially imposed on her, therefore making her a less interesting character in hindsight. But that's exactly what Vriska does: she steals certain intangible qualities from others. She steals luck, valor, agency, credit, and above all, relevance. By making Jade sleep all the time, she literally diminishes the relevance of Jade in the story. And in doing so, Vriska absorbs that stolen relevance directly into herself, as if to say, See? I did this. I'm responsible for this thing about her you thought was special. It was me all along, and now you're forced to focus on me more than her, and also more than everyone else.

AG: The guardian is not going to attack the agents who engineered him in the first place.
AG: Or who I should say were "encouraged" (lol) to engineer him.

AG: I was striking a mutually 8eneficial arrangement! This is often the most effective way to manipul8 others.
AG: I just sort of gave them an idea. Nudged them along in the direction of seizing more power, which they wanted to do anyway.
AG: Remem8er, I already have a lot of experience getting these simple minded agents to march to my drum 8eat.
AG: I was exiling them left and right in our session! I'm an expert at this 8y now.
AT: wHY WOULD YOU DO THAT,

AG: Tavros, at this point it should 8e o8vious.
AG: I am the unseen hand 8ehind every major event in their session, and to some extent, their whole lives.
AG: At least those events not happening 8y the volition of their own natural incompetence!
AG: Don't you think this is how it should 8e? Shouldn't the greatest player leave her fingerprints on every step of the rise to power of her ultim8 nemesis?
AT: wOW, nO, tHAT'S,
AT: i DON'T EVEN KNOW HOW TO SAY ALL THE WAYS i THINK THAT IS CRAZY,

And then, in case it wasn't totally clear Vriska's about to launch into a villainous monologue, she starts tossing out hammy stuff like "I AM THE UNSEEN HAND!" This moment sort of does have the feel of when the villain dramatically explains all their dastardly plans in front of a trembling protagonist. So maybe we instinctively start siding with Tavros, because generally we're supposed to side with those on the receiving end of villainous diatribes. There are just a couple problems with this. First of all, he's Tavros, so we shouldn't be siding with him on anything. Second of all, many of the points Vriska's making are actually right? Tavros objects and calls her plans crazy, but she's correct in pointing out how he was trying to do exactly the same thing, just less effectively. And not to mention for selfish reasons—he was trying to control Bec to pump up his own self-esteem and use that swagger to horrendously flirt with a girl he barely knew. So he has no real credibility to object to Vriska's intervention. She calls him out on that, and she's totally right. Even though she's sort of insane, Vriska has a way of being right much of the time and often has a fairly practical analysis of certain situations, usually tactical ones. It can be frustrating when a villainous individual is right about a lot of things, because it can lead to some internal dissonance over whether or not you should be considering them villainous at all. In the case of Vriska, the dissonance is so strong that you really have no choice but to completely reverse your perception of her as a villain and fully embrace her as the true hero of the story. You also have no choice but to completely disregard all her flaws, basically fall in love with her, and then propose to her if you ever get the chance.

AG: 8ut you must agree, 8ecause you were copycatting my idea.
AT: nO i WASN'T,
AG: You were 8razenly inserting yourself into Jade's history. The self-insertion plan was my idea, and it's revolting and cowardly for you to deny it.
AT: tHAT WAS, FOR A GOOD THING THOUGH,
AG: Hahahaha, sure. Whatever you say.
AG: It's incredi8ly sad how outclassed you are. It's actually depressing that you thought you could 8eat me at my own game. And then most sickeningly of all, you don't own up it!
AG: I have every angle covered already. The human session is on full Serket lockdown. Any effort you make to disrupt my plans will 8e laugha8le, just like everything you have ever done in your life.
AG: The only thing left to do now is prepare to kill Jack myself, and save everyone's ungrateful asses.
AG: It's a shame you're not strong enough to take him on with me. Too 8ad you spent so long sleeping instead of tur8o-leveling like me.
AG: We might have made a pretty awesome team.
AG: Oh well.

> Page: Retrieve arms.

AT: oKAY, tHEN,
AT: aLL OF YOUR USUAL INSULTING THINGS ASIDE, mY TAKE ON THIS IS,
AT: tHAT YOU CREATED OUR IMPOSSIBLY HARD BAD GUY, wHO WANTS TO KILL US,
AT: aND BY ASSOCIATION, i GUESS THAT MAKES,
AT: yOU THE BAD GUY TOO,
AT: iNSTEAD OF A GOOD GUY WHO'S JUST MEAN,
AG: Nice deduction!
AG: Wrong, excruci8tingly linear, and laced with the sort of a8solutes morons like to throw around........
AG: 8ut nice!
AT: aND THAT BEING THE CASE,
AT: eVEN THOUGH i'M TERRIFIED OF YOU,
AT: aND nOT AS STRONG,
AT: oR REAL CONFIDENT,
AT: oNLY MOSTLY FAKE CONFIDENT,
AG: Yeeeeeeees?
AG: Go on.
AT: i THINK,
AT: i AM GOING TO HAVE TO STOP YOU,
AG: Yeah! That's the spirit.
AG: Pretty weakslime threat there, 8ut it's a start.
AG: Tell you what.
AG: If you can find me in this la8, you can have at me.
AG: I'll even give you a free shot! No funny 8usiness or anything.
AT: oK,
AT: tHEN,
AT: hERE i COME,
AG: I'll 8e w8ing. <3

Here are some more correct statements by Vriska, along with a reiteration of her attitude toward Tavros, which is, despite her bullying, that all she really wants is for him to become a strong, assertive guy who's willing to stand up to her. But he can never really do it, despite this feeble showing here. A lot of their relationship at this point in the story orbits around this hidden traumatic event that took place in their session, which has been implied but won't be shown for a while. Namely, the gruesome quest cocoon botched euthanasia fiasco. The fact that Tavros blew that final "test" seems to have exacerbated Vriska's hostility toward him. He has no way of knowing it, but that was his last chance to prove himself as sufficiently assertive or ruthless enough to be worth her time. Trying to prove himself at this point is just walking into a trap.

> AH: Ride.

This is a high-quality transition. Vriska is destroying Tavros from the comfort of her beloved Cage shrine. She checks on Jade, who is investigating the lab at the top of her house, which contains her stuffed, dead dream self, Grandpa's dog Harley, and the missing Fourth Wall he apparently stole from Jack for some reason. The Fourth Wall is a window into the real world, and by real, I mean still pretty fake. But it's the fake real world that contains my self-insert, who engages in shenanigans and fools around in his mansion situated on a cliff top populated by many beautiful horses. It's a good time to check in with me, to see how I'm doing after my previous meltdown in the scary attic. Looks like I've rebounded nicely. The makeup is mostly worn off. I still have my shitty, one-horned headband. I bought one of those cool red-sleeved Dave shirts that were popular with the kids those days. Add in the shades and I'm cosplaying Dave, which was also en vogue and will probably go down in history as the laziest cosplay tradition ever. Oh, I'm also being controlled by Vriska apparently. And why not? We just learned that Vriska is retroactively behind almost everything, so for all intents and purposes, she might as well just be controlling me as I write the story as well. Isn't that basically an apt description of what's going on when an author starts obsessing over his favorite OC and starts shoving her in the spotlight repeatedly, uses her as his go-to tool for stirring the pot, inflating the drama, and rewarding her endlessly for pretty much just existing? What's the real difference between becoming obsessed with a favored OC and the possibility that she's literally hijacked the author's mind as a sort of powerful, conjured muse? Maybe you find it surprising I admit to all this so freely. Perhaps others would be embarrassed, or pause before acknowledging such subservience to a figment of authorial whim. But not me. There is no limit to the ways in which I will degrade and humiliate myself, all in the name of my beautiful waifu.

Yes.

> Hell yes.

> Hell.

> Fucking.

> Yes.

Falcor has rapid-cycling pool balls for eyes, which is part of the device in the story where I just keep messing with you about the identity of Lord English right up until the point when he's finally revealed. This is a good thing to tease the reader with now, since **[S] Jade: Enter** debunked the idea that the invincible demon who attacked the trolls was English. It turns out to be Jack, who just happens to have powers of omnipotence related to English's powers. So now it's like, well if *that* wasn't English, then *who is* English?! As usual, I'm not really in any hurry to give you critical information. But that doesn't mean you can't be roundly messed with along the way. Also, in case you didn't know, these panels reference the film *The NeverEnding Story*. Actually, and not many people realize this, these panels precisely duplicate the compositions and subject matter of one scene in that film, where Falcor literally vomits on some bullies. You might want to watch the movie and keep an eye out for this scene. I think you will agree my attention to detail is even more impressive than usual.

And so came to an end the most heroic thing that ever happened in the history of metafiction.

Let's move on.

> Heir: Level up.

THE WINDY THING subsides, and clear skies prevail. You soar to the highest rung, and rule over your echeladder as the HEIR TRANSPARENT.

Boondollars fly.

> Air: Cloud up.

The clouds have returned. The fireflies are still trapped. The spell remains unbroken.

There is commotion behind you. A nearby village, perhaps?

> [S] John: Enter village.

There's an upper limit to the rungs of the echeladder. Which is a thing I guess I decided not long before this panel. It's my way of saying, we're done with this silly thing. We're moving to a new logic for advancing levels. We've got to get to the god tier stuff soon. People don't know that yet, but we do. What they do know is those dang blue pajamas John was wearing earlier still need to be explained. Don't worry, Vriska (who else?) will be all over this soon. There's always been something a little childish about the echeladder aesthetic, like it's a leveling system meant for a little kid. Part of it is the toy-like design, but it's also conveyed through some of the names, like Riptike, Kneehigh Pilgrim, or Cool Buckaroo. The time for juvenile nonsense is over. Soon John must put aside his childhood ways and embrace his destiny as a very serious adult. Which apparently involves spending literally every moment of your life from now on in some ridiculous pajamas while still being mostly useless.

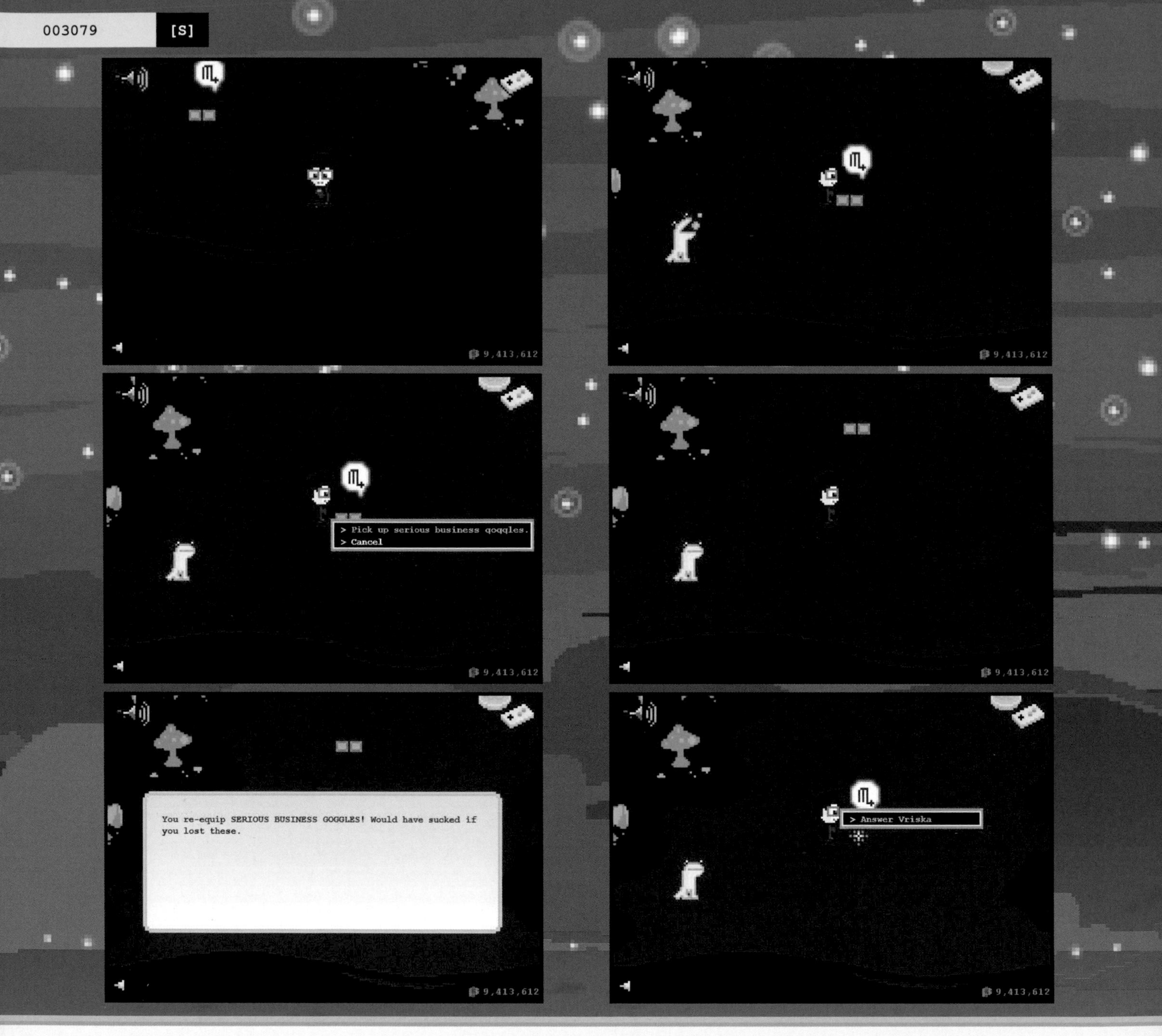

We're already doing another one of these playable RPG pages. **[S] Past Karkat: Wake up.** was posted on 10/25, and this page was posted on 12/15, not even two months later. That's how bonkers the pace was, back in this frenzied era of ceaseless content. The minigame turned out to be a compelling format, everyone was ecstatic about it, so the general feeling in the air was: why not do more of these? Might as well keep riding the wave. The game fosters these feelings of exploration and freedom, and brings a sense of enormity to the world and story just by adding a fun little sprite-based salamander village you could discover. An impression that you're directly helping John work his way toward finding his Quest Bed instead of just passively clicking through the pages until it happens. As you've seen already, these RPG games get *kind of* long when translated to book pages. So this game lasts for the rest of this book. Meaning that, in a way, this is the final page of the book. It's over already, I know. Isn't it crazy how the pages fly by when you're captivated by my tendency to preposterously over-explain my great story to you? But don't worry, I'll stay down here to keep you company during this home stretch, cracking wise, keeping it loose. Except for the pages where I decide to delete the gutter, because I don't particularly feel like devising commentary about a fucking mushroom John finds in a chest or something.

The game gets off to a strong start, because it gives you exactly what you were craving after reading a ton of Vriska's megalomaniacal bullshit: more Vriska. Her talksprite is being reused from the previous game because, why not. It was there, it was fine, and the dev cycle was literally several days long. We did need a new John talksprite, though. I think these sprites tended to get better and more consistent-looking as more of these games got made. John seems really on-point here. The outfit he got when Vriska was treating him like a dress-up doll is still pretty silly, I guess. He won't have to wear it for much longer, though. And no, that's not me lewdly insinuating he's about to seduce one of these salamanders. Good grief. Is that REALLY the first place your mind has to go??? Disgraceful.

003079 [S]

VRISKA: FOR GAINING ALL THE LEVELS!!!!!!!! ::::O

JOHN: oh, right! i got to the top of my echeladder somehow. i didn't even really think it had a top, or that i would get there so fast.

JOHN: so i guess that's it, then! don't have to worry about leveling up anymore. that's pretty neat.

VRISKA: Don't 8e ridiculous, John.

VRISKA: While you may have technically gained all the levels just now, you did not truly gain ALL of them just yet.

VRISKA: In a way, this is really just the 8eginning.

Vriska gets down to business by saying what I already said, which is that gaining all the levels on your echeladder is kid's stuff. There are much bigger and cooler fish to fry, involving blue pajamas, pseudo-immortality, and a sword through the chest. She's the one to guide John through this process, not only because she's his patron troll, or because she wants to be responsible, but because she's the only one who's already done it herself.

JOHN: it is?
VRISKA: Yes. You are now ready to 8egin your ascent through the god tiers.
VRISKA: No8ody I know was a8le to progress this far anywhere near as fast and you, John. Not even me! I can't tell you how proud I am.
JOHN: wow, really?
JOHN: ok, what do i do?
VRISKA: The thing is, from this point on, you can't make any progress while you're awake. So you've got to get to sleep!

This exchange probably creates some nomenclature ambiguity. Vriska says "ascent through the god tiers," plural. Yet later on in the story god tier is referred to as more of a binary status, a cool mode you can achieve, and you stay that way forever once you do. The latter is a more apt way of describing it, but both ways are technically correct. There are multiple "tiers" to progress through after the initial transformation takes place. But they don't actually matter that much—just like the echeladder rungs, but with more serious-sounding tier names like "REVENGE OF DOCTOR RAGNAROK" and "SAYONARA KANSAS." New grown-up branding, same useless results.

003079 [S]

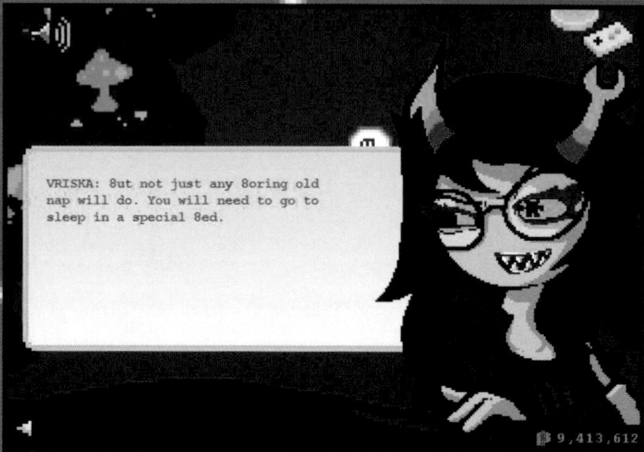

VRISKA: 8ut not just any 8oring old nap will do. You will need to go to sleep in a special 8ed.
9,413,612

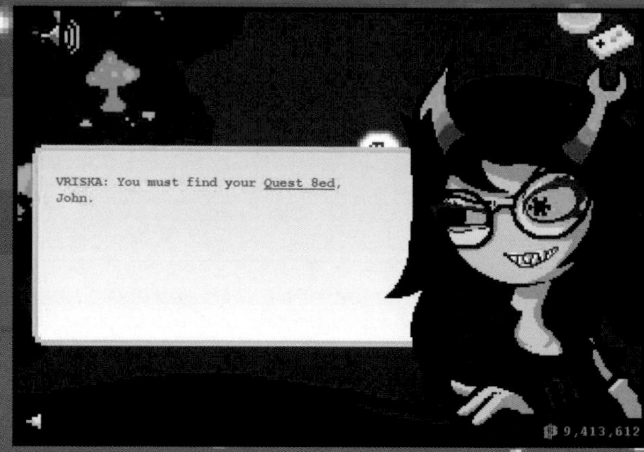

VRISKA: You must find your Quest 8ed, John.
9,413,612

JOHN: that sounds pretty cool. where is it?
9,413,612

VRISKA: Not too far away! 8ut rather than me telling you, why don't you talk to the locals and ask around?
9,413,612

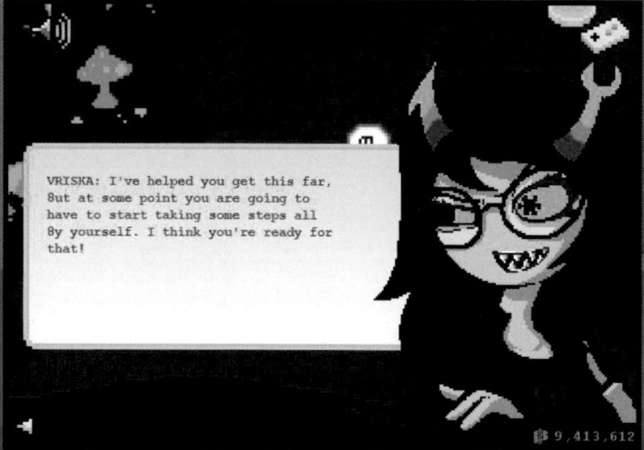

VRISKA: I've helped you get this far, 8ut at some point you are going to have to start taking some steps all 8y yourself. I think you're ready for that!
9,413,612

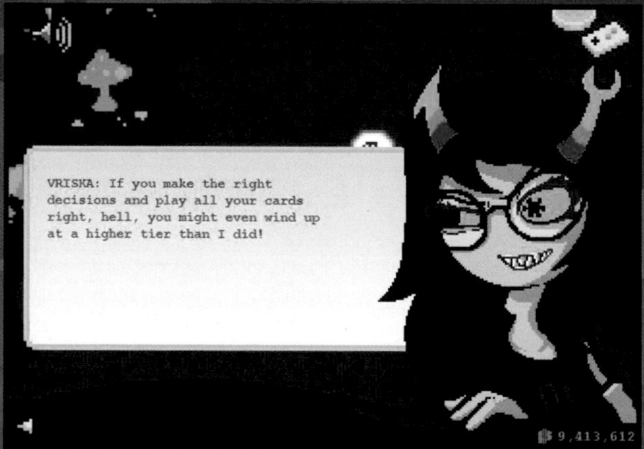

VRISKA: If you make the right decisions and play all your cards right, hell, you might even wind up at a higher tier than I did!
9,413,612

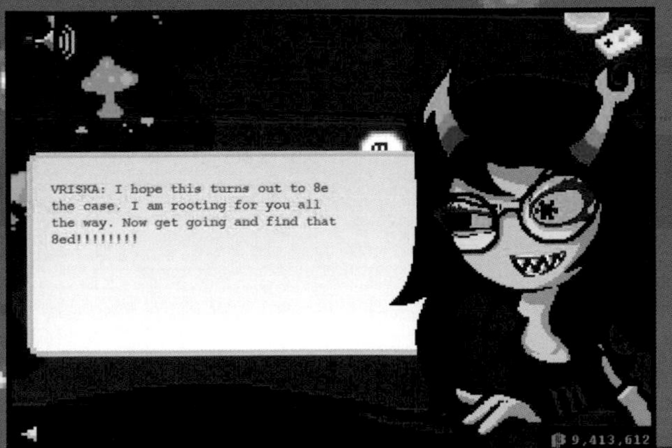
VRISKA: I hope this turns out to 8e the case. I am rooting for you all the way. Now get going and find that 8ed!!!!!!!!
9,413,612

JOHN: ok, i will! thanks a lot, vriska!
9,413,612

9,413,612

SALAMANDER: Did you see it??? It was there, after the Windy Thing!
9,413,612

JOHN: see what?
9,413,612

SALAMANDER: Oh gosh, I can't think of the word. The big flat thing thats as wide as possible, and up.
9,413,612

003079 [S]

JOHN: um...
9,413,612

SALAMANDER: The dark colored ceiling that clouds stay under.
9,413,612

JOHN: you mean... the sky?
9,413,612

SALAMANDER: YES! It was so beautiful. I hope to witness its miracle again one day before the end of my sadly short amphibious lifespan.
9,413,612

9,413,612

Open Pyxis
> Cancel
9,413,612

9,413,612

You got a MINITABLET
9,413,612

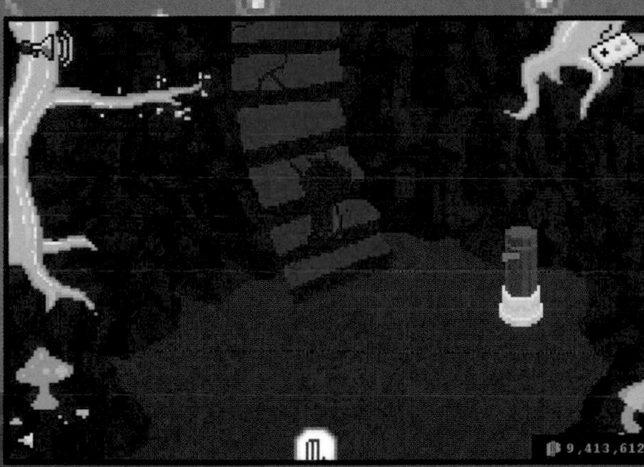
9,413,612

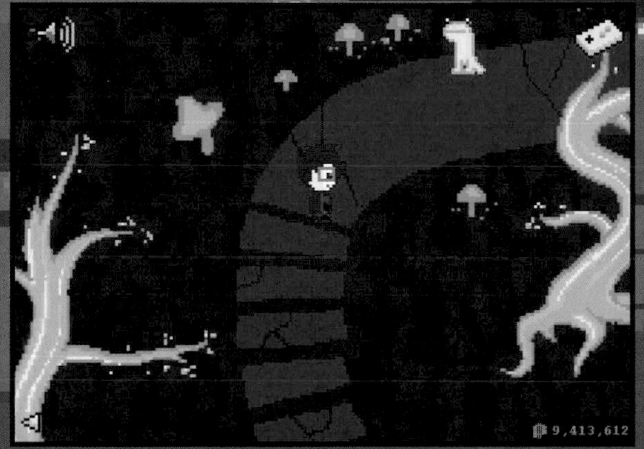
9,413,612

9,413,612

SALAMANDER: That was quite a bluster, wouldn't you say? It really had us all whipping around here, our little legs flailing every which way.
9,413,612

Even though it's in a different format, all this still feels pretty similar to the earlier walkaround Flash where John explores LOWAS and talks to salamanders. They say the same brainless NPC sort of things to continue filling out your understanding of the lore. They also bafflingly continue not to recognize John as the figure of legend they've heard about in their myths. There's nothing that significant about this fact. It's just always been my impression that in a lot of RPGs the NPCs tend to be kind of dumb, and tell tall tales about heroes right to your face, without realizing you were involved with the heroic exploits they're babbling about. It almost seems like a subset of dramatic irony that is specific to RPGs.

Also we're learning new points of lore from the villagers, because of course a lot more stuff has happened since we last explored a LOWAS environment. They've even had some time to come up with new mythical names for recent events, because giving lofty names to any big thing that happens in the game is probably in their DNA as NPCs. The Green Tragedy is a pretty good euphemism for having your village burned down by a lot of green fire. This really wasn't even that long ago, either. Easily less than an hour? The same temporal principle still seems to be in play in the Medium, where once something happens, it's as if it's been that way for a long time already. But then again, this may have little to do with temporal mechanics and more with the simple type of brains the consorts have, which make them born NPCs.

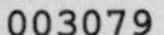

003079 [S]

SALAMANDER: Luckily the Heir saved us! I'm going to pop a big friendly bubble in his face if I am ever lucky enough to meet him.

JOHN: wow...

JOHN: sounds like he's in for a treat!

SALAMANDER: We must all come together and unify as a people after the terrible Green Tragedy.

SALAMANDER: This harmonious union will mostly entail a lot of standing around and fidgeting hyperactively... together!

My sense is that NPCs say a lot of dumb things due to the basic reason that when games are designed, the people who make the maps and position the sprites are just trying to fill the environments out a lot of the time. Then the writers have to give those sprites some dialogue, and there's not always amazing things for random guys loitering around to say, so the writers just end up making them say dumb stuff that comes across as kind of funny. That's part of the charm of RPG-style environments like this. Not everything is a big deal. You just wander around at your own pace. A few people say intriguing things, but most just spout nonsense to provide environmental color.

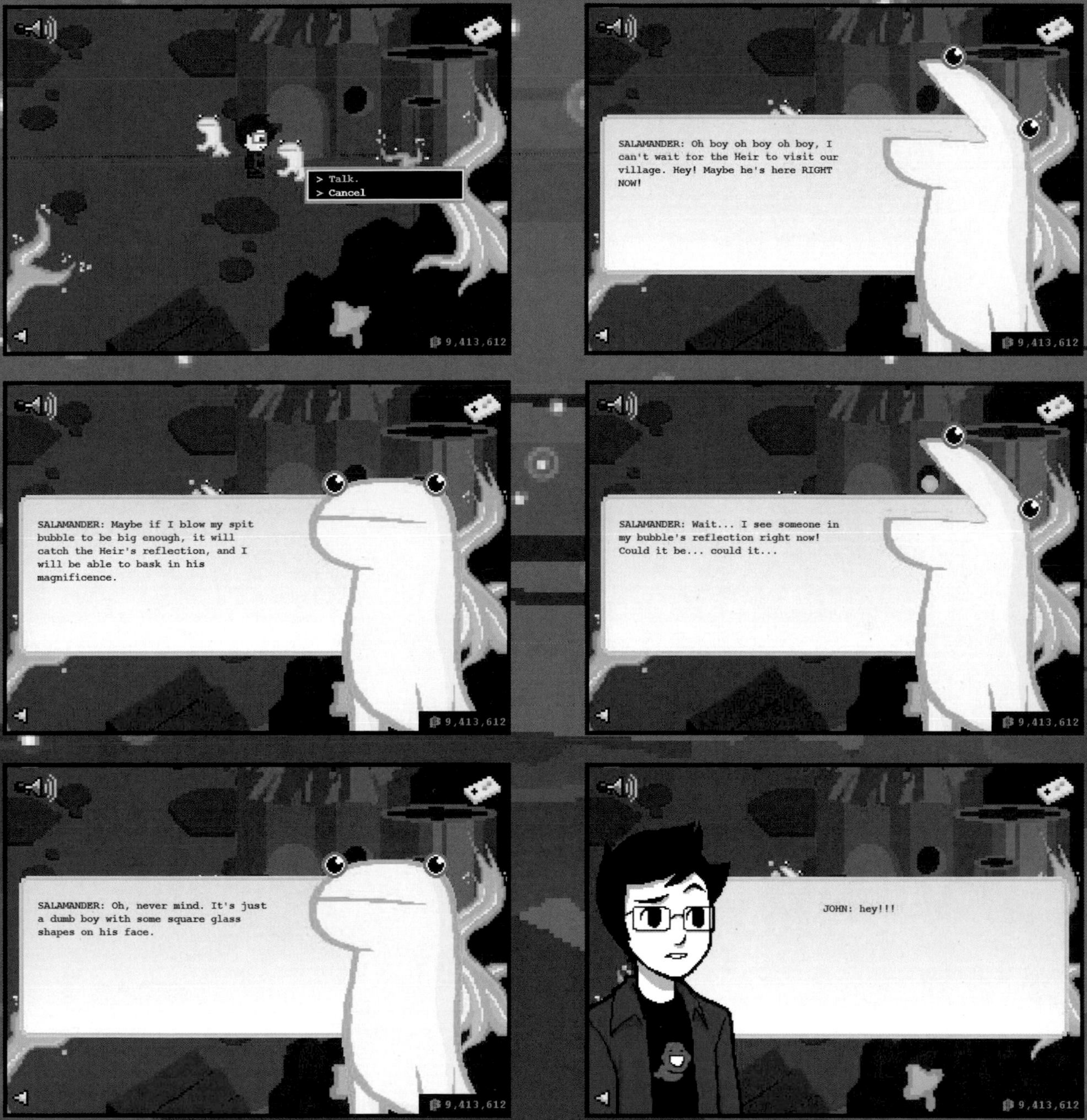

> Talk.
> Cancel

9,413,612

SALAMANDER: Oh boy oh boy oh boy, I can't wait for the Heir to visit our village. Hey! Maybe he's here RIGHT NOW!

9,413,612

SALAMANDER: Maybe if I blow my spit bubble to be big enough, it will catch the Heir's reflection, and I will be able to bask in his magnificence.

9,413,612

SALAMANDER: Wait... I see someone in my bubble's reflection right now! Could it be... could it...

9,413,612

SALAMANDER: Oh, never mind. It's just a dumb boy with some square glass shapes on his face.

9,413,612

JOHN: hey!!!

9,413,612

The Heir has been gravely disrespected. John should shove this ignorant bastard down a parcel pyxis.

9,413,612

9,413,612

9,413,612

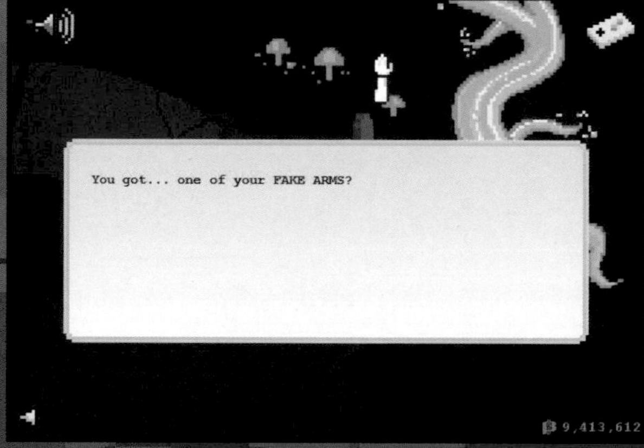
You got... one of your FAKE ARMS?
9,413,612

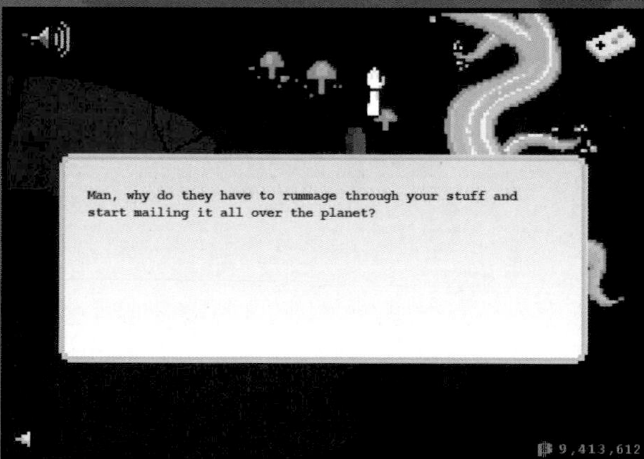
Man, why do they have to rummage through your stuff and start mailing it all over the planet?
9,413,612

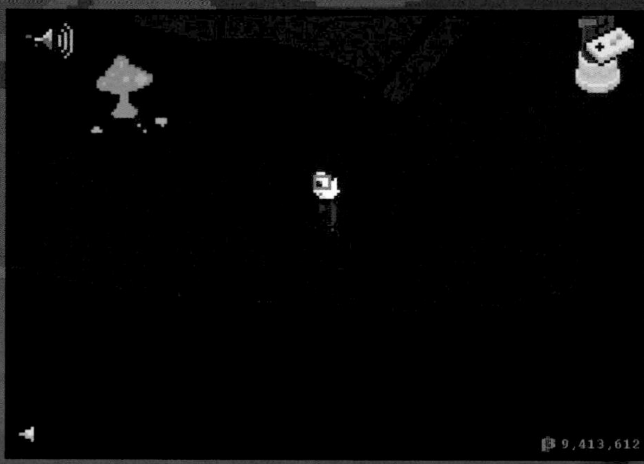
9,413,612

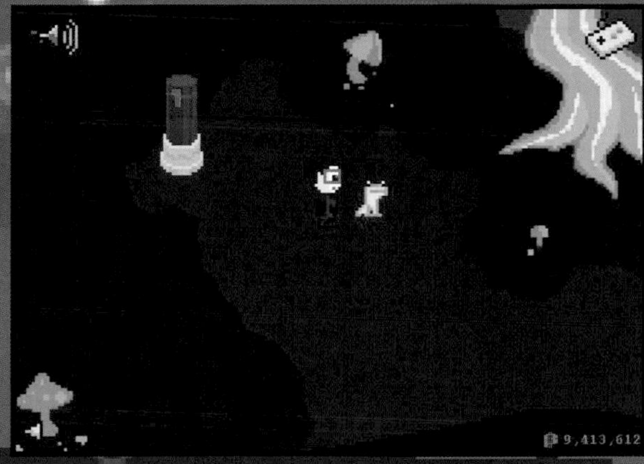

JOHN: hey little fella, where are your parents?

JOHN: do salamanders even have parents?

JOHN: oh, duh, of course they do. i guess what i mean is do you have a family or anything?

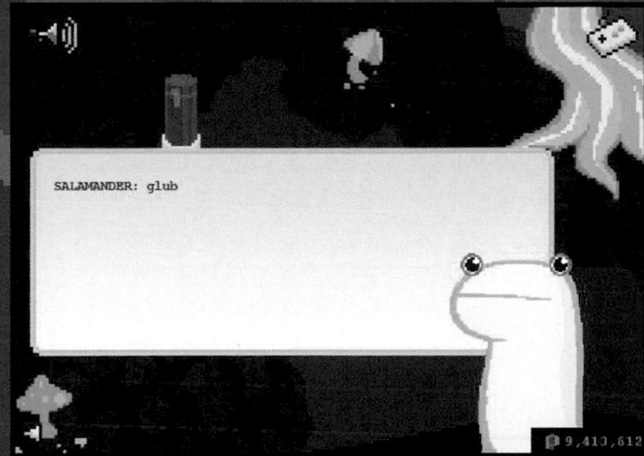
SALAMANDER: glub

JOHN: hmm, i already adopted one young salamander today. but, then i left her at my friend's house...
9,413,612

JOHN: so i think i'll let you be. i dunno if i'm cut out to be a dad!
9,413,612

JOHN: i mean, i don't even have a tie, or a pipe, or a really serious looking wallet or anything.
9,413,612

JOHN: thinking about it is making me miss my dad. hey, i wonder if i'll see him when i sleep on my quest bed? i hope so.
9,413,612

JOHN: anyway, thanks for listening. see you, little guy!
9,413,612

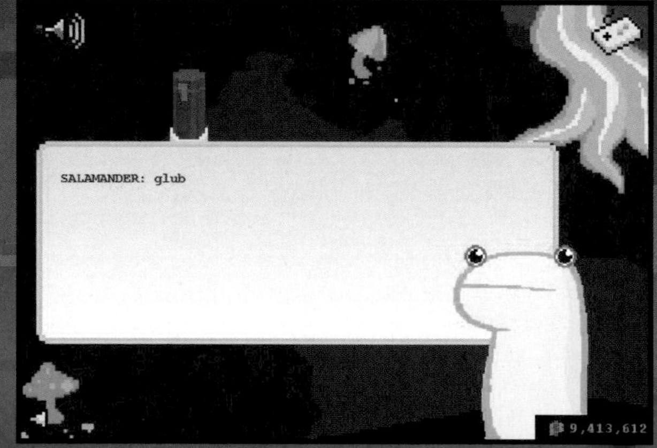
SALAMANDER: glub
9,413,612

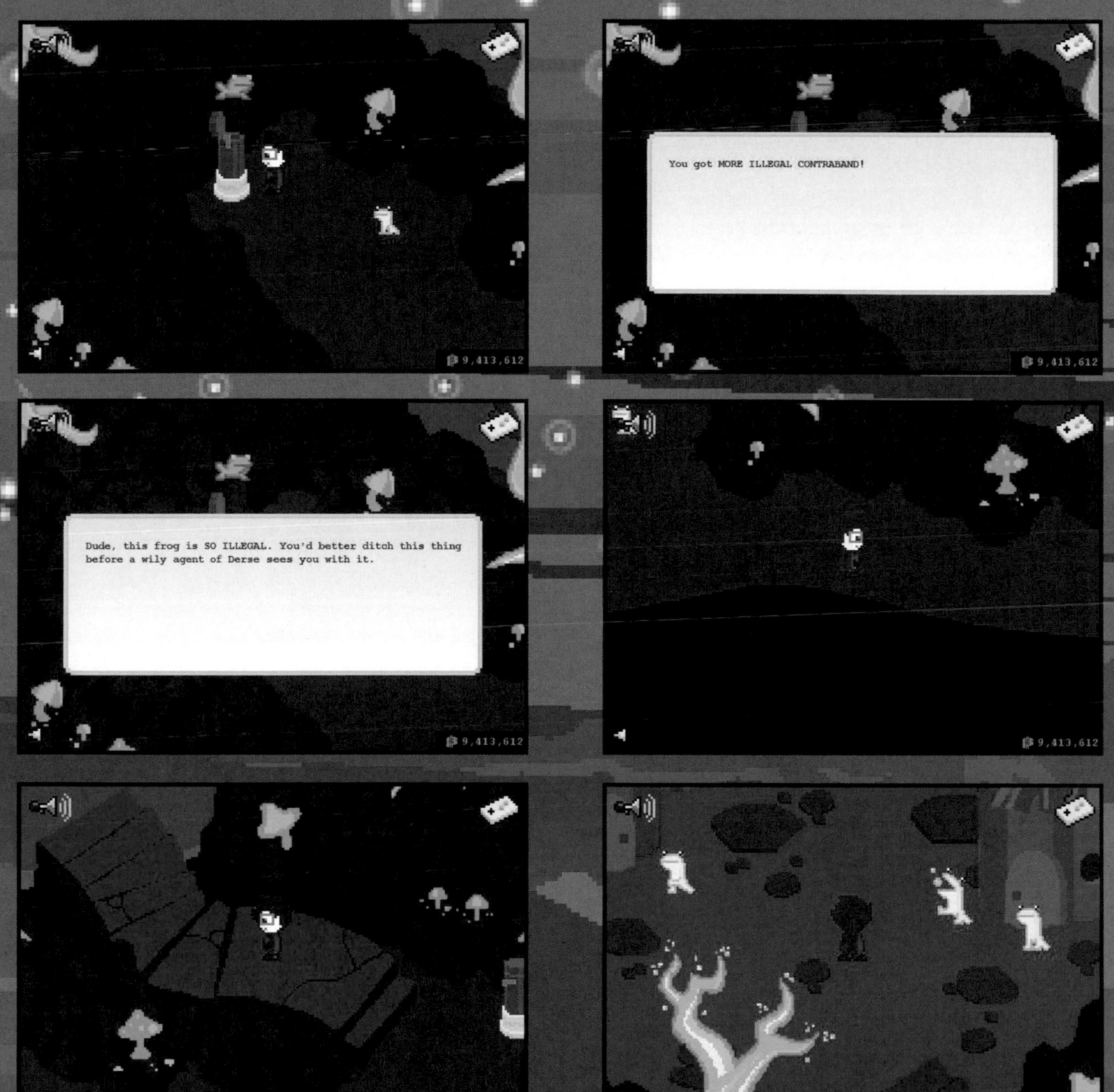
9,413,612
You got MORE ILLEGAL CONTRABAND!
9,413,612
Dude, this frog is SO ILLEGAL. You'd better ditch this thing before a wily agent of Derse sees you with it.
9,413,612
9,413,612
9,413,612
9,413,612

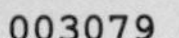

You got a CAN OF TAB!

Oh yes, you have been dying to try this beverage for a long time. Perfect timing too, since you are in need of a good sugar kick. This can should be JAM PACKED full of real, actual sugar.

Blech. This stuff sucks.

I feel obligated to point out any instance of the running gag where I imply Tab has sugar. I don't know if I've ever mentioned it before, but...Tab is bad? It sucks. Faygo is all right. Not good, not awful. But Tab is just plain bad. I always want to like it. I try to, because I like the can design. I've probably purchased Tab no less than half a dozen times just because I like the can. And yet, each time I am left with regrets.

Mushrooms don't grow in fucking orchards.

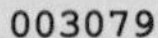

003079 [S]

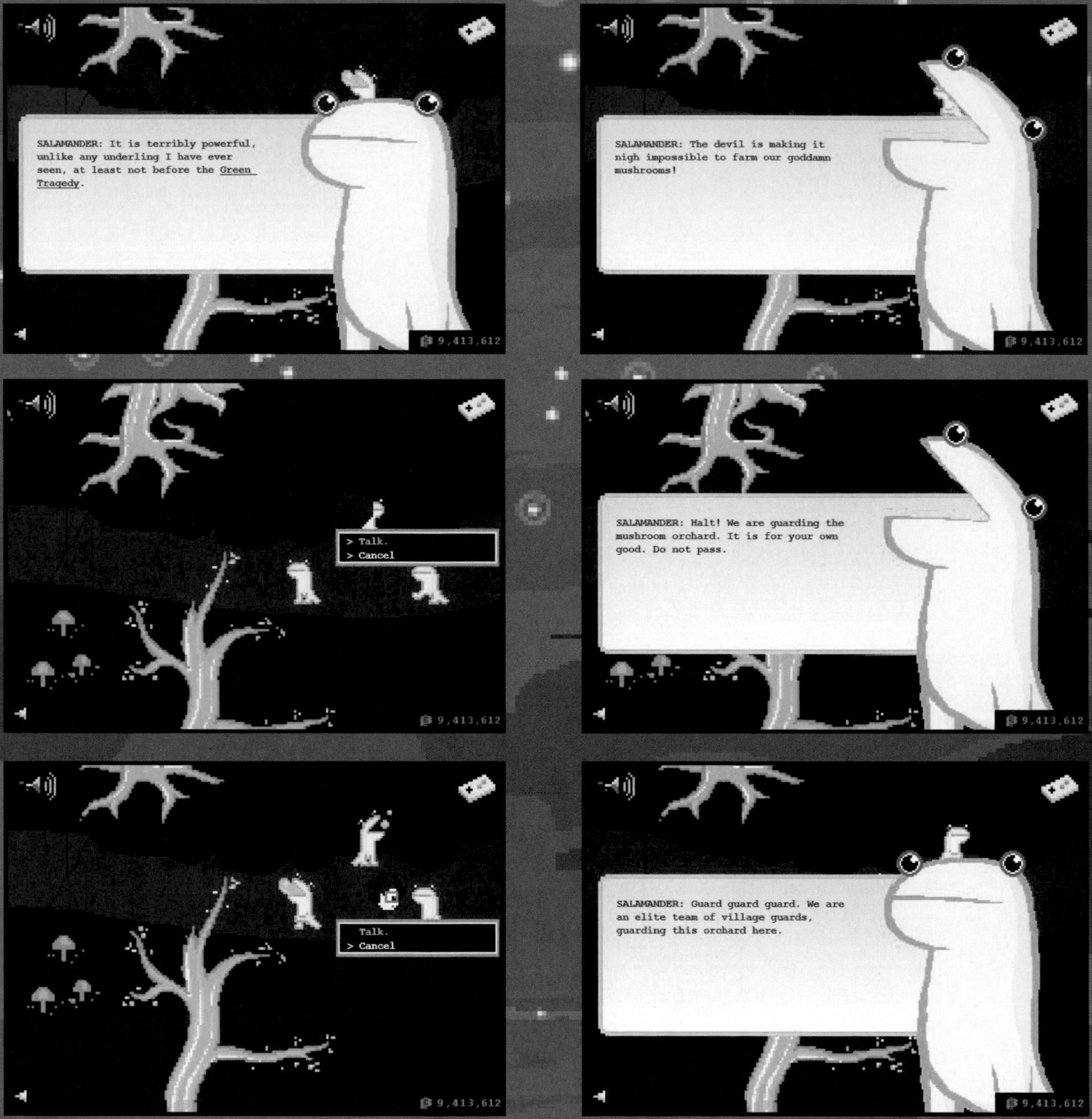

SALAMANDER: It is terribly powerful, unlike any underling I have ever seen, at least not before the Green Tragedy.

SALAMANDER: The devil is making it nigh impossible to farm our goddamn mushrooms!

> Talk.
> Cancel

SALAMANDER: Halt! We are guarding the mushroom orchard. It is for your own good. Do not pass.

Talk.
> Cancel

SALAMANDER: Guard guard guard. We are an elite team of village guards, guarding this orchard here.

There is a minor joke here about how the salamaders are supposed to be guarding the orchard and not letting anyone through. Yet they're all scattered about, blowing bubbles, sort of lost in their own worlds, easily providing the space for John to wander through. These guys just don't have their shit together at all. No wonder their village burned down.

The return of the Mushroom Farmer is a very emotional moment. We missed him so much, along with his dedication to farming all these goddamn mushrooms. Notice how we've switched game logics here, which is a nice twist to this RPG Flash. We're switching back to standard sprite mode, which allows you to battle a Bec imp and try your hand at a much more powerful adversary than the ones you fought in the first LOWAS game.

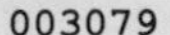

[S]

SALAMANDER: SOMEONE'S got to be farmin' all these goddamn fuckin' mushrooms, pain in the ass though truly it be.

9,413,612

SALAMANDER: So that's what I'm doing.

9,413,612

SALAMANDER: Standing around here

9,413,612

SALAMANDER: farmin' all these

9,413,612

SALAMANDER: goddamn

9,413,612

SALAMANDER: fuckin'

9,413,612

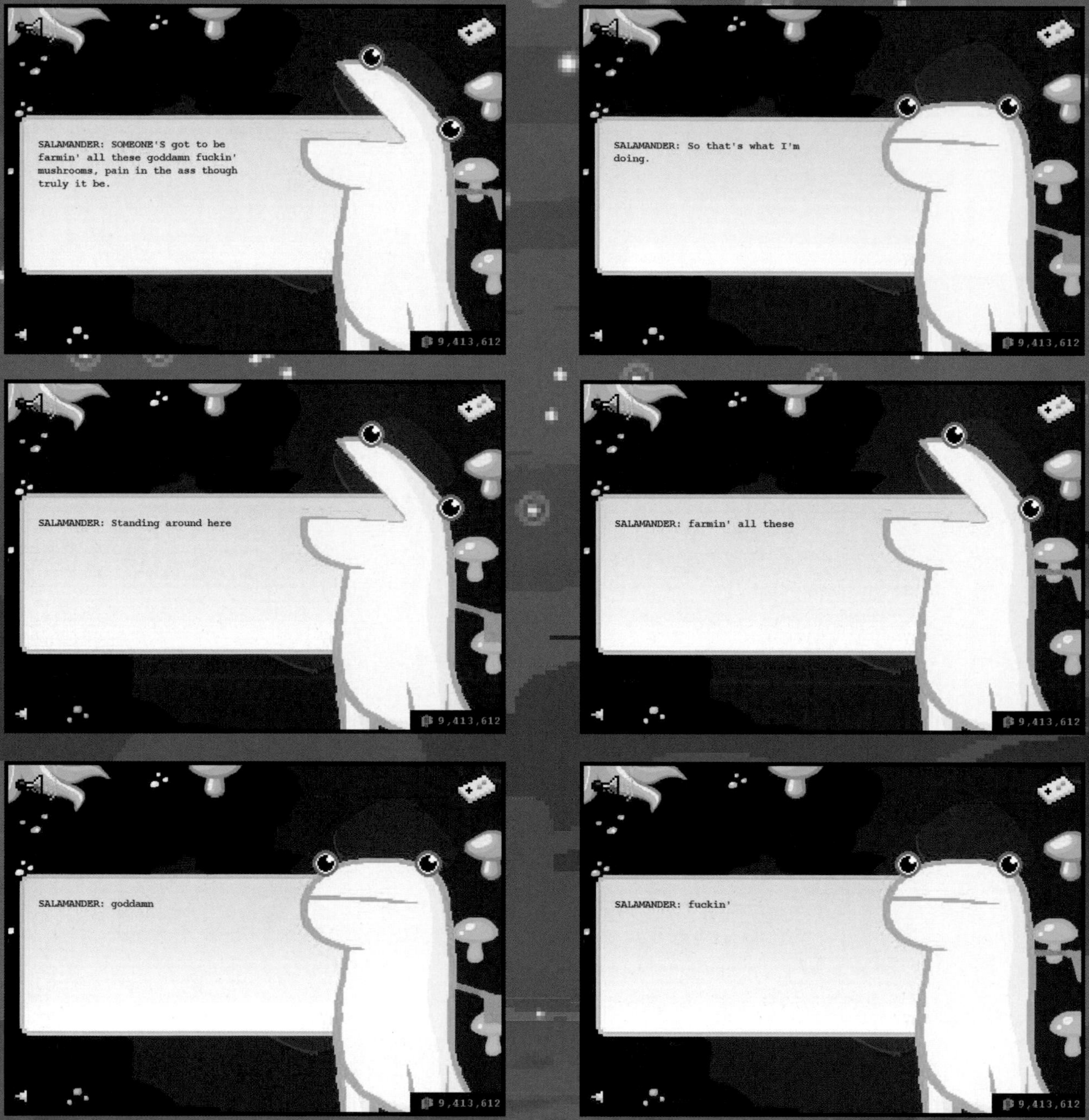

You almost get the sense that the Mushroom Farmer considers his agricultural duties burdensome? Quite a salty attitude he's showing here about harvesting delicious mushrooms. I like to think this is less a reflection on his enjoyment of his work and more an indication of the no-nonsense, rough-and-tumble persona of a seasoned farmhand. He's just gonna give it to you straight, see? This guy won't blow bubbles up your ass.

I have another confession to make: this battle serves no purpose. Few of them do, really. It's just that the game logic was already there, so it was easily adaptable for this game, with a couple of updated sprites. It is a more challenging battle, though, and you get to try out your cool, new time-freezing hammer while you're at it. Which, to be fair, isn't just a fun thing for you to try out. It actually does help defeat this much tougher imp in a tactical sense.

003079 [S]

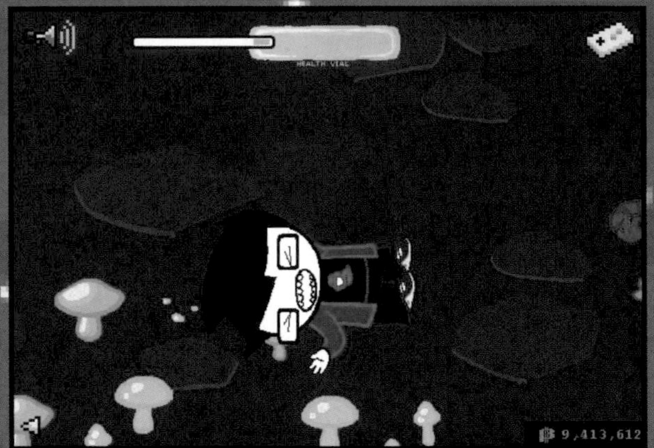

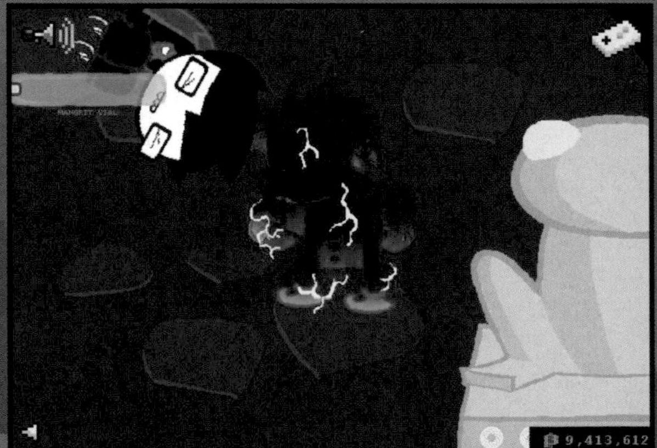

[S] 00307

9,413,612

9,413,612

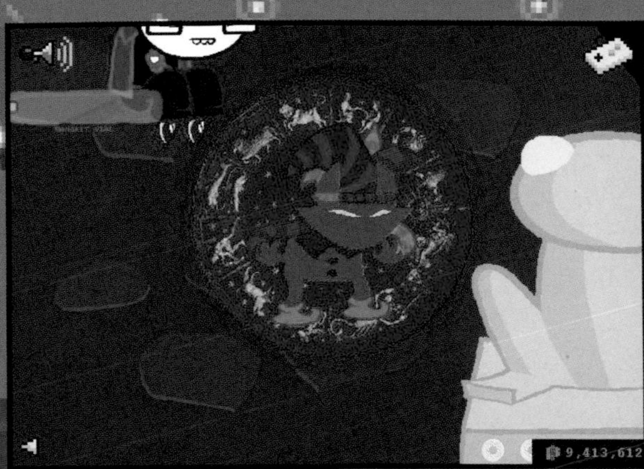

9,413,612

9,413,612

+1
Uranium
9,413,612

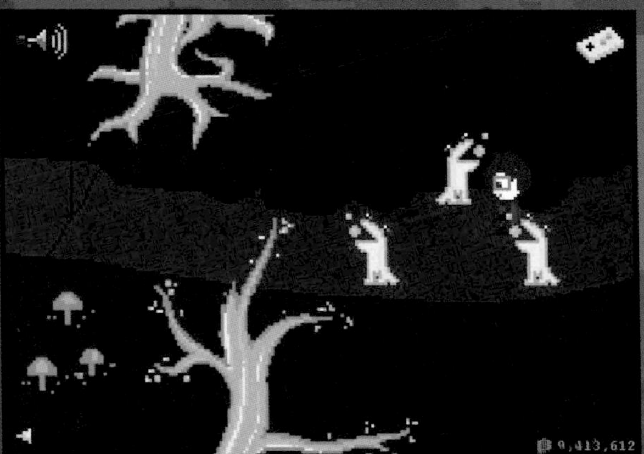

9,413,612

> Talk.
> Cancel

SALAMANDER: I thought the spell was broken there for a moment! The clouds went away, and the fireflies were all buzzing around, acting disoriented.

SALAMANDER: But then the clouds came back! To be honest, I was a little relieved. I have grown fond of them. And if the fireflies were to escape from above, I would miss them dearly!

SALAMANDER: They're really pretty, and they're my friends.

JOHN: aw...

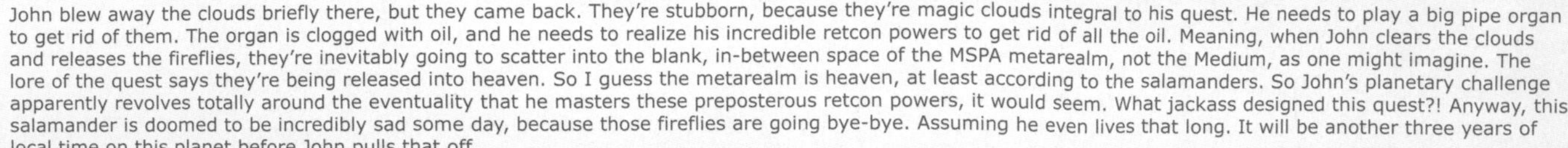

John blew away the clouds briefly there, but they came back. They're stubborn, because they're magic clouds integral to his quest. He needs to play a big pipe organ to get rid of them. The organ is clogged with oil, and he needs to realize his incredible retcon powers to get rid of all the oil. Meaning, when John clears the clouds and releases the fireflies, they're inevitably going to scatter into the blank, in-between space of the MSPA metarealm, not the Medium, as one might imagine. The lore of the quest says they're being released into heaven. So I guess the metarealm is heaven, at least according to the salamanders. So John's planetary challenge apparently revolves totally around the eventuality that he masters these preposterous retcon powers, it would seem. What jackass designed this quest?! Anyway, this salamander is doomed to be incredibly sad some day, because those fireflies are going bye-bye. Assuming he even lives that long. It will be another three years of local time on this planet before John pulls that off.

SALAMANDER: Our village has the best snack stand in the land! It offers the juiciest bugs and most succulent onions!
9,413,612

SALAMANDER: I'm so hungry. Alas, I have not a single boondollar to pop my bubble with.
9,413,612

What's the point of exploring a village if you can't do a little shopping? What stands out the most about this snack stand is how expensive the grasshopper is. I think that raises a lot of important questions... "DOES it, though?" Okay, who said that. WHO FUCKING SAID THAT? Fine, hot shot. You think you're so cool? Why don't YOU write the author note for this page? Here, I'll get you started. "Hi, I'm a random clown, and I think my opinions are sooooo much better than those of the guy who made this thing. I'm not even the slightest bit curious about that grasshopper, or its exorbitant cost, because apparently I think I'm too cool for school. Most things aren't really a big deal to me? I kind of shrug my way through life, even when I see amazing shit. Like when a great webcomic man shares his deeply insightful thoughts about his work, or when I encounter expensive grasshoppers that have no explanation at all. I guess that's just how I roll as a person? In summary, I guess you could say, I'm not a piece of shit at all." Wow, great work, man. People are going to love it. And here I was, all set to write a master's thesis on all the secrets of the snack stand grasshoppers, but I guess there's no need to do that anymore. The fans will like what you had to say so much better!

John, you son of a bitch. You could easily afford to buy this hungry salamander 100 grasshoppers. And yet you torment him, with precisely the amount of money that will result in probably hours of agonizing indecision for this poor sap. You're a thirteen-year-old kid, for Christ's sake. You're going to stand here and use your extravagant wealth to teach this simple-minded amphibian a harsh lesson in money management? How quickly one slips into the mindset of the upper class upon finding a bit of money in one's pocket. What's next, John? Will you be preaching the virtues of conservative economic policies to the citizens of this poor, working-class village? Or maybe John is just playing one of his funny pranks here. That could be it. Maybe the truth is that wealthy conservative individuals are really just great pranksters. Ah, I see you would like some of my money? Well, the joke's on you, because...you can't have it! ;-)

The other salamander should have taken some tips from this guy. It turns out John is incredibly easy to trick into giving up all his money, if you know the right hustle. But this salamander made the mistake of low-balling John out of the gate, and then raised the price when he realized he had a sucker on the line. But not even John is that dumb. Still, this guy did an awful lot better than the other guy, who will probably die of starvation before he decides how to spend that measly 100 boondollars.

John continues to be a prickly bastard, showing no appreciation for the incredible purchase he just made. Sure, he hates smuppets, and sure, it probably isn't *really* worth 10,000 boondollars. But it's all about the *perceived* value, John. It automatically becomes more valuable simply because you paid a fortune for it, like designer clothing. If it only cost you one boondollar, then maybe you'd be right in regarding it as something that belongs in a toilet. But for 10K? Suddenly now it feels like something that belongs in a museum.

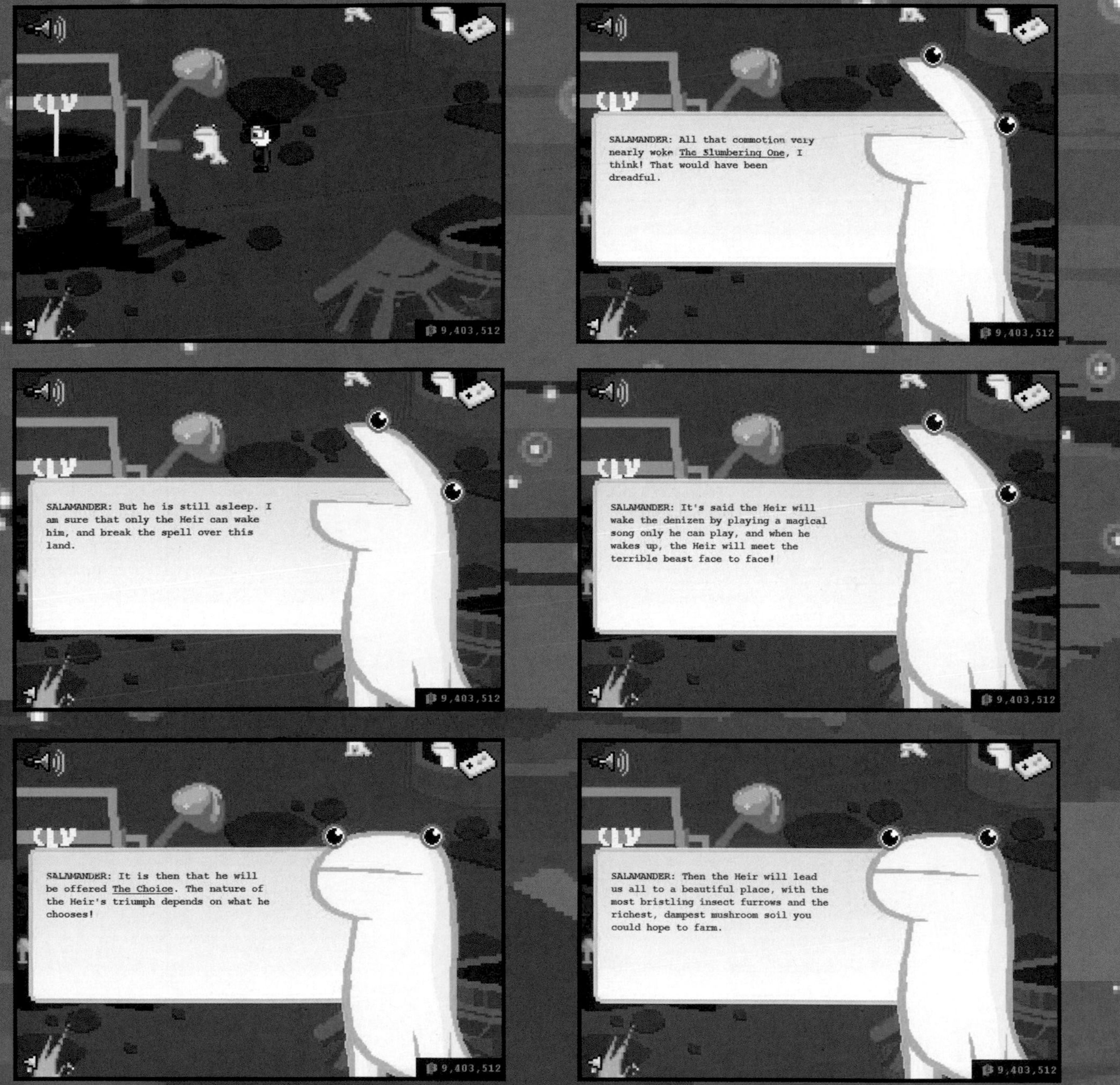

This consort says that the Heir will lead them all to a "beautiful place." Now that we know the full arc of this legend, we have to wonder what place he's talking about. The metarealm (i.e. "heaven") where John releases the fireflies? Or the universe the kids create, resulting in a home for the "paradise" planet, Earth C? Like most prophesies, you can make more than one answer fit. Allowing more than one viable answer for any given prophecy is very important to prophetic practice, because it provides a variety of escape hatches to ensure that the prophet does not get bit in the ass by his own egregious bullshit.

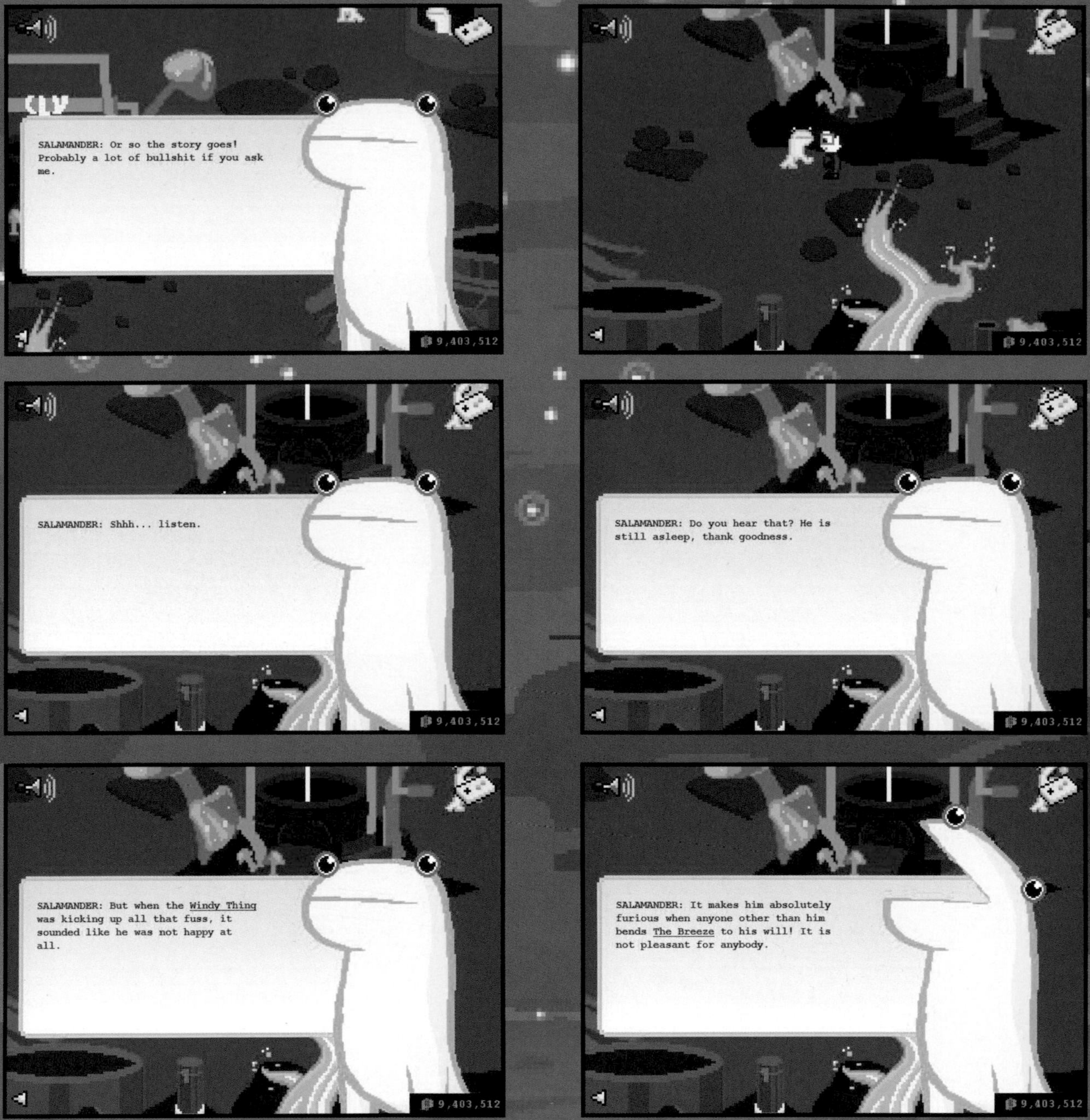

003079 [S]

SALAMANDER: Or so the story goes! Probably a lot of bullshit if you ask me.

SALAMANDER: Shhh... listen.

SALAMANDER: Do you hear that? He is still asleep, thank goodness.

SALAMANDER: But when the Windy Thing was kicking up all that fuss, it sounded like he was not happy at all.

SALAMANDER: It makes him absolutely furious when anyone other than him bends The Breeze to his will! It is not pleasant for anybody.

At one point, we could also examine the well and look inside, which was a panel that didn't make the cut here. It zoomed into the dark hole and we could hear ominous Typheus sounds, which were just orca noises. What was the point, you ask? Don't ask. If we go down that road, I'd probably have to just admit this entire RPG page didn't serve much of a purpose, and we probably could have skipped right to the Quest Bed scene without losing much. And then, where does it stop? We could probably dispense with the entire story. It's not like it's ever done anyone any good. Has *Homestuck* ever fed a hungry person? Cured a disease? Hell, no. It is settled then. Let's do away with all stories. Pack it in, folks. Art is canceled. All because you were curious about some orca noises.

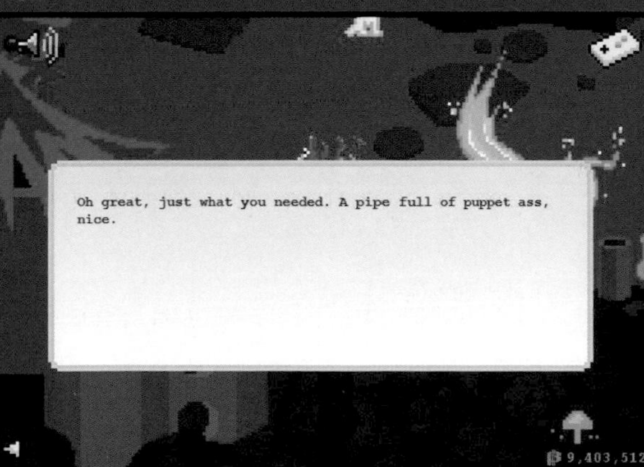

John is really raking in the puppet ass today. I wonder what Vriska is thinking as she watches all these time-wasting shenanigans? The question is ridiculous, of course, because there's no way she isn't fast-forwarding through all this nonsense to get to the Quest Bed part. She likes John and all, but not *this* much.

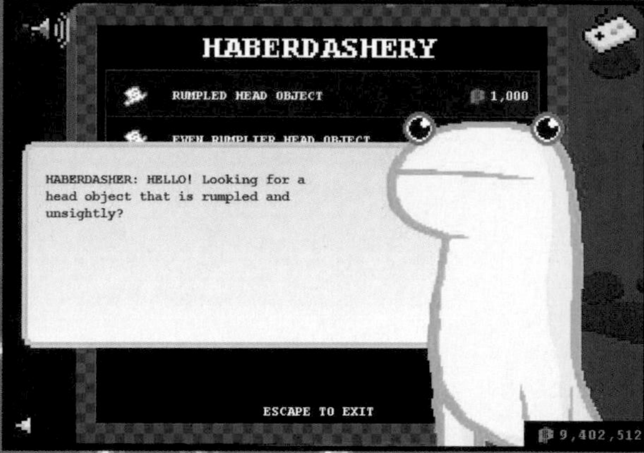
HABERDASHERY
RUMPLED HEAD OBJECT 1,000
HABERDASHER: HELLO! Looking for a head object that is rumpled and unsightly?
ESCAPE TO EXIT
9,402,512

HABERDASHERY
RUMPLED HEAD OBJECT 1,000
HABERDASHER: All of our head objects are rumpled and unsightly, fortunately!
ESCAPE TO EXIT
9,402,512

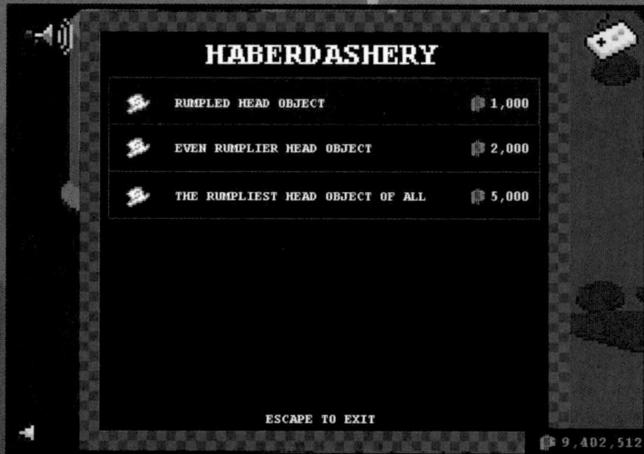
HABERDASHERY
RUMPLED HEAD OBJECT 1,000
EVEN RUMPLIER HEAD OBJECT 2,000
THE RUMPLIEST HEAD OBJECT OF ALL 5,000
ESCAPE TO EXIT
9,402,512

9,402,512

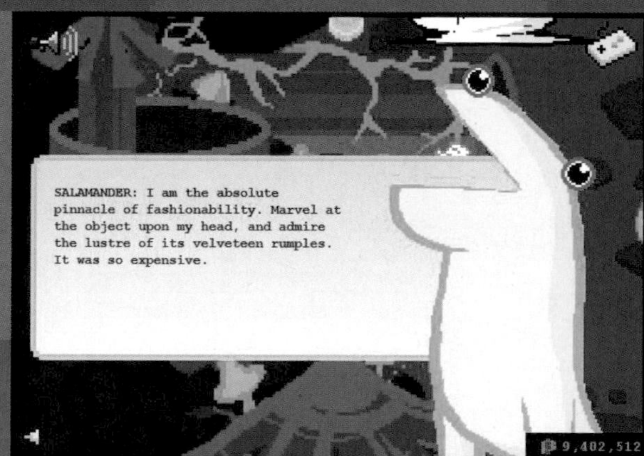
SALAMANDER: I am the absolute pinnacle of fashionability. Marvel at the object upon my head, and admire the lustre of its velveteen rumples. It was so expensive.
9,402,512

9,403,512

Part of checking back on LOWAS activity now and then is just noticing how some of John's mundane objects seeded around the countryside have essentially taken hold as memes. One guy put on John's shitty, rumpled top hat, and now hats are all the rage, not to mention lavishly marked up for retail. This trend sort of continues in the alpha session, when Derse under the Condesce regime starts following similar viral fashion trends. This probably means there's something inherently alluring about the idea of rumpled headwear to simple-minded beings.

Here John goes again, being a cheap bastard. It's almost easy not to notice what a tightass he is, because you get distracted by the nice gesture and how much the salamander appreciates it. But if you're alert, you notice John gives only 1,000 boondollars, which is just barely enough for the cheapest Rumpled Head Object in the store. Just 2,000 boondollars would have bought an Even Rumplier Head Object, and a measly 5,000 would have snagged The Rumpliest Head Object Of All. John could have sprung for a top-of-the-line head object for this guy without breaking a sweat. But he didn't. So disappointing.

003079 [S]

SALAMANDER: oh my god oh my god oh my god
9,402,512

SALAMANDER: THANK YOU SO MUCH, I LOVE MY NEW RUMPLED HEAD OBJECT, AND I LOVE YOU.
9,402,512

JOHN: heheheh. you're welcome.
9,402,512

9,413,612

9,413,612

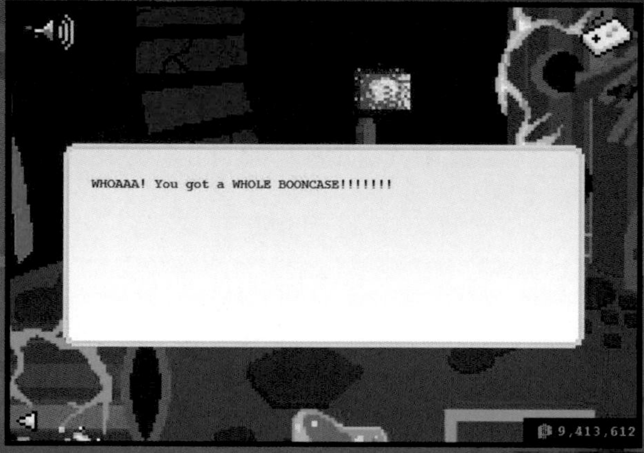

WHOAAA! You got a WHOLE BOONCASE!!!!!!!
9,413,612

....
9,413,612

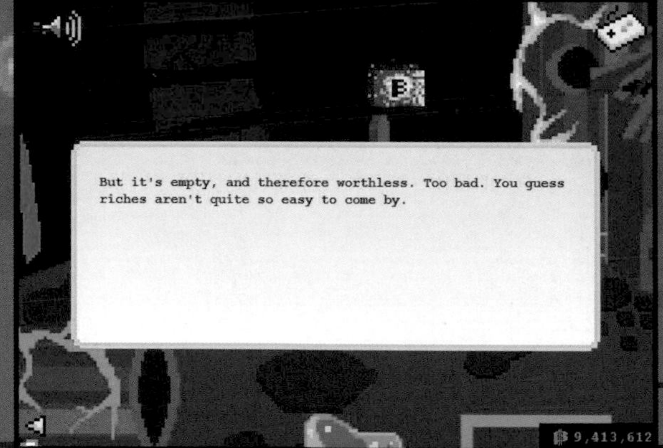
But it's empty, and therefore worthless. Too bad. You guess riches aren't quite so easy to come by.
9,413,612

9,413,612

Shop.
> Cancel
9,413,612

FRAYMOTIF SHOP
FEATHERCADENCE 10,000,000
MERCHANT: What will it be today?
ESCAPE TO EXIT
9,413,612

FRAYMOTIF SHOP
FEATHERCADENCE 10,000,000
PNEUMATIC PROGRESSION 100,000,000
BREATHLESS BATTAGLIA 1,000,000,000
IVORIES IN THE FIRE 10,000,000,000
MIXOLYDIAN MAELSTROM 200,000,000,000
FANTASIA'S INHALE 1,000,000,000,000
ESCAPE TO EXIT
9,413,612

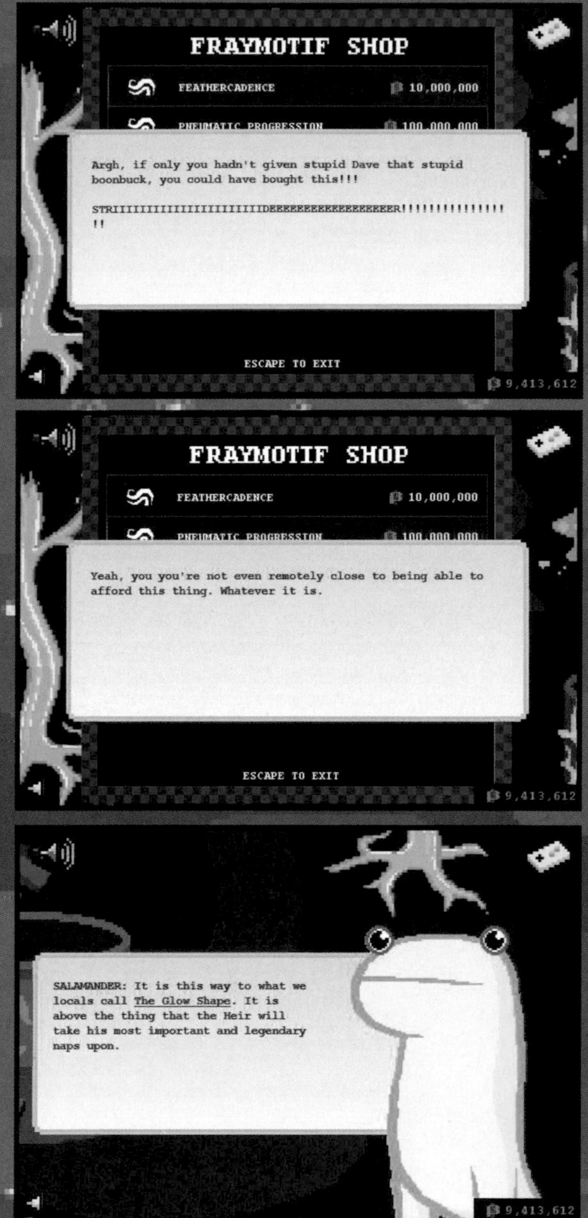

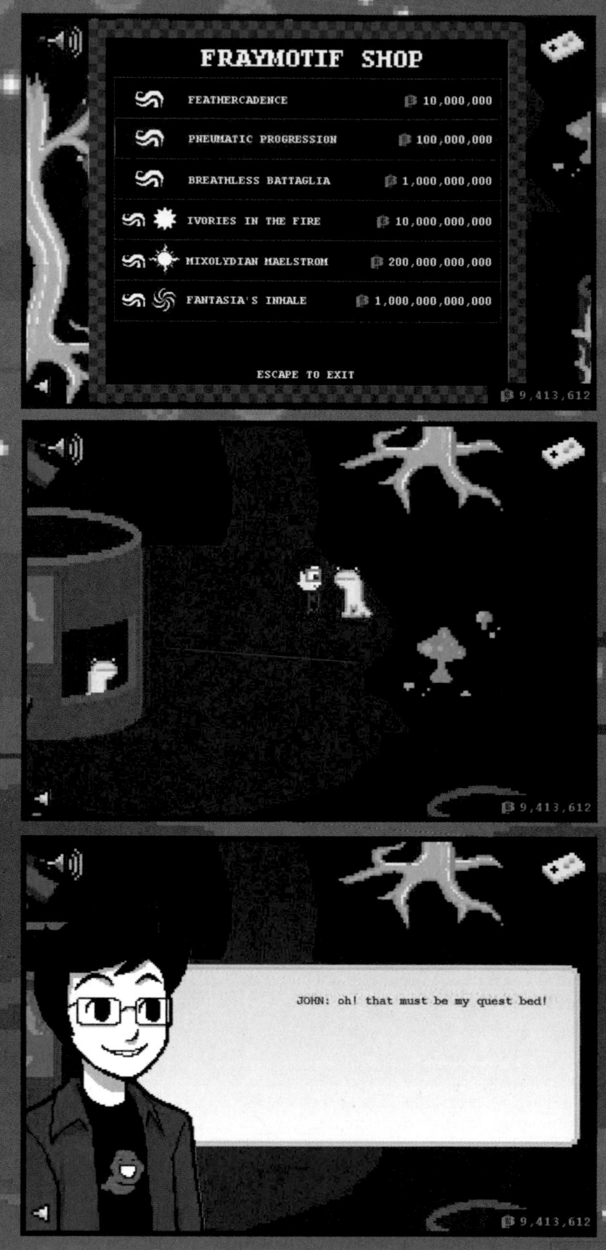

Here's the first concrete evidence that fraymotifs are actual game constructs that players can acquire and use. I believe they were mentioned at least once earlier, though when things are mentioned offhand, you can frequently write them off as whimsical gags or small points of worldbuilding that might not receive further development. But these do, and are presumably some sort of cool spells or battle techniques that you can buy in a shop. The astronomical prices suggest they're late-game maneuvers you can start incorporating into your tactics once you can afford them. And the dual aspect symbols in the shop menu imply the stronger ones are combination attacks. I think I imagined this battle concept much earlier in the story, when the kids' musical interests were more pertinent, and conceived some vague idea that combined their aspect powers with something musical in nature, like playing a song that results in a strong magical attack. Aside from this little shop menu here, mentions of fraymotifs throughout the story are exceedingly rare. There's a brief shot in a smaller panel of Dave and Jade using one later in this act, and that's it. You have to wait until **[S] Collide** to see a few of them in action, in an actual animated setting. Frankly, they were never even invented to be shown on-screen in an explicit way. I considered their appearance in **Collide** as sort of bonus material, like throwing a bone to anyone who remembered these were a thing. The point of hinting at a system like this is to capture the imagination—to let readers speculate about what these mysterious things could be and how they might be used in a typical session—and not so much to provide a concrete indicator of what's to come. In short, it's more background lore in a story where stuff like this is fun to think about, but not the real focus.

Dude still doesn't get it, even when John blurts it out. The truth is, the consorts are probably programmed to recognize the Heir only once they see him in the full pajama getup. Otherwise, he could beat them over the head with a log and shout "I AM THE LEGENDARY HEIR OF BREATH!" and they would still be like, "Gosh, I can't WAIT for the Heir to arrive and save us from this log-wielding hooligan!" I think this makes sense, as it provides a better NPC environment for the player and encourages him to keep growing, keep striving to advance through his quest and fully realize his role as an Heir. If the villagers started celebrating his Heir status too early, it might go to his head.

> John: Proceed to Quest Bed.

This is the end of the game. Unlike the first RPG minigame, which was somewhat open-ended and directionless, this one has a clear endpoint. From now on, the main goal of playing these games all the way through is to achieve the practical purpose of knowing what note they end on, so that when you turn the page, it actually makes sense and you know what's going on. If you got fed up with this nonsense only halfway through and clicked the next page, you wouldn't really have any context for John sitting down on that stone, bed-like slab. Playing through an entire game becomes the process for consuming an entire page, resulting in unbroken continuity. For the most part, this leads to a pretty decent and fun media experience that slows down the standard pacing a little but otherwise isn't too clunky. Of course, this all breaks down once the Meenahbound monsterpieces start dropping like bombs in the heart of the Act 6 badlands.

> John: Take legendary nap.

EB: ok, i think i'm ready to take this legendary nap!
EB: and then climb the god tiers, i guess?
AG: Yes, exactly! Pretty exciting, isn't it?
EB: yeah...
EB: maybe it is a little TOO exciting.
AG: What's that mean?
EB: i am not sleepy at all!
EB: also, this is not much of a bed. more like a really hard slab of rock.
EB: i don't see how i will be able to sleep.
AG: John.
AG: Would you like me to put you to sleep?
EB: um...
EB: you mean, you're asking me this time, instead of just doing it?
EB: what happened to you wanting to be responsible for me becoming a hero!
AG: John, I am clearly involved in your rise to power now regardless. That can't 8e changed!
AG: I am giving you the option, 8ecause at some point a hero has to start making choices.

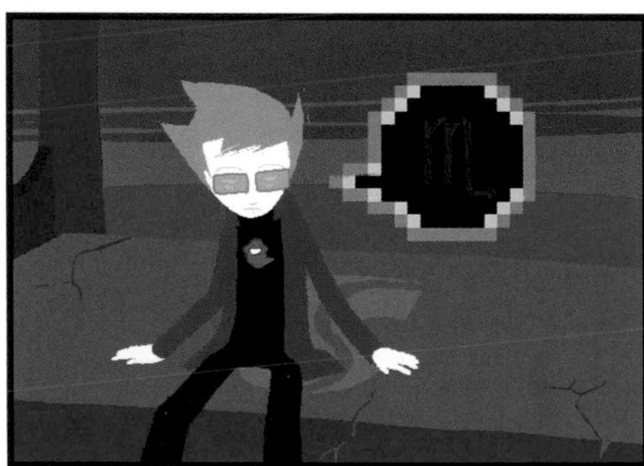

AG: Once you take a 8r8k from hunting treasure and stop getting distracted 8y side quests, you eventually realize that's what this game is all a8out.
AG: The choices you make affect the destiny of the universe you cre8te, as well as the type of hero you 8ecome.

Yet another scene wherein Vriska does the thing where she repeatedly violates someone's free will without consent, and then later offers the consent back as a gesture to show how thoughtful and magnanimous she really is. And then it stupidly seems to be effective as such a gesture, because we just can't seem to stay mad at Vriska. Nor should we.

AG: It would have 8een nice if someone was around to explain all this to me, and let me have some control over my own f8.
AG: I had to do this a much less pleasant way. I'm sparing you that indignity.
AG: 8esides, it's not like you're some loser who doesn't know how to make tough decisions.
AG: So what'll it 8e, John?
EB: well...
EB: i'm supposed to go to sleep to realize my destiny...
EB: and you have the ability to make me do that, so...
EB: i don't really see the harm in that.
EB: it sounds like it is just the practical thing to do.
AG: Am I hearing a "yes," John?
EB: yes, that is my decision.
EB: vriska, please put me to sleep!
AG: You got it. <3

Viriska sounds a little bitter about the fact that when she "had to do this," it involved slowly bleeding out while still conscious, psychically demanding that Tavros kill her, and when he hesitated, psychically controlling him to spell out the command to kill her in her own blood, and then eventually in his own blood too when his fingers got raw and wounded from painting too many blood-letters on a rough stone surface. Which probably wasn't at the top of her list of "fun activities for couples." She knows John basically needs to be euthanized for this to work. Quietly in his sleep is a nice way to go about it. See? She's trying to be nice and is working on being a better person. We should give her points for this. But in fairness, we should also give her points for when she isn't.

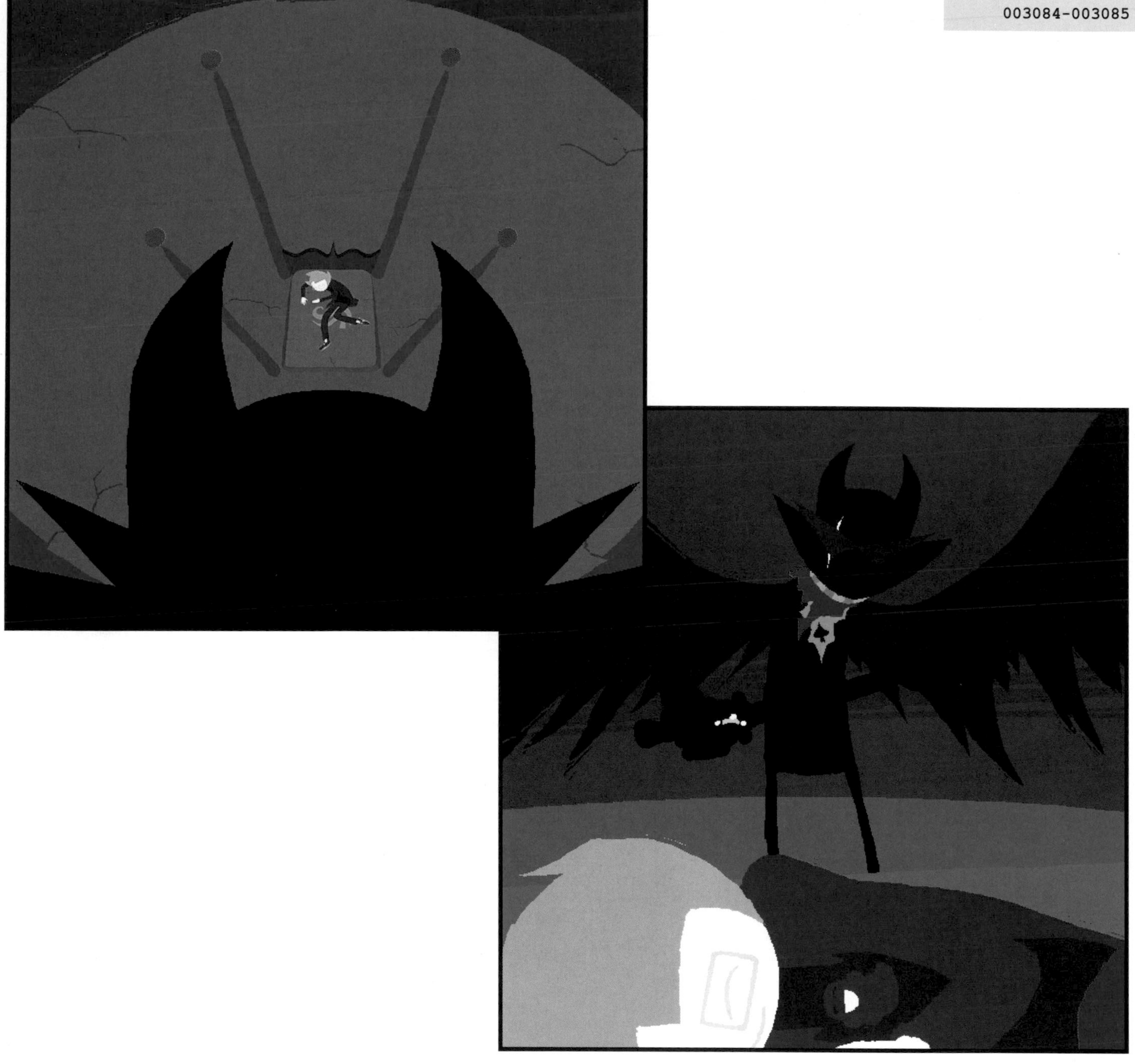

It wasn't long ago that Jack had his ridiculous clown form, which had way too much going on visually. Tentacles, a jester hat... It was all a bit silly. Luckily, Bec prototyped himself, which simplified Jack's form into something a little more badass, so that we could take him more seriously as a villainous threat. But even more luckily, I started quickly dispensing with that idea and began making him ridiculous again. Jack likes taking souvenirs, and he took one from Bro after defeating him. Now the chief antagonist is a dog wearing sunglasses. I always lost sleep at night any time I sensed a great enough deficiency in the overall silliness factor of the villains of this story, and I was careful to correct the problem whenever it surfaced.

003086

AG: 8888)

R.I.P. John Egbert. The death of John seems like a good note to end this book on and cap off roughly the first half of Act 5 Act 2. I'm guessing the next book should take us all the way through to **[S] Cascade**, or the End of Act 5. I sure hope it does, because having the second of two sub-acts end up spanning THREE books frankly sounds like the height of idiocy. And the LAST thing I want *Homestuck* to be associated with is the height of idiocy. As a closing thought, if I may remark upon the death of John here, some believed that killing off the protagonist of the story at this stage was quite a bold choice. And they were absolutely right. But it's one of those things you can only pull off if you're truly an avant garde storyteller who fearlessly defies narrative formula and all the safe choices in media. But as the loyal fans would see, it made perfect sense to kill John here. The surrounding narrative and cast are more than strong enough to stand without him. They use his memory as a motivating force to drive them to triumph, glory, personal growth, and overwhelmingly satisfying character arcs. At the end of the story, they would all look back on this moment, as would the readers, and see it as kind of an emotional turning point. A massive tone shift in the story, where it was casting off the safety of the known and charging deep into the thick underbrush of the storytelling wilderness. Every now and then we'd get a little flashback, of Rose for Instance, remembering some heartfelt and uplifting advice John once gave her. It seemed so crazy to everyone that I would coldly take John out here, without ceremony or even much surrounding explanation. But in hindsight, you'll scarcely be able to find a single reader who wouldn't admit that when all was said and done, it just plain *worked*. Tune in next book, when we take our first cautious steps into this brave, new Johnless *Homestuck*. And if you feel nervous or afraid, just remember that I will be with you, holding your hand every step of the way down here in the laugh gutter. Except it won't be the laugh gutter anymore, because it's time to get serious. From now on, it will be the sobbing trough, a deep recess for our most potent feelings of melancholy and sorrow. No more jokes, no more goofs, just a bunch of stone-faced, hard-hitting shit, as Act 5 Act 2 hits a new tonal gear. I'm preparing myself as we speak. My life coach and priest have finally caught up with me, and they've brought along a brand-new friend: my exorcist. I hit the Yankee Candle store earlier and bought a few dozen wax fatties, borrowed a straightjacket from my former psychiatrist's widow, and now I'm ready for whatever happens next. Are you?

ART CREDITS

[S] Past Karkat: Wake up.
Brett Muller, Eyes5, Jessica Allison, M Thomas Harding, Paige Turner, Richard Gung, SaffronScarf, Vivus

[S] Jade: Wake up.
Brett Muller, Eyes5, Jessica Allison, M Thomas Harding, Paige Turner, Richard Gung, SaffronScarf, SkepticArcher, Tavia Morra, Vivus

[S] Jade: Enter.
Brett Muller, Eyes5, Lexxy, M Thomas Harding, Nic Carey, Richard Gung, SaffronScarf, Sockpuppy, Vivus

[S] John: Enter village.
Eyes5, Lexxy, M Thomas Harding, Richard Gung, Tavia Morra

SBURB CLIENT

SBURB version 0.0.1

SKAIANET SYSTEMS INCORPORATED. ALL RIGHTS RESERVED.

SBURB client is running.

Homestuck
Book 5
Part 2: Act 5 Act 2 Part 1

VIZ Media Edition

By Andrew Hussie

Cover Art - Adrienne Garcia
Book Design - Christopher Kallini
Cover & Graphic Design - Adam Grano
Editor - Leyla Aker

© 2011 Andrew Hussie. All rights reserved.

The stories, characters and incidents mentioned in this publication are entirely fictional.

No portion of this book may be reproduced or transmitted in any form or by any means without written permission from the copyright holders.

Printed in China

Published by VIZ Media, LLC
P.O. Box 77010
San Francisco, CA 94107

10 9 8 7 6 5 4 3 2 1
First printing, October 2019

PARENTAL ADVISORY
HOMESTUCK is rated T+ for Older Teen and is recommended for ages 16 and up. This volume contains sordid receptacles, flighty broads and their snarky horseshitometers, a Fruity Rumpus Asshole Factory, and a million rambunctious gross tentacle mutants.

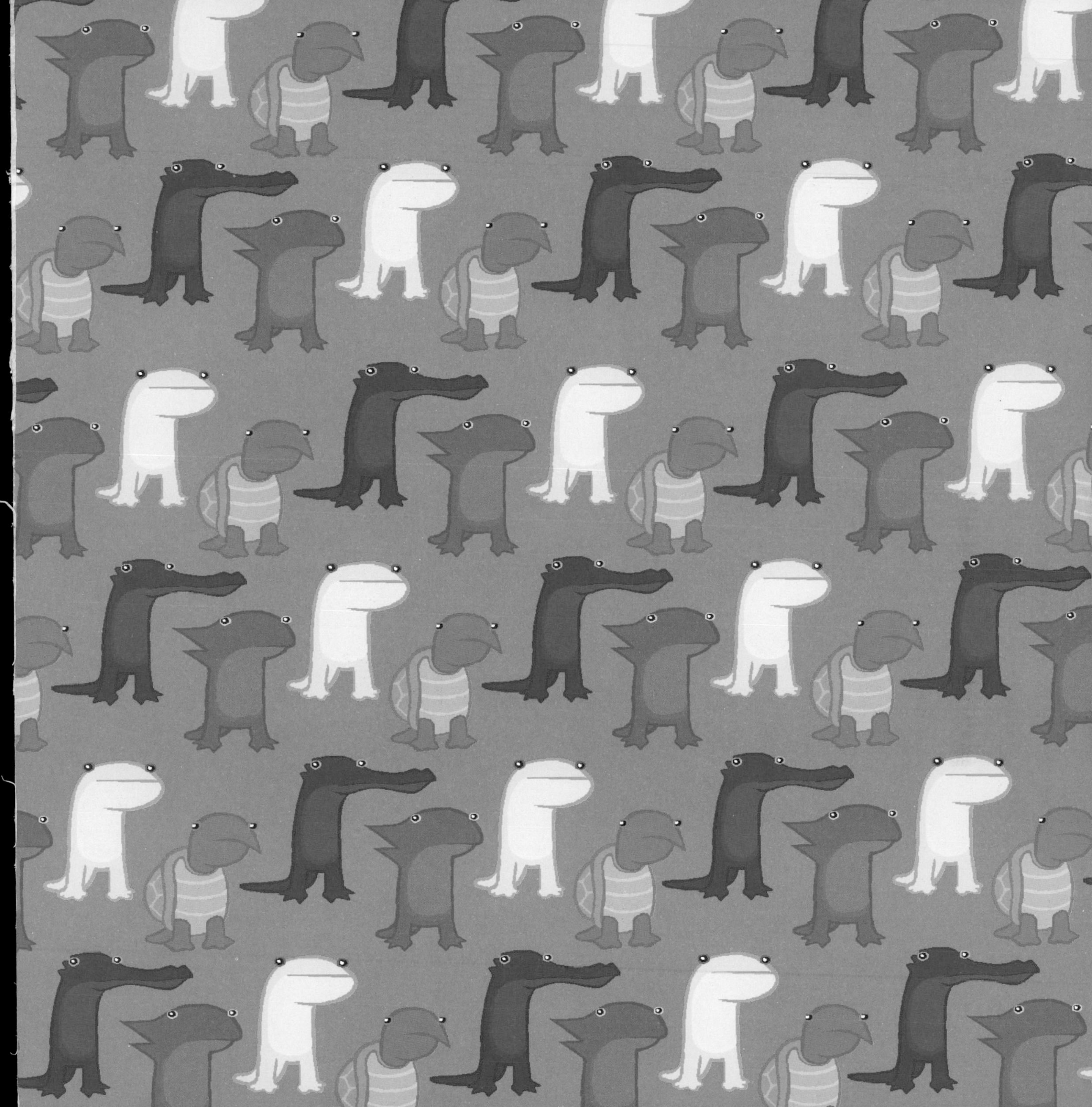